WARS OF ATTRITION

Wars of Attrition

Vietnam, the Business Roundtable, and the Decline of Construction Unions

MARC LINDER

Fănpìhuà Press
Iowa City
1999

331.88124
L74w

Suggested Library of Congress Cataloging
Linder, Marc, 1946—
        Wars of attrition: Vietnam, the Business Roundtable,
and the decline of construction unions/by Marc Linder.
            p. cm.
        Includes bibliographical references and index.
        ISBN 0-9673899-0-9
          1. Construction industry—U.S. 2. Industrial relations—U.S.
        3. Construction unions—U.S. 4. Construction workers—U.S.
        5. Employers' associations—U.S.
        HD9715.U52L498
        338.4'7'6900973—dc21   Library of Congress Catalog Card Number: 99-95101

Recent construction settlements will raise earnings levels for many craftsmen to those of doctors and lawyers unless moderation is achieved.[1]

You cannot increase...construction wages 50 to 60 percent in 3 years...without changing the nature of the United States. ... The No. 1 domestic problem of the country is the effect of the wage push on the total lives of everyone.[2]

[W]age rate wars can break out, much as gasoline price wars do. ... I don't view it as equity that when one chicken gets out of the coop, all the others have to be let out, too.[3]

---

[1]"Finding a Formula with which to Test the Reasonableness of Settlements" at 1 (Oct. 14, 1969) (no author), in NACP, RG 174: General Records of the Labor Dept., Office of the Secretary, Records of the Secretary of Labor George P. Shultz, 1969-1970, Box No. 58: Councils, Folder: 1969 Committee: Cabinet Committee on Construction.

[2]*Economic Prospects and Policies: Hearings Before the Joint Economic Committee*, 92d Cong., 1st Sess. 380 (1971) (testimony of Roger Blough).

[3]Arthur Okun, "Discussion," *BPEA* 3:1971 at 765, 766.

Contents

Tables

Abbreviations

AA	*Applied Anthropology*
AAAPSS	*Annals of the American Academy of Political and Social Science*
AABN	*American Architect and Building News*
ABC	Associated Builders and Contractors
AC	*American Contractor*
AD	*Architectural Design*
AER	*American Economic Review*
AF	*American Federationist*
AFL-CIO	American Federation of Labor-Congress of Industrial Organizations
AGC	Associated General Contractors of America
AJS	*American Journal of Sociology*
AL	*American Labor*
AP	*American Plan*
ASQ	*Administrative Science Quarterly*
ASS	*Archiv für Sozialwissenschaft und Sozialpolitik*
BBL	*Bulletin of the Bureau of Labor*
BCTB	*Building and Construction Trades Bulletin*
BCTD	Building and Construction Trades Department
BEA	Bureau of Economic Analysis
BHR	*Business History Review*
BJA	*Building: A Journal of Architecture*
BJELL	*Berkeley Journal of Employment and Labor Law*
BJIR	*British Journal of Industrial Relations*
BLR	*Buffalo Law Review*
BLS	Bureau of Labor Statistics
BMP	*Bricklayer, Mason and Plasterer*
BPEA	*Brookings Papers on Economic Activity*
BR	Business Roundtable
BSR	*Business and Society Review*
BTC	Building Trades Council
BW	*Business Week*
CB	*Carpenter and Builder*
CC	Coordinating Committee/Construction Committee
CCC	Cabinet Committee on Construction
CCE	Council of Construction Employers
CCH	Construction Committee History
CCI	*Census of Construction Industries*

CCPS	Cabinet Committee on Price Stability
CICEP	Construction Industry Cost Effectiveness Project
CISC	Construction Industry Stabilization Committee
CL	*Construction Lawyer*
CLLJ	*Comparative Labor Law Journal*
CLR	*Construction Labor Report*
CMA	Contractors Mutual Association
CPR	Current Population Reports
CPS	Current Population Survey
CPWR	Center for the Protection of Workers' Rights
CQ	*Congressional Quarterly*
CR	*Construction Review*
CT	*Chicago Tribune*
CUAIR	Construction Users Anti-Inflation Roundtable
CUH	*Construction User Headlines*
CWC	*Compensation and Working Conditions*
CWD	*Current Wage Developments*
DLR	*Daily Labor Report*
DOL	United States Department of Labor
DW	*Daily World*
EE	*Employment and Earnings*
EJ	*Economic Journal*
EO	Executive Order
EWJ	*Electrical Workers' Journal*
F	Federal Reporter
FR	*Federal Register*
FW	*Financial World*
HBR	*Harvard Business Review*
HLR	*Harvard Law Review*
HM	*Harper's Magazine*
IBEW	International Brotherhood of Electrical Workers
IHCBLJ	*International Hod Carriers and Building Laborers' Journal*
ILO	International Labour Organisation
ILR	*International Labour Review*
ILRR	*Industrial and Labor Relations Review*
IOE	*International Operating Engineer*
IR	*Industrial Relations*
IRLJ	*Industrial Relations Law Journal*
IRRA	Industrial Relations Research Association
IST	*International Science & Technology*
IUOE	International Union of Operating Engineers
JAH	*Journal of American History*

JASA	*Journal of the American Statistical Association*
JB	*Journal of Business*
JBMP	*Journal of the Bricklayers, Masons and Plasterers International Union of America*
JCEM	*Journal of Construction Engineering and Management*
JEBH	*Journal of Economic and Business History*
JEWO	*Journal of the Electrical Workers and Operators*
JH	*Journal of Housing*
JIE	*Journal of Industrial Economics*
JLR	*Journal of Labor Research*
JNH	*Journal of Negro History*
JPE	*Journal of Political Economy*
JSH	*Journal of Social History*
JW	*Jahrbuch für Wirtschaftsgeschichte*
LAT	*Los Angeles Times*
LCP	*Law and Contemporary Problems*
LH	*Labor History*
LLJ	*Labor Law Journal*
LRR	*Labor Relations Reporter*
LSJ	*Labor Studies Journal*
LT	*Labor Today*
MARBA	Mid-America Regional Bargaining Association
MCAA	Mechanical Contractors Association of America
MDB	*Monatsberichte der Deutschen Bundesbank*
MLR	*Monthly Labor Review*
MR	*Monthly Review*
MSC	*Merit Shop Contractor*
NAB	National Association of Builders
NACP	National Archives at College Park
NAHB	National Association of Home Builders
NAM	National Association of Manufacturers
NB	*Nation's Business*
NCA	National Constructors Association
NCEC	National Construction Employers Council
NCSA	National Construction Stabilization Agreement
NECA	National Electrical Contractors Association
NICA	National Industrial Construction Agreement
NJ	*National Journal*
NLRA	National Labor Relations Act
NLRB	National Labor Relations Board
NPMS	Nixon Presidential Materials Staff
NY*DN*	New York *Daily News*

NYP	*New York Post*
NYRB	*New York Review of Books*
NYT	*New York Times*
NZ	*Neue Zeit*
NZZ	*Neue Zürcher Zeitung*
PATJ	*Painters and Allied Trades Journal*
PJ	*Painters Journal*
PK	*Probleme des Klassenkampfs*
PM	*Personnel Management*
PPPUS	*Public Papers of the Presidents of the United States*
PRWET	*Pacific Research & World Empire Telegram*
QJE	*Quarterly Journal of Economics*
QREB	*Quarterly Review of Economics and Business*
RD	*Reader's Digest*
RES	*Review of Economics and Statistics*
RG	Record Group
RR	*Roundtable Report*
SCB	*Survey of Current Business*
SF	Subject Files
SP	Soutar Papers
UA	United Association
UAJ	*United Association Journal*
UAQ	*Urban Affairs Quarterly*
UBS	*University of Buffalo Studies*
UCPE	*University of California Publications in Economics*
UCWN	*United Construction Workers News*
UISSS	*University of Illinois Studies in the Social Sciences*
USBC	United States Bureau of the Census
USDC	United States Department of Commerce
USDL	United States Department of Labor
USNWR	*U.S. News and World Report*
WHCF	White House Central File
WLR	*Wayne Law Review*
WP	*Washington Post*
WSJ	*Wall Street Journal*
WZHABW	*Wissenschaftliche Zeitschrift der Hochschule für Architektur und Bauwesen Weimar*

Preface

Nowhere else...is there to be found so cogent a proof of the axiom that unionism in America is merely the other side of capitalism's coin. It is the same coin. It is not a token of any other minting.[1]

The decline of the once quasi-monopolistic construction unions during the last quarter of the twentieth century has, according to activists, "shaken the building trades' wing of the House of Labor to its foundations...."[2] To be sure, construction unions have not been alone in suffering huge losses. In the steel, automobile, rubber, clothing, and other industries unions have also experienced severe decreases in membership.[3] But unlike industrial unions, the building trades were not victims of cheap imports from an inexorably globalizing economy: high-wage union pipefitters building petrochemical and power plants in Texas and Michigan did not lose their jobs to low-paid construction workers in or from China, El Salvador, or Indonesia.[4] Instead, their jobs were taken by compatriots, some of them until recently union brothers, employed by cut-rate antiunion construction firms—some of which had been union firms in good standing. Indeed, some nonunion contractors are subsidiaries of long-time respectable union contractors.[5]

Despite advances in prefabrication and modularization, today, as in the

---

[1]Herbert Harris, *American Labor* 150 (1939) (referring to the United Brotherhood of Carpenters).

[2]Jeff Grabelsky & Mark Erlich, "Recent Innovations in the Building Trades," in *Which Direction for Organized Labor?* 167-89 at 167 (Bruce Nissen ed., 1999).

[3]Leo Troy & Neil Sheflin, *U.S. Union Sourcebook: Membership, Finances, Structure, Directory* B-1-B-17 (1985); *Directory of U.S. Labor Organizations: 1987-87 Edition* 61-65 (Courtney Gifford, 1986); *Directory of U.S. Labor Organizations: 1997 Edition* 81-82 (C. Gifford ed., 1997)

[4]"In many industries, the main reason why labor and management are worried about productivity is that productivity has been growing faster...in Japan or Germany or some other trading partner than in the United States, and that has led to a rising volume of imports. That sort of concern, in the direct sense is really not relevant to the construction industry. We are not worried about Japanese contractors coming in and building American roads or American buildings." Albert Rees, "Measuring Productivity in Construction: An Overview," in National Commission on Productivity and Work Quality, *Measuring Productivity in the Construction Industry* 5-10 at 7 (n.d. [ca. 1973]).

[5]Throughout "open shop" is used interchangeably with "nonunion" and "antiunion." Although employers in this sector assert that they are literally "open shop" because they do not discriminate against individual workers who happen to be union members and who wish to work for them, this meaning is Pickwickian since such employers are vociferously antagonistic to the members' unions and tolerate the individual workers only so long as they refrain from organizing. The disingenuousness of employers' claims to indifference or impartiality became manifest in the 1980s when unions began their "salting" campaigns: employers fired or refused to hire qualified construction workers who were known to be union organizers. See below chapter 15. Historically, unions have taken the position that all shops are closed—either to unionists or nonunionists. William Haber, *Industrial Relations in the Building Industry* 241-45 (1930).

past, buildings largely remain nontransportable commodities so that buyers in one locality must pay the going rate there regardless of cheaper rates elsewhere.[6] However, unlike the situation earlier in the century, the growth of national firms with mobile workforces has meant that industry is no longer so localized that unions can assume that monopolizing the local labor market will also shield the local product market from competition by lower-wage firms.[7] And although a corporate owner requiring a building for a site in Chicago must still have it built in Chicago, it may choose to shift the site to Alabama if construction costs are too high, just as it might close an existing manufacturing plant and open another one in Alabama (or Malaysia) if it decides that the plant workers' demands interfere with profitability.

Unlike their counterparts in manufacturing industries, where employment has plummeted in tandem with unionization, construction workers have significantly increased in number.[8] Moreover, whereas the world market did not begin intimidating U.S. industrial workers until the latter half of the 1970s, construction unions became subject to economic and political attacks a decade earlier during the Vietnam War. This asynchronous development is curious because competitive pressure on the construction industry was largely derivative. As Roger Blough, the leader of the Roundtable, told Congress in 1971: "It is not the direct kind of competition..., but there is definitely indirect competition between construction costs abroad and construction costs in this country" in the sense that "[e]very time you sell a pair of shoes, you are selling a piece" of the factory in which it was manufactured.[9] Since the primary source of these attacks was large industrial owner-customers, which complained that exploding construction wages were driving new plant construction costs to levels at which the products produced in them were becoming less competitive, it is remarkable that manufacturing corporations chose to focus first not on their own employees, but turned instead to construction workers, whose wages represented only a small share of the costs of manufactured products. And finally, much more so than their industrial colleagues, construction workers were attacked by a complex coalition of employers, the state, industrial customers, and the media, intent on breaking unions' control of the supply of skilled building tradesmen.

Construction unions in the early 1970s were subject to the first wave of

---

[6]But see Marc Linder, *Projecting Capitalism: A History of the Internationalization of the Construction Industry* 9-13 (1994) (discussing the export of prefabricated structures).

[7]Royal Montgomery, *Industrial Relations in the Chicago Building Trades* 4 (1927).

[8]From 1979 to 1997, production or nonsupervisory workers in construction rose 23 percent (from 3,565,000 to 4,361,000) whereas those in manufacturing fell 15 percent (from 15,068,000 to 12,809,000). Calculated according to *Handbook of U.S. Labor Statistics* 139 (2d ed.; Eva Jacobs ed. 1998).

[9]*Economic Prospects and Policies: Hearings Before the Joint Economic Committee*, 92d Cong., 1st Sess., pt. 2, at 374 (1971).

demands by employers for concessionary bargaining based on allegedly untenable union-nonunion wage gaps (and productivity-inhibiting work rules).[10] To be sure, similar developments had emerged in the mid-1950s in textiles and in the late 1950s and early 1960s in meatpacking.[11] But those industries differed from construction in that textile wage differences were rooted in North-South differentials, while the newly emerged nonunion meatpacking firms were able to lower wages because they had opened operations in rural areas with capital-intensive technologies that increasingly eliminated the need for large numbers of skilled workers.[12] Nonunion construction firms, in contrast, competed solely on the basis of lower wages and benefits and elimination of union work rules. Wage differentials offered nonunion firms considerable latitude for competitive underbidding: between 1967 and 1975, the union-nonunion wage gap for building craftsmen varied between 30 and 42 percent, while that for laborers ranged between 40 and 48 percent. In contrast, the average in manufacturing industries ranged between -1 and 10 percent and 14 and 24 percent, respectively.[13]

The only roughly comparable developments with regard to wage cuts in 1971-72 in manufacturing took place sporadically except in the rubber industry and at General Motors' Frigidaire division against the background of employers' complaints about a productivity squeeze. Firestone Tire and Rubber Company first threatened to (and later did) open a new plant in Tennessee rather than in Akron unless its union workers accepted the equivalent of a $1.14 (or 19 percent) per hour wage cut. At the Frigidaire plant in Dayton, workers, represented by the International Union of Electrical Workers, worked under collective bargaining agreements similar to those at GM automobile plants; consequently their wages were $2 an hour higher than those at competing appliance manufacturers.

---

[10]The claim that construction was "the first major industry case" of big capital's "union-busting" following management's offensive at the end of the 1950s and beginning of the 1960s, which almost unleashed "a raw re-opening of the class struggle," is exaggerated. Mike Davis, *Prisoners of the American Dream: Politics and Economy in the History of the US Working Class* 132, 123 (1987).

[11]Daniel Mitchell, *Unions, Wages and Inflation* 74 (1980). Even partly unionized firms, such as General Electric, had begun developing strategies in the late 1940s to avoid unions including relocation to the South and opening nonunion parallel production plants duplicating operations in unionized plants in order to counteract strikes. Barry Bluestone & Bennett Harrison, *The Deindustrialization of America: Plant Closings, Community Abandonment, and the Dismantling of Basic Industry* 164-70 (1982).

[12]Hervey Juris, "Union Crisis Wage Decisions," 8 (3) *IR* 247-58 (May 1969). Of the 23 manufacturing industries surveyed by the BLS in the first half of the 1960s, meat packing recorded by far the largest union-nonunion wage gap (66 percent). Vernon Clover, "Compensation in Union and Nonunion Plants, 1960-1965," 21 (2) *ILRR* 226-33 (Jan. 1968).

[13]Orley Ashenfelter, "Union Relative Wage Effects: New Evidence and a Survey of Their Implications for Wage Inflation," in *Economic Contributions to Public Policy: Proceedings of a Conference held by the International Economic Association at Urbino, Italy* 31-60, tab. 2.3 at 37 (Richard Stone & William Peterson eds., 1978).

Following major layoffs, some workers were recalled at wages reduced by 25 cents per hour. As early as 1971, some labor relations analysts perspicaciously viewed Frigidaire as a harbinger of the wage squeeze to which rising imports would sooner or later subject other manufacturers. Nevertheless, at the same time, as construction unemployment rose sharply, union electricians near Cleveland acquiesced in $4 an hour (or 50 percent) wage cuts for one- and two-family housing construction.[14]

Construction employers remained leaders of the norm-breaking wave of union wage concessions in the first half of the 1980s in conjunction with unprecedented depression-level rates of unemployment: the industry accounted for 39 percent of all concessionary collective bargaining settlements between 1981 and 1985.[15] Again, construction differed from most of the other industries being pressed for concessions. Unlike the metals, machinery, lumber, and automobile industries, construction was not subject to foreign competition; and unlike the airlines and trucking industries, it had not been plunged into deregulation. By the time of the depression of the early 1980s, however, construction was no longer unique: not only were other industries (such as retail food stores and printing-publishing) exposed to low-wage nonunion competition, but the demonstration effect,[16] especially among weakly unionized firms, impelled some employers to seek to eliminate unions altogether. Incredibly, 19 percent of large corporation executives polled by *Business Week* in 1982 openly admitted: "Although we don't need concessions, we are taking advantage of the bargaining climate to ask for them."[17] Even while the magazine was editorially condemning such companies as "simply bent on taking unfair advantage of the unions' current weakness,"[18] it noted a paradox: "Despite staggering job losses, building trades unions are still demanding and winning double-digit wage settlements where they have leverage."[19]

And the anomaly continues: despite the decades-long multi-pronged assault, at century's end, hundreds of thousands of construction workers remain highly paid union members. Average hourly union pay scales (including fringe benefits) in 20 large cities reached $34.78 for electricians, $33.90 for plumbers, $28.94 for carpenters, and $23.03 for building laborers in September, 1998. In New

---

[14]Jim Hyatt, "Some Workers Accept Pay Cuts as Alternative to Losing Their Jobs," *WSJ*, July 23, 1971, at 1, col. 6, at 23 col 5; Everett Groseclose, "Increasingly, Workers Give Up Some Benefits So as Not to Lose Jobs," *WSJ*, Jan. 26, 1972, at 1, col. 6, at 27, col. 2.

[15]Daniel J. B. Mitchell, "Shifting Norms in Wage Determination," *BPEA*, No. 2, 1985, at 575-99, tab. 4 at 582.

[16]Mitchell, "Shifting Norms in Wage Determination" at 582-83.

[17]"A Management Split over Labor Relations," *BW*, June 14, 1982, at 19 (Lexis). The poll discerned a divide between firms less than 40 percent and more than 70 percent organized.

[18]"The Best Deal for Labor," *BW*, June 14, 1982, at 128 (Lexis).

[19]"Concessionary Bargaining: Will the New Cooperation Last?" *BW*, June 14, 1982, at 66 (Lexis).

York City, they reached heights barely imaginable to millions of sweatshop and service sector workers: $53.80, $55.66, $50.96, and $36.19, respectively.[20]

The analysis of construction unions' decline during the last quarter of the twentieth century begins with the Vietnam War. One economic consequence of that war's unpopularity—inscribed in Congress's failure to declare war, and the Johnson administration's refusal to subject the economy to formal militarization—was that for the first time in the twentieth century, a "full-employment" wartime economy was not accompanied by wage-price controls.[21] Part I focuses on the contradictory effects of the tight labor market during the Vietnam War. While Chapter 1 deals with employers' disenchantment with the labor militance spawned by diminished fear of unemployment, Chapter 2 documents how heightened power and swiftly rising wage rates misled some unions and workers to overlook that once the boom became a recession, firms employing lower-waged workers might oust some unionized employers. Part II turns to the rhetoric and reality of charges that greedy and tyrannical construction unions had undermined the economy by enabling their members to be grotesquely overpaid and underworked. Chapter 3 dissects the employer-inspired media campaign, while Chapter 4 presents a detailed empirical account of construction workers' wages, unemployment, and annual incomes. The unique underlying sources and most prominent manifestations of construction unions' unusually formidable labor market and workplace power are studied in Chapter 5.

Part III shifts attention to employers. Chapter 6 introduces construction employers' most important organizations and the positions that they adopted on the role of unions, while Chapter 7 is devoted to the extraordinary impact that the Roundtable, an organization of large industrial construction users, exerted on the development of construction labor-management relations. This account is uniquely enriched by first-time-ever access to Roundtable minutes and internal memoranda

---

[20]*ENR*, Sept. 28, 1998, at 31. Despite the severe setbacks sustained by construction unionism overall, John T. Dunlop, the doyen of construction labor relations analysts, insists that, at least in big cities like Detroit, Chicago, New York, and Boston, unions in the mechanical trades, such as electricians and plumbers, are virtually as strong at the end of the twentieth century as they were in the 1960s. Telephone interview with Prof. John T. Dunlop, Harvard University, Cambridge, MA (Jan. 7, 1999). Dunlop appears to stand utterly alone in this view, which all other union and management informants treated derisively. One example of the hyperbolic character of Dunlop's assertion: whereas in 1979 unions could still repel employers' demand for lower wage rates in residential construction in the Chicago area, by 1982 they were forced to make the concession. Richard Schneirov & Thomas Suhrbur, *Unions Brotherhood, Union Town: The History of the Carpenters' Union of Chicago 1863-1987*, at 153-54 (1988). Grabelsky & Erlich, "Recent Innovations in the Building Trades" at 169, note that large commercial and industrial projects in those cities are still "largely union built," but add that even in the immediately surrounding suburbs "union labor can often be found only on megaprojects."

[21]Daniel Quinn Mills, *Industrial Relations and Manpower in Construction* 275 (1972).

relating to the construction industry. Part IV offers an account of the strategies formulated and implemented by the Nixon administration and employers to contain construction unions. Chapter 8 analyzes the first tentative measures taken by the federal government in 1969 and 1970. Efforts by the Nixon administration and employers to use the legal attack on construction unions' racially discriminatory membership policies to weaken their control over the labor market form the substance of Chapter 9, while Chapter 10 examines a similarly structured but less successful program to promote the industrialization of residential construction in order to undermine the role of skilled workers and their unions. The unions' counterattack is scrutinized in Chapter 11, which interprets the pro-war and pro-Nixon demonstrations on Wall Street in May 1970 as a building trades' strategy for luring the administration away from its alliance with anti-construction union employers. Chapter 12 treats the intra-employer debate over and failure to enact national legislation imposing geographically broader collective bargaining units on construction in order to strengthen contractors' negotiating position.   An examination of the Nixon administration's most decisive intervention, the direct wage controls implemented by the Construction Industry Stabilization Committee from 1971 to 1974, constitutes Chapter 13.

The tentative outcome of constructive labor-capital struggles during the last quarter of the twentieth century is taken up in Part V. Unions' failure to enact legislation during the brief Ford administration that might have contained the dynamic of the antiunion movement is studied in Chapter 14, while Chapter 15 extensively views that movement's progress and unions' resistance. Finally, Chapter 16 provides a comparative historical perspective of earlier open-shop movements in construction.

Research for this book began in May 1970 and continued intensively throughout the 1970s and intermittently during the 1980s before becoming full-time again in the 1990s. The vantage point of the end of the century makes it a much more interesting study than it could have been in the early 1970s, when no one foresaw the vast expansion of the nonunion sector. Not even the Roundtable itself, to judge by its initial pessimistic analysis, predicted such a rapid deterioration of construction unionism: "Nor can the prospects for a more effective utilization of non-union construction labor be expected, realistically, to result from any lessening of union membership or allegiance to unions where these are already established...."[22]

Pat Anderson of the Nixon Presidential Materials Staff, Tab Lewis, Textual Archives Service Division, and Clarence Lyons, Jr., Chief, Civilian Records,

---

[22]Anthony Alfino, Algie Hendrix, & Carl Oles, "Manpower Supply in the Construction Industry" 46 (Aug. 11, 1970), in BR, CCH: 1970.

Textual Archives Service Division, of the National Archives and Records Administration at College Park, were all supremely resourceful in locating documents. Linda Seelke at the Lyndon B. Johnson Library in Austin made available additional archival documents. Richard Strassberg, Director of the Kheel Center for Labor-Management Documentation & Archives at Cornell University, was extraordinarily helpful in making available the materials on the Roundtable contained in Douglas Soutar's papers. James Gross, who is responsible for having acquired these papers for the Kheel Center, also made the initial contacts to arrange for their use. Connie Bulkley, a former archivist at the Kheel Center, helped select appropriate materials. The Business Roundtable provided access to the minutes of all its Coordinating/Construction Committee meetings, internal memoranda, and the entire run of its otherwise unavailable *Report* and *Construction User Headlines* as well as access to many former members. Jane Seegal at the Building and Construction Trades Department Center to Protect Workers' Rights provided hard to find materials. Kenneth Hedman, vice president for labor relations at Bechtel Corporation, Ted Kennedy, chairman, BE&K, Inc., Robert McCormick, president of the National Constructors Association, and Douglas Soutar, formerly a key member of the Roundtable, filled in numerous parts of the puzzle. Daniel Quinn Mills, who played an important role in managing federal controls of construction wages in the early 1970s, helped recreate the parties' mindset, while John Dunlop, the institutional memory of construction labor-management relations since World War II, provided useful background information.

Part I

Employer Resentment and Union Overestimation of the Vanishing Reserve Army of the Unemployed

What was wrong with 1968 and 1967? We had full employment. But at what cost? 300 Americans dead every week. That is too high.[1]

---

[1]Richard Nixon, "Remarks to the AFL-CIO Ninth Constitutional Convention of the AFL-CIO in Bal Harbor, Florida, November 19, 1971," in *PPPUS: Richard Nixon: 1971*, at 1118-25 at 1120 (1972).

Military-Industrial Prologue

A major part of the problem in this sector is that there is no central decision group with which a confrontation can accomplish anything. The labor force is highly organized, but in terms of particular craft groups in limited areas. The national leadership has not been eager to be cooperative, but even if it were, it has no power to make California plumbers moderate their claims.[1]

The monumental strategic importance of U.S. economic, especially wage, policies, during the Indochina war loomed over the annual Godkin lectures that Walter Heller delivered at Harvard University in March 1966. As chairman of the Council of Economic Advisers (CEA) under Presidents Kennedy and Johnson, he had been centrally involved in formulating those policies. Heller sketched three ways in which they served the administration's "international aims":

(1) Materially, they provide the wherewithal for foreign aid and defense efforts and for financing Vietnam on a both-guns-and-butter basis.

(2) Ideologically, a vigorous American economy is a showcase of modern capitalism for all the world to see.

(3) Strategically, an expanding economy and a shrinking external payments deficit strengthen the President's hand in international policies. The doubling of our growth rate in the past five years...has strengthened not only the dollar but our strategic position in dealing with our free-world partners.[2]

Generating adequate profits for accumulating productive capital and producing the world's most destructive military machine while maintaining a standard of living that would not undermine workers' acquiescence in the conduct of that war were the crucial goals of the first U.S. administration willing to use "the full range of modern economic tools...."[3] Heller boasted that the "discouraging pattern of recessions every two or three years between 1949 and 1960 has been broken...by a tight coupling of measures to boost demand with measures to boost productivity and hold costs in check." The key was "sizable and sustained productivity advances...." Between 1961 and 1965 this "'great reconciler'...made it possible largely to satisfy the rising income claims of business and labor while holding, or even cutting, unit costs of output. Moderation in wages and profits becomes more bearable when higher productivity, bigger volume, and lower taxes keep take-home pay and profits rising merrily."[4] Specifically, during the first half

---

[1]John Sheahan, *The Wage-Price Guideposts* 39 (1967).

[2]Walter Heller, *New Dimensions in Political Economy* 11 (1967 [1966]).

[3]Heller, *New Dimensions in Political Economy* at 1.

[4]Heller, *New Dimensions in Political Economy* at 73-74.

of the decade, after-tax corporate profits doubled, while the average weekly take-home wage in manufacturing rose by 18 percent compared to a 1 percent decline in the latter half of the 1950s.[5]

The material and legitimacy-sustaining foundations of the prosperity phase of the business cycle, Heller told his Harvard audience, could, however, easily be jeopardized in "an economy overheated by the demands of the war in Vietnam...." If the national government were forced to "take some of the inflationary steam out of private spending on plant and equipment," the untoward results might include: a slower increase in manufacturing capacity for a "Vietnam-charged economy"; a reduction in employment; interruption of plant modernization and expansion; and loss of business confidence. And the Hobson's choice confronting the federal government meant that if it decided that this set of possible outcomes was too risky, it might nevertheless face the following costs of inaction: inflation, "intensified labor shortages, and growing delivery lags in machinery, equipment, and construction"; "reinforcement of wage demands leading to increases in unit labor costs"; and the "creation of future excess capacity to bedevil a post-Vietnam economy."[6]

Heller articulated these contradictory forces before he could foresee either the multidimensional debacle that the war would soon become for the United States or the crucial role that construction workers would play in frustrating the military-industrial game plan. In May 1964, when asked at a press conference about what had become the longest upswing in peacetime, President Johnson had cautioned: "We would not say for a moment...that recessions are not possible."[7] Two weeks later Heller wrote him a memorandum titled, "Thinking Ahead to the Next Recession," reminding Johnson: "It may seem a bit strange to talk about the next recession when there's none in sight and we're in the midst of a lusty, lean, and lively expansion--but expansions do eventually peter out."[8] Yet just a few months later, against the background of the "unparalleled economic achievements of these past four years," Johnson in his 1965 *Economic Report of the President* boasted: "*I do not believe recessions are inevitable.* Up to now, every past expansion has ended in recession or depression—usually within three years from its start. But the vulnerability of an expansion cannot be determined by the calendar. ... In principle, public measures can head off recessions before they start."[9]

---

[5]Heller, *New Dimensions in Political Economy* at 77.

[6]Heller, *New Dimensions in Political Economy* at 6.

[7]"The President's News Conference Held on the South Lawn of the White House," in *PPPUS: Lyndon B. Johnson: 1963-64*, Book I, 615-22 at 622 ([May 6, 1964] 1965).

[8]"Walter Heller, "Memorandum for the President: Subject: Thinking Ahead to the Next Recession" 1, EX FG 11-3 (5/21/64-7/20/64), LBJ Library (May 21, 1964).

[9]*Economic Report of the President* 5, 10 (1965).

The hubris that characterized U.S. policy[10] was poignantly on display in January 1967 when Secretary of Defense Robert McNamara testified before the Senate Committees on Armed Services and Appropriations. A skeptical senator engaged him in the following colloquy:

> Senator SYMINGTON: My question is, how long can this Nation afford to continue the gigantic financial cost incident to this major ground war in Asia, without its economy becoming nonviable?
>
> Secretary MCNAMARA: I think forever, and I say it for this reason: That there are many things, many prices we pay for the war in South Vietnam, some very heavy prices indeed, but in my opinion one of them is not strain on our economy.[11]

Because "forever" is such a long time that even a Vietnam war booster could imagine that senators might regard his claim as "completely incomprehensible," McNamara found it prudent to make it sound more plausible. He observed that the Department of Defense budget, which had amounted to $50 billion in 1963, would in any event have risen to $55 billion by 1967 by virtue of pay increases. The actual increase to $68 billion represented 8.9 percent of GNP, compared to 8.7 percent in 1963, because GNP itself had risen so "dramatically." Consequently:

> I don't see how it can be said that the defense burden, heavy as it is, is distorting our economy. I don't think it is. That is why the price increase was as small as it was. That is why we are able to carry on these operations without materiel controls, and that is why we don't have either wage or price controls planned. ...
>
> What I am really saying to you gentlemen is that with as serious a problem as we are having in Vietnam, and God knows it is serious, it isn't money that is worrying me. [I]t is not at the moment an insuperable financial burden for us. Nor do I think that in the future a defense budget as high as 9 percent of our GNP would constitute such a burden. I think we

---

[10]By 1969, a former member of Johnson's CEA, arguing that the continued absence of recession had rendered Johnson's belief uncontroversial, spoke of "the obsolescence of the business cycle pattern." Consequently: "Today few research economists regard the business cycle as a particularly useful organizing framework for the overall analysis of current economic activity, and few teachers see 'business cycles' as as appropriate title for a course to be offered to their students." Arthur Okun, *The Political Economy of Prosperity* 37, 33 (1970).

[11]*Supplemental Military Procurement and Construction Authorizations, Fiscal Year 1967: Hearings Before the Senate Committee on Armed Services and the Subcommittee on Department of Defense of the Senate Committee on Appropriations*, 90th Cong., 1st Sess. 96 (1967). See also Arnold Weber & Daniel Mitchell, *The Pay Board's Progress: Wage Controls in Phase II*, at 258 (1978): "During World War II and the Korean War considerable emphasis had been placed on maintaining labor peace as well as on economic stabilization. The Phase II venture in controls took place in quite a different context. The requirements of the Vietnam conflict did not necessitate the concerted mobilization of the nation's resources."

can sustain that kind of load in the future.[12]

Contrary to McNamara's assurances, however, in 1965 the Johnson administration had "massively escalated the war at the worst possible moment for the economy, just as the country was completing a long, hard climb toward the economists' nirvana—full employment without inflation." Johnson, "[d]etermined to have both guns and butter...set in motion the most virulent inflation in the country's history."[13] In consequence, labor markets in 1966-1968 "became disorganized...under the impact of the sudden, unexpected upsurge" of war spending. The two million workers siphoned off into the "war effort"—about two-fifths of the total increase in the labor force—lowered the unemployment rate to 3.8 percent. This forced achievement of a rate below the 4 percent set as a target by the CEA in 1962 "set off a sharp increase in wages and prices."[14]

As U.S. military forces in Vietnam expanded to well over a half million by 1968,[15] the total cost of the war rose almost 300-fold from $100 million in 1965 to $28.9 billion in 1969, the year of peak expenditures.[16] By 1968, war expenditures alone consumed 3.2 percent of GNP,[17] while total military outlays at $78 billion exceeded 9 percent of GNP.[18] Once Johnson had committed the United States to a massive land war, military purchases, at seasonally adjusted annual rates, increased from $50.3 billion in the third quarter of 1965 to $72.5 billion by the second quarter of 1967.[19] When GNP increased by the largest amount in history in the last quarter of 1965 and unemployment fell to 4 percent, economists recognized that inflation was "inevitable." Significantly, however, the initial inflationary pressure arose in "highly competitive" "unorganized labor-intensive, low-wage sectors" such as raw materials and services and not in sectors dominated by "monopolistic firms and big

---

[12]*Supplemental Military Procurement and Construction Authorizations, Fiscal Year 1967*, at 97. The AFL-CIO Executive Council agreed with McNamara; see "Economy Has Ability to Meet Both Military, Social Needs," *AFL-CIO News*, Mar. 2, 1968, at 7. The sovereign disregard of the war repeated itself during the Nixon administration, when the August 15, 1971 wage-price controls were called the country's first peacetime control even though the "war still raged in Vietnam." Hugh Rockoff, *Drastic Measures: A History of Wage and Price Controls in the United States* 200 (1984).

[13]Robert Stevens, *Vain Hopes, Grim Realities: The Economic Consequences of the Vietnam War* 6 (1976).

[14]Stevens, *Vain Hopes* at 79.

[15]USBC, *Statistical Abstract of the United States: 1972*, tab. 421 at 260 (1972).

[16]Expenditures amounted to $5.8 billion, $20.1 billion, and $26.5 billion in 1966, 1967, and 1968, respectively. Anthony Campagna, *The Economic Consequences of the Vietnam War*, tab. 5.2 at 83 (1991).

[17]Stevens, *Vain Hopes*, tab. 8-6 at 99.

[18]Calculated according to *Economic Report of the President 1973*, tab. C-1 at 193 (1973).

[19]Committee for Economic Development, *The National Economy and the Vietnam War*, Appendix A, tab. 4, at 75, chart 3 at 22 (1968). See also Center for Strategic Studies, *Economic Impact of the Vietnam War* 72-75 (1967) (written by Murray Weidenbaum)

unions."[20]

To be sure, mainstream and administration economists strove to portray these changes in a relatively harmless light. For example, Arthur Okun, who had been a member and chairman of Johnson's CEA, described the major problem facing the federal government between 1961 and mid-1965 as "inadequate total demand" and the main task as "invigorat[ing] the economy." At that juncture, however, once "noninflationary prosperity" had been achieved, "the normal challenges of high employment," Okun conceded at his Crawley Memorial Lectures at the Wharton School in April 1969, "became immensely complicated by the upsurge in defense spending."[21]

The economic and political obstacles to controlling a low-unemployment militarized economy without traditional wartime controls made themselves felt soon enough. In this context, one of the salient differences between manufacturing and construction is symbolized by a memo that Heller wrote to President Johnson a few days after the assassination of President Kennedy in 1963. Relating the substance of a long meeting with the president of the United Automobile Workers (UAW), Heller reported that Walter Reuther had told him "in the most emphatic terms possible" that the union would be "going for a whopping wage increase" in 1964, especially from General Motors:

He mentioned no numbers, but it is clear that what he's after would give a big shove to the price-wage spiral. He says they're going to "unburden" GM (whose after-tax profits in the 12 months ending in September were $1.6 billion) of the biggest chunk of profits any company ever parted with.

Our arguments about socially responsible collective bargaining, the need for price stability, and so on, made no apparent dent. He claims rank-and-file pressures require a dramatic settlement; that the AFL-CIO have been good boys long enough; that labor's share of income has been slipping while the corporations have been racking up unwarranted price increases.

He's confident he'll have a good case with the public. ... And he's tired of remaining moderate while the irresponsibles in the labor movement like Hoffa and the Building Trades are pushing inflationary wage increases with impunity.

We have been hoping the "good unions" could be persuaded to take it easy for at

---

[20]Okun, *Political Economy of Prosperity* at 66. The chairman of Johnson's CEA, Gardner Ackley, insisted that the administration's wage "guideposts weren't intended to hold down wage increases of unorganized or weakly organized workers" that were brought about not by union power, but by employers' need to attract more labor. Ackley stressed, however, that if such low-wage workers' wage increases exceeded the national trend in productivity increases, while unionized workers' wage increases matched productivity increases, "there is an unavoidable inflationary bias in the economy." *Congressional Review of Price-Wage Guideposts: Hearing Before a Subcommittee of the House Committee on Government Operations,* 89th Cong., 2d Sess. 110 (1966).

[21]Okun, *Political Economic of Prosperity* at 43, 44, 62.

least another year while the economy was getting back toward full employment.[22]

In early 1966, the new CEA chairman, Gardner Ackley, sounded a similar theme. In a memo to Johnson bearing the ironic title, "The Solid Gold Cadillac," Ackley explained the UAW's renewed push for strong wage increases: "The source of the problem is fantastic automobile profits." GM's more than $2 billion in profits amounted to "a 26% after-tax return on equity (a figure more reasonably associated with a newly opened gold mine). There has never been a profit record like this in the history of American industry." Because such profits revealed how the administration's wage-price guideposts had failed: "If we can't pull their prices down, Reuther will go after their profits in 1967 with a huge wage demand. And he will get it. Workers in other industries will surely try to follow him, touching off a massive wage-price spiral."[23]

In contrast, redistributing excess profits to wages rarely played a part in justifying construction unions' demands for higher wages.[24] It had been a long time since the Carpenters' union monthly magazine had published "What We Earn and What Our Bosses Pocket," using the 1880 census data to calculate wages, capital, and profits[25]—followed two months later by the front-page announcement of Karl Marx's death.[26]

---

[22]Walter Heller, "Memorandum for the President: Subject: Prices and Wages in 1964" at 1, Dec. 6, 1963, EX FI, 11/22/63-12/14/63, LBJ Library.

[23]Ackley to the President, "The Solid Gold Cadillac," Mar. 6, 1966, Papers of Stanley W. Black; quoted in James Cochrane, "The Johnson Administration: Moral Suasion Goes to War," in *Exhortation and Controls: The Search for a Wage-Price Policy 1945-1971*, at 193-293 at 248 (Craufurd Goodwin ed., 1971).

[24]Danel Quinn Mills, *Industrial Relations and Manpower in Construction* 78 (1972), found no statistically significant correlation between changes in profit rates and wage rates.

[25]"What We Earn and What Our Bosses Pocket," 3 (2) *Carpenter* 4 (Feb. 1883).

[26]3 (4) *Carpenter* 1 (Apr. 1883).

1

The Vietnam War and the Labor Market: The Johnson Administration

The construction industry must be able to react to labor market conditions on an instantaneous basis. The work force is highly transient and it responds immediately to a better offer, even if only for a few cents per hour.[1]

We have flexibility unknown anywhere else in the Western world. When we need another 10, 20 or 100 pipefitters, we call the union hall, and within a reasonably short period we have these men working. Conversely, when our volume drops, these men are sent back to their labor depository to be called to work by some other contractor.[2]

Disputes between labor and capital, as organized by trade unions operating to secure for their members "an improved status in the existing economic order," come down to "a struggle over the supply of labor...." Workers seek to create "'social arrangements'" that make labor scarce and dear, whereas employers want labor that is plentiful and cheap. From such a direct confrontation resulted, according to the eminent economist Alvin Hansen, "an unavoidable conflict of interest and an inevitable struggle."[3] In spite of decades of experience with cycles of such conflicts, employers and the state in the late 1960s reacted as if they had never before been exposed to the realities of a tight labor market.

At the end of 1950s, when the rate of unemployment in construction ran as high as 13 to 15 percent, unions had not been in a position to take full advantage of locally favorable circumstances. Their moderation on the St. Lawrence Seaway project, for example, resulted from the insight that the "only realistic wage policy" on such projects was "one which will enable them to preserve their bargaining power in the long run by consistently attempting to fulfill their labor-contractual obligations to employers in the short run." Because local contractors had a "limited ability to pay, union policy is to keep those employers competitive in the labor market by forgoing high wage rates on the large projects."[4] The absorption of the

---

[1]Letter from Nello Teer, president, Associated General Contractors, to Donald Irwin, administrator, Office of Wage Stabilization, Cost of Living Council, Mar. 25, 1974, in *CLR*, No. 964, Apr. 3, 1974, at G-1.

[2]D. Quinn Mills, "Chapter 2: Construction," in *Collective Bargaining: Contemporary American Experience* II-22 (Gerald Somers ed., 1979), quoting Walter Kardy, executive vice-president, Mechanical Contractors Association of America, speech before the 17th Annual Construction Conference of the Builders Exchange of Columbus, Ohio, Feb. 17, 1977, mimeo.

[3]Alvin Hansen, "The Economics of Unionism," 30 (4) *JPE* 518-30 at 519 (Aug. 1922).

[4]D. Cullen, "Union Wage Policy in Heavy Construction," 49 (1) *AER* 68-84 at 77 (Mar.

reserve army of the unemployed in construction and the economy at large in the late 1960s, however, prompted workers to ignore mediating the long and short runs.

High unemployment in the late 1950s and early 1960s prompted renewed interest in such phenomena as technological and structural unemployment brought on by automation, foreign competition, and plant relocation. Congress responded by enacting the Manpower Development and Training Act of 1962[5] to subsidize training or retraining to "forestall" potential "resistance and unrest among the affected workforce."[6] When the country's first official *Manpower Report* estimated in 1963 that 2.4 million additional construction journeymen would be needed by 1970,[7] building trades unions were not impressed by the accompanying "wave of hysteria" calling for "fragmentation of our crafts" and government take-over of the "time-tested" apprenticeship programs, jointly administered by unions and management, that had "produced the journeymen who built America." After all, they argued, with the unemployment rate in construction at 18 percent in 1963 and never below 12 percent since 1957, and "our high mobility rate, no job in years had suffered from lack of available skilled labor."[8] Moreover, localized shortages typically resulted from contractors' "notorious[] nonchalance" about planning: even on large projects, they often bid without surveying labor availability, letting unions "worry" about recruitment.[9]

As early as March 1965, the president of the National Constructors Association (NCA), the organization of the largest firms building the largest industrial plants, declared that for the first time (apart from the Korean War) since World War II "acute manpower shortages" in some trades in some localities were "'almost certain'" to develop. Speaking at the NCA's annual dinner in honor of its collective bargaining partners, the officers of the AFL-CIO Building and Construction Trades Department (BCTD)[10] and the presidents of its affiliated

---

1959). See also Donald Cullen, "Labor Market Aspects of the St. Lawrence Seaway Project," 68 (3) *JPE* 232-51 (June 1960).

[5]Pub. L. No. 87-415, 76 Stat. 23 (1962).

[6]Saul Blaustein, *Unemployment Insurance in the United States: The First Half Century* 30 (1993) (quote); Paul Brinker, *Economic Insecurity and Social Security* 281-91 (1968).

[7]*Manpower Report of the President* tab. F-6 at 198 (1963).

[8]BCTD Executive Council, "Manpower Needs in the Construction Industry" (Nov. 1963), in Subcommittee on Employment and Manpower of the Senate Committee on Labor and Public Welfare, 88th Cong., 2d Sess., 3 *Selected Readings in Employment and Manpower: The Role of Apprenticeship in Manpower Development: United States and Western Europe* 1157, 1158 (Comm. Print 1964). For an overview of apprenticeship programs, see DOL, Labor-Management Services Adm., *Admission and Apprenticeship in the Building Trades Unions* (1971).

[9]Daniel Mills, "Factors Determining Patterns of Employment and Unemployment in the Construction Industry of the United States" 241 (Ph.D. diss., Harvard U., 1967).

[10]The BCTD, which dates back to 1908, arose as a response to jurisdictional disputes among interdependent trades and their unions in an era of rapid technological change. Robert Christie,

unions, William Sheets complained that tightening of skilled labor supplies associated with the rapid increase in industrial plant construction might not be so "readily overcome by the automatic influx of workers from areas of labor surplus because labor mobility" had declined considerably in recent years. The reason for this new construction labor market structure, according to Sheets, was both a material increase in unemployment benefits and an enhanced economic status for the craftsman: "'He has developed interest in his community resulting in more permanent roots. As a result the average worker now tends to wait awhile between jobs at home instead of going far afield in search of work.'" Locally established benefits such as vacation plans and health and welfare funds, because they require workers to work in their local union's jurisdiction to remain eligible, tended "'to immobilize the construction worker and remove him from the boomer class.'"[11]

Hypermobility had long been the hallmark of the construction labor force in the United States. As far back as 1880, the Census Office, discussing the ramifications of "the well-known tendency to the concentration of labor and capital in large shops and factories," referred to "the immense extension of the contract system of erecting buildings, the effect of which is to disconnect an increasing proportion of the working carpenters of every city or large town from actual shops and constitute them a movable, readily disposable force, to be hired now by this contractor and now by that...."[12] Whether large industrial construction employers really preferred the structure of a bygone period when, because of his high degree of mobility, the building worker "tend[ed] to develop a more cosmopolitan outlook," "d[id] not identify himself with any local section or group," and was "disinterested in purely local affairs,"[13] no longer mattered. Although the NCA saw no easy way out of the predicament of spatially balkanized construction labor markets, which left an employer "'hamstrung by a lack of men'" in San Francisco

---

Empire in Wood: A History of the Carpenters' Union 120-36 (1956). The BCTD was founded to promote the formation of local building trade councils, make more uniform demands on employers, and mediate in local and national disputes between unions and local councils and employers. Albert Helbing, *The Departments of the American Federation of Labor* 13-39 (1931); William Spencer, "The Building Trades as Organized Prior to the Formation of the Building Trades Department," 23 *AF* 558-63 (1916). On an earlier national federation of local councils, which resulted from the rise of large inter-city construction firms, the National (and later International) Building Trades Council, and the short-lived Structural Building Trades Alliance, see William Kirk, *National Labor Federations in the United States* 79-105 (1906); George Barnett, "The Dominance of the National Union in American Labor Organization," 27 *QJE* 455-81 at 474-80 (May 1913); Theodore Glocker, "Amalgamation of Related Trades in American Unions," 5 (3) *AER* 554-75 at 556 (Sept. 1915).

[11]"Acute Shortage of Skilled Craftsmen in Some Areas Looming This Year, President Sheets of NCA Asserts," *CLR*, No. 496, Mar. 24, 1965, at A-5-A-6.

[12]Census Office, *Compendium of the Tenth Census (June 1, 1880)*, pt. II at 926, 927 (1883).

[13]Richard Myers, "The Building Workers: A Study of an Industrial Sub-Culture" 39 (Ph.D. diss., U. Michigan, 1945).

without access to an abundant supply of unemployed workers in New York
"'unwilling to travel,'" Sheets warned that "'wasteful overtime'" was not the
solution because their customers, large industrial corporations, would not pay for
it. Finally, the NCA president cautioned that if the industry failed to solve the
problem of an adequate labor supply through apprenticeship and other programs,
the government would intervene: "'Gentlemen, as you know, there are strange
forces in the land. The winds of social, political and economic change are blowing.
Shortly, Title VII of the Civil Rights Act will become effective.'"[14]

Analysts had long emphasized construction unions' unique function as a
labor supply agency and "as a means of moving labor away from areas of surplus
to areas in short supply."[15]   Indeed, labor historians identified geographic labor
mobility as the basis in the nineteenth century of (initially weak) national building
trades unions in an industry lacking a national market.[16] In the nineteenth century,
before the rise of a national union, travelling journeymen were considered an
important source of the oversupply of labor and strikebreakers.[17] In the 1920s, too,
"[m]ost of the heavy construction...was still being performed by large nonunion
contractors who recruited crews in low-wage areas, transported them to the job site
where they were housed in tent camps surrounded by barbed wire, and patrolled by
armed guards, if necessary, to keep union organizers out. When the job was
finished, the contractor often dumped his crew on the local community and
recruited another for his next job."[18] By the 1960s, however, employers, however,
were unanimously of the opinion that the construction worker no longer "must be
prepared to be a nomad."[19]

Three months after the NCA dinner, a leader of another major construction
employers' organization, Associated General Contractors of America (AGC),

---

[14]"Acute Shortage of Skilled Craftsmen in Some Areas Looming This Year, President Sheets of NCA Asserts," at A-5-A-6.

[15]John Dunlop, "Labor-Management Relations," in *Design and the Production of Houses* 259-301at 262 (Burnham Kelly ed., 1959).

[16]Lloyd Ulman, *The Rise of the National Trade Union: The Development and Significance of Its Structure, Governing Institutions, and Economic Policies* 45, 52 (1966 [1955]). As early as the 1880s, some of these migrations were induced by the multistate operations of large construction firms. Mobility was also a product of the seriatim building of boom towns in the West: following the intitial construction period, the oversupply of workers migrated to the next one. *Id.* at 55-56, 59-60.

[17]Martin Segal, *The Rise of the United Association: National Unionism in the Pipe Trades, 1884-1924,* at 22, 35 (1970).

[18]Garth Mangum, *The Operating Engineers: The Economic History of a Trade Union* 251-52 (1964).

[19]ILO, Building, Civil Engineering and Public Works Committee, 7th Sess., Report II: *Technological Changes in the Construction Industry and Their Socio-Economic Consequences* 8 (1964). For a novelistic account of nationwide migration by the unemployed during the 1930s to build a tunnel in West Virginia, see Hubert Skidmore, *Hawk's Nest* (1941).

deployed the diametrically opposed claim to explain why unionized building tradesmen, "'an elite corps within the house of labor,'" were successfully demanding wage increases so out of line with productivity that they were creating an imbalance with the rest of the economy, which ultimately came "'out of the pockets of workmen in other industries for housing and other construction services.'" The reason, according to Carl Halvorson, was simple: local union leaders, possessing what "'amounts to a legal monopoly...can shut down an entire city or state by simply calling a strike or by putting pickets on jobs.'" And whereas the NCA was protesting that workers created artificial labor market shortages by refusing to move, the AGC ascribed their power to their ability during a strike to "'go elsewhere [while] the construction job shuts down.'" To dampen this "'wave of irresponsible wage demands,'" Halvorson urged Congress not to repeal the provision in the Taft-Hartley Act authorizing state "right-to-work" laws, which sustained the "'open-shop threat.'"[20]

By the first days of 1966, as the Vietnam war began to shape the national economy, the federal "government [wa]s starting to worry publicly about developing shortages of labor and point[ed] to the construction industry as one area where the manpower situation is tight." The Commissioner of Labor Statistics, Arthur Ross, observed that this "undersupply" would be exacerbated during the coming year by "increased defense production and absorption of greater numbers of men into the military service."[21] At the same time, the CEA, noting the above-average increase in construction prices and wages as partly reflecting prosperity, urged: "Ways must be found to expand more quickly the supply of skilled construction labor" as well as to promote geographic mobility. Overall the Council warned: "Construction is clearly an industry that raises serious problems for wage-price stability."[22]

Secretary of Labor Willard Wirtz, concerned about recent high construction wage settlements, dropped a hint to John Dunlop, the impartial chairman of the Construction Industry Joint Conference—which assembled national labor organizations and contractor associations to resolve common problems—that

---

[20]"AGC Views 'Spiraling Wage-Fringe Increases' with Alarm, Says They Are Far Outrunning Rise in Productivity," *CLR*, No. 510, June 30, 1965, at A-6, A-7. A few years later, Halvorson sugested teaching building trades in high schools to break the union "monopoly." "Construction Problems are Political, Sociological," *ENR*, Mar. 27, 1969, at 28.

[21]"Concern Voiced over Tightening Supply of Labor," *CLR*, No. 538, Jan. 12, 1966, at A-5. For more detailed contemporaneous labor market analyses by Ross and Secretary of Labor Willard Wirtz, see *January 1966 Economic Report of the President: Hearings Before the Joint Economic Committee of the Congress*, 89th Cong., 2d Sess. 273-385 (1966). The federal government (chiefly the Department of Defense) was itself the country's largest employer of construction craft workers, employing 72,400 in 1967 and 64,500 in 1972. Arthur Gartagnis, "Trends in Federal Employment, 1958-72," 97 (10) *MLR* 17-25 at 21, 23 (Oct. 1974).

[22]*Economic Report of the President* 78, 85-86 (1966).

industry self-control would be preferable to government intervention. Supported by the AGC, Dunlop drafted a proposal that would have authorized national unions and national contractor associations to mediate local disputes. In addition to the unsurprising resistance of local unions at a time when labor markets were favorable to workers, the national unions themselves unanimously rejected the administration's proposal as calculated to "produce unjustified limitations on wage increases." The president of the BCTD, C.J. Haggerty, second-guessing his own decision, conceded that the unions' rejection might induce the federal government to consider direct wage controls, but also expressed hope that the government would not retaliate by withholding funds from federal construction projects.[23]

The BCTD also publicly expressed its irritation with the administration's wage guidelines, which the CEA had established in 1962 in principle by reference to the annual economy-wide productivity increase, and then quantified at 3.2 percent in 1966.[24] At the same time, the BCTD suggested that the U.S. Department of Labor (DOL) might have been trying to pressure the unions to comply with the guidelines when it influenced the Department of Justice to file a discrimination suit against the Building and Construction Trades Council of St. Louis for having walked off a federal construction project in response to the presence of a black plumber and two black helpers.[25] The construction unions' open declaration that they would ignore the guidelines prompted *The New York Times* to suggest that the

---

[23]"National Machinery to Mediate Local Contract Disputes Goes to Union Chiefs for Discussion Later This Month," *CLR*, No. 543, Feb. 9, 1966, at A-11; Damon Stetson, "Building Trades Bar U.S. Efforts to Curb Pay Rises," *NYT*, Feb. 18, 1966, at 1, col. 3; "National Settlement Plan Vetoed by Union Presidents as Unwarranted Attempt to Impose Wage Restrictions," *CLR*, No. 544, Feb. 23, 1966, at A-7, A-8; William Burke, "Hammering on Guideposts," Federal Reserve Bank of San Francisco, *MR*, Apr. 1966, at 87-94 at 93-94. The national unions also buttressed their rejection with the claim that the Landrum-Griffin Act had undermined their power over the locals, leading to an increasing number of contract settlement rejections by the rank and file—a claim that the Chamber of Commerce conveniently resurrected in 1975 (a time of high unemployment) when employers' organizations opposed legislative enactment of a similar plan, which the national unions supported. "Halvorson, Haggerty at Odds over Factors Underlying President's Cutback Directive," *CLR*, No. 729, Sept. 10, 1969, at A-2; "Landrum-Griffin Viewed as Fomenter of Rank-and-File Unrest in Unions," *CLR*, No. 732, Oct. 1, 1969, at A-11. The Department of Commerce also published an article on missile site construction arguing that transient labor's "independence of spirit" made resolution of labor problems through existing local union leadership more difficult. Local union control over the individual crafts was further weakened by the relatively high proportion of transient workers who constituted the effective local craft union membership at any one time. Wayne Howard, "The Missile Sites Labor Commission," 16 (2) *CR* 4-15 at 5 (Feb. 1970).

[24]*Economic Report of the President* 189 (1962); *Economic Report of the President* 92 (1966).

[25]Damon Stetson, "Labor Chiefs Increasingly Irked by Administration Pay Guideline," *NYT*, Feb. 16, 1966, at 47, col. 1. Haggerty claimed that the walk-out did not constitute racial discrimination, but merely unwillingness to work with persons not members of AFL-CIO unions. See below chapter 9.

rest of labor might follow these "most persistent flouters...."[26]

In March, *The Manpower Report of the President* pointed to the looming tight construction labor markets.[27] At the same time, Secretary Wirtz was informing President Johnson that employers would support a proposed tax increase "'because they think it will restore enough unemployment to be a buffer against extreme wage demands and labor shortages.'"[28] The AGC took advantage of the opportunity to repeat longstanding demands to fortify managerial power. To insure "the maximum utilization of skilled workers," it urged an end to featherbedding and the use of skilled workers to perform unskilled tasks, and the training of specialists and shorter training periods.[29]

A *New York Times* front-page report in late March on its survey of 20 major labor markets revealed employers' disenchantment with the consequences of the decline in the unemployment rate to 3.7 percent. As the coercive fear of unemployment disappeared: "The shortage of workers is leading to greater opportunities for many employes [sic], and an increasing number of them seem to be showing more independence." The high quit rate prompted one employer to complain that employees "'can select the shift they want, write their own ticket on things like this.... They'll leave now at the drop of a hat.'" A laundry company official lamented that workers "'[w]alk out at lunch or leave at night and you don't see them any more.'" The tight labor market extended even to unskilled labor, pushing its cost up 30 percent in Chicago, where the unemployment rate was only 2.5 percent. One state employment agency official likened the job market to that prevailing during World War II.[30]

The ostensibly labor-friendly Johnson administration[31] could not overtly bemoan the collapse of the class-disciplinary function of unemployment, but was, according to the *Times* report, "worried...because manpower shortages can force employers to bid against each other for the same workers"; since the government assumed that employers' product market power enabled them to maintain profit levels, it saw higher wages as promoting inflation. Ironically, the solution lay in

---

[26]"Tottering Guideposts," *NYT*, Feb. 19, 1966, at 26, col. 2 (editorial).

[27]*The Manpower Report of the President* 17, 42 (1966).

[28]Cathie Martin, *Shifting the Burden: The Struggle over Growth and Corporate Taxation* 83 (Chicago: U. Chicago P., 1991) (citing Memo, Secretary of Labor to LBJ, "The Economy and the Government," 3/17/66, CF F111, Taxation, LBJ).

[29]"AGC Urges Steps to Ease 'Acute' Manpower Shortages, Asks Joint Machinery to Moderate Wage Settlements," *CLR*, No. 548, Mar. 23, 1966, at A-1, A-2.

[30]David Jones, "Manpower Needs Grow Across U.S.," *NYT*, Mar. 27, 1966, at 1, col. 2, at 82, col. 4-7.

[31]On the Johnson administration's frustration of labor's best chance to repeal the provision in the NLRA permitting states to enact statutes banning union shops and its acquiescence in big business's opposition to repeal, see Thomas Ferguson & Joel Rogers, *Right Turn: The Decline of the Democrats and the Future of American Politics* 61-63 (1986).

dismantling discriminatory restrictions of the labor supply: Johnson "asked employers to reconsider requirements so that jobs normally done by adult men could be done by women, teen-agers, the handicapped and immigrants"; and in the South some industrial employers apparently preferred the wage-depressing impact of hiring blacks for the first time to the ideological benefits of workplace segregation.[32]

Shortages led to "pirating of manpower": firms in Chicago, for example, recruited craftsmen away from competitors with promises of premium overtime. The Builders Association of Chicago obligated its members to avoid scheduled overtime because it "'leads to a cut-throat rat race that isn't good for the industry.'"[33] Despite the Pickwickian application of "cut-throat" to a boom that warranted paying above-average wages, employers' self-help measures appeared inadequate to deal with the labor market turbulence.[34] A big business consultant observing the industry in 1968-69—when unemployment rates fell as low as 1.6 percent for electricians, 2.0 percent for plumbers and pipefitters, and 3.2 percent for structural metalworkers and bricklayers[35]—portrayed employers' worst nightmare of "the virtually absolute control unions have over the supply of manpower" coupled with low unemployment:

> Skilled craftsmen, knowing that they are so much in demand that they can always find work, have no qualms about not reporting for work whenever they please, or leaving one job for another if they don't like their working conditions or anything else about a job. The manpower shortage also leads some employers to offer skilled craftsmen non-contract benefits as an inducement to leave another job for their own, which compounds the problem of turnover and absenteeism.
>
> As a result...it is extremely difficult to discipline an employee for absenteeism or any rule violation, because the employee is likely to quit and go to another job where he is desperately needed.[36]

Haplessly exposed to insubordination they perceived as verging on anarchy,

---

[32]Jones, "Manpower Needs Grow Across U.S.," at 1, col. 2, at 82, col. 4-7.

[33]"Chicago Employer Groups Impose Overtime Ban in Effort to Restrain 'Pirating' of Workers," *CLR*, No. 546, Mar. 9, 1966, at A-3.

[34]Lloyd Reynolds, "Cutthroat Competition," 30 *AER* 736 (1940). By the end of 1966, a NASA official offered a much more intelligible critique of overtime—namely, that it makes labor less efficient. By the same token, "curtailing it in a skill-shortage market merely stimulates moonlighting, with the same loss of efficiency." His proposed solution was to couple opposition by union leaders to the extra work that members liked with increases in the work force at which point further increases in hourly rates would "make sense." "Blame for Rising Construction Costs Pinned on Both Management, Labor," *CLR*, No. 588, Dec. 28, 1966, at A-1, A-2.

[35]Mills, *Industrial Relations and Manpower in Construction*, tab. 11 at 90.

[36]M. R. Lefkoe, *The Crisis in Construction: There Is an Answer* 5 (1970).

employers, who had come to regard their panoply of managerial powers and prerogatives as second nature, urgently called for state intervention to restore normalcy. Institutional memories of tight labor markets were short: earlier in the century a study of construction labor relations in Chicago had concluded that despite an agreed-upon principle that "there should be no limitation upon the amount of work a man should do during a given day,...it has always been found impossible in this industry—and in a majority of industries for that matter—to keep up production standards during a period when there is a paucity of workers."[37]

Construction workers hardly viewed themselves as taking advantage; rather, they were merely gaining a respite from what seemed like the facts of work life. Looking back at these boom conditions, especially in large cities, one Boston union carpenter recalled the late 1960s as "one of those rare periods when individual workers held the upper hand as employers competed for a limited pool of skilled labor. Supervisors often looked the other way at a slip-up, a mistake, a curse hurled at a foreman...." What had once been "unthinkable"—leaving a project before it was over—"became an option as men hunted overtime pay and better working conditions. 'If a foreman looked at you cross-eyed...you'd pick up your tools and go to another job down the street.'"[38] An NCA survey of its members in the late 1960s revealed that 20 percent of their construction dollar volume was done on an overtime basis; two-thirds of those overtime schedules were created expressly to attract labor, the rest to maintain or speed up completion dates.[39]

Contractors may have been thriving too,[40] but they still searched for ways to avoid an unfavorable labor market. One method for dealing with shortage-induced wage increases that the construction firms shared with their counterparts in other industries was "increased mechanization in all phases of the construction industry." When, for example, the introduction of heavy earth-moving equipment led to a shortage of skilled machine operators, demands were "placed on the machinery industry to increase the size and productive capacity of its products, and to develop machinery that reduces the number of operatives needed to complete a project."[41] Another example was the precast concrete structures, which "so greatly reduced the need for bricklayers that in many parts of the country there is a surplus of these tradesmen."[42] Laborers' work was also subject to "rapid mechanization" as huge

---

[37]Royal Montgomery, *Industrial Relations in the Chicago Building Trades* 179 (1927). Montgomery also reported that contractors "generally say that in busy times the men work more leisurely than in dull periods, when idle men are walking the streets looking for jobs." *Id.* at 152-53.

[38]Mark Erlich, *With Our Hands: The Story of Carpenters in Massachusetts* 156-57 (1986).

[39]BR, "Scheduled Overtime Effect on Construction Projects" 5-6 (Rep. C-2, Nov. 1980).

[40]Erlich, *With Our Hands* at 157.

[41]USDC, *Growth Pace Setters in American Industry, 1956-68*, at 28 (1968).

[42]Edward Young, "Low Productivity: The Real Sin of High Wages," *ENR*, Feb. 24, 1972, at 18-23 at 19.

cranes, fork-lift trucks, automatic lifts, conveyor belts, powered wheelbarrows, and large earth-moving equipment raised their productivity.[43] Overall, however, labor-saving innovations could not overcome the shortage of skilled building tradesmen.

The monetary expression of a labor market unfavorable to employers became the focus of attention. Economic policy makers in the Johnson administration tried to persuade militant construction business unionism that extracting the maximum from a tight labor market was not only pointless but also self-destructive because wage increases in excess of productivity increases would not shift income from capital to labor, but merely unleash an inflation that would put an end to the upswing.[44] As early as May 1964, CEA chairman Heller, in a memo titled, "Construction Wages: A Tough Nut to Crack," warned President Johnson that they were

high and rising too fast, to the dismay:
--of home-buyers and home-makers, who have to pay through the nose for plumbers, carpenters, electricians, etc.;
--of other workers, who feel these decentralized unions are getting away with murder.[45]

Since bills from small building contractors for home repairs never formed the central concern of national labor policy, Heller's focus on them verged on the demagogic, but he quickly proceeded to berate the building trades unions for their "'fat and sassy'" wage and fringe boosts going back as far as 1960, when they had averaged 5.2 percent; their wage settlements beyond the guideposts remained the rule rather than the exception, rejections of employers' offers of increases in excess of 5 percent in Cleveland being only the most recent examples. Heller lamented that the atomized collective bargaining process made it "hard to lay a finger of responsible restraint on them," but to encourage Johnson to act anyway he added parenthetically: "Apart from wages, they're tough -- as you know -- on minority groups." What he sought from Johnson as a first step was a "Presidential statement pointing the finger straight at them" by contrasting the building trades with the rest of organized labor. On the one hand, "<u>labor generally is to be complimented</u> for its

---

[43]Mills, "Factors Determining Patterns of Employment and Unemployment" at 123.

[44]For an analysis of this reasoning, see Marc Linder, "From Surplus Value to Unit Labor Costs: The Bourgeoisification of a Communist Conspiracy," in *idem, Labor Statistics and Class Struggle* 3-55 (1994). Construction unions had earlier been accused of pricing themselves out of non-tight labor markets: in 1939 Sumner Slichter argued that with regard to housing they had "seriously misjudged their market and [we]re pursuing a policy that [wa]s not only injuring their members but [wa]s substantially reducing the ability of private industry to absorb the savings of the community." Sumner Slichter, "The Changing Character of American Industrial Relations," 29 (2) pt. 2, Supp. *AER* 121-37 at 133 (Mar. 1939).

[45]Chairman of the CEA Walter Heller, "Memorandum for the President, Subject: Construction Wages: A Tough Nut to Crack" at 1, May 23, 1964, EX FG 11-3, 5/21/64-7/20/64, LBJ Library.

moderation and respect for the national interest" because generally wage increases had approximated productivity increases during the Kennedy-Johnson administration. On the other hand, "[s]ome of the <u>building trades are a regrettable exception</u>" because their wage increases violated the productivity guideposts. Finally Heller wanted the president to state that building craft unions "should not take advantage of the high level of construction activity to push for excessive wage increases -- because that would be the surest way to slow down or reverse construction, lose jobs, and hurt the whole economy."[46]

Against the backdrop of, but never alluding to, the intensifying militarization of the economy, Secretary of Labor Wirtz also cautioned the BCTD that increases in construction union scales in 1965 had exceeded those in virtually all other industries and that the prospect of even larger increases in 1966 might disrupt macroeconomic wage-price stability.[47] Building trades unions sought to rebut the accusation of outsize increases. The president of the United Association of Journeymen and Apprentices of the Plumbing and Pipe Fitting Industry (UA), Peter Schoemann, while expressing his union's pride in "our nation's no-nonsense reply to Communism" in Vietnam, rejected the notion that wage increases should be confined to productivity increases without taking into account those in the cost of living.[48] The following week, however, the U.S. Bureau of Labor Statistics (BLS) reported that major construction contract settlements for 1966 were averaging 6.4 percent wage increases—twice the level of the Johnson administration's 3.2 percent wage guideposts, well above those negotiated in other industries, and also in excess of the the cost of living increases mentioned by Schoemann.[49]

Early 1966 also witnessed the federal government's first successful imposition of pressure on a construction union to moderate its wage demands. After the AGC of New Jersey had reached an agreement with a local of the International Union of Operating Engineers (IUOE) to increase the pay scale by 15 percent to $7.75 per hour, in February the contractors met with the CEA staff in Washington "as the Government's efforts to curb inflationary forces in the industry intensified" by confining wage increases to 3.2 percent annually. The employers' association president told the staff that he "felt the climate was pro-labor.... Labor has pretty well had its way over the past few years.'" But referring to the government's success in rolling back steel prices in 1966, he added that "'if they can handle U.S. Steel they

[46]Chairman of the CEA Walter Heller, "Memorandum for the President, Subject: Construction Wages: A Tough Nut to Crack" at 1-2, May 23, 1964, EX FG 11-3, 5/21/64-7/20/64, LBJ Library.

[47]"Wirtz Urges Wage-Price Stabilization in Construction," *CLR*, No. 548, Mar. 23, 1966, at A-7, A-8.

[48]"UA President Schoemann's Convention Keynote Address," *CLR*, No. 658, Aug. 10, 1966, at C-1, C-2, C-3.

[49]"Construction Wage Settlements Twice Guidepost Figure, BLS Reports," *CLR*, No. 569, Aug. 17, 1966, at B-1.

ought to be able to handle this union situation.'" At the same time, the national AGC issued a statement expressing its concern with "'the ever-growing power of the building and construction trades unions.'"[50]

At this point *The New York Times* inserted itself into the dispute, which was emblematic of the conflicts triggered by tight labor markets: intensifying mechanization caused operating engineers to experience the industry's most explosive employment growth as their numbers rose 40 percent between 1962 and 1970.[51] A week after the newspaper reported these events, its chief national news commentator, Arthur Krock, devoted his entire column to warning that, compared to the breaches of the administration's anti-inflation guidelines created by recent wage increases in the automobile and steel industries, execution of the New Jersey Operating Engineers' contract would sweep away "a vital and already crumbling dike against ruinous inflation...." He urged President Johnson to withhold funds from federal highway construction—a significant source of employment for operating engineers—to restrain the union's demands. Krock's urgent tone was prompted by his prediction that the Operating Engineers' wage increase "would put irresistible pressure on all the other construction unions in the huge New York City area to demand the same in order to maintain their traditional wage relationship.... And the demand would as inevitably spread to" all the other construction unions nationally. Quoting John Garvin, a construction labor relations consultant, Krock characterized the New Jersey case as "'the Munich of wage-price restraint.'"[52]

Initially, the president of Local 825, Peter Weber, announced that "he would not reduce the size of a huge contract he had won, regardless of how much pressure the Johnson administration applied against him." To pressure the union to settle for a smaller increase, the administration considered cutting off $200 million of federal highway funds to New Jersey.[53] A few days later the workers struck because the employers, advised by their contractor associations not to pay the rates agreed upon, refused to meet the terms of the agreement, which they had not yet signed. The employers also "angrily laid plans to retaliate with a statewide lockout that would stop more than $100-million worth of projects." After a five-day strike, both sides agreed to binding arbitration by Wirtz and Raymond Male, the

---

[50]Edwin Dale, Jr., "U.S. Economic Advisers Seek to Curb Jersey Building Pay," *NYT*, Feb. 8, 1966, at 21, col. 2-3.

[51]Calculated according to Mills, *Industrial Relations and Manpower in Construction*, tab. 11 at 90. See also Mills, "Factors Determining Patterns of Employment and Unemployment" at 69.

[52]Arthur Krock, "In the Nation: A Crumbling Dike Against Inflation," *NYT*, Feb. 15, 1966, at 38, col. 3-6.

[53]"Jersey Union Head Resists President on Settlement Cost," *NYT*, Mar. 17, 1966, at 24, col. 3. The news prompted Krock to repeat his warning that this settlement might become "a standard objective of organized labor." Arthur Krock, "In the Nation: The Thumb that Could Save the Dike," *NYT*, Mar. 17, 1966, at 38, col. 3 at 4.

New Jersey Labor Commissioner: "It was the first time that the White House has publicly succeeded in forcing a union to roll back its wage demands since Presidential wage guidelines of 3.2 per cent were instituted. It marked one of the very rare occasions in the history of collective bargaining that a union has left it up to state and Federal labor officials to arbitrate a wage dispute."[54] *The New York Times* reported that employers and unions were watching the case closely because it was the first time that the administration had "been in a position almost to dictate a settlement in line with the guideposts."[55]

The New Jersey dispute remained the administration's focal point for moderating construction wage increases into the summer. In June, Labor Secretary Wirtz set forth a plan calling for contractors to guarantee at least 1,600 hours or 40 weeks of work annually to employees who had worked at least 700 hours as operating engineers the previous year and were substantially attached to the industry; employers would deposit 20 cents an hour per worker to fund public works employment for those whom they could not employ for the minimum period. The plan's "basic aim" was to deprive construction unions of their preeminent justification for larger than average wage increases—seasonality; smaller building trade wage increases would, in turn, deprive other unions of one of their favored arguments for their own wage demands.[56] However, the New Jersey contractors opposed the plan on the grounds that, together with the wage increases proposed by Wirtz, it would cost them even more than the 9 percent increase demanded by the Operating Engineers.[57] This rejection, which was reinforced by the national AGC, which characterized the plan as an effort to "force a guaranteed annual wage on the construction industry" that would encourage absenteeism among workers who had already worked their 700 hours, triggered a series of selective three-week strikes by

---

[54]"Wirtz's Aid Asked in Jersey Dispute," *NYT*, Mar. 27, 1966, at 85, col. 4; "Jersey Union Agrees to U.S. Arbitration," *NYT*, Mar. 29, 1966, at 1, col. 1, 14, col. 6 (quotes). A 35-cent per hour wage increase went into effect immediately; other provisions of the three-year contract were entrusted to the arbitrators. Weber's retreat may have been related to the fact that he was under indictment on kickback charges.

[55]"Labor Pact Study Is Set for Jersey," *NYT*, Apr. 7, 1966, at 28, col. 6. Protests by the Building Contractors Association of New Jersey, the state's largest, were instrumental in bringing about the review of the terms of the agreement between Local 825 and the AGC. "New Jersey Builders Ask Change to Comment on Proposed Annual Wage Guarantee," *CLR*, No. 563, July 6, 1966, at A-3, A-4.

[56]David Jones, "Guaranteed Pay Proposed by U.S.," *NYT*, June 27, 1966, at 35, col. 1. For the full text, which did not specify the amount per hour to be paid into the fund, see "Determination of Secretary of Labor and New Jersey Commissioner of Labor and Industry in Matter of Contract of IUOE Local 825 and Contractors (Official Text)," *CLR*, No. 564, July 13, 1966, at C-1-C-5.

[57]"Jersey Builders Oppose Wirtz's Plan for a Work Guarantee," *NYT*, July 11, 1966, at 20, col. 4.

Local 825.[58] (Nevertheless, the union president's support for the "revolutionary proposal" ultimately led to its adoption and the accumulation of several million dollars in the fund, which both sides, however, decided to convert instead into supplemental unemployment compensation.)[59]

In March 1966, the national AGC complained that "severe manpower shortages...were encouraging unions to seek inflationary wage settlements."[60] By August, the AGC proclaimed the existence of critical local labor shortages in certain trades.[61] The AGC saw the unfavorable labor market as partly caused by governmental "do-gooders" and "super-planners," who failed to understand that unemployment benefits ("rocking-chair money") actually reduced workers' mobility, making them less willing to move where there was more work. Unions' "irresponsible" demands such as children's summer camp benefits also helped account for the excessive rise in wages.[62] By autumn, the president of the AGC announced that the labor market "'surely must be the worst ever in the memory of our oldest member.'"[63]

That October, the *Wall Street Journal* permitted consultant John Garvin to elevate the rhetoric of crisis to a kind of *Götterdämmerung*. In a opinion piece, Garvin predicted that a continuation of the pattern of collective bargaining "might well destroy the industry." He conceded that such a prediction might seem to "border on the absurd" at a time when wage settlements that "soar far beyond" the administration's wage guideposts seem "readily recoverable in higher prices...." But, he asserted, intensified competition had depressed the rate of profit on the increased volume of business; when that volume inevitably declined, buyers' insistence on the new, lower "markup" would make it difficult for contractors to "adjust" it. If that scenario were, further, accompanied by continuing wage increases, "the industry would face a disastrous profit squeeze." At this point, Garvin transmitted a warning from users that soon gained in salience: contractors' inability or unwillingness to resist "excessive union demands" "is reaching the stage where the customers' own, non-construction union contract demands are being influenced by the rapid advances in construction union wages." Garvin's call

---

[58]"'Extended Earnings Opportunity Plan' Offered Construction Industry," *CLR*, No. 564, July 13, 1966, at A-12, A-13; "New Jersey Engineers End Strikes, AGC Attacks 'Extended Earnings Opportunity' Plan," *CLR*, No. 565, July 20, 1966, at A-1, A-2 (quote).

[59]"Operating Engineers Strike New Jersey Builders, Controversial Work Opportunities Plan at Stake," *CLR*, No. 567, Aug. 3, 1966, at A-5 (quote); A. H. Raskin, "Unused Inflation Curb," *NYT*, Mar. 1, 1971, at 29, col. 1 at 2-3.

[60]"Wirtz Minimizes Labor Shortage," *NYT*, Mar. 15, 1966, at 1, col. 7, at 22, col. 7.

[61]"AGC's 1966 Manpower Survey Reveals Critical Shortage," *CLR*, No. 570, Aug. 24, 1966, at A-7.

[62]"Labor, Government, and Management Accused for Critical Manpower Shortage," *CLR*, No. 570, Aug. 24, 1966, at A-9, A-10.

[63]"AGC President Calls Labor Situation Worst Ever," *CLR*, No. 576, Oct. 5, 1966, at A-1.

for more centralization or at least regionalization of collective bargaining anticipated another point that large construction users began stressing: national contractors "can wreak havoc with local collective bargaining relationships" when they agree to pay whatever local rates local contractors pay without becoming involved in negotiations; since local unions know that the national contractors will provide employment even during a strike against local contractors, they are relieved of the normal constraints imposed by strikes.[64] Construction employers' initial reaction to Garvin's proposal was mixed.[65]

By year's end, the National Association of Manufacturers (NAM) catapulted the shortage of skilled construction workers out of its narrow industry-specific context and into a cause of macroeconomic and macrosocietal catastrophe:

> For want of a nail, a kingdom was lost....
>
> For want of someone to hammer nails, America...may have some serious difficulties in reaching the potential its advancing technology and enormous output of finely educated young workers indicate to be possible.
>
> For it is evident that a combination of circumstances is generating a shortage of workers in the building trades at the very moment that industry is formulating vast capital spending plans, affluent families are seeking new and better homes, and Washington is embarking on the vast program of rebuilding all our cities.[66]

One of the consequences that the NAM predicted was: "Upward pressure on all wage scales as the building trades get contracts reflecting demand and other unions strive to match the scales." The scarcity of skilled building workers was exacerbated by institutional labor market phenomena. Journeymen "do not journey anymore, but wait for the work to come to them. There may be a shortage in a trade in Manhattan and unemployed in that trade in the Bronx, but some local unions would no more allow the Bronx workers to enter and share the work than they would allow Yugoslavs...." But even if such exclusive unions opened admissions, the number of applicants would be insufficient because youth no longer performed (even skilled) manual labor voluntarily. To be sure, this proclivity did not distinguish them from their predecessors: "But earlier generations had less choice," and the supply of those with the least choice, immigrants, had declined.[67]

Oddly, 1966 closed with a BLS report "that the anticipated shortages not only failed to materialize, but that unemployment in construction has risen

---

[64] John Garvin, "Construction Fault," *WSJ*, Oct. 4, 1966, at 18, col. 4.

[65] "Garvin Outlines New Idea for Bargaining," *ENR*, Nov. 24, 1966, at 67-68. Garvin also warned that failure to heed his call for regional bargaining would prompt the government gradually to nationalize the construction industry. "A Choice: Federate of Be Nationalized," *ENR*, Mar. 2, 1967, at 66.

[66] "Some Vanishing Americans," *NAM Reports*, Dec. 19, 1966, at 6-8 at 6.

[67] "Some Vanishing Americans" at 6.

substantially since spring, to a seasonally adjusted rate of 9.3 percent in November." This reversal was attributed to a sharp drop in residential building, which accounted for one-third of total summer employment. The BLS predicted that in the wake of a decline in military inductions, the labor market would loosen during the winter of 1966-67.[68]

Despite this forecast, by April 1967 the White House launched a trial balloon in response to a suggestion by a national specialty contractors group that a labor-management conference be convened to study how to moderate wage cost pressures. Agreeing that the "problem of excessive wage increases in construction has long been of concern to" the Johnson administration, the president's special assistant stressed "the highly decentralized structure of collective bargaining" as a principal obstacle to lower wage settlements.[69] For Garvin, the construction management labor relations consultant, however, the very fact that a single contractors association submitted this suggestion without industry-wide coordination was emblematic of the deleterious decentralization and disarray that plagued building employers.[70]

One of the most remarkable efforts to undermine construction workers' bargaining power was the unique[71] decision in June 1967 by the U.S. Steel Corporation—of which the future Roundtable leader Roger Blough was chairman and CEO—to stop construction work that it was carrying out (both as its own general contractor and through out-of-town contractors) in the Pittsburgh area "to deny jobs to craft-union members on strike against local contractors." The company's refusal to "'be an economic crutch to striking building trades unions'" was not motivated solely by solidarity with other construction employers. Rather, its president, Leslie Worthington, explained that the purpose was "to exert pressure on the unions and thus, presumably, lessen anticipated increases in construction-labor costs." Failure to reduce those costs would defeat the purpose of building the modern plants that the firm was "in 'desperate need' of...to compete with lower-priced imports."[72]

The background to this user intervention, which became an inspiration to

---

[68]"Report Notes Reversal of Manpower Situation," *CLR*, No. 588, Dec. 28, 1966, at A-10.

[69]"White House Receptive to Suggestion of Wage Conference for Construction," *CLR*, No. 602, Apr. 5, 1967, at A-1, A-2. Mills argued that "the incapacity of the national leadership of the industry to act without governmental assistance was apparent after 1966." D. Q. Mills, "Construction Wage Stabilization: A Historic Perspective," 11 (3) *IR* 350-65 at 352 (Oct. 1972).

[70]"Garvin Says Uncoordinated Call for White House Conference Points Up Disarray of Management," *CLR*, No. 603, Apr. 12, 1967, at A-5.

[71]"'The Case Against National Agreements': Remarks of Leon B. Kromer, Executive Vice President, Mechanical Contractors Assn.," *CLR*, No. 687, Nov. 20, 1968, at D-1, D-2.

[72]"U.S. Steel Supports Struck Contractors by Halting Some Work," *WSJ*, June 5, 1967, at 14, col. 3.

the Roundtable when it was formed two years later, was U.S. Steel's experience with collective bargaining in connection with a mill it was having built near Cleveland. As building trades contracts were about to expire on April 30, 1967, all parties were aware that a high settlement was inevitable: a shortage of workers, the concentration of several projects by national contractors in the area, and large increases in recent settlements in neighboring large cities unambiguously pointed to it. The $1.45 per hour increase over three years to which the parties were on the verge of agreeing became $2.32 at the last minute when the Mechanical Constructors Association of Cleveland announced that increase with the Plumbers and other employers were unable to mobilize support from owners or national contractors to resist the higher rate. In contemplation of similar increases in the Pittsburgh area as the June 1 contract expiration date approached, U.S. Steel informed the Master Builders Associations of Pittsburgh of its interest in the negotiations and its intention to support local construction firms by waiving its rights under national contracts to continue building during strikes. U.S. Steel was also able to become directly involved through its American Bridge division, which was a national contractor. With the additional support of large area employers such as Westinghouse and Jones & Laughlin, the contractors considered themselves victorious in holding the major unions to a $1.50 increase over three years.[73]

Unspoken by U.S. Steel, but furnished by Garvin, was its related concern with "the impact on [its] production labor of high wage settlements granted by this industry to construction industry labor. No production worker is going to be satisfied with 5 percent, or even 6 and 7 percent, wage settlements—when he sees the construction industry unions easily obtaining 10 percent, 20 percent and even 30 to 40 percent, and higher, settlements."[74] Unfortunately, from the perspective of those calling for united action to hold down wages, U.S. Steel's "isolated action here and there [wa]s not enough."[75]

A few weeks later, Garvin drew attention to the relationship between construction wages and wage-price-profit developments in automobile production, explaining to several Detroit contractors groups: "There has probably never been a time when wage settlements in the construction industry have so strongly

---

[73]CUAIR, "A Statement of Program: Preliminary - Confidential" at 23-26 (July 15, 1969), in SP, Box 5, CUAIR 1969-70. Blough presented this version at the July 22, 1969 meeting to which he had invited corporate executives to recruit them to the Roundtable. Notes taken of the meeting mentioned the Pittsburgh events as an example of "self help." SP, Box 5, File-CUAIR 1969-1970. This "Pittsburgh Case Study" illustrating how users can intervene was deleted from a later version: CUAIR, "A Statement of Program" (Mar. 18, 1970), in SP, Box 5, File-Construction Committee.

[74]"Address Prepared by John C. Garvin for Presentation June 15, 1967, New Mexico Building Branch, Associated General Contractors of America," *CLR*, No. 612, June 14, 1967, at C-1, C-2.

[75]"Remarks of Winston M. Blount, President, Chamber of Commerce of the United States, at Construction Industry Labor Conference," *CLR*, No. 661, May 22, 1968, at C-1, C-3.

influenced the wage demands and negotiations of the manufacturing industries."
The impact was particularly acute on the auto industry, in which contractors had
"allowed wages and, thus, the cost to construct to escalate to a point where the auto
people have to consider other ways to construct, alter, maintain and repair their
plant requirements." Similarly, "exorbitant wage settlements" in construction
exerted a significant influence on the UAW's wage negotiations.[76]

The new BLS forecasts of a more favorable labor market may have inspired
the AGC to change its tack: by August 1967 it blamed "the paradox of a manpower
shortage in the midst of unemployment" not only on union policies to "maintain a
shortage," but also on "too many contractor 'freeloaders,'" who failed to train new
workers.[77] The admission was hardly novel: as far back as the 1920s, construction
employers admitted that their failure to offer continuous employment was
responsible for the shortage of apprentices and the absence of a training system.[78]
In 1961, the U.S. Department of Commerce projected that of the 2.3 million new
construction workers needed in the 1960s apprenticeship would provide only 10
percent; this low proportion was exacerbated by the fact that changing technology
made increased apprenticeship imperative.[79]

The residential construction industry soon weighed in as well. The
National Association of Home Builders (NAHB) predicted that from 1966 to 1975
218,000 jobs for skilled construction workers would open up annually through
expansion, retirement, death, and exit from the industry. In contrast, government
apprenticeship programs would train only 3,600 workers annually or 1.59 percent
of the requisite number.[80] This inexorably opening scissors overlooked, to be sure,
the fact that the perennial shortage of construction apprentices was largely an
illusion: most new skilled construction workers did not go through formal
apprenticeship programs because not only were they not the sole route to training,
but, in the view of many, were in fact superfluous; their real purpose was to train
supervisors and foremen.[81]

---

[76]John Garvin, "The Need is Great and the Time Is Now," *CLR*, No. 617, July 19, 1967, at
D-1, D-4.

[77]"Unions, Contractors Share Blame for Manpower Shortages," *CLR*, No. 619, Aug. 2, 1967,
at A-1.

[78]BLS, *Apprenticeship in Construction* 9-10 (Bull. No. 459, 1928); "Apprenticeship in
Building Construction," 26 (6) *MLR* 15-28 (June 1928).

[79]"Construction Comments: Construction Manpower Needs in the Sixties," 7 (4) *CR* 4-5
(Apr. 1961). For projections for individual trades, see DOL, Apprenticeship & Training Bureau,
Manpower Requirements and Training Needs in Construction Occupations, 1960-1970, tab. 1 (1959).
Alone almost one million additional carpenters were projected.

[80]"Training Programs Falling Short of Needs for Skilled Craftsmen, NAHB Asserts," *CLR*,
No. 625, at B-1.

[81]George Strauss, "Apprenticeship: An Evaluation of the Need," in *Employment Policy and
the Labor Market* 299-332 at 308-13 (Arthur Ross ed., 1965). Strauss, one of the leading academic

The labor market conditions prompted even the NCA, the organization of large unionized national industrial construction firms, to address the issue of "exorbitant wage boosts in construction." A sudden realization that "the law of supply and demand" on the labor market sometimes favored workers in the short run caused the NCA to reverse course and adopt the AGC's analysis of the underlying cause:

The recently-striking workers in the Ford Motor Company could not go down the street and get temporary jobs with General Motors or Chrysler. The average UAW striker was simply out of a job and without income. So it became only a matter of time before the financial pain of both the striker and the management had reached a point at which an agreement could be reached.

The skilled construction worker has a much more favorable position than his automotive counterpart. He works not for a single employer but for many contractors; in fact for the entire industry. If there is no work at home, because of a strike or any other reason, and if he wants to continue in construction, he goes to a neighboring or even distant community. ... For this reason a strike or the threat of a strike is a more serious matter to the construction employer than to those of other industries.

In addition to the special bargaining advantages enjoyed by building trades unions due to the nature of the industry, these unions have also benefitted from the law of supply and demand. Because of the record high levels of construction volume in recent years, the supply of skilled men is simply not adequate....[82]

For good measure, the NCA president also apportioned a large share of the responsibility for unfavorable labor markets to his member-firms' large industrial customers, which selected sites based on the availability of water, power, and raw materials, but gave no attention to labor market conditions; consequently, "the pyramiding of industrial projects in congested areas" spawned higher costs through overtime.[83] Conflict among NCA's national construction firms, local contractors, and industrial customers over national agreements, labor supply, and labor relations sharpened during the late 1960s. The focus was on the plumbing trade because the Plumbers Union (UA) supplied about 40 percent of national industrial constructors' on-site labor, which in turn represented about 12 percent of that union's entire membership. The NCA defended national agreements on the grounds that without them national constructors would have to sign numerous local agreements that did

---

writers on the construction industry, nourished a jaundiced view of apprenticeship, the expansion of which he regarded "as a means of training the skilled tradesmen needed to win the cold war." Moreover, he argued that even plumbers "are not noted for high mentality (after all, in some circles to be a 'plumber' is slang for being dumb)." *Id.* at 299, 310.

[82]"NCA Chief Advocates National Arbitration System Within Framework of Jointly Developed Wage Code," *CLR*, No. 635, Nov. 22, 1967, at A-1.

[83]"NCA Chief Advocates" at A-2.

not meet the needs of large-scale industrial projects; if labor disputes arose, national firms would be subject to local grievance procedures that they did not help formulate; and, finally, if labor shortages arose, national unions would not be able to help secure workers from other labor markets. Local construction firms opposed to national contracts emphasized that the only pressure that they could bring to bear against striking workers—the cessation of wages—frequently disappeared when the no-strike clause in national agreements permitted local workers to find employment during local strikes.[84] Yet even a former president of the NCA acknowledged that its member-firms "cannot enter a locality with manpower requirements which represent half or sometimes even more than the entire membership of local unions without having a detrimental effect on local labor relations." How they would implement his call for creating "an industrial work force apart from the rest of the industry work force" he did not explain.[85]

In the chapter of its February 1968 *Annual Report* devoted to "The Problem of Rising Prices," the CEA singled construction workers out for special mention. That the rise in construction prices had exceeded that in most other sectors "by a substantial margin" was "due principally to the fact that wages of construction workers have been rising more rapidly than those of other industrial workers while the improvement in construction practices and techniques has lagged seriously." It blamed restrictive union entry rules for the inadequate supply of skilled workers, which accounted for the unions' great bargaining strength, which was reinforced by the construction contract bidding system: since all employers in a given area operated under the same wage rates, they had little incentive to resist high wage demands. Finally, the CEA attributed flagging productivity growth to antiquated building codes, which precluded the use of new materials and methods; unions were joined by smaller specialty contractors in resisting change in these codes.[86]

On April 29, when construction was "perhaps the most heavily unionized sector in the economy,"[87] Okun, the chairman of the CEA, wrote a memorandum to Johnson seeking approval to issue a statement expressing concern "about prospective inflationary wage settlements in the construction industry." The statement was to be issued by the Cabinet Committee on Price Stability (CCPS)—consisting of the Treasury, Commerce, and Labor Secretaries, the Budget Bureau director, and CEA chairman—which Johnson had created in February to study long-term structural price problems and to inform business, labor, and the public of the "consequences of irresponsible wage and price behavior." Despite the

---

[84]George McGuire, "The Case for National Agreements," *CLR*, No. 687, Nov. 20, 1968, at C-1; Leon Kromer, "The Case Against National Agreements," *id.* at D-1.

[85]John Graney, "Misplaced Responsibilities," *CLR*, No. 687, Nov. 20, 1968, at E-1, E-2.

[86]*Economic Report of the President* 118 (1968).

[87]A.J. Grimes, "Personnel Management in the Building Trades," 43 (1) *Personnel J.* 37-47 at 37 (Jan. 1968).

directive that the CCPS "will not...become involved in specific current wage or price matters,"[88] Okun was eager to become involved in a specific current wage matter—namely, an impending strike-lockout in the Detroit building trades:

We face the the threat of a <u>major jump in the already excessive level of construction settlements.</u>

- These averaged 7-1/2% in the first quarter, far above the 6% average of all industries.
- Now the Detroit-Toledo building trades unions are demanding a fantastic rise of <u>roughly 30% a year</u>. If they succeed, this will set a pattern for other settlements scheduled later this spring.
- The <u>contractors could complain</u> justly if we were to remain silent in the face of this inflationary danger.
- Even the <u>national labor leaders recognize</u> the outrageous character of these local wage demands.[89]

Mindful of the president's directive, Okun assured Johnson that the "wording of the statement focusses on an industrywide situation, not a specific negotiation. Of course, our timing is influenced by the fact that the Detroit contract expires May 1." The other advantage that Okun saw in the release was providing himself with "a useful opportunity to background the press on just how bad the wage demands in construction are...."[90]

The statement that the CCPS did in fact release to coincide with the Detroit action expressed "its strong concern that that construction wage increases which might be negotiated prior to the peak building season of 1968 could imperil efforts to regain price stability." The CCPS also warned that collectively bargained construction wage increases that had been accelerating since 1964 and exceeded those in other sectors by one-third "threaten to harm the economy seriously and raise sharply the cost" of the whole gamut of public and private construction output. Moreover, the committee could foresee no productivity gains that could even "begin to offset such large wage increases." Finally, the CCPS sought to justify its deviation from its assigned long-term task by stressing the urgency of alerting the world to the possibility that untoward developments in construction, including "the acceleration in the inflationary spiral that could arise from negotiations" in Detroit and elsewhere, "could set back the goal of price stability immeasurably." The

---

[88]*Economic Report of the President* 20-21 (1968). See also "Memorandum Establishing the Cabinet Commision on Price Stability," Feb. 23, 1968, in *PPPUS: Lyndon B. Johnson: 1968-69*, Book I, at 265 (1970).

[89]Arthur Okun, "Memorandum for the President: Subject: Proposed Statement on Construction Costs" at 1, Apr. 29, 1968, EX LA 8, 1/1/68-, LBJ Library.

[90]Arthur Okun, "Memorandum for the President: Subject: Proposed Statement on Construction Costs" at 1, 2, Apr. 29, 1968, EX LA 8, 1/1/68-, LBJ Library.

committee's solemn request that labor and management "give particular attention to the President's urgent request that 'unions and business firms exercise the most rigorous restraint in their wage and price determinations in 1968'"[91] fell on ears deafened by mass action in Detroit.

Curiously, the analysis that appeared in the *Wall Street Journal* just hours after the strike in Detroit had begun and already spread to the rest of the state of Michigan, halting two-thirds of all major construction, included deep background information from unidentified administration officials that undercut the message that Okun had so ardently wished to send. After quoting officials citing informal reports that construction unions' general goal for 1968 was to equal or break the 10 to 18 percent wage increases that had been obtained in Ohio in 1967, the *Journal* noted that one administration official cautioned that these data were "only from the employers' side and could be 'puffed up' for bargaining purposes...." The newspaper also heard from a government source that "he had heard from construction unions in many areas an equally unconfirmed report that their employers' profits are so 'bloated' that they can afford to grant outsized settlements without increasing their own charges."[92]

The struggle over wages in Detroit in 1968 was instructive because, although employers acted cohesively, secured a national audience for their complaints over wage demands, elicited users' interest, and fought back, analysts regarded the resulting regional wage contour embracing the Detroit-Toledo-Cleveland-Akron-Columbus as having generated a wage spiral.[93] As the April 30th expiration date of contracts covering 53,700 construction workers approached, the trade press reported that union wage demands had "soared to an all-time high," ranging up to 77 percent "over the next 13 months." Cement masons, for example, whose then hourly wage rate (including fringe benefits) amounted to $5.63, had demanded an increase of $4.33 over the next two years. Contractors were especially outraged because productivity had allegedly fallen by 25 percent during the previous two years. It is unclear how employers had been able to overcome the complicated methodological problems of comparing heterogeneous outputs over time to measure productivity changes,[94] but a spokesman sarcastically adverted to

---

[91]"High Wage Demands Worry Cabinet Committee," *CLR*, No. 659, May 8, 1968, at A-1, A-2. Later the CCPS was concerned lest the industry be unable to build the housing needed for the children of the baby-boom generation." Address by Merton J. Peck, Member of CEA, on 'Economic Policy and the Construction Industry,'" *CLR*, No. 683, Oct. 23, 1968, at D-1.

[92]"Presidential Panel Asks Building Unions to Cut Pay Demands; Peril to Prices Seen," *WSJ*, May 2, 1968, at 5, col. 1-4. *The New York Times* published a very small, perfunctory article hidden at the back of the newspaper. "Cabinet Unit Warns on Building Wages," *NYT*, May 2, 1968, at 52, col. 1.

[93]D. Q. Mills, "Wage Determination in Contract Construction," 10 (1) *IR* 72-85 at 75 (Feb. 1971).

[94]National Commission on Productivity and Work Quality, *Measuring Productivity in the*

"'an inverse ratio between the amount of wages paid and the will to work.'" Although the alleged magnitude of the decline appears implausible during such a short period, employers attributed it to the loss of discipline associated with full employment: "critical labor shortages...lead to complacency on the part of workers." The fact that industrial customers, including the all-important automobile manufacturers, claimed to have begun to understand that, if obtained, such wage increases would both increase their construction costs and infect their own employees, gave construction firms hope that their bargaining power would be fortified by striking building tradesmen's inability to find alternative jobs.[95]

The Detroit AGC could take credit for having inspired the CCPS's warning about the inflationary impact of construction unions' wage settlements, which was apparently based on information it had furnished. The federal government was especially concerned about the situation in Detroit "because of the close geographic relationship between construction workers and those in manufacturing industries, implying that high craft settlements would induce bigger demands from skilled factory workers in Detroit." Not surprisingly, the CCPS failed to include in its formal statement its caution that "'unions in many areas claim construction profits are bloated and there is no need for higher prices.'"[96]

On May 1, Detroit construction workers began striking; two days later more than 100,000 were on strike throughout the state of Michigan and 10,000 more in Toledo. Nevertheless, owing in part to public opinion, which the AGC believed it had mobilized against the "patently unreasonable" demands, unions, according to *ENR*, the leading trade magazine, had "become a little less cocky"; cement masons, for example, had cut their demands by more than half—from $4.33 to $2.10.[97] After a 73 day strike, which was intensified by a statewide lockout that closed down 95 percent of construction work, the two-year settlements included increases of $1.90 per hour for carpenters and $1.92 for bricklayers and operating engineers.[98] Though much lower than the original demands, these increases, which exceeded the federal minimum wage of $1.60, prompted *ENR* to report that they had "begun to

---

Construction Industry (n.d. [ca. 1973]).

[95]"Detroit Groups Fight High Demands," *ENR*, Apr. 25, 1968, at 75-76. For an example of how large industrial capital supported construction companies against their employees to prevent the latter's wage demands from infecting industrial workers during the Weimar republic, see Dagmar Schwab, "Unternehmerverbände gegen Bauarbeiter," 12 (3) *WZHABW* 199-203 (1965).

[96]"Wage Demands Are Far Too High," *ENR*, May 9, 1968, at 25.

[97]"Thousands Strike in Michigan," *ENR*, May 9, 1968, at 66. See also "Bargaining: Success, Chaos and Dismay," *ENR*, May 16, 1968, at 78; "Recognition at Last," *id.*, at 92 (editorial).

[98]"Detroit Carpenters Settle with All But AGC on Two-Year Contract with Raises of $1.90," *CLR*, No. 667, at A-11-A-12 (July 3, 1968); "Striking Bricklayers Settle in Detroit; AGC Comes to Terms with Area Carpenters," *CLR*, No. 669, at A-6-A-7 (July 17, 1968); BLS, *Analysis of Work Stoppages, 1968*, at 11, 22 (Bull. 1646, 1970).

threaten if not destroy the aims and concept of management unity in Detroit."[99] In fact, however, the events served as a catalyst in the formation of a regional congress of construction associations.[100]

Despite these gains, as late as September 1968 the president of the BCTD was still claiming that construction wage increases were "just keeping up with the cost of living increases."[101] Such attestations made little impression on the NCA, whose president told an Ironworkers union convention that construction wage rates were "rising out of all proportion to...cost-of-living standards...or wage increases in other industries." As a result, large industrial customers had begun awarding bids to nonunion contractors. He warned that failure to deal with these wage increase might bring about mandatory government controls.[102]

At the same time, the NAM created a study group, headed by a vice-president of U.S. Steel, to examine construction labor problems.[103] In late 1968, a conference on construction problems organized by the U.S. Chamber of Commerce struck a similar note, calling on customers actively to support contractors by not operating through local strikes, thus depriving strikers of alternative employment. Significantly, even the industrial relations manager of Dow Chemical, a major customer, chided project owners for working through strikes.[104]

As the Johnson administration drew to a close, the CCPS issued its final report, which added a new dimension to the by then common complaints about outsize wages. It not only alluded to the "views expressed in other industries over the impact of construction wages on maintenance wage scales" as "symptoms of this malaise," but also noted the dual impact of tighter nonconstruction labor markets on construction—preventing "some of the normal inflow of labor into construction jobs" and prompting construction workers to seek the "steadier" work that other sectors offered. The committee also observed that the hothouse economy of the late 1960s generated overtime and high wages for skilled workers in all industries as a result of which: "As individuals they have become much more independent of both their employers and labor organizations."[105] This militance spawned by a worker-friendly labor market that made skilled employees semi-

---

[99]"New Pacts Test Detroit Unity," *ENR*, July 4, 1968, at 54.

[100]"Regional Group Gets Management Unity," *ENR*, Aug. 29, 1968, at 100.

[101]"Bricklayers Vote Down Contract Ratification Demand, Haggerty Answers Critics of Construction Wage Bargaining," *CLR*, No. 678, Sept. 18, 1968, A-1, A-2.

[102]"NCA President Collins Asks Industry Action on Wage Costs, Jurisdictional Disputes," *CLR*, No. 682, Oct. 16, 1968, at A-10.

[103]"NAM to Look into Construction Labor Problems," *CLR*, No. 679, Sept. 25, 1968, at A-7.

[104]"Management Conference Backs Wide-Ranging Program to Curb Construction Labor Costs," *CLR*, No. 687, Nov. 20, 1968, at A-9, A-11. On the conference, see below chapter 7.

[105]"Staff Study Report of Cabinet Commitee on Collective Bargaining Arrangements," *CLR*, No. 702, Mar. 5, 1969, at C-1, C-2.

autonomous of organizational structures was reflected in the report's pessimism stemming from the decline both in cohesion and cooperation among national contractor associations and unions and in their "joint capacity at the industry level to respond constructively to difficult problems."[106] Finally, the CCPS urged removal of construction bottlenecks by increasing the availability of sufficient skilled workers by means of nondiscriminatory manpower training programs and increasing mobility through pension vesting.[107]

---

[106]"Report Cites Need for Continuing Dialogue on Reforming Industry's Bargaining Set-Up," *CLR*, No. 702, Mar. 5, 1969, at A-1.

[107]"The Report to the President from the Cabinet Committee on Price Stability," *CLR*, No. 693, Jan. 1, 1969, at E-3.

2

What Did Unions Know About the Open-Shop Threat and When Did They Know It?

Its leaders are experienced business men bargaining to sell the products of its members for a higher price.[1]

Of all the myriad problems besetting the American economy today, perhaps the most serious is the inflationary effect of the high cost of labor settlements in the construction industry.[2]

Paradoxically, even at the height of union power and a seller's labor market in the 1960s, violent protests by construction unionists against nonunion projects[3] as well as repeated litigation over collective bargaining provisions and strikes in support of union workers' right to refuse to work on the same site with nonmembers[4] revealed that a nonunion sector steadily loomed as a threat. Indeed, as early as 1954, the Memphis building trades unions, which had long monopolized the labor market, began to lose their hold in a deunionizing industry.[5]

National union leaders constantly warned the membership of these perils. The Carpenters union, for example, was acutely aware of the dangers. As early as 1962, its president, Maurice Hutcheson, pointed to "a vast pool of small operations that need organization and should be organized." He was especially wary of residential construction, which "must be organized if our Brotherhood is to grow and prosper." Hutcheson warned that housing contractors would be difficult to organize once they branched out into general contracting. To be sure, he could not yet discern the overriding long-run threat: "The days of organizing large blocs of men working for a large contractor...are past. With a few exceptions, here and there, the large employers have been organized."[6] Four years later, Hutcheson

---

[1]William Haber, "The United Brotherhood of Carpenters and Joiners: A Study of Conservative Trade Unionism" 284 (B.A. thesis, U. Wisconsin, 1923).

[2]"Statement of Edwin H. Gott of U.S. Steel Corp on Impact of High-Cost Construction Settlements," *CLR*, No. 762, Apr. 29, 1970, at D-1.

[3]E.g., "A Nonunion Project Is Damaged in Lansing," *NYT*, Nov. 20, 1965, at 18, col. 1.

[4]E.g., John Pomfret, "Bricklayers Lose Labor Board Case," *NYT*, May 8, 1965, at 23, col. 6; NLRB v. Local No. 2, United Association of Journeymen and Apprentices of Plumbing, 360 F.2d 428 (2d Cir, 1966); NLRB v. Muskegon Bricklayers Union 5, 378 F.2d 859 (6th Cir. 1967).

[5]That year five ironworkers were shot by nonunion workers when they tried to shut down a nonunion project. Michael Honey, *Southern Labor and Black Civil Rights: Organizing Memphis Workers* 263 (1993).

[6]*Proceedings of the 29th General Convention of the United Brotherhood of Carpenters and*

stressed that the large volume of nonunion work not only was responsible for much of the union's loss of membership—which, in turn, was exacerbated by locals' reluctance to admit new members lest they become competitors when jobs become scarce—but also put downward pressure on wages that would be difficult to resist.[7] By 1973, the union's new president, William Sidell, had made recruitment of the half-million nonunion carpenters and halting the nonunion contractors' penetration of the union sector his highest priority.[8]

Other unions also warned their members about the spreading nonunion sector in the 1960s. The Bricklayers' president, Thomas Murphy, declared in 1968 that "we must recognize the facts of life. The non-union condition is growing...."[9] In his opening remarks at a conference the next year devoted to discussing "problems," Murphy announced: "'We have to do something about this non-union membership—I cannot stress this too emphatically. In our negotiations now, all we are doing is upgrading the non-union membership. I don't want a million members, but I do want the non-union bricklayer in our organization.'" One of the reasons that organizing the unorganized was the union's "greatest challenge" lay, as in other construction unions, in the locals' reluctance to accept new members.[10] By 1972, Murphy was still admonishing members that, often when locals turned down applicants for membership on the grounds that the hiring hall had no work to offer, "the rascal then finds a job at our trade." Indeed, the point of organizing the unorganized was precisely "to combat the menace of the non-union worker."[11] Later that year, a specialty trade contractors association issued a plea for joint action with the Bricklayers "to combat the inroads of open shop competition...."[12]

The NCA, the all-union employers group, brought the nonunion threat to the attention of Ironworkers at their 1968 convention. Introducing the NCA president, George Collins, union president John Lyons pointed to the "tremendously increased rate of competition in the last six years...from open-shop contractors who

---

Joiners of America 100 (1962).

[7]*Proceedings of the Thirtieth General Convention of the United Brotherhood of Carpenters and Joiners of America* 11, 107-108 (1966).

[8]Walter Galenson, *The United Brotherhood of Carpenters: The First Hundred Years* 355 (1983) (citing United Brotherhood of Carpenters, Official Circular, Sept. 10, 1973).

[9]Thomas Murphy, "Obtaining a Fair Contract," 72 (7) *BMP* n.p. [inside front cover] (July 1968). A year later he referred back to and repeated this warning. Thomas Murphy, "Averting Work Stoppages," 73 (7) *BMP* n.p. [inside front cover] (July 1969).

[10]"Lengthy Agenda Tackled at Washington, D.C. Conference," 73 (6) *BMP* 124-26 at 125, 126 (June 1968).

[11]Thomas Murphy, "Our Primary Function Is Organizing," 76 (5) *BMP* n.p. [inside front cover] (May 1972). See also Thomas Murphy, "Organizing the Unorganized," 76 (6) *BMP* n.p. [inside front cover] (June 1972).

[12]"Tile Contractors Urge Union Contractor Action to Fight Open Shop Competition and Protect Work Jurisdiction," 77 (1) *JBMP* 6 (Jan. 1973).

have, in certain areas of the country, developed a high degree of competency to compete with" the NCA.[13] Collins called on the Ironworkers to "face the plain fact" that their increasing wage rates led to an inevitable loss of markets, which he illustrated by reference to the recent awarding of the contract for a large chemical and petrochemical complex to a nonunion contractor by a client who had historically dealt with union labor and firms. In addition to outsize wage increases, Collins adduced jurisdictional disputes—accounting for 60 percent of all work stoppages on NCA projects—as another cause of client dissatisfaction with union workers.[14] The president of the BCTD, Frank Bonadio, reinforced the message that "we cannot afford to lose any more jobs to non-union." He warned of the dangers inherent in his estimate that in the jurisdiction of 15 percent of local building trades councils 95-100 percent of an ongoing "million-billion-dollart works program" would be union, in 15-20 percent of the councils 10-15 percent of the work would be union, while in the remainder 40-60 percent would be union.[15]

At the Ironworkers next convention in 1972, Lyons changed his approach. He confirmed that during the intervening four years nonunion construction had undergone "phenomenal growth...." For example, "owners who in the entire history of their corporation, or utility, had never had major construction work done any other way than by union contractors, have turned to open shop contractors and in some areas of the country even refuse to accept bids from union contractors." However, in seeking an explanation, Lyons asserted that: "Without any question, the greatest single contributing factor is the Denver Building Trades decision.... This...has made picketing of unfair contractors almost impossible without running into situations that the courts have held to be in violation of the law."[16]

This explanation, however, carried little weight. To be sure, in 1951, the U.S. Supreme Court had ruled that construction unions had engaged in an unlawful secondary boycott and thus committed an unfair labor practice under the Taft-Hartley Act by striking and picketing in order to force a unionized general

---

[13]"Thirty-Third Convention of the International Association of Bridge, Structural and Ornamental Iron Workers: Third Day," 58 (11) *The Ironworker* 6 (Nov. 1968) (special insert).

[14]"Thirty-Third Convention of the International Association of Bridge, Structural and Ornamental Iron Workers: Third Day," 58 (11) *The Ironworker* 7 (Nov. 1968) (special insert). President Lyons the following year confirmed that jurisdictional disputes were "becoming one of the greatest deterrents and obstacles to the promotion of 100 per cent union construction. It is an absolute fact that in the past few years many construction projects scheduled to be built in areas...plagued by jurisdictional work stoppages have been handed by plant owners to the nonunion contractor for the sole purpose of avoiding the costly delays to the owner that unauthorized jurisdictional work stoppages bring about." "The President's Page," 59 (10) *The Ironworker* n.p. [inside front cover] (Oct. 1969).

[15]Thirty-Third Convention of the International Association of Bridge, Structural and Ornamental Iron Workers: Fourth Day," 58 (11) *The Ironworker* 4 (Nov. 1968) (special insert).

[16]"General President John H. Lyon's Address to the 34th Convention," 72 (9) *The Ironworker* 10-14 at 10, 11 (Sept. 1972).

contractor at a building site to terminate its contract with a nonunion subcontractor.[17] At the time the BCTD had plausibly asserted that the "decision is a severe blow to building trades unions and destroys the right they have always had, to refuse to work wirh non-union men."[18] But the growth of the open-shop movement was primarily driven by the expansion of large general contractors who hired nonunion specialty contractors; consequently, because the typical situation on such industrial building sites, unlike that in *Denver Building and Construction Trades Council*, involved no union contractors at all, no union workers were employed there and thus no secondary action would have been implicated. Moreover, the timing suggested by Lyons' argument made little sense: for more than a decade after that prohibition had been in effect, the antiunion movement made no discernible headway.[19]

The national leadership of the Plumbers union was also well aware of the nonunion threat. The president, Peter Schoemann, urged his members in 1969 not to "make overtime an inducement for employment": "If we do not quickly realize we are killing that golden goose, the client/owner will find another labor market."[20]

Examining how nonunion plumbing firms gained ground in Columbus, Ohio, is instructive. In the late 1960s, when Local 189 virtually monopolized the supply of skilled plumbers for large commercial, industrial, and residential projects, nonresidential work had become so plentiful and lucrative that union contractors gradually stopped bidding on large residential and smaller commercial projects. Nonunion firms filled this vacuum during the late 1960s "[l]ike a metastasizing cancer.... A high $850 initiation fee tended to keep out new journeymen.... The nonunion sector accelerated its growth..., and then, and only then, did the union wake up. But it was too late. Once nonunion contractors had proven their competence to builders, they established a foothold that was difficult to dislodge." By the fall of 1970, when the nonunion share of large projects approached one-half

---

[17]NLRB v. Denver Building and Construction Trades Council, 341 U.S. 675 (1951).

[18]"Supreme Court Rules Against Labor on Secondary Boycott," 4 (6) *BCTB* 1 (June 1951). The attainment and maintenance in the late nineteenth century of the joint closed shop, in which no union would work at any building site if unionists were employed at jobs normally filled by union members, called into being city building trades councils. Frank Stockton, *The Closed Shop in American Trade Unions* 98-106 (1911).

[19]Nevertheless, legislative repeal of this decision has been at or near the top of construction unions' political agenda during the entire second half of the twentieth century. Indeed, during the early Eisenhower administration the prospect of legislatively overturning the ruling impelled the AFL unions to seek to cut a special deal with the Republicans, some of whom, in turn, were desirous of union support so that the party could shed its image as the businessman's party. James Gross, *Broken Promise: The Subversion of U.S. Labor Relations Policy, 1947-1994*, at 78, 81, 89-91 (1995).

[20]"Schoemann: 'Save the Goose,'" *ENR*, Mar. 27, 1969, at 66. Two years later the CUAIR cited Schoemann as having told his members that the open shop was growing at an alarming rate. CUAIR, CC, Minutes, May 4, 1971, at 3, in BR, 1971-Vol. II: Minutes.

and one-third of the union's active membership was unemployed, Local 189 offered to help the union contractors association regain the lost residential market by agreeing to a $4.36 per hour cut from their regular wage of $10.52 (including fringe benefits) on houses up to three stories. Moreover, journeymen were prohibited from quitting the job for higher paying commercial or industrial work once they had accepted employment; and if the union was unable to find union workers for an employer within 48 hours, it was free to hire temporary workers. When signed in October 1971, the agreement was the first of its kind in the United States, but the low profit margins on such small jobs deterred all but a few contractors from bidding on them. The following year, on September 13, hundreds of plumbers and other journeymen, "frustrated" by the declining living standards brought on by the expanding nonunion sector, destroyed more than $600,000 worth of structures and equipment at nonunion building sites in Columbus. While the press denounced the "rampage" and "violence," many building unionists, according to Local 189's historian, imbued with the "traditional rough-and-tumble code of ethics that had long governed the behavior of construction workers," were concerned only with the action's effectiveness, "not its morality." But this manifestation of their "determination to defend their livelihoods" quickly backfired: in the wake of a multimillion dollar lawsuit against the unions, nonunion contractors, who until then had not been militantly antiunion, "frightened by their vulnerability to mass action, joined the militantly antiunion" Associated Builders and Contractors, which soon consolidated the nonunion sector. By the mid-1970s, straits were so dire that Local 189 began encouraging its own members to become small contractors both to deprive nonunion firms of the small jobs and to provide more work for members.[21]

The president of the Painters union also admonished members about "Meeting the Non-Union Threat," which by 1972 was claiming "[m]ore and more jobs...."[22] Frank Raftery pointed to the more than 100,000 full-time painters' jobs in the single-family home market: "Who represents these 100,000 painters? We surely don't. With our 140,000 painters, mostly in the commercial and industrial and multi-family dwelling markets we couldn't have more than 15,000-20,000 men in the new residential field. This leaves an organizing potential of 80,000."[23]

---

[21]Richard Schneirov, *Pride and Solidarity: A History of Plumbers and Pipefitters of Columbus, Ohio 1889-1989*, at 112-19 (quotes at 113, 117, 118) (1993). Shifting into petty self-employment has long been common among unemployed skilled construction workers, but the union's encouragement of the practice was unusual. See Marc Linder, "Self-Employment as a Cyclical Escape from Unemployment: A Case Study of the Contruction Industry in the United States during the Postwar Period," in 2 *Research in the Sociology of Work: Peripheral Workers* 261-74 (1983).

[22]S. Frank Raftery, "Meeting the Non-Union Threat," 86 (6) *PATJ* n.p. [inside front cover] (June 1972).

[23]S. Frank Raftery, "From the General President," 87 (1) *PATJ* n.p. [inside front cover], at 27 (Jan. 1973).

Although the "war" between unions and non-union firms was an old one, it had, according to the Painters union in 1973, "escalated seriously over the past few years. Until recently, a division between commercial and residential work was generally accepted by both sides. But lately that division has been increasingly challenged by non-union contractors." What had started as a trend in the South and rural areas, "is now national in breadth, entering even the big-city strongholds of unions. Non-union construction, mostly maintenance work so far, is even to be found in tightly organized New York city." To be sure, the Painters' explanation of the union response was self-contradictory: "The trend is blamed on the supposed high price and allegedly low productivity of union labor. Building trades union leaders are trying to combat this fiction through agreements easing work rules and practices and by emphasizing to craftsmen the urgency of giving a fair day's work for a fair day's pay."[24]

How it was possible or why it was necessary to combat a "fiction" became even more mysterious when President Raftery tried to convince members that increasing productivity no longer imposed physical or economic hardships on them:

> Productivity is sometimes considered a dirty word among workers. They remember what it was like to be forced to work harder and faster, without just compensation. And, often, increased productivity meant less hours of work and fewer jobs.
>
> But now the situation is different. We can increase productivity simply by working more efficiently. And...there is more than enough work for everyone, if only we make some adjustments in our priorities. We must recognize that long-range gains in work opportunities are worth a few short-term sacrifices.[25]

Regardless of the correctness of his analysis, by 1974, Raftery declared at the union's general convention that "We Organize or We Perish."[26]

The clarity and urgency with which the president of the Electricians' union (IBEW) presented the threat of the expanding antiunion sector would be hard to surpass. In May 1970, Charles Pillard published an editorial in the union journal conveying a warning from the NCA to the BCTD that "if the old head-in-sand policy regarding the very real problems facing the building trades unions are [sic] continued, disastrous days lie ahead for organized tradesmen." The billions of dollars of construction lost to nonunion firms included "all types of industrial and manufacturing projects which they could not touch previously because

---

[24]"Winning the Battle Against Non-Union Contractors," 87 (2) *PATJ* 16-17 at 16 (Feb. 1973).

[25]S. Frank Raftery, "Meeting the Non-Union Threat," 86 (6) *PATJ* n.p. [inside front cover] (June 1972).

[26]"We Organize or We Perish," 88 (9) *PATJ* 14-17 (Sept. 1974). See also "Redirecting Our Organizing Efforts," 89 (4) *PATJ* 2-3 (Apr. 1975).

of...manpower availability, engineering, designing, and lack of know-how and good supervision." Nonunion contractors had not only for the first time been awarded contracts to build nuclear power plants, but were also "capable of choosing and taking almost any job anywhere, because the union contractors cannot compete with them." Nor were "'scabby' wages...the total reason": unionists could compensate for their higher wages by doing better work in less time—but not if they continued to drive owners away with strikes and jurisdictional disputes. Pillard's comments culminated in this warning: "What is even more shocking and stunning was the message that these large contractors would not hesitate, if forced, to go open-shop to stay in business. And, they certainly intend to stay in business!"[27]

Later the IBEW published the most ruthlessly honest account of the failings of a construction union when it commissioned a history by a labor historian.[28] The chapter devoted to construction electricians recounted that the union's members had gravitated toward large industrial projects where it was "[f]ully in control of the skilled work force"; but by abandoning commercial and residential work, they opened a niche for nonunion contractors. Despite warnings from the NECA as early as 1954, full-employment through the 1960s blinded members to the threat: "Confident that they could never price themselves out of the market as long as their unions restricted access to the trade, many construction workers practiced what came to be called country-club unionism, for their locals still refused to admit new members or even train apprentices to keep up with industry demand." With locals "at the peak of their bargaining power in the 1960s...they asserted their autonomous rights whenever the international tried to rein them in." But this "celebration of local autonomy and raw economic power brought unintended results" as the forces that coalesced into the Roundtable enabled nonunion contractors to "restructure the process of construction work itself, undermining the union concept of craft by breaking down various trades into 'subspecialties' and then hiring semiskilled men and helpers to work under the direction of a few skilled mechanics. By the mid-1970s, construction unions as a whole had lost their "monopoly on skilled craftsmen...." After the fact, the restructuring made it clear that members' "economic strength...had always been tied to the construction industry's decentralized structure and not to their militant autonomy...."[29]

---

[27]Charles Pillard, "Building Trades Unions Must Find Proper Solutions to Major Problems to Avert Loss of Job Opportunities," 69 (5) *EWJ* 2 (May 1970). See also "IBEW Construction Branch Convenes in Nation's Capital," *id.* [n.p.].

[28]For a typically uncritical paid-for union history with a similarly uncritical foreword by John Dunlop, see Thomas Brooks, *The Road to Dignity: A Century of Conflict: A History of the United Brotherhood of Carpenters and Joiners of America, AFL-CIO, 1881-1981* (1981).

[29]Grace Palladino, *Dreams of Dignity, Workers of Vision: A History of the International Brotherhood of Electrical Workers* 258, 259, 261, 262, 263 (1991). Nevertheless, building trades unions were able to hold on to their monopoly much longer than Friedrich Engels would have

Operating Engineers' president Hunter Wharton bluntly told the 1,000 delegates at the union's 1972 convention that construction workers' failure to increase their productivity in tandem with their wage increases had resulted in a shift to nonunion operations. Consequently, unions could "'no longer demand...standby labor on the job so as to create a job for those who have no desire to work for their pay.'"[30] Wharton's remarks were inserted into the *Congressional Record* after they had been reported in *U.S. News & World Report.*[31] Bechtel's representative at the Roundtable referred to Wharton's admission that the building trades unions had all "'reached beyond our grasp'" as evidence that open-shop competition was having an effect.[32]

Nor did construction workers lack for outside voices warning of disastrous consequences if they maintained their policies. When the Secretary of Housing, George Romney, addressed the national legislative conference of the BCTD in May 1969, the 3,000 delegates cheered his admonition that their wage increases since 1962 were "'four and five times higher'" than any other union's. They then jeered him for urging them to end restrictive work practices and reform apprenticeship programs. Over the crescendo of boos, Romney warned: "'There's nothing more vulnerable than entrenched success.'"[33] Editorially *The New York Times* rebuked the "monopolistic unions" for their "mocking reception" of Romney, and warned them that they "lived in a private world of their own," in which they negotiated wage increases twice as large as the minimum wage. And although the newspaper traced the unions' "arrogance" to "their serene assurance that there is no ceiling to the capacity of their contractors to pass on to the consumer increased costs for housing, factories, office buildings and public projects," it did concede that government calls for wage restraint would be ignored as long as living costs continued to rise.[34]

---

imagined possible. In 1885 he wrote to the German socialist leader August Bebel: "You people believe perhaps that any worker in the branch can join up with the machinists, carpenters, masons, etc. without further ado? Not at all. Whoever wants to join has to have been attached as an apprentice for a series of years (mostly 7) to a worker who belongs to the union. ... This lasted until 1848. Since then, however, the colossal upswing in industry has produced a class of workers just as numerous as or even more numerous than the 'skilled' workers of the trade unions, who do as much work or even more but can never become members.... But do you think that the unions would ever consider doing away with all this old rot? Not in the least. ... The fools want to reform society according to their own views, but do not want to reform themselves in accord with society's development. They stick to their traditional superstition which only injures them instead of getting rid of this stuff, thus doubling their numbers and power and in fact again becoming what theyr emain less and less, namely unions of all workers of the trade against the capitalists." Letter from Friedrich Engels to August Bebel, Oct. 28, 1885, in Karl Marx [&] Friedrich Engels, 36 *Werke* 377 (1967).

[30]"Building Union Chief Is Critical of Labor," *NYT*, Apr. 25, 1972, at 16, col. 5.

[31]118 Cong. Rec. 19141-42 (1972).

[32]CUAIR, CC, Minutes, Apr. 28, 1972, at 5-6, in BR, 1972: Vol. II-Minutes.

[33]"Romney Jeered at Union Parley," *NYT*, May 13, 1969, at 42, col. 3.

[34]"Two Faces of Labor," *NYT*, May 15, 1969, at 46, col. 1.

Significantly, the *Times* adumbrated no role for private capital groups to confront construction unions' "extortionate" and "insatiab[le]" demands; instead, it despaired of the political parties' ever taking "the risk of alienating these A.F.L.-C.I.O. power centers" and using federal, state, or local government construction contracting counterstrength to assert the public interest.[35]

At the 1971 BCTD convention, union leaders conceded that the expansion of nonunion contractors and recession were forcing unions to raise productivity.[36] The next year, the BCTD focused on the growing problem in the South and Southwest, but by 1973, the shrinkage of the union sector had become so patent that the BCTD approved a four-cent per capita tax to finance a program to combat "'open shop'" contractors. Not included in this campaign but coordinated with it was the execution of a new national work rules agreement with the NCA designed to make union contractors "more competitive with open-shop firms."[37]

To impress upon construction users that unions would not acquiesce in the shift to nonunion contractors, in 1972 the Philadelphia Building & Construction Trades Council organized picketing, mass protests, and consumer boycotts when the Sheraton Hotel chain, a subsidiary of International Telephone and Telegraph, hired the nonunion Altemose Construction Company to build a suburban hotel.[38] The dispute reached a high point on June 5, 1972, when a thousand people engaged in "'a virtual military assault'" on the Valley Forge site, inducing the state supreme court to lament that the "violence and destruction reflect[] little improvement in the state of labor relations during the three quarters of a century since the Pullman and Homestead strikes."[39] The violence and lengthy litigation surrounding the project moved the struggle between unions and the antiunion employers to a new stage of direct confrontation, prompting open-shop backers to accuse unions of resorting to violence when the market had adjudged them failures.[40]

Despite the avalanche of warnings from union leaders about the increasingly urgent need to counteract the growing antiunion sector, building tradesmen may have left the impression of being more interested in assaulting than organizing their nonunion competitors. This neglect was congruent with the

[35]"Reckless Spiral," *NYT*, July 1, 1969, at 40, col. 1 (editorial).

[36]Jerry Flint, "Building Unions Urged to Spur Output," *NYT*, Nov. 15, 1971, at 81, col. 4.

[37]Damon Stetson, "Building Trades' Leaders Voice Worry as Nonunion Hiring Rises," *NYT*, Feb. 10, 1972, at 29, col. 3.; "Building Trades Department to Mount Campaign Against 'Open-Shop' Contractors," 77 (10) *BMP* 16 (Nov.-Dec. 1973); "Organizing Is Major Theme at Building Trades Convention," 27 (11) *Laborer* 7 (Nov. 1973).

[38]"Philadelphia Construction Unions Battle Non-Union Contractor, Injunction," 26 (7) *Laborer* 12 (July 1972).

[39]Altemose Construction Co. v. Building & Constr. Trades Council of Philadelphia, 296 A.2d 504, 507 (Pa. 1972). See also Altemose Construction Co. v. NLRB, 514 F.2d 8 (3d Cir. 1975).

[40]Herbert Northrup & Howard Foster, *Open Shop Construction* 192-203 (1975).

extraordinary complacence displayed by the leadership of the AFL-CIO. As background for a report examining why union membership was not growing at the same rate as the labor force,[41] *U.S. News & World Report* interviewed president George Meany at great length early in 1972. He sliced the Gordian knot by challenging the legitimacy of the question: he neither knew nor cared because union density had never been so high in the United States as in Western Europe. Indeed, he did "not necessarily" even prefer a higher proportion because "[w]e've done quite well without it" and "made tremendous strides...under Gompers, and his percentage of the labor force was very tiny compared with what we've got now." Meany then encapsulated the cavalier laisser-faire attitude toward organization that soon came to haunt both the building trades unions and the entire labor movement.

> Why should we worry about organizing groups of people who do not appear to want to be organized? If they prefer to have others speak for them and make the decisions which affect their lives without effective participation on their part, that is their right. ...
>
> Frankly, I used to worry about membership, about the size of the membership. But quite a few years ago I just stopped worrying about it, because to me it just doesn't make any difference.[42]

The Indochina boom created highly favorable economic conditions for unions firmly in control of labor markets. Despite the information with which international union and NCA presidents repeatedly confronted members about the untoward consequences for the union sector of unabated wage increases, national union leaders, who regarded locals' tactics as counterproductive "guerilla unionism,"[43] proved incapable, in the teeth of atomized collective bargaining, to restrain their members. Long experience with a highly cyclical industry had apparently taught skilled construction workers that since neither employers nor owners practiced moderation at the height of prosperity, they too should exert their full leverage before the next depression phase of the building cycle inevitably disemployed them. The unions were "riding so high" in terms of labor market control and capacity to strike successfully in the late 1960s and early 1970s that, in the view of some management-side labor relations officials, even with the benefit of hindsight, no imaginable institutional arrangement realistically could have induced them to exercise self-restraint.[44]

---

[41]"Is Labor Movement Losing Ground?" *USNWR*, Feb. 21, 1972, at 22-26.

[42]"U.S. Needs '30,000 New Jobs a Week Just to Break Even,'" *USNWR*, Feb. 21, 1972, at 27-34 at 27-28.

[43]Royal Montgomery, *Industrial Relations in the Chicago Building Trades* 41 (1927).

[44]Telephone interview with Kenneth Hedman, vice president, labor relations, Bechtel Corp., San Francisco (Mar. 12, 1999).

Part II

Rhetoric and Reality

"The tight supply of labor in the trades in New York hasn't helped the productivity picture...."[1]

[T]he current business slump has revived all the depression-consciousness that makes building tradesmen fearful even in the best of times.[2]

---

[1]Alan Oser, "Building Costs Push Steadily Upward," *NYT*, June 14, 1970, sect. 8, at 1, col. 1, at 9, col. 1 (quoting Howard Turner, president, Turner Construction Co.).

[2]A. H. Raskin, "Unused Inflation Curb," *NYT*, Mar. 1, 1971, at 29, col. 1.

3

The Press's Production of Public Perceptions of Rapacious Construction Unions and Workers

Between a President who seemingly has little respect for blue-collar workers, minority groups which are determined to break down the whole concept of apprenticeship training, and a press that pictures construction workers as feather-bedding millionaires, the need for solidarity is unprecedented.[1]

In the midst of an unprecedentedly unpopular undeclared war, while the state, employers, and the press decried their wage increases as undermining the economy and society, construction workers and their unions managed to project themselves as pro-war patriots,. In contrast, during World War II and the Korean War, both conducted with the help of elaborate statutory regulation, construction unions were shining examples of voluntary compliance with state wage controls.[2]

The chief basis for concentrating attacks on wage increases on construction unions was their allegedly ubiquitous demonstration effect: "the large number of building trades workers in every major community," argued *The New York Times* editorially in 1971, "makes their high settlements a source of envy and emulation for all other unions."[3] The following year, the construction industry's leading trade magazine, *Engineering News-Record,* conceding that "[n]ot every construction worker is party to the organized thievery that contrives to extract higher and higher hourly wages for less and less work," narrowed the group of macroeconomic trouble-makers to the 10 percent of the three million union members who "take an active part in establishing union policies."[4] Alternatively estimating the circle of culprits as the 5 or 10 percent who regularly attended local union meetings, *ENR* observed that "the economy of the entire nation and its 80 million workers may be

---

[1] M. A. Hutcheson, "If Hard Hats Stand for Hard-Working Old-Fashioned Patriotism, So Be It," 91 (5) *The Carpenter* 40 (May 1971).

[2] Emergency Price Control Act of 1942, Pub. L. No. 421, 56 Stat. 23; Act of Oct. 2, 1942, Pub. L. No. 729, §§ 4, 5, 56 Stat. 765, 766, 767; Defense Production Act of 1950, Pub. L. No. 774, 64 Stat. 798. For example, the Operating Engineers union was "praised for its efforts to prevent work stoppages during the Second World War and the Korean conflict...." Garth Mangum & John Walsh, *Union Resilience in Troubled Times: The Story of the Operating Engineers, AFL-CIO, 1960-1993*, at 54 (1994). Construction unions, however, were far from satisfied with their role in the Korean War stabilization programs; see "What Place Is Labor to Have in Defense?" 4 (1) *BCTB* 2 (Jan. 1951); "Labor in the Defense Program," 4 (2) *BCTB* 2 (Feb. 1951).

[3] "Checking the Pay-Price Spiral," *NYT*, Mar. 28, 1971, sect. 4, at 14, col. 1.

[4] "The Trouble with Labor Is Management," *ENR*, Feb. 24, 1972, at 64 (editorial).

adversely affected by 150,000 to 300,000 construction union members."[5]

Just as vociferously, however, *ENR* denied that announcing that it was "time to break the strangle hold these 300,000 active unionists have on construction" was in any way to "suggest union-busting." Rather, "curbs on featherbedding don't demand [unions'] destruction. The spread of open shop contracting across the south and into some northern states offers a welcome new, third force in the struggle between union contractors and unions."[6] Whether the ultimate aim was destroying, busting, decimating, or merely weakening, a survey of the contemporary daily and business press undeniably revealed the existence of an anti-construction union campaign. The importance that big business attached to shaping public opinion on this subject can be gauged by the fact that its most potent national lobbying organization, the Roundtable, held a series of meetings in the summer of 1970 with the *Reader's Digest* "resulting in agreement to prepare an article detailing specifics of some of the construction industry's labor related problems."[7] In January 1971 *Reader's Digest* published "Wage Madness in the Construction Industry," parts of which appeared to have been taken from some of the statements of the Roundtable's leader, Roger Blough, who in turn commended the piece to his members.[8] Two years later the Roundtable worked closely on a three-article series, by the same author, attacking construction unions in *Reader's Digest*, which, unbeknownst to the public, was itself a Roundtable member.[9]

The most prominent broadsides appeared in *Fortune*, which began focusing on construction in the late 1960s. The first in the series, from December 1968, "The Unchecked Power of the Building Trades," echoing traditional descriptions of the power of capital, fashioned an image of construction unions designed to deconstruct any sympathies that these organizations might have nurtured: "The most powerful oligopoly in the American economy today is the loose confederation of craft unions known as the building trades. ... Their collective economic power...is the single most important direct contribution to the current wage-price spiral." The magazine ignored both the inflationary impact of the Vietnam War and

---

[5]Edward Young, "Low Productivity: The Real Sin of High Wages," *ENR*, Feb. 24, 1972, at 18-23, at 19.

[6]"The Trouble with Labor Is Management," *ENR*, Feb. 24, 1972, at 64 (editorial).

[7]"1970 Summary CUAIR Coordinating Committee" at 2, in BR, 1970: CCH.

[8]Charles Stevenson, "Wage Madness in the Construction Industry," 98 (585) *RD* 47-51 (Jan. 1971); Letter from Roger Blough to the Roundtable Members (Dec. 21, 1970), in SP, Box 5, File-CUAIR 1969-1970.

[9]James Gross, *Broken Promise: The Subversion of U.S. Labor Relations Policy, 1947-1994*, at 235 (1995); Charles Stevenson, "The Tyranny of Terrorism in the Building Trades," 102 *RD*, June 1973, at 89-94; *idem*, "The Construction Unions Declare War," 103 *RD*, July 1973, at 79-83; *idem*, "Labor Violence—A National Scandal," 103 *RD*, Aug. 1973, at 153-58. *Reader's Digest* had also zealously joined in this attack earlier; Edward Young, "The Scandal Behind Soaring Construction Costs," *RD*, July 1972, at 66-70.

the fact that construction unions' power not only had been greater earlier in the century without triggering employer claims of outrageous wage increases, but had actually declined during the 1960s.[10] Before the depression of the 1930s, construction unions' power in cities with quasi-total organization was reputedly so "arbitrary and dictatorial" that real collective bargaining did not even take place.[11] Undeterred, *Fortune* rushed on to make construction workers also responsible for any possible housing shortage.[12] In case any of its own numerous readers had missed the piece, the Sunday *New York Times* published a lengthy resume.[13]

Such causal accusations were continuous with the period's managerial public relations approach. During the late 1960s and early 1970s, when worker alienation was perceived as threatening profitability, large corporations generally sought to divide and conquer workers and consumers. Thus the chairman of GM "warned that public sympathy for factory workers, based on 'misconceptions,' may result in rising labor costs prices—and rising consumer prices. The public, he said, doesn't realize that shorter work-weeks and greater worker control over tasks 'almost always involve an extra cost...which must inevitably be reflected in the price of the product...."[14]

In September 1969 *Fortune* returned to the theme of union construction workers as quasi-criminal infectious wreckers, this time editorially urging measures adequate to a situation that had in the meantime become more threatening:

> The latest round of wage increases in the construction industry signals once again that something drastic must be done to bring this conglomeration of monopolies back to economic reality before it wrecks us all. [E]ven more ominous, the construction contracts, won in special circumstances by murderous bargaining power, are generating pressures for the rank and file of the industrial unions for similar exorbitant increases.
>
> The inflationary settlements recently made in New York demonstrate that a handful

---

[10]Mills, *Industrial Relations and Manpower in Construction* at 29, 57.

[11]Haber, *Industrial Relations in the Building Industry* at 513.

[12]Thomas O'Hanlon, "The Unchecked Power of the Building Trades," *Fortune*, Dec. 1968, at 102-107, 209-14 at 102. On the inflationary impact of the war, see Benjamin J. Cohen, "Vietnam: The Impact on American Business" at 23-26 (mimeo, Dept. of Economics, Princeton U., Dec. 10, 1969). A left-wing architect misconstrues "the public" in arguing that it should give pause that the public "does not begin to take notice of the problems of the mode of production of this branch until they—mediated through the circulation sphere (construction cost inflation)—appear in the distribution sphere (rising rents)." Rolf Rosenbrock, "Bauproduktion," in *Architektur und Kapitalverwertung: Veränderungstendenzen in Beruf und Ausbildung von Architekten in der BRD* 85-124 at 100 (Klaus Brake ed., 1973). Since capitalist production as such is not accessible to the public, this information mechanism is precisely adequate.

[13]Joseph Fried, "Union 'Stranglehold' Is Charged," *NYT*, Dec. 18, 1968, sect. 8, at 1, col. 6.

[14]Laurence O'Donnell & Walter Mossberg, "UAW Will Emphasize Escape from 'the Job' in 1973 Contract Talks," *WSJ*, Dec. 8, 1972, at 1, col. 1.

of powerful business agents, representing a small number of workers, can set in motion a wage patterns for industries employing millions.[15]

From beneath the bombast of rhetoric conjuring up thugs run amok surfaced a concern that transcended the building industry itself: capital interests sought to prevent the spread of wage increases obtained by means of union militance in one industry to others. *Fortune* held construction firms themselves in part responsible for this contagion because they operated on a cost-plus basis and theretofore had only insufficiently undertaken to meet exorbitant wage demands with an entrepreneurial united front. The magazine also pointed to three groups (the NAM, the Chamber of Commerce, and "a number of top corporation executives" led by the former chairman of United States Steel, Roger Blough) calling for the revision of federal labor legislation to reinvigorate employers' bargaining power and "protect management's right to introduce laborsaving methods and materials"; these groups were also urging adoption of a new apprenticeship system that would fully integrate minorities. Finally, the editors put the rest of the working class on notice that it had nothing but its chains to lose by ignoring the unsustainable wage patterns set by the building trades: "No workingman...gains anything at all from monopoly union practices in a key industry. These only rob him of his higher right to share in the growth of a productive and efficient economy."[16]

The *Fortune* editorial was supported by an article in the same issue illustrating the deleterious power of the construction unions, whose members were building the GM Vega factory at Lordstown, Ohio. The article's editorial message was clear: "The explosive inflationary pressures generated by labor conditions" in construction, and especially "the unconscionable rise in labor costs," confronted "the business community with what is probably its most serious and urgent problem." Because Ford was already selling a similar automobile, GM feared that any delay in production would endanger its position in the increasingly important market for small cars; consequently, GM was willing to accept higher construction costs. The sudden absorption of a large number of skilled building tradesmen created a tight regional labor market; the resulting wage increases provoked the ire of construction firms not involved in the Lordstown project.[17]

---

[15]"Editorial: Breaking Up a Labor Monopoly," *Fortune*, Sept. 1969, at 85.

[16]"Editorial: Breaking Up a Labor Monopoly" at 85-86.

[17]Don Sider, "The Big Boondoggle at Lordstown," *Fortune*, Sept. 1969, at 106-109, 196. Sheahan, *Wage-Price Guideposts* at 40, stated, without offering examples or sources, that "attempts of the Defense Department to rush through large-scale construction projects in areas unable to supply the required labor readily...resulted in extraordinary wage increases that spread by example even to sections in which the labor supply is adequate." Clinton Bourdon & Raymond Levitt, *Union and Open-Shop Construction: Compensation, Work Practices, and Labor Markets* 106 (1980), argued that

In December 1968, a regional group of construction employers requested some accommodation from GM; instead, GM and its general contractor accused each other of bearing responsibility for premium overtime costs. The group charged that "the 'welfare state'...on the project will saddle the multistate area with adverse working conditions and affect union demands in future labor contract negotiations."[18] Local construction firms complained to GM that, by offering 70-80 hour workweeks, its general contractor "was monopolizing the supply of building tradesmen" and making it impossible for firms in eastern Ohio, western Pennsylvania, and northern West Virginia to compete; as a result, many other projects would have to be abandoned or performed with nonunion workers.[19] The dispute was serious enough to induce the AGC executive director to request GM's president to eliminate the overtime regime.[20]

The adverse publicity prompted GM to offer self-exculpatory data while defending its practices at a project requiring a peak construction force of 1,800 workers and employing 20 to 30 percent of all locally registered workers in several crafts. GM argued that overtime had been an absolute necessity: "It takes overtime to bring out-of-town and out-of-state tradesmen to such a wide place in the road like Lordstown for a relatively short construction period." Moreover, GM stated that 70-hour weeks had prevailed only in late 1968, whereas later hours varied between 40 and 60 for various trades. Indeed, when hours were cut from 60 to 54, jurisdictional strikes followed, which the general contractor stopped by threatening to call off all Saturday work in any week marked by work stoppages.[21]

Fortune's bias-forging purpose was manifest in the Lordstown article's layout: two of its five pages were completely given over to large color photographs of eight Lordstown construction workers next to large bolded labels with their horrifying hourly overtime rates (including pension and other social wage payments), which "soar[ed]" to between $10.58 and $14.76.[22] Some Lordstown

---

major strikes in the late 1960s and early 1970s were a major factor making union construction "less attractive to many...industrial users. ... Uncertainty in schedule is intolerable to industrial clients, when they are building revenue-producing facilities in competitive markets." Although this point may be valid, it may not bear much explanatory weight since these firms must have been equally sensitive to strikes by their own union production employees, and yet firms such as GM did not seek to replace them with nonunion workers temporarily, let alone permanently.

[18]"GM Hit on Overtime," *ENR*, Mar. 6, 1969, at 14.

[19]"Further Meeting Held with GM Officials on Overtime Controversy at Ohio Site," *CLR*, No. 705, Mar. 26, 1969, at A-10, A-11.

[20]"AGC's Dunn Urges General Motors President to Personally Investigate Overtime Dispute," *CLR*, No. 707, Apr. 9, 1969, at A-5.

[21]"GM Figures Rebut Lordstown Project Critics," *ENR*, July 10, 1969, at 28-29.

[22]Sider, "The Big Boondoggle at Lordstown" at 107-108. At the other extreme, the Socialist Workers Party, despite admitting the lack of productivity data, gratuitously claimed: "Construction workers are already among the most highly exploited and not much more can be squeezed out of them

workers had "flocked from as far away as California and Louisiana to try to get in on what they knew would be easy pickings. ... At one time or another...most of the crafts have worked a seventy-hour work." What was so easy about performing hard physical labor in the cold or heat ten hours a day seven days a week 2,000 miles from home *Fortune* did not explain in its rush to the punch line—that a mere laborer might gross $563.50 some week, while a carpenter's weekly wages reached $661.[23] One photograph showed a smiling black man in a hard hat next to his $11.13 hourly overtime rate, prompting *Fortune* to remark that he "has good reason to smile." Of a bricklayer who commuted from 30 minutes away and whose overtime wage was $13.35, the magazine remarked that the "drive is well worth while." That a plumber received a wage of $14.76 per hour of overtime explained "why plumbers are rather choosy about making house calls."[24]

Unsurprisingly, *Fortune* found no space for photographs of GM's highest executives grinning at their desks paired with calculations of their vastly higher per-work-hour annual incomes and sneering comments on the "easy pickings." For example, the chairman of General Motors, James M. Roche, was for several years the highest paid business executive in the United States; even if he had worked all 8,760 hours of 1967, his estimated compensation of $950,000 would have merited a caption of $108.45 per hour; if he put in 40 hour weeks, his hourly salary would have amounted to $475. The photos that *Fortune* did publish in its articles on executives' emoluments and perquisites were dignified and the comments bereft of any hint of unearned income.[25] Manifestly, the magazine believed that times had changed radically since 1887, when the *American Architect and Building News* had opined: "Speaking generally, the workm[a]n can never escape from his daily toil and cannot rise in the social scale. The aggregation of capital which characterizes the present age...has robbed him of the flattering unction with which he once nourished his soul that he could enter the class above him."[26]

The cost of the Lordstown plant proved to be twice the projected figure of $75 million. Whether as a consequence of the construction costs or not, GM ultimately priced the Vega several hundred dollars higher than expected and also

-----

except lower wages. This is where the open-shoppers come in...." Nat Weinstein, "The Open-Shop Drive in the Building Trades," in Nat Weinstein, Frank Lovell, & Carol Lipman, *Construction Workers Under Attack: How to Fight Back and Rebuild Unions* 11-16 at 14 (1974 [1973]).

[23]Sider, "The Big Boondoggle at Lordstown" at 106.

[24]Sider, "The Big Boondoggle at Lordstown" at 107-108. *Fortune*'s jibe was a red herring since many plumbers employed by plumbing contractors performing small residential jobs lack the skills required for technologically sophisticated and specialized industrial construction.

[25]Jeremy Main, "An Expanding Executive Pay Package," 77 *Fortune*, June 15, 1968, at 166-69, 356, 362, 365, at 167. In 1969, Roche's compensation dropped to only $790,000. "How the Top Men Fared in 1969," *BW*, June 13, 1970, at 59-68.

[26]"Trade-Unions in America," 22 (603) *AABN* 29-30 at 29 (July 16, 1887).

considerably above its German and Japanese competitors' small cars.[27] *Fortune* assigned co-responsibility to GM for the untoward wage developments—especially since it had incorporated a large number of overtime hours into the construction plans "not so much to get the job done but to ensure that contractors could be recruit an ample supply of workers."[28] *Fortune* conceded that the options open to GM—and, by implication, other large construction industrial users—were problematic.[29] Thus it pooh-poohed several "novel" suggestions offered by the disgruntled area contractors and their customers. First, GM could buy a construction company and do its own construction work (amounting to more than $1 billion annually), but, for unexplicated reasons ("in the auto industry it is an accepted maxim that you get into trouble when you get into another man's business"), vertical integration was suboptimal. In a variant move, GM could hire its own construction labor force and move it from site to site to avoid creating tight local labor markets, but that strategy would be inefficient. Alternatively, GM could avoid greedy U.S. unions altogether by building its plants outside the country, "but G.M.'s own sense of national responsibility, not to mention its fear of government disapproval, would prevent that extreme move." Finally, GM "could demand a nonunion or open shop on its jobs, but for a company and an industry which is so thoroughly unionized that could be disastrous."[30]

The first two of the contractors' suggestions were hardly "novel": numerous industrial companies, such as duPont, maintained their own so-called force account construction divisions. Whether such vertical integration was as rational as contracting with construction firms depended largely on scale and specialization efficiencies.[31] The last two, antiunion, suggestions, however, anticipated future events. For the time being, however, *Fortune* sighed, GM, "rather than lead the

---

[27]Jerry Flint, "Hard Hats Finding Fat Raises Do Not Help," *NYT*, Feb. 6, 1971, at 28, 50.

[28]Sider, "The Big Boondoggle at Lordstown" at 109.

[29]The Roundtable asserted that in 1968 66 percent of overtime offered on projects carried out by NCA members was paid to attract labor and 34 percent to accelerate or maintain schedules. "Builders Put a Lid on Overtime Pay," *BW*, June 19, 1971, at 38. This claim was repeated in BR, *Coming to Grips with Some Major Problems in the Construction Industry* 7 (1975 [1974]).

[30]Sider, "The Big Boondoggle at Lordstown" at 196.

[31]Within a few years such possibilities became reality in the utility industry. Lefkoe, *Crisis in Construction* at 8; "A Different Way to Build," *ENR*, Mar. 20, 1975, at 184 (editorial) (in-house construction enabled Dayton Power & Light Co. to reduce labor costs by one-half); "Utilities Try Building Own Facilities to Control Costs and Raise Productivity," *WSJ*, July 15, 1975, at 38, col. 1. Such force account workers were generally nonunion and received below-average wages; management was able to increase its control over the production process. In the mid-1960s, nonconstruction firms accounted for about 30 percent of all construction activity. John Cambern, "Profile of the U.S. Contract Construction Industry," *CR*, Sept. 1964, at 4. Although in the 1970s some major manufacturers had their own construction forces in the thousands, by the 1990s the trend toward outsourcing eliminated most of them. BR, "The Business Stake in Effective Project Systems" 4 (1997).

anti-inflation battle itself...has chosen to join" the aforementioned corporate users group run by Roger Blough; it would encourage contractors associations to take "tough" bargaining positions, monitor agreements, and "may chastise any company that forces a contractor to capitulate to the extreme demands of the building trades' unions." But the magazine left little doubt that stronger measures would eventually be needed: "it remains to be seen whether this alliance of sympathy is sufficient to correct the imbalance of union power at collective-bargaining sessions."[32]

Fortune's observations suggested that for the time being large industrial capital was not considering the possibility that it might restructure the building industry in order to lower costs. Industrial users appear to have been willing to countenance the industry's subrational organization, turning their attention instead to labor-management relations within construction. This strategy, however, presupposed a community of interests whose existence was not demonstrated. In particular, it presupposed that competing industrial corporations (the construction industry's customers) could stop seeking extra profits at the expense of their competitors, and that construction firms could be mobilized as a united front.

The monitoring and policing functions that the Blough group was to fulfill were analogous to those of a state-like aggregate capitalist, but *Fortune* assigned no role to the state. This private enforcer was designed to impose on individual firms behavior that would yield them short-term (inflation-suppressing) and long-term (improved international position) advantages, but only disadvantages to construction workers and unions (except in the Pickwickian sense that anything that fosters capital accumulation ultimately benefits the working class). This program thus seemed to embody a repressive function rather than one insuring the maintenance of the working class. Whether such a strategy was possible without direct state involvement appears implausible. In any event, George Meany was not far from the mark in charging that Blough "runs an organization...dedicated to bringing wages down."[33]

In contrast, the editorial page of *ENR* offered its specialized audience a more sober and nuanced analysis of Lordstown and the larger issues it raised. The magazine's point of departure was that in the short run the interests of GM and construction firms were bound to clash: the higher, overtime-driven, building costs were "but a small part of the manufacturer's tooling and production costs" and would all be recouped in the automobile prices. Moreover, since GM would probably not engage in similar construction projects in the region in the near future, "its present impact on future wages in the region is of remote concern, if any." Equally remote to GM, the magazine concluded, was the effect that higher

---

[32]Sider, "The Big Boondoggle at Lordstown" at 196.

[33]1 *Proceedings of the Ninth Constitutional Convention of the AFL-CIO: Daily Proceedings and Executive Council Reports* 22-23 (1971).

construction wages "must eventually have on wages its production workers will demand." *ENR* hoped that this "horrible example" would serve as a lesson that a more far-seeing organization, such as a U.S. Chamber of Commerce task force, could bring to bear to make large users understand that their short-term self-regarding actions could have a disastrous impact wage inflation in construction. In any event, the Ohio-Pennsylvania Regional Congress of Construction Employers, "at its present stage of development," was not in a position to deal with the problem without their large customers' support.[34] The debacle at Lordstown did in fact exert precisely the domino impact that employers had feared: it "contributed significantly to large wage settlements" in neighboring Akron, Cleveland, Pittsburgh, and by 1969 in Buffalo.[35]

In October 1970 *Fortune* continued its assault. "The Building Trades versus the People" levelled charges at construction workers reminiscent of those hurled at the robber barons at the turn of the century. *Fortune* accused their unions of having forged an "apparatus for redistributing wealth by force. Construction workers, whose incomes are already inflated far above the national average, siphon away billions a year from the whole public as consumers. [T]he industry discriminates against labor with less monopoly power: since average output per employed American is less than $12,000 a year, unduly high wages in construction inexorably result in unduly low wages somewhere else." Not only were building trades unions exploiting everyone else, their "fantastic...wage trajectory...threatens to tear apart the intricate functional distinctions in incentives and rewards that make an economy dynamic and help it use its resources efficiently." In short, "Unskilled work, executive pay" was a recipe for disaster that "[e]ven the Communist countries" had learned to avoid. Predicting that by 1972 the incomes of a substantial proportion of skilled building tradesmen would reach $20,000, *Fortune* calculated that at that point they would surpass "the income of many talented young executives and professional people who have invested many thousands of dollars and years of their lives in preparing themselves for their jobs." The magazine warned that people with ability could not be motivated to undergo long training "unless there is a considerable spread between top and bottom income levels." Although none of this rhetoric explained why the army of mid-level corporate white-collar employees were somehow more deserving of their salaries than plumbers and electricians of their wages, *Fortune* overlooked the possibility that if so many unmotivated executive apprentices found plumbing more lucrative, the labor market would soon take care of the alleged shortage of skilled tradesmen that

---

[34]"What's Good for GM...," *ENR*, Mar. 13, 1969, at 80.

[35]DOL, Labor-Management Services Adm., *The Bargaining Structure in Construction: Problems and Prospects* 42 (1980) (prepared by Donald Cullen & Louis Feinberg).

allegedly was driving wages up.[36]

The magazine strove to characterize public sympathies for labor as misguided. *Fortune* expressly eschewed the class context that had seemed appropriate enough when rallying industrial employers to protect their profits from encroachments by construction workers: "Most Americans as consumers...all too often...sentimentally take sides with the workers against the bosses.   In construction, however, the real conflict is not between labor and capital, but between labor and consumers, with the employers serving as a medium for passing labor's exactions on to the public at large."[37] (Roger Blough of the Roundtable was especially taken with this piece, sending copies to all members.)[38] Employers favored this argument when the business cycle and/or conditions specific to the industry in question permitted passing on the costs so that increased wage costs appeared as the sole cause of the increased prices. When such shifting was not possible, the conflict appeared as a profit squeeze within the branch or firm; when shifting was successful, leading to increased profits at the expense of consumption, the conflict was merely displaced to the aggregate social level. In the case of factory construction, where the consumer was not "the public at large" but industrial firms, their profits could be reduced for the benefit of construction firms to the extent that they were unable to pass their increased costs on to final consumers. In this case a conflict between firms of different industries could be transformed into one between construction firms and construction workers/unions and/or industrial firms and construction firms on the one hand and construction workers/unions on the other.

The same issue of *Fortune* devoted yet another piece to wily and unruly construction workers, which also carried an implicit caution that words and deeds may not only conceal essentials, but even make them appear as their opposite. The magazine reported on a strike in Kansas City in which 4,000 striking laborers were supported by 18,000 skilled trademen: "According to a candid union leader, the major reason the craftsmen backed the strikers is that 35 percent of the strikers were black. The craftsmen reckoned that if the blacks made a lot of money as laborers, 'they won't have too much of a motive to crash the trades.'"[39] The reasoning seemed a tad strained since black workers were already overrepresented in the

---

[36]Gilbert Burck, "The Building Trades versus the People," 82 (4) *Fortune* 94-97, 159-60, at 95, 96 (Oct. 1970).

[37]Burck, "The Building Trades versus the People" at 95. Sylvester Petro, "Unions, Housing Costs and the National Labor Policy," 32 (2) *LCP* 319-48 at 329 (Spr. 1967), also argued that construction unions' efforts to secure control over labor functions for their members were merely a struggle between workers, not between labor and capital.

[38]Letter from Roger Blough to Members of the Roundtable (Oct. 20, 1970), in SP, Box 5, File-CUAIR 1969-1970.

[39]"In Kansas City They Couldn't Go As Far As They Wanted," *Fortune*, Oct. 1970, at 98.

unions of the bricklayers, cement masons, and lathers, who struck for 197 days allegedly to keep laborers at bay.[40]

If the image cultivated by the press and prominent economists of the standard of living of "the" construction worker during those years was to be credited: "Construction workers are fast becoming members of the U.S. middle class."[41] The *Wall Street Journal* in a lead front-page article on the "relatively high standard of living" of an electrician whose projected before-tax income of $18,000 including overtime required him to go "heavily in debt" to buy a $28,500 house, quoted his employer as calling "'[t]he construction worker...a man who's moving very rapidly into the upper middle class.'"[42] These class-conscious claims may seem quaint from the vantage point of late-twentieth-century supraclass public opinion, but they were contested even in 1970. The *Wall Street Journal* may have editorialized that the "bribes that have been going to the nation's 3 million building trades workers are getting out of hand,"[43] but *The New York Times* provided an emblematic account of the modest and unchanging standard of living of a union plumber in Chicago whose major worry was that blacks were living only six blocks away.[44] Indeed, the *Times,* in contradicting contemporaneous depictions of construction workers' luxurious living standards, may have dissolved the paradox by suggesting that rising consumer prices cancelled out their wage increases: "Hard Hats Finding Fat Raises Do Not Help."[45] Presumably, then, other workers, unable to obtain equally high wage increases, must have been experiencing a decline in real wages.

Remarkable, too, was the indignation with which journalists, professors, and corporate executives not only pointed to the mere existence of manual workers with annual incomes between $15,000 and $25,000, but created the impression that this range represented the normal case.[46] In the 1973 edition of his introductory economics textbook—a work that "has gone along way toward giving the world a common economic language"[47]—Paul Samuelson knew no better way to ridicule "New Left college students...eager to join the picket line in a display of fraternal

---

[40]In fact, the trowel trades obtained a $4.50 per hour wage increase over four years, while the laborers received $4.15. BLS, *Work Stoppages in Contract Construction, 1962-73*, at 51 (Bull. 1847, 1975).

[41]"Be a Construction Worker—Make $26,000 a Year," *ENR*, Sept. 17, 1970, at 55.

[42]Everett Groseclose, "Construction Workers Chafe at Claim They're 'Villains' of Inflation," *WSJ*, Aug. 11, 1971, at 1, col. 6.

[43]"Bribing the Building Trades," *WSJ*, Dec. 14, 1970, at 14, col. 1 (editorial).

[44]Seth King, "Plumber Discounts His Paper Victory Over Inflation," *NYT*, July 18, 1970, at 14, col. 1.

[45]Flint, "Hard Hats Finding Fat Raises Do Not Help" at 28.

[46]E.g., A. Raskin, "Unused Inflation Curb," *NYT*, Mar. 1, 1971, at 29; Everett Groseclose, "Construction Workers Chafe at Claim They're 'Villains' of Inflation," *WSJ*, Aug. 11, 1971, at 1, col. 6; "Construction Pay Is Raising the Roof," *BW*, Apr. 18, 1970, at 74, 76.

[47]"Theorist with a Best Seller," *BW*, Feb. 14, 1959, at 73, 74.

unity against the exploiting bosses" than to ask what such "a revolutionist ha[d] in common with...plumbing or construction union...members who get wages of more than $20,000 a year...."[48]

Even when such attacks were unfounded, proponents, judging by statements not meant for public consumption, appear to have believed them. For example, at a Roundtable meeting in 1972, Roger Blough mentioned a recent *New York Times* article on "individual workers who receive up to $76,000 a year in overtime pay, pushing the cost of the World Trade center from something like 300 million to somewhere in the neighborhood of 700 million dollars."[49] In fact, the article nowhere suggested the arithmetically preposterous claim that the few shop stewards holding such sinecures were responsible for the $350 million cost overrun.[50]

The image of construction workers and unions that the press forged raises several questions.[51] This antiunion campaign did not represent a journalistic whim, but a movement, which was already in an organizationally advanced stage and encompassed both the largest industrial firms and the Nixon administration; the extent of the cooordination of these efforts, remains to be elucidated. The motive for industrial users' extraordinary interest in the construction industry was not only the above-average rise in building costs, which affected industrial customers, but also the fear that construction unions' militance might spread to industrial employees. To this end, employers and the federal government developed a strategy to strengthen organizationally weak construction capital vis-à-vis the unions. How they imagined this re-equilibration process was as yet unclear. The danger was in any event immediate enough to galvanize unions into undertaking the effort to divide and conquer their enemies by allying themselves with President Nixon. To contextualize these complex political maneuverings it is necessary to scrutinize the reality content of the image of greedy and grasping construction workers and powerful construction unions, and to analyze the peculiar economic structure of the construction industry.

---

[48]Paul Samuelson, *Economics* 138 (9th ed. 1973).

[49]CUAIR, CC, Minutes, Sept. 15, 1972, 4, in BR, 1972-Vol. II, Minutes.

[50]Robert Tomasson, "$76,000 Pay in Overtime Indicated in Contract," *NYT*, Sept. 3, 1972, sect. 8, at 1, col. 6, at 4, col. 7-8. Indeed, just a few months later, Saul Horowitz, Jr., the CEO of HRH Construction Company and a member of the Contractors Advisory Committee, sympathetically explained that "creation of shop steward, master mechanic and other types of do-nothing jobs is attributable to the desires of the union leadership to meet the needs of older, security-oriented members of their unions." He suggested that management propose alternative responses to older members' needs that were more productive than "this galaxy of non-productive posts." Here Horowitz mentioned the possibility of four-day weeks or five or six-hour days. BR, CC, Minutes, Feb. 1, 1973, at 9, in BR, 1973-Vol. II, Minutes.

[51]For a suggestion that the scholarly and journalistic pictures more or less coincide with each other, see Howard Foster, "Labor in Construction: Recent Research and Popular Wisdom," in *Labor & Manpower* 104-19 at 119 (Richard Pegnetter ed., 1974).

4

Reality: Wages and Unemployment

There was considerable discussion about how the Roundtable could answer Mr. Meany's assertion that the average construction worker only realized an income of $8,000 per annum. Various suggestions were made for developing meaningful statistics in this regard.... However, it was pointed out that good statistics on income of individual construction workers was [sic] difficult to come by and that in view of the shortage of workers and their migratory tendencies, the trend in wage rates, on which the Roundtable has been concentrating so far, is the important statistic.[1]

The experience of the pressure exerted by the industrial reserve army can...even strengthen the false notion that the law of supply and demand is the essential law of the capitalist economy.[2]

How accurate were the accusations of the press, employers, and the government that construction workers' wages during the Vietnam war represented unsustainable overreaching? This chapter confronts rhetoric and reality by presenting a broad variety of wage data. Journalistic reports implicitly assumed that relatively high hourly wages were associated with 2,000 hours of work annually. Because hourly wage rates, however, may reveal little about standards of living, the impact of the intervening variable of unemployment on annual incomes is also examined in depth.

WAGES

The inclusive nature of the craft union culture has allowed the continuation of one of the most astounding characteristics of the industry—the uniform wage for *all* journeymen in the union setting. In a society that reveres pay-scale hierarchies and provides status rewards on the basis of income differentials, union carpenters and other organized building trades workers have offered a distinctive and almost subversive model for compensation systems.[3]

The concerted attacks on construction union, workers, and wages during the late 1960s and early 1970s must be viewed against the business cycle movements of those years: in December 1969 the U.S. economy reached the peak of the boom

---

[1]CUAIR, CC, Minutes, Feb. 16, 1971, at 3, in BR, 1971-Vol. II: Minutes.

[2]Christel Hopf & Wulf Hopf, "Gleichgültigkeit und Identifikation als Kategorien der Analyse von Klassenbewußtsein," 6 (1) *PK* No. 22, 67-100 at 92 (1976).

[3]Mark Erlich, *With Our Hands: The Story of Carpenters in Massachusetts* 19 (1986).

phase of a long upswing (which had begun in February 1961), after which it fell
into a steep recession, bottoming out in November 1970, and reaching another peak
in November 1973 and yet another trough in March 1975.[4] The rise in the wage
level associated with the partial absorption of the reserve army of the unemployed
during the boom phase contributes—as a result of the temporary impossibility of
using the methods of increasing the productivity and intensity of labor to counteract
the rising price of labor power—to an acceleration of the passage through the
conjunctural phases by permitting profits and investments to decline. If, at the
beginning of an upswing, special industry-level developments give militant unions
the opportunity to enforce wage increases beyond what is "justified" (in relation to
the volume of unemployment), firms and/or the state may seek to prevent the spread
of this militance threatening the revival of profits. It is in the context of this threat
of union militance that the attacks on building trade unions can be understood.

The course of profitability in the construction industry, like that in
manufacturing, during the Vietnam era is unambiguous (virtually regardless of how
the numerator and denominator are defined): the before-tax rate of profit among
construction corporations rose monotonically from a low of 8.4 percent in 1960 to
a high of 13.9 percent and 14.0 per cent in 1965 and 1966, before falling to 10.5
percent in 1970.[5] After tax profits, in the words of the Business Roundtable, peaked
in 1966 following "an outstanding performance in the early Sixties." In April 1970,
the chairman of U.S. Steel publicly declared that, given the downturn in profits,

---

[4]U.S. BEA, *Handbook of Cyclical Indicators*, tab. 10 at 178 (1984).

[5]In manufacturing, the rate of profit rose from 14.6 percent in 1961 to a high of 19.6 and
19.2 percent in 1965 and 1966, before falling to 9.6 percent in 1970. The profit rate in this particular
series, which covers all corporations, is defined as total profits (=total receipts minus total deductions)
divided by total net capital assets (=depreciable, depletable, and amortizable assets minus accumulated
depreciation, depletion, and amoritzation, plus inventories and land). The data, which were not
available for 1962, are all taken from IRS, *Statistics of Income* for the years in question. Use of
numerous other definitions did not affect the trend. Other investigators using other data bases have
also shown that manufacturing profitability peaked in 1965-66. E.g., William Nordhaus, "The Falling
Share of Profits," *BPEA* 1: 1974, at 169-208, tab. 5 at 180, fig. 3 at 181; Michael Lovell, "The Profit
Picture: Trends and Cycles," *BPEA* 3:1978, at 768-88, fig. 1 at 776; Daniel Holland & Stewart Myers,
"Profitability and Capital Costs for Manufacturing Corporations and All Nonfinancial Corporations,"
70 (2) *AER* 320-25, tab. 1 321 (May 1980) (Papers & Proceedings). For similar results for the entire
economy, see Fred Moseley, *The Falling Rate of Profit in the Postwar United States* 88 (1991).
Calculating the profitability of the largest construction firms on the basis of their published annual
income accounts is made difficult by the fact that some were not publicly traded, while others either
maintained nonconstruction divisions or were themselves subsidiaries of larger nonconstruction firms.
The data on net income (only component of the profit rate) of one large firm not subject to any of these
problems, Morrison-Knudsen Company, did not conform to the aforementioned macro-trends: its net
income was stagnant to falling despite more than doubling its operating revenues. Fluor Corporation's
net income moved more in synch with those trends. *Moody's Industrial Manual* 776, 625 (1968);
Moody's Industrial Manual 823, 747 (1970); *Moody's Industrial Manual* 2: 2384, 1:278 (1972);
Moody's Industrial Manual 2: 2430, 1:593 (1974).

"skyrocketing" construction costs were jeopardizing economic recovery.[6]

Table 1 compares the median hourly increases (in cents) in negotiated wages in manufacturing and construction from 1962 to 1974. The gap between them was stable until 1966; from then until 1970 it increased strongly; from 1970 to 1974 the gap closed as construction increases declined and those in manufacturing continued to rise. When the gap peaked in 1970, hourly construction wage increases reached 90.5 cents compared to 23.3 cents in manufacturing. This increase of 14.7 percent over the previous year compared to 6 percent in manufacturing prompted one Roundtable leader to speak of "wage madness."[7]

Table 1: Median Hourly Wage Increases in Collective Bargaining Agreements in Manufacturing and Construction, 1962-1974 (in cents)		
Year	Manufacturing	Construction
1962	6.6	12.4
1963	7.0	14.9
1964	6.8	15.3
1965	8.0	17.5
1966	10.2	19.8
1967	13.1	34.9
1968	15.7	49.6
1969	19.9	70.2
1970	23.3	90.5
1971	27.0	68.1
1972	21.1	38.3
1973	24.6	39.8
1974	30.3	49.9

Source: *CLR*, No. 852, Jan. 26, 1972, at B-2; *CLR*, No. 954, Jan. 23, 1974, at B-4; *CLR*, No. 1005, Jan. 22, 1975, at B-11.

---

[6]BR, "The Business Roundtable: Its Purpose and Program," n.p. [slide 19], in BR, CCH: 1973; United States Steel, untitled (Apr. 14, 1970), in SP, Box 5, File-CUAIR 1969-1970.

[7]CUAIR, Members Meeting, June 3, 1971, Minutes at 7, in SP, Box. 5. On the percentage data, see *id.* at 11.

The preoccupation of government officials, economists, journalists, and employers with the widening gap between construction and manufacturing wages during the Vietnam War was accompanied by a tendency to generalize this differential wage movement for the entire post-World War II period.[8] Table 2 shows the development over this period.

The excess in the rate of increase of construction over manufacturing wages was relatively small until 1965. Only during the Vietnam War years, 1965-71, did the gap open widely. In contrast, during the operation of the Nixon administration wage controls between 1971 and 1974, manufacturing wages rose faster than those in construction. The existence of the differential as such throughout the postwar period (and in fact since the nineteenth century) is adequately accounted for by such differences as skill levels and unemployment and injury rates.[9]

An aspect that constituted the real brisance of construction union successes compared with wage struggles in other industries was disposable weekly real wages—net of inflation, federal income taxes, and social security contributions. Table 3 shows the development during the Vietnam War period.

The disposable real weekly wage of the average worker at the end of this ten-year period fell below the level recorded at the outset. The vast bulk of the gap between the 62.5 percent increase in nominal gross wages and the 0.4 percent decrease in real net wages was accounted for by inflation; real gross wages rose by only 4.0 percent.[10]

---

[8]See, e.g., Howard Foster, "Wages in Construction: Examining the Evidence," 11 (3) *IR* 336-49 at 337 (Oct. 1972).

[9]The differential varied by wage series; for hourly earnings, it varied between 27 (1947) and 59 percent (1971); for weekly earnings between 19 (1947) and 49 percent (1971); for real spendable weekly earnings between 17 (1947) and 46 percent (1971); for annual "full-time" wages and salaries between 1 (1947) and 18 percent (1971). From 1947 to 1975, real hourly construction wages rose at a compounded annual rate of 2.4 percent compared to 1.8 percent in manufacturing; the increases for the more comprehensive series were lower. This difference is modest in light of the 2.8 percent annual compounded growth rate of the deflated output per hour of all persons in the private sector rose during the same period. BLS, NEWS: "Productivity and Costs in Nonfinancial Corporations: Annual Data for 1975," tab. 1 & A (USDL 76-129, Feb. 25, 1976).

[10]*MLR*, 98 (6):94. See generally, David Freedman, "Inflation in the United States, 1959-1974: Its Impact on Employment, Incomes and Industrial Relations," 112 (1-2) *ILR* 125-47 at 136-42 (Aug.-Sept. 1975).

Table 2: Rate of Change in Construction and Manufacturing Earnings, 1947-1974 (in %)

Period	Average hourly earnings of production or nonsupervisory workers		Gross average weekly earnings of production or nonsupervisory workers		Real spendable weekly earnings of production or nonsupervisory workers with 3 dependents		Annual wages & salaries per full-time equivalent employee	
	Construction	Mfg	Construction	Mfg	Construction	Mfg	Construction	Mfg
1947-74	338.7	261.5	323.7	257.9	69.8	43.7	331.0	228.2
1947-57	75.6	68.4	70.3	65.9	28.1	23.9	81.0	76.4
1957-65	36.5	27.3	38.0	31.8	22.3	16.2	35.2	33.2
1965-71	53.8	36.8	53.0	32.5	15.1	0	51.3	35.3
1971-74	18.8	23.2	17.8	23.6	-5.8	0	16.4	22.1

Sources: Hourly, weekly, and real spendable weekly earnings: BLS, *Handbook of Labor Statistics 1975—Reference Edition*, tab. 98 at 248, tab. 104 at 258 (Bull. 1865, 1975); annual wages and salaries per full-time equivalent employee: BEA, *The National Income and Product Accounts of the United States, 1929-82: Statistical Tables*, tab. 6.8A at 279-81 (1986).

Table 3: Average Disposable Real Weekly Earnings (in constant 1967 $) of Private-Sector Workers, 1965-1974			
Year	Wages	Year	Wages
1965	91.32	1970	89.95
1966	91.21	1971	92.67
1967	90.86	1972	96.64
1968	91.44	1973	95.73
1969	91.07	1974	90.97

Source: 98 (6) *MLR* 94 (June 1975). Data refer to nonagricultural workers with three dependents.

Whereas the increase in nominal weekly gross manufacturing wages during this period (from $107.53 to $176.40) amounted to 64.0 percent, the corresponding rise in construction was 80.0 percent (from $138.38 to $249.08).[11] Table 4 shows the development in real spendable weekly earnings for these two sectors.

Whereas real weekly earnings in manufacturing were absolutely stationary, in construction they recorded a modest overall increase of 8.3 percent; through the year 1972, the corresponding increases were 5.6 percent and 17.4 percent respectively. Emphasis of this differential should not conceal the fact that construction workers' average real weekly wage increase during this decade amounted to only $1.08 per year.[12] And even this trivial sum presupposes that the workers were actually employed year-round.

Although the course of hourly wages is even less indicative of real wages than weekly wages, they are introduced here to compare developments in construction and elsewhere. Table 5 shows the relation of gross hourly earnings in construction to those in the whole private sector and manufacturing.

The development of the gap between construction and other hourly nonsupervisory workers breaks down into three periods: from 1965 to 1968 the gap widened slowly; between 1968 and 1971, it widened more rapidly, 1969-70 being the high point; and from 1971 to 1974 the gap closed somewhat. The turning point (1971) coincides with the introduction of wage controls in construction and in the total economy.[13]

---

[11]BLS, *Employment and Earnings, United States, 1909-75*, at 748, 749-50 (Bull. 1312-10, 1976).

[12]See also "Haggerty Urges Action on Three Fronts," *ENR*, Sept. 19, 1968, at 253 (calculating that average construction worker's real weekly wage rose by 50 cents between June 1967 and June 1968); Andrew Levison, *The Working Class Majority* 109 (1974).

[13]A similar pattern prevailed with respect to individual manufacturing industries: the ratio

Table 4: Average Disposable Real Weekly Earnings (in constant 1967 $) of Manufacturing and Construction Workers, 1965-1974					
Year	Mfg	Construction	Year	Mfg	Construction
1965	102.41	129.98	1970	99.66	142.78
1966	102.31	131.05	1971	102.42	149.58
1967	101.26	134.33	1972	108.19	152.62
1968	102.45	134.34	1973	107.59	149.62
1969	101.49	139.16	1974	102.40	140.78

Source: BLS, *Employment and Earnings, United States, 1909-75,* at 749, 751. The data refer to workers with three dependents.

Table 5: Ratio of Gross Hourly Earnings in Construction to Those of All Private-Sector and Manufacturing Employees, 1965-1974 (in %)					
Year	Total Private	Manufacturing	Year	Total private	Manufacturing
1965	151	142	1970	163	156
1966	152	143	1971	165	159
1967	153	145	1972	164	158
1968	155	147	1973	163	157
1969	158	150	1974	160	154

Source: *MLR*, June 1975, at 89. The data refer to production or nonsupervisory workers.

That hourly wages outside of—unlike those in—construction rose more quickly from 1971 to 1974 than from 1968 to 1971 was due to inflation; real hourly wages stagnated in the second period, whereas they recorded a small increase in the first. To be sure, real construction wages per hour fell during the years after 1971. With 1967=100, the index for deflated hourly construction wages evolved as follows: 1971—113.8; 1972—116.7; 1973—116.1; 1974—110.8.[14]

That construction workers' weekly wages fared better than their hourly

---

between average hourly earnings in construction on the one hand and basic steel and motor vehicles on the other rose from 1.06 and 1.11 for 1962-66 to 1.25 and 1.23, respectively, in 1970; Mills, *Industrial Relations and Manpower in Construction*, tab. 5 at 58.

[14]27 (7) *CWD* 42 (July 1975). See also BLS, NEWS, at 15 [no pagination] (USDL, 75-411 July 25, 1975).

wages resulted from the fact that their workweek was cut by fewer hours than that of other workers. Thus whereas the average workweek in construction declined by 1.3 percent from 37.4 hours in 1965 to 36.9 hours in 1974, the decline in the total private economy and manufacturing amounted to 5.7 percent and 2.9 percent—from 38.8 to 36.6 hours and from 41.2 to 40.0 hours—respectively.[15]

The foregoing wage data refer to all construction workers—both union and nonunion members. Since controversy centered on the deleterious impact of building trades unions, it is necessary to differentiate between the two groups with regard to wage growth rates. As to the gap between their absolute levels, BLS surveys in 1972 and 1973 revealed union hourly premiums ranging between 35 percent and 70 percent in various trades; in 1977, the median premium in various trades ranged between 26 percent and 56 percent.[16] In 1974, construction recorded the largest union-nonunion differential in median weekly earnings—67.8 percent.[17]

From 1965 to 1975, nominal hourly wages of all construction workers rose from $3.70 to $7.25 or 95.9 percent, while union building trades wage rates increased from $4.42 to $8.88 or 100.9 percent.[18] Thus during this tumultuous period, when critics pilloried building trades unions as the chief cause of U.S. economic decline, union wage rates barely rose faster than those of the industry at large.[19]

This surprising result calls for a reexamination of traditional analyses that explained the above-average wage increases in construction exclusively in terms of union power. For although this parallel course in wages does not refute the thesis concerning building trade unions' extraordinary negotiating position—a uniform wage evolution might merely reflect unorganized employers' desire to keep unions and their control over the methods of production at bay by conceding higher wages—it is nevertheless necessary to search for possible explanations as to why the wages of construction workers as a whole improved relative to that of other workers.

---

[15]*MLR*, June 1975, at 89.

[16]BLS, *Industry Wage Survey: Contract Construction September 1972*, at 6 (Bull. 1853, 1975); BLS, *Industry Wage Survey: Contract Construction September 1973*, at 1 (Bull. 1911, 1976); BLS, *Compensation in the Construction Industries in Large Metropolitan Areas* 4 (Rep. 610, 1980). In contrast, near the beginning of the century: "In almost all the building trades and in many others, the wages of the non-unionists are the same as those of the Trade Unionists. This is not because the employers are generous; it is simply that no employer in a well organized trade dares to beat down the wages of the unorganized." Robert Hunter, *Labor in Politics* 195-96 (1915).

[17]Thomas Bradshaw & John Stinson, "Trends in Weekly Earnings: An Analysis," 98 (8) *MLR* 222-32 at 30 (Aug. 1975). See generally, Judith Gross, "Union-Nonunion Wage Differentials in the Construction Industry" (Ph.D. diss., Princeton U., 1975).

[18]Calculated according to 99 (6) *MLR* tab. 14 at 85 (June 1976); BLS, *Union Wage Rates and Hours: Building Trades July 1, 1974*, text tab. 2 at 4 (Bull. 1889, 1975); BLS, *Union Wage Rates and Employee Benefits in the Building Trades, July 1, 1975*, tab. 1 at 4 (Summary 76-3, Mar. 1976).

[19]The ratio between the absolute levels has been stable for many years. BLS, *Compensation in the Construction Industry*, tab. 26 at 53 (Bull. 1656, 1970).

The relevant macroeconomic processes, such as the accumulation of capital and its constant quantitative and qualitative recomposition, that underlie shifts in the sectoral and branch demand for labor assert themselves by means of workers' mobility.[20] One possible objection to this approach would emphasize that such mobility could not come into play with regard to short-term conjunctural variations especially in construction where skilled labor predominates; after all, the average worker cannot be turned into a skilled worker from one day to the next. Although this objection seems plausible, the building trades refute it not only cyclically, but year-in and year-out: "From its low in February to its peak in August, contract construction...adds enough workers to staff the entire motor industry vehicle manufacturing industry. Six months later employment will have dropped by approximately the same number."[21] This mechanism forms part of the background for the movement of construction wages during the Vietnam war era.

The most detailed and persuasive contemporaneous effort to explain these wage developments was undertaken in 1967 by Daniel Quinn Mills in a doctoral dissertation, under the direction of John Dunlop, which was itself part of the federal government's study of the construction industry; both Dunlop and Mills played important parts in the formulation and execution of wage control policy in the Nixon and Ford administrations.[22] In the book version of his study, published five years later, Mills rejected union-power-centered explanations of rising wages. He objected that during this period construction employment grew faster than union membership, producing a decline in union density.[23] Instead, Mills emphasized that:

high settlements in construction were the result of the interaction of two major factors. One was a set of favorable economic conditions. In the late 1960s, there occurred a large increase in the volume of private and industrial work and public building work—sectors of the industry that are highly unionized, involve the more skilled mechanics and intricate work, are the domain of the larger contractors, and are the least price-elastic of all construction markets. Relative price changes among all construction inputs were favorable to more labor-intensive production.... These inflationary demand conditions were reinforced by a major drain-off of the labor supply available to construction, a result of the boom in other sectors of the economy. Aggregate construction employment grew only slowly in the 1960s, for the

---

[20]In turn, this mobility presupposes the real existence of average or abstract labor. 1 Karl Marx, *Das Kapital* 668 (1962 [1867]); Stephen Sobotka, "Union Influences on Wages: The Construction Industry," 61 (2) *JPE* 127-43 at 136 (Apr. 1953).

[21]Robert Myers & Sol Swerdloff, "Seasonality and Construction," *MLR*, 90:2 (Sept. 1967). See also Dunlop & Mills, "Manpower in Construction" at 246. See also 1 Marx, *Das Kapital* at 58: "This change in form may not come off without friction, but come it must."

[22]Daniel Mills, "Factors Determining Patterns of Employment and Unemployment in the Construction Industry of the United States" ii (Ph.D. diss., Harvard U., 1967). Mills assisted in the preparation of BLS, *Seasonality and Manpower in Construction* iii (Bull. 1642, 1970).

[23]D. Q. Mills, *Industrial Relations and Manpower in Construction* 57 (1972).

rapid growth of nonresidential building work was offset to a large extent by declining activity in residential and highway construction. It was rather the generally low unemployment of the late 1960s that, by putting pressure on labor markets generally, led to historically low unemployment rates in construction.[24]

This focus on cyclical shifts in aggregate and sectoral employment and unemployment as the driving forces behind wage movements calls for a discussion of these factors.

UNEMPLOYMENT

The short duration of the typical construction job vitally affects industrial relations in the construction industry. ... Discharge cannot hold the same fears to the construction worker who is in the habit of losing many jobs each season.[25]

Before the war the building industry, even in periods of prosperity and expansion, operated with a large proportion of unemployment, and the existence of this reserve of labour meant that the fluctuating demands for the various types of workers could be met easily as they arose. At the same time, the fear of unemployment gave a sharp stimulus to effort. Thus a high margin of unemployment provided both a means of solving the organisational problems of the industry and also a disciplinary sanction.[26]

Building labor is more productive, assuming the same labor-capital ratio, in periods of depression. The scarcity of jobs at such times means that the more productive workers receive employment preference, and that, once employed, workers strive to attain high levels of output in order to retain their jobs. ... The attempt of the less efficient workers to compete under such conditions may take a toll in terms of length of working life or general physical condition.[27]

Mills took as his point of departure shifts in accumulation—which find expression in fluctuations in the volume of unemployment—from which he derived the special situation of the construction industry. The relatively strong upward pressure on construction wages is illustrated by trends in the ratio of the aggregate unemployment rate to that in construction, which has generally been higher in most capitalist economies.[28] This ratio, as seen in Table 6, decreased precisely in the years

---

[24]Mills, *Industrial Relations and Manpower in Construction* at 60.

[25]John Dunlop & Arthur Hill, *The Wage Adjustment Board* 2 (1950).

[26]Ministry of Works, *Working Party Report Building* 83 (1950) (written by C. G. Allen).

[27]Richard Scheuch, "The Labor Factor in Residential Construction" 161, 161 n.4 (Ph.D. diss., Princeton U., 1951).

[28]See, e.g., Société des Nations, *Situation économique mondiale 1932-33*, at 119 (1933);

after 1966 to its post-World War II low, falling (and remaining) below 2:1 for the first time; in other words, during the Vietnam war boom years construction unemployment declined faster than in the economy as a whole. The Indochina war years also represented the first time since the Korean war that construction unemployment dropped below 10 percent and the first time in the post-World War II period that the proportion of total unemployment accounted for by the construction industry fell below the same figure.

				Unemployment in
Table 6: Unemployment Among Construction Workers and All Workers, 1948-75				
Year	Unemployment rate in construction industry (%)	Total unemployment rate (%)	Ratio of construction to total unemployment rate	Unemployment in construction industry as share of total unemployment (%)
1948	8.7	3.8	2.3	10.1
1949	13.9	5.9	2.4	10.4
1950	12.2	5.3	2.3	10.6
1951	7.2	3.3	2.2	10.6
1952	6.7	3.0	2.2	11.6
1953	7.2	2.9	2.5	12.3
1954	12.9	5.5	2.3	10.9
1955	10.9	4.4	2.5	11.8
1956	10.0	4.1	2.4	11.4
1957	10.9	4.3	2.5	12.2
1958	15.3	6.8	2.2	11.4
1959	13.4	5.5	2.4	12.5
1960	13.5	5.5	2.5	12.0

ILO, *Yearbook of Labour Statistics* 394-429 (1974). Even Lenin believed that construction workers faced worse conditions than industrial workers generally and had to earn in a few months enough to feed their families during the whole year. V.I. Lenin, "Stroitel'naia promyshlennost' i stroitel'nie rabochie," *idem, Polnoe sobranie sochinenii* 23:151-52 (1961 [1913]).

Table 6: Unemployment Among Construction Workers and All Workers, 1948-75			
1961	15.7	6.7	2.3	11.5
1962	13.5	5.5	2.5	11.9
1963	13.3	5.7	2.3	11.2
1964	11.2	5.2	2.2	10.3
1965	10.1	4.5	2.2	10.8
1966	7.1	3.8	1.9	9.9
1967	6.6	3.8	1.7	9.1
1968	6.9	3.6	1.9	9.2
1969	6.0	3.5	1.7	8.3
1970	9.7	4.9	2.0	9.3
1971	10.4	5.9	1.8	8.5
1972	10.3	5.6	1.8	9.2
1973	8.8	4.9	1.8	9.3
1974	10.6	5.6	1.9	9.4
1975	18.1	8.5	2.1	10.2
Av.	10.8	4.9	2.2	10.6

Source: *Employment and Training Report of the President*, tab. A-22 at 172 (1977).

An industry such as construction, which relies heavily on methods of extensive accumulation, meets the increased demand in the prosperity phase of the next business cycle by absorbing additional workers, whereas manufacturing industries to a much greater degree implement labor-saving rationalization. As a result, the level of employment in manufacturing in the last year before a crisis is generally not regained for several years, whereas the construction industry achieves this level considerably earlier.[29] For the same reason, the construction industry, which has been characterized by extraordinarily high rates of unemployment for as long as records have been kept in the United States,[30] is much more heavily reliant

---

[29]BLS, *Handbook...1974*, at 106-108.

[30]Among members of the Bricklayers, the unemployed as a proportion of the unemployed and employed never fell below 19.8 percent and rose as high as 67.9 percent between 1888 and 1904.

on the existence of a—in relation to the 'normal' level of employment—larger pool of permanently available workers.[31] These considerations also largely explain why cyclical unemployment plays a larger role in construction. This insight only seemingly contradicts the fact that the ratio of the rate of construction unemployment to that in manufacturing customarily decreases in crisis years.[32] The average unemployment rate in construction is, in other words, so high that its increase during the crisis and depression phases of the business cycle appears modest compared to the changes in manufacturing.[33]

Calculated according to the data in each year's *Proceedings of the Annual Convention of the Bricklayers' and Masons' International Union of America*. See also *Eighteenth Annual Report of the [Massachusetts] Bureau of Statistics of Labor* 280-84 (1887); D. Smelser, "Unemployment and American Trade Unions" 18 (Ph.D. diss., Johns Hopkins U., 1919); Stanley Lebergott, *Manpower in Economic Growth* 182 n.66 (1964). Decennial census data revealed unemployment rates for building tradesmen much higher than the aggregate average. In 1890, when the average for all males was 15.6 percent, the weighted average for the building trades reached 32.3 percent, ranging from 13.4 percent for plumbers to 42.9 percent for masons and plasterers; in 1900, when the aggregate average was 22.0 percent, the weighted average for the building trades reached 42.2 percent, ranging from 22.0 percent among plumbers to 56.1 percent among plasterers. Calculated according to Bureau of Census, *Special Reports: Occupations at the Twelfth Census*, tab. 88 at ccxxvii-ccxxx (1904). According to a special survey in New York City in 1914, unemployment among building tradesmen amounted to 32.1 percent compared to 16.2 percent for all occupations; again, plumbers recorded the lowest rate (23.1 percent) and bricklayers the highest (43.9 percent). BLS, *Unemployment in New York City, New York* 8-14 (Bull. No. 172, 1915). See also BLS, *Unemployment in the United States* 9-11 (Bull. No. 195, 1916).

[31]During the years under review, the unemployment rate in construction exceeded the average in all developed capitalist countries (except France) for which the ILO published data for 1964-73 making comparisons possible: Austria, Belgium, Spain, Finland, Ireland, Netherlands, Sweden, UK, US, and Canada. ILO, *Yearbook of Labour Statistics* 270-96, 394-429 (1974). See also U.N., Economic Commission for Europe, 1 *Proceedings of the Seminar on Changes in the Structure of the Building Industry Necessary to Improve Its Efficiency and to Increase Its Output* 108, 110 (1965). Construction also displayed the highest unemployment rates during the Depression of the 1930s and the worldwide economic crisis of 1974 to 1976. Société des nations, *Situation économique mondiale 1932-33*, at 119 (1933); International Federation of Building and Wood Workers, *Building and Wood*, No. 1 1975, at 9-13.

[32]BLS, *Handbook...1974*, at 167; *MLR*, June 1975, at 82.

[33]Cyclical fluctuations in construction may be greater than official unemployment figures suggest because both a greater share of disemployed workers reappears under other rubrics such as "self-employed" and a part of the reserve army is displaced by new enrollees. See Marc Linder, "Self-Employment as a Cyclical Escape from Unemployment: A Case Study of the Construction Industry in the United States During the Postwar Period," in 2 *Research in Sociology of Work: Peripheral Workers* 261-74 (1983). For a phenomenology of the "'floating surplus'" or casual fringe of construction laborers, see Norman Dearle, *Problems of Unemployment in the London Building Trades* 94, 97-98 (1908). A skilled building tradesman's capacity for establishing a business of his own varies among trades. In the 1920s Mencken commented on this fact and its relationship to political views: "It will be a long, long while, perhaps, before such workingmen as electricians...turn to the Left, for all that one needs to go into business for himself is a set of simple tools, but in other trades the thing is growing more nearly impossible as year chases year. Not many...of the plumbers will ever become

This mechanism provides a partial explanation for the oft-observed phenomenon that the increase in employment during the prosperity phase of the cycle considerably exceeds the decline in unemployment.[34] The difference between these two magnitudes may be accounted for by: (1) "self-employed," who abandon their businesses to become wage workers again; (2) wage workers from other industries; and (3) those who had previously left the ranks of the employed and enter into production without having been unemployed in the immediately preceding period. By the same token, the reserve army is replenished by "chronically" unemployed who, at the peak of the business cycle temporarily find and then lose employment again.[35]

The importance of seasonal unemployment, which is not unique to, but is especially prominent in, construction, is illustrated by the fluctuations in employment between the low point in February and the high point in August, which during the post-World War period ranged between 15 percent and 45 percent and far exceeded the average year-to-year changes in employment.[36] The absolute size of this work force, reaching as high as one million workers, constitutes a huge labor supply and recruitment problem, which is in part solved by means of the enforced unemployment of more than a half-million workers during the winter in addition to those unemployed during the summer.[37] These imposing numbers should not distract attention from the fact that seasonal unemployment alone scarcely explains the above-average unemployment rates in construction since construction unemployment

---

boss plumbers, and not many of the carpenters will ever be contractors." H. L. Mencken, "Labor in Politics," in *idem, On Politics: A Carnival of Buncombe* 90, 93 (Malcolm Moos ed., 1960 [1924]).

[34]This observation applies, to be sure, most predictably to seasonal fluctuations within a year; Howard Foster, "Labor Force Adjustments to Seasonal Fluctuation in Construction," 23 (4) *ILRR* 528-40 (July 1970). The relationship can be seen clearly for 1950/1951, 1955/1956, 1959, 1962/1966, 1968/1969, and 1972-1973; BLS, *Handbook...1974,* at 103, 168.

[35]In contrast, during recession years, the increase in unemployment exceeded the decrease in employment, for example, in 1949, 1954, 1958, 1961, and 1970. Some support for the argument that the disemployed from other sectors seek employment in construction during recessions is embedded in the fact that, unlike movements in construction and the economy as a whole, the reduction in employment during recession years regularly exceeded the increase in unemployment in manufacturing and trade—sectors that accounted for about three-fifths of all those who shifted from other sectors to construction. BLS, *Handbook...1974,* at 27, 103, 168; BLS, *Seasonality and Manpower in Construction,* tab. 69 at 64. In terms of BLS data collection, however, it is unclear how such workers would have been recorded as being in construction. Despite the prominence of the contrary movements of construction unemployment and employment, they were not statistically correlated—for the period 1950 to 1968 the correlation was 0.05—because the quantitative changes, as distinguished from those in direction, did not agree with each other.

[36]BLS, *Employment and Earnings: United States, 1909-72,* at 23 (Bull. 1312-9,1973); BLS, *Seasonality and Manpower in Construction* at 31.

[37]BLS, *Seasonality and Manpower in Construction,* tab. 53 at 52.

in the summer also far exceeded that of the economy as a whole.[38] This point is especially important since overemphasis of seasonal factors is often coupled with references to weather conditions, which transmogrify societal phenomena into ineluctable facts of nature. Yet as President Calvin Coolidge's Committee on Seasonal Operation in the Construction Industries pointed out in 1924: "bad weather is not the principal cause of seasonal idleness. Rather customs fixed before present techniques had been developed."[39]

The societal character of seasonal unemployment emerges from the way in which the problem has developed historically. Through the first third of the twentieth century, the supply of construction labor in most capitalist countries "consisted mainly of persons who regularly found employment in other sectors during the winter, had other sources of income (e.g. small landholders and owners of small family businesses) or remained unemployed." To be sure, this phenomenon did not become relevant for social politics until these countries became thoroughly capitalist: "Increased urbanization made the construction labour force more dependent on full-time employment in the industry, as alternative complementary work became more difficult to find in urban centres."[40] Not until the 1920s did significant public discussion of the problem take place in the United States, which then waned unter the weight of mass unemployment during the 1930s.[41]

A question arises here as to why construction firms did not over time adopt methods for keeping their growing investment in machines and equipment profitably occupied year round. U.S companies lagged far behind their European counterparts in availing themselves of winter construction technologies.[42] The backwardness of U.S. practices—which also extended to state promotion[43]—may have been linked to

---

[38]Jan Wittrock, *Reducing Seasonal Unemployment in Construction* 23 (1967), at times neglects this circumstance. But see Robert Myers & Sol Swerdloff, "Seasonality and Construction," 90 (3) *MLR* 3 (Sept. 1967). The BLS estimated that seasonality accounted for about one-third to two-fifths of construction unemployment. BLS, *Seasonality and Manpower in Construction* at 43, 100.

[39]USDC, *Seasonal Operation in the Construction Industries: Summary of Report and Recommendations of a Committee of the President's Conference on Unemployment* vi (1924).

[40]Wittrock, *Reducing Seasonal Unemployment in Construction* at 17, 19.

[41]"Irregular Employment in the Building Industry," 13 (1) *MLR* 165-68 (July 1921); "Equalizing Production in the Building Industry," 14 (1)*MLR* 162-64 (Jan. 1922); Committee on Seasonal Operation in the Construction Industries [of the] President's Conference on Unemployment, *Seasonal Operation in the Construction Industries: The Facts and Remedies* (1924); Wittrock, *Reducing Seasonal Unemployment in Construction* at 19.

[42]Wittrock, *Reducing Seasonal Unemployment in Construction*; "Reducing Seasonal Unemployment," 89 (9) *MLR* 990-93 (Sept. 1966); BLS, *Seasonality and Manpower in Construction* at 24-30; *Seasonal Unemployment in the Construction Industry: Hearings Before the Select Committee on Labor of the House Committee on Education and Labor,* 90th Cong., 2d Sess. (1968); William Delaney, "Winter Construction Weather Or Not," *Manpower*, May 1970, at 2-7.

[43]See, e.g., the West German Arbeitsförderungsgesetz, §§ 74-89, Bundesgesetzblatt, I, 582

U.S. firms' relatively small fixed capital stock.[44] U.S. building firms also relied on the rental market to avert economic pressure to valorize their capital year round: in 1967 and 1972 they spent 92 percent and 80 percent, respectively, as much on rental payments for machinery and equipment as they did on capital expenditures for new machinery and equipment.[45] Although this flexibility reduced the compulsion to build year round, it alone cannot resolve the issue of causality—namely, whether seasonal methods of building led to the peculiarities of the capital structure or vice versa.[46] That the latter at least in part explain the former emerges from the fact that: "Seasonal employment patterns of large construction firms have less amplitude than those of smaller firms. Large firms may be better able to take advantage of cold weather materials and equipment and, therefore, tend to maintain their work forces during off-season periods."[47] The significance of seasonality may be gauged by the fact that only about half of all construction workers who received the major part of their annual earnings from construction were employed in all four quarters compared to four-fifths of their counterparts in manufacturing.[48]

So-called frictional unemployment, which in the first half of the 1960s was estimated as accounting for 15 to 24 percent of annual construction unemployment,[49] is likewise a form particularly prominent in construction that can be explained by the industry's special firm structure, which potentially casualizes a large part of the construction work force. Except for the relatively small core of especially valued employees in many firms as well as the small number of large firms that manage their

---

(June 25, 1969) ("Promotion of Year-round Employment in the Construction Industry"); Wittrock, *Reducing Seasonal Unemployment in Construction* at 230-32.

[44]In 1972 the net value of depreciable assets per employee was $2,793 compared to DM 13,500 in West Germant. Calculated according to USBC, *CCI, 1972: Industry Series: United States Summary—Statistics for Construction Establishments With and Without Payroll*, tab. B2 at 1-10 (1975); 27 (11) *MDB* 19 (Nov. 1975); *Statistisches Jahrbuch der BRD 1974*, at 261 (1974).

[45]Calculated according to USBC, *CCI, 1972: Industry Series: United States Summary—Statistics for Construction Establishments With and Without Payroll*, tab. B2 & B3 at 1-10, 1-11 (1975).

[46]Firms could also submit to the compulsion outside of construction by "turning their idle equipment to coal strip mining operations." "Constractors Make Idle Rigs Pay on Strip Mining Operation," *ENR*, May 8, 1975, at 10-11; see also "The Steelworkers Try to Organize a Mine," *BW*, Aug. 11, 1975, at 22 (mine owned by Nello Teer, a leading antiunion contractor) .

[47]BLS, *Seasonality and Manpower in Construction* at 27. That seasonal fluctuations are very mild in Florida, Arizona, and California, which are warm year round, should not divert attention from the insight that "the industry's expectation of normal seasonal weather has more direct influence on construction activity and employment than actual weather conditions for a particular period of time." *Id.* at 35, 29.

[48]BLS, *Seasonality and Manpower in Construction*, tab. 32 at 36. Cf. Howard Foster, "The Labor Market in Nonunion Construction," 26 (4) *ILRR* 1071-85 (July 1973).

[49]BLS, *Seasonality and Manpower in Construction* at 44 n.42.

own personnel departments, construction workers are hired for one project at a time, after which they again must seek a new project or firm to which they can sell their labor power. Weeks or months can pass between such jobs.

The flexibility that thereby accrues to firms with regard to their wage costs permits them, especially since their fixed capital burden is relatively small, to adjust to the industry's cyclicity in a much different way than is demanded of the workers, who revealed the highest mobility of all groups: in 1961, for example, 25 percent of construction workers changed their jobs compared with 10 percent of all manufacturing employees and 11 percent of all workers. Moreover, 55 percent of all construction workers, compared with only 37 percent of all workers, who changed jobs did so more than once. Particularly enlightning were the reasons for the job change: whereas 66 percent of construction workers sought a new job because they had lost their old one, only 42 percent of manufacturing employees and 38 percent of all workers indicated the same reason. Conversely, only 17 percent of construction workers pointed to "improvement in status" as the basis for their job change compared to 37 percent of manufacturing employees and 34 percent of all workers.[50]

This extraordinary mobility was, as far as employers were concerned, not without its adverse consequences. The BLS echoed employers' complaints that a flagging propensity to move exacerbated frictional unemployment, although it recognized that because this form of unemployment was "strongly associated with job termination," it might "not be particularly reduced in size by a high level of aggregate demand."[51] In 1971 the new Nobel laureate, Paul Samuelson, also commiserated with employers, observing at a Brookings symposium: "[N]o employer has successfully taken a construction strike in recent years, and employers have learned through bitter experience that it is disastrous to take a strike. Apparently, one key reason is that any construction worker with an automobile can hunt work in a nearby area when a strike shuts down building in his city.[52] Such reasoning, bordering on a moral reproach, is ironic in light of the importance that economists and government officials have attached to labor mobility as a means of reducing unemployment and achieving a more balanced industrial structure. Thus despite economists' preference for the fiction of a universal rationality of economic behavior valid for owners of all factors of production as well as for consumers, they were manifestly disturbed by a mobility merely aimed at rational income optimization.

That complaints about "manpower shortages" did not begin to disappear until construction unemployment reached one million does not contradict unemployment's function of providing a readily available supply of workers during

---

[50]Gertrude Bancroft & Stuart Garfinkle, "Job Mobility in 1961," 86 (8) *MLR* 897-906 at 903-905 (Aug. 1963).

[51]BLS, *Seasonality and Manpower in Construction* at 44.

[52]Paul Samuelson, "Discussion," *BPEA* 3:1971 at 767.

the upswing and boom phases of the business cycle.[53] The composition of skills in the reserve army may have been suboptimal because the extremely splintered structure of firms frustrated a rational training system, as firms themselves have admitted.[54] Construction employers have not been reticent about applauding the positive impact of high unemployment. The leading trade journal quoted one in 1946 as noting that "low productivity will be alleviated only by unemployment reservoirs, making jobs difficult to get, coupled with weeding out of inefficient personnel."[55] The next year *ENR* was able to report that increased unemployment had brought increased productivity in its wake: "So long as workers are waiting to take jobs, the men holding those jobs have a real incentive for more and better work."[56]

Unemployment may have fulfilled its function with regard to labor supplies during the post-World War II period, but what about its classical function as a wage-depressant? The expectation of a high negative correlation between movements in unemployment and wage rates presupposes a mechanistic linkage between unemployment and unions' strength and willingness to strike. Moreover, in the age of permanent inflation, a study of nominal wages alone would not suffice to evaluate the overall impact of the reserve army.[57] But despite the conclusion by economists in the 1960s that because changes in unemployment rates no longer "take one very far in an effort to explain" movements in collectively bargained wage rates it had become necessary to rethink traditional wage theory's understanding of the links, increases in industrial wage rates clearly fell in recession years in which unemployment rates peaked (1949, 1954, 1958, 1961).[58] In construction, the decline in the growth rate in nominal hourly wages also continued in the year following the recession when the unemployment rate exceeded 10 percent (1950, 1955, 1959, and 1962). Indeed, unemployment remained so high among construction workers after 1958 that the growth rate continued to decline through 1963. That this phenomenon was absent in manufacturing puts in a revealing light building trades unions' allegedly uninhibited power. Conversely, the growth rate in nominal hourly wages in construction rose uninterruptedly from 1963 to the end of the decade as the

---

[53]"Manpower Shortages Have Nearly Disappeared," *ENR*, Mar. 20, 1975, at 171; *ENR*, June 12, 1975, at 3.

[54]BLS, *Apprenticeship in Building Construction*.

[55]"Construction Workers—How Many and at What Wages?" 136 (6) *ENR* 187-90 (Feb. 7, 1946).

[56]"What Can Be Done About High Construction Costs?" 138 (22) *ENR* 885 (May 29, 1947).

[57]Only three times (1922 and 1932-1933) during the whole period after 1907 did hourly wage rates of organized building trades workers decline. BLS, *Union Wages and Hours: Building Trades July 1, 1974*, at 6 (Bull. 1889, 1975); BLS, "Union Wage Rates and Employee Benefits in the Building Trades, July 1, 1975" (Summary 76-3, March 1976).

[58]Richard Lester, "Negotiated Wage Increases, 1951-1967," 50 *RES* 173-81 at 180 (quote), 175, 179 (May 1968).

unemployment rate declined continuously.[59]

The pattern changed during the 1970s. The growth rate of wage increases continued to rise despite the fact that the unemployment rate began to increase again in 1970; only after a time lag of a year did unemployment begin to exert its impact on wages, which lasted during 1972 as the unemployment rate remained above 10 percent. When the crisis of 1974 erupted, no time lag was necessary to brake (nominal) wage increases.

The course of real hourly wages ran largely parallel to that of nominal wages. During the period after 1963, when money wages rose uninterruptedly, real wages rose only at a rate continuous with that of the postwar period as a whole. The first real wage declines finally took place in the years following 1973.

Any discussion of construction unemployment must deal with the question of whether its wage-depressing function is neutralized by the fact that building tradesmen's higher hourly wage can be conceptualized as containing a premium for unemployment. This built-in increment, together with state unemployment insurance benefits, should, so the argument goes, deprive unemployment of its coercive impact: "After all, the construction worker who earns the same in nine months as the manufacturing worker earns in twelve months is, other things equal, receiving the equivalent of a three-month vacation."[60] *The New York Times* editorial board went even further. In support of the Carter administration's drive to tax the unemployment compensation of "highly paid seasonal workers" in order to heighten their incentive to "go back to work," the newspaper asked its readers in 1978 to "consider the situation of a skilled construction worker who can earn $20,000 in just nine months. The other three months make a tempting sabbatical, partciularly with a tax-free $115 a week...thrown in at the unemployment office." Such a revision was needed, the *Times* opined, to maintain a system that was "not intended to preserve the perquisites of the good life led by those at the top of the economic heap...."[61]

To be sure, not even building trades unions deny that their members' above-average hourly wages are designed to compensate them for their heightened exposure to unemployment. (If construction workers were not predominatly skilled they would

---

[59]BLS, *Handbook of Labor Statistics 1974* at 241, 251. Of the almost 10 million workers who were unemployed at least 5 weeks in 1961, 13.7, 16.8, and 15.3 percent were employed as construction workers between 1957 and 1962 in their first, best, and current or last job. Robert Stein, "Special Labor Force Report: Work History, Attitudes and Income of the Unemployed," 86 (12) *MLR* 1405-13 at 1408 (Dec. 1963).

[60]Howard Foster, "Wages in Construction: Examining the Arguments," 11 (3) *IR* 336-49 at 346 (Oct. 1972).

[61]"The Benefits of Unemployment," *NYT*, Feb. 6, 1978, at A18, col. 1, at 2. In an unpublished task force report, by General Dynamics officials, the Roundtable even proposed capping the earnings on the basis of which unemployment compensation was paid to prevent a build-up of very high annual earnings resulting from overtime payments. Anthony Alfino, Algie Hendrix, & Carl Oles, "Manpower Supply in the Construction Industry" 25 (Aug. 11, 1970), in BR, CCH: 1970.

not receive this premium, which serves to insure their availability when demand for their labor reappears; this type of premium is superfluous for the unskilled, such as farm workers, who are always available in the United States.) But the argument, in addition to overlooking the heightened insecurity and anxiety associated with patching together those nine months of work and income, misleadingly implies that an unemployed construction worker compares his lot with that of an industrial worker, who has to work the entire year to receive the same annual income. But with respect to the intimidating impact of unemployment, an unemployed construction worker would more plausibly compare himself with his employed co-worker. And here most construction workers would presumably prefer the difference between wages and unemployment compensation to the additional "vacation": this preference is not a matter of marginal pain and pleasure calculations, but is, instead, rooted in the fact that average real disposable annual wages did not permit any significant latitude for workers with families. In 1964, for example, a total of $425 million was paid out to unemployed construction workers, increasing their income "slightly."[62] In this sense the reserve army retained its intimidating effect.

Mills's analysis was noteworthy for locating the chief cause of the declining construction unemployment rates not so much in this sector—since mutually opposing tendencies produced stagnating employment—but in the attraction of workers away from construction to other sectors. One counter-argument reads: "[T]he question of why tight labor markets elsewhere should divert manpower from construction when construction wages were much higher to begin with is not clear."[63] Though plausible, this objection betrays an untenable view of the connection between demand for labor as determined by capital accumulation and the wage formation process and/or the supply of labor. It entails that rising wages quasi-independently of the level and/or the severity of the variations in the demand for labor determine the supply side; it neglects the possibility that suppliers of the factor of production labor are not attracted by higher or rising wages where it is clear that the level of employment will be increased only marginally, especially since the building trades unions are to some extent in a position to control access.[64]

Thus it still must be explained why the wage level in construction increased relatively quickly in the face of a relatively moderate increase in employment. Here Mills's analysis, which focused on the varying tendencies in the various construction branches, remains suggestive.[65]

---

[62]BLS, *Seasonality and Manpower in Construction* at 56.

[63]Howard Foster, "Labor in Construction: Recent Research and Popular Wisdom," in *Labor & Manpower* 104-19 at 118 (Richard Pegnetter ed., 1974).

[64]Sobotka, "Union Influences on Wages" at 136.

[65]In contrast, Howard Foster, "Wages in Construction: Examining the Arguments," *IR*, 11 (3):336-49 at 349 (Oct. 1972), merely resigns: "We are then apparently left with a notion which begs more questions than it resolves, namely, that the construction unions have lately discovered that they

The other counter-argument to Mills's explanation of the declining unemployment rates relates to the composition of the employment sectors that in the late 1960s recorded higher growth rates than construction. Table 7 shows the development of employment in the aggregate as well as in selected sectors from 1965 to 1969.

Construction thus showed the smallest absolute increase and the second smallest relative increase of all employment sectors. The largest sector, manufacturing, also experienced below-average growth. The largest relative and absolute increases were recorded in government and services. These differential growth rates are important because those sectors with the strongest demand for labor were ones to which construction workers, based on their qualifications, probably had below-average access.[66] Since a large share of newly hired construction workers were recruited from among unemployed construction workers, it is plausible that the reduction in the number of the latter can be traced back not so much to the macroeconomic pull, but rather to the increased demand for labor within the construction industry itself. The explosive growth in the number of soldiers was to some extent an exception inasmuch as many younger construction workers doubtless were drafted into or joined the military. Overall, then, the causes of the below-average growth of construction employment must be sought in that industry itself.

It is, therefore, necessary to examine the shifts in the shares of the various sub-branches of construction in total output and of the accompanying shifts in employment. Mills's statement that growth during these years was concentrated in those sub-branches building commercial and public buildings, whereas residential and highway construction declined, stands in need of correction and supplementation.

There is no doubt that during the 1960s industry output shifted toward commercial, industrial, and other nonresidential building and public utility construction and away from residential construction. From 1960 to 1970, private residential construction increased (in current dollars) 39 percent from $23.0 billion to $31.9 billion, while nonresidential building and public utility construction rose 116 percent from $15.8 billion to $34.1 billion and 77 percent from $15.9 billion to $28.1 billion, respectively.[67] The added demand for skilled workers for electricians, iron workers, plumbers, and sheet metal workers created by the expansion of nonresidential building heightened their bargaining power.[68]

---

possessed more market power than they thought and thereupon decided to exploit more aggressively."

[66]But see BLS, *Seasonality and Manpower in Construction* at 64-65.

[67]Calculated according to *Economic Report of the President*, table C-38 at 236 (1973).

[68]BLS, *Work Stoppages in Contract Construction, 1962-73*, at 10. (Bull. 1847, 1975).

Table 7: Sectoral Employment Growth, 1965-69 (in 000)

Sector	1965	1966	1967	1968	1969	Increase 1965-69	
Total labor force	77,178	78,893	80,793	82,272	84,240	7,062	9.2%
Armed forces	2,723	3,123	3,446	3,535	3,506	783	28.8%
Total civilian labor force	74,455	75,770	77,347	78,737	80,734	6,279	8.4%
Unemployed	3,366	2,875	2,975	2,817	2,832	-534	-15.9%
Total employed	71,088	72,895	74,372	75,920	77,902	6,814	9.6%
Nonagricultural wage/salary workers	60,815	63,955	65,857	67,951	70,442	9,607	15.8%
Manufacturing	18,062	19,214	19,447	19,781	20,167	2,105	11.7%
Construction	3,186	3,275	3,208	3,306	3,525	339	10.6%
Transportation & utilities	4,036	4,151	4,261	4,311	4,435	399	9.9%
Trade	12,716	13,245	13,606	14,099	14,704	1,988	15.6%
Finance	3,023	3,100	3,225	3,381	3,562	539	17.8%
Services	9,087	9,551	10,099	10,622	11,228	2,141	23.6%
Government	10,074	10,791	11,398	11,846	12,202	2,128	21.1%

Source: Economic Report of the President, tab. B-27 at 218, B-32 at 224 (1977).

During the latter part of the 1960s, as Table 8 reveals, all sub-branches recorded an increase in the value of new construction in place in current prices, although the mini-recession in 1966-67 witnessed some declines.[69]

Table 8: Changes (in %) in the Value of New Construction Put in Place, 1964-69		
Subsector	Current $	Constant (1972) $
Private residential	19	-5
1-unit structures	7	-14
Private nonresidential buildings	63	26
Industrial	90	47
Commercial	74	34
Public utilities	90	57
Public	37	8
Highway	30	2
Total	39	10

Source: 23 (8) *CR*, tab. A-2 at 6-12 (Dec. 1977).

The growth rates of private residential construction and highway construction were below average, the former, adjusted for inflation, turning negative. In particular the reduction in the share of residential construction (and especially single-unit structures) in total output from 41 to 35 percent (and 23 to 17 percent) is relevant since union density in this sub-branch was also below average.[70] The highest growth rates (in current dollars) were recorded in private industrial nonresidential buildings (90 percent), public utilities (90 percent), commercial buildings (74 percent)—the most heavily unionized subsectors requiring the most highly skilled workers using the most advanced technology and the least sensitive to price increases.[71]

---

[69]*SCB*, July 1966 and July 1968 at S-9; BLS, *Seasonality and Manpower in Construction* at 134-35.

[70]Foster, *Manpower in Homebuilding*; BLS, *Labor and Material Requirements for Construction of Private Single-Family Houses* 8 (Bull. 1755, 1972). Within this sub-branch, one-family housebuilding is a stronghold of nonunion firms. Foster, *Manpower in Homebuilding* at 43. It also recorded the sharpest decline in its share of total construction output—from 21.3 to 17.5 percent between 1965 and 1969.

[71]An interpretation of these varying growth rates calls for a brief methodological account of the heterogeneous composition of construction demand, which is a principal basis of the peculiar

Mills's conclusions concerning wage developments dealt largely with these three sectors. It is, rather, his remarks on the underlying conditions of production and valorization that are in need of discussion precisely because in the long run they can lead to a situation that could turn around the short-run tendencies at issue. Mills's thesis that these growth sectors were characterized by the most advanced technology

---

structure of construction cycles. The traditional tripartite classification, residential, commercial, and public construction, is relevant to the extent that it expresses the upward and downward oscillations that contribute to a construction cycle that deviates from the aggregate business cycle. A few suggestive comments must suffice here. The decline in residential construction was, in light of the widening gap between income and construction costs, hardly surprising. John O'Riley, "The Outlook," *WSJ*, Jan. 11, 1971, at 1, col. 5; *NZZ*, Sept. 21, 1974, at 15; "The Ivy-Covered Cottage, Nearly an Impossible Dream," *NYT*, May 11, 1975, § 4, at 9; "The No-Frills American Dream," *BW*, June 16, 1975, at 17-18. That school and hospital construction, whose growth rate was 56 percent, were the pillars of public construction was related to the Johnson administration's expansion of the education and health sectors. Analysis of private nonresidential construction would require a much more differentiated study of industrial capital on the one hand and commodity and money capital on the other, which roughly coincide with the subdivision into industrial and commercial buildings. With regard to industrial capital, two aspects are of overriding significance. First, the alternating phases of intensive and extensive expanded accumulation correspond more or less to a rising or constant organic composition of capital. During periods of extensive reproduction, production is chiefly increased by duplicating existing facilities; intensive reproduction entails increasing productivity, which is achieved by a rising organic composition of capital, which presumably is more closely associated with machines and equipment than with structures: "An industrial building is only a casing for the manufacturing process. The layout of machinery within a building can often be completely altered and modernized without altering the building itself." Patricia Hillebrandt, *Economic Theory and the Construction Industry* 64 (1974). Second, the long-term tendency of technical progress is to increase the share of machines and equipment and to reduce that of buildings of total industrial investment as firms conserve on floor space and improve design and engineering of buildings and equipment. USDC, *U.S. Income and Output* 9, fig. 6 at 10, fig. 30 at 65, tab. V-12 at 196-97 (1958); Donald Kemmerer & C. Jones, *American Economic History* 332 (1959); Simon Kuznets, *Capital in the American Economy* 154-55, 166-73 (1961); E. Howenstine, *Compensatory Employment Programmes: An International Comparison of Their Role in Economic Stabilisation and Growth* 235 (OECD 1968); Robert Katzenstein, *Technischer Fortschritt: Kapitalbewegung—Kapitalfixierung* 68-73 (1971); Ernest Mandel, *Der Spätkapitalismus* 182 (1973). The share of structures declined especially after 1965. *Economic Report of the President 1974*, at 250 (1974); USBC, *Statistical Abstract of the United States: 1974*, at 400-401 (1974). The increase in industrial construction in 1965 resulted from nearly full utilization of manufacturing capacity, peak profits, and availability of adequate investment funds. "New Construction Outlook for 1966," 11 (11) *CR* 4-6 (Nov. 1965); Nancy Hoover, "Record New Construction Boosts 1965 Economy," 12 (4) *CR* 4-9 (Apr. 1966). The decline in industrial construction between 1970 and 1972 was "obviously reflecting an overall excess plant capacity." Abraham Goldblatt, "Construction in 1972," 19 (4) *CR* 4-9 at 5 (Apr. 1973). The boom in commercial office building was already at the time explained by "the growing extent and complexity of private and public administrative work." As production and nonproduction workers became increasingly spatially separated, the latter increased in number rapidly while the former stagnated; moreover, average floor space per office employee rose with the proliferation of computers and other machinery. Robert Fisher, "The Boom in Office Building: Demand, Financing, Leasing and Operation," 14 (6) *CR* 4-7 at 4 (June 1968). See also Robert Fisher, "The Boom in Office Building: Supply and Increasing Scale," 14 (5) *CR* 4-7 (May 1968).

and the highest proportion of skilled workers must be examined.[72] Mills also argued that changes in factor prices, especially interest rates, favored labor intensive methods of production. To be sure, there is no absolute correlation between the share of skilled workers and the state of technological development because even relatively unskilled workers can operate highly automated equipment; tendentially, however, it is plausible that the proportion of skilled workers does decline in the course of technological development. It is not coincidental, then, that the construction sub-branch that has come closest to creating industrial conditions of production by substituting machines for human labor, highway construction,[73] also exhibited the highest proportion of unskilled and semi-skilled workers. Table 9 shows the composition of the labor force in various types of construction based on skill level.

Table 9: Skill Composition (in %) of On-Site Labor in Selected Sub-Branches, 1959-62			
Sub-branch	Skilled	Semiskilled/unskilled	Administrative/supervisory
Private housing	71	26	3
Hospitals	66	30	4
Schools	61	35	4
Public housing	58	38	4
Federal office bldgs	47	37	6
Highways	39	51	10

Source: Claiborne Ball, "Employment Effects of Construction Expenditures," 87 (2) *MLR* 154-58 at 156 (Feb. 1965)

Significantly, exactly the same number of construction workers were employed in highway construction in 1959 and 1968, while their deflated output rose by 26.2 percent; in construction as a whole, 8.5 percent more workers produced only 18.8 percent more output.[74] Such an increase in productivity linked to an increase

---

[72]Mills, *Industrial Relations and Manpower in Construction* at 62-63.

[73]Helga Fassbinder et al., "Zur Berufspraxis des Architekten: Entwicklung von Bauindustrie, Bauauftraggebern und staatlicher Planungstätigkeit als Bestimmungsmomente der Architektenarbeit," *ARCH +*, No. 18, at 1-73 at 16-17 (July 1973). On the increasing use of labor-saving mechanization in highway construction and the concomitant increase in the number of skilled operating engineers at the expense of unskilled workers in connection with the interstate highway program, see Adela Stucke & Edward Gordon, "Manpower Impact of the Proposed $101 Billion Highway Program," *CR*, Feb. 1955, at 5-8.

[74]BLS, *Seasonality and Manpower in Construction* at 135-36.

in the organic composition of capital also seems to be a method of checking wage costs despite the fact that union density in this sub-branch was 51.3 percent.[75] That other sub-branches did not proceed along similar lines cannot be explained by reference to rising interest rates.[76] In light of the continuous stream of complaints about rising wage costs and the enhanced control that skilled workers concededly exert over the production process—revealingly, the share of administrative and supervisory personnel in highway construction was twice as high as in other sub-branches—this phenomenon deserves more attention than it can be afforded here.

Developments in productivity shape trends in construction employment. The lack of a procedure for comparing heterogeneous use-values over time means that no firm statistical measure is available,[77] but there can be no doubt that a significant increase in construction productivity took place during the post-World War II period. Largely it derived from the growth of mechanization. The principal lines of progress encompassed earth movement, materials handling, concrete mixing, and the spread of the use of prefabricated materials.[78] Although much of the actual assembly process remains largely a set of craft operations, these developments attained such a wide scope of application that the notion of stagnant productivity is unrealistic.

The dispersion of growth rates in the sub-branches cannot be explained by any grand theory: although the various demand-impulses—which on another level are to be understood as accumulation processes—played a considerable part, the sub-branch-specific productivity increments, which eventually expressed themselves in varying needs for labor, cannot be left out of the account. That capital-for-labor substitution-driven productivity increases did not, during the period in question, reach the desired levels,[79] may be explained as follows: customers in these various

---

[75]BLS, *Compensation in the Construction Industry* at 51; BLS, *Employee Compensation and Payroll Hours: Heavy Construction Industry, 1971,* at 16 (Rep. 428, 1974).

[76]For a critical approach to interest rates as an overarching explanatory variable in construction, see Clarence Long, Jr., *Building Cycles and the Theory of Investment* 29 (1940).

[77]For an example of the type of research underway, see Sara Behman, "Measuring Trends in Output Per Manhour for Specific Craft Operations," in *Measuring Productivity* at 31-48.

[78]P. A. Stone, *Building Economy* 9 (1966); H. Weber & W. Berthold, "Fließfertigung in der Bauelementenproduktion," *Industrialisierung des Bauens*, No. 2, 1970, at 1-100; "Prefabs' Uphill Fight," *BW*, July 4, 1964, at 74-77; "Packaged Buildings Go Up Fast," *BW*, Apr. 9, 1966, at 47-48, 50; Charles Field & Steven Rivkin, *The Building Code Burden*, 9-32 (1975); Leo Grebler, *Large Scale Housing and Real Estate Firms* (1973); C. A. Grubb & M. I. Phares, *Industrialization: A New Concept for Housing* (1972); William Meyer, *The Building Trades Versus Building Prefabrication* (Princeton U. Research Center for Urban & Environmental Planning, Working Paper 10, 1974); William Keating, *Emerging Patterns of Corporate Entry into Housing* (U. California at Berkeley Center for Real Estate and Urban Economics, Spec. Rep. 8, 1973).

[79]But such increases, as expressed in the decline in hours of labor per constant $1,000 of contract cost, did take place in several sub-branches during the 1960s and 1970s. Diane Finger, "Labor Requirements for Federal Highway Construction,"98 (12) *MLR* 31-36 (Dec. 1975); John Olsen, "Decline Noted in Hours Required to Erect Federal Office Buildings," 99 (10) *MLR* 18-22 (Oct. 1976);

sub-branches (especially commercial capital, public utilities, and governments) were temporarily in a position to finance the relatively greater construction price increases. Their ability to do so was related to the fact that they themselves were scarcely exposed to foreign competition—governments and public utilities not at all, whereas banks and commercial capital were only beginning to be subject to such influences. But such a situation was not sustainable: on the one hand, the fiscal crisis narrowed state investment latitude; on the other hand, the increased costs of the sphere of circulation (of money and commodity capital) as well as of the general conditions of production embodied in public utiltities had to make themselves felt at some point for capital in general. But the construction firms involved in these sub-branches were not in a position to undertake a comprehensive restructuring that would have offered a long-term solution of the productivity problem.

Under these circumstances the short-term strategy of a part of large industrial capital (organized in the Business Roundtable) as well as of the federal government to attack wage costs by means of juridical and administrative means becomes plausible.[80] Less plausible were contemporary apocalyptic leftwing assertions that the basic objective of Nixon's economic program was "eventually to destroy...collective bargaining as it exists now in the United States by eliminating bargaining between labor and management based upon any criteria except that of 'productivity': in other words, to eliminate collective bargaining based upon the traditional criteria of profitability, comparability, cost of living, low-wage...."[81]

Robert Ball & Joseph Finn, "Labor and Materials Requirements for Sewer Works Construction," 99 (11) *MLR* 38-41 (Nov. 1976). Based on new price indexes, several economists during this period concluded that construction productivity increases during the post-World War II were on a par with those of the economy at large. Douglas Dacy, "Prices and Productivity in the Construction Industry, 1947-1961" (Ph.D. diss., Harvard U., 1962); *idem*, "A Price and Productivity Index for a Nonhomogeneous Product," 59 *JASA* 469-80 (1964); *idem*, "Productivity and Price Trends in Construction Since 1947," 47 (4) *RES* 406-11 (Nov. 1965); Robert J. Gordon, "A New View of Real Investment in Structures, 1919-1966," 50 (4) *RES* 417-28 (Nov. 1968); Christopher Sims, "Efficiency in the Construction Industry," in 2 *The Report of the President's Committee on Urban Housing: Technical Studies* 145-76 at 149-50 (1968).

[80]Nevertheless, a typical contemporaneous leftwing analysis that saw an exit from every crisis in wage cuts improperly absolutized this aspect while neglecting the methods of relative surplus value production. Pacific Studies Center, "Black Monday," *PRWET*, Nov.-Dec. 1969, at 18. See also Marc Weiss, "The Construction Industry," *Leviathan*, Dec. 1969, at 29. The continuously falling share of wage costs in total construction costs indirectly confirms that the methods of relative surplus value production also prevail in construction. Even in single-family-housing construction, whose level of productivity is relatively low, the proportion of wage costs declined from 32.7 percent in 1947 to 20.4 percent in 1969. BLS, *Labor and Material Requirements for Construction of Private Single-family Houses* 8 (Bull. 1755, 1972).

[81]Jack Rasmus, "Workers' Control and the Nixon Economic Program," in *Workers' Control: A Reader on Labor and Social Change* 395-428 at 413 (Gerry Hunnius et al., eds., 1973).

ANNUAL WAGES

[T]he speed that gives the most output per lifetime is not necessarily the optimum speed. Suppose that if men produce at a given rate, they are not compelled to retire until they are 65...and that they then have a normal life expectancy for that age, which is...12 years. Suppose, however, that if these same men produced at a 15 per cent higher rate, they would be compelled to retire at 62 and that, as a result of the faster speed of work, their life expectancy would be only 6 years. If work in each case began at 20..., the faster rate of output would yield 7.3 per cent more product per lifetime but the men would live on the average 9 years less. Is 7.3 per cent more output worth 9 years of life? That is the type of question that must be answered in order to determine the optimum speed of work.[82]

If work in a certain industry, say building..., is of a fluctuating character..., average yearly earnings will tend to be below those for comparable work in other industries.... The hope that *he* will be lucky and get some of the employment that is to be got, will keep many a man in the industry who could have moved to another one had it been merely a matter of comparing the actual long-term earnings in the two industries. Too many men will therefore hang around, and this reserve army will depress average earnings unless positive steps are taken to "decasualize" the industry.[83]

"Sure, we've got a dollar or a dollar-and-a-half raise for the last two or three years, and people see that $8.60 an hour and wonder if we aren't living high. But that kind of pay doesn't amount to spit. I made $7,200 last year."[84]

[I]t's hard to begrudge that an operating engineer can make $100,000 in a good year, when Goldman, Sachs partners may pocket a billion from their company's public stock offering. Operating engineers run the big rigs, the shovels, cranes and bulldozers.... What Goldman, Sachs partner can do anything as useful?[85]

The discussion of the extraordinary levels of unemployment in construction strongly suggests that high hourly wage rates may not translate into similarly high annual incomes. Indeed, the fact that the course of annual wages resembled that of hourly wages is misleading because this series is constructed by abstracting from unemployed and short-term workers. If these factors are taken into account, annual wages declined absolutely during recession years. Construction wages would show even sharper declines because: (1) the share of part-time workers was greater than in all other industries; (2) even full-time construction workers, on average, worked only three-fourths of the hours or weeks of the average worker in the economy as a whole;

[82]Sumner Slichter, *Union Policies and Industrial Management* 165 n.5 (1941).

[83]K. Rothschild, *The Theory of Wages* 77 (1965 [1954]).

[84]"Construction Men Seem Confused on Wage Order," *NYT*, May 4, 1971, at 26, col. 3 (quoting Chicago ironworker).

[85]Charles Morris, "Rage of the Rank and File," *NYT*, July 9, 1998, at A25, col. 2 (nat. ed).

and (3) construction workers not only had the highest unemployment rate, but on average were three to four time more likely to be unemployed several times per year and also remained unemployed for longer periods of time.[86]

Scrutiny of the available data on annual wages is crucial to test the validity of the contemporary claim that outrageously high hourly wages also translated into outlandish annual incomes and living standards for "the" building tradesman.[87] Noteworthy in terms of the continuity of employers' rhetorical warfare for public consumption is their use of the same statistical legerdemain. Thus in connection with the lockout of 50,000 to 60,000 construction workers in Chicago in 1900, the president of the Chicago Bricklayers' Union testified to the U.S. Industrial Commission that employers, who were attacking unions' control over working conditions, had "gone so far as to post notices in the [street] cars to mislead the general public, that we receive $4 a day." In fact, averaged over an entire year, bricklayers' wages failed to reach even $1.75.[88]

In the most thorough study of the issue of annual wages in construction, the BLS observed in 1970 that:

> Generally, there is a high correlation between rates of pay and annual wage and salary earnings in most industries because the work year for a large proportion of the employees is relatively uniform. In construction, however, employment is seasonal, projects are frequently completed within relatively short periods of time, and some of the workers cannot find other employment immediately after their job on a project has been completed.

---

[86]Robert Bednarzik, "Involuntary Part-Time Work: A Cyclical Analysis," 98 (9) *MLR* 14 (Sept. 1975); BLS, *Seasonality and Manpower in Construction* at 68-72, 46; BLS, *Compensation in the Construction Industry* at 23; Sol Swerdloff, "Manpower Facts in Labor-Management Negotiations," 90 (1) *MLR* 10 (Jan. 1967). In 1961, for example, when the unemployment rate reached 15.7 percent, 43.9 percent of construction workers were unemployed at some time that year. BLS, *Seasonality and Manpower in Construction* at 148.

[87]The available data are deficient; comparable data for construction workers are available only for a few scattered recent years. Some older data series are not comparable because they were adjusted for full-time employees, thus neglecting the point of overriding importance—whether construction workers work fewer hours than other employees. A good example is provided by the congressional testimony of Bureau of the Census statistician Herman Miller, who presented data on lifetime earnings of various occupations including construction trades; because they were projections, they neglected precisely what should have been studied. *Hearings Before the Subcommittee on Employment and Manpower of the Senate Committee on Labor and Public Welfare on Bills Relating to Equal Employment Opportunity*, 88th Cong., 1st Sess. 325-74 (1963).

[88]Industrial Commission, 8 *Reports: Chicago Labor Disputes of 1900 with Especial Reference to the Disputes in the Building and Machinery Trades*, H. Doc. No. 177, 57th Cong., 1st Sess. 225 (1901) (testimony of George Gubbins). A contractor testified that his payroll records showed that laborers earning $2 per day had higher higher annual wages than bricklayers at $4 per day because their work was steadier: "The average earnings of a bricklayer in Chicago last year, I am sure, were not more than $400." *Id.* at 100 (testimony of Thomas Nicholson). On the background to the lockout, see Royal Montgomery, *Industrial Relations in the Chicago Building Trades* 24-32 (1927).

In addition, unemployment in the industry is high, inclement weather robs workers of days of work, and many days of work are lost because of work stoppages and industrial injuries. As a result, the actual annual earnings of construction's major earners—those who earn the largest part of their annual earnings in the industry—are substantially below those of their counterparts in the mining industries; most manufacturing industries; the transportation, communication and public utility industries; wholesale trade; and about one-fourth of the finance, insurance and real estate industries.[89]

Data from 1964 illustrate the below-average attachment of construction workers to their industry: the proportion of workers with some earnings from manufacturing who worked in all four quarters in manufacturing ranged from 45 to 73 percent in various industries; the corresponding proportion among construction workers ranged from 27 to 37 percent in various branches. Even among employees with the major proportion of their earnings from construction, the corresponding shares ranged between 45 and 57 percent, compared with 60 to 83 percent in manufacturing.[90] By 1971, 54.3 percent of all workers with the major proportion of their income from construction worked all four quarters in that industry; the corresponding figures for the total private economy and manufacturing were 65.8 and 70.3 percent.[91] The same pattern is reflected not only in the higher unemployment rate in construction, but also in the ratio of available workers to the number of full-time jobs. Thus, in 1963, 5.4 million construction workers competed for 3.0 million full-time jobs; this ratio of 1.8:1 exceeded that of 1.3:1 in manufacturing.[92]

That not even half of all those construction workers who received the major share of their income from construction worked there all four quarters suggests that the average construction worker worked considerably fewer than 2000 hours. In the absence of precise and comprehensive data, a 1964 study is useful which revealed that operating engineers worked on average 1,476 hours; for the years 1960-64, the highest level, 1698 hours, was recorded in 1962.[93] A study conducted in four areas of thirteen trades in 1966-67 found that the median number of annual hours was 998.5. If all those working fewer than 700 hours are excluded as casual workers, the

---

[89]BLS, *Compensation in the Construction Industry* at 65.

[90]BLS, *Annual Earnings and Employment Patterns, Private Nonagricultural Employment, 1964*, tab. 7 at 11 Report 330, 1969).

[91]BLS, *Annual Earnings and Employment Patterns of Private Nonagricultural Employees, 1971 and 1972*, tab. A-49 at 352 (Bull. 1928, 1976).

[92]J. Dunlop & D. Mills, "Manpower in Construction: A Profile of the Industry and Projections to 1975," in 2 *The Report of the President's Committee on Urban Housing: Technical Studies* 239-86 at 246 (1968). See generally, D.Q. Mills, "A Study of Manpower Utilization in the Construction Industry: Intermittency of Employment, Unemployment and Labor Shortages" (May 1969).

[93]Sol Swerdloff, "Manpower Facts in Labor-Management Negotiations," 90 (1) *MLR* 10 (Jan. 1967).

median for all crafts and cities amounted to only 1,535 hours.[94]

Another 1964 BLS study shed light on the median annual earnings of construction and other workers. Among those who worked four quarters, earnings from construction ranged from $5,776 in general building construction to $6,562 in heavy construction. The corresponding highest median annual wage and salary earnings in manufacturing were as follows: petroleum ($7,399); ordnance ($7,227); transportation equipment ($6,987); primary metals ($6,754); chemicals ($6,591); nonelectrical machinery ($6,420). Other relatively highly paid nonmanufacturing industries included: pipeline transportation ($7,533); airline transportation ($6,886); public utilities ($6,713); oil and gas extraction ($6,565); trucking and warehousing ($6,555); metal mining ($6,363); coal mining ($6,188).[95] Thus although the annual wages of construction workers working all four quarters were, as gauged by the ratio of their wages to those of their counterparts in other industries, considerably higher than those who worked any quarters in construction, they did not belong to the highest reaches among production workers: well organized workers in oligopolized large-scale industries secured higher incomes.[96]

These patterns roughly persisted throughout the Vietnam war years. In 1970, for example, when the median annual earnings of year-round construction workers amounted to $8,835, their counterparts in the following manufacturing branches recorded higher earnings: ammunition ($8,987); industrial chemicals ($9,649); petroleum refining ($10,263); tires ($9,215); blast furnace/basic steel workers ($9,091); office and computing machines ($9,346); aircraft ($9,445). In addition, railroads ($9,554), trucking ($8,860), and air transportation ($10,199), as well as

---

[94]BLS, *Seasonality and Manpower in Construction* at 69.

[95]BLS, *Annual Earnings and Employment Patterns, Private Nonagricultural Employment, 1964*, tab. 1 at 5. This study was based on the Social Security Administration's 1-percent continuous work history sample.

[96]This hierarchy differs somewhat from that prevailing at the end of the nineteenth and in the early twentieth century, when state labor bureau surveys revealed that plumbers (and often bricklayers) generally received high daily wages which translated into relatively high annual wages, which were, however, exceeded by those of a few smaller groups of artisans such as locomotive engineers, glassblowers, iron rollers; most of the building trades recorded annual wages closer to the average for all workers. Massachusetts, *Sixth Annual Report of the Bureau of Labor Statistics* 365 (1875); Missouri, Labor and Industrial Inspection Dept., *First Annual Report of the Bureau of Labor Statistics for the Year Ending January 1, 1880*, at 54-62, 67, 75, 91, 104, 634 (1880); Bureau of Statistics of Labor and Industries of New Jersey, *Eighth Annual Report for the Year Ending October 31, 1885*, at xxxv (1885); State of Indiana, *Eighth Biennial Report (Fourteenth Volume) of the Indiana Department of Statistics for 1899 and 1900*, tab. V at 198-99 (1900); State of Kansas, *Sixteenth Annual Report of the Bureau of Labor and Industry for 1900*, at 5, 33, 59-79 (1901); *Eighteenth Annual Report of the Commissioner of Labor, 1903: Cost of Living and Retail Prices of Food*, tab. II.B at 264-82, tab. II.C at 283 (1904); Robert Chapin, *The Standard of Living Among Workingmen's Families in New York City* 46, 47, tab. 6 at 50 (1909); Clarence Long, *Wages and Earnings in the United States 1860-1890*, tab. 42 at 98 (1960).

public utilities ($9,275) all reported higher earnings. To be sure, the two highest-paid construction specialty trades, plumbing ($10,005) and electrical work ($10,737), rested at the top of the earnings pyramid.[97]

Further evidence that construction workers did not deserve their reputation for living in luxury comes from the same study: only about one-fifth of construction workers employed four quarters in 1964 recorded annual earnings in excess of $9,000.[98] This pattern is corroborated by data from the 1967 CPS, which showed that: "Full-time year-round construction workers earned more than the all-industry median for full-time workers, but less than their counterparts in most of the industries for which separate data are available."[99] Thus median total earnings of construction craftsmen and operatives ($7,077) were lower than those of their counterparts in transportation, communication, and public utilities ($7,505) and all durable goods manufacturing ($7,117).[100]

Trends for the Vietnam war period can be gleaned from the relevant absolute and distributional income figures based on social security data. The median annual incomes from construction of construction workers who worked all four quarters and whose major source of income was construction is contrasted with those of their manufacturing counterparts in Table 10.

Over the entire ten-year period, the median annual earnings in manufacturing of those who worked all four quarters and whose major industry was manufacturing rose 79.6 percent compared with 84.8 percent for their counterparts in construction. The gap in annual earnings between the two groups rose from 1966 to 1970 and then fell during the remainder of the period as manufacturing wage increases exceeded those in construction. If Roger Blough testified to Congress in 1971 that a 50- to 60-percent increase in construction wages in three years had to change the character of the United States, no such change in annual earnings took place even for the minority of construction workers fortunate enough to secure year-round employment. With 1967 as the starting point, such an increase took almost eight years.

The distribution of these earnings underscores the modest incomes even of year-round full-time construction workers, which led the BLS to conclude "that the relatively high hourly wage rates for construction workers generally are not translated into high annual earnings."[101]

---

[97]BLS, *Annual Earnings and Employment Patterns of Private Nonagricultural Employees, 1970*, tab. B-1 at 51-52 (Bull. 1842, 1975).

[98]BLS, *Compensation in the Construction Industry*, tab. 34 at 78.

[99]BLS, *Compensation in the Construction Industry* at 70.

[100]BLS, *Compensation in the Construction Industry*, tab. 35 at 79.

[101]BLS, *Seasonality and Manpower in Construction* at 56.

Table 10: Annual Earnings from Their Industry of Major Earnings of Four-Quarter Workers in Construction and Manufacturing, 1965-75					
Year	Construction		Manufacturing		Excess of construction above manufacturing earnings (%)
	$	% Increase	$	% Increase	
1965	6,348	-	5,770	-	10.0
1966	6,699	5.5	6,155	6.7	8.8
1967	7,151	6.7	6,286	2.1	13.8
1970	8,835	7.8	7,345	5.6	20.3
1971	9,377	6.1	7,835	6.7	19.7
1972	9,753	4.0	8,572	9.4	13.8
1973	10,435	7.0	9,133	6.5	14.3
1974	10,994	5.4	9,642	5.6	14.0
1975	11,731	6.7	10,365	7.5	13.2

Calculated according to BLS, *Annual Earnings and Employment Patterns of Private Nonagricultural Employees-1965*, tab. 1 at 9 (Bull. 1675, 1970); BLS, *Annual Earnings and Employment Patterns of Private Nonagricultural Employees, 1966-67*, tab. A-1 at 19 (Bull. 1765, 1973); BLS, *Annual Earnings and Employment Patterns of Private Nonagricultural Employees, 1970*, tab. A-1 at 21 (Bull. 1842, 1975); BLS, *Annual Earnings and Employment Patterns of Private Nonagricultural Employees, 1971 and 1972*, tab. A-2 at 23, tab. B-2 at 436 (Bull. 1928, 1976); BLS, *Annual Earnings and Employment Patterns of Private Nonagricultural Employees, 1973-75*, tab. A-1 at 6, tab. B-1 at 132, tab. C-1 at 258 (Bull. 2031, 1979). Because the BLS did not publish the data for 1968 and 1969, the increase for 1970 is the average for the preceding three years.

Table 11 shows the proportion of such four-quarter construction workers and their manufacturing counterparts whose annual earnings exceeded $10,000 and $15,000 in the late 1960s and early 1970s. From 1965 to 1972, both year-round construction and manufacturing workers experienced a quadrupling of the proportion with annual incomes from their major industry of earnings in excess of $10,000 (unadjusted for inflation), although the absolute level among the former remained about 30 percent higher. By 1972, one in five construction workers and one in nine manufacturing workers recorded annual earnings above $15,000.

Table 11: Percentage of Four-Quarter Workers in Construction and Manufacturing Whose Annual Earnings from Their Industry of Major Earnings Exceeded $10,000 and $15,000, 1965-72				
Year	Construction		Manufacturing	
	>$10,000	>$15,000	>$10,000	>$15,000
1965	12.4		9.7	
1966	16.4		12.3	
1967	20.0		13.9	
1970	36.0		23.2	
1971	45.7	16.8	29.6	8.6
1972	48.3	20.1	36.1	11.4

Calculated according to BLS, *Annual Earnings and Employment Patterns of Private Nonagricultural Employees-1965*, tab. 8 at 23; BLS, *Annual Earnings and Employment Patterns of Private Nonagricultural Employees, 1966-67*, tab. A-15 at 47, tab. 16 at 49; BLS, *Annual Earnings and Employment Patterns of Private Nonagricultural Employees, 1970*, tab. B-8 at 72; BLS, *Annual Earnings and Employment Patterns of Private Nonagricultural Employees, 1971 and 1972*, tab. A-40 at 289, tab. B-40 at 702. For the years 1973-75 the BLS failed to publish comparable distributional data.

At the other end of the annual income spectrum, 1963 Social Security Administration data revealed that 41 percent of the two million workers who earned more in construction than in any other industry earned less than $3,000. Even among those who worked all four quarters that year in general building construction, 20 percent earned less than $3,000. These figures prompted Mills to observe that "a considerable number of persons strongly attached to the contract construction industry...were poor persons, as defined by federal government sources."[102]

The most significant data on annual wages from this period stem from two surveys carried out by the Census Bureau for 1966 and 1970, which unearthed theretofore inaccessible data disaggregated for union and nonunion workers. In 1966, among year-round full-time male private wage and salary workers in construction, 43.3 percent of carpenters, 59.6 percent of other craftsmen, and 43.0 percent of laborers were union members compared to 33.5 percent of all year-round full-time male private wage and salary workers and 53.6 percent of all male operatives and kindred workers. The median earnings for the union non-carpenter craftsmen (the highest paid blue-collar group) were $8,701—40 percent higher than

[102]Mills, "Factors Determining Patterns of Employment and Unemployment" at 138, 140 (quote).

those of their nonunion carpenters and only 10 percent lower than the median earnings of the highest paid group (nonunion male managers, officials, and nonfarm proprietors). In terms of distribution, 30.6 percent of union noncarpenter craftsmen reported annual earnings of $10,000 or more compared to only 6.0 percent of nonunionists. The median earnings of union carpenters, $8,311, were 51 percent higher than those of their nonunion counterparts; whereas 20.8 percent of union carpenters earned $10,000 or more in 1966, no nonunionists did.[103]

In 1970, when the Census Bureau conducted a larger and more complete survey, on an occupational basis, 46.0 percent of 415,000 carpenters, 57.4 percent of 1,190,000 construction craftsmen except carpenters, and 33.6 percent of 360,000 construction laborers were unionists compared to 25.0 percent of all year-round full-time wage and salary workers and 45.4 percent of blue-collar workers. The median earnings of the largest and highest paid group, non-carpenter craftsmen, for 1970 were $11,212—43 percent higher than those of their nonunion counterparts and 29 percent higher than the average for all blue-collar union occupations among which they were the highest. (If only white men are compared, these craftsmen's $11,359 median earnings exceeded the average for blue-collar unionists by 24 percent.) In terms of distribution, 61.6 percent of union noncarpenter construction craftsmen recorded annual earnings in excess of $10,000 while 13.7 percent received more than $15,000; for union carpenters and laborers the figures were 45.9 and 6.3 percent and 29.8 and 1.0 percent respectively. Among the nonunionist craftsmen, carpenters, and laborers, the corresponding shares were 20.4 and 2.9 percent, 17.3 and 3.0 percent, and 5.6 and 0.6 percent respectively. To put these figures in perspective: the 129,671 construction workers with annual wages in excess of $15,000 in 1970 accounted for only 6.6 percent of all year-round full-time construction workers and 10.7 percent of the unionists among them.[104]

The union wage premium was also much higher in construction than in manufacturing. Indeed, on an occupational basis, "[t]he widest earnings margins were achieved by skilled workers in the building trades. Union construction craftsmen and carpenters...surpassed the median earnings of their nonunion counterparts by...more than 40 percent." Similarly, on an industrial basis, construction also recorded the widest differential—at least 50 percent higher.[105]

[103]USBC, "Labor Union Membership in 1966," tab. 2 at 10 (CPR, Ser. P-20, No. 216, 1971). The sample of year-round full-time construction laborers was not large enough to meet the Census Bureau's reliability criteria with respect to subgroups. For the larger group of those whose occupation of longest job in 1966 was construction laborer, unionists' annual earnings were 3.19 times as high as nonunionists'. *Id.* tab. 1 at 8. Carpenters formed the largest group of construction craft workers, but their share declined from 38.1 percent in 1950 to 24.7 percent in 1970. *Employment and Training Report of the President*, tab. 3 at 62 (1976).

[104]BLS, *Selected Earnings and Demographic Characteristics of Union Members, 1970*, tab. 6 at 13 (Rep. 417, 1972).

[105]BLS, *Selected Earnings and Demographic Characteristics of Union Members, 1970*, at

The conclusion from these data is that organized skilled building tradesmen's top median annual income just sufficed to secure them budget expenditures "at an intermediate level of living for a 4-person family."[106] Even this modest standard of living, however, was confined to a limited group: more than 40 percent of skilled unionists in addition to virtually all the nonunionists and unskilled workers failed to reach the annual wage necessary to sustain this level. And even that relatively small group was scarcely relieved of all the fears concerning unemployment, injuries, and illnesses associated with loss of income that are inherent in working-class existence.

To put the unionized construction craftsmen's economic standing in further relational perspective: their median income in 1970 ($10,957) placed them only in the middle point of the third quartile of the distribution of wage and salaries among year-round full-time male workers.[107]

2, 3. The wage differential between skilled and unskilled construction workers fell from 1.47 in 1953 to 1.30 in 1964 before rising again to 1.35 by 1970. See A. Gustman & M. Segal, "The Skilled-Unskilled Wage Differential in Construction," 27 (2) *ILRR* 261-75 (Jan. 1974); Martin Personick, "Wage Differentials Between Skilled and Unskilled Building Trades," 97 (10) *MLR* 64-66 (Oct. 1974).

[106]BLS, *Handbook of Labor Statistics 1971*, tab. 127 at 291 (Bull. 1705, 1971). The threshold annual budget for an intermediate level of living in urban areas was $10,664 in Spring 1970.

[107]Peter Henle, "Exploring the Distribution of Earned Income," *MLR*, 95 (12):16-27, tab. 1 at 17 (Dec. 1972). The median income for construction craftsmen subsumed that of the carpenter and noncarpenter cratfsmen.

5

Sources of Power of Militant Business Unionism

> When making an investment, about the only thing that concerns the investor is: Will it pay? ... We as investors are not concerned about whether the company is an insurance company, a stock or other corporation....
>
> When we become members of Organized Labor, we are investors in the biggest paying proposition that we could have chosen for our investments. We looked over the available information, sized up our chances, became satisfied of the solvency of the organization...and decided...that here was a good investment.[1]

> Like the old-style competitive businessman, whose historical shadow he is, the business unionist pursues his particular narrow interests with no thought for the interests of society or even for his own industry, much less for workers as a class.[2]

> I don't think any special-interest group is qualified to run the Government. I don't think General Motors should run the Government, and I don't think the AFL-CIO should run the Government.[3]

Building trades unions have long been regarded as representing the archetypical business or pure and simple unionism, which focuses exclusively on the interests of the workers of a particular craft or industry by engaging in the business of supplying their labor to employers at the best possible prices secured by contracts, while disregarding the structure and distribution of class power, the welfare of nonmembers, or perhaps even the long-range interests of the union's own members.[4] Unions can neglect these more encompassing goals without visibly losing their legitimacy under only certain historical conditions: the dominant socioeconomic

---

[1] Heber White, "Membership—An Investment," 48 (8) *Carpenter* 24-26 at 24 (July 1928).

[2] C. Wright Mills, *The New Men of Power: America's Labor Leaders* 117 (1948).

[3] "U.S. Needs '30,000 New Jobs a Week Just to Break Even," *USNWR*, Feb. 21, 1972, at 27-34 at 31 (interview with George Meany).

[4] Robert Hoxie, *Trade Unionism in the United States* 45 (2d ed. 1966 [1923]); Selig Perlman, *A Theory of the Labor Movement* 131 (1928); Bernard Mandel, "Gompers and Business Unionism, 1873-90," 28 *BHR* 264-75 (1954); Bernard Mandel, *Samuel Gompers: A Biography* 225-26 (1965 [1963]); Philip Taft, "On the Origins of Business Unionism," 17 (1) *ILRR* 20-38 (Oct. 1963); H. Gitelman, "Adolph Strasser and Origins of Pure and Simple Unionism," 6 (1) *LH* 71-83 at 72 (Winter 1965). According to Herbert Harris, *Labor's Civil War* 39-41 (1940), the AFL executive council was dominated by the building trades, which were interested in local affairs and politics as a result of local wage competition, and not in the national politics that affected industrial unions.

trends do not adversely affect members; no technological or organizational changes are looming that would render the indefinite continuation of union policies implausible—in other words, there is no reason to believe that long-run interests diverge from short-run interests; and the exclusion of some workers from membership is not viewed as harming organized workers' interests.[5]

Even if "trade-unions," as President Samuel Gompers reported to the AFL annual convention in 1896, "are the business organizations of the wage-earners,"[6] construction workers' intransigent self-regarding militance may have jeopardized the stability of the societal status quo to which they were allegedly committed. Whether construction unionists have in fact acted as good businessmen in organizing the sale of their labor power remains to be seen.[7]

CONSTRUCTION UNIONS' ORGANIZATIONAL STRENGTH

Trade unionists have construed solidarity to mean an exchange of services: "You help me to get more wages, and I assist you in turn." But this is very far from touching the real solidarity of interest of the working class.[8]

The experienced builder...sees the prematurely aged building mechanic, sometimes a pathetic figure, standing on the sidewalk week after week, in the furtive hope that a job commensurate with his now narrowed abilities is available for him. Unionism seems to have done little or nothing toward the solution of this, the most vital of problems.[9]

The construction industry has never been universally organized—not until the end of the 1930s, for example, did unions enter the traditionally open-shop highway construction sector and only after World War II did they make concerted efforts to organize the sector—but since the end of the nineteenth century, building trades unions have constituted the largest segment of the organized labor movement

---

[5]If the quotation is accurate, business unionism was taken to its absurd logical conclusion in the following statement by an unidentified union negotiator: "'If we have only ten men out of a thousand working, that is all right, provided they are the ten highest paid men ever.'" Gilbert Burck, "The Building Trades Versus the People," 82 (4) *Fortune* 94-97, 159-60 at 96 (Oct. 1970).

[6]*Report of the Proceedings of the 16th Annual Convention of the American Federation of Labor* 19 (1896).

[7]That their business partners take the metaphor seriously is clear from the high praise that Bechtel's vice president for labor relations bestowed on the new president of the Carpenters—an excellent businessman who could have succeeded in any business. Telephone interview with Kenneth Hedman, San Francisco (Mar. 12, 1999).

[8]*Proceedings of the Ninth Annual Convention of the Socialist Labor Party* 26 (n.d. [1896]) (Delegate Vogt on behalf of the Socialist Trade and Labor Alliance).

[9]W. A. Starrett, *Skyscrapers and the Men Who Build Them* 295 (1928).

in the United States.[10] From 1897-98 into the Great Depression (1929-31), they accounted for 15 percent to 27 precent of all union members and 14 percent (1898) to 33 percent (1929-30) of all AFL members.[11] During the next three decades, construction unions increased their representation within the union movement.[12]

Table 12, based on a different criterion, shows construction union members who actually worked in contract construction as a proportion of all U.S. union members from 1956 to 1978. The membership so classified amounted to about two-thirds of the total membership of the construction unions. Throughout the Vietnam war period, then, construction unions accounted for about one-sixth of the total AFL-CIO membership and a little less than one-seventh of the entire unionized labor force in the United States.

The degree of unionization among construction workers is, for several reasons, difficult to calculate. First, the membership figures published by unions include a large number of workers who worked in Canada or outside of the construction industry.[13] Second, these published data include all dues-paying members even if they were retired. Third, the figures do not make it clear whether the members were unemployed at the time they paid dues. This point is especially relevant because this particular overcount means that the degree of organization would automatically rise during recessions as a constant membership is divided by declining employment. And fourth, since the average annual employment represented about one-half of those who work in construction in the course of a year, a question arises as to the appropriate denominator.[14]

---

[10]Walter Galenson, *The CIO Challenge to the AFL: A History of the American Labor Movement 1935-41*, at 529 (1960); Garth Mangum, *The Operating Engineers: The Economic History of a Trade Union* 249 (1964).

[11]Calculated according to data in Leo Wolman, *The Growth of American Trade Unions* 110, 120 (1924); Leo Wolman, *Ebb and Flow in Trade Unionism* 172-75, 198-99, 232-33 (1936); U.S. Bureau of the Census, *Historical Statistics of the United States: Colonial Times to 1970*, Pt. 1, ser. D 944 at 177 (1975). According to John Commons, "Is Class Conflict in America Growing and Is It Inevitable?" 13 (6) *AJS* 756-83 (May 1908), unions had practically disappeared in trustified industries and were still found only in the building trades, railroads, mines, docks, and the fringes of trusts.

[12]Calculated according to data in Leo Troy, *Trade Union Membership, 1897-1962*, tab. A-1, A-2, and A-3 (1965). The data in Wolman and Troy are not comparable since the former are based on union reports whereas the latter used per capta tax payments as an indicator of membership; they also differ with regard to the unions selected as belonging to building and construction. On the building trades as the core of the AFL, see Philip Taft, *Organized Labor in America* 203-205 (1964).

[13]In the Carpenters union, for example, only slightly more than half of all members worked in the construction industry in 1936. Galenson, *The CIO Challenge to the AFL* at 519.

[14]BLS, *Directory of National Unions and Employee Associations 1971*, at 104-106, 116-17 (Bull. 1750, 1972); Daniel Quinn Mills, *Industrial Relations and Manpower in Construction* 90 (1972); BLS, *Compensation in the Construction Industry* 9 (Bull. 1656, 1970); William Hahn, "Construction Manpower Needs by 1980," 94 (7) *MLR* 12 (July 1971).

Table 12: Building and Construction Trade Union Membership, 1956-1978			
Year	Total	% total union membership	% total AFL-CIO membership
1956	2,123,000	12	13
1958	2,324,000	13	15
1960	2,271,000	13	15
1962	2,417,000	14	16
1964	2,323,000	13	15
1966	2,463,000	13	15
1968	2,541,000	13	16
1970	2,576,000	12	16
1972	2,752,000	13	16
1974	2,738,000	13	16
1976	2,694,000	13	15
1978	2,884,000	13	16

Sources: 1956-64, 1968-72: BLS, *Handbook of Labor Statistics 1975—Reference Edition*, tab. 155 at 382-86 (Bull. 1865, 1975); 1966: BLS, *Handbook of Labor Statistics 1968*, tab. 126 at 296 (Bull. 1600, n.d. [1968]); 1974-76: BLS, *Handbook of Labor Statistics*, tab. 162 at 406-408 (Bull. 2070, 1980).

One way of dealing with these methodological problems is to subtract these misleading subgroups, insofar as they can be quantified, and to set the remainder in relation to the average annual employment in construction. The final result is still subject to great uncertainties, but the deficiencies in the sources are unavoidable. Table 13 presents an illustrative calculation of the membership of the 17 member unions of the BCTD for the year 1970.

If half of the Canadian and retired members are subtracted from the estimated number of construction union members working in construction, the total number of organized workers was about 2.4 million in 1970. They represented about 85 percent of the average annual employment of 2,820,000 that year.[15] Even this adjusted proportion appears excessively high, especially since it would have approached 100 percent in the winter months.

---

[15]BLS, *Handbook of Labor Statistics 1974*, at 106. Only one-half of the Canadian and retired members are subtracted to avoid double counting those who not working in construction.

Table 13: Membership in U.S. Construction Unions, 1970				
Union	Members	Members employed in construction (estimated)	In Canada	Retired
Asbestos workers	17,936	17,750	2,436	
Boilermakers	138,000	92,500	7,200	
Bricklayers	142,751	142,751	9,346	
Carpenters	820,000	715,000	77,000	36,000
Electricians	921,722	175,000	56,305	
Elevator constructors	16,938	16,938	2,184	
Granite cutters	3,500	0		300
Iron workers	177,857	108,000	14,791	5,300
Laborers	580,000	460,000	50,000	
Lathers	14,856	14,856*	. 1,529	
Marble polishers	8,000	8,000*	353	
Operating engineers	392,783	320,000	26,378	
Painters	210,000	160,000	11,868	15,000
Plasterers	68,000	67,000	319	
Plumbers	311,550	220,000	32,144	
Roofers	24,362	24,362		
Sheet metal workers	120,000	40,000	13,616	
Total	3,967,985	2,581,887	305,469	56,600

Sources: BLS, *Directory of National Unions and Employee Association 1971*, at 22-43, 104-106;
Mills, *Industrial Relations* at 90. * Unknown: assumed that all work was in construction

   Although other data sets, not strictly comparable with Table 13, confirm the
skepticism about such quasi-universal unionization, they nevertheless underscore

high rates of organization.[16] The first survey of union membership conducted by the Census Bureau revealed that in 1966 43.7 percent of all male private wage and salary workers in construction were unionists. Among those for whom construction was the occupation of longest job in 1966, 53.3 percent of construction craftsmen (46.1 percent of carpenters and 56.6 percent of other construction craftsmen) and 30.5 percent of construction laborers were union members. For the narrower group of year-round full-time construction workers, 54.8 percent of craftsmen (43.3 percent of carpenters and 59.6 percent of other craftsmen) and 43.0 percent of laborers were members.[17]

According to the 1970 Census Bureau survey, 969,000 or 38.3 percent of 2,532,000 year-round full-time wage and salary workers in the construction industry were union members. The share amounted to 41.1 percent among white men, but only 32.1 percent among black men. Among the 4,975,000 wage and salary workers whose longest held job in 1970 was in the construction industry, 1,948,000 or 39 percent were unionized. Of the 4,040,000 workers whose occupation of longest held job was in construction, 1,847,000 or 46 percent were in unions. On an occupational basis the difference in unionization rates beteween skilled and unskilled workers was large—52 percent and 30 percent respectively. Among the smaller group of 1,965,000 construction craftsworkers and laborers whose year-round full-time job was a construction occupation, 995,000 or 51 percent were union members. The difference in the degree of unionization as between skilled and unskilled workers was large here too: 55 percent of year-round full-time construction craftsmen were union members compared with 34 percent of construction laborers. A much higher proportion of white than black male laborers was organized—37 percent versus 24 percent. Ironically, the total number of black craftsmen was too small to generate statistical reliability. Regional differences were even more prominent: 54 percent of male workers (whose longest job held was in construction) in the West were members, but only 25 percent of those in the South and 17 percent of black males in the South.[18]

Other studies found similar rates of organization. A 1965 BLS study revealed that 45 percent of building construction workers were employed by firms in which bargaining agreements covered a majority of workers. BLS contrasted this

---

[16]Irving Bernstein, "The Growth of American Unions," 2 (2) *LH* 131-57 at 138 (Spr. 1961), estimated union density in the building trades at 77, 84, 73, and 86 percent in 1939, 1953, 1956, and 1958, respectively; in transportation, membership exceeded 100 percent.

[17]USBC, "Labor Union Membership in 1966," tab. B at 2, tab. 1 at 8, tab. 2 at 10 (CPR, Ser. P-20, No. 216, 1971). Because the sample in this Survey of Economic Opportunity was intentionally selected to oversample blacks and other nonwhites, the reliability of of estimates not tabulated by race was reduced. *Id.* at 6.

[18]BLS, *Selected Earnings and Demographic Characteristics of Union Members, 1970*, at 13-21, 26-27 (Rep. 417, 1972).

minimum coverage estimate with the "maximum...established by the proportion of workers who are union members," which averaged 80 percent in 1966, ranging between 98 percent in February and 73 percent in August.[19] In 1969, more than three-fifths of construction workers working for special trade contractors were employed by firms in which a majority was covered by collective bargaining agreements. In the three branches with the largest employment, plumbing, electrical work, and masonry, the rate of unionization was highest: 77, 67, and 60 percent respectively. In the other branches, the combined rate of organization was 57 percent.[20] In 1971, 55 percent of workers in heavy construction and 51 percent in highway construction were unionized.[21]

Several BLS industry wage surveys in the 1970s also reported very high union membership rates, which were skewed by being heavily weighted toward large metropolitan areas and excluding contractors with fewer than eight employees. A survey of 21 areas with one-sixth of all contract construction workers revealed that contractors whose collective bargaining agreements covered a majority of their nonsupervisory construction workers employed four-fifths of the work force in 1972. In the North and West this share exceeded 95 percent among contractors with 250 or more workers.[22] Such figures underlay A. H. Raskin's claim that Taft-Hartley's "ban on the closed shop has been almost meaningless in the urban strongholds of the construction...crafts."[23] A similar 1973 survey of a different set of areas found an overall unionization share of three-fourths.[24] Yet another survey in 1977 revealed that 65 to 69 percent of nonsupervisory construction workers in 17 large metropolitan areas worked under labor-management agreements, rising to 80-84 percent in firms of 250 or more workers.[25]

The BLS's estimate that in the latter part of the 1960s about 60 to 70 percent of construction workers were employed in firms with collective bargaining agreements covering a majority of their workers—a level similar to that in 1936 when 68 percent of employed construction workers were unionists—should be

---

[19]BLS, *Compensation in Construction* at 9, 82.

[20]BLS, *Employee Compensation and Payroll Hours: Construction—Special Trade Contractors, 1969*, at 1, 15 (1972).

[21]BLS, *Employee Compensation and Payroll Hours: Heavy Construction Industry, 1971*, at 16 (Rep. 428, 1974).

[22]BLS, *Industry Wage Survey: Contract Construction September 1972*, at 3-4 (Bull. 1853, 1975).

[23]A. H. Raskin, "Taft-Hartley at 25—How It's Worked," *NYT*, June 18, 1972, sect. 3 at 1.

[24]BLS, *Industry Wage Survey: Contract Construction September 1973*, at 3-4 (Bull. 1911, 1976).

[25]*BLS, Compensation in the Construction Industries in Large Metropolitan Areas*, text tab. 3 at 9 (Rep. 610, 1980).

supplemented in two respects.[26] First, construction craftsmen outside of housing construction were even more highly organized.[27] And second, the degree of unionization in construction in the late 1960s and early 1970s was, as it had been for decades, considerably higher than in manufacturing, although certain individual industries, such as metals, automobiles, and railroads, were more highly organized. This differential was particularly important in view of the size structure of construction firms: comprised of hundreds of thousands of mostly small companies scattered all over the United States, the industry was subject to fragmented collective bargaining.

THE SIZE-STRUCTURE OF CONSTRUCTION FIRMS

The reason why the striking bricklayers cannot win is that it is not in reality the contractors with whom they have to deal, but with the men who employ these contractors to do their work for them—with the capitalists who put up the big buildings that give work to the vast mass of the workingmen.[28]

Even Marx clearly recognized the capitalist dynamic that promotes cost-reducing innovations, although he mistakenly predicted that workers would not share in productivity gains....[29]

Construction employment is much less concentrated than in manufacturing because firms are much smaller. This peculiar size-structure undergirds the argument that unions are able to dominate collective bargaining because employers

---

[26]BLS, *Compensation in Construction* at 10; Edward Sanford, "Wage Rates and Hours of Labor in the Building Trades," 45(2) *MLR* 291, 297 (Aug. 1937). See also Leo Wolman, *Growth of American Trade Unions* at 46-47, 86, 92, 95, 110-11, 120-21, 130-61; *idem*, "Labor," in *Recent Economic Changes: Report of the Committee on Recent economic Changes of the President's Conference on Unemployment* 2:480, 482 (1929); Mark Perlman, "Labor in Eclipse," in *Change and Continuity in Twentieth-Century America: The 1920's*, at 109, 111 (1968); *To Amend the National Labor Relations Act, 1947, with Respect to the Building and Construction Industry: Hearings Before the Subcommittee on Labor and Labor Management Relations of the Senate Committee on Labor and Public Welfare*, 82d Cong., 1st Sess. 57-58 (1951) (statement of Richard Gray, president of the BCTD, estimating a 90 percent degree of organization). Gray also recounted that the Bureau of the Census reported 3,100,000 building tradesmen as of Aug. 1, 1951, while the building trades unions paid per capita tax to the AFL on that date of 2,872,067 members (which was about 93 percent). "Death of S. 1973," 4 (10) *BCTB* 6-7 (Oct. 1951).

[27]Foster & Northrup, *Open Shop Construction*, estimated that 50 to 60 percent of all construction work was carried on by nonunion firms—80 to 90 percent in homebuilding, but only 25 percent of commercial construction.

[28]"Anxious to Arbitrate," *CT*, June 17, 1887, at 1, col. 4-6.

[29]John Kendrick, *Productivity Trends in the United States* 4 (1961).

are numerous, small, and atomized. Table 14 displays the distribution of establishments and employment by size classes for 1967 and 1972. No significant changes occurred between 1967 and 1972: the modal size class was 20 to 49 employees, while the mean number of employees per establishment was 9.3 and 9.5. About one-fourth of the employees worked in establishments with fewer than 10 employees, which in turn accounted for more than four-fifths of all establishments. One-third worked in establishments with 10 to 49 employees, which accounted for one-sixth of all establishments. A further one-fourth worked in establishments with 50 to 249 employees, which accounted for one-fortieth of all establishments. And finally, one-sixth to one-seventh worked in the largest establishments with 250 or more employees, which accounted for less than 0.3 percernt of all establishments.[30] In contrast, in manufacturing, 32.8 percent of employees in 1967 worked in establishments with 1,000 or more employees. On average, manufacturing establishments employed 60 employees in 1967—almost seven times as many as their construction counterparts.[31]

Even greater in number than establishments with payroll were those without payroll: the 426,067 and 482,865 such establishments in 1967 and 1972 were 16 percent and 10 percent, respectively, more numerous.[32] The absence of payroll in these establishments does not necessarily mean that only self-employed owners worked in them: they may, instead, have unlawfully or lawfully employed workers whom they classified as nonemployees. Self-bossed workers operating mini-businesses may have put additional downward pressure on bids, prices, and wages; where they employed workers as nonemployees, they shaped labor relations by precluding collective bargaining and atomizing the workforce. The existence of such a large sector of quasi-self-employment also imparted a different tone to labor relations by creating the rhetoric and, to some extent, the reality of temporary escape from lifelong wage labor.[33]

---

[30]A quarter-century later, employment was even less concentrated: the mean size of establishments with payroll was 8.1 employees, while establishments with 250 or more employees accounted for only 10.7 percent of all employees. Calculated according to USBC, *1992 CCI: Industry Series: United States Summary*, tab. 8 at 27-12 (1995).

[31]USBC, *Statistical Abstract of the United States: 1976*, at tab. 1308 at 763 (97th ed., 1974).

[32]USBC, *CCI, 1967: Type of Operation and Legal Form of Organization*, tab. 1 at 1-3 (1970); USBC, *1972 CCI: Industry Series: United States Summary*, tab. A1 at 1-2.

[33]Marc Linder, "Self-Employment as a Cyclical Escape from Unemployment: A Case Study of the Construction Industry in the United States During the Postwar Period," in 2 *Research in the Sociology of Work: Peripheral Workers* 261-74 (1983); George Strauss, *Unions in the Building Trades: A Case Study* 69 (1958). Unionization is difficult when workers expect to work themselves out of wage-earning status by becoming foremen and then business owners, but it is unclear that this barrier was serious in the late twentieth century. John Dunlop, "The Development of Labor Organization: A Theoretical Framework," in *Insights into Labor Issues* 163-93 at 184 (Richard Lester & Joseph Shister eds., 1948).

Table 14: Size Distribution of Employment in Construction Establishments with Payroll, 1967 and 1972

Establishments with...employees	1967 Establishments Number	1967 Establishments %	1967 Employees Number	1967 Employees %	1972 Establishments Number	1972 Establishments %	1972 Employees Number	1972 Employees %
1-4	238,595	64.7	434,528	12.6	271,974	62.1	506,696	12.2
5-9	62,992	17.1	423,436	12.3	79,520	18.2	520,084	12.5
10-19	35,148	9.5	488,915	14.2	45,965	10.5	617,471	14.9
20-49	21,772	5.9	656,842	19.1	27,972	6.4	837,355	20.2
50-99	6,419	1.7	434,472	12.6	7,991	1.8	541,614	13.1
100-249	2,966	0.8	437,188	12.7	3,481	0.8	508,679	12.3
250-499	589	0.2	199,397	5.8	737	0.2	249,728	6.0
500-999	203	0.06	139,291	4.1	220	0.05	147,042	3.5
1,000+	87	0.02	222,196	6.5	81	0.02	217,110	5.2
Total	368,771	100.0	3,436,265	100.0	437,941	100.0	4,145,779	100.0

Sources: U.S. Bureau of the Census, *CCI, 1967: U.S. Summary*, tab. B3 at 16-5 (1970); U.S. Bureau of the Census, *1972 CCI: Industry Series: United States Summary*, tab. B4 at 1-12 (1975).

The use of "establishments" for gauging employment size-classes may be assailed on the grounds that it underestimates the real concentration of employees. In terms of the employer's economic power vis-à-vis its employees, this objection is appropriate: if a firm maintains several establishments, its overall strength is obviously distorted by the choice of this reference point by the Bureau of the Census. On the other hand, the establishment basis gives a better sense of the size of the group within which workers interact.[34]

The quinquennial Economic Census also generates data on an enterprise basis, which reveal that, at least in construction, the concentration of employment is not vitally affected by which organizational basis is used as the standard. Table 15 shows the same size-class employment data on an enterprise basis.

Shifting the focus to the company level reveals 50 percent and 100 percent, respectively, greater concentration of employment in the largest size-class: 9.6 percent of all employees were employed in companies with 1,000 or more employees in 1967 and 10.9 percent in 1972.[35] This concentration, however, is dwarfed by that in manufacturing: in 1972, 45.2 percent of all manufacturing employees were employed in companies with 10,000 or more employees compared to only 2.9 percent in construction. Construction companies, on average, employed only 10 workers in 1972 while their manufacturing counterparts employed 86. This minimal concentration conceals the presence of large firms in the industrial, power plant, and civil engineering subsector. There three firms with 72,186 employees accounted for 12.9 percent of all employment and 16.6 percent of all sales and receipts in 1972.[36] Companies of such size, probably NCA members, held much stronger bargaining positions.

---

[34]The definition reveals the extent to which an establishment may actually approximate a construction site: "[A] 'construction establishment' is defined as a relatively permanent office, or other place of business at which or from which the usual business activities related to construction are conducted. ([A] relatively permanent office is one which has been established for the management of more than a single project or job and which has been or is expected to be maintained on a continuing basis.) Such 'establishment' activities include (but are not limited to) estimating, bidding, scheduling, purchasing, supervision, and operation of the actual construction work being conducted at one or more construction sites. ... Separate construction reports were not required for each project or construction site. ... An establishment is not necessarily identical with the 'company' or 'enterprise' which may consist of one or more establishments." USBC, *1972 CCI: Industry Series: United States Summary*, at vi.

[35]The figures for the two size-classes that are blank were withheld by the Census Bureau. In 1992, the proportion had dropped to 6.8 percent. USBC, *1992 Economic Census—Enterprise Statistics* (1997) (data emailed by the Bureau of the Census).

[36]USBC, *1972 Enterprise Statistics*, Pt. 1: *General Report on Industrial Organization*, tab. 5 at 144, 148 (1977). The subsector is "heavy construction, except highway." For further detail, see Linder, *Projecting Capitalism* at 177-81.

Table 15: Size-Distribution of Employment in Construction Companies, 1967 and 1972

Companies with...employees	1967 Companies		1967 Employees		1972 Companies		1972 Employees	
	Number	%	Number	%	Number	%	Number	%
1-4	201,814	60.8	433,070	12.7	235,591	59.4	502,813	12.1
5-9	63,907	19.2	420,172	13.2	78,551	19.8	513,549	12.3
10-19	35,786	10.8	478,741	14.0	44,852	11.3	601,403	14.4
20-49	21,053	6.3	626,414	18.3	26,492	6.7	790,743	19.0
50-99	5,887	1.8	397,799	11.6	7,269	1.8	491,049	11.8
100-249	2,730	0.8	404,761	11.8	3,054	0.8	446,187	10.7
250-499	587	0.2	198,831	5.8	664	0.2	225,640	5.4
500-999	191	0.06	131,978	3.9	220	0.06	143,389	3.4
1,000-2,499	72	0.02	104,331	3.0	99	0.02	150,809	3.6
2,500-4,999	15	0.01	54,623	1.6	18	0.01	180,657	4.3
5,000-9,999	16	0.01	106,113	3.1	16			
10,000-24,999	4		65,983	1.9	6		121,533	2.9
Total	332,062	100.0	3,422,816	100.0	396,832	100.0	4,167,772	100.0

Sources: USBC, *1967 Enterprise Statistics,* Pt. 1: *General Report on Industrial Organization,* tab. 3-1 at 166 (1972); *idem, 1972 Enterprise Statistics,* Pt. 1: *General Report on Industrial Organization,* tab. 5 at 144 (1977).

Other economic indicators underscore the huge size differences between construction and manufacturing firms. The average sales and receipts among all 265,052 manufacturing companies in 1972 was $3.1 million compared to $182,000 among 893,933 construction companies.[37] In 1970, manufacturing corporations with assets in excess of $50 million accounted for 67 percent of total corporate manufacturing receipts and 79 percent of assets compared to only 8 percent and 14 percent, respectively, in construction.[38] In 1975 and 1976, when Fluor Corporation was the country's largest construction company, it ranked only 283rd and 254th, respectively, among the 500 largest publicly owned corporations in terms of annual profits. Fluor's 1975 net earnings of $47.4 million amounted to only 1.5 percent of first-ranked AT&T's $3.147 billion or 3.8 percent of fourth-ranked General Motors' $1.253.1 billion.[39]

CAUSES AND CONSEQUENCES OF CONSTRUCTION UNIONS' STRONG POSITION

By the infirmity of human nature it happens, that the more skilful the workman, the more self-willed and intractable he is apt to become, and, of course, the less fit a component of a mechanical system, in which...he may do great damage to the whole. The grand object therefore of the modern manufacturer is, through the union of capital and science, to reduce the task of his work-people to the exercise of vigilance and dexterity,—faculties, when concentred to one process, speedily brought to perfection in the young.[40]

[W]here did the practical knowledge come from for conducting the industries of the country? All the skill in the building trades had come from the bench side, and the masters in this business had been working-men.[41]

---

[37]USBC, *1972 Enterprise Statistics*, Pt. 1: *General Report on Industrial Organization*, tab. 5 at 144, 148 (1977).

[38]IRS, *Statistics of Income—1970, Corporation Income Tax Returns* 35-36 (1974). This huge gap understated the real difference between manufacturing and construction firms because corporations accounted for 98 percent of manufacturing's receipts compared to only 76 percent in construction. IRS, *Statistics of Income—1970, Business Income Tax Returns* 5-6 (1973).

[39]"The Bottom-Line Directory," *FW*, July 15, 1976, at 13, 15, 21, 26; "The Bottom-Line Directory," *FW*, July 15, 1977, at 13, 27. The only other construction company appearing on the magazine's list of the 500 corporations with the largest annual profits was Stone & Webster, which ranked 453rd in 1975, when it was the seventh largest construction firm in terms of contracts awarded.

[40]Andrew Ure, *The Philosophy of Manufactures: or, An Exposition of the Scientific, Moral and Commercial Economy of the Factory System of Great Britain* 20-21 (3d ed. 1861 [1835]).

[41][Robert] Applegarth, "Discussion," in W. Stanley Jevons, "On Industrial Partnership," in *idem, Methods of Social Reform and Other Papers* 122-55 at 153 (1883 [1870]). Applegarth was the secretary of the Amalgamated Society of Carpenters and Joiners.

[T]he contractor knows where he is going to get his labor supply. He doesn't have to have it laying in his backyard on his own payroll. He has got a collective bargaining contract and the labor supply is there.[42]

A number of the peculiarities of the construction industry in the United States must be explained by reference to skilled workers' special position in a technologically backward sector. To be sure, firms welcomed some aspects of the extraordinary power of skilled building trades unions, which, given the structure of the industry, were almost indispensable.[43] The fact that the structure of the construction industry was in part still preindustrial was the basis of organized skilled workers' enhanced opportunities for control and defense. In most branches of the industry, hand tools occupied a central position, and where they had been supplanted by machines, they were generally—highway construction being the chief exception—not part of a continuous flow of production, but rather of individual partial operations. This preautomated stage of the productive forces, in which the proliferation of specialized detail workers associated with *Manufaktur* was not fully developed, was correlated with a merely formal, and not yet fully substantive, subordination to capital.[44]

It is precisely this preservation of a large number of skilled workers with a relatively broad competence within an industry composed of an above-average proportion of small firms with relatively low capital intensity that made possible construction workers' control. This combination is unique among the larger industries of material production: "After 1900, mechanization and minute sub-division of labor...became widespread in almost every phase of American industry, with the exception of the building industry."[45]

---

[42]"Remarks by President George Meany of AFL-CIO on Philadelphia Plan for Minority Employment," *CLR*, No. 747, Jan. 14, 1970, at F-1, F-3.

[43]The converse proposition is that retaining responsibility for certain aspects of production may incline skilled workers, despite their heightened autonomy, to be committed to purposes that ultimately bind them even more tightly to their employers than is the case in other industries precisely because the shared responsibility makes it more difficult for them to perceive an antagonistic relationship. This production-centered approach to class conflict differs sharply from those that focus on exchange relations, which, for example find expression in collective bargaining. See, e.g., Lionel Robbins, *The Economic Basis of Class Conflict* 7 (1939): "The clue to a successful approach to the problem...lies in the analysis of markets. In the exchange society the market is, as it were, the reflection of the whole network of economic relations."

[44]See, e.g., Grimes, "Personnel Management in the Building Trades" at 42-43. Grimes added that specialization, with the exception of that among carpenters and iron workers, was more task- than person-oriented. That industrialization accompanied the spread of such phenomena associated with the development of *Manufaktur* in construction creates a complicated mixed-form industrial structure.

[45]Philip Foner, 3 *History of the Labor Movement in the United States: The Policies and Practices of the American Federation of Labor, 1900-1909*, at 178 (1964).

Building trades unions thus were the only significant group of skilled manual workers able to expand their membership without having to devote their resources to coming to grips with employment-reducing or -limiting technological innovations. The effect of most mechanical innovations in late nineteenth and early twentieth-century construction was not the substitution of unskilled for skilled labor, but that of power-driven machines for unskilled labor.[46] Whereas some unions' long-term viability was undermined by such changes, and other unions to a greater or lesser degree accommodated themselves to mechanization and the division of labor, construction unions were neither menaced nor accommodating. As a result, their energies were freed to engage in other activities.

A considerable portion of these energies was devoted to jurisdictional disputes with other unions. In a sense, such disputes were substitutes for struggles that other unions were forced to conduct with employers.[47] Building trades unions attended to the distributive effects of the use of new building materials on employment not so much by opposing their introduction as by seeking to preserve members' jobs by indulging in costly internecine strife over new occupations within the changing division of labor to oust other unions and ward off encroachments.[48] The building trades' uniquely uninterrupted existence as organizations of the skilled was thus largely a function of "The Business Capitalism Forgot."[49]

Implementation of this workers' control presupposed not only that the skilled workers possessed the knowledge to manage production as individuals, but could also bring this knowledge to bear as a cohesive group. To the extent that the knowledge they were striving to withhold from employers was rooted in a certain developmental stage of the productive forces, it would lose its basis when the latter

---

[46]For example, the introduction around 1895 of the power hoist eliminated large numbers of hod carriers from brick construction; the use of power shovels and trenching machines dsiplaced many unskilled workers in excavation and highway construction, while cement mixers replaced still more. W. C. Clark, "The Construction Industry," in *Representative Industries in the United States* 182-223 at 198-99 (H. Warshow ed., 1928); Harry Jerome, *Mechanization in Industry* 137, 140 (1934); Haber, *Industrial Relations in the Building Industry* at 16-35.

[47]As Raymond Postgate, *The Builders' History* 355 (1923), noted for Britain: "The pugnacity which the members were not allowed to exercise against their employers they seemed to turn against their fellow workers."

[48]N. Whitney, *Jurisdictions in American Building-Trades Unions* (1914); E. Cummins, "The National Board for Jurisdictional Awards and the Carpenters' Unions," 19 (3) *AER* 363-77 (Sept. 1929); John Coyne, "Jurisdictional Disputes in the Building Industry," 46 (12) *AF* 1298-1302 (Dec. 1939); "Document: The Agreement Establishing a National Joint Board for the Settlement of Jurisdictional Disputes in Building and Construction Industries," 2 (3) *ILRR* 411-15 (Apr. 1949); Kenneth Strand, *Jurisdictional Disputes in Construction: The Causes, the Joint Board, and the NLRB* (1961).

[49]"The Industry Capitalism Forgot," 36 (2) *Fortune* 61-67, 167-70 (Aug. 1947) (on residential construction).

were revolutionized even if unions could prolong such processes.

One of scientific management's most important goals, therefore, was to transfer such knowledge to management so that increases in productivity would not be reserved for workers' control. Unions largely succeeded in fending off the relatively few attempts to introduce scientific management into the building trades.[50] In bricklaying, however, in some localities motion studies inspired by Taylorism did make some headway in the early twentieth century.[51] To be sure, John R. Commons reported in 1906 that employers had specialized the bricklayer's work in New York , "arranged an unremittent flow of brick and mortar, and lays him off at any half-hour. Not a minute of his precious time is wasted, nor a stroke of his arm permitted to lag."[52] As a result, bricklayers could no longer sustain the pace after the age of 45.[53] Generally, however, the body of building tradesmen remained in "unique possession of craft knowledge and craft skill," while their employers remained unable to gather up, systematize, and concentrate scattered craft knowledge in order to "dol[e] it out again only in the form of minute instructions" for a minute task.[54] Significantly, construction workers and their unions, unlike their major industrial counterparts, did not enter into the grand historical compromise with employers after World War II in which union leadership ceded relatively uncontested control over working conditions back to management in exchange for productivity-linked wage increases.[55]

The available data on skilled construction workers are not always mutually consistent, but they all agree that the proportion of skilled workers far exceeds that

---

[50]Haber, *Industrial Relations in the Building Industry* at 226, supported this claim by arguing that union rules in many places prohibited time and motion studies, but he offered only one obscure example.

[51]Frederick Taylor, *The Principles of Scientific Management* 77-85 (1916), explicitly developed this position with respect to bricklaying, relying on the work of Frank Gilbreth. See Frank Gilbreth, *Concrete System* (1908); Frank Gilbreth, *Bricklaying System* (1909); Frank Gilbreth, *Motion Study: A Method for Increasing the Efficiency of the Workman* 71-73, 96-97 (1911); 4 *Evidence Taken by the Interstate Commerce Commission in the Matter of Proposed Advances in Freight Rates by Carriers, August to December, 1910*, at 2776-87 (S. Doc. No. 725, 63d Cong, 3d Sess, 1911) (testimony of Frank Gilbreth); "Refuse to Lay Bricks by Rule: Scientific Management Ideas of a New Yorker Cause a Strike at Glenn Falls," *NYT*, Mar. 29, 1911, at 11, col. 4; "Bricklaying Yields to Science for the First Time," *NYT*, Apr. 2, 1911, sect. 6, at 9, col. 1-7; Edna Yost, *Frank and Lillian Gilbreth: Partners for Life* 54, 56, 71, 159, 163-75, 190 (1949); Milton Nawordny, *Scientific Management and the Unions: A Historical Analysis* 54-55 (1955).

[52]John R. Commons, "Restrictions by Trade Unions," in *idem, Labor and Administration* 120-34 at 134 (1913 [1906]).

[53]*Eleventh Special Report of the Commissioner of Labor: Regulation and Restriction of Output* 293 (1904)

[54]Robert Hoxie, *Scientific Management and Labor* 131-32 (1921).

[55]Kim Moody, *An Injury to All: The Decline of American Unionism* 27-28 (1996 [1988]).

of industry at large. A study published at the end of the 1950s estimated that the proportion of skilled and supervisory workers in construction was 49.8 percent compared to 19.6 percent in manufacturing. The building trades accounted at that time for one-third of all skilled workers in the United States.[56] Studies from the 1960s estimated that there were two to three craftsmen for every unskilled worker in construction.[57] The ratios in the branches from which this aggregate average was formed varied significantly—from more than three to one in one-family housebuilding to less than one to one in highway construction.[58]

Significantly, the proportion of supervisory personnel was especially high in branches, such as highway and underground construction, in which unskilled workers predominated.[59] This structure supports the thesis that the production process and the content of apprenticeship were oriented toward workers who supervised themselves.[60] (The fact that the ratio of journeymen to foremen was five to ten times higher in union than nonunion construction strongly supports the

---

[56]BLS, *The Construction Worker in the United States* 28 (1959). Because the data were derived from the census, they did not necessarily reflect the annual average qualification structure of those employed in construction.

[57]William Hahn, "Construction Manpower Needs by 1980," 94 (7) *MLR* 12-18, tab. 1 at 14 (July 1971); BLS, *Compensation in the Construction Industry*, tab. 3 at 13.

[58]These data are derived from special surveys conducted by BLS. On their origin, see BLS, *Handbook of Methods* 235-38 (Bull. 1711, 1971). For a summary of the results until the mid-1960s, see Claiborne Ball, "Employment Effects of Construction Expenditures," 88 (2) *MLR* 156 (Feb. 1965). Later studies included: BLS, *Labor and Material Requirements for Hospital and Nursing Home Construction* 8 (Bull. 1691, 1971); BLS, *Labor and Material Requirements for Construction of Private Single-family Houses* 6 (Bull. 1755, 1972); BLS, *Labor and Material Requirements for Public Housing Construction 1968*, at 6 (Bull. 1821, 1974); Robert Ball, "Labor and Material Requirements for Apartment Construction," 98 (1) *MLR* 70-73 (Jan. 1975). The developmental tendencies were not uniform: in some branches the proportion of skilled declined, in others it rose.

[59]E. Jay Howenstine, "Compensatory Public Works Programs and Full Employment," 73 (2) *ILR* 112-13 (Feb. 1956); Ball, "Employment Effects of Construction Expenditures." An above-average proportion of laborers worked in construction—19.4 percent compared with 6.7 percent in manufacturing. BLS, *The Construction Worker in the United States* at 28. However, to characterize construction laborers as unskilled "can be misleading. ... Many type [sic] of construction-laborer...jobs require training and experience, as well as a broad knowledge of construction methods, materials, and operations. Rock blasting, rock drilling, and tunnel construction are examples of work in which 'know-how' is important. Construction laborers...must know the effects of different explosive charges under varying rock conditions...to prevent injury and property damage. Construction laborers...do all the work in the boring and mining of a tunnel, including operations which would be handled by craftsmen if the job were located above ground." BLS, *Occupational Outlook Handbook: 1970-71 Edition* 374 (Bull. No. 1650, n.d.). On the division of labor, see also BLS, *Conciliation and Arbitration in the Building Trades of Greater New York* 57 (Bull. 124, 1913); Arch Mercey, *The Laborers Story 1903-1953: The First Fifty Years of the International Hod Carriers', Building and Common Laborers' Union of America (AFL)* 27 (1954).

[60]Mills, *Industrial Relations* at 183-84.

argument that higher union journeymen wages in part "represent embodied supervisory skills.")[61] These craftsmen may then have found themselves in a contradictory situation because they were enabled to attain greater control over the production process, but at the same time were entrusted with responsibility for a production process that always remained profit driven for owners and managers. Thus whereas manufacturing workers immediately experienced capital's self-regarding control over their working conditions, construction craftsmen may have been more actively engaged in their own exploitation. This contradiction was embodied, for example, in the fact that foremen not only alternated on various projects between being supervisors and workers, but were also sometimes autonomously appointed by unions.[62]

From employers' perspective, supervision was another area of union power undermining their control that had long been a focus of managerial concern.[63] Particularly the Roundtable criticized contractors for permitting themselves to be deprived of the kind of command structure common to other industries:

> Most foremen and general foremen have risen from journeymen ranks in union construction. As a result, foremen and general foremen typically are members of the same union as the employees they supervise, and are covered by the same labor agreements. It is logical, therefore, that such foremen view the union as their de facto employer and agent, responsible for negotiating their wages, hours and conditions of employment; for pursuing their grievances; and for arranging their next job. ... Actions that antagonize a large percentage of the people working for them, or the union business agent, could jeopardize the jobs of these supervisors. ... This difficult situation is peculiar to...unionized construction....[64]

Especially contractors that operated nationally with widely varying workloads in given localities had, according to the Roundtable, "few options other than to draw such supervisors from local unions" because they are "concerned with the high cost of retaining and relocating first- and second-level supervisors from project to project...."[65] Indeed, so entrenched was this dual rule that the Roundtable

---

[61]Bourdon & Levitt, *Union and Open-Shop Construction* at 49.

[62]Grimes, "Personnel Management in the Building Trades" at 43. For a partial analogy in France, which, however, undermined collective bargaining, see Maurice Parodi, "Wage Drift and Wage Bargaining: A Case Study of the Building Industry in Marseilles," 1 (2) *BJIR* 225-27 (June 1963).

[63]Unions' "limitations on the foreman's power restrict his supervisory initiative and deprive the employer of much of the value of his services." Haber, *Industrial Relations in the Building Industry* at 218.

[64]BR, "Contractor Supervision in Unionized Construction" 6 (Rep. C-3, Dec. 1987 [Feb.. 1992]).

[65]BR, "Contractor Supervision in Unionized Construction" at 7.

itself had to concede that "realistically" the goal of "returning all supervision to management control" could be achieved only in the long term.[66]

Such coerced coresponsibility was linked to so-called restrictive practices that management accused craftsmen of upholding. The power that arose here and its conversion into militance could appear as part of a struggle for the preservation of narrow vested interests, especially since they proceeded from the orthodox economic position that labor is but one factor of production among several, which its owner must protect against any and all threats.[67] In this sense skilled building trades unions were indistinguishable from industrial unions in the United States, which also rejected "the participation in every general activity of the working class as class."[68] If construction unions achieved greater material gains for their members, such successes were largely rooted in the industry's backward structure.

A building trades journeyman was generally understood to be "a craftsman who mastered his trade by serving an apprenticeship."[69] The length of this apprenticeship varied according to trade and union.[70] To be sure, some critics doubted both whether the demand for highly qualified journeymen was as large as traditionally assumed and whether journeymen were as skilled as defenders asserted. To many critics the real purpose of the institution of apprenticeship was to train supervisory personnel. Others argued that craft training in part served to produce journeymen who could largely supervise themselves.[71] Finally, skeptics throughout the nineteenth and twentieth century observed that a large proportion of building trades workers picked up their craft knowledge without going through a

---

[66]BR, "Contractor Supervision in Unionized Construction" at 10-11.

[67]In contrast, turn-of-the-century German Social Democracy took the position that although competition with the "iron slave 'machine'" would not be "pleasant" for some construction workers, "in the interest of cultural progress" the use of technology to make construction work easier was desirable. P. M. Grempe, "Technische Fortschritte im Bauwesen," 19 (2) *NZ* 58 (1900-1901).

[68]Draft letter from Friedrich Engels to Eduard Bernstein, June 17, 1879, in Karl Marx [&] Friedrich Engels, *Werke* 34:378 (1966).

[69]BLS, *Compensation in the Construction Industry* at 6 n.10.

[70]U.S. DOL, *Admission and Apprenticeship in the Building Trades Unions* (1971).

[71]E.g., George Strauss, "Apprenticeship: An Evaluation of the Need," in *Employment Policy and the Labor Market* 299-332 at 313 (Arthur Ross ed., 1965). A survey of apprentices revealed that six years after completing an apprenticeship, 19.7 percent of former apprentices still in construction were foremen or supervisors. Joseph Schuster, "Career Patterns of Former Apprentices in the Construction Trades," 5 (5) *CR* 4-8 at 5 (May 1959). Bill Haywood, president of the radical Western Miners Federation, rhetorically asked at the founding of the International Workers of the World why the skilled had thrown a wall around unions and demanded that entrants undergo apprenticeships: "For the benefit of the union? No, but for the benefit of his employer, who is a member of the Citizens' Alliance (applause), and who is trying to crush out of existence that same union that has endeavored to develop skilled mechanics for the benefit of the capitalist class. (Applause)." *Proceedings of the First Convention of the Industrial Workers of the World* 576 (1905).

formal apprenticeship.[72]

"Skill" assumes different meanings over time as the content of particular skills becomes restricted in the wake of a deepening division of labor.[73] A tendency toward specialization and introduction of labor-saving machinery among carpenters, for example, dates back to the nineteenth century; indeed, deskilling was the immediate motive for the formation of the United Brotherhood of Carpenters and Joiners in 1881.[74] Again, in the 1920s, a close observer of the building industry

---

[72]James Motley, *Apprenticeship in American Trade Unions* 22 (1907); F. Wolfe, *Admission to American Trade Unions* 37-38 (1912).

[73]On the debate over the social construction of skill, see Charles More, *Skill and the English Working Class, 1870-1914* (1980). The socially constructed nature of construction skills has more recently appeared on the feminist agenda as some have attributed the higher wage level in construction to the fact that the industry employs largely skilled adult men. Clarence Long, *Wages and Earnings in the United States 1860-1890*, at 109 (1960). A female carpenter underscored this link in arguing that male workers opposed women in the building trades because they feared that their work would be devalued in their own (and their employers') eyes if women could perform it. "MacNeil-Lehrer Report," PBS, Aug. 22, 1977, channel 9, Austin, TX, 6:00-6:30 p.m. CDST. In 1970, only 1.2 percent of construction workers were women; fifteen years after the DOL issued hiring goals for women, the share had risen to only 1.9 percent. Georgia Dullea, "Women Fight for More Construction Jobs, Less Harassment," *NYT*, Aug. 23, 1977, at 30, col. 1; "U.S. Rules Will Push for More Women's Jobs in Construction," *WSJ*, Apr. 10, 1978, at 3, col. 4; "Women in Construction Still Waiting for Respect," *NYT*, Sept. 29, 1992, at B12, col. 1 (nat. ed.).

[74]P. J. McGuire, "A Chapter of Our History," 6 (9) *Carpenter* 2 (Sept. 1886). A leading nineteenth-century British construction journal noted that a general joiner (saws, planes, etc.),worked by two lads, could replace 30 skilled joiners. "Labour Saving Machines for Builders," 27 (1384) *The Builder* 640 (Aug. 14, 1869). By the 1880s, the introduction of woodworking machinery in planing mills in the United States shifted some carpentry work to factories. Consequently, towns became filled with "a small army of idle members of the trade, ready to 'scab' in their or other towns. At the same time the work of the carpenter...had been minutely subdivided. For this reason the annual influx of relatively unskilled country carpenters assumed large proportions." Theodore Glocker, *The Government of American Trade Unions* 34 (1913). Wm. Godwin Moody, *Land and Labor in the United States* 145 (1883), stated that in building and carpentry, the circular saw did the work of 12 men, while the planing machine replaced 15 to 20. In the mid-1890s a state labor bureau found that carpentry had been "practically revolutionized in the past fifty years by the introduction of machinery and subdivision of labor." *Fourth Biennial Report of the Bureau of Labor of the State of Minnesota: 1893-1894*, at 214 (1895). See also *Third Annual Report of the Bureau of Industrial Statistics of Maryland: 1895*, at 119 (1895); *Fifth Annual Report of the Bureau of Industrial Statistics of Maryland: 1896*, at 39 (1897). Nevertheless, according to one contemporary scholar, in the building trades "there is not now, and is not likely soon to be, enough subdivision and use of machinery to render special training unnecessary." Edward Bemis, "Relation of Trades-Unions to Apprentices," 6 *QJE* 76-93 at 76 (Oct. 1891). And a U.S. carpentry journal stated that, because machinery had had little impact, 20 house carpenters could not do much more than 100 years earlier. 7 (5) *CB* 81 (May 1885). Another scholar found in the early twentieth century that despite the advances in machinery and subdivision, the "all-round workman" was not only still needed but preferred by employers. James Motley, "Apprenticeship in the Building Trades," in *Studies in American Trade Unionism* 263-91 at 264 (Jacob Hollander & George Barnett eds., 1912). By the 1920s it was estimated that at least

noted that whereas at the turn of the century a painter had to have an elementary knowledge of pigments, mixing lead, and color schemes, once paint manufacturers prepared paint in laboratories and shipped it to contractors ready to be applied, skill became "incidental." The demand for rapid building and speed meant that even after a four-year apprenticeship, a painter was "hired on the basis of 'how many acres he can smear in a week.'" Similarly, mechanization, subdividing and deskilling had gripped other occupations, too, as the carpenters ceased being all-round mechanics and spent most of their time on form work.[75] In the late 1930s and early 1940s, the introduction of power tools (such as saws and drills) brought about an "increased number of simplified operations in the carpenter's trade, with at least some jobs limited to a few operations which can be performed with a single tool. There is a tendency where modern power equipment is available, for certain carpenters to become saw operators, or hammer operators almost exclusively."[76]

By the 1960s, especially under the influence of suburban tract housing, firms built hundreds of identical housing units with crews of carpenters specializing in narrow tasks such as laying concrete foundations or door installation, for some of which employers prescribed the amount of time required. By the mid-1960s, when demand for higher quality single-family housing increased, this deepening of the division of labor had proceeded to the point at which some locals became "hard pressed to supply old-style general carpenters to contractors."[77] Bricklayers, pipefitters, and electricians underwent similar specialization by the 1960s.[78] A history of the Carpenters Union in Chicago, where union strength in the residential sector far exceeded the national average, revealed that the general all-round skill level continued to decline as more than a score of subspecialities such as shingling, carpeting, resilient floor building, and insulating made long forbidden piecework and a nonunion labor force an ever more threatening reality. By the 1970s, drywall installation, paid by the square foot, even attracted union members from Chicago in search of work. The approximately one-quarter of that city's membership who by the 1980s remained highly skilled general carpenters formed "a persistent hedge

---

half of all carpenters were "'hatchet and saw'" men. J. Cowper, "Apprenticeship Education in the Construction Industry Discussed from the Standpoint of a General Contractor," in Federal Board for Vocational Education, *Apprenticeship Education in the Construction Industry* 9-15 at 11 (Bull. No. 92, 1924). See also Frank Shaw, *The Building Trades* 18-19 (1916). Cyril Jackson, *Unemployment and Trade Unions* 50 (1910), stated that unemployment in the British building trades was caused in part by overspecialization even among laborers such as scaffolders, hoisters, and plumbers' mates.

[75] William Haber, "Craftsmanship in Building," 33 (12) *AF* 1446-51 at 1446 (Dec. 1926).

[76] Richard Myers, "The Building Workers: A Study of an Industrial Sub-Culture" at 167-68 (Ph. D. diss., U. Michigan, 1945).

[77] Richard Schneirov & Thomas Suhrbur, *Union Brotherhood, Union Town: The History of the Carpenters' Union of Chicago 1863-1987*, at 152 (1988).

[78] Morris Horowitz, *The Structure and Government of the Carpenters' Union* 5 (1962).

against the tendency of carpentry to degenerate into a semiskilled occupation."[79]

Even in broad generic ways various building trades' skills differ sharply. The skill of bricklayers, painters, and roofers "consists largely of the ability to perform a difficult physical task for several hours a day at an acceptable pace." In contrast, carpenters, plumbers, and pipefitters may face physically less demanding tasks, but must master several specialties and possess the "capacity to lay out and perform a job." Of yet another variety is operating engineers' central skill: manipulating large, powerful, and complicated machinery efficiently and safely.[80]

One of the most important bases of workers' control in construction is that U.S. building trades unions, "in contrast to construction practices in any other country, have long served as a source of labor supply, as an agency to furnish men of an established skill on request of the contractor, and as a means of moving labor away from areas of surplus to areas of short supply."[81] Today, as in the past, the vast majority of contruction firms do not employ sufficient workers year round "to meet their average needs"; instead, unions furnish workers when needed and take them off contractors' hands (and payrolls) as soon as a project is completed.[82] The reasons for this peculiar labor supply system lie, as one of its strongest opponents stressed, in construction firms' size structure: "[I]f the industry is to be composed of smaller firms, then it makes economic sense to use temporary employees and to rely heavily on a union hiring hall."[83] Consequently, most construction firms[84] are

---

[79]Schneirov & Suhrbur, *Union Brotherhood* at 152, 162 (quote).

[80]Mills, *Industrial Relations and Manpower in Construction* at 184.

[81]John Dunlop, "Labor Management Relations," in *Design and the Production of Houses* 259-301 at 262 (Burnham Kelly ed., 1959).

[82]Montgomery, *Industrial Relations in the Chicago Building Trades* at 8.

[83]M. R. Lefkoe, *The Crisis in Construction: There Is an Answer* 34 (1970). Lefkoe noted that the mobility problem would become moot if firms shifted to a system of employing workers year round. *Id.* at 159-70. Interestingly, mobility—rather than the absence of national markets—has historically been made responsible for the rise of national trade unions in construction while also making local unions relatively autonomous vis-à-vis the central unions. Lloyd Ulman, *The Rise of the National Trade Union* 45, 52 (1966 [1955]).

[84]Grimes, "Personnel Management in the Building Trades" at 38, 40, excepted the very largest firms from this pattern. Bechtel, for example, employs a core group of key workers year round. Telephone interview with Kenneth Hedman, vice president for labor relations, Bechtel Corp., San Francisco (Mar. 12, 1999). Gordon Bertram and Sherman Maisel, *Industrial Relations in the Construction Industry* 47 (1955), adduced small firms in residential construction as another exception because they "tend to maintain a more stable relationship with their employees. Each develops particular techniques and procedures and as a result they find that their costs fall as workers become accustomed to their special jobs." These authors were referring to the same phenomena of spcialization that Grimes, "Personnel Management in the Building Trades" at 42-43, observed. Manifestly, such tendencies weakened skilled building trades unions.

prepared or forced to leave the risks of or the control over labor supply to unions.[85]

If this system, which is functional from construction firms' standpoint, contained certain dangers insofar as a prerequisite of production flexibility became a union task, the power that arises in this context was also subject to two decisive contraints, which secured the maintenance of management prerogatives in production and the free play of market forces in the wage formation process. One was rooted in employers' "right" to discharge workers whom unions referred. In 1973, for example, half of 769 collective bargaining agreements under which 1,213,317 construction workers were employed guaranteed employers the right to reject workers whom unions recommended. A typical clause read: "The employer may choose not to employ workers who have proven ineffective in the past or have insufficient qualifications for existing work."[86]

Even in the heyday of the closed shop: "Whatever the power of a local union, and regardless of labor market conditions, a contractor's authority to discharge at will was seldom challenged or abridged. ... As a general rule, having once secured the closed shop, construction unions 'yielded' to employer freedom in employing and discharging his men so long as they knew that only union men at union wages would be employed in place of those discharged."[87] After the Taft-

---

[85]On the history of hiring halls, see Philip Ross, "Construction Hiring Halls: Origins and Development," 11 (3) *IR* 366-79 (Oct. 1972); CUAIR *Report*, No. 72-8, at 2-3 (July 28, 1972). On the role of the business agent as a labor broker, see George Strauss, *Unions in the Building Trades: A Case Study*, chs. 3 & 6, in *UBS* 24 (2) (June 1958). See also *idem*, "Business Agents in the Building Trades," 10 (2) *ILRR* 240-46 (Jan. 1957). Bourdon & Levitt, *Union and Open-Shop Construction* at 62-63, offer a more nuanced view of hiring halls, stating that the "overall impact of the unions on referrals is much less than is usually assumed." They are centrally involved when employers require large numbers of workers, but at times of high unemployment they are "not needed. Men continually come to the offices or gates of projects looking for work...."

[86]BLS, *Contract Clauses in Construction Agreements* 14 (Bull. 1864, 1975). See also *id.* at 12-16.

[87]Ross, "Construction Hiring Halls" at 371-72. On the closed shop in the building trades in the nineteenth century, see Frank Stockton, *The Closed Shop in American Trade Unions* 38-40, 43 (1911). Even during the period (1896-1921) when the Building Trades Council of San Francisco dominated industrial relations, one of the unions' governing principles was employers' freedom to hire or fire "any man, within the limits imposed by union shop conditions...." Ryan, *Industrial Relations in the San Francisco Building Trades* at 110. At the turn of the century, the U.S. Commissioner of Labor observed that "in so far as a union does not interfere with the employer's right to 'hire and fire,' just so far does it fail to enforce its rules.... Usually it is found that the unions which do not contest this freedom of the employer, except in matters of union membership and union activity, are the older and stronger unions (compositors, bricklayers, molders). Such unions, having established the union shop, yield to the employer freedom in employing and discharging his men so long as they know that only union members at union wages will be employed in the place of those discharged." Commissioner of Labor, *Eleventh Special Report of the Commissioner of Labor: Regulation and Restriction of Output* 21 (1904). The consequence of this policy among bricklayers was a work pace with which men could not keep up after the age of 45; the outright defense of vested interests in

Hartley Act prohibited the closed shop in 1947, some observers suggested that construction firms possessed in this regard even greater freedom than employers in other industries: "rigidity in hiring is to some extent balanced by an extraordinary (for union firms) flexibility in firing. By and large, contractors are free to dismiss workers whenever they desire without regard to seniority or any other criterion. Except for disciplinary dismissals, unions do not challenge the choice of an employer as to whom to retain and whom to let go. The employer is also the sole judge of whether a worker's performance is satisfactory...."[88]

Union acquiescence can at best be interpreted as meaning that unions, in order to justify their existence in view of the enormous problems of seasonal and frictional unemployment, were above all interested in securing employment for their members. The price that members had to pay for this employment was exposure to employers' heightened power. Workers presumably defended their counter-controls tenaciously to resist reduced aggregate employment and/or growth in employment.[89]

The second of the aforementioned limitations of the building trades' enhanced power associated with their domination of the labor market[90] is firms'

Britain meant that a bricklayer's working life there was five to ten years longer. *Id.* at 286-93. For a similar assessment of the speed of bricklayers' work, see John Commons, "Restrictions by Trade Unions," in *idem, Labor and Administration* 120-34 at 134 (1964 [1906]).

[88]Howard Foster, "Labor in Construction: Recent Research and Popular Wisdom," in *Labor & Manpower* 112 (Richard Pegnetter ed., 1974). Bourdon and Levitt, *Union and Open-Shop Construction* at 39, regard the expansive right to hire and fire as enabling union employers to "adjust worker quality to fit the [rigid] wage," whereas nonunion employers typically adjust the wage to fit their skill and productivity criteria. The union model "may be better suited to a labor market...where numerous workers continually move between firms."

[89]Haber, *Industrial Relations in the Building Industry* at 222, went so far as to assert that it was this "unlimited right to 'hire and fire'...which has brought in many other rules as protective devices. If building-trades employers were willing to restrict their right to discharge and would guarantee tenure of job somewhat, it seems probable that many of the restrictive practices would be eliminated." John Leggett, *Class, Race and Labor: Working Class Consciousness in Detroit* 57 (1968), described the AFL craft unions as understanding themselves as a "business which monopolized prized skills and sold labor at a certain price to an employer." A CIO-type industrial unions, in contrast, "simply maintained that it organized workers...but it never considered itself an organization designed to sell labor to management. In fact, industrial unions have generally accepted technological innovation—despite the consequent loss of union membership—as 'progress,' a stance incomprehensible to a craft union." Margaret Chandler, "Craft Bargaining," in *Frontiers of Collective Bargaining* 54 (John Dunlop & Neil Chamberlain, eds., 1967), offered a similar judgment: "In a sense the crafts are the union equivalent of the management-rights-oriented company."

[90]Chandler, "Craft Bargaining" at 58, noted: "As crafts have confronted weaker markets for their services, they have had the choice of either not organizing them or of formally or informally adjusting craft rules and wage rates to fit their specific requirements. Thus, some construction crafts have little interest in organizing the home-building industry. They prefer that smalll home builders find in the nonunion market the lower wages and flexibility that craft lines deny. For the union man,

ability to hire cheaper nonunion workers in response to union attempts to limit the supply of labor in order to drive up wages.[91] Focusing exclusively on wages scarcely does justice to firms' concerns. As one study determined, many employers were willing to pay for being relieved of the necessary and expensive function of labor recruitment "provided that the price is not excessive—that is, provided union wages (and the cost of restrictive practices) do not depart so far from the structure and level of wages characteristic of a 'free market' that it would clearly profit employers to do their own labor contracting."[92] Consequently, the hypothesis here is that it was both the reduction of wage rates and the elimination of worker control that formed the decisive aspect of the antiunion open-shop movement.[93]

In summary, then, these labor market functions were not acquired by unions through struggle, but were, rather, either forced on them—as in the case of directing workers' mobility, in the absence of which the unions' existence would have been threatened—or devolved on them in the absence of more adequate institutions, in part spontaneously and in part with employers' tacit cooperation. The bilateral

---

the nonunion sector serves as a buffer. ... Such buffer arrangements also provide flexibility in bargaining with management, for the craft world provides a variety of escape hatches."

[91]Cf. Foster, "Labor in Construction" at 109; Gordon Bertram, *Consolidated Bargaining in California Construction: An Appraisal of Twenty-Five Years' Experience* 63, 185 (1966). That the prevalent reaction to higher wages in manufacturing—namely, increasing capital intensity by means of labor-saving innovation—is not so widespread in construction is merely another aspect of worker control.

[92]D. Cullen, "Union Wage Policy in Heavy Construction," 49 (1) *AER* 68-84 at 82 (Mar. 1959). Cf. Garth Mangum, *The Operating Engineers: The Economic History of a Trade Union* 261 (1964).

[93]Neglect of the various capital groups within construction in favor of a monolithic picture of "capital" can lead to a false understanding of the antiunion movement. For example, a pamphlet published by the Socialist Workers Party asserted that "[t]he building contractors shunned union labor" during the period (beginning in 1971) ushered in by the Nixon administration's labor market measures, while it explained unions' restriction of membership on the grounds that fewer and fewer firms wanted to hire union members. Frank Lovell, "Introduction," in Nat Weinstein, Frank Lovell, and Carol Lipman, *Construction Workers Under Attack: How to Fight Back and Rebuild the Unions* 3 (1974). One of these Trotskyist authors then reached this result: " Construction workers are already among the most highly exploited and not much more can be squeezed out of them except lower wages." Nat Weinstein, "The Open-Shop Drive in the Building Trades," in *Construction Workers Under Attack* 11-16 at 14 (1973). Apart from omitting to explain how he measured and compared this exploitation, the author missed precisely the most important aspect of the open-shop movement—namely, the effort to squeeze more labor out of construction workers—even though he confirmed this point in the previous sentence by accusing union leaders of acquiescing in speedup. This isolated view of the income of a factor of production underlies the criticism directed at construction unions during the interwar period—that the wage increases resulting from their monopolization of the labor market were responsible for the increased unemployment. Gustav Cassel, *Teoretisk Socialekonomi* 317-19 (2d ed., 1938). Cf. the more realistic analysis by Howard Foster, "Unions, Residential Construction and Public Policy," 12 (4) *QREB* 45-55 (Winter 1972).

advantages of this system are manifest: construction firms could rely on a relatively efficient labor supply, which made its year-round employment unnecessary, while unions gained legitimation vis-à-vis their membership, especially since members were dependent on them for their labor exchange activities. The system became disadvantageous for employers only if unions succeeded in bringing about an 'artificial' scarcity of labor in order to drive up wages. Yet the permanently large pool of unemployed reduced this risk.

To perform their labor supply functions unions had to use their knowledge about production—otherwise they would have been unable to provide an adequate supply of labor differentiated according to the requisite qualifications.[94] In this sense worker control and labor supply functions were intertwined. The real struggle surrounding this control took place not in collective bargaining negotiations, but already at the time of organizing: once a firm was unionized, it quasi-automatically abdicated its labor market functions to the unions.

WORKER CONTROL

[T]he commodity labor power can really become a commodity when its seller is no longer compelled to dispose of it at any moment and under any condition. Paradoxically expressed: only the supersession of "free competition" makes free competition possible.[95]

The building trades have probably had the greatest success in opposing labor-saving changes.[96]

[A] major problem for construction labor markets is unemployment caused by the fact that 6 million craftsmen are seeking to fill 3.4 million jobs. ... As a consequence, many of the construction unions' procedures are based on efforts to protect the conditions of workers who have made heavy investments in their skills and jobs in a very fluid labor market.[97]

The phenomena summarized under the label "worker control" are generally treated in the scholarly literature from a sociological perspective with an emphasis

---

[94]This task is much less urgent for unskilled laborers. Historically, craft unions were interested in organizing a helpers' union in order to avoid the consequences of integration. John Ashworth, *The Helper and the American Trade Unions* 87-89 (1915); Haber, *Industrial Relations in the Building Trades* at 160-61, 307.

[95]N. Auerbach, *Marx und die Gewerkschaftren* 27-28 (1972 [1922]).

[96]Sumner Slichter, *Union Policies and Industrial Management* 214 (1941).

[97]DOL, Manpower Administration, *Training and Entry into Union Construction* 27 (Manpower R&D Monograph 39, 1975) (by Ray Marshall, Robert Glover, & William Franklin).

on the theory of bureaucracy.[98]   A remarkable exception was the effort by Stinchcombe in 1959 to incorporate aspects of the production process into the analysis.[99] Stinchcombe argued that "professionalization of the labor force in the construction industry serves the same functions as bureaucratic administration in mass production industries and is more rational than bureaucratic administration in the face of economic technical constraints on construction projects."[100] In mass production, "both the product and the work process are planned in advanced by persons not on the work crew." Among the components of the labor process are: the place at which the work is carried out; the movement of tools, materials, and workers as well as their "most efficient arrangement"; the individual operative movements; and schedules and quality controls. In construction, in contrast to industrial mass production, "all these characteristics of the work place are governed by the worker in accordance with the empirical lore that makes up craft principles. These principles are the content of workers' socialization...." To be sure, he saw no threat to firms emanating from this autonomy: "control of pace, manual skill, and effective operative decision (the essential components of industrial discipline) is more economical if left to professionally occupational standards."[101]

Stinchcombe's analysis is applicable to those situations in which the traditional methods of production still prevail. Where, however, they were supplanted by industry-like methods, new labor-management relations formed.[102]

---

[98]For a typology of "inherent management functions" and discussion of the few—job content, size of the work force, policies affecting selection of employees, scheduling of operations and the number of shifts—that have been limited by collective bargaining agreements, see Raymond Rowley, "Labor Unions' Encroachment on Contractors' Right to Manage" (Stanford U. Dept. of Civil Engineering, Technical Memorandum No. 1, June 12, 1962, rev. Julian Sabbatini, June 1, 1969).

[99]A.L. Stinchcombe, "Bureaucratic Craft Administration of Production: A Comparative Study," 4 (2) *ASQ* 168-87 (Sept. 1959). Cf. Grimes, "Personnel Management in the Building Trades" at 37; Richard Myers, "Interpersonal Relations in the Building Industry," 5 (2) *AA* 1-7 (Spr. 1946); Jeffrey Riemer, "Worker Autonomy in the Skilled Building Trades," in *Varieties of Work* 225 (Phyllis Stewart & Muriel Cantor eds. 1982).

[100]Stinchcombe, "Bureaucratic Craft Administration of Production" at 169.

[101]Stinchcombe, "Bureaucratic Craft Administration of Production" at 170, 169.

[102]The international literature on this subject includes: ILO, Civil Engineering and Public Works Committee, 7th Sess., Report II: *Technological Changes in the Construction Industry and Their Socio-Economic Consequences* (1964); *idem*, Eighth Sess., Report II: *Social Aspects of Prefabrication in the Construction Industry* (1968); UN, Economic Commission for Europe, *Industrially Made Building Components* (1969); *idem, Progressive Methods of Design, Organization and Management in Building* (1971); R. B. White, *Prefabrication: A History of Its Development in Great Britain* (1965); R. E. Jeannes, *Building Operatives' Work* (1966); Joseph Carreiro et al., *The New Building Block: A Report on the Factory-Produced Dwelling Module* (Research Rep. No. 8, Center for Housing & Environmental Studies, Cornell U., 1968); *Bauforschung—Rationalisierung—Industrialisierung* (Schriftenreihe des Bundesministers für Wohnungswesen und Städtebau, Vol. 25, 1969); Norbert Gangl, *Die Engpässe für eine konsequent industrialisierte Wohnbauwirtschaft Ansätze zu einem*

This picture underscores the extent to which craft workers can be functionalized for employers' interests clothed as mere requirements of production. These aspects may be understudied, but the associated "restrictive practices" have been intensively examined. Employers have complained about them since the nineteenth century. In the early years of the twentieth century, for example, an NAM publication made these invidious comparisons: closed-shop bricklayers laid 800 to 1,000 bricks in hours compared to 3,000 per day a few years earlier; closed-shop structural iron workers made 75-100 rivets a day, whereas their nonunion counterparts made 200 to 400; and whereas carpenters hung one door per hour before they gained a monopoly, in closed shops they hung only four per day.[103]   In 1970 the Construction Users Anti-Inflation Roundtable defined them unabashedly from the nineteenth-century my-business-is-my castle viewpoint as "any practice that prevents the employer from utilizing his employees, his equipment or his technical know-how in what he feels is the most efficient fashion."[104]

Such union practices can be considered from two perspectives: first, as an attempt to maintain aggregate employment; and second, as resistance against employer efforts to intensify labor and/or labor processes that threaten workers' health. Orthodox economists are wont to treat the first aspect, constructing it above all as inhibiting productivity.[105]   Some academic specialists have provided much more realistic analyses. A dissertation on apprenticeship in the building trades in the mid-1920s concluded that "limitation [of output] by labor unions has in many cases served to protect the workman from conditions bordering upon servitude."[106] In his book on industrial relations in the Chicago building trades, Montgomery, who took the position that "collective bargaining always involves a certain amount of...sacrifice of autocratic prerogatives," observed, in seeking to differentiate legitimate union regulatory rules from antisocial restrictions, that working rules designed to prevent "unhealthful 'rushing' and 'pacesetting'" and subcontracting that amounted to "little more than piecework detrimental to the maintenance" of union wage scales "may have added something to the cost of building construction; but unless one denies the responsibility of industry for the maintenance of the standard of living and of decent working conditions for its workers, the cost cannot

---

Modell der industrialisierten Wohnbauwirtschaft (1970).

[103]Walter Drew, *Closed Shop Unionism* 10 (NAM No. 16, n.d. [ca. 1911]).

[104]H. Edgar Lore, John Oliver, & J. Warren Shaver, "Restrictive Work Practices in the Construction Industry" 1 (CUAIR, mimeo, 1970).   The authors were high-ranking officials of construction and construction-user firms.

[105]See, e.g., "Restrictive Labor Practices Smother Productivity," *ENR*, Nov. 26, 1970, at 98, reporting that the AGC viewed "emulating human relations approach of open shop builders" as a solution. For a critique of such views, see Marc Linder et al., *Der Anti-Samuelson* 3:297-98 (1975).

[106]Frederick Horridge, *The Problem of Apprenticeship in the Six Basic Building Trades* 16 (1926).

be considered other than one that industry should be called upon to assume."[107] Likewise, William Haber's 1930 history of construction labor relations offered a bluntness lacking in later works: "An analysis of the working rules of unions which employers classify under the term 'restriction of output,' shows that these seek to curb the dictatorship of the employer and to assert the workers' right to participate in determining 'working conditions.'"[108] And even *Fortune*, in an early postwar issue devoted to housing, conceded that "[m]ost builders agree" with the president of the Carpenters union, William Hutcheson, that the extent and importance of restrictive rules had been "vastly distorted."[109]

In the only post-World War II national study of construction labor relations, Mills focused on the pluralistic element: "The concept of a restrictive practice is often ambiguous and elusive. A crew size rule may be seen as a safety rule by some and a restrictive practice by others. There are genuine differences among workers and employers over the pace of work, the existence of health hazards, flexibility in administering work rules and craft assignments, the normal quality and skill of the work force...., the scope and content of jobs, the rate at which technological changes should be introduced, and preferences of security in employment."[110] However the practices were conceived, they were a vital issue to unionized contractors, who were wont to say: "'We're not concerned with the men earning what they do, we're concerned with conditions that make you hire more than we need.'"[111]

To be sure, at times it is difficult to distinguish between the two bases of these union objections to technological innovations. The difficulty is in part objective (for example, when labor-saving innovations intensify labor), but is in part also a function of the propagandistic purposes to which the demands are put. The distinction is real in the narrowly economic sense, but also politically important because it draws a line between, on the one hand, potentially corporate-like or "antisocial"[112] demands, which not only stood in the way of the development of the

---

[107]Royal Montgomery, *Industrial Relations in the Chicago Building Trades* 186, 148-49 (1927). Ryan, *Industrial Relations in the San Francisco Building Trades* at 82, plagiarized Montgomery. Intriguingly, even under the strictly antiunion regime of the Industrial Association of San Francisco during the 1920s and 1930s, the campaign against restrictive work practices was conditioned on "always having due regard for the health, safety and well-being of the individual." *Id.* at 168.

[108]Haber, *Industrial Relations in the Building Industry* at 198-99. Haber added that: "The indirect result of these rules has been to stimulate efficiency in the contracting organization, which must meet competition and competitive costs in spite of these rules." *Ibid.* at 236.

[109]"Boss Carpenter," 33 (4) *Fortune* 119-23, 276-82, at 121 (Apr. 1946).

[110]Mills, *Industrial Relations* at 258-59.

[111]Alan Oser, "Building Costs Push Steadily Upward," *NYT*, June 14, 1970, sect. 8, at 1, col. 1, at 9, col. 2-3 (quoting Saul Horowitz, Jr., president, HRH Construction Co., in New York City).

[112]Ryan, *Industrial Relations in the San Francisco Building Trades* at 100.

productive forces—although empirical studies found that the extent of productivity-inhibiting union practices was, journalistic images notwithstanding, slight[113]—but also necessarily supported the economically most regressive employer factions, and, on the other, demands directed against the health consequences of the specific capitalist development and deployment of technology. This ambiguity makes it difficult to assess construction unions' success in this area.[114]

A good illustration of a multivalent union work practice from the period under review was a resolution adopted by New York District Council No. 9 of the International Brotherhood of Painters in 1968 that no journeyman member performing New York City Housing repaint work paint more than 10 rooms weekly. The union characterized the purpose of the rule as relieving "pressure on painters to work quickly so as to reduce the number of violations of trade rules, increase the health and safety of union members, and improve the quality of their work." Their collective bargaining agreement included no production quotas, but did prescribe a 7-hour day, 5-day week. Because the painters, on average, had been painting 11.5 rooms per week, some of them, at the union's urging, simply stopped work after completing 10 rooms even when they had not worked 35 hours. The employers, members of the Association of Master Painters and Decorators of the City of New

[113]Haber & Levinson, *Labor Relations* at 196-97; Allen Mandelstramm, "The Effects of Unions on Efficiency in the Residential Construction Industry: A Case Study," 18 (4) *ILRR* 503-21 (July 1965). An influential survey conducted in the late 1970s found that "[r]estrictions on an employer's use of the tools of the trade are irrelevant for multimillion dollar firms," while "[r]equirements on crew size or work distribution also rarely constrain large firms which undertake projects of a scale that can efficiently sustain the activity of many journeymen in one trade...." The impacts on small firms were less benign. Bourdon & Levitt, *Union and Open-Shop Construction* at 65. For examples of the journalistic counterposition, see Thurman Arnold, *The Bottlenecks of Business* (1940); Robert Lasch, *Breaking the Building Blockage* 95-99 (1946). A survey of construction collective bargaining agreements found: "Most agreements place no limitations on the employer's right to employ tools and equipment of his choice on the job, or to introduce new laborsaving devices or technological improvements." Restrictions were concentrated among painters. BLS, *Contract Clauses* at 24. An older study came to similar conclusions. BLS, *Union Wages, Hours, and Working Conditions in the Building Trades, June 1, 1941* (1942). For a description of the resistance by the plumbers unions against certain innovations at the turn of the century, see Walter Weyl & A. Sakolski, "Conditions of Entrance to the Principal Trades," in *BBL*, No. 67, Nov. 1906, at 732. On the situation in postwar Britain, see Frank Knox & Josselyn Hennessy, *Restrictive Practices in the Building Industry* (1966).

[114]In this sense it is difficult to understand Erlich's view of carpenters' resistance to portable power tools after World War II in the wake of their memories of the huge unemployment preceding it: "In retrospect, it is hard to believe that the circular saw and electric drill, now such integral parts of the construction process, created such a controversy. Indusrtrial workers had long since been forced to accept technological marvels that dwarfed the invention of the circular saw. ... But the pace of technological change is a relative...phenomenon. [C]arpenters had experienced no challenge on this scale to their work methods since the inception of factory-produced millwork in the late nineteenth century." Mark Erlich, *With Our Hands: The Story of Carpenters in Massachusetts* 146 (1986).

York, Inc., successfully charged the union before the NLRB with an unfair labor practice for having modified a term of the collective bargaining agreement without having complied with its statutory duty to negotiate with the employer over the modification. The appellate court therefore enforced the NLRB's order that the union cease and desist from unilaterially enforcing a production quota.[115]

Typically construction unions' employment-oriented demands prevailed, which served only the limited interests of their members. Unions' success in this area has been traced back to several causes:

One reason is that most of the changes opposed by these unions affect only a small part of the work done by the skilled craftsmen. The employer needs these men for other parts of the work. A second reason is that no single restriction imposed by these unions on labor-saving methods greatly increases the total labor cost of building. ... This means that employers cannot afford to incur large expenses in order to prevent the restriction.... A third reason...is...that the areas of competition are so small that the unions are able to impose restrictions on all the employers in the area. Hence the competition of non-union employees does not compel the unions to give up their prohibitions upon labor-saving methods.[116]

Especially this last consideration points to a crucial aspect of union power—local unions' extraordinary authority vis-à-vis the national union and smaller local firms.[117] Important, too, is the influence that members exerted over union policies.[118]

---

[115]New York District Council No. 9, Int'l Bhd Painters v. NLRB, 453 F.2d 783 (2d Cir. 1971). Although the dissenting judge noted that a wages and hours provision "cannot be magically transformed into provisions specifying the rate of speed at which employees are to work or the amount they are to produce," this insight applied only to painters who worked the full 35 hours but so slowly that they painted only 10 rooms; it failed to deal with painters who simply quit before having worked 35 hours. *Id.* at 788. For the Communist Party's glowing description of District Council 9, see A Rank & File Painter, "N.Y. Painters Face Crucial June Election," *DW*, May 21, 1970, at 5, col. 1. The difference between working slowly and stopping early has at times had real-world consequences. In Chicago in the 1920s, Lathers, able to complete their quota of work in 6.5 to 7 hours, had formerly packed their tools and left. "More recently this practice has been dropped and instead the policy of going more slowly throughout the day has been adopted. So long as the former practice was held to, the union had little even superficial justification for its contention that the limitations upon output were for the practice of protecting the older workers. While an elderly and slower man was insured by the rule against competition with younger pace-setters, he was not helped greatly by being left on the job to complete his quota when the younger men left; on the contrary, his inability to compete...was being advertised." Montgomery, *Industrial Relstions in the Chicago Building Trades* at 160.

[116]Slichter, *Union Policies and Industrial Management* at 214.

[117]Ulman, *The Rise of National Trade Unions* at 345-46; George Barnett, "The Causes of Jurisdictional Disputes in American Trade Unions," 9 (4) *HBR* 404-406 (Apr. 1931).

[118]George Strauss, "Controls by the Membership in Building Trade Unions," 61 *AJS* 527-35 (May 1956). But see Scott Greer, *Last Man In: Racial Access to Union Power* 130 (1959); Frank Tannenbaum, "The Social Function of Trade Unionism," 62 (2) *PSQ* 161-94 at 170-71, 175-79 (June

It would be premature, however, to see unions as solely responsible for this orientation since their policies were forged within the limits imposed by the development of the construction industry.[119] This development gave rise to the craft unions' special functions, which enabled members to exert extraordinary control, but only so long as such controls were adequate to the prevailing construction methods and/or firm size structure. This structural determination of union functions in favor of employers' interests was not, however, monolithic: leeway also existed for a system-maintaining union policy. Moreover, certain characteristics of the construction industry disadvantaged employers vis-à-vis their counterparts in other industries such as their lack of control over the location of production and the inability to threaten recalcitrant workers, despite the enormous mobility demanded of them, with shifting production elsewhere in the United States let alone abroad.

COMPARATIVE ALIENATION

The trend of employers, assisted by combined capital, is to debase labor and deny its lawful and just share of what it produces.[120]

[T]he term Marxist is an accusation not of disloyalty but of intellectual sterility. Many of Marx's assumptions, not least the one about workers being "alienated," have been called into question by the repeated postponement of the fall of capitalism. But he still is a powerful intellectual influence today, even among Republicans....[121]

The operation of the GM Lordstown plant, the building of which had catalyzed capitalist outrage at construction workers' exorbitant wage rates,[122] triggered in early 1972 what the editors of *The New York Times* called a "rank-and-file rebellion"[123] that startled many observers as a throwback to the nineteenth century.[124] At Lordstown, "the engineering values of a hypermodern and super-

---

1947).

[119]Cf. Sumner Slichter, *The Impact of Collective Bargaining on Management* 259 (1960).

[120]Preamble, *Constitution and Rules of Order of the Bricklayers, Masons and Plasterers International Union of America* n.p. (inside front cover) (1972) (first inserted in 1897).

[121]"The HEW Encyclical," *WSJ*, Feb. 2, 1972, at 8, col. 1, 2 (editorial).

[122]See above chapter 3.

[123]"Revolt of the Robots," *NYT*, Mar. 7, 1972, at 38, col. 2 (editorial). See also Agis Salpukas, "Young Workers Disrupt Key G.M. Plant," *NYT*, Jan. 23, 1972, at 1, col. 4.

[124]For contemporary news reports, see Charles Camp, "Utopian GM Plant in Ohio Falls from Grace Under Strain of Balky Machinery, Workers," *WSJ*, Jan. 31, 1972, at 28, col. 1; "General Motors, UAW Make Progress in Talks over Struck Vega Plant," *WSJ*, Mar. 6, 1972, at 4, col. 3; Agis Sapulkas, "Workers Increasingly Rebel Against Boredom on Assembly Line," *NYT*, Apr. 2, 1972, at

automated assembly line experienced a head-on collision with the values of a hypermodern and unusually young workforce.... Expressing...disgust for GM's hard-driving, high-speed (101 cars an hour) production philosophy, the workers responded with soaring absentee rates, sabotage, and finally a bitter twenty-two-day strike." The "sullen resentment" of workers protesting "the militaristic precision and dehumanizing character" of the assembly line created a "disaster" for GM[125] at a plant where managers complained "that expensive seconds [we]re being wasted in the crevices of the working day."[126]

Whereas earlier in the post-World War II period, the fashionable academic preoccupation with rediscovering Marx's "theory of alienation" had taken the form of abstracted history of ideas,[127] sociologists and politicians suddenly recognized that it was no longer merely intellectuals who were alienated.[128] Within a few months of the Lordstown strike, the Senate Subcommittee on Employment, Manpower, and Poverty held hearings on *Worker Alienation, 1972*, at which the lead witnesses, workers from the Lordstown plant, testified about the alienation produced by their unrelentingly fast, repetitive, monotonous, and boring work.[129]

Following the hearings, four committee members, including Ted Kennedy and liberal Republican Jacob Javits, introduced the Worker Alienation Research and Technical Assistance Act of 1972. The bill included findings that: "the alienation of American workers because of the nature of their jobs is a problem of growing seriousness for the national economy and to individual workers"; alienation often resulted in lessened productivity, and frustration and social dissatisfaction among workers; and "it is in the national interest to encourage the humanization of working conditions and the work itself so as to increase worker job satisfaction...; insofar as possible, work should be designed to maximize potentials for democracy, security, equity, and craftsmanship." The bill would have authorized the Secretaries of Labor and Health, Education, and Welfare to conduct research on methods already

---

34, col. 3-8; Lawrence O'Donnell, "General Motors' Plan to Increase Efficiency Draws Ire of Unions," *WSJ*, Dec. 6, 1972, at 1, col. 6. For left-wing accounts, see Barbara Garson, "Luddites in Lordstown," *HM*, June 1972, at 68-73; Stanley Aronowitz, *False Promises: The Shaping of American Working Class Consciousness* 21-50 (1974 [1973]); Ken Weller, *The Lordstown Struggle and the Real Crisis in Production* (1974). The best and most detailed account of the plant and the 1972 strike is David Moberg, "Rattling the Golden Chains: Conflict and Consciousness of Auto Workers" (Ph.D. diss., U. Chicago, 1978).

[125]David Jenkins, *Job Power: Blue and White Collar Democracy* 11, 198 (1974 [1973]).

[126]Emma Rothschild, "GM in More Trouble," *NYRB*, Mar, 23, 1972, at 18-25 at 21.

[127]E.g., Lewis Feuer, "What Is Alienation? The Career of a Concept," in *idem, Marx and the Intellectuals: A Set of Post-Ideological Essays* 70-99 (1969 [1962]).

[128]Feuer, "Introduction" in *idem, Marx and the Intellectuals* 1-8 at 1-2.

[129]*Worker Alienation, 1972: Hearings Before the Subcommittee on Employment, Manpower, and Poverty of the Senate Labor and Public Welfare Commitee*, 92d Cong., 2d Sess. 10-19 (1972).

being used to "meet the problems of work alienation" such as shorter working days, job rotation, "worker participation in the decisionmaking process with regard to the nature and content of his job," and redesign of jobs and production patterns. Finally, the bill would have authorized the appropriation of $10 million annually for two years to develop and conduct pilot demonstration projects to make significant contributions to the knowledge in the field concerning the aforementioned methods as well as job enrichment and guaranteed employment.[130]

In the midst of this congressionally acknowledged, system-threatening uproar at the point of production, one large group of workers could be identified who were not afflicted with Marxist alienation. Construction workers may have been wreaking another kind of havoc with their wage demands, but they were at least craftsmen who enjoyed and took pride in their work instead of assaulting modern methods of production and the notion of work altogether. Indeed, the major empirical study of alienation in the United States during the 1960s noted that construction, "based largely on a traditional craft technology and traditional manual skill, is the single largest employer of blue-collar workers."[131] In particular the AFL-CIO began to propagate the thesis of the unalienated building tradesman. Here is merely one example of the genre by John Joyce, the secretary of the Bricklayers, Masons and Plasterers International Union:

The building tradesman sees his job through from start to finish. He—not an inspector at the end of an assembly line—supervises its quality. He sets his own pace. One is tempted to think that he has been neglected by sociological fashion because he controls his work himself, through his union. He is not dependent on "sophisticated" management or academic consultants to advise him on how to soothe his alienation.[132]

How accurate was Joyce's picture of the nonalienated construction worker? The first point—that he "sees his job through from start to finish"—suggests that the division of labor in the building trades was less detailed than in manufacturing. Though true, this claim should not be exaggerated: a bricklayer or carpenter on a huge industrial or commercial project in the second half of the twentieth century was hardly a manual Renaissance man, who made an entire product himself.[133]

---

[130]S. 3916, §§ 2, 3(a)(2) & (4), & § 6, 92d Cong., 2d Sess. (1972). Representative Bella Abzug filed an identical bill three days later. H.R. 16441, 92d Cong., 2d Sess. (1972).

[131]Robert Blauner, *Alienation and Freedom: The Factory Worker and His Industry* 168 (1973 [1964]).

[132]John Joyce, "Construction in 70s," *AF*, Oct. 1973, at 12.

[133]How remote the precapitalist artisan was from the twentieth-century construction worker can be gauged by Sombart's observation that the artisan viewed his products exclusively as use values that were a manifestation of his own essence. Werner Sombart, *Der moderne Kapitalismus* 2:59 (2d ed., 1917).

After all, as early as the 1870s, the advent of various woodworking machines made possible the production of standardized windows, doors, and other building parts ready for installation, which in turn facilitated the subdivision of carpentry into door hanging, floor laying, stair building, and many other specialties performed by workers paid only half the wage of a carpenter.[134] Indeed, it is the enormous size and complexity of twentieth-century megaprojects, which dwarf any individual worker's minuscule contribution, that instill craft workers with pride: "working on a unique and individuated product is almost inherently meaningful."[135] Robert Blauner, the author of the major U.S. study of alienation in the 1960s, went so far as to exempt unskilled construction workers from industrial meaninglessness: "Even the unskilled laborer shoveling cement on a building site is making a contribution toward the construction of a particular and tangible structure. His work is organized by the building problems of the individual site...."[136]

If the hallmark of industry is the application of a "system of machines and apparatuses in which the labor process is approximately automatic and is performed continuously with respect to the connection of the subprocesses,"[137] construction, with the exception of highway construction, did not pass muster as industrialized.[138]

---

[134]Robert Christie, *Empire in Wood: A History of the Carpenters' Union* 26-27 (1956); Ryan, *Industrial Relations in the San Francisco Building Trades* at 7.

[135]Blauner, *Alienation and Freedom* at 23. Earlier in the century, some in the building industry proposed that in an effort to revive the spirit of craftsmanship plaques be erected in public recognition of construction. E. J. Mehren, "How Can the Spirit of Craftsmanship Be Revived in the Building Industry?" 93 *ENR* 837-38 (Nov. 20, 1924).

[136]Blauner, *Alienation and Freedom* at 172.

[137]Walther Hoffmann, *Stadien und Typen der Industrialisierung: Ein Beitrag zur quantitativen Analyse historischer Wirtschaftsprozesse* 1 (1931).

[138]The three main areas of mechanization have been earth movement, materials handling, and concrete mixing. Despite successes especially in the first area, "[n]o real success has so far been achieved in mechanising craft processes, although a number of mechanical aids to craftsmen have been developed." P. A. Stone, *Building Economy: Design Production and Organisation* 8-9 (1966). The increase in construction machines per worker was not synonymous with the replacement of living labor power by machine tools, which characterizes the transition from *Manufaktur* to industrial production. Only highway construction used machines that combined machine tools and means of transportation, whereas in building construction machines (such as cranes) replaced the labor of moving heavy objects without integrating the individual labor operations. Cement mixers did represent a transition to industrial production, but only as one phase within an otherwise craft-oriented structure. Helga Fassbinder et al., "Zur Berufspraxis des Architekten: Entwicklung von Bauindustrie, Bauauftraggebern und staatlicher Planungstätigkeit als Bestimmungsmomente der Architektenarbeit," *ARCH+*, No. 18, July 1973, at 1-73 at 16-17. See also Projektgruppe Branchenanalyse des Bauhauptgewerbes TU Berlin, "Industrialisierung des Bauens unter den Bedingungen des westdeutschen Kapitalismus," *Kursbuch*, No. 27, May 1972, at 99-136; Rolf Rosenbrock, "Bauproduktion: Entwicklungstendenzen der Bauwirtschaft," in *Architektur und Kapitalverwertung: Veränderungstendenzen in Beruf und Ausbildung von Architekten in der BRD* 85-124 (Klaus Brake ed., 1973).

Instead, it "is still largely in the era of hand craftsmanship supplemented by powered hand tools, the lowest form of mechanization...."[139] Nevertheless, despite the higher skill level and more 'organic' activity of modern construction workers, they, too, were subject to technological and socioeconomic pressures common to all wage workers.[140] For example, the "pre-assembly of as many elements as possible on a factory basis" meant that a carpenter who "can install six to ten prefabricated door assemblies, pre-hung in the frames with hardware already in place, in the time it takes to hang a single door by conventional methods...becomes a doorhanger and ceases to be a carpenter."[141] In spite of this deepening division of labor, its less complex character and the lack of automation meant that construction workers had still not become and did not experience themselves as mere appendages of the means of production in the same way that factory workers did. For these reasons construction workers retained, as Joyce argued, greater control over the pace of work and the way they worked.[142]

In a broader sense, however, construction firms had for several decades been introducing the "industrialization of building" by means of "the model of industrial manufacturing":

> This change seems to have originated with the emergence of large-scale building contractors, both commercial and residential, with the large public works projects of the Depression, the demands for large-scale building in World War II and the pressures on the industry to provide mass housing in the years following World War II. Out of these events and other social processes associated with them, came entrepreneurs in building activity on the model of entrepreneurs of large-scale manufacturing processes in industry. They brought with them and stimulated adoption of a variety of managerial and production techniques—cost analysis, job analysis, time and motion study, prefabrication, on-site mass production, etc.—which boil down to treating building as a manufacturing process. ... As a consequence of this new approach to the building process, efficiency in use of labor and materials was increased, costs were lowered, speed of construction was greatly increased....

---

[139]Harry Braverman, *Labor and Monopoly Capital: The Degradation of Work in the Twentieth Century* 208 (1974).

[140]A contemporaneous analysis of trends in the industrialization of residential construction observed: "The one-sided mechanization of residential construction is characterized by the fact that the machine to an ever greater degree...penetrates the productions methods of residential construction. The machinery is expanded to an ever greater degree; the amount of horse power per employee is augmented to an increasing degree. But despite this mechanization the methods of production remain...in principle craft-oriented work sequences." Gangl, *Die Engpässe für eine konsequent industrialisierte Wohnbauwirtschaft* at 15-16.

[141]Braverman, *Labor and Monopoly Capital* at 208-209.

[142]For earlier confirmation for the building trades generally, see Milton Derber, "Building Construction," in *Labor Management Relations in Illini City* 1: 659-785 at 677 (W. Chalmers et al. eds., 1953).

Along with these changes in management and methods came a series of building techniques, components and materials which adapted themselves to the concept of building as a manufacturing process—to the idea of the house or building as a product. ... Much of the building operation was moved off-site into the factory itself; on-site activity was made as much like factory work as possible. New power tools and equipment were adapted, both on-site and in-factory, to replace previous craft operations.[143]

Not so surprisingly, then, construction employers were engaged in a less public struggle to eliminate the very conditions that underwrote their employees' comparatively unalienated state. While employers and the state, during the Vietnam war years, trained their criticism on construction unions' and workers' wages and their macroeconomic consequences, they also sought to introduce methods of production that would reduce the objective and subjective control that enabled workers to resist subordination to employers. The reason for the tension in construction employers' attitudes towards their employees is not hard to discern. Like other skilled craftsmen, building tradesmen

are relatively independent of their companies, since the market demand for their skills gives them mobility in an industrial structure made up of large numbers of potential employers. The occupational structure and economic organization of craft industries thus make the work force autonomous from management, rather than integrated with it or alienated from it. This autonomy is expressed in the skilled craftsman's characteristic (and characterological) resentment of close supervision. Since the management control structure has little effective power and since craft technology is too undeveloped to be coercive, the locus of social control in these work settings is the journeyman's own internalization of occupational standards of work excellence and norms of "a fair day's work." Work discipline in craft industries is therefore essentially self-discipline.[144]

Construction firms' ambivalence about the self-contradictory ends that they were pursuing—the employment of unalienated but nonmilitant workers—is readily documented. The intensity and peculiar qualities of labor struggles in the construction industry were rooted in craft workers' greater powers of resistance. Joyce's reference to self-supervision with respect to the quality of output and the pace of work reflects, at least on the surface, a degree of independence from the mechanisms of capitalist discipline unknown to most industrial workers.[145] Construction employers, on the one hand, traditionally welcomed the fact that they could in part dispense with a separate layer of supervisory personnel: "The

---

[143]Donald Schon, *Technology and Change* 157-58 (1967).

[144]Blauner, *Alienation and Freedom* at 175.

[145]For example, skilled maintenance workers, even and perhaps especially at the Lordstown plant, "who have mastered a large number of machines or are expert electricians have enormous power over production." Aronowitz, *False Promises* at 47.

journeyman is trained to perform much of the supervisory and planning functions that in other industries are the role of management."[146] On the other hand, many employers were also eager to deprive their employees of this autonomy. For example, the AGC's 1974 proposal to revamp apprenticeship training programs appeared to be a step in this direction. Under this plan, "a worker would receive...proficiency in one subskill of a trade. Examples: framer, rough carpenter, drywall taper, pipe caulker, asbestos shingle roofer." The plan, to be sure, left open the possibility of accumulating sufficient subskills to become a master craftsman, but the goals of cutting down training time and producing qualified workers "when and where needed" suggested that such an outcome would at best have been an unintended by-product.[147]

Autonomous self-management by craftsmen contained its own ambiguities. On the one hand, where work rules define employers as dependent on workers' personal skill, a "certain psychological ascendancy is...established in favor of the worker which virtually eliminates any general feeling of deference toward the contractor class."[148] On the other hand, those who perform management's role may also have internalized its function as enforcer of the self-valorization demands of the employer's capital investment.[149] The same ambiguity extends to the role of supervising co-workers: "It has long been customary for foremen in the construction industry to be regular members of the union whose members they direct. The practice arises in part from the fact that there is a good deal of interchange, from job to job, between the status of foreman and worker. A craftsman may be a foreman on one job today and a worker on another job tomorrow."[150] To the extent that worker-foremen's overall dominant experience was that of being a wage worker, the possibility of divided loyalties, compounded by the supervisees' extraordinary scope for self-direction, created significant potential for conflict for employers.

The Roundtable identified one of the sources of construction unions' enhanced power in

---

[146]Mills, *Industrial Relations and Manpower in Construction* at 183-84.

[147]"New Way to Meet Manpower Needs Unveiled," *ENR*, Oct. 17, 1974, at 85.

[148]Myers, "The Building Workers" at 269.

[149]Though less prevalent today than earlier in the century, the transition between union worker and employer-business owner may also exert its impact. In Chicago in the 1920s, when unionism had been an accomplished fact for 50 years, "perhaps more than half of the subcontractors...were once building-trades workers. Many of them still carry the union card. Unless too unreasonable demands are made by the workers, the employer is not willing to sacrifice the services of his union workers, more efficient on the whole, he thinks, than the non-union men...." Montgomery, *Industrial Relations in the Chicago Building Trades* at 7.

[150]John Dunlop & Arthur Hill, *The Wage Adjustment Board: Wartime Stabilization in the Building and Construction Industry* 15 (1950).

the fact that the hiring hall is usually the source from which the contractor draws his Foremen and General Foremen. These levels of supervision...are typically craftsmen who, for one reason or another, are assigned to a given construction project in a supervisory role. Whether or not they will assume that role on the projects in the future is largely left to the whim of the hiring hall and union officials. This situation leaves little doubt as to where the loyalties of supervisory employees are likely to lie, or as to what factors are likely to have a primary influence on their actions and decisions as members of supervision.[151]

Possibly the most subversive impact of the hiring hall—through which, Roger Blough estimated, two million of 3.4 million construction workers were hired[152]—from the Roundtable's perspective, was its mitigation of the disciplinary function of firings. Even when employers exercised their contractual right to reject or dismiss workers sent by the union, "discharge from the job is not likely to have much effect on a construction worker. He probably will return to the hiring hall for prompt reassignment to another construction project"[153] with another employer. Thus the long tradition of militance and violence in construction labor struggles strongly suggests that the other possibility—namely, workers' internalization of management's conception of discipline—was not representative enough to undermine unions' special powers of resistance.

Despite Joyce's disparaging reference to sociologists, their overwhelming focus on the effects of the micro-division of labor on workers' consciousness overlapped with his approach. As Gavin Mackenzie, author of one of the most frequently cited contemporaneous sociological studies of craftsmen in the United States, asserted: "It would seem...that we must focus on the *nature of the job itself* in explaining...the relatively high level of satisfaction found amongst the craft workers.... This means that the intrinsic satisfaction inherent in craft jobs, rooted in the amount of freedom and control the craftsman has over his work situation, as well as in the nature of the tasks he is asked to perform, provide virtually *the* explanation of the degree of job satisfaction found among these blue collar workers."[154] Ironically, Mackenzie found that precisely bricklayers, one of the groups he interviewed, had little "scope for variety or individuality. The vast majority of the people we talked to simply laid bricks, blocks, or stone. To be sure, buildings differ from one another in form, but the actual tasks involved in bricklaying do not."[155]

---

[151]BR, *Coming to Grips with Some Problems in the Construction Industry* at 52.

[152]CUAIR *Report*, No. 72-8, at 2 (July 28, 1972).

[153]BR, *Coming to Grips with Some Problems in the Construction Industry* at 52.

[154]Gavin Mackenzie, *The Aristocracy of Labor: The Position of Skilled Craftsmen in the American Class Structure* 41 (1973).

[155]Mackenzie, *Aristocracy of Labor* at 14.

Regardless of this substantive defect, to conceptualize and measure "job satisfaction" by means of a questionnaire administered to an individual worker artificially isolated and atomized vis-à-vis the researcher-interrogator cannot capture the manifold layers of meaning of the capital-labor relationship.[156] The most striking example was Mackenzie's interpretation of the answers he received to this question: "Do you think it is more realistic to look at a large firm somewhat like a football team—with each person doing his bit toward the success of the enterprise—or is it more realistic to see it composed of two opposed parts—managers on the one side and workers on the other?"[157] That 72 percent of the craftsmen fell into the group of "'footballers'" was less interesting to Mackenzie than "the almost complete absence of ideological responses"[158] justifying their views of large firms: the great majority—who, he fails to add, were not employed in such firms[159]—"gave as their reasons the fact that simply this was the only way a firm could get things done. ... For these people, to discuss a firm in terms of conflict relationship between management and workers is silly and meaningless. The large firm and teamwork are, by definition, inseparable." Even where craftsmen stated that "[t]hrough intervention of unions for the workers we get higher pay and higher benefits," Mackenzie interpreted the attitude toward unions "purely and simply as an instrumental and personal one." He completely stripped the sale of labor power of its fundamental structural peculiarity by imputing to his interviewee the notion that unions bargain with employers to "get the best deal for union members" in exactly "the same way as he will bargain with the car salesman to get the best deal he can on a new car." The relationship between unions and employers thus was conflictual "only insofar as any commercial relationship is..., and it is questioning the existing form of social structure only as much as the man buying a new car is questioning the concept of a money economy."[160]

Even if workers, as consumers, share with employers the illusions of the sphere of circulation, as producers they become acutely conscious of the fact that commerce rests on production, which in turn may be taken out of their hides in various health-, welfare-, and life-threatening forms. It is ironic that precisely during those years when the employing class as a whole and the state were denouncing unionized construction craftsmen's militance as subverting the economy and society, Mackenzie concluded that they were doing nothing more than bargaining for a lower car price.

---

[156]See Hartwig Berger, *Untersuchungsmethode und soziale Wirklichkeit* 55-68 (1974).

[157]Mackenzie, *Aristocracy of Labor* at 179. For a critique of the football team approach, see Ursula Schumm-Garling, *Herrschaft in der industriellen Arbeitsorganisation* 40 (1972).

[158]Mackenzie, *Aristocracy of Labor* at 139.

[159]Mackenzie, *Aristocracy of Labor,* tab. 2 at 16.

[160]Mackenzie, *Aristocracy of Labor* at 139, 140, 144, 145.

STRIKES

In a state of society founded upon the antagonism of classes, if we want to prevent Slavery..., we must accept war. In order to rightly appreciate the value of strikes and combinations, we must not allow ourselves to be blinded by the apparent insignificance of their economical results.... Without the great alternative phases of dullness, prosperity, over-excitement, crisis and distress, which modern industry traverses in periodically recurring cycles, with the up and down of wages resulting from them, as with the constant warfare between masters and men closely corresponding with those variations in wages and profits, the working-classes...would be a heart-broken, a weak-minded, a worn-out, unresisting mass, whose self-emancipation would prove as impossible as that of the slaves of Ancient Greece and Rome.[161]

Under certain circumstances, there is for the workman no other means of ascertaining whether he is or not paid to the actual market value of his labor, but to strike or to threaten to do so.[162]

Construction workers' extraordinary control was inscribed in their leading position as strikers.[163] Looking back from the mid-1970s, two labor economists concluded that construction "may be the most strike-prone industry"; it had been the site of almost 25,000 strikes, or about one-fifth the national total, during the post-World War period.[164] During the Vietnam war, however, strike activity reached unprecedented levels. In 1969 and 1970, almost 1000 strikes took place during contract negotiations, accounting for 36 percent of all collective bargaining agreement renewals—up from 20 percent between 1960 and 1967. The settlements finally reached at the end of some long strikes exceeded the unions' original demands.[165] As Tables 16a and 16b, which present basic strike indicators for the three decades after World War II, impressively demonstrate, during the 10 years from 1962 to 1971, construction workers, while representing only 4 percent of the

---

[161]Karl Marx, "Russian Policy Against Turkey—Chartism," in Karl Marx [&] Friedrich Engels, *Collected Works* 12: 163-73 at 169 (1979 [1853]).

[162]Karl Marx, "Panic on the London Stock Exchange—Strikes," in Karl Marx [&] Friedrich Engels, *Collected Works* 12: 329-34 at 333 (1979 [1853]).

[163]On the building trades unions' leading position as strikers in the late nineteenth and early twentieth century, see *Third Annual Report of the Commissioner of Labor, 1887: Strikes and Lockouts* 15, 28 (1888); 1 *Tenth Annual Report of the Commissioner of Labor, 1894: Strikes and Lockouts* 18 (1896); *Sixteenth Annual Report of the Commissioner of Labor, 1901: Strikes and Lockouts* 31 (1901); BLS, *Strikes in the United States 1880-1936*, at 30 (Bull. No. 651, 1937).

[164]David Lipsky and Henry Farber, "The Composition of Strike Activity in the Construction Industry," 29 (3) *ILRR* 389-404 at 389 (Apr., 1976).

[165]Mills, *Industrial Relations and Manpower in Construction* at 69.

civilian labor force, accounted for one-fifth of all strikes, 17 percent of all strikers, and 19 percent of all striker days.[166]

The indicators displayed in Table 16a and 16b illustrate several components of strike activity: the number of strikes; number of strikers; total number of worker-days on strike; and average number of days each striker was on strike. In addition, the tables report on construction strikes, strikers, and strike days as a proportion of the aggregate national data. Finally, they also reveal the proportion of construction workers participating in strikes as well as the percentage of total construction working time accounted for by strike time. The Bureau of Labor Statistics, the official national strike data collection agency, uniformly uses the terms "idleness" and "days idle" to describe the amount of time during which workers are on strike. This curious word choice carries obvious pro-production and pro-employer ideological freight. An ancient word, "idle" means empty, useless, vain, worthless, serving no useful purpose, not engaged in work, doing nothing, and unemployed. The word buries the insight that struggles vital to the development of society may be taking place during strikes.[167]

From the middle of the Korean War—during which the federal government did not even ask unions to give a no-strike pledge[168]—on, the number of strikes attained a much higher level than at any time since the BLS initiated its modern set of strike statistics in the 1920s.[169] But an even higher plateau was reached during the years from 1964 through 1970 culminating in the all-time record of 1,137 strikes in 1970. The combined force of government intervention, Roundtable support for the nonunion sector, and mounting unemployment then took hold: within three years the number of strikes plummeted 53 percent to 539.[170] Once the Construction Industry Stabilization Committee (CISC) was established in 1971, "unions could not help but realize the futility of striking for excessive wage increases which would later be rejected by the CISC." By the same token, construction firms "were reluctant to hold the line against costly union bargaining demands and thus incur a lengthy strike when they expected the committee to ultimately roll back any wage settlement not in keeping with CISC guidelines."[171]

---

[166]BLS, *Work Stoppages in Contract Construction, 1962-73*, at 1.

[167]5 *Oxford English Dictionary* 22-23 (1961 [1933]).

[168]Benjamin Aaron, "Controls During World War II and the Korean War," IRRA, *Proc. of the Fiftieth Annual Meeting*, 1:160-67 at 161 (1998).

[169]*Work Stoppages in Contract Construction 1946-66*, tab. 1 at 4 (Rep. No. 346, 1968).

[170]Lipsky & Farber, "The Composition of Strike Activity in the Construction Industry" at 401, deny that rising unemployment reduced the number of strikes, but admit that it did limit their size and duration.

[171]BLS, *Work Stoppages in Contract Construction 1946-66*, at 22. Dunlop, the chairman of the CISC, had predicted that: "'A strike or lockout against the program by significant organizations will cause it to collapse.'" Byron Calame, "Construction-Industry Panel May Be Model for Stabilizing

Despite the strong increase in the number of strikes, construction was overtaken by other industries as is shown by Table 16a: construction strikes as a percentage of all strikes reached their high point (26 percent) in 1964, and then fell almost continuously for the next decade to a low of 10 percent in 1973.

The trend in the number of striking workers was similar to that of strikes, but showed greater fluctuations; and unlike the strike indicator, the number of strikers, after reaching a peak of 621,000 in 1970, fell sharply but rose to a new peak of 630,000 in 1974 (chiefly after the expiration of the CISC on April 30). The fact that construction worker strikers as a proportion of all strikers fluctuated at a lower level than in the case of strikes indicates that construction strikes were smaller than in the national economy as a whole. Finally, the proportion of construction workers participating in strikes exceeded 11 percent from 1966 to 1972, reaching a peak, once again in 1970, of 18 percent, which, however, was lower than the high point of 24 percent during the Korean War.[172]

The category of worker-days on strike, shown in Table 16b, synthesizes the number of strikes, the number of workers per strike, and the duration of strikes. Nationally, construction ranked first in worker-days on strike, averaging 6.6 million annually between 1962 and 1971. This indicator rose almost eightfold—from less than 2 million days in 1963 to a postwar high point of more than 15 million in 1970.[173] The more than 25 million striker-days in 1969 and 1970 exceeded the next highest consecutive two years by a large margin. Although construction accounted for almost one-fourth of all striker-days in the United States in 1969-70, the peak of 29 percent was reached in 1972, when the absolute volume had fallen by half. As unemployment rose higher, construction's share of total striker-days fell further: by 1976 it was only 8 percent.[174] 1970 was also the peak year for the number of days on strike per striker (25) and striker-days as a percentage of total estimated working time in construction (1.76 percent)—a level almost five times higher than the national average (0.37 percent) and much higher than the industry average in the rest of the post-World War period.[175]

Pay, Prices After Nov. 12," *WSJ*, Aug. 18, 1971, at 30, col. 1, 3.

[172]The data on strikers may include double counting of workers who participated in more than one strike in a given year. BLS, *Work Stoppages in Contract Construction, 1962-73*, at 81.

[173]BLS, *Work Stoppages in Contract Construction, 1962-73* at 1.

[174]BLS, "News: Work Stoppages, 1976," tab. 4 [n.p.] (USDL: 77-76, Jan. 26, 1977).

[175]For the calculation of overall striker-days as a proportion of total working time, see BLS, *Analysis of Work Stoppages, 1975*, tab. 1 at 10 (Bull. 1940, 1977); on the methodology, see Howard Fullerton, "'Total Economy' Measure of Strike Idleness," *MLR*, October 1968, at 54-56. The proportion for construction is understated because the BLS assumes a standard year of 255 working days, whereas construction workers on average work only 200 days. BLS, *Work Stoppages in Contract Construction, 1962-73* at 1.

Table 16a: Strikes and Strikers in Construction, 1946-1975

Year	Work stoppages				Workers involved			
	Number	Index (1967=100)	% of U.S. total		Number (000)	Index (1967=100)	% of U.S. total	% of construction employment
1946	351	40	7		146.0	48	3	9
1947	382	44	10		175.0	57	8	9
1948	380	44	11		108.0	35	6	5
1949	615	71	17		197.0	65	7	9
1950	611	70	13		237.0	78	10	10
1951	651	75	14		232.0	76	10	9
1952	794	92	16		634.0	208	18	24
1953	1,039	120	20		574.0	188	24	22
1954	804	93	23		437.0	144	29	17
1955	733	85	17		204.0	67	8	7
1956	784	90	20		231.0	76	12	8
1957	785	91	21		308.0	101	22	11
1958	844	97	23		326.0	107	16	12
1959	771	89	21		251.0	82	13	8
1960	773	89	23		269.0	88	20	9

Table 16a: Strikes and Strikers in Construction, 1946-1975

1961	824	95	24	216.7	71	15		8
1962	913	105	25	284.2	93	23		10
1963	840	97	25	208.0	68	22		7
1964	944	109	26	247.8	81	15		8
1965	943	109	24	301.4	99	19		9
1966	977	113	22	455.2	149	23		14
1967	867	100	19	304.5	100	11		9
1968	912	105	18	364.2	120	14		11
1969	973	112	17	433.1	142	17		12
1970	1,137	131	20	621.0	204	19		18
1971	751	87	15	451.3	148	14		12
1972	701	81	14	454.2	149	26		12
1973	539	62	10	367.4	121	16		9
1974	688	79	11	629.8	207	23		16
1975	600	69	12	308.0	101	18		?

Table 16b: Worker-Days on Strike in Construction Strikes, 1946-1975

Year	Number (000)	Index (1967=100)	% of all worker-days on strike in U.S.	% of all working time in construction	days on strike per worker involved
1946	1,450	28	1	0.40	10
1947	2,770	54	8	0.66	16
1948	1,430	28	4	0.29	13
1949	2,760	54	5	0.53	14
1950	2,460	48	6	0.44	10
1951	1,190	23	5	0.18	5
1952	6,700	130	11	1.03	11
1953	8,000	155	28	1.22	14
1954	4,800	93	21	0.71	11
1955	1,810	35	6	0.28	9
1956	2,680	52	8	0.35	12
1957	3,970	77	24	0.51	13
1958	4,790	93	20	0.71	15
1959	4,120	80	6	0.58	16
1960	4,470	87	23	0.63	17
1961	3,491.4	68	21	0.48	16
				0.56	15

Table 16b: Worker-Days on Strike in Construction Strikes, 1946-1975

1963	1,932.2	37	12	0.25		9
1964	2,788.3	54	12	0.35		11
1965	4,627.5	90	20	0.57		15
1966	6,135.9	119	24	0.73		13
1967	5,155.4	100	12	0.63		17
1968	8,722.9	169	18	1.03		24
1969	10,385.8	201	24	1.18		24
1970	15,240.4	296	23	1.76		25
1971	6,849.6	133	14	0.79		15
1972	7,843.7	152	29	0.88		17
1973	3,663.4	71	13	0.39		10
1974	12,721.0	247	27	1.27		20
1975	7,307.3	142	23	0.84		24

Sources: BLS, *Work Stoppages in Contract Construction, 1962-73*, tab. A-1 at 39 (Bull. 1847, 1975); BLS, *Handbook of Labor Statistics 1974*, at 367-68 (Bull. 1825, 1974); BLS, "Work Stoppages, 1974," tab. 4 at 5 (Nov. 1975); BLS, "Work Stoppages 1975," tab. 5 at 6 (Summary 76-7; Aug. 1976).

Construction strikes accounted for a much smaller volume of nonworking days than injuries or unemployment, but the figure for 1970 was impressive even on an international scale of labor-capital turbulence: it exceeded the levels achieved by Italian industrial workers in the late 1960s and early 1970s, if not in the year of the "hot autumn," 1969, when 4.7 percent of hours were lost to "labor unrest."[176]

The average duration of construction strikes was markedly lower than in the economy as a whole. It rose from 14 days in 1962 to a high of 21 days in 1970, but at no time exceeded the lowest value for all industry (22 days). The chief reason for this deviation was the large number of brief jurisdictional strikes involving relatively few workers in construction. 3,451 such strikes took place from 1962 through 1971, accounting for 37 percent of all construction strikes but less than 4 percent of all striker-days.[177] This subordinate role contrasts sharply with the situation in the 1920s when jurisdictional disputes "constitute[d] the single largest cause of work stoppages" in construction, accounting for 95 percent of strikes and 75 percent of striker-days.[178]

The concentration of strike activity, both regionally and with respect to a few large and long strikes, was not unique to construction, but nevertheless quite prominent. What the BLS calls "major strikes," involving more than 10,000 workers, accounted for an increasing proportion of striker-days during the Vietnam war. Although major strikes represented fewer than 1 percent of all construction strikes, they accounted for almost 40 percent of all strikers and half of all striker-days between 1965 and 1972. Whereas 485,000 workers participated in such strikes between 1962 and 1966, almost twice as many (857,000) did so between 1967 and 1971. The average number of strikers in major strikes also doubled from 15,700 in 1966 to 31,400 in 1971.[179]

Table 17 sets out the concentration of major strikes in the construction industry between 1965 and 1975, which accounted for almost three-tenths of all

---

[176]Roberto Franzosi, *The Puzzle of Strikes: Class and State Strategies in Postwar Italy*, tab. 5.17 at 181, tab. 5.18 at 182 (1995).

[177]BLS, *Work Stoppages in Contract Construction, 1962-73*, tab. 8 at 21, 27, tab.14 at 33. Yet in 1975, the mean duration of construction strikes was 34 days compared with 22 for all industries. BLS, *Analysis of Work Stoppages, 1975*, at 5. In addition, an unusually high proportion of construction strikes occurred during the term of the contract and were short. Between 1961 and 1966, 59 percent of all construction strikes occurred during the term of a contract. BLS, *Work Stoppages in Contract Construction 1964-66*, at 2. Strikes following expiration of an agreement are often long and large. Mills, *Industrial Relations and Manpower in Construction* at 49.

[178]Haber, *Industrial Relations in the Building Industry* at 152 (quote), 153.

[179]BLS, *Work Stoppages in Contract Construction, 1962-73* at 25. Major strikes in the economy at large also accounted for about one-half of all striker-days. *Ibid.*

Table 17: Strikes with More Than 10,000 Strikers, 1965-1975					
Year	Strikes			Strikers		
	All	Construction	Construction as % of all	All	Construction	Construction as % of all
1965	21	4	19	387,000	75,700	20
1966	26	12	46	600,000	191,300	32
1967	28	4	14	1,340,000	70,100	5
1968	32	5	16	994,000	101,000	10
1969	25	8	32	668,000	160,000	24
1970	34	9	26	1,653,000	243,000	15
1971	29	9	31	1,901,000	282,500	15
1972	18	9	50	390,000	217,000	56
1973	25	5	20	713,000	173,600	24
1974	27	11	41	835,000	329,700	39
1975	20	7	35	474,000	100,000	21
All	285	83	29	9,955,000	1,943,900	20

Sources: BLS, "Work Stoppages, 1974," tab. 3 at 4 (1975); BLS, *Work Stoppages in Contract Construction, 1962- 73*, tab. A-4 at 57 (Bull. 1847, 1975); BLS, "Work Stoppages in Contract Construction, 1946-73: Addenda to Bulletin 1847"; BLS, *Analysis of Work Stoppages, 1975*, tab. 6 at 17 (Bull. 1940, 1977).

strikes.[180] The almost two million construction workers who participated in such

---

[180]A few large construction strikes bulked large in the industry's total strike activity. In 1969, two strikes in Missouri for wage increases and benefits accounted for more than half of major strike striker-days that year; 37,000 workers took part in a 119-day strike in Kansas City, while in St. Louis 20,000 workers struck for 84 days. The following year two strikes accounted for more than half of major strike striker-days: in Kansas City 27,000 workers struck for 197 days, while 15,000 workers struck for 135 days in Birmingham. In 1971 two California strikes in support of striking teamsters at construction sites, the number of strikers in each of which exceeded that of any other construction strike in recent decades, towered over all others: in one, 65,000 workers struck for 33 days, while in the other 116,000 struck for 15 days. Two large strikes dominated the picture in 1972: 50,000 struck for 39 days in support of cement masons and iron workers in Minneapolis, while 22,600 struck the Building Trades Employers Association in New York City for 110 days over seniority provisions for elevator constructors. In 1975, 26,000 iron workers, laborers, carpenters, and plumbers struck the North Texas Contractors Association for 154 days. BLS, *Work Stoppages in Contract Construction, 1962-73* at 25-26; BLS, *Analysis of Work Stoppages, 1975*, tab. 5 at 14 (Bull. 1940, 1977).

strikes represented one-fifth of the ten million strikers in those strikes. The figures for 1972 underscore construction union militance: when the CISC was applying "all the pressure it could muster to reduce conflict in the industry,"[181] major construction strikes accounted for half of all such strikes and construction workers 56 percent of all such strikers.

---

[181]Lipsky & Farber, "The Composition of Strike Activity" at 393.

Part III

Capital Fractionated and United

Q. [D]o you think that...employers...understand when a union man is employed he engages himself subject to this reserved right of his to quit the employment...because non-union men are also engaged in the same work? A. I don't know what the employers think. They are rather a stupid set. They never learn anything until it is very late, and they have to be taught through a strike or two in nearly every case.[1]

---

[1] 1 *Report of the Committee of the Senate Upon the Relations Between Labor and Capital* 354 (1885) (Senator Wilkinson Call of Florida questioning P.J. McGuire, general secretary of the Brotherhood of Carpenters and Joiners).

6

Construction Employer Organizations

You know that in our industry it is entirely different from the cotton industry, and the steel industry in this respect. Our employers are not capitalists in the sense that these large organizations are. We meet our employers every day, call them Tom, Dick and Harry; we meet them from time to time when we have a little trouble. They understand our troubles and we understand theirs. You know we have a lot of members in our trades union movement in the building industry who get up and preach about capitalism and all that kind of thing, and who would have us at one another's throats with our employers, who say we have nothing in common with them. Gentlemen, we have everything in common with them....[1]

The extraordinary number and variety of employer initiatives for restructuring labor relations in the construction industry in the late 1960s and early 1970s was bewildering, at times coalescing into a confused mass. The intersecting aims of rapidly shifting coalitions were often only roughly discernible; similarly, the bases of conflicting proposals were not always readily identifiable. This chapter introduces the most important employers associations and analyzes their specific plans.

The construction industry's heterogeneity was expressed in the absence of an industry-wide umbrella organization of all associations and a corresponding fragmentation of collective bargaining, which resulted in many thousands of contracts. This decentralized structure was reflected in the fact that the typical or modal collective bargaining agreement encompassed the work performed by a single trade at all the organized construction sites in a locality and was negotiated between one or several locals of a national union and an employer organization representing most or all building contractors based in that area and employing members of the unions in question.[2] Before exploring the positions of these associations, it will be useful to sketch the history of construction employers organization.

---

[1] *Proceedings of the Nineteenth General Convention of the United Brotherhood of Carpenters and Joiners of America* 344 (1916) (speech of William Dobson, president of Bricklayers union).

[2] DOL, Labor-Management Services Adm., *The Bargaining Structure in Construction: Problems and Prospects* 4 (1980) (prepared by Donald Cullen & Louis Feinberg).

BRIEF HISTORY OF CONSTRUCTION EMPLOYER ORGANIZATIONS

In a number of cases the contractors insured themselves against their competitors' being able to get men at lower rates during slack periods by such provisions as: "Party of the second part agrees that during the life of this agreement no member of its organization shall work for any persons not parties to this agreement for any sum per day less than that stipulated in this agreement."[3]

Modern building employer groups arose in the mid-1880s. Just as local trade unions antedated this period, local mechanics' exchanges and master builder associations had also existed earlier in the nineteenth century.[4] Not until the end of the century, however, did the construction market begin to be coterminous with the national economy's market. Such consolidation implies that production and the labor market had broken down the existing local and regional limits. An incipient national construction and construction labor market emerged in the form of "a unique example of employer-induced migration in the operations of several large firms, each of which contracted for work over a wide area. These interstate firms apparently arose after the depression of 1873-1879 and might be considered the counterparts in the construction industry of the large-scale, multiple-plant concerns elsewhere.... They generally specialized in large-scale projects, such as state or municipal buildings...."[5] The emergence of national building firms and national labor mobility gave rise to national construction unions.[6]

The closing years of the nineteenth century also witnessed a number of innovations in building materials and machinery—wrought iron, structural steel, reinforced concrete, elevators, power hoists and derricks, pneumatic riveters, and steam shovels—that made possible the erection of tall buildings.[7] The rapid growth of the largest cities coincided with the rise of

---

[3]Royal Montgomery, *Industrial Relations in the Chicago Building Trades* 36 (1927).

[4]John R. Commons et al., *History of Labour in the United States* 1:69, 71-72 (1918); William Ham, "Associations of Employers in the Construction Industry of Boston," 3 *JEBH* 55-80 at 60-62 (1930-31); Clarence Bonnett, *History of Employers' Associations in the United States* (1956).

[5]Lloyd Ulman, *The Rise of the National Union* 55 (1966 [1955]).

[6]Ulman, *Rise of the National Union* at 59-60. By the turn of the century, large structures were being built chiefly by large firms headquartered in New York City. James Motley, *Apprenticeship in American Trade Unions* 103 (1907).

[7]Luke Grant, *The National Erectors' Association and the International Association of Bridge and Structural Ironworkers* 5 (1971 [1915]); W. Clark, "The Construction Industry," in *Representative Industries in the United States* 188-223 at 194-200 (H. Warshow ed., 1928); Haber, *Industrial Relations in the Building Industry* at 16-35; W. Clark & J. Kingston, *The Skyscraper: A*

the great corporations and trusts and the locating of their head-quarters—together with those of financial- and distribution-sector firms—in the central areas of these cities, especially New York City and Chicago. The existence of ground rent then made the advent of the skyscraper almost inevitable.[8]

The end of the nineteenth and the beginning of the twentieth century thus gave birth to a number of large building firms with the technological and financial capacity to undertake the construction of these large projects. Concentrated as they were in the largest cities, these firms were confronted with the already relatively well-organized skilled building trades workers on whom they were by and large compelled to rely as a source of labor supply. Data for the nineteenth century are lacking, but in the early twentieth century building tradesmen in the major cities were highly organized and represented a large proportion of total union membership in these cities. In 1912, the approximately 90,000 organized building tradesmen in New York City alone accounted for 18 percent of the nationwide total of 509,000. New York accounted for more than 30 percent of of all organized elevator constructors and more than half of all unionized asbestos workers.[9] In 1920, when about 50 percent of all bricklayers were organized, the rates for the large cities all lay well above this level with some approaching complete unionization.[10] By 1936, 82 percent of all skilled workers in nonresidential construction were union members. In New York City, Boston, Cleveland, St. Louis, and Washington, D.C., organization was almost complete.[11]

The rise of a limited number of large building firms competing with

Study in the Economic Height of Modern Office Buildings (1930); Ham, "Associations of Employers in the Construction Industry of Boston" at 57-58; Harry Jerome, *Mechanization in Industry* 135-37 (1934); Harold Faulkner, *The Decline of Laissez Faire* 1897-1917, at 128 (1951). According to Motley, *Apprenticeship in American Trade Unions* at 102-103 n.94, these changes also brought about a substitution of unskilled for skilled workers: "With the introduction of ferro-concrete as a building material, the superintendant and foremen, aided by hatchet and saw carpenters and ordinary laborers, are able to construct the entire framework of the building."

[8]Clark & Kingston, *Skyscraper.*

[9]BLS, *Conciliation and Arbeitration in the Building Trades of Greater New York* 10, 44-94 (Bull. 124, 1913) (written by Charles Winslow); Leo Wolman, *The Growth of American Trade Unions 1880-1923*, at 111 (1924).

[10]Wolman, *Growth of American Trade Unions* at 92, 95.

[11]Edward Sanford, "Wage Rates and Hours of Labor in the Building Trades," 45 (2) *MLR* 281-300 (Aug. 1937); *Investigation of Concentration of Economic Power: Hearings Before the Temporary National Economic Committee*, Pt. 11: *Construction Industry*, 76th Cong., 1st Sess. 5574-86 (1940).

one another in the largest cities—AFL president Gompers estimated in 1911 that a dozen or so large building contractors built almost all the modern buildings[12]—and all similarly dependent on the same largely unionized supply of craftsmen brought about the need for new organizational forms adapted to the changing structures of competition among firms as well as between capital and organized labor. These interrelationships were complicated by the fact that certain alliances of convenience, when extended beyond a certain point, began to generate unintended consequences, which in turn called forth counter-campaigns and counter-alliances. For example, once a few large firms had begun to struggle for control over an urban construction market, the closed shop could become "a convenient instrument"[13] to exclude unwelcome competition or to bring insubordinate contractors back into line.[14]

But the relative power that local unions achieved and consolidated was not so easily manipulable as the large firms may have imagined since, once set in motion, it gained a certain autonomy. In particular, the unions' control over the skilled labor supply and the consequent 'infringement of management prerogatives' constituted "unbearable conditions" for local employers associations. Conditions varied from city to city, but one feature was common to most at the turn of the century: "The rapid growth of cities throughout the United States during this period was in part the result of unrestricted immigration and the growth of concentrated large-scale industry. The building demands created by the movement of workers to the cities placed building workers in a unique bargaining position."[15]

These "unbearable conditions" were often similar to those that had originally given rise the employer associations. For example, the Master Builders' Association was established in Boston in 1885 as a reaction to

---

[12]R. Christie, *Empire in Wood: A History of the Carpenters' Union* 81 (1956).

[13]Rasmus Berg, *Blikkenslagersvenden gennem tiderne: Festskriftet udgivet af Blikkenslagerforbundet in Danmark i Anledning af dets 50 aars Jubilæum* 80-81 (1940) (term describing the use that master plumbers made of the plumbers' union in Denmark ca. 1880).

[14]William Haber, *Industrial Relations in the Building Industry* 252, 255 (1930); Gordon Bertram & Sherman Maisel, *Industrial Relations in the Construction Industry* 40 (1955).

[15]Sen. Rep. No. 1150, Pt. 2: *Violations of Free Speech and Rights of Labor, Employers' Associations and Collective Bargaining in California*, Part II: *Organized Antiunionism in California Industry Prior to the Passage of the National Labor Relations Act*, 77th Cong., 2d Sess. 84 n.46 (1942). Since large employers supported unrestricted immigration explicitly as a means of keeping wage rates down, its contribution to unions' strong position is an example of how pro-business policies can turn against their initiators. Albion Taylor, *Labor Policies of the National Association of Manufacturers* 121 (1927).

workers' demands for the nine-hour day.[16] In other cities, employers' associations arose as a general response to union efforts to enforce the closed shop.[17] A number of these organizations were formed under the auspices of the National Association of Builders (NAB), which was founded in 1887. Although a year or two earlier building trades workers had been defeated in the biggest building strike ever in Boston, the NAB's secretary later told aggressive employers: "We do not want to lick them. We want to adopt a more businesslike way."[18] The cooperation of local employers vis-à-vis their unionized labor supply was a reaction to the possible advantages accruing to unions, which previously had had to deal with relatively small firms on an individual level. William Haber, the leading historian of construction labor relations, argued that employers were organizationally 30 years behind unions: "It is possibly no exaggeration to say that the unorganized individual employer in the building trades was at a greater disadvantage in dealing with the union than the unorganized worker in his relations with an employer."[19]

The dissolution of the NAB by the turn of the century—the depression of 1893 had eliminated many of the local exchanges—underscored an "absence of homogeneity in interests and in stability" as the organization's fundamental weakness.[20] That the NAB's antiunion stance, though supported by employers, was unrealistic for many members in New York City and Chicago[21] suggests that it was precisely the largest firms that were least interested in a direct confrontation with organized labor despite the fact that they may have been in the best position to conduct such a campaign successfully. The emphasis placed by employers' associations on obligating unions contractually to supply them with tradesmen "even though the union must take such men from shops of employers not members of the association

---

[16]Ham, "Associations" at 63.

[17]Haber, *Industrial Relations in the Building Industry* at 448; Commons et al., *History* 2:424; Bates, *Bricklayers' Century of Craftsmanship* at 72, 92.

[18]Industrial Commission, 7 *Reports: On the Relations and Conditions of Capital and Labor Employed in Manufactures and General Business* 851 (H. Doc. No. 495, 56th Cong., 2d Sess, 1901) (W. H. Sayward).

[19]Haber, *Industrial Relations in the Building Industry* at 442, 446 (quote).

[20]Haber, *Industrial Relations in the Building Industry* at 449, 443 (quote). Attached to the last issue of the NAB's quarterly *Bulletin: Devoted to the Ethics of Associated Effort*, at the University of Wisconsin at Madison library is a letter, dated Jan. 11, 1900, from its secretary, William Sayward, stating that *Bulletin* had been discontinued about a year ago. 4 (5) *Bulletin* (Oct. 1898).

[21]Haber, *Industrial Relations in the Building Industry* at 450.

of employers,"[22] indicates the competitive advantages inhering in such quasi-exclusive agreements.[23] Since union responsibility for the labor supply was an integral element of a branch characterized by unusually unstable employment, management control over the supply would have implied a capacity to finance more or less year-round employment. The capital stock, however, had not yet reached a magnitude that would have pressured firms to seek continuous capacity utilization in order to spread their overhead costs. Where, as in the exceptional case of iron erectors, "expensive equipment had to be constantly employed so that the overhead should not consume the profits,"[24] firms were able to offer steadier employment. Not coincidentally, the erectors' national association favored the open shop.[25]

Despite these unfavorable conditions for employers, lockout statistics for the years 1881-1905 reveal the existence of a sector of firms capable of combating united labor. During that period, the building trades, ranking first in all categories, accounted for 16 percent of all lockouts, 55 percent of all affected establishments, and 31 percent of all locked-out employees. Construction lockouts were also larger than the all-industry average: they encompassed more than three times as many establishments and almost twice as many employees. Whereas lockouts affected two and one-half times more workers than strikes in industry at large, in construction lockouts were nine times larger; at 105 days, they were also longer than average. Employer militance was also reflected in the fact that employers prevailed in two-thirds of all lockouts.[26] The spatial concentration of lockouts in Illinois and New York underscores the importance of a sector of organized employers in Chicago and New York City.[27] Characteristically, in the majority of establishments affected by lockouts the major cause or object of the action

---

[22]BLS, *Conciliation and Arbitration in the Building Trades of Greater New York* at 36 (quoting an umpire's decision within the framework of the General Arbitration Board regulating labor relations between building trades unions and the Building Trades Employers' Association of New York City during the first decade of the twentieth century).

[23]Courts had held illegal exclusive agreements which pledged employers' associations and unions to deal only with each other. F. Hilbert, "Employers' Associations in the United States," in *Studies in American Trade Unionism* 183-217 at 187-88 (J. Hollander & G. Barnett eds., 1906).

[24]Haber, *Industrial Relations in the Building Industry* at 278.

[25]Grant, *National Erectors' Association* at 80.

[26]Calculated according to *Twenty-First Annual Report of the Commissioner of Labor 1906*, at 16-17, 21-22, 52-53, 81-82 (1907).

[27]*Third Annual Report of the Commissioner of Labor, 1887: Strikes and Lockouts*, tab. XIII at 882-85 (1888); *Sixteenth Annual Report of the Commissioner of Labor, 1901: Strikes and Lockouts*, tab. XV at 642-48 (1901).

was not reducing wages or increasing hours, but rather the key issues of union power—the closed shop, union recognition, and building trades councils.[28]

The divergence of interests between large and small employers with respect to unionism—a heterogeneity that in the 1960s and 1970s still exacerbated their inability to speak with a "single voice"—has often been advanced as an explanation of the failure of several early national organizations such as the National Building Trades Employers' Association, which was founded in 1903 and again in 1919.[29] This organization arose in response to the founding of the Structural Building Trades Alliance of unions, which proved to be weak.[30] This sequence of events confirms the general observation that employers' organizations develop "only after organizations of employees have become strong enough to gain advantages in the making of the labor contract."[31]

Prior to the depression of the 1930s, employer groups coalesced and wielded power from time to time in large cities such as Chicago (in 1900 and 1921) when construction firms concluded that the local building trades council had wrested too much control from them. But at that time only in New York City had employers succeeded in maintaining their organization continuously for more than 25 years.[32]

CONSTRUCTION INDUSTRY EMPLOYERS ASSOCIATIONS

An employer, as a rule, is not an unfair man, and generally it is a business proposition with him, and it is just as much of a business proposition with us. We should not look upon him as a thief.[33]

The most important construction employers associations that

---

[28]2 *Tenth Annual Report of the Commissioner of Labor, 1894: Strikes and Lockouts*, tab. XXV at 1897 (1896); *Sixteenth Annual Report of the Commissioner of Labor, 1901*, tab. XXI at 705-706.

[29]Haber, *Industrial Relations in the Building Industry* at 456-57, 461; Hilbert, "Employers' Associations" at 205-207.

[30]Haber, *Industrial Relations in the Building Industry* at 334-35.

[31]Hilbert, "Employers' Associations" at 185.

[32]Montgomery, *Industrial Relations in the Chicago Building Trades*; Clarence Bonnett, *Employers' Associations in the United States: A Study of Typical Associations* 153-204 (1922); Haber, *Industrial Relations in the Building Industry* at 346.

[33]"Report of the Proceedings of the Fourth Annual Convention, Utica, January 8-14, 1906," 3 (1) *IHCBLJ* 3 (Jan. 1906) (James Kirby, president, Structural Building Trades Alliance).

articulated their own plans for dealing with labor during the Indochina war period were the National Constructors Association, Associated General Contractors, and Associated Builders and Contractors. Differences among these groups were preordained by their formal positions vis-à-vis unions: whereas the NCA operated 100 percent union, the AGC, whose members at one time had been heavily closed or union shops, was in transition toward bifurcation between union and nonunion factions, and the ABC was militantly antiunion.

National Constructors Association

Employers associations are..., strictly economically speaking, nothing but purchasing cartels.... But purchasing cartels of a very special kind, because the commodity labor power...after all cannot enter totally into entrepreneurs' possession.[34]

The NCA was the most influential group in terms of its members' own concentrated capital power and their crucial role in building the factories, refineries, and power plants for the country's largest industrial corporations. Formed in 1947, it proved to be the most significant construction organization to emerge from World War II. The NCA was established by 21 of the largest national general contractors engaged in building oil refineries and steel and chemical plants "to improve field labor relations."[35] The origin of the NCA was linked to the very large industrial projects that developed during and after the war and made it necessary for these firms to establish labor relations staffs.[36] Since NCA members employed about 50,000 workers (in 1950)[37] and had long relied on the

---

[34]Emil Lederer, "Sozialpolitische Chronik: Die Unternehmerorganisationen," 30 *ASS* 848-70 at 868 (1919).

[35]*To Amend the National Labor Relations Act* at 126, 128 (NCA folder submitted in evidence by its vice-president, J. J. O'Donnell). A rich source of information, the NCA *Bulletin*, has apparently been lost: a fire at the NCA office in the 1980s destroyed all of its back issues; no library appears to hold it and no NCA member appears to have retained issues from the 1960s and 1970s; Bechtel Corporation, for example, disposed of its holdings in 1979. Telephone interview with Robert McCormick, NCA president, Washington, D.C. (Mar. 11, 1999); telephone interview with Kenneth Hedman, vice president and labor relations manager, Bechtel Corp., San Francisco (Mar. 12, 1999).

[36]Daniel Quinn Mills, "Factors Determining Patterns of Employment and Unemployment in the Construction Industry of the United States" 21 (Ph.D. diss., Harvard U., 1967).

[37]*To Amend the National Labor Relations Act* at 130.

building trades unions as a "source of highly skilled personnel,"[38] it was scarcely surprising that the strong increase in strike activity in the early postwar period motivated these large firms to improve their bargaining position vis-à-vis organized labor as quickly as possible. The "NCA's initial goal was to head off potential chaos threatened by the end of wage stabilization after World War II and to do this through improved labor contract bargaining at the local and national levels."[39]

That the war had fostered close union collaboration was visible in the fact that unions and firms unanimously agreed to a fifteen-month extension of wartime controls. After the repeal of all controls in 1946, the unions adopted a similar position. "They would have preferred a policy of moderate increases through a government agency. But the unions could hardly tolerate a condition in which wage controls had been removed in all areas of the economy except construction. It would have been impossible to justify or explain before the membership."[40] The firms shared this view, although they would have been publicly obliged by employers' call for a repeal of all controls. The fears expressed by the union leadership were apparently well founded.[41]

Composed of forty-four general contractors, the NCA in 1973 included nine of the country's ten largest construction firms. They accounted for a large proportion of all industrial building in the United States, although they also performed much of their work abroad. Of special importance here is that their employees were 100 percent unionized.[42] NCA members employed a large proportion of certain unions' membership—for example, one-fourth to one-half of union plumbers.[43] Because the core of year-round union workers was employed by these firms—their 75,000 to 150,000 employees in addition to 100,000 working for subcontractors accounted for

[38]*To Amend the National Labor Relations Act* at 126.

[39]"NCA Increases the Pressure to Cut the Fat Out of Labor Costs," *ENR*, Mar. 1, 1973, at 18.

[40]John Dunlop & Arthur Hill, *The Wage Adjustment Board: Wartime Stabilization in the Building and Construction Industry* 43, 47 (quote) (1950).

[41]John Dunlop, "The Decontrol of Wages and Prices," in *Labor in Postwar America* 3-23 at 5 (Colston Warne ed., 1949).

[42]"The ENR 500," *ENR*, May 16, 1974, at 57-70 at 58; "NCA Members Ply the World and Find Jobs on Every Continent," *ENR*, Dec. 5, 1974, at 14; "NCA Increases the Pressure to Cut the Fat Out of Labor Costs," *ENR*, Mar. 1, 1973, at 18-22.

[43]Mills, *Industrial Relations and Manpower in Construction* at 35 n.22.

80 to 90 percent of heavy industrial construction[44]—developments in this sector had a disproportionate impact on the structure of labor relations in the whole industry.

NCA members preferred (and in many instances had no alternative but) to employ union members because unions could furnish them with the requisite number of workers with the proper mix of skills at all of their myriad far-flung building sites, but they were not unconditionally committed to the unions. The limit of that commitment was marked by the point at which union wage increases could no longer be compensated for by productivity advantages. At that point, the NCA members could: (1) depress the wage level down to that of the nonunion sector; (2) roll back the defensive controls that union workers had built up against management and that blocked productivity growth from capital's perspective;[45] or (3) hire nonunion workers.

By the late 1960s and early 1970s firms increasingly asserted that the aforementioned limit had already been reached. As early as 1966, one NCA member complained that 90 percent of $175 million spent on plant expansion by the natural gas industry would flow to open-shop contractors.[46] In 1967, the NCA president, J. M. Graney (who two years later joined the Roundtable), began warning: "'We have no monopoly, and there are other ways in which these services can be provided.'"[47] He insisted that the industry's most pressing problems were all labor-related: declining productivity, excessive wage increases, labor shortages, and local union irresponsibility. Graney's principal recommendation called for dismantling union hiring halls and creation of independent referral systems operated by professional personnel administrators. The NCA president, however, also charged industrial owners with responsibility for labor shortages; in selecting

---

[44]Damon Stetson, "Builders and Unions Sign an Accord to Curb Strikes," *NYT*, Feb. 15, 1971, at 46, col. 5.

[45]An indirect suggestion of this resistance against labor intensification measures is found in an older study, which revealed that productivity in southern states almost uniformly exceeded that in the North and unit wage costs were significantly lower in the South. Since northern unions were much stronger, the differential productivity, especially in such technologically backward occupations as bricklaying, the capital equipment in which was presumably similar everywhere, may have reflected differential intensity. E. Stewart, "Labor Productivity and Costs in Certain Building Trades," 19 (5) *MLR* 1-15 (Nov. 1924).

[46]M. Lefkoe, *The Crisis in Construction: There Is an Answer* 8 (1970). Lefkoe did not identify the firm, which he apparently interviewed. Since Lefkoe did not begin his research until 1968, it is unclear why the firm referred to 1966 as in the future.

[47]"Graney Urges Contractor Unity," *ENR*, June 29, 1967, at 53.

new plant sites, they failed to pay attention to the labor market: "They overlook the fact that the mere availability of jobs will no longer attract skilled craftsmen from long distances...."[48]

The BCTD agreed in early 1970 to take unspecified steps to "strengthen the competitive positions" of its NCA-member employers, which had lost $7.5 billion in work to nonunion contractors in the previous two years.[49] But in mid-1970, the NCA joined the AGC and several specialty contractor associations in asking President Nixon to impose wage controls to "cool union demands" and protect the rest of the rest of the economy from "the spillover effects of exorbitant wage increases in construction." (The BCTD replied that it would accept wage controls if they were combined with those on prices, profits, and all incomes.)[50] By year's end, the NCA repeated the request.[51] In May 1972, R. Eric Miller, the president of the NCA, a vice-president of Bechtel, and the NCA's liaison with the Roundtable, warned the Operating Engineers convention that "the nonunion contractor in manhours per unit of work beats us [Bechtel] from 20 to 30 percent. That is not the wage rates—that is the number of manhours that it takes to do the work." Against the background of $36 billion in nonunion construction in 1971, he limned the possibility of future contracts providing for "effective grievance machinery to completely eliminate strikes and lockouts."[52]

These facts—or at least such perceptions—were a major reason for the expansion of the nonunion sector. The question here is whether similar tendencies were also observable within the NCA. In the first instance, its members focused on overcoming union resistance at the workplace. Thus in 1971, the NCA and the BCTD concluded an agreement to increase productivity through "uniform work rules" and to eliminate "costly and disruptive strikes and picketing." In March 1971, the NCA and each of its

---

[48]"Graney Calls for Impartial Hiring Halls," *ENR*, Nov. 30, 1967, at 103. *ENR* editorially supported Graney's proposal to remove hiring halls from unions' unilateral control: "Hiring and Wage Reform," *ENR*, Nov. 30, 1967, at 116.

[49]"General Presidents Seek to Develop Program to Strengthen Competitive Positions of Union Contractors and Craftsmen," 23 (2) *BCTB* (Feb. 1970) [no pagination] (quote); "'Summit Committee' Formed by Building Trades Department to Halt Spread of Nonunion Industrial Construction Work," *CLR*, No. 752, Feb. 18, 1970, at A-4.

[50]"Contractors Advocate Wage-Profit Curbs in Wire to President," *CLR*, No. 771, July 1, 1970, at A-1, A-2.

[51]"NCA Again Urges President to Impose Wage-Price Controls in Construction," *CLR*, No. 796, Dec. 23, 1970, at A-3.

[52]"NCA Chief Tells Engineers Convention Open Shop Contractors Are Making Headway," *CLR*, No. 866, May 3, 1972, at A-2, A-3.

member companies and the BCTD and its member unions entered into an agreement under which each union "shall as soon as practical incorporate" eleven specified work rules into its agreements with any of the NCA members, and "shall use its best efforts to require its affiliated local unions" with such collective bargaining agreements to incorporate these rules. Prominent among the work rules were: prohibitions on slowdowns, standby crews, featherbedding, illegal strikes and work stoppages, nonworking stewards, "limit on production by workmen" or "restrictions on the full use of tools or equipment" or "on the number of men assigned to any crew or any service; discouragement of overtime; and a requirement that "workmen shall be at their place of work at the starting time and shall remain at their place of work until quitting time."[53] Unions characterized the agreement as promoting organizing efforts "by making union shop contractors more competitive."[54]

To be sure, Postmaster General Winton Blount, himself a major contractor, quickly informed the Cabinet Committee on Construction that the agreement was not the "'historic breakthrough'" that the parties claimed it to be. Blount emphasized that the work rules had been written national union policy since 1958, which the national leadership had been unable to induce the locals to incorporate into their agreements; the internationals' lack of leverage gave Blount little reason to expect more success now.[55] This view was common. Two weeks later, John O'Connell, an official with Bechtel and the NCA, reported on the agreement to the CUAIR Coordinating Committee, emphasizing that "while the NCA would prefer to to be free to make assignments solely from the employers' points of view, they saw no alternative to the craft system in the construction industry and to try to make it work as efficiently as possible." To be sure, O'Connell insisted that the NCA had, as a result of owner surveys, diluted its demands with respect to closing down all relevant work during strikes for economic advantage and eliminating overtime except for emergencies. Predicting that some unions would resist complying, O'Connell explained that contractors and owners had to stand up to them: "Either these agreements will be made to work or the

---

[53]"Agreements with National Constructors Association on Uniform Work Rules and Jurisdictional Disputes," *CLR*, No. 806, Mar. 3, 1971, at C-1.

[54]Philip Shabecoff, "Builders, Unions to Revamp Rules," *NYT*, Mar. 3, 1971, at 1, col. 2, at 63, col. 1.

[55]Memorandum from Winton Blount to Members of the CCC (Mar. 5, 1971), in NACP, RG 174: General Records of the Labor Dept., Office of the Secretary, Records of Sec. James D. Hodgson, 1970-72, 1971, Box No. 105: Committees to Interdepartmental (Misc. to Construction Industry Stabilization), Folder: 1971-Committee: CCC.

NCA is out of business."[56] However, when the Plumbers union became the first to implement the incorporation in November 1971, the NCA president, Benjamin Frost, expressed disappointment that progress had been so slow.[57] Although the NCA refrained from joining the open-shop movement, it did at times use the threat.[58]

The following year, the NCA and the Plumbers entered into a new agreement designed to make the firms more competitive vis-à-vis nonunion companies. National firms were, for example, free to stop work to support local contractors involved in labor disputes. In explaining the union's reasons for acquiescing in the new realities, its general president, Martin Ward, came as close as anyone to predicting the future correctly when he observed that "many NCA members 'have begun to express a desire to return to the condition of the 1940's when the bulk of their operations were nonunion, or when they conducted a dual operation, building union only upon request of their clients.'" Ward suggested that his members' efforts to increase their productivity would determine "'whether this will be our last agreement or whether this work will continue to be done 100 percent by union craftsmen.'"[59] Later in 1972, Ward had become such a believer that he confided to a conference sponsored by *Business Week* that the increasingly cooperative relationship between industry and unions was in large part attributable to the new work rules. When "asked about the stress the construction unions have been putting on 'a fair day's work for a fair day's pay,' the president of the BCTD 'said it has been adapted from labor's slogan at the turn of the century when "a fair day's pay for a fair day's work" was the rallying cry for working men seeking increased pay. He said the present one is to encourage workers to put in their full eight hours at work, and not to extend lunch or coffee breaks.'"[60]

---

[56]CUAIR, CC, Minutes, Mar. 23, 1971, at 3, 5, in BR, 1971-Vol. II: Minutes.

[57]"NCA and UA Sign Addendum to Agreement Establishing Set of National Work Rules," *CLR*, No. 843, Nov. 17, 1971, at A-1. Five years later, the NCA was still urging adoption of a single national agreement for all major industrial projects to combat the open shop by combating work stoppages and setting high standards for skill and productivity." Building Trades, NCA Seek New Labor Pact Approaches," *ENR*, Aug. 26, 1976, at 49.

[58]Damon Stetson, "Builders and Unions Sign an Accord to Curb Strikes," *NYT*, Feb. 15, 1971, at 46, col. 5; "NCA Increases the Pressure to Cut the Fat Out of Labor Costs," *ENR*, Mar. 1, 1973, at 18.

[59]"National Constructors, United Association Execute Revised National Piping Agreement," *CLR*, No. 873, June 21, 1972, at X-1, X-2.

[60]"Construction Industry, Union Spokesmen Agree Cooperation Best in Years, Aids Productivity," *CLR*, No. 890, Oct. 18, 1972, at A-8, A-9.

Yet by the end of 1972, after three consecutive years of declining industrial construction "obviously reflecting an overall excess plant capacity,"[61] the NCA announced that the work rule agreement had lapsed because the majority of union presidents, though favoring the pact, deferred to the one or two who refused to execute the contract without modifications.[62] The agreement's potential for staving off nonunion competition was, however, too great for either side to permit it to die. Thus in 1973 the parties signed a new agreement obligating the unions to incorporate the work rules by May 31, 1974 into all contracts with NCA members, which covered 500,000 workers. Despite the inroads into worker control embodied in the new rules, the NCA president told the BCTD: "It is not the case of taking something out of the hide of labor. What we seek in making these agreements is simply a way of doing the job better."[63] Yet the 1973 National Productivity Pact between the NCA and the Laborers' International Union expressly prohibited "any organized coffee breaks, rest periods or other non-working time...during working hours."[64] To what extent the paper agreements were implemented was contested. At any rate, the NCA's dissatisfaction with the international unions' inability to impose the agreement on unwilling locals was bluntly expressed by its vice president: "'In this industry we do not enforce our agreements; until we do, we are not going to make any progress.'"[65]

More remarkable still was the statement by the BCTD president at the Council of Construction Employers' 1974 Construction Industry National Conference that employers should stop blaming unions for all their productivity problems. Frank Bonadio asserted: "Many of these problems...stemmed from business conditions during the Second World War and after, when contractors actually made money by hiring unnecessary manpower and making the government pay for it. 'You are the people who agreed to coffee breaks and high time,' he said to employers. 'We're both to blame for this condition. You gave it to us and we were happy to run with

---

[61] Abraham Goldblatt, "Construction in 1972," 19 (4) *CR* 4-9 at 5 (Apr. 1973).

[62] "NCA Calls Off Work Rules, Jurisdictional Pacts," *CLR*, No. 899, Dec. 20, 1972, at A-13.

[63] "Revised Work Rules Agreement Ratified by NCA and Building Trades Department," *CLR*, No. 941, Oct. 17, 1973, at A-21-A-23. Unlike the earlier agreement, it provided for final and binding arbitration of disputes. "Construction Accord Signed," *NYT*, Oct. 11, 1973, at 52, col. 5. See also "NCA-Union Pact in Houston Is Aimed at Open Shop," *ENR*, Nov. 15, 1973, at 85.

[64] "National Productivity Pact Ratified by National Constructors Association and Laborers Union," *CLR*, No. 948, Dec. 5, 1973, at F-1, F-2.

[65] *RR*, No. 74-5, at 4 (June 1, 1974).

it.'" But in the past few years, he added, "the unions have been active in knocking out coffee break and high time provisions in local agreements, and trying to make their employers more competitive in the face of open shop inroads. 'The unions have got to get off their rumps and do something about the nonunion contractor...but you contractors have to help.'"[66]

NCA members' dependence on union hiring halls may explain why the NCA failed to adopt more rigorous measures toward unions; these firms' extraordinarily heavy reliance on low-wage projects in the Third World may also have contributed to their relatively relaxed attitude toward unions in the United States.[67] Nevertheless, they did not abstain from urging the federal government to intervene against unions. The most eloquent testimony in this regard stemmed from Stephen Bechtel, the senior director of Bechtel Corporation, the largest and best known industrial and power plant construction firm in the United States and the world. At a meeting of the influential Business Council he argued that "the construction unions should be 'opened up.'" Such a course "included the elimination of racial restrictions in the construction unions and the use of the union card as a prerequisite for employment. It also meant doing away with restrictions on the types of jobs some unions are allowed to perform and with restrictions on prefabricated construction."[68]

These four issues reappeared again and again: (1) incorporating minorities into the construction labor supply; (2) eliminating union control over the labor market; (3) relaxing the rigid boundaries between skilled trades and/or unions; and (4) undermining union resistance to industrial construction methods. The last two points were geared toward preserving the sphere of management prerogatives, which employers regarded as especially beleaguered. As mechanisms for yielding extra profits for individual firms, the measures that would have implemented these developments could also have triggered concentration and centralization processes as well as disemployment, all of which could have depressed wages.

The NCA placed itself at odds with other leading management associations such as the NAM and Chamber of Commerce in late 1973 when

---

[66]"Construction Employers Discuss Legislation, Ending of Controls at Washington, D.C. Meeting," *CLR*, No. 965, Apr. 10, 1974, at A-7, A-10.

[67]Marc Linder, *Projecting Capitalism: A History of the Internationalization of the Construction Industry* 192 (1994).

[68]Albert Hunt, "Business Council's Inflation Gripes May Renew Nixon Leadership Issue," *WSJ*, Oct. 19, 1970, at 4, col. 1.

it called for a continuation of wage controls in construction through 1974 even after they had been removed in all other sectors. The NCA predicted that termination of the CISC would lead to "an inflationary...spiral of wages equal to or in excess of that during...1968-70." The organization argued macroeconomically that "industrial construction activities involving large scale energy facilities, environmental and pollution control facilities, and other heavy technological processes, in which NCA companies are primarily involved, may increase along with a rise in commercial construction in 1974, thereby placing new pressures on the wage structure."[69]

Government control of wages was not the only subject on which the NCA differed with other large employers' groups. The advantages and drawbacks of union hiring halls created such a complicated cost-benefit structure for employers that the NCA firms themselves could not formulate and adhere to a unitary position. Despite many members' view of hiring halls as indispensable, the NCA president in 1967 characterized as an urgently needed reform the removal from local union control of hiring halls and their reassignment to professional personnel administrators responsible to joint labor-management trustees.[70]

The NCA members were also at odds with their biggest customers, the members of the Roundtable, which in 1970 recommended that contractors vindicate their management rights by replacing union hiring halls with their own arrangements for gaining control over the labor supply. (The following year contractors began running a nonunion hiring hall in Houston.)[71] The union hiring hall admittedly relieved contractors of the need to operate their own personnel offices, but at what the Roundtable deemed an unacceptable price—enabling unions to become "the *de facto* employers with respect to most of the hiring, training, and placement functions, as well as the administration of non-wage benefits."[72] The principal managerial functions that construction unions, according to the Roundtable, had assumed encompassed:

---

[69]"Continuation of Wage and Price Controls Urged by National Constructors Association," *CLR*, No. 944, Nov. 7, 1973, at A-24, A-25.

[70]"Professional Administration of Hiring Halls Under Trusteeship Urged by NCA President," *CLR*, No. 614, June 28, 1967, at A-7, A-8.

[71]"Houston Contractors Use Nonunion Hiring Program," *NYT*, Aug. 28, 1976, at 24, col. 1.

[72]CUAIR, "Restoration of the Management Role in the Construction Industry" at 2 (Mar. 1970), in SP, Box 5, File-Construction Committee. The Roundtable self-published this report unchanged; BR, *Coming to Grips with Some Major Problems in the Construction Industry* 51-58 (1974).

a. Recruiting and selection of manpower, typically referred to as the "hiring function."

b. Identification of the training and development needs of the work force, often including the providing of training programs and other activities designed to meet those needs.

c. Assignment of employees to the tasks required to accomplish the operating objectives, or the "placement function."

d. Determination of the type and amount of work to be accomplished within a given period of time.

e. Compensation of employees for work performed or time committed, including both monetary and benefit forms of compensation.

f. Provision and administration of a disciplinary system to administer the penalty side of the "reward and penalty" system.

g. Direction of the work force through an established supervisory organization.[73]

In 1973 the NCA, once again declaring its commitment to unionized operations, opposed the replacement of union hiring halls by employer-controlled systems on the grounds that the Roundtable had failed to take into account the divergent circumstances under which national construction firms operate. On large and complex projects "in remote areas, far from established sources of manpower," the broadest forms of staffing were required, for which the NCA had found "the top officials of organized labor...to be the most effective and reliable" sources. Even in local labor markets 25 to 75 miles from a metropolitan center, NCA member-firms "'rarely have the luxury of having adequate numbers of local workers available due to the project size and tight schedule of requirements.'" The "'terrific'" labor turnover on long-term projects taking as long as ten years to complete was an exacerbating factor according to the NCA.[74] In contrast, the Roundtable not only encouraged large users such as utility companies to create their own construction subsidiaries, but welcomed nonunion contractors' efforts to improve their workers' training sufficiently to bid for large industrial projects.[75]

Underscoring its willingness to work with unions—which boasted that they were, "in effect, a 'hiring hall' run for the employer free of charge"[76]—the NCA in 1974 announced that it and the Plumbers had

---

[73]CUAIR, "Restoration of the Management Role in the Construction Industry" at 1 (Mar. 1970), in SP, Box 5, File-Construction Committee.

[74]"NCA Prefers Hiring Halls over Proposed Employer-Controlled Referral Arrangements," *CLR*, No. 945, Nov. 14, 1973, at A-12.

[75]"Industrial Construction Users Study Methods to Get Better Construction Value, Efficiency," *CLR*, No. 1000, Dec. 11, 1974, at A-20, A-22.

[76]"The Laborers' Champion: Through Five Fateful Decades," 3 (5) *Laborer* 5-7, 24 at 7 (May, 1949). For the thesis that hiring halls were not widely adopted in construction until the 1950s,

undertaken the first comprehensive national labor supply survey for the electrical utility construction sector, which accounted for about 5 percent of all construction workers, and lent itself to a seven-year projection because power plant construction required long lead times.[77] At the same time, the NCA announced a cooperative agreement with another group of union-shop contractors, the Contractors Mutual Association (CMA), to work toward wide-area coordinated collective bargaining, strengthening local contractors' bargaining position, and eliminating restrictive work practices.[78] *ENR* prematurely praised the link as "A Turning Point in Labor Relations," cautioning that the organizations were "not out to crack down on organized labor, whose future is inextricably tied to that of union contractors." Rather, the members were merely seeking "more economic labor relations policies and practices" that would make it possible for them to "stay in business as union contractors."[79]

The NCA belonged to various committees or groups whose aim was to strengthen employers' negotiating position vis-à-vis unions.[80] In 1975 the NCA urged a merger of the CMA and the Council of Construction Employers. (CCE). By dropping engineering-design capability as a criterion, the NCA made national industrial general contractors eligible to become members.[81] The CMA, a so-called horizontal organization of individual contractors, had been formed in May 1971 with support from the Roundtable and Blough, who wished to create an organization that would deal with all unionized sectors. The CMA, which was chaired by John O'Connell of Bechtel, was never able totally to remove the taint of being the users' creature. The CCE, a vertical organization of 10 associations representing 50,000 contractors, was founded in 1972 to become the counterpart of the BCTD. Viewed as the CMA's mainstream rival, it was dissolved in 1978

---

when the closed shop, which had been the chief vehicle for union control over hiring, was outlawed. Philip Ross, "Construction Hiring Halls: Origins and Development," 11 (3) *IR* 366-79 (Oct. 1972).

[77] "Study Shows 120,000 Construction Workers Needed to Build Power Plants Through 1980," *CLR*, No. 993, Oct. 23, 1974, at A-9.

[78] "CMA, NCA Announce Joint Cooperative Agreement, Plans to Unify Contractors," *CLR*, No. 994, Oct. 30, 1974, at A-6, A-7.

[79] "A Turning Point in Labor Relations," *ENR*, Nov. 7, 1974, at 68 (editorial).

[80] "Contractors Mutual Association Points Way to Contractor Unity," *ENR*, Sept. 12, 1974, at 16-17; "New Board Hopes to Improve Labor Relations," *ENR*, Oct. 10, 1974, at 61; "CMA, NCA Pioneer New Industry Group," *ENR*, Oct. 31, 1974, at 10.

[81] "NCA Ratifies CMA Relationship; Pulls Out of CCE," *ENR*, Feb. 6, 1975, at 221; "NCA President William R. Jones Seeks Better Labor Cost Control," *ENR*, Nov. 27, 1975, at 22-23.

after the creation of the National Construction Employers Council (NCEC), which the CMA supported. The AGC declined to join the CMA-NCA in 1974 because it viewed them as trying to expand the union sector at the expense of the nonunion sector, which would have placed the AGC as a mixed organization in a difficult situation; in 1976, however, a new AGC leadership led it into a trial participation, which resulted in the formation of the NCEC to develop policies concerning collective bargaining.[82]

National agreements, which by 1967 were increasingly coming under attack, were another important area in which the NCA was at loggerheads with other construction employers associations. One manifestation of such opposition was the proposed multi-employer certification bill, which would have given exclusive NLRA bargaining rights to a grouping of local contractors and would have barred any such contractor from honoring any national agreement with deviant provisions. Despite the fact that national contractors might employ a large majority of the local union's members, they would have lost all right to codetermine working conditions. When special trade contractors associations induced a Republican Senator to introduce the bill in 1967 making it an unfair labor practice under the NLRA for a construction industry employer having or seeking contractual relations with a local union to bargain outside the multi-employer representative selected by so-called area resident employers employing the largest number of workers in a particular trade, the NCA opposed it as "a direct attack on national agreements."[83]

In 1976, for the first time ever, the NCA participated directly in local bargaining. NCA members, users, and other national contractors—building a billion dollar nuclear powerplant at Hanford and othe projects—had locked out members of a UA pipefitters' local in Washington state to support the negotiating position of that state's Mechanical Contractors Associations. The NCA finally intervened to enter into the first nationally negotiated, multiproject agreement covering wages and working conditions because of the prolonged and total breakdown of local bargaining and requests by local

---

[82]DOL, *The Bargaining Structure in Construction* at 20-34; BR, CCH: 1971 (on O'Connell).

[83]"NCA Suggests Countermeasures to Fend Off Number of Attacks on National Contracts," *CLR*, No. 607, May 10, 1967, at A-8; S. 2796, 90th Cong., 1st Sess. (1967); "Multi-Employer Certification Bill Thrown into Congressional Hopper," *CLR*, No. 639, Dec. 20, 1967, at A-9, A-10 (quote). According to "Contractors Will Try to Change the Law on Bargaining," *ENR*, Dec. 8, 1966, at 68-69, the bill was also designed to prevent unions from engaging in whipsaw strikes. On multiemployer and regional collective bargaining legislation, see below chapter 12.

contractors. Significantly, at the end of the lockout, the UA continued its strike against local mechanical contractors into its sixth month.[84]

By the mid-1970s, despite all the innovative agreements with and concessions from unions, NCA members' competitive position was deteriorating rather than improving. In 1965, seven NCA members accounted for 69 percent of all domestic contracts awarded to the ten largest U.S. firms; ten years later, this share had fallen to 41 percent.[85] Whereas the organization reported that members had lost to open-shop firms 181 contracts worth $8.5 billion from 1969 to 1971—even declining to 78 and $7.2 billion between 1971 and 1973—by 1978 the figures had risen to 270 and $28.1 billion. Ominously, nonunion firms were gaining ground with respect to the NCA's biggest and technologically most sophisticated projects—petro-chemical and power plants. Most menacing of all was the geographic aspect: whereas until the mid-1970s the open shop firms' gains were largely confined to the Gulf Coast and Southeast, by the latter half of the 1970s they had invaded the West Coast, Mid-continent, and Great Lakes regions, leaving only the East Coast largely unscathed.[86]

Associated General Contractors of America

Our chief concern is to protect the local contractors who comply with the union scale against the unequal competition of employers who bring men from the country to work below it.[87]

The AGC was founded in 1918 by firms interested in war construction. The AGC formally supported the open shop as early as 1920, but the nature of its membership precluded enforcement: "Opportunism and expediency eclipsed principles in a very short time. Chicago and New York general contractors, working under ironclad closed-shop agreements, obviously disregarded such declarations...." The AGC's practical recognition of the closed shop was dictated by its support of the National Board for Jurisdictional Awards, "a premise of whose very existence was the principle

---

[84]"Nationally Negotiated Wage Pact Ends Five-Month Lockout," *ENR*, Dec. 16, 1976, at 49.

[85]Linder, *Projecting Capitalism* at 192.

[86]Northrup, *Open Shop Construction Revisited* at 209-11. Although Northrup published chronologically continuous data in graph form, his tables states that data were lacking for 1973-77.

[87]"Building Trade Mechanics," 8 (21) *BJA* 165 (May, 26, 1888) (from a N.Y. *Daily News* interview with a walking delegate of the United Order of American Carpenters and Joiners).

of the closed shop." As a result, the AGC restricted itself in its early years to codes of ethics, trade practices, standardization, the elimination of day labor on public works, and reforming mechanics' lien laws.[88] Even during the 1930s, the AGC was more focused on the question of government competition in construction than on labor relations.[89] Its ability to form alliances with the building trades unions was nicely captured by their cooperation in the early 1950s to combat attempts by industrial unions to promote vertical integration by limiting the volume of construction that industrial firms contracted out so that such work could be preserved for their own members.[90]

At the 1968 National Conference on Construction Problems, John Garvin, a labor relations consultant, observed that the AGC had undermined its own efficacy in forging labor policies by virtue of its dual union and nonunion membership. Since the latter actually gained from instability in the organized sector, he suggested that the organization be bifurcated.[91] The following year, when the AGC held its first national open shop conference, its membership was already 35 percent nonunion.[92] By the early 1970s, as the AGC established an open-shop labor relations service, its members numbered over 9,000 firms, of which the nonunion section had recently risen sharply. Many of these nonunion firms originated from the practice of double breasting—that is, unionized firms' "setting up a separate non-union or open-shop company run by the same management that's running the unionized firm."[93] In the 1970s and 1980s these dual-shop firms became major streams of the open shop movement, which unions had little success in combating as unfair labor practices under the NLRA.[94]

An important determinant of the AGC's increasingly nonunion orientation derived from the competitive pressures to which its members were exposed. In terms of size, AGC firms occupied a position between the NCA

---

[88]Haber, *Industrial Relations in the Building Industry* at 455-56, 88.

[89]Booth Mooney, *Builders for Progress* 54, 64, 78, 82 (1965).

[90]"Vertically-Formed Unions Industry Threat," 34 (10) *The Constructor* 33 (Oct. 1952); Mooney, *Builders for Progress* at 130.

[91]"Management Conference Backs Wide-Ranging Program to Curb Construction Labor Costs," *CLR*, No. 687, Nov. 20, 1968, at A-9-A-14 at A-13.

[92]"The Open Shop Voice Grows Loud and Clear," *ENR*, Nov. 27, 1969, at 44-46.

[93]"AGC Prods Nixon and Paves Way to Industry Labor Reform," *ENR*, Mar. 18, 1971, at 55, 56; Bill Paul, "Nonunion Contractors Winning Sizable Share of Construction Work," *WSJ*, July 7, 1972, at 1 col. 6, at 15, col. 1.

[94]See below chapter 15.

members and the industry-wide average. Deprived of the advantages of scale and scope of the NCA firms, on the one hand, and of the lower wage costs and expanded managerial prerogatives of the growing nonunion sector on the other, the AGC's higher-profile antiunion position became more and more rational especially as it own nonunion membership grew. That the typical AGC member was not a national firm, as was the case with the NCA, brought about a readiness and/or necessity to demand decisive state intervention; for it was precisely the locally operating firms, which were embedded in splintered collective bargaining units, vis-à-vis which well-organized workers often enjoyed a certain negotiating advantage, that stood in greatest need of state assistance.

The self-paralyzing fissures within the AGC were amply on display in 1968 when a group of AGC chapters, representing 30 percent of the total membership and 50 percent of union-firm membership, sought to persuade the organization to support multiemployer regional bargaining. These contractors, initially based in the Northeast and Midwest, opposed national or project agreements (such as the NCA's) and proposed requiring AGC union-firm members to "join with the historically established multi-employer bargaining unit in the local, state or regional area in which the work is being performed." The group also wanted to create a permanent committee to keep the NAM, as an organization of users, informed of "unrealistic wage settlements and onerous conditions in the construction industry" and to secure their "cooperation and support in achieving fair and equitable settlements."[95] This group failed to become a majority within AGC, but the Roundtable soon arose to offer the cooperation and support it had imagined coming from the NAM. The AGC at its 1968 annual convention declined to go farther than endorsing a multiemployer construction industry congressional bill and only with regard to its ban on unions' "whipsaw tactics"; the AGC voted to censure, but not to punish, members that continued to operate during local AGC strikes pursuant to no-strike clauses in national agreements.[96]

Without accusing the local building trades unions of engaging in a national conspiracy to demand large wage increases, the AGC in 1969 proposed the adoption of a national stabilization agreement under which unions would pledge not to strike.[97] By 1971 the AGC adopted the position

---

[95]"Local Groups Seek Management Unity," *ENR*, Mar. 14, 1968, at 87, 88 (quote); "AGC Leaves Biggest Issue Hanging," *ENR*, Apr. 4, 1968, at 29.

[96]"AGC Leaves Biggest Issue Hanging," *ENR*, Apr. 4, 1968, at 29.

[97]"AGC Seeking National Stabilization Agreement to Curb Threat of 'Run-Away Wage

"that the strike and the picket line to enforce wage demands 'are no longer acceptable in this country.'" It sought to support this demand through a common expiration date for all construction labor agreements and binding arbitration.[98] This objective it shared with the Regional Congress of Construction Employers, a group formed in 1969 of 700 contractors in western New York, western Pennsylvania, northern West Virginia, southern Michigan, and all of Ohio. It believed that a common expiration date for all collective bargaining agreements would prevent unions from playing one employer off against another or from finding work for their members during strikes. They claimed to welcome the attendant risk of very large strikes: whereas hundreds of small strikes failed to capture public attention, one "big regional strike, crippling construction over a wide area," might prompt beneficial federal intervention.[99]

The AGC president in 1973, Nello Teer, Jr., a nonunion contractor, praised "fear of nonunion competition [a]s the major factor in keeping wage demands down." For Teer the "[o]pen shop has become a viable and essential component of our national AGC, and is the only proven restraint we have to the irresponsible greed of organized labor. While CISC is due much credit for cooling off the gross demands of the building trades, we know the only truly effective long-range influence has been the prospect of loss of jobs due to open shop operations."[100] This evaluation was similar to, if not identical with, that of the Roundtable[101] and of D. Quinn Mills, a leading academic-bureaucrat wage regulator: "It cannot be doubted that the growth of nonunion construction contributed to an economic environment...favorable

Inflation,'" *CLR*, No. 709, Apr. 23, 1969, at A-1.

[98]"AGC's Healy Calls Strike Outmoded Weapon, Offers Six-Point Settlement Plan," *CLR*, No. 835, Sept. 22, 1971, at A-14.

[99]James Gannon, "Industry Quietly Forms Group to Curb Spiral of Construction Costs," *WSJ*, Aug. 14, 1969, at 1, col. 6, at 16, col. 1. See also "Plan to Develop Regional Congress of Management Groups is Launched," *CLR*, No. 675, at A-1 (Aug. 28, 1968); "Regional group Gets Management Unity," *ENR*, Aug. 29, 1968, at 100. One of the group's chief goals by late 1969 was cooperating with the CUAIR. "Regional Congress Sets 1970 Goals, Returns Officers for Another Term," *CLR*, No. 745, at A-6-A-7 (Dec. 31, 1969).

[100]"AGC Convention Stresses 'Contractor Power,' Job Site , More Open Shop Services," *CLR*, No. 911, Mar. 21, 1973, at A-6, A-7.

[101]In a letter sent to its entire membership, the Roundtable stated that the decline in collectively bargained first-year wage and benefit increases in construction from 14.1 percent in 1971 to 6.9 percent in the first half of 1973 was "due principally to the efforts of the...CISC..., the continued growth of open shop competition, the rising influence of local user groups, and the spread of coordinated industry bargaining endorsed by the Roundtable." Letter from John Harper and G. Wallace Bates (Oct. 5, 1973), in SP, Box 6, File-Business Roundtable General.

to wage restraint and thereby to CISC's activities. However...it is unlikely that the impact of nonunion construction was, in the absence of a controls program, of sufficient magnitude to restrain increases in average hourly earnings to a large extent."[102]

The AGC also staked out a different position than the NCA with regard to contracts between owner and contractor giving the former the right to require the latter to work through strikes. Although the AGC advocated project agreements giving the contractor the right to shut down construction affecting workers from unions on strike against a local employer bargaining group, the growing popularity among owners of the first kind of agency agreement was seen as eventually resulting in "AGC members being forced to employ strikers while their chapter is taking a strike. Each owner...makes a determination whether the position of the local employer bargaining group is justified in light of his own interests." The AGC was concerned with the increase in the number of "owners taking over the right of the contractor to determine his own course of action should a strike against the local employer bargaining group occur."[103] And more generally, the AGC, while urging users to aid contractors, "warned against users combining to 'dictate the terms of the relationship between the contractor and his employees.'"[104]

The increasingly antiunion composition and orientation clearly imprinted itself on the organization's refusal to join the CMA-NCA alliance in 1974: "'AGC cannot support any plan which has as one of its main purposes the enlargement of the market for unionized contractors at the expense of those contractors who work without collective bargaining agreements.'"[105]

The AGC's ambivalence toward unions prompted Labor Secretary Dunlop to call it a "'schizoid organization' in which its member union contractors are overruled by its member nonunion builders."[106] This

---

[102]D.Q. Mills, "Explaining Pay Increases in Construction: 1953-1972," 13 (2) *IR* 196-201 at 200 (May 1972).

[103]"Associated General Contractors Staff Report on Current Labor Activities," *CLR*, No. 962, Mar. 20, 1974, at F-1, F-2-F-3.

[104]CUAIR, *Report*, No. 72-2, at 3 (June 22, 1972) (William Dunn, exec. vice pres., AGC, at CUAIR's annual meeting).

[105]*ENR*, Nov. 14, 1974, at 3.

[106]"Dunlop Statement on H.R. 5900," *CLR*, No. 1052, Dec. 17, 1975, at AA-12. The occasion was the AGC's opposition to enactment of the situs picketing bill. See below chapter 14. Two decades later, the Arizona AGC chapter finally put an end to this state of affairs by consolidating with the ABC chapter. Mary Powers, "Groups Grappling with Training," *ENR*, Feb. 26, 1996, at 9.

ambivalence toward unions extended to state intervention as well. In 1966 the AGC did "not want more federal controls but [wa]s fearful of the 'unrestrained power' exercised by local unions." Because the AGC "didn't think the union internationals [we]re 'in sympathy' with the 'excessive' wage demands made by their local affiliates," it urged the implementation of binding adjudication of local contract disputes by the AGC and the international unions—a plan that had been thwarted since 1961 by the resistance of local unions.[107]   Yet in 1975, when Congress passed a Construction Industry Collective Bargaining bill along very similar lines, the AGC's opposition helped induce a fatal presidential veto.[108]

Associated Builders and Contractors

It is the profit that is achieved during the eight hour working day that allows the worker not to work during the remaining sixteen hours of the day.[109]

The Associated Builders and Contractors, which was founded in the early 1950s, was (and remains) the principal organizational expression of the open-shop movement.[110]   From a few hundred members in the 1950s, it expanded rapidly to almost 5,000 by 1972 and more than 10,000 by 1976.[111] The antiunion movement had originated largely as a southern phenomenon,

---

[107]"National Machinery to Mediate Local Contract Disputes Goes to Union Chiefs for Discussion Later This Month," *CLR*, No. 542, Feb. 2, 1966, at A-11, A-12.

[108]"AGC Prepares for Senate Floor Fight over Situs Picketing Bill," *CLR*, No. 1042, Oct. 8, 1975, at A-22, A-23. See below chapter 14.

[109]Joseph LaMonaca, "The President's Letter," *The Contractor*, Nov. 1972, at 2. This article was enclosed in a letter that J. M. Graney, the Roundtable's executive director-construction, sent to Roger Blough, Virgil Day, Douglas Soutar, William Murphy (chairman of the Roundtable), and John Post (executive director). One paragraph of the printed version of the article, which was written by the president of the ABC and appeared in its magazine, was marred by a typographical error; Graney's letter consisted almost exclusively of the corrected version quoted in the text. Letter from J. M. Graney (Dec. 7, 1972), in SP, Box 5, File-CUAIR.

[110]"The Open Shop Voice Grows Loud and Clear," *ENR*, Nov. 27, 1969, at 44-46; Northrup & Foster, *Open Shop Construction* at 18-20; John Trimmer, "Talk to American Subcontractors Association, Mar. 19, 1976, Atlanta, Georgia"; *idem*, "ABC: Profile of Philosophy," *MSC*, Jan. 1976, at 15-16, 30; Feb. 1976, at 10-12; Mar. 1976, at 10-13; Apr. 1976, at 4-6, 25; May 1976, at 8-10; June 1976, at 8-9, 21; July 1976, at 27, 29; Aug. 1976, at 25-26; Sept. 1976, at 9, 28-29; Oct. 1976, at 23-25.

[111]Bourdon and Levitt, *Union and Open-Shop Construction* at 115. By 1998, membership exceeded 21,000 firms. http//:www.abc.org.

but as early as 1967 the BCTD declared that if the nonunion sector's rapid growth continued, it would gain national scope.[112] By 1971 nonunion firms accounted for approximately 32 percent of all nonresidential industrial construction activity—a doubling in just two years.[113]

By mid-1972, the business press frequently reported that union labor's high wages and productivity restraints had enabled nonunion contractors to push beyond their southern and southwestern rural origins into northern suburbs and even well-organized cities,[114] although even later in the decade nonunion construction remained far more entrenched in the South.[115] The movement's openly political and quasi-conspiratorial side was conspicuous when some chemical and petroleum company users, especially in the South, "not wanting unionized personnel on the premises, limit[ed] their bids to open shop contractors as a means of encouraging the plant employees to remain nonunion."[116] The open shop's 1974 move into such a "union stronghold" as Westchester County bordering on New York City was ominous.[117]

Its expansion into the key sector of technologically sophisticated large-scale industrial construction outside the South was one of the greatest achievements of the Roundtable and its corporate members.[118] The

---

[112]"Union-Government Consultation, Not Conflict, on Tough Issues Urged at BTD Convention," *CLR*, No. 637, Dec. 6, 1967, at A-1, A-6.

[113]Bill Paul, "Nonunion Contractors Winning Sizable Share of Construction Work," *WSJ*, July 7, 1972, at 1, col. 6; "Asserting the Public Interest," *WSJ*, July 31, 1973, at 20, col. 1 (editorial). See also "Situs Picketing Legislation Faces Some Obstacles," *ENR*, June 12, 1975, at 8. On the predominantly nonunion residential sector, see Howard Foster, *Manpower in Homebuilding* (1974).

[114]"Labor Letter," *WSJ*, May 30, 1972, at 1, col. 5; "Open Shops Build Up in Construction," *BW*, July 1, 1972, at 14-15; Bill Paul, "Nonunion Contractors Winning Sizable Share of Construction Work, *WSJ*, July 7, 1972, at 1, col. 6.

[115]In 1975, the ratio of open shop contract volume to open and union volume was 69 percent in the South; the next highest ratio, 22 percent, was recorded for the area from Mississippi River to the Rockies, while the Midwest and Far West recorded 4 and 5 percent respectively. "Open Shop Survey Shows Penetration at the Top," *ENR*, May 27, 1976, at 8-9.

[116]Northrup, *Open-Shop Construction Revisited* at 221.

[117]*ENR*, Nov. 7, 1974, at 3. See also "Union Contractors Sound Alarm on Open Shop Growth," *ENR*, Apr. 4, 1974, at 41 (nonunion firms had pervaded many urban areas in New York).

[118]Asked to identify the greatest contributory factor to the unions' decline, Mills unhesitatingly named the Roundtable and its success in inducing industrial firms to use nonunion contractors to build their facilities outside the South. Telephone interview with Daniel Quinn Mills, Harvard Business School (Jan. 4, 1999). Dunlop appears to be unique in responding "not much" to a question as to what the Roundtable had achieved with regard to combating construction unions. Telephone interview with John T. Dunlop, Harvard University (Jan. 7, 1999).

movement received an especially crucial initial boost when du Pont, which until 1970 had performed its construction under union shops, concluded that its construction costs were too high and began awarding contracts to three large and old antiunion firms, Brown & Root, Daniel International, and H. B. Zachry. By 1973-74, nonunion firms accounted for half of du Pont's $700 million of construction, which employed 10,000 employees.[119] Du Pont also promoted the open-shop's long-term viability by working with nonunion contractors to develop local training programs.[120]

As the "largest amalgam of nonunion employers in the country," ABC experienced "phenomenal growth" that "forced the unionized sector of the industry to make changes and concessions that might not otherwise have happened." Since this movement originated as a reaction against rising labor costs, it is hardly surprising that the underlying wage and productivity factors were the targets: "A.B.C. uses the so-called merit shop, under which the employer pays workers according to their skill and productivity instead of giving an equal wage to all workers in a certain trade, as is done under union contracts."[121] Indeed, ABC's chairman proudly announced the open shop's attraction: "owners have begun to realize that in today's construction market the only flexible cost left is labor."[122] Although "[o]pen-shop contractors emphasize that their success doesn't come from exploiting workers," their proof was Pickwickian: their wages and benefits were lower, but "annual take-home pay generally runs higher" because they provide more hours of work.[123]

---

[119]"Open Shop Contractors Gird to Meet Growing Demand," *ENR*, Nov. 22, 1973, at 43; Northrup, *Open-Shop Construction Revisited* at 220. See also "ABC Convention Unwraps New Manpower Programs," *CLR*, No. 945, Nov. 14, 1973, at A-8, A-9. Even when it used union-shop firms, DuPont was "probably unique" in designing its own plants, managing its own construction, and designing its own technology. *RR*, No. 74-11, at 2 (Nov. 1974). Only about one-quarter of du Pont's own employees were unionized. Corporate Date Exchange, *Labor Relations: A Company-Union Guide* 14 (1982) (data from late 1970s).

[120]*CUH*, May 1975, at 5.

[121]"'Merit Shop' Fight Ends in Michigan," *NYT*, July 22, 1973, at 32, col. 3-5 at 5.

[122]"ABC Says Inflation Is a Factor in Its Rapid Growth," *ENR*, Oct. 10, 1974, at 12 (quoting Philip Abrams)..

[123]Gilbert Burck, "A Time of Reckoning for the Building Trades," *Fortune*, June 4, 1979, at 82, 85. "A Fair Day's Pay for No Work," *WSJ*, Apr. 23, 1973, at 12, col. 1 at 2 (editorial), argued that "the most conscientious, productive union worker...inevitably will find it more rewarding to work full time in a nonunion shop, coming out ahead financially even at a lower hourly rate of pay." The Bricklayers union opposed an annual wage plan in the 1930s because it would have guaranteed only (say) 300 days work for $2,000 instead of $1,500 for 150 days. "The Annual Wage Plan," 41 (6) *BMP* 91-93 (June 1938).

By 1973, charging that the BCTD unions were enagaged in a nationwide conspiracy to use coercion and to force ABC members out of business, the organization filed complaints with the NLRB seeking injunctions and compensation on behalf of their members' employees who had allegedly lost wages.[124]   That year ABC achieved one of its most important victories in northern Michigan, where a Houston, Texas nonunion firm gained a contract to build a $12 million natural gas processing plant for Shell Oil Company.   After construction unions established an informational picket at the site of the first major industrial contract performed in Michigan by a nonunion contractor in many years, battles broke out between pickets and the workers, half of whom were from the South and Southwest. The building trades' fading position was underscored by the UAW's decision not to supplement its moral support with money or staff. *Business Week* linked this decision to the fact that the UAW's vice president Douglas Fraser had recently "smothered a demand by his own skilled workers for wage parity with outside building tradesmen by pointing out that construction unions have opened the door to nonunion contractors by pricing themselves out of the market."[125] ABC's injunction suit was resolved on the basis that "in the most heavily unionized state in the nation, a union group has agreed to let hard-hats work alongside what they have denounced as 'scab' labor at less than union scale.   Normally union members doing this would be subject to union disciplinary action."[126]

ABC's unabashedly proemployer view of the NLRA's purpose is exemplified by its claim that: "'All we ask for is that an employer and a worker have the right to choose.'"[127] In fact, labor law, even the lopsidedly proemployer Taft-Hartley Act, accords the employer no right to choose whatsoever: if its employees choose a union, the employer must recognize and bargain with it.

How the open-shop movement contemplated securing the requisite labor emerges from its challenge to the ABC members to orient their

---

[124]"Open Shop Lawsuit Seeks Labor Board Curb on Union Violence," *ENR*, May 24, 1973, at 8-9; "Halting Violence at Building Sites," *BW*, July 13, 1974, at 68 (NLRB dismissed charges); "Union Violence Heads for Trial After NLRB Charges Reduced," *ENR*, June 27, 1974, at 8.

[125]"Builders Fight the Federation," *BW*, July 7, 1973, at 54.

[126]"'Merit Shop' Fight Ends in Michigan," *NYT*, July 22, 1973, at 32, col. 3 at 4. On early concessions by unions on work rules in response to open-shop advances, see "Building Trades Take a New Tack," *BW*, Oct. 20, 1973, at 106.

[127]Sherrie Winston, "Building Trades Sharpen Skills, Toughen Tactics and Organize," *ENR*, Sept. 1, 1997, at 28 (Lexis).

employment policy toward "a new breed of workers whose goals and needs are substantially different from those of the previous generation. No longer...are young men interested in job and economic security. Rather...they view work as a necessary evil or a means toward achieving other self-oriented goals. At the same time...this group of 18 to 25-year-olds can be more quickly trained and are promotable at a faster pace than the old steeds of the earlier workforce."[128] The construction industry accommodated the demand for such workers by producing a large mass of unemployed—"a reserve of crafts willing to work 'temporarily' on nonunion projects." Decisive in this context was not so much the direct pressure on wages as the increased "productivity," which stemmed from the fact the new workers forwent "the ordinary contractual limits on what and how much a craftsman can do."[129] Here the insecurity triggered by increasing unemployment fostered productivity. During the 1957-58 recession, for example, "many construction workers have, in fact, been working more assiduously...thus increasing their productivity. Builders regard this as an incidental benefit of the current economic dip and a reflection of the efforts of each worker to demonstrate his individual skill and value, and thus minimize his chances of being laid off if construction work suffers any marked decline in volume."[130]

Such short-sighted recruitment and employment practices shed light on the coordinate wage strategies. U.S. labor economists tend to regard the craft wage formation process as an exception: "Historically, craft wage rates have been governed by the general value of a skill rather than by the economic circumstances of a particular industry or by the actual work performed. The employer is essentially paying for the whole reservoir of talents possessed by a qualified journeyman. From the management point of view this practice has made it difficult to realize savings from technological change when crafts monopolize certain work; for while the job content may be altered, the price of labor remains the same."[131] This description may

[128]"The Open Shop Voice Grows Loud and Clear," *ENR*, Nov. 27, 1969, at 44-46 at 45.

[129]"Open Shops Building Up in Construction," *BW*, July 1, 1972, at 14.

[130]Stephen Thompson, "The Rise of Building Productivity," 108 (5) *Architectural Forum* 104 (May 1958). See generally, Sumner Slichter, *Union Policies and Industrial Management* 165 (1941). The unemployment rate among construction workers rose to 13.7 percent in 1958. BLS, *Compensation in the Construction Industry: Employment Patterns, Union Scales and Earnings* 27 (Bull. 1656, 1970); *idem, The Construction Worker in the United States* 31 (1959). Some employers openly admitted the therapeutic effect of the reserve army of the unemployed; e.g., "Construction Workers—How Many and at What Wages?" *ENR*, Feb. 7, 1946, at 187-90 at 189.

[131]Margaret Chandler, "Craft Bargaining," in *Frontiers of Collective Bargaining* 60 (John

simply reflect the fact that the dequalification processes associated with the development of the productive forces in other industries failed to dominate construction; in other words, construction unions' "monopoly power" was able to prevent the devaluation of their members labor power because "the job content" was not transformed.

The chief competitive advantage that union-free construction firms have claimed is precisely the compression of the wage structure by eliminating the new production of or ceasing to recognize the existence of the "whole reservoir of talents" in their employees. By specializing and deskilling their workers, employers are in a position to pay only for a much narrower range skills that cost less to produce. The open-shop movement then took the logically next step in this cost-saving program—the transition to piece rates. Building trades unionists, who throughout the twentieth century successfully combated piece-rate work because it "destroys that feeling of comradeship between man and man, which is the corner stone of true brotherhood and manhood,"[132] regarded uniform time wages as "the ultimate expression of solidarity within the trade," because piecework, "[w]ithout any built-in limit on earnings," induced workers to "drive themselves mercilessly...." The accompanying unsustainable celebration of younger workers' present strength over their long-term health insured the high turnover rates and labor shortages that have continued to plague nonunion employers.[133]

Dunlop & Neil Chamberlain eds., 1967).

[132]"Piecework Is Wasteful and Dishonest," 27 (12) *BMP* 266 (Dec. 1924). See generally, David McCabe, *The Standard Rate in American Trade Unions* 190-99 (1912). As early as 1890, only 5 percent of painters, fewer than 2 percent of carpenters and masons, and and fewer than 1 percent of plumbers were pieceworkers compared to 18 of all industrial workers and 13 percent of all males over sixteen years. U.S. Census Office, *Report on Manufacturing Industries in the United States at the Eleventh Census: 1890*, pt. I, tab. 4 at 94-107 (1895). The argument that the non-standardized output in construction precludes piece rates is refuted by its use in a number of Western European countries. See Ludwig Bernhard, *Die Akkordarbeit in Deutschland* 69-91 (1903); Walter Galenson, *Labor in Norway* 218 (1949); "Payments by Results in the Building Industry," 63 (1) *ILR* (Jan. 1951); V. Allen, "Incentives in the Building Industry," 62 (147) *EJ* 595-608 (Sept. 1952); P. A. Stone & W. Reiners, "Organisation and Efficiency of the House-Building Industry in England and Wales," 2 (2) *JIE* 118-34 (1953-54); R. C. Sansom, *Organization of Building Sites* 55-76 (Nat. Bldg. Studies, Spec. Rep. No. 29, 1960); Georg Meyer-Keller, *Leistungslohn im Baubetrieb* (1967); *Murerforbundet I Danmark gennem 75 år* 51 (1962). Unions' preference for piece wages in some European countries casts doubt on the claim that unions there were simply not strong enough to forbid it. John Dunlop, *Industrial Relations Systems* 260 (1958).

[133]Erlich, *With Our Hands* at 226, 191. But see John Dunlop, "Labor-Management Relations," in *Design and the Production of Houses* 275 (Burnham Kelly ed., 1959): "The flat hourly

Even a brief account of the open-shop movement makes clear that its proposals for restructuring the construction industry would have to be significantly different from those emanating from the sectors working with unions. Whereas the NCA and AGC demanded measures that strengthened their negotiating position vis-à-vis unions, the ABC sought to impede union countermeasures, for merely ignoring them would have tended to bring about violent reactions. Consequently, what antiunion firms required in the first instance was not so much new state initiatives, but judicial rulings that would put an end to the physical offensive that union workers had organized at many open-shop building sites. To be sure, the police anticipated the judges.[134]

These contradictory tendencies were expressed, for example, in the fact that, on the one hand, the various groupings found a common basis in the creation of a "single voice" for construction—the National Construction Industry Council founded in 1974-75.[135] As early as 1972 the CCE, formed by national employer associations, had warned: "'Before controls on our industry are lifted we must find ways to improve the balance between management and labor, and ways to improve productivity and to stabilize our labor relations.... The industry cannot survive chaos revisited."[136] On the other hand, serious difference of opinion among the members emerged at the

---

rate tends to create dissatisfactions in a work crew composed of men of varying skill, experience and pace of work because the lower productivity of the newer or less skilled groups limits the earnings of the more experienced."

[134]On these actions and their judicial sequels, see "Labor Letter," *WSJ*, May 30, 1972, at 1, col. 5; "Open Shop Lawsuit Seeks Labor Board Curb on Union Violence," *ENR*, May 24, 1973, at 8-9; "Builders Fight the Federation," *BW*, July 7, 1973, at 54; "Halting Violence at Building Sites," *BW*, July 13, 1974, at 68; "Union Violence Heads for Trial After NLRB Charges Are Reduced," *ENR*, June 27, 1974, at 8; "Violence Strikes an Open Shop Project," *ENR*, Sept. 5, 1974, at 9; "Michigan Building Trades Agree to Halt Violence," *ENR*, Feb. 13, 1975, at 9; "Rebutting Lawsuits, AGC Denies Promoting Open Shop," *ENR*, Feb. 27, 1975, at 41; *WSJ*, June 3, 1975, at 8; "Labor Riots Kill One, Injure Four," *ENR*, Jan. 22, 1976, at 19. The current president of the NCA argues that although some violence did occur, it never became a significant obstacle to the expansion of nonunion employers, who blew it out of proportion for propagandistic purposes. Telephone interview with Robert McCormick, Washington, D.C. (Mar. 11, 1999).

[135]"The Construction Industry May Soon Develop a Single Voice,"*ENR*, Aug. 8, 1974, at 17.

[136]"Industry Paves Way to Management Unity," *ENR*, May 10, 1973, at 55. Among the members of the CCE were the AGC, NAHB, and various special trade associations such as the National Roofing Contractors Association. See also "CCE Is Helping Local Bargaining Groups," *ENR*, Nov. 28, 1974, at 45.

very first meetings with regard to labor relations.[137] Shortly before the AGC had rejected collaboration with the NCA on the grounds that it could not support any plan that was designed to expand the unionized market at the expense of nonunionized firms.[138]

Only the intervention of large industrial capital could break such an impasse.

Wage-Intensity and Employer Organization

"Remember, we can only command our present wage levels as long as we dominate the labor market with adequate numbers of better skilled workers with a higher productivity factor."[139]

To reach conclusions concerning the formation and behavior of employers' associations in the various construction sectors it is instructive to examine how large wages bulked in the total production costs of firms in the industrial construction sector. It is plausible, for example, that a firm/branch with a relatively low share of wage costs could afford to be 'generous' toward its workers since wage increases would 'force' price rises less than would equal percentage wage increases in firms/branches with higher wage shares; conversely, high-wage-share branches would be more vulnerable to wage increases and might be expected to adopt a hard-line approach toward unions.[140]

Table 18 shows wages paid to production workers in construction as a share of production costs.

---

[137]"National Construction Industry Council Is Born in Washington," *ENR*, Jan. 30, 1975, at 8-9.

[138]*ENR*, Nov. 14, 1974, at 3. See also "Federal Construction Office Gets NCIC Backing," *ENR*, Feb. 27, 1975, at 8-9; "NCIC Rejects Liaisons with Unions," *ENR*, May 27, 1976, at 9-10.

[139]"Haggerty Cites Manpower Needs," *ENR*, Aug. 28, 1969, at 109 (BCTD president speaking at Painters convention).

[140]Accounts of German construction employers' organizations confirm this point for the nineteenth and twentieth century. E. Reuss, *Die Verbände der Bauindustrie, ihr Werden, Wesen und Wirken* 24-25 (1966); Karl-Gustav Werner, *Organisation und Politik der Gewerkschaften und Arbeitgeberverbände in der deutschen Bauwirtschaft* 203-204 (1968).

			Assets
Sub-Sector	Wages (%)	Workers	($000)

Table 18: Construction Worker Wages as a % of Production Costs, and Construction Workers and Gross Book Value of Depreciable Assets per Establishment, 1972

Sub-Sector	Wages (%)	Workers	Assets ($000)
All	35	8	53
Single-family houses	21	4	27
Other residential	29	12	52
Highway-street	32	26	504
Special trades	41	7	29
Heavy	36	29	265
Industrial	33	15	73
Commercial	34	13	58

Source: USBC, *1972 CCI, Industry Series: United States Summary*, tab. B1 & B2, and tab. 2 of Industry Series Reports. Production costs include total payroll of all workers, depreciation charges on fixed assets, rental payments for machinery and equipment, and materials, components, and supplies; only establishments with payroll are included.

The average for all sectors was 35 percent and overall the subsectors displayed little dispersion with regard to wage-intensity. Even the heavy (not elsewhere classified) and industrial sectors, in which NCA members operated, were located close to the average at 36 and 33 percent respectively. Only single-family housing (21 percent) and special trades (41 percent) lay far from the other sectors, whose clustering between 29 and 36 percent was unlikely to explain any differences in labor policies. Indeed, the single-family housing sector was the least organized although its major building contractor association, the National Association of Home Builders, did not play a conspicuous role in the open-shop movement and generally maintained a low labor relations profile since unions displayed little interest in organizing residential building workers.[141] In the special trades, whose wage share was highest, the degree of unionization was also high—more than 60

---

[141]Michael Sumichrast & Sara Frankel, *Profile of the Builder and His Industry*, tab. 60 at 203 (1970); Foster, *Manpower in Building* at 42-48; Northrup & Foster, *Open Shop Construction* at 49-71, 19-20.

percent in 1969, reaching as high as 67 percent in plumbing and 77 percent in electrical work[142]—and a number of national contractor associations traditionally employed union members under firmly institutionalized collective bargaining mechanisms.[143]

One of the explanatory difficulties is the complex interaction between cause and effect. The low degree of unionization in residential building, for example, contributed to the sub-sector's below-average wages. In 1972, the average payroll expenditure per construction worker amounted to 73 percent of the industry-wide average,[144] and it is largely this wage differential that is statistically responsible for the low wage share.[145] Since residential construction was not a primary battleground between unions and antiunion employers, but rather was abandoned to nonunion employers by default, it would be difficult to draw any specific conclusions concerning employer militance on the basis of low wage shares.[146] By the same token, special trade contractors' dependence on one type of highly skilled labor that had long been largely organized left this sector little alternative to banding together in employers' associations in order to increase individual small firms' bargaining power. Because most special trade work took place in highly organized sectors, these unions were well placed to exert pressure on subcontractors to recognize them.[147]

In spite of the fact that average payroll outlays per worker were

---

[142]BLS, *Employee Compensation and Payroll Hours: Construction—Special Trade Contractors, 1969*, at 1, 15 (Rep. 413, 1972).

[143]Dunlop & Hill, *Wage Adjustment* at 12; Northrup & Foster, *Open Shop Construction* at 16; Charles Pitcher, "A Directory of National Trade Associations, Professional Societies, and Labor Unions Involved in the Construction and Building Materials Industries," 21 (1) *CR* 4-22 at 7-8 (Jan.-Feb. 1975).

[144]USBC, *1972 CCI*, Industry Ser., U.S. Summary, tab. B1.

[145]Although BLS, *Labor and Material Requirements for Construction of Single-family Houses*, tab. 7 at 15 (Bull. 1755, 1972), indicated that this sector had the lowest wage share in total costs, it is not clear that it can be identified with the lowest labor input unless the skill level were lower, which was not the case. *Id.* at 8; Claiborne Ball, "Employment Effects of Construction Expenditures," 88 (2) *MLR* 154-58 at 156 (Feb. 1965). The relatively large share going to "overhead and profit" suggests that proprietors' labor may have been classified under this heading.

[146]When the CIO tried to organize residential construction beginning about 1940, it stressed the AFL unions' neglect of this sector; despite offering contractors conditions reminiscent of "open-shop" demands, it failed to organize many workers or employers. "C.I.O. Makes Sortie in Building Field," *NYT*, Mar. 21, 1940, at 1, col. 3, at 20, col. 3; 1 (3) *UCWN* 4 (Sept. 1, 1940); Miles Colean, *American Housing* 152-53 (1944); Bates, *Bricklayers' Century* at 244-45.

[147]In 1972, 56 percent of total payments to subcontractors were recorded in the commercial, industrial, and heavy construction sectors. USBC, *1972 CCI*, Industry Ser.: U.S. Summary, tab. B1.

significantly above average in the relatively well organized nonresidential and heavy construction sectors, wages as a share of total costs were only average in these subsectors.[148] If wage cost shares were not decisive in determining the degree of organization or employer counter-organization, the other two factors from Table 18, average number of workers and assets per establishment, are more promising explanatory variables. For establishments with relatively large numbers of workers and fixed assets[149] were also relatively well organized on both sides. Whereas the relatively large number of workers concentrated at work sites may have fostered collective action, the concentrations of fixed capital that would have been vulnerable to strikes and other actions may have motivated employers to recognize unions rather than combat them.[150] Though plausible, these ad hoc arguments do not allow of greater generalization. Wage shares thus do not appear to have been decisive and show a very weak correlation with the number of workers and amount of assets per establishment.[151] The most plausible conclusion, therefore, is that employer organizations were formed primarily as a reaction to prior organization by construction workers.[152]

---

[148]In heavy construction (not elsewhere classified), per capital payroll outlays at $12,318 about one-third higher than the industry average of $9,232. USBC, *1972 CCI*, Industry Ser.: *U.S. Summary*, tab. B1.

[149]The Spearman rank correlation for all sectors is 0.96 and the correlation coefficient 0.84; both are significant at the .01 level.

[150]A good example is the highway sector once it began mechanizing in the 1920s and 1930s. Garth Mangum, *The Operating Engineers* 249 (1964).

[151]The correlation coefficients are 0.32 and 0.11 respectively.

[152]The process by which each step toward organizational centralization on the part of one side fostered or even compelled a parallel step on the other side was much less prominent in the United States, where centralized collective bargaining was far from complete, than elsewhere. For a lucid description of the early development in Germany, see Otto Liebich, *Organisations- und Arbeitsverhältnisse im Baugewerbe* (1922).

7

Industrial-Capitalist Customers' Counterattack— The Business Roundtable

[O]ur experience covering a period of over twenty years clearly indicates that having to deal with unionism in the building industry was unavoidable primarily because the average owner is unwilling to have his building operation made a battle ground for deciding the issue as between a union and a non-union operation; ...whereas a manufacturer, if he is opposed to unionism, might justify a battle for two or three years to gain the open shop, the average building owner, who builds but one operation, is unwilling to wage a battle for posterity.[1]

The most powerful big business organization devoted to restructuring the construction industry was forged by the latter's largest industrial customers. The group's origins can be traced to efforts by larger general contractors during the waning months of the Johnson administration, as *ENR* reported, to "move toward an organized counterattack on soaring wage demands and declining productivity." At a two-day national labor conference sponsored by the AGC in Washington, D.C. in May 1968, the organization painted a "dire picture of construction negotiations" by predicting 1,400 strikes and 10 million lost man-days for the year compared to 1,200 and 8 million in 1967; it also forecast an increase in collectively bargained wage rates of 8 to 10 percent compared to 6 to 8 percent the previous year. Winton Blount, the owner of the country's 54th largest construction company (Blount Brothers Corporation in Montgomery, Alabama) and president of the Chamber of Commerce of the United States, declaring that "'It's time for a showdown,'" proposed as one possible solution restructured bargaining on the state, regional, and national levels. Another reason for more centralized collective bargaining was offered by John Healy, also a construction company owner and future AGC president: "'such bargaining by a unified management group will even help save the unions from themselves. The insatiable demands of the craft unions are usually generated on the local level by people not versed in economics and the effects of such demands on the industry. The inernationals by and large know better but are afraid to buck the locals.'" Blount also endorsed the proposal by NCA president J. M.

---

[1]"Part Ways with Award Enforcement," 44 (35) *AC* 21(Sept. 1, 1923) (printing letter of L. J. Horowitz, president, Thompson-Starrett Co.).

Graney that "[w]e...get rid of exclusive hiring halls...." The assembled employers also heard William Chartener, assistant secretary of commerce for economic affairs, describe some building trades wage demands as making "previous settlements look like an offer of free donuts during a coffee break." He warned that such trends might price the industry out of its market.[2]

The first concrete step to create the requisite organized management cooperation took place on August 7, 1968, when Blount and AGC executive director William Dunn met "with top executives from some of the largest U.S. construction firms and their customers on ways to keep down construction costs." In contrast to virtually all later accounts of the origins of the Business Roundtable, *ENR* depicted the contractors, and not their large industrial customers, as having taken the initiative: "A long-standing contractor complaint is that owners often worry more about finishing a project on time than higher cost caused by expensive labor settlements. So owner pressure—if any—is on the contractor to settle, and finish the job. Contractors seek owners' support in resisting union demands." *ENR* reported that those present had agreed that Blount's Chamber of Commerce "should be the vehicle to bring together" all the parties influencing costs.[3]

The immediate organizational catalyst for the Roundtable's formation was a two-day National Conference on Construction Problems sponsored by the Chamber of Commerce of the United States two weeks after Richard Nixon had been elected president in November 1968.[4] The list of registrants included representatives of several NCA members such as Bechtel and Fluor, as well as numerous major users such as Ford, U.S. Steel, Monsanto, and First National City Bank.[5] In highlighting the steps that owners and builders could take to "improve the state of the art of the contractors' labor relations," the Chamber pursued the "ultimate goal" of "slow[ing] the construction cost spiral."[6] Blount, soon to become Postmaster General in the new administration, set the agenda rhetorically by pronouncing construction labor

---

[2]"Attacking the Bargaining Crisis," *ENR*, May 30, 1968, at 11 (quotes); "Builder Heads Chamber of Commerce," *ENR*, May 2, 1968, at 36.

[3]"Washington Observer," *ENR*, Aug. 29, 1968, at 27.

[4]"U.S. Chamber to Be 'Catalyst' for Problems Among Builders," *NYT*, Nov. 24, 1968, sect. 1, at 114, col. 3.

[5]Registration List, in *Papers Presented at the National Conference on Construction Problems* (Nov. 18-19, 1968).

[6]Letter from [   ]Chamber of Commerce, to Douglas Soutar (Oct. 22, 1968), in SP, Box 5, File Construction-National Conference on Construction Problems-US CoC.

relations "chaotic at best—despotic or unbelievable may be better terms...." But Blount also identified the core substantive agenda by asserting that labor problems "in many instances are beyond the ability of the industry itself to handle alone and some drastic changes are needed so that some semblance of order can be restored." The nub of those changes was quickly revealed by consensus to be the active involvement of industrial customers in supporting construction firms to limit "outsized settlements and labor practices which hamper productivity."[7]

The proposal met with an especially eager reception from representatives of industrial companies operating large facilities in the Houston-Gulf Coast area, who agreed that they could no longer "afford the luxury of standing by idly with open checkbooks and insist on scheduled completion of their industrial construction projects at any price." Indeed, some had already created a participatory role for themselves through membership in the major contractors associations' Employers Council in Houston; customers and builders reported to each other during labor contract negotiations especially with respect to the former's support for the latter during strikes. The arrangement, according to B. J. Kinsel, Dow Chemical's industrial relations manager in Freeport, Texas, helped moderate wage settlements.[8]

Kinsel also sparked an intense debate over national contracts (between large national construction firms and industrial customers) and their provisions calling for work to continue during local strikes in the area by asserting that users failed to understand that undermining local contractors had repercussions for themselves: the inferior "settlement that the local contractor comes up with is going to affect the economics of doing business in your neighborhood forever." The Dow representative then pointed out that if an owner wanted construction to continue during a local strike, it could accomplish that end without weakening local contractors' bargaining position by doing "the entire job open shop...."[9] Kinsel, who argued that national agreements represented a coalition between national contractors and unions

---

[7]"Management Conference Backs Wide-Ranging Program to Curb Construction Labor Costs," *CLR*, No. 687, Nov. 20, 1968, at A-9-A-14 at A-11. Blount later became a Roundtable member.

[8]"Management Conference Backs Wide-Ranging Program to Curb Construction Labor Costs" at A-11.

[9]"Management Conference Backs Wide-Ranging Program to Curb Construction Labor Costs" at A-12-A-13.

designed to give national contractors steady employment while weakening local contractors' bargaining power, offered a preview of big business's union-free construction sector. Dow had built what was probably the largest chemical producing plant in the United States with union workers, but was currently building a plant in the same area with open-shop contractors as were two other chemical companies. "The reason," he added, was "strictly economics."[10]

After Shell Chemical Company's representative agreed with Kinsel, the NCA vice president defended the national agreements that his members frequently entered. In addition to observing that such contracts shielded industrial contractors and their customers from provisions of local agreements that were inappropriate to such projects, George McGuire made two empirical assertions: instances of working through local strikes were few, and as employers of only 1.5 to 2 percent of the construction labor force, nothing NCA members did could plausibly affect the problem of "wage escalation" one way or the other. Regardless of whether this latter argument was sound in an industry allegedly characterized by lock-step, coercively comparative wage bargaining, a representative of a specialty contractors association insisted with respect to the first argument that even where no strike took place, "the mere fact that a national agreement holder is working in an area where negotiations are taking place can transform a normally reasonable business agent into a demanding and belligerent negotiator."[11]

Just how seriously the large unionized firms took the restructuring campaign was evident in the remarks by J. M. Graney, labor relations manager at Ebasco Services, a former NCA president, and future Roundtable consultant and executive director for construction. Arguing that the deterioration in labor relations had progressed to the point at which "'tinkering'" would no longer work, Graney developed his earlier proposal for ousting the union hiring hall: for the industrial construction sector, he suggested a separate work force, "nonunion if necessary," that would be "computerized, inventoried, recruited, trained referred and managed by national hiring halls operated by professionals as a personnel office for industrial contractors." In a similar vein, the director of industrial relations

---

[10]B. J. Kinsel, "The Bargaining Process—Can We Bargain Better?" at 5 in *Papers Presented at the National Conference on Construction Problems* (Washington, D.C., Nov. 18-19, 1968).

[11]"Management Conference Backs Wide-Ranging Program to Curb Construction Labor Costs" at A-12-A-13.

at the American Iron and Steel Institute, an organization of large consumers, proposed the formation of a national human resources center. Others astutely noted that "the civil rights issue could be used as a lever to force labor reforms."[12]

The overall mood of the conference was captured by participants who complained of an "industry dominated by unions...protected by a government the unions hold captive." To deal with this alleged systemic bias, "most agreed on the need for major labor law reforms to help contractors retrieve, then exercise, the management rights they have given or lost to unions."[13] Herbert Northrup went so far as to propose repeal of the Norris-LaGuardia Act, which since before the New Deal had protected the labor movement from injunctions issued by a class-biased judiciary.[14] These labor-law related complaints were curious since even at the height of labor influence during the Johnson administration, unions had failed to induce Congress to enact their highest-priority legislation—repeal of Taft-Hartley's authorization of state anti-union-shop laws and legalization of union picketing of whole construction sites to pressure general contractors not to hire nonunion subcontractors.[15]

Leaving little trace of an open-shop crusade, the Conference Resolution recognized the "need for immediate action to...preserve the free collective bargaining process...." First among the resolution's desiderata was an inventory of manpower skills and requirements together with programs to recruit "disadvantaged and minority groups" and make the labor force more mobile. To strengthen collective bargaining it would be necessary to gain "the full support of owners." The resolution was less forthcoming with regard to decoding the proemployer content of the "legislation tailored to the needs of the construction industry," but its call for eliminating restrictive work practices required no explanation.[16] The resolution created a task force charged with formulating a program to strengthen contractors' bargaining

[12]"Labor Problems May Find a Cure," *ENR*, Nov. 28, 1968, at 31, 32.

[13]"Labor Problems May Find a Cure," *ENR*, Nov. 28, 1968, at 32.

[14]Herbert Northrup, "Restrictive Practices and Racial Barriers" at 11, in *Papers Presented at the National Conference on Construction Problems.*

[15]"Labor Expects Little from New Congress," *ENR*, Nov. 24, 1966, at 68. Whatever the reality-content of the claim of union legislative dominance, more realistic employers recognized that it was "a direct result of its solidarity and its ability to speak with one voice." "Local Groups Seek Management Unity," *ENR*, Mar. 14, 1968, at 87.

[16]"Labor Problems May Find a Cure," *ENR*, Nov. 28, 1968, at 32.

position.[17]   Editorially, *ENR* applauded Blount and the Chamber of Commerce for having facilitated the unprecedented gathering of customers and constructors and union and open-shop firms; however, the magazine's assurance that the Chamber "has no desire to step on anyone's toes, or to usurp anyone's prerogatives" was premature.[18]

Further evidence that employers had begun to forge a consensus on the construction industry was furnished by the NAM's publication in April 1969 of its provocatively entitled report, "Chaos in the Construction Industry." The NAM underscored the importance of contractors' undercapitalization for their inability to endure strikes or lockouts and chastised industrial customers for undermining contractors' bargaining position by insisting that they work through local strikes. It also appealed to users' narrow economic self-interest by explaining: "Industrial employees will no longer remain content with contract settlements which do not provide for the inflationary increases won by their counterparts in the construction field."[19]   The NAM, which, in contrast to the Roundtable, purported to represent small and medium-sized firms, established a special task force to "promote programs to solve labor-management problems in construction." This allegedly clear line between big and small business was clouded by the fact that a vice president of U.S. Steel became chairman of the task force.[20]

The task force met during the following months "with the intention of bringing owners and contractors together...." The Roundtable's own history then adds the non sequitur: "It was obvious to the task force that an owner organization was necessary." (One of the ways industrial users set out to bring contractors together was to warn them that "major clients would move independently if the industry did not get its house in order.")[21] Among the 23 people attending the first task force meeting in December 1968 were

---

[17]"Management Conference Backs Wide-Ranging Program to Curb Construction Labor Costs" at A-9.

[18]"A Salute to the Chamber," *ENR*, Nov. 28, 1968, at 164.

[19]NAM, "Chaos in the Construction Industry," *CLR*, No. 710, Apr. 30, 1969, at C-1, C-2, C-5. The NAM argued: "Project owners and developers should facilitate a favorable contract settlement by not insisting that work at a struck facility be recommenced at the cost of meeting unreasonable union demands." "Chaos in the Construction Industry: Analysis and Recommendation," *NAM Reports*, Apr. 21, 1969, at 10.

[20]"NAM Moves in on Construction," *ENR*, Sept. 18, 1969, at 246.

[21]BR, "Chapter 2: Prologue--The U.S. Construction Industry 1968-1982" at 7-8 (mimeo, n.d.); "Regional Congress Meets in Cleveland, over 200 Attend from Seven States," *CLR*, No. 696, at A-4 (Jan. 22, 1969) ("house in order").

David Luckenbill of Shell, Weldon McGlaun of Procter & Gamble, and Jack Turner of Dow, who were all to play vital roles in the 1970s; together with the executive secretary of the NCA they served on the Committee on Collective Bargaining.[22]

Another Task Force meeting in February 1969 focused on ways to overcome the owners' fragmentation and divergent interests, which were as great as construction companies'. The unifying theme was that users, "not the contractor, ultimately pay the bill." A subcommittee also proposed that owners could strengthen contractors' negotiating position by shutting down all projects in a geographic area and influencing the news media to bring about early settlements. Moreover, it recommended consolidated, wider-area bargaining and common expiration dates for agreements to deprive unions of the leverage to play one firm off against another.[23]

Despite this activity, the next few months witnessed little progress. In an illuminating letter to his boss, S. D. Bechtel, Jr., R. Eric Miller, vice president in charge of labor relations at Bechtel and its liaison with the task force, reported as late as April 1969 that the participants until then had "tended to 'spin their wheels'.... We really need a new 'leader' such as Blough to get us 'off the dime' and working toward the definition of goals and the accomplishment of these. Otherwise, I say let's not expend our Bechtel efforts on a treadmill, rather, let's turn them totally to the pure Bechtel problems." One of the obstacles, according to Miller, was the reluctance of some owners in the refinery, chemical, and utility equipment industries to participate for fear of antitrust liability: "However, I am pleased to hear some of them (Shell, Dow, G.E.) say that they intend to find the 'proper legal advice' which will sell their firm on taking a continued part...."[24]

A few days later, Virgil Day, who was in charge of labor relations at

---

[22]Construction Committee Summary of Dec. 9, 1968 Task Force on Construction Problems Meeting, in BR, 1968: CCH.

[23]National Chamber of Commerce Task Force on Construction Problems, Meeting of Feb. 14, 1969, in BR, 1969: CCH.

[24]Letter from R. Eric Miller to S.D. Bechtel, Jr. (Apr. 11, 1969), in BR, 1968: CCH. According to another internal account, two months were wasted trying to persuade Fred Kappel, the former CEO of AT&T, to replace Blount. Peter J. Pestillo, "Construction Problems: In Search of a Solution" 16 (Mar. 14, 1969), in BR, 1969: CCH. GE's intense involvement in the Roundtable's formation was in part a function of its status as a general contractor for nuclear power plants, which were allegedly not profitable because the firm had failed to gauge construction inflation accurately. Peter J. Pestillo, "Construction Problems: In Search of a Solution" at 1 (Mar. 14, 1969), in BR, 1969: CCH.

GE, wrote his boss that the "chemical people have been out front on this project. They've organized owner groups in some areas already.... Shell and Dow have taken substantial losses to bring about some stability." More significant still was Day's revelation that Steve Bechtel had been "instrumental in an effort to recruit Roger Blough to this venture."[25] Later, David Luckenbill, Shell Oil's manager of construction relations, informed the firm's vice president that GE and Bechtel had been "the prime corporate forces which precipitated the action" to form the CUAIR, Shell and U.S. Steel being "the principal supporting companies...."[26] The fact that the world's largest construction company and staunch union employer, the key member of the NCA, was not merely accommodating its largest customers, but was actively promoting the formation of the Roundtable, suggests that at least Bechtel early on had welcomed big business's assistance in enhancing its bargaining power with unions. To be sure, Stephen Bechtel was a unique hybrid figure: one of the richest capitalists in the United States and a member of the board of directors of J. P. Morgan & Company, he had long invested a substantial proportion of his family's capital in industries outside of construction.[27]

The other cause of delay, as Miller noted in a report to Bechtel, was Blount's acceptance of Nixon's offer of a cabinet position. Some progress was achieved, however, on April 1, when the task force met with the NAM and the Labor Law Reform Group, which were vitally interested in the same problems. They agreed both on the need to form a single group and that: "A leader of national stature (Blough or equal) is required to give overall direction to the activities...and to 'sell' these recommendations at 'top board levels' and 'top government levels'...." Leading top executives of a cross-section of important industries would be needed to "assist the 'leader.'" That Bechtel was primarily interested in dealing with rather than eliminating unions was clearly visible in Miller's conclusion that "at some point in time" a labor counterpart "certainly has to become a partner...." Miller judged that unions could probably "buy" "something unusual and big...more readily...than 'patches on patches.'" For the long term, Miller could envision a National Construction Industry Council, consisting of contractors, owners, government, and labor, to establish ground rules for working projects during

---

[25]Letter from V. B. Day to F. J. Borch at 2, 4 (Apr. 21, 1969), in BR, 1969: CCH.

[26]Letter from D. B. Luckenbill to A. C. Hogge (Jan. 26, 1970) (Private and Confidential), in BR, CCH: 1970.

[27]Linder, *Projecting Capital* at 131.

local bargaining breakdowns, and to deal with jurisdictional disputes and manpower utilization, but for the immediate future the main point was to "glue the contractor/owner segments together and to tie down our leader."[28]

The Roundtable was "formed as a result of presentations and discussions at the May 1969 meeting of the Business Council at the Homestead," in Hot Springs, Virginia, at which "a group of...Chief Executive Officers convinced Roger M. Blough that he was the appropriate person to lead such an owners organization." He had been the board chairman of the United States Steel Corporation between 1955 and 1969 as well as chairman of the elite Business Advisory Council and Business Council during the Kennedy administration; after his retirement from U.S. Steel he became associated with the Wall Street law firm of White & Case. The Roundtable's founding members were Fred Borch, the president of General Electric, J. K. Jamieson, president of Standard Oil of New Jersey, Birny Mason, Jr., chairman of Union Carbide, Frank Milliken, president of Kennecott Copper, James Roche, chairman of GM, and H. I. Romnes, chairman of AT&T. Blough, who had retired as CEO of U.S. Steel in January, agreed to overcome his reluctance only on the condition that "all CEOs present in the meeting would support the organization and would personally participate on a Policy Committee...." The new organization met for the first time at the Wall Street offices of White & Case on June 3 (the so-called vice presidents' meeting) with representatives of 15 major corporations agreeing to serve on a coordinating committee. Having adopted the name Construction Users Anti-Inflation Round Table, the group, consisting solely of users, "quickly recognized the need for contractor advice and input...." It therefore set up a Contractor Advisory Council, made up of CEOs of large construction firms and designed to work with the policy committee, and a Contractors Task Force, consisting of construction and labor relations experts, who worked with the coordinating committee. During the summer, the new group, as yet unknown to the public, held a series of meetings with "high level members" of the Nixon administration, including the Attorney General, Labor Secretary, the chairman of the Council of Economic Advisors, and Postmaster General Blount, "to insure their support and understanding of the Anti-Inflation Round Table's purpose." Interestingly—in light of a report in the *Wall Street Journal* that the group did not want unions to have advance knowledge of its

---

[28]Report from R. Eric Miller to S.D. Bechtel, Jr., "Chamber of Commerce Task Force on Construction Labor Problem" at 3-5 (Apr. 11, 1969), in BR, 1968: CCH.

formation—"[m]eetings were also held with George Meaney [sic] and Lane Kirkland of the AFL-CIO."[29]

In early July, John Harper, the chairman of Alcoa, sent telegrams to his counterparts at large corporations inviting them to an introductory meeting. The telegram to Edward McL. Tittmann, the chairman of American Smelting & Refining Company (ASARCO), read: "Accelerated costs in the construction industry are of deep concern to all of us. To this end a Construction Users Anti-inflation Round Table has been formed. You are urged to attend a presentation on this matter by Roger Blough on...July 22...in the Links Club, New York. The meeting will also be of interest to your industrial relations officer."[30]

Blough's paper, "Construction Users Anti-Inflation Roundtable: A Statement of Program," which formed the core of the testimony that he was to give to the Joint Economic Committee of Congress in January 1971, focused on the impact that "unbelievable" construction wage increases would inevitably have on industrial employers—the gap between the two sectors was "certain to 'suck up' all wages"—and the risk that the compulsory arbitration or wage controls suggested as possible remedies for construction "could soon permeate the entire economic system." After sharing an example of how U.S. Steel had successfully cooperated with construction firms in Pittsburgh to hold down union wages, Blough nevertheless insisted that the

[29]BR, "Chapter 2: Prologue--The U.S. Construction Industry 1968-1982" at 7-8 (mimeo, n.d.) (BR files); "The Construction User Anti-Inflation Roundtable" at 2 (undated [ca. Nov. 1969]), in SP, Box 5, File-Construction Committee ("Business Council"); Jim Heath, *John F. Kennedy and the Business Community* 17-19 (1969) (on Blough); James Gannon, "Industry Quietly Forms Group to Curb Spiral of Construction Costs," *WSJ*, Aug. 14, 1969, at 1, col. 6, at 16, col. 1. On the vice presidents meeting, see CUAIR, CC, Minutes, June 3, 1969, at 3, in BR, 1969: Vol. II-Minutes. Blough reported to the Coordinating Committee on his August 19 meeting with Meany and Kirkland. CUAIR, CC, Minutes, July 25, 1969, at 3,in BR, 1969: Vol. II-Minutes. The Roundtable wrote its history for a history of the Construction Industry Institute (CII) at the University of Texas, which was itself in part financed by the Roundtable. The Roundtable furnished a copy of the manuscript. Because the published version made several deletions, the original is quoted here. See Robert Jortberg & Thomas Haggard, *CII: The First Ten Years* 7-8 (1993). The history singles out David Luckenbill of Shell, R. Eric Miller of Bechtel, Mike Graney of Ebasco, Weldon McGlaum of Procter & Gamble, Jack Turner of Dow Chemical, and Peter Pestillo of the Labor Law Committee of the U.S. Chamber of Commerce as having contributed to forming the CUAIR in early 1969. Business Roundtable, "Chapter 2" at 8.

[30]Telegram from John Harper to Edward Tittmann (July 4, 1969), in SP, Box 5, File-CUAIR 1969-1970. A membership list date June 20, 1969 included 20 firms including U.S. Steel, Dow Chemical, Goodyear Tire & Rubber, International Paper, B. F. Goodrich, General Dynamics, Sheel Oil, Procter & Gamble, and Owens-Corning Fiberglas. Construction Roundtable, "Members of Roundtable -- June 20, 1969, in SP, Box 5, CUAIR Membership.

Roundtable was "in no sense a union-busting group. Many intelligent union leaders are as concerned as we are." According to the CUAIR's organizational chart, its highest operating level was the Policy Committee, consisting of "a few of those who participated in the early discussions.... They, in turn, will seek advice from some of the leading executives in the construction industry who form a Contractors' Advisory Committee," to which in turn was subordinated a Contractors Task Force, consisting of those executives' subordinates. Similarly, operating under the Policy Committee was the Roundtable Coordinating Committee to which "[f]ifteen of the principal members of the Roundtable have assigned competent men of stature in their organizations...." This working committee, in turn, supervised several task forces covering the following areas: expanding supply of skilled craftsmen, eliminating restrictive work practices, strike insurance, seasonality, legislative reform, overtime, and improving contractor bargaining. While promising that the Roundtable would not interfere with any member's freedom to act, Blough urged the assembled executives to join in a "united front." Among the most important steps that they could take were: refraining from scheduling overtime; not interfering with local contractors' strikes by continuing to build; supporting expansion of supply of skilled labor by including minorities; and supporting stronger collective bargaining by contractors.[31]

What the vice president for industrial relations at one of the CUAIR members chose to take notes on is worth mentioning. He set an exclamation point after the datum that only 1,200 of 870,000 contractors had more than 100 employees, adding that the balance of power was the "real culprit." Without drawing any negative conclusions, the official jotted down that Blough had met with leading Nixon administration economic policy officials (such as George Shultz, Arthur Burns, and Paul McCracken), who reported

---

[31]Roger Blough, "Construction Users Anti-Inflation Roundtable: A Statement of Program" 1, 2, 9, 23-26, 28-29, 34-35 (Preliminary-Confidential, July 15, 1969), in SP, Box 5, File-CUAIR 1969-1970. An attorney at Blough's law firm sent Soutar a copy the day after the meeting, stressing that it was "still quite confidential...." Letter from [ ] to D. H. Soutor [sic] (July 23, 1969), in SP, Box 5, File-CUAIR 1969-1970. By Aug. 1, 1969, three other Coordinating Committee task forces were added—restoration of management to contractors, jurisdictional disputes, and compilation of statistics. Each task force was chaired by a coordinating committee member. For example, J. Warren Shaver, U.S. Steel vice president for labor relations, chaired the task force on restrictive work practices, while Virgil Day, GE vice president for industrial relations, headed that on legislative reform. Construction Roundtable, "Coordinating Committee Task Forces" (Aug. 1, 1969). SP, Box 5, File-CUAIR Membership.

that they had political problems with Labor, while the construction unions had given the administration "more support than others." From the ensuing discussion the industrial relations manager noted a question by William F. May, the chairman of American Can Company, as to the legality of a construction company formed by a number of larger companies. Such a radical restructuring of the construction industry, however, never entered the Roundtable's agenda. Frank Milliken, the president of Kennecott Copper and one of the Roundtable's founding members, also explored an issue that the Roundtable, for all its propagandistic references to the harm done to home buyers, never took up: what pressure could be put on residential construction? Replying that the best route was through banks, Blough added that he had met with the five top bank executives including David Rockefeller, who had explained that they could not make joint agreements not to make loans.[32] But Rockefeller and the officials of First National City Bank, Morgan Guaranty Trust, Metropolitan Life Insurance, and New York Life Insurance all expressed "considerable interest in the project and offered to be of help if feasible wasys [sic] could be found."[33]

The note-taking industrial relations manager, a well-connected link in the increasingly dense national network of big business's antiunion groups, doubtless spoke for many of his colleagues in a confidential memo to his boss characterizing the Roundtable as a "worthwhile project and a major problem and factor in the inflation equation. ... This is one of our nation-wide industry participation projects like the Labor Law Reform project, utilizing the same talent."[34]

In early August, the well-informed *Construction Labor Report* reported that, following a seven-month study, the task force, consisting of representatives of some of the largest industrial project owners, power companies, the American Iron & Steel Institute, the AGC, NCA, various subcontractors associations, Bechtel, and the Chamber of Commerce, recommended the creation of an organization of users and construction firms to promote cooperation in coordinating labor relations policies and inventorying manpower skills to combat "extravagantly inflationary" wage settlements, artificially created labor shortages, and restrictive work practices

---

[32]Untitled notes, in SP, Box 5, File-CUAIR 1969-1970.

[33]CUAIR, CC, Minutes, July 21, 1969, at 4, in BR, 1969: Vol. II-Minutes.

[34]Memo from [　] to EMT (July 25, 1969), in SP, Box 5, File-CUAIR 1969-1970.

while strengthening collective bargaining.[35]

CUAIR's policy committee was composed of the top executives of eight of the largest U.S. corporations, including General Motors, Standard Oil (N.J.), AT&T, and GE. The CUAIR's 17-member coodinating committee also included executives of Dow Chemical, Texaco, Shell, Procter & Gamble, Goodrich, Alcoa, du Pont, U.S. Steel, and International Paper. In addition, Graney, a former NCA president, served as a consultant. Focusing on the "'astronomical'" wage increases that it saw as underlying the "alarming" rate of construction cost increases, the CUAIR initially projected itself as a research group designed to promote "wider public understanding of the industry's problems and the inflationary threat they present to our economy."[36] Such a role was necessary because big business's ignorance of the construction industry had caused it "unwittingly to accelerate the rise in building costs"; Blough's group intended to "stiffen resistance to additional union wage increases...."[37]

The Roundtable's choice of an educational public image was, according to the *Wall Street Journal*, dictated by fear that a group of the country's largest firms collectively seeking to lower their costs might prompt the government to initiate an antitrust investigation. The *Journal*, in a perceptive front-page scoop published shortly before the CUAIR was formed, not only waxed ironic about Blough—who had provoked President Kennedy in 1962 by raising steel prices—as "inflation fighter," but stressed that the organization had "kept quiet" about its formation largely to preclude early union opposition; after all, the *Journal* surmised, "union leaders' normal instincts probably would prompt them to view the Round Table as a sinister big-business conspiracy against them." In "mustering tremendous economic pressure" to de-escalate construction costs, the organization was as focused on keeping its own members in line as construction unions and firms. Any member that tried to pressure a contractor to acquiesce in a high wage

---

[35]"Task Force Asks Creation of Construction Buyers Group to Help Solve Industry's Labor Problems," *CLR*, No. 724, Aug. 6, 1969, at A-1, A-2; "Report of Contractor-Client Task Force on Meeting Construction Labor Problems," *id.* at C-1-C-5. On Bechtel's size, see "Contractors Set Volume Record as '68 Domestic Work Takes Off," *ENR*, Apr. 10, 1969, at 70-84 at 73.

[36]"Announcement Released by Roger Blough on Construction Users Anti-Inflation Roundtable," *CLR*, No. 727, Aug. 27, 1969, at D-1 (quotes); "Owners Use New Vehicle to Fight Inflation," *ENR*, Aug. 21, 1969, at 14-15; BR, *Report*, No. 73-3, at 1-2 (Mar. 23, 1973).

[37]"New Blough Panel to Fight Increase in Building Costs," *NYT*, Aug. 21, 1969, at 12, col. 8.

settlement or provided work to unionists on strike elsewhere would be subject to the organization's "'collective displeasure'.... They will monitor each other in a sort of internal police system." Exactly how members would make violations "'more painful'" without imposing some tangible penalties, for example, by withholding intercorporate business, the *Journal*'s inside informant failed to confide.[38]

Like employers' resentment of the consequences of a free labor market at the height of a boom, the Fortune 100's preemptive approach to one another's competitive optimum profit strategies seemed to view the free market as an evil to be avoided by oligopolists. In practice, however, Roundtable companies rarely if ever refrained from pushing for as rapid completion as possible of their plants in favor of a shut-down to undermine construction unions' long-run control of the labor market and negotiating leverage.[39]

The type of public education that the Roundtable envisioned was exemplified by a press release from Blough's successor as chairman of U.S. Steel, Edwin Gott, in April 1970. Blough quickly circulated it to the Roundtable members, calling it a "good example" of the kind of public statement by user executives that could be especially effective in connection with local negotiations.[40] Gott's statement highlighted a recent contract in Kansas City, which provided that "the annual employment cost of an unskilled highway construction laborer working forty hours per week will

---

[38] James Gannon, "Industry Quietly Forms Group to Curb Spiral of Construction Costs," *WSJ*, Aug. 14, 1969, at 1, col. 6, at 16, col. 1. A copy of this article is found in SP, Box 5, File-Construction Committee. The BCTD president, Frank Bonadio, characterized the building trades unions as "'victims of a conspiracy'" with the Roundtable as one of chief conspirators. "Building Trades Seek the Best of Two Worlds," *ENR*, Jan. 11, 1973, at 22. When the Roundtable was strongly urging members to refrain from scheduling overtime for construction projects, its Coordinating Committee noted that one company (Commonwealth Edison) that had not gone over to the 40-hour basis, "will be approached to discuss this matter further." BR, CC, Minutes, June 26, 1970, at 3, in BR, 1970-Vol. II: Minutes.

[39] Telephone interview with Robert McCormick, president, NCA, Washington, D.C. (Mar. 11, 1999). The Roundtable's objective was not unprecedented: in 1887 building owners in New York City had permitted delays so that master plumbers could continue their ultimately successful struggle against the plumbers union over control of the apprenticeship system. "The Strike in the Plumbing Trade," 6 (10) *BJA* n.s. No. 62, at 85 (Mar. 5, 1887). When the Plumbers abandoned the strike ("systematic warfare against the bosses") in favor of "incessant guerrilla warfare" in each shop, the union (incorrectly) predicted that people erecting buildings would insist that the plumbing work be done promptly. "Really But Not Officially Ended," *NYT*, Apr. 10, 1887, at 7, col. 3.

[40] Letter from Roger Blough to Members of the Roundtable (Apr. 24, 1970), in SP, Box 5, File-CUAIR 1969-1970.

increase to almost $20,000" by 1971. He urged the public: "Contrast this to the incomes of the millions of highly skilled men and women with years of costly preparation behind them and it becomes obvious that something is critically wrong when an industry can get to a point where such an imbalance could occur."[41]

As a public educator, Gott, who apparently saw nothing wrong or imblanced about his own $309,834 annual compensation,[42] omitted to mention that virtually no construction laborers worked year round. Even the laborers' employers in Kansas City contended that they worked on average only 1,700 hours, while their union put the figure at closer to 1,200.[43] Special surveys that the BLS published just as Gott spoke impressively documented how few hours they (or their colleagues in any other construction occupation) worked annually. In Detroit, Omaha, and Milwaukee, the average number of hours that laborers worked in a twelve month period amounted to 765, 626, and 590, respectively; even excluding all laborers working fewer than 700 hours raised the averages only to 1,540, 1,467, and 1,416, respectively. Those working more than 1,800 hours accounted for only 14.4, 10.0, and 8.9 percent, respectively, of all laborers in those cities.[44] An unprecedentedly detailed BLS study for 1970 revealed how low construction laborers' annual wages were. The median earnings of year-round, full-time union construction laborers were only $8,730, and exceeded $15,000 only for 1.2 percent of them; the corresponding figures for nonunionists were only $5,419 and 0.9 percent.[45]

Later the Roundtable portrayed its original raison d'être as having been the "terrible shape" in which construction found itself in the later 1960s and early 1970s: "the industry was becoming increasingly noncompetitive in the world marketplace."[46] To be sure, this claim was untenable: at that time U.S. construction firms dominated the world market, very few non-U.S. firms operated in the United States, and any labor problems in the form of high union wages or work rules did not apply in the world market since by this

---

[41]United States Steel, untitled (Apr. 14, 1970), in SP, Box 5, File-CUAIR 1969-1970.

[42]"How the Top Men Fared in 1969," *BW*, June 13, 1970, 59-68 at 68.

[43]"One City's 'Ordeal by Strike,'" *USNWR*, Sept. 14, 1970, at 64.

[44]BLS, *Seasonality and Manpower in Construction*, tab. 78 and 79 at 71 (Bull. 1642, 1970). The data were collected in the latter part of the 1960s.

[45]BLS, *Selected Earnings and Demographic Characteristics of Union Members, 1970*, tab. 6 at 14 (Rep. 417, 1972).

[46]Business Roundtable, "Overview" (http://www.brtable.org/document.cfm/89).

time U.S. firms operating abroad employed very few U.S. workers, instead recruiting third-world workers.[47]

Even if construction customers yielded to competitive pressures in their own product markets by disregarding construction costs for the sake of quick completion of projects, they soon understood the untoward ramifications. GM's president may have apologized to his fellow Roundtable members for the construction contretemps at Lordstown by referring to his firm's problems,[48] but GM's vice president and director of labor relations (and Roundtable participant) explicitly articulated its interest in the struggle against construction unions:

> "Prior to our auto negotiations in 1970, the construction industry got extravagant salary increases.... There's no damn way we can afford to raise salaries 18 percent for construction or any other group and remain competitive.
> "We have building trade union members rubbing shoulders with our own auto worker union skilled mechanics who perform the same jobs. The building trade people are not above saying: 'Hey, buddy. If you were a member of the electrical workers union instead of the auto workers, you'd have this kind of check.' They jab them and they irritate them, so that our electrician goes down to his UAW local and says, 'Goddamn. How come that guy gets $8.50 an hour and I get $5.80?"[49]

That the CUAIR Coordinating Committee took its mission seriously is obvious from the fact that it met 63 times (twice a month) from the time of its establishment until the merger that created the Business Roundtable in 1972. Blough, according to the Roundtable's self-history, "attended all but one of these meetings, providing dynamic leadership...."[50] He addressed various employers association meetings to mobilize their support for the CUAIR's "fight against...runaway wages and restrictive work practices in construction." If the mere mention of $19,000 annual incomes for laborers failed to galvanize members of the American Textile Manufacturers Institute, Blough's assertion of their "'magnet-like pull' on the general level of industrial wages" may have provoked managers to join the struggle.[51]

The access that the Roundtable was able to secure quickly became

---

[47]Linder, *Projecting Capitalism.*

[48]Haynes Johnson & Nick Kotz, *Unions* 144 (1972).

[49]Haynes & Kotz, *Unions* at 137 (quoting George B. Morris, Jr.).

[50]Business Roundtable, "Chapter 2" at 9.

[51]"Blough Cites Jump in Costs of Building as Inflation Factor," *NYT*, Mar. 22, 1970, sect. 1, at 66, col. 4-5.

apparent. Blough and others met with John Dunlop on October 1 and with
the Cabinet Committee on Construction on October 23, 1969.[52] In December
Under Secretary of Labor James Hodgson sent a memo to Secretary Shultz
informing him that he had just learned that the first half hour of the next
meeting of the Cabinet Committee on Construction would be "devoted to
giving Roger Blough an audience."[53]   In his review of the industry's
problems, Blough included among possible long-term solutions (in addition
to strengthening constractors' bargaining power by means of multi-employer
bargaining units) two suggestions to which the CUAIR otherwise gave no
prominence: binding arbitration of disputes and creation of a Labor Court of
Justice.[54]

By February 1970, the Construction Roundtable numbered 106
members—many of the country's largest manufacturing, extractive, utilities,
communications, transportation, and retail firms—all of whom were
represented by the president, chairman of the board, and/or CEO.[55] Member-
companies paid annual dues based on their combined gross sales and
stockholders equity; in 1971, these dues, which ranged from $2,500 for those
with less than $500 million combined sales and equity to $35,000 for those
with more than $6.5 billion, totalled between $1.5 and $2 million.[56]

On June 10, 1970, Roundtable officials met with Paul McCracken,
chairman of the CEA and of the Cabinet Committee on Construction, and
Secretary of Housing George Romney. Blough, Virgil Day, Peter Pestillo,
and J. M. Graney urged a three-point program: suspension of the Davis-
Bacon Act; creation of a Construction Manpower Procurement Agency
within the U.S. Employment Service to "reform" union hiring halls; and

---

[52]CUAIR, CC, Minutes of Oct. 13 and 27, 1969, in BR, 1969: Vol. II-Minutes.

[53]Memorandum from Hodgson to Shultz (Dec. 20, 1969), in NACP, RG 174: General
Records of the Labor Dept., Office of the Secretary, Records of the Secretary of Labor George P.
Shultz, 1969-1970, Box No. 58: Councils, Folder: 1969 Committee: CCC.

[54]Minutes of CCC Meeting, Dec. 22, 1969, in NACP, RG 174: General Records of the Labor
Dept., Office of the Secretary, Records of the Secretary of Labor George P. Shultz, 1969-1970, Box
No. 58: Councils, Folder: 1969 Committee: CCC.

[55]Construction Roundtable, "Members of Roundtable" (Feb. 1, 1970), in SP, Box 5, File-
CUAIR Membership.

[56]"Messrs. Murphy, Blough and Borch: Dues Schedule Based on Combined Gross Sales Plus
Stockholders Equity" (Oct. 6 [1971?]), in SP, Box 5, File-CUAIR. The total amount of dues has been
estimated because, although this schedule includes the number of companies falling into the brackets,
the number of companies in at least one bracket was omitted and the number in the highest bracket was
too indistinct to be deciphered. See also "Dues Schedule Based on Combined Gross Sales Plus
Stockholder Equity" (Oct. 16, 1972), in BR, CCH: 1972.

creation of a Temporary National Construction Review Panel to improve productivity, reduce collectively bargained-for wage increases, and restructure construction industry organization. Suspending the Davis-Bacon Act, "that depression-born anachronism," which caused the federal government to underwrite and propagate "excessive settlements," would not only "show decisively that the White House means business" in controlling inflation, but as an administrative act would not require congressional action. The proposed government-operated system of referral offices, based on computerized listings of all construction workers by classification and special skill, was designed to weaken unions' control of the labor market and collective bargaining position. The Construction Review Panel was intended to obviate the need for a general incomes policy, of which there was much talk in Washington at the time. Its first mission was to improve productivity by laying the "foundation for handling unnecessary work restrictions, job maintenance attitudes, methods of introducing modern equipment, and utilization of skills on the job." How the panel would have gone about implementing such a highly intrusive plan, which would have encroached on unions' defensive controls as well as managerial prerogatives, Blough did not explain. Nor did the proposal set forth what the panel would be empowered to do in considering recommendations for "restructuring the basic make-up of bargaining, the organization of unions and contractors..., work policies, and similar matters."[57] A half-year later Nixon did suspend the Davis-Bacon Act for a few weeks, but the Roundtable's other proposals were both too radically invasive and vague to persuade a president who just a few days earlier had sworn everlasting gratitude to the leaders of the rampaging hard hats.[58]

The Roundtable's legislative agenda was in fact much broader and radical than these few proposals, although it recognized that the make-up of the House and Senate Labor Committees made it very unlikely that such

---

[57]CUAIR, "Report to Members: Roundtable Group at White House Meeting; Urges Three-Point Program" (July 15, 1970) ("Confidential - Not For Publication"), in SP, Box 5, File-CUAIR 1969-1970. According to the current NCA president, the Roundtable's proposal to create a government hiring hall was merely rhetorical because it would have interfered too severely with private enterprise; moreover, it would have lacked the hiring hall's flexibility of providing a contractor with the craftsperson with the required skilled at the right place the next morning. Telephone interview with Robert McCormick, Washington, D.C. (Mar. 11, 1999).

[58]See below chapter 11.

changes would be enacted during the first Nixon administration.[59] Together with the Fair Labor Law Study Group, with which it would merge in 1972, it supported outright repeal of the Davis-Bacon Act as well as of the Norris-LaGuardia Act—which had been enacted during the Hoover administration to put an end to decades of judicial discrimination against unions—because employers were frustrated by its ban on the issuance of injunctions against strikes in violation of collective bargaining agreements. Big business also sought to amend the NLRA to strengthen already existing prohibitions on publicity picketing and strikes to protest use of prefabricated materials. In contrast, the Roundtable was unable to agree with contractors groups regarding several other issues. For example, whereas the AGC wished to eliminate union members' right to reject labor agreements negotiated by their leaders, "[m]any in industry feel that this element of union democracy should be retained despite occasional hardships."[60] In terms of litigation, in mid-1970 Blough met with legal scholars and others to discuss legal action against craft unions' augmentation of their labor market monopoly by means of violating labor relations and civil rights laws.[61]

A month after its meeting with administration officials, the CUAIR had gained a sufficiently high profile to prompt *The New York Times* to offer Blough a 1,000-word op-ed column on the front page of its Sunday real estate section to repeat his message that the "'astronomical'" "'inflationary impact of skyrocketing settlements in the construction industry...is a national problem of paramount importance.'"[62]

At the same time Blough circulated to the members a report by one of the Coordinating Committee's task forces, "Restoration of the Management Role in the Construction Industry," which starkly underscored the Roundtable's fundamentalist position. Focusing on the union hiring hall as the root problem, the report characterized unions as "the de facto employers" with respect to hiring, training, placement, and administration of non-wage benefits. Apparently believing that management's unfettered prerogative to disemploy was designed as a kind of capital punishment, the

---

[59][ ], "Report - Legislative Issues" at 1 (n.d. [ca. 1970]), in SP, Box 5, File-CUAIR 1969-1970.

[60]CUAIR, "Report - Legislative Issues" (n.d. [ca. Nov. 1969]), in SP, Box 5, File-CC.

[61]CUAIR, CC, Minutes, June 26, 1970, in BR, 1970-Vol. II: Minutes.

[62]"Roger Blough, "Rising Labor Costs Are Seen [sic] Road to 'Disaster,'" *NYT*, July 12, 1970, sect. 8, at 1 col. 5. Here Blough conceded that such annual incomes presupposed year-round work.

Roundtable perceived the hiring hall as nullifying the employer's power to fire because the discharged worker merely returns to the hiring hall "for reassignment to another construction project in the area." Even more "regrettable" from the Roundtable's perspective was the fact that many contractors maintained a "stronger bond" to the unions than to their customers or "the proper common interest relationships among members of the same industry."[63]

      Undergirding the task force's proposal to "strengthen collective bargaining" was a precept that the CUAIR soon turned on its head: "It is of prime importance to demonstrate that there is no anti-union character to these programs to 'strengthen collective bargaining.' While it is recognized that there are important segments of the world of construction where the work is performed by non-represented employees, this does not detract from the conclusison that the road to improvement—or the road block against improvement—will be found at the collective bargaining table."[64] By August 1970, the Roundtable Policy and Coordinating Committees invited a group of open-shop contractors to their joint meeting.[65] At the Coordinating Committee meeting on October 6, after Donald Grant of Atkinson Company, a union shop member of the Contractor Task Force, mentioned that open-shop activity was increasing, Blough asked whether any committee member opposed the view that the Roundtable had not taken a position on the open-shop question: "No such opposition was made known."[66] In sharing the results with all the members, Blough, after having chanted his by now talismanic disavowal of any antiunion sentiments, effectively gave the nonunion construction firms free advertising and privileged access to the Fortune 100. Blough reported the nonunion contractors' unanimous assertion that their productivity level exceeded that of their union counterparts because they retained more of their freedom to manage. In an apparent effort to create a snowball effect, Blough conveyed the nonunion firms' claim that "the major barrier to the spread of open shop work is the unwillingness of industrial companies to permit contractors to bid on work. It was stated,

[63]CUAIR, "Restoration of the Management Role in the Construction Industry" at 2, 3 (Mar. 1970), in SP, Box 5, File-CC. The Roundtable self-published this report unchanged in BR, *Coming to Grips with Some Major Problems in the Construction Industry* 51-58 (1974).

[64]"Report of Contractor-Client Task Force on Meeting Construction Labor Problems" at C-2.

[65]BR, CC, Minutes, Aug. 18, 1970, at 2, in BR, 1970: Vol. II-Minutes.

[66]BR, CC, Minutes, Oct. 6, 1970, at 3, in BR, 1970: Vol. II-Minutes.

however, that during the last few months some large companies were reappraising their contracting policies and some were now inviting bids on an open shop basis."[67]

That same month Blough made common cause with the antiunion ABC. At its annual convention, Blough observed: "The competitive principle is at work and users will not be tied to an uneconomic form of work."[68] ABC members' "sweatshop with substandard wages and working conditions" had already begun to alarm the NCA and the construction unions by taking away 150 projects worth $7.5 billion in 1969-70.[69] Blough reported to the Coordinating Committee on November 4 that the open shop appeared to do well without the hiring hall.[70] Much of the Coordinating Committee's November 17 meeting was devoted to the open shop. Consultant Weldon McGlaun submitted a memorandum on an open-shop contractor's satisfactory performance in Tennessee. Luckenbill of Shell noted that owner pressure was bringing about cooperation between general contractors and smaller open-shop builders. The CUAIR's two-track approach to construction labor relations was then nicely captured by a colloquy between R. Eric Miller of Bechtel, who reminded the committee that it was not the Roundtable's purpose to advocate the open shop or to take antiunion action, and J. Warren Shaver, vice president for labor relations at U.S. Steel, who added that the group's "purpose was to use the pressure of these events to improve the union structure...."[71] One of the leading member of the CUAIR's coordinating committee invidiously compared the two sectors at the organization's second annual members meeting in 1971. The nonunion segment, which claimed productivity advantages as great as 40 percent, had over the previous five years doubled its annual volume to $25 billion: "about the only radical thing they do is run their own businesses."[72]

In January 1971, Blough told Congress's Joint Economic Committee that a "hard crackdown on construction unions"[73] was needed to avoid a

---

[67]Roger Blough, "Open Shop Contracting" at 1, 2, 5 (Oct. 23, 1970), in SP, Box 5, File-CUAIR 1969-1970.

[68]"Open Shop Builders Gird for Greater Challenges," *ENR*, Oct. 22, 1970, at 81.

[69]"ABC and the Open Shop Stir Up an Industry Searching for Change," *ENR*, Oct. 15, 1970, at 22-24 (quote at 23).

[70]BR, CC, Minutes, Nov. 4, 1970, at 8, in BR, 1970: Vol. II-Min.

[71]BR, CC, Minutes, Nov. 17, 1970, at 3-5, in BR, 1970: Vol. II-Min.

[72]CUAIR, Members Meeting, June 3, 1971, Minutes at 8, in SP, Box 5 [ ].

[73]"Blough Outlines Suggested Remedies to Restrain 'Wage-Push' Inflation," *CLR*, No. 802,

"colossal economic bust." Declaring that "the inflationary impact of skyrocketing settlements in the construction industry has been almost unbelievable in magnitude," but denying that his labor-supply-oriented proposals were antiunion, he urged the U.S. Employment Service to replace union hiring halls—"[t]he source" of flagging productivity and inadequate management—in order to break unions' power, and customers to explore the possibilities of nonunion contractors. Blough also used this national forum to announce that among the remedies available to users was "increasingly [to] give open shop operators a fairer chance to contract new projects." He reported that those firms claimed that unburdened by unions, they could pay the same wages, offer more continuous employment, and bid lower prices. Finally, just a few weeks before Nixon acted, Blough urged the president to suspend the Davis-Bacon Act to demonstrate the government's serious pursuit of economic stabilization.[74]

The CUAIR's advocacy of suspension was linked to its opposition to an incomes policy and its preference for a government-appointed panel that would, inter alia, help improve productivity and hold hearings on unacceptable collective bargaining settlements, which could then not be used on government projects.[75] Reinforcement for this attack on the Davis-Bacon Act came from Assistant Secretary of Labor Arthur Fletcher, who was invited to address the CUAIR Coordinating Committee in February. Agreeing that the prevailing wage law should be revised, Fletcher "made suggestions for political action by concerned citizens."[76] A few months later, the Coordinating Committee, taking note of bills introduced to repeal the act, stressed that they "need support at the grass roots level."[77]

Virgil Day spoke for the Roundtable in calling the hiring hall "the root of all evil in the construction industry."[78] The task force on hiring halls that the CUAIR formed in 1972 grew out of a construction users meeting in

---

Feb. 3, 1971, at A-11.

[74]*Economic Prospects and Policies* at 337, 340, 342, 361, 369.

[75]CUAIR, CC, Minutes, June 9, 1970, in BR, 1970-Vol. II: Minutes.

[76]CUAIR, CC, Minutes, Feb. 16, 1971, at 6-7, in BR, 1971-Vol. II: Minutes.

[77]CUAIR, CC, Minutes, Feb. 4, 1972, at 3, in BR, 1972: Vol. II-Minutes. Blough cited figures to the Coordinating Committee showing that 40 percent of new construction in 1971 was subject to the Davis-Bacon Act or related prevailing wage laws. CUAIR, CC, Minutes, Apr. 28, 1972, at 6, in BR, 1972: Vol. II-Minutes.

[78]"U.S. Chamber Conference Discusses Repeal or Suspension of Davis-Bacon," *CLR*, No. 802, Feb. 3, 1971, at A-17, A-18.

Biloxi, Mississippi, at which, according to Blough, almost all the participants agreed that union hiring halls, which he estimated to be the source of three-quarters of all construction workers, were "'the single most serious impediment to solving the problems of manpower supply, restoration of management rights and balanced collective bargaining....'"[79]

The antiunion thrust was again on display at a meeting of the CUAIR Coordinating Committee—which consisted of 19 members, most of whom were vice presidents in charge of labor relations[80]—in March 1972, also attended by representatives of several NCA members serving on the Contractors Task Force. Blough raised the question as to whether the Roundtable should issue a study on project agreements: "After considerable discussion, it was the sense of the meeting that project agreements were not in and of themselves panaceas...." Far more interesting was the only reason adduced for this skepticism:"it may commit all work on the project, even for a period as long as 10 years, to be performed pursuant to collective bargaining agreements and, therefore, may freeze out future open-shop competition."[81] Presumably, the Roundtable expected a good deal more of such competition during the 1970s and into the 1980s. One of the invited speakers at CUAIR's annual meeting in 1972 was the executive vice president of Brown & Root, the country's largest antiunion construction company, who was part of the segment, "Changes Ahead for Construction and Their Effect on the User."[82]

By 1972, CUAIR membership included about 120 firms: "Essentially all of the major companies in the oil, chemical, metals, automobile and rubber industries were Round Table members." In addition to corporations in the paper, textile, glass, building materials, and equipment industries, one-fourth of the membership consisted of electrical utilities, which were especially large construction users. Given the organization's origins, purpose, and interests, it should not have been surprising, but "[u]nfortunately, there

---

[79]"Roundtable Casts Critical Eye at Hiring Halls," *Iron Age*, Aug. 17, 1972, at 19, in SP, Box 5, File-CUAIR. Construction firms voluntarily availed themselves of hiring halls, but the National Utility Contractors Association urged outlawing them."National Utility Contractors Urge Legislation for Control of Unions," *CLR*, No. 819, June 2, 1971, at A-11.

[80]CUAIR, "Coordinating Committee" (Aug. 1, 1972), in SP, Box 5, File-CUAIR.

[81]CUAIR, CC Minutes, Mar. 17, 1972, at 5, in BR, 1972-Vol. II: Minutes.

[82]CUAIR, "Membership Meeting, June 12, 1972, Program," in SP, Box 5, File-CUAIR. No nonunion construction firm appears to have been represented on the Contractors Advisory Committee until 1982 when a Brown & Root official joined. BR, "Construction Committee History—Summary," in BR, 1970: CCH.

was a relatively low level of activity by the Contractor Advisory Council and by the Contractor Task force." What contacts the CUAIR was able to maintain with major contractors were based primarily on "personal associations of members of the Coordinating Committee with senior contractor executives." Despite the considerable time that Blough devoted to the matter in the latter part of 1970, the CUAIR also failed in its effort to forge a separate organization, which would have focused on labor relations problems and embraced general, specialty, and national contractors. The Contractors' Mutual Association (CMA), which he initated in the spring of 1971, attracted fewer than 50 members, in large part because the AGC advised its membership not to join. The Roundtable traced this failure to a lack of understanding of the CMA's objectives. The CUAIR suffered another defeat in 1975-76 when it failed to merge the CMA with the AGC's chosen vehicle, the Council of Construction Employers (CCE); as a result, the CMA failed to make a major contribution to dealing with labor issues.[83]

Nor was the Roundtable invincible in labor-management struggles. Even the Roundtable's key policy of user-contractor solidarity did not always succeed. Despite customer acceptance of delays "in a common cause" and effective marshalling of public opinion against "extravagant union demands," employers proved unable to defeat construction workers during long strikes in Kansas City in 1969 and 1970.[84] Moreover, in 1972, the Mid-America Regional Bargaining Association (MARBA), an organization of 14 regional employers' groups, which the CUAIR believed owed its existence to support by local user groups, demanded that the Carpenters Union in Chicago accept a large number of work rule changes in exchange for a large wage increase. In June, authorizing its first strike since 1919, the Carpenters Chicago District Council was able to shut down almost all building in a three-county area. The union magnified its leverage by finding employment for most of its striking members with 3,000 small contractors, most of whom still held union cards. After subjection to selective picketing throughout the rest of 1972,

---

[83]BR, "Chapter 2" at 8-11. By mid-1972, CUAIR numbered 119 members, a few of whom were vice presidents of the firms they represented. CUAIR, "Members" (July 1, 1972), in SP, Box 5, File-CUAIR,

[84]"In Kansas City They Couldn't Go As Far As They Wanted," 82 (4) *Fortune* 98-101 (Oct. 1970). In 1970, the Cleveland Mechanical Contractors Association thanked the local user group for its help during a four-month strike by pipefitters: although the monetary settlement was "extremely high," the contractors were able to resist demands for restrictive practices. CUAIR *Report*, Dec. 7, 1970, at 1.

MARBA retracted its demands when the 1973 building season began.[85] Nevertheless, CUAIR's Coordinating Committee was informed in July that MARBA "feels that the price of the wage increases was worth union recognition of consolidated bargaining."[86]

Nor was the Roundtable able to gain unchallenged supremacy even within the Nixon administration. The building trades unions' successful strategy of preempting administration attacks visibly irritated the CUAIR. Thus at the Coordinating Committee's October 5 meeting just a month before the 1972 presidential election, Blough, called on by its chairman, Virgil Day, to comment on current events, referred to newspaper reports of union support for Nixon and an interview with the Secretary of Labor attributing to him the view that the second Nixon administration would neither permit antiunion legislation nor undertake massive intrusions into collective bargaining.[87]

At the Coordinating Committee's meeting on September 15, 1972, Blough confidentially raised the possibility of a merger with the Labor Law Study Group and the Links Club group of 25 top executives who met bimonthly to review and report on labor conditions. Some members initially questioned the wisdom of such a combined group, which was tentatively called the Employers Roundtable, "lest the effectiveness of the Roundtable be diluted."[88] In order to prevent such dilution, it was made clear at the committee's October 5 meeting, the new organization's Construction Committee would carry on the work of the Coordinating Committee, which would continue to invite its Contractors Task Force members to some of its meetings. The minutes made no reference to the facial expressions accompanying "the sense of the meeting that the Construction

---

[85]Schneirov & Suhrbur, *Union Brotherhood* at 154-55; CUAIR, CC Minutes, Oct. 5, 1972, at 4, in BR, 1972-Vol. II: Minutes. MARBA invited user support. CUAIR, CC, Minutes, Feb. 4, 1972, at 4, in BR, 1972: Vol. II-Minutes. The strike of 75,000 workers lasted two weeks. "Unions OK Building Strike," *CT*, June 23, 1972, at 1, col. 3; "Builders, Union Sign New Pact," *CT*, July 8, 1972, sect. 1, at 15, col. 3. See also "Unions Urged to Join in Regional Bargaining, " *ENR*, Apr. 20, 1972, at 16. In particular, the Cement Masons Union rejected employers' proposal for a flexible lunch break to be scheduled some time between 11:30 a.m. and 1 p.m. permitting the uninterrupted pouring of concrete. Employers offered to pay double time if a worker was not permitted to eat lunch during this period and to permit him to eat later on company time; under the then existing rule employers had to pay masons double time who were required to work during the fixed lunch break from noon to 12:30. "Strike-Lockout Stalls Chicago Construction," *ENR*, July 6, 1972, at 43. On the formation of MARBA, see "Construction Gets a New Regional Bargaining Group," *ENR*, Dec. 2, 1971, at 33.

[86]CUAIR, CC Minutes, July 27, 1972, at 7, in BR, 1972-Vol. II: Minutes.

[87]CUAIR, CC Minutes, Oct. 5, 1972, at 2, in BR, 1972-Vol. II: Minutes.

[88]CUAIR, CC Minutes, Sept. 15, 1972, at 8-9, in BR, 1972-Vol. II: Minutes.

Committee...should endeavor to preserve for the combined group the reputation which the Roundtable has enjoyed, of having no anti-labor bias."[89] On October 16, 1972, the CUAIR merged with the Labor Law Study Group to form the Business Roundtable-For Responsible Labor-Management Relations. The new organization's Policy Committee appointed an executive committee, which in turn supervised two primary committees, the Construction Committee (formerly the CUAIR's Coordinating Committee), and the Labor Law Committee (formerly the Labor Law Study Group).[90]

One of the principal motives for the merger had been laid out by GE vice president Virgil Day several months earlier. He invidiously compared unions' ability to exercise restraint and leadership and to present a "single unified theory of the case properly supported by research" regarding labor law change with businessmen's multitude of diverse voices. Moreover, Day bemoaned the fact that the proposals issued by the NAM and Chamber of Commerce were worked out by their staffs and thus did not necessarily represent the views of CEOs or business in general.[91] Big Business, in other words, needed its own organization for articulating and propagandizing its views on labor.

The new Construction Committee initially consisted of 18 members. Day was chairman and Rex Reed, vice president in charge of labor relations of AT&T, vice chairman. In addition to J. M. Graney, the former NCA president, who served as the Roundtable's Executive Director-Construction, the other 15 members represented very large industrial corporations and one power company.[92]

The Labor Law Study Group, 39 of whose 60 members also belonged to the CUAIR,[93] was a big business organization created in the 1960s to undo NLRB decisions that had, according to Francis O'Connell, Jr., vice president

---

[89]CUAIR, CC Minutes, Oct. 5, 1972, at 5, in BR, 1972-Vol. II: Minutes.

[90]CUAIR, CC Minutes, Nov. 2, 1972, at 6-7, in BR, 1972-Vol. II: Minutes. For 1973, the Litigation Committee, which had asked for $331,000, was budgeted $200,000, which was found "a bit too tight." The Public Information Committee's budget was reduced from $400,000 to $350,000. BR, CC, Minutes, Dec. 19, 1972, at 4, 5, 8, in BR, 1972-Vol. II: Minutes.

[91]CUAIR, CC, Minutes, Apr. 28, 1972, at 4-5, in BR, 1972: Vol. II-Minutes (R. Eric Miller).

[92]The companies were Texaco, Georgia Power, Kaiser Industries, Humble Oil, General Dynamics, International paper, Shell Oil, Goodrich, Alcoa, GM, du Pont, U.S. Steel, American Smelting and Refining, Dow Chemical, and Owens-Corning Fiberglas. BR, Executive Committee Meeting, Nov. 13, 1972, Minutes at 3, in SP, Box 6, 1st folder. The new name, Construction Committee, was first used in the minutes of the Dec. 5, 1972 meeting. BR, CC, Minutes, Dec. 5, 1972, in BR, 1972-Vol. II: Minutes.

[93]BR, "Chapter 2" at 11.

of Olin Mathieson Chemical Corporation and a key corporate labor relations official, covertly imposed "socialistic...codetermination" on free enterprise.[94]

Big business's labor law bête noire was a 1962 NLRB decision holding that an employer had committed an unfair labor practice by refusing to bargain with a union over its decision to subcontract out work that bargaining unit employees had been performing.[95] The nub of employers' animus was expressed by the histrionic dissent of NLRB member Philip Rodgers, a Republican and Eisenhower appointee: by declaring subcontracting a mandatory subject of collective bargaining, the majority had "thrust the entire question squarely into the arena of economic struggle and industrial turmoil where strikes, picket lines,...protracted litigation, and many other aspects of economic power possessed by a union are 'protected' by this Board and are, therefore, legally available to a union to compel a complete abandonment by management of its proposal, on pain of suffering irreparable damage to every aspect of its business."[96] At a Senate hearing on congressional oversight of administrative agencies, an attorney representing the Chamber of Commerce asserted that under the Wagner Act, "the boss was still the boss." After *Fibreboard*, however, "overnight, management found that it no longer had the exclusive right to manage...." When one senator finally managed to get into the record that the Supreme Court had unanimously upheld the Board, the management attorney demanded that Congress amend the NLRA to exclude "basic management judgments" from collective bargaining.[97]

---

[94]*Congressional Oversight of Administrative Agencies (National Labor Relations Board): Hearings Before the Subcommittee on Separation of Powers of the Senate Committee on the Judiciary,* 90th Cong., 2d Sess. 683 (1968) (statement of Francis O'Connell, Jr., vice president, Olin Mathieson Chemical Corp. and representing the NAM) (quote); Haynes Johnson & Nick Kotz, *Unions* 112-29 (1972); "Construction Users Roundtable Announces Modification of Name, Extended Functions," *CLR*, No. 897, Dec. 6, 1972, at A-1; Peter Slavin, "The Business Roundtable: New Lobbying Arm of Big Business," *BSR*, No. 16, Winter 1975-76, at 28-32; Mark Green & Andrew Buchsbaum, *The Corporate Lobbies: Political Profiles of the Business Roundtable and the Chamber of Commerce* 79-83 (1980); Kim McQuaid, "The Roundtable: Getting Results in Washington," *HBR*, May-June 1981, at 114 (Lexis); James Gross, *Broken Promise: The Subversion of U.S. Labor Relations Policy, 1947-1994*, at 201-36 (1995).

[95]Fibreboard Paper Products Corp., 138 NLRB 550 (1962). The Kennedy Board reheard this case, which the majority holdover-members of the Eisenhower Board had dismissed, after it had decided another case expressly overruling Fibreboard I. Fibreboard Paper Products Corp., 130 NLRB 1558 (1961); Town & Country Mfg. Co., 136 NLRB 1022 (1962).

[96]Fibreboard, 138 NLRB at 558.

[97]*Congressional Oversight of Administrative Agencies (National Labor Relations Board)* at 357, 377 (statement and testimony of Leonard Janofsky).

Reading in the *Wall Street Journal* that the UAW's vice president had told automobile workers, to "thunderous applause," that "'the only prerogatives management has left are the ones we haven't gotten round to taking away from them yet,'"[98] doubtless did little to allay big business's apprehensions. The zealousness with which Roundtable executives pursued these claims is underscored by their statements not meant for external consumption. Speaking to CUAIR's annual members meeting in 1971 on behalf of the Labor Law Reform Group, Frederick Atkinson, a vice president of R. H. Macy and Company, insisted that "in the field of labor law business has been 'backing down aggressively for the last 25 years.'"[99] That Atkinson identified the beginning of this era of employer spinelessness as antedating Taft-Hartley suggested a breathtakingly radically reactionary program. After all, Douglas Soutar, one of the key corporate figures in shaping postwar labor-management relations labor figures and a founder of the Labor Law Study Group and the Roundtable, characterized the relationship with unions in the late 1960s and early 1970s as "civil war."[100]

The perceived need for a merger between the two corporate organizations was based on the realization that legislative reform of labor law along the lines favored by big business "was probably not possible or practical. They felt," as the Roundtable's own history observed, "that reform by litigation offered greater opportunities, but such an approach required a larger and broader base and greater support from CEO's...."[101]

The March Group, yet another organization of CEOs of large corporations such as GE and Alcoa, who were concerned about declining U.S. competitiveness and sought to create consensus on certain public policy issues, merged into the Business Roundtable in 1973.[102] The Roundtable, in

---

[98]Walter Mossberg, "Factory Bordeom: How Vital an Issue?" *WSJ*, Mar. 23, 1973, at 10, col. 4 at 5-6.

[99]CUAIR, Members Meeting, June 3, 1971, Minutes at 17, in SP, Box 5.

[100]Telephone interview with Douglas Soutar, Litchfield Park, AZ (Jan. 8, 1999). When asked about Robert Georgine's repeated attacks in the 1970s on the Roundtable for engaging in a "terrible conspiracy" to "break" construction unions, Soutar laughed and observed that corporations had a right to get together to defend their interests so long as they did not violate the antitrust laws. Telephone interview with Soutar. For one of the early versions of Georgine's attacks (containing the preceding quoted words), see Haynes Johnson & Nick Kotz, *Unions* 138 (1972). Other authors try to meld such a "conspiracy theory" with "the 'just desserts' theory," according to which construction workers brought on the open shop movement by securing wage increases far in excess of inflation or productivity gains. Mangum & Walsh, *Union Resilience in Troubled Times* at 169-70.

[101]"1972 Summary CUAIR CC" n.p. [6], in BR, CCH 1972.

[102]John Harper, Alcoa chairman, who had been cochair of the March Group, became cochair

the words of Francis O'Connell, Olin Corporation's representative on the CUAIR and the Labor Law Study Group, "sprang from two organizations formed out of concern over the excessive power of organized labor and the abuse of that power."[103] *ENR* engaged in extraordinary understatement when it predicted in 1974 that in the year 2000 the Roundtable would be "the most articulate, influential and effective lobbyists for legislated reforms in construction labor relations."[104] Indeed, by 1976, *Business Week* had already certified it as "Business' Most Powerful Lobby in Washington."[105] If in 1969 the Roundtable sought to shield its very existence from scrutiny, by 1976 it was forced to witness its entire membership, matched up with the corresponding Fortune 500 rankings, listed by Representative Wright Patman in the *Congressional Record*.[106] Some irony attaches to Patman's method: in 1969-1970 the Roundtable actually checked the list of the top *Fortune* 200 companies to determine which large construction users had not yet received an invitation to join.[107]

The CUAIR's objectives continued to be promoted by the merged organization's labor management and construction committees, which assisted local construction user councils. As articulated by the Roundtable, those objectives included: support for contractors in labor negotiations; expanding the construction labor force, "particularly through the employment of minorities"; increased use of helpers and other non-journeymen; eliminating work restrictions; "promoting the contractor's right to manage";

---

of the Roundtable. BR, *Report*, No. 73-5, at 1 (May 23, 1973); BR, "The History of the Business Roundtable" (http://www.brtable.org); Thomas Ferguson & Joel Rogers, "The Knights of the Roundtable," *Nation*, Dec. 15, 1979, at 620-25 at 624. According to BR, "Chapter 2" at 11, the March Group had been part of the 1972 merger.

[103]Francis O'Connell, "Too Cozy with Labor?" *Fortune*, May 22, 1978, at 24 (Lexis). In this letter to the editor, O'Connell complained that soon the Roundtable "began to shy away from open engagement in the battles against organized labor power."

[104]Charles Harding & James Fullilove, "Future of the Labor Force," *ENR*, Apr. 30, 1974, at 313-22 at 320.

[105]"Business' Most Powerful Lobby in Washington, *BW*, Dec. 20, 1976, at 60. Yet by 1997 *Fortune* reported that the Roundtable, "like a vacuum-tube operation struggling to survive in a digital age," had become an "also-ran" because CEOs were "too busy restructuring, reengineering, merging or acquiring to dabble in public policy." Jeffrey Birnbaum, "Washington's Power 25: Which Pressure Groups Are Best at Manipulating the Laws We Live By?" *Fortune*, Dec. 1997, at 144 (Lexis).

[106]122 Cong. Rec. 4074-75 (1976).

[107]CUAIR, CC, Minutes, Dec. 2, 1969, in BR, 1969: Vol. II-Minutes; CUAIR, CC, Minutes, Jan. 6, 1970, in BR, 1970: Vol. II-Minutes.

and lobbying for legislative reform.[108] For 1973, the Construction Committee's highest legislative priorities related to the Davis-Bacon Act and secondary boycotts.[109]

The Roundtable's impact, according to Douglas Soutar, a vice president of the American Smelting and Refining Company, a founder of the Labor Law group, member of the Roundtable's Construction Committee, and chairman of its Labor-Management Committee, lay above all in the "coordinated effect" that it was able to bring about by virtue of the money its immensely wealthy corporate members could contribute: "the Roundtable funded everyone." The Roundtable project that, in Soutar's view, achieved most was the litigation that it financed to counteract "union power unvarnished." Remaining hidden in the background, the Roundtable funded cases, nominally brought, according to Soutar, by a "poor devil" of a small construction contractor, in which the Chamber of Commerce of the United States appeared as an amicus represented by Gerard Smetana, at the time an attorney with Roundtable member Sears, Roebuck, and co-chairman of the Roundtable's Litigation Committee, who during the remainder of the twentieth century participated in a large volume of appellate litigation seeking to roll back union rights, or, in the Roundtable's words, to achieve "more equitable labor relations in America." The cases, largely dealing with secondary boycott and picketing issues, were designed to establish proemployer precedents that the Roundtable believed could not be expected from a prolabor NLRB or the Congress. In 1973, for example, one of the Litigation Committee's priorities was to expand the antitrust laws to cover union violence against open-shop contractors intended to fix prices by means of forced union rates. In retrospect, Soutar ranked these litigational results as the Roundtable's most important accomplishments.[110]

---

[108]BR, "Chapter 2" at 12-13.

[109]BR, "The Business Roundtable: Its Purpose and Program," n.p. [slide 42] (Apr. 4, 1973), in BR, CCH: 1973.

[110]Telephone interview with Douglas Soutar, Litchfield Park, AZ (Jan. 8, 1999); BR, *Report*, No. 73-5, at 4 (May 23, 1973); BR, *Report*, No. 73-10, at 6 (Oct. 29, 1973); BR, "The Business Roundtable: Its Purpose and Program," n.p. [slide 46] (Apr. 4, 1973), in BR, CCH: 1973. Included among the many cases were George Koch Sons, Inc. v. NLRB, 490 F.2d 323 (4th Cir. 1973); Connell Construction Co. v. Plumbers and Steamfitters Local Union No. 100, 421 U.S. 616 (1975); NLRB v. Enterprise Association, Local 638, 429 U.S. 507 (1977); Altemose Construction Co.v. Building and Construction Trades Council of Philadelphia, 443 F. Supp. 492 (E.D. Penn. 1977); Chamber of Commerce of the United States v. NLRB, 574 F.2d 457 (9th Cir. 1978). Other litigation focused on unions' antitrust liability and lawfulness of government payment of public welfare benefits to strikers.

The focus on litigation resulted from the Roundtable's perception in 1969 that "the makeup of Congress (and particularly of the Labor Committee of the Senate and House) is unfriendly to management, tools of labor, and could block anything we tried to do."[111] Four years later this judgment remained unchanged. In a letter to Virgil Day, the president of a research organization consoled the Roundtable official with the thought that despite "the 'Mexican standoff' aspect to the legislative reform matter"—meaning that if labor introduced any prolabor bills, the Roundtable's issues would be added on as amendments—"the litigation program is sawing away with mounting success, and 'law' is being written which is just as effective as equivalent legislation itself."[112]

The Business Roundtable went to some verbal lengths to assure the world that it was not out to destroy unions. One of its "most important" activities was promoting the formation of local users groups or "local Roundtables" throughout the United States, which were designed to be primarily responsible for overcoming the imbalance between construction

---

BR, *Report*, No. 73-10, at 6 (Oct. 29, 1973). Before *Koch*, which dealt with the Plumbers union's right to refuse to install certain pipes, which GE, the customer, required the construction firm to use, but which violated the terms of the labor agreement between the construction firm and the union because they had been cut and threaded offsite, was argued before the NLRB, Blough sent two letters to the membership alerting them to the case's importance and enclosing amicus briefs. Letter from Blough (June 8 and July 20, 1972), in SP, Box 5, File-CUAIR. The amicus brief filed by Roundtable member American Electric Power Service Corporation argued that at stake was whether owners were free to design their plants as their architects and engineers specified or whether local building trade unions would be permitted to "dictate design and construction. ... To take away this last measure of protection will purely and simply place all authority over the construction of plants at the mercy of the Building Trades Unions." Amicus Curiae Brief of the American Electric Power Service Corp., at 8, 14, Local Union No. 438, United Association of Journeymen and Apprentices of the Plumbing and Pipe Fitting Industry, 201 NLRB 59 (1973). SP, Box 5, File-CUAIR. The employers prevailed on the grounds that the union's action was a secondary boycott because the members' employer had no power to give them the work that they demanded and therefore their boycott was designed to put pressure on the decision maker, which was a neutral employer. On the historical aims of such boycotts, which included elimination of low-paid unskilled work, see Leo Wolman, *The Boycott in American Trade Unions* 49-59 (1916). On collective agreements with the Plumbers in which such shop work was banned, see Montgomery, *Industrial Relations in the Chicago Building Trades* 168-69. Haber, *Industrial Relations in the Building Industry* at 220, found that many unions were aware that "most building operations will eventually be mechanized, and ...recognize[d] that opposition to the spread of shop work [wa]s futile."

[111][   ] to Frederick Atkinson (Nov. 12, 1969), in SP, Box 6, File-Business Roundtable Annual Mtg-DS Report 6/16/75 (summarizing the sense of a Fair Labor Law Study Group meeting).

[112][   ] to Day (June 27, 1973), in SP, Box 6, File-Business Roundtable Annual Mtg-DS Report 6/16/75.

labor and management.[113] The Roundtable had organized dozens, many of which were chaired by the highest executives of some of the largest corporations in the city or region.[114] At a meeting of one such users group in October 1973 John Harper, the Roundtable's chairman (and CEO of Alcoa), insisted, in a non sequitur, that the organization "would neither accept nor deserve a stamp of anti-union bias...because it is devoted to improving the performance of the business system for the benefit of all the American people." This misleading rhetoric was echoed by Soutar, who ranked high among the Roundtable's objectives "'a consistent, continuing endeavor to give the organization the accurate stamp of being pro-business, pro-public, and not anti-union.'"[115] And Virgil Day repeated the self-denying sentiment at the 1975 annual conference of local user groups: "It should be clearly understood that the Roundtable has no position on the open shop as against unionized construction; the Roundtable is concerned with every facet of the industry."[116]

The Roundtable also minced words in describing the objective of its general labor law reform program. It protested that its goal was not to develop "a punitive thrust against organized labor, but to safeguard the worker's right to decide whether or not to join a union, and, if he does, to have a union responsive to his needs...."[117]

Chief among the Roundtable's non-antiunion activities was promoting bad publicity for construction unions and sympathetic attention for the industry's nonunion sector. The grant that it bestowed on Herbert Northrup's *Open Shop Construction*, which was funded entirely by contributions from businesses, including both a large antiunion construction firm, H. B. Zachry Company, and the increasingly antiunion user and Roundtable member E. I. du Pont de Nemours, was well spent: the book spawned enormous positive media coverage of the nonunion construction

---

[113]Letter from Roger Blough to E. McL. Tittman [sic], chairman, ASARCO (Dec. 5, 1969), in SP, Box 5, File-CUAIR 1969-1970 (quote); "Preliminary: Construction Users Anti-Inflation Roundtable" at 3 (Dec. 8, 1969), in SP, Box 5, File-CC (quote).

[114]The chairman of Inland Steel Company was chairman of the Chicago Construction Users Council, while the president of the New York Telephone Company presided over the New York Construction Users Council. Business Roundtable, "Area with Local User Group Activity" (June 1, 1973), in SP, Box 5, File-CUAIR Membership.

[115]BR, *Report*, No. 73-10, at 2, 6 (Oct. 29, 1973).

[116]*CUH*, May 1975, at 4.

[117]*RR*, No. 74-4, at 2 (Apr. 26, 1974).

sector and put unions on the defensive.[118] Northrup turned to "industry circles" for financing after the DOL in 1971 had rejected his proposal to study manpower training in nonunion construction firms.[119] At its August 22, 1972 meeting, CUAIR's Coordinating Committee discussed the proposal that Northrup had submitted for a $50,000 18-month study. The committee agreed that the study was needed, but concluded that since "anti-inflation activity" was its "general purpose," it "should not become a Roundtable study." Instead, it decided that Northrup's proposal "will be brought to the attention of various member companies which will be able to decide on a company-by-company basis whether or not to participate in sponsoring it." As Northrup himself conceded: "The Roundtable does not campaign for open shop construction as such. It does, however, encourage alternatives to the union shop where it is feasible, and this, of course, involves opening up bid opportunities to open shop contractors."[120]

The Roundtable also supported the explicitly open-shop ABC in its struggle for "honest law and order"—that is, against union "violence."[121] In 1972, Leon Altemose, perhaps the highest-profile nonunion target of union violence, attended a Coordinating Committee meeting together with his attorney to discuss the problems of open-shop contractors who use union subcontractors.[122] Gerard Smetana, the Roundtable's chief labor lawyer, was co-counsel for Altemose and others who sued 50 unions for violating the

---

[118]E.g., "50 to 60% of U.S. Construction May Be Open Shop," *ENR*, Sept. 18, 1975, at 41.

[119]Northrup & Foster, *Open Shop Construction* at iv (acknowledging Roundtable grant).

[120]CUAIR, CC, Minutes, Aug. 22, 1972, at 4, in BR, 1972-Vol. II: Minutes; Northrup & Foster, *Open Shop Construction* at 21. Three years later the Roundtable without dissent declined another request from Northrup for $20,000 to study minority employment in construction. In that context, Edgar Lore, vice chairman of Dravo, made the interesting comment that since Robert Georgine had become BCTD president, unions had acquiesced more in minority employment. BR, CC, Minutes, Oct. 21, 1975, at 7, in BR, CCH: 1975.

[121]Northrup & Foster, *Open Shop Construction* at 203. In his history of the Operating Engineers, Mangum explains the background to violent confrontation in the industry: in the 1920s and 1930s, "contractors were...tough, and organizational success or failure often rested on the relative abilities of contractor and business agent in physical combat." Large nonunion firms performing most of the heavy construction "recruited crews in low-wage areas, transported them to the job site where they were housed in tent camps, surrounded by barbed wire, and patrolled by armed guards, if necessary, to keep union organizers out. When the job was finished, the contractor often dumped his crew on the local community and recruited another for his next job. Local labor leaders eager to protect local working conditions replied in kind." Garth Mangum, *The Operating Engineers: The Economic History of a Trade Union* 251-52 (1964). See also *id.* at 243: "Those whose work is of a physical nature are likely to react physically to displeasure or in pursuit of their goals."

[122]CUAIR, CC, Minutes, July 6, 1972, in BR, 1972-Vol. II, Minutes.

antitrust laws.[123]   In 1974, its Construction Committee also gave John Trimmer, the executive vice president of the ABC, the opportunity to attend one of its meetings to address it.[124]

The Roundtable "worked closely with the author in developing" a series of three articles that *Reader's Digest* published with intense propagandistic fervor on this subject in three consecutive issues in 1973. In addition to the "initial circulation of some 18 million copies," the Roundtable "plan[ned] to distribute re-prints to editorial people and opinion leaders."[125] The Roundtable also sought to influence general public opinion. In early 1974 the Construction Committee reported that *Reader's Digest* would publish, over three years, "with Roundtable sponsorship and major financing,...monthly articles (labeled advertisement, but identical with other textual material in the magazine) that would depict the many aspects of business's contributions to society."[126] It then spent alone in 1975 $1.2 million for 136 pages of advertsting in *Reader's Digest* that was written as a "joint venture" by the magazine's staff as if it were editorial material.[127] The Roundtable's growing influence was reflected in the request for help from leading CBS documentary producers who were planning to develop a program to show the obstacles to increased productivity and management's exercise of control: "The producer has asked the Roundtable staff for guidance and for identification of a major project, at any location in the U.S., where he could depict all of the productivity-inhibiting practices that prevail in the industry."[128] Anecdotal evidence that the "Roundtable's message has even affected the ideas of the men themselves. I've often heard people say that 'We priced ourselves out of the market,' or 'We have to give up

---

[123]*RR*, No. 73-5, at 4 (May 23, 1973).

[124]BR, CC, Minutes, July 16, 1974, in BR, CCH: 1974.

[125]Letter from [ ], Public Information Committee, to the Roundtable's Policy, Construction, Labor-Management, and Public Information committees (June 4, 1973), in SP, Box 6, File: BR-General; Charles Stevenson, "The Tyranny of Terrorism in the Building Trades," 102 *RD*, June 1973, at 89-94; *idem*, "The Construction Unions Declare War," 103 *RD*, July 1973, at 79-83; *idem*, "Labor Violence—A National Scandal," 103 *RD*, Aug. 1973, at 153-58.

[126]BR, CC, Minutes, Feb. 19, 1974, at 5, in BR, CCC: 1974. *Reader's Digest* staff was to write the ads. BR, CC, Minutes, Mar. 1, 1974, at 7, in BR, CCH: 1974.

[127]"Business Roundtable, Reader's Digest Would Brainwash College Students," 95 (4) *Carpenter* 18 (Apr. 1975); Gross, *Broken Promise* at 235; Mark Erlich, *Labor at the Ballot Box: The Massachusetts Prevailing Wage Campaign of 1988*, at 26 (1990); BR, *Report*, No. 75-2, at 2-3 (Mar. 1975) (quote).

[128]BR, CC, Minutes, Feb. 19, 1974, at 5, in BR, CCH: 1974.

something.'"[129]

Because CUAIR "has long seen the need for, and has worked for legislation curbing the excessive power of union officials," the National Right to Work Committee invited Blough in June 1972 to an "unpublicized conference" of organizations sharing this common goal.   Although scheduling conflicts precluded his attendance, Blough, who agreed that there was "considerable need for legislative change," referred the group to the Labor Law Study Group, which was responsible for legal reforms in construction.[130]   At the Business Roundtable's first annual meeting in June 1973, its Construction Industry Panel heard Nello Teer, Jr., owner of a nonunion construction firm, both praise the Roundtable for its salutary effect on the industry and call for two extraordinarily radical changes that would have restored the blatantly proemployer biased legal framework for labor-management relations that had prevailed before the 1930s: a national right-to-work law (which would have made union shop agreements between employers and unions an unfair labor practice under the NLRA) and application of antitrust laws to unions.[131]   Such federal action would, presumably, not have qualified as part of the "Niagara of new labor legislation" with which the Roundtable's Labor-Management Committee was "deeply concerned...."[132]

The Roundtable devoted special attention to union hiring halls, which form "a major base of union power"[133]:

An increase in demand for labor encourages an increase in supply in most industries. Not necessarily so in construction. A union-administered work referral system establishes an environment conducive to artificial shortages. These shortages, in turn, have enabled the unions to achieve stronger bargaining positions, and thereby to obtain inflationary wage increases, excessively restrictive work practices, and other costly conditions of employment. In his role as hiring hall administrator, a union official is often torn between the longer term interests of the industry and the union members on the one hand and the political appeal of

---

[129] Robert Cook, "Work in the Construction Industry: A Report from the Field," in 2 *Research in Social Problems and Public Policy* 207-41 at 233 (1982).

[130]Letter from National Right to Work Committee [ ] to Roger Blough (June 5, 1972), and Roger Blough to Reed Larson (June 14, 1972), in SP, Box 5, File-CUAIR.

[131]*RR*, No. 73-6, at 2-3 (June 15, 1973).

[132]*RR*, No. 73-6, at 3 (June 15, 1973).

[133]"The Hiring Hall in the Construction Industry," in BR, *Coming to Grips with Some Major Problems in the Construction Industry* 15-23 at 16 (1974).

maintaining a surplus of job opportunities and additional income through overtime.[134]

The Roundtable regarded as "[t]he most promising solution...a management operated referral system," which itself "could be operated for profit...."[135] The one fundamental characteristic of the hiring hall that the Roundtable saw no need to mention, let alone alter, was its throw-away treatment of workers, who under all of these systems lacked even a modicum of employment security. What the Roundtable meant by contractors' regarding the hiring hall as "the most convenient means of meeting the constantly changing labor force requirements"[136] was that they employed few permanent employees, being free to discharge all their workers at the end of each project. To be sure, the Roundtable was unable to reach agreement with the NCA firms on labor sourcing. For although they were similarly unmotivated to restructure the industry to create year-round employment, they insisted that the fact that many of their projects were "gigantic, complex, and in remote areas" made it too risky to implement any of the Roundtable's proposals.[137]

The subordination of the contractor to the industrial user that the Roundtable envisioned emerged with great clarity from the second volume of its *Coming to Grips with Some Major Problems in the Construction Industry*, one of whose chapters was devoted to the contribution that contract language between owner and contractor could make to dealing with unions' "[a]buse" of their excessive power during the negotiation and administration of collective bargaining agreements. The Roundtable explained its members' unusual interest in the relations between construction firms and unions by reference to the demonstration effect: "[i]nflationary" construction wages influence industrial wages; similarly, building trades unions' restrictive practices "set targets for industrial workers and unions," who may be drawn into the former's strikes and other "counterproductive practices...."[138] Among the provisions that the Roundtable recommended to its members for inclusion

---

[134]"Report on 'The Hiring Hall in the Construction Industry' by Task Force of Construction Committee of the Business Roundtable," *CLR*, No. 920, May 23, 1973, at E-1, E-2.

[135]BR, *Coming to Grips with Some Major Problems in the Construction Industry* 16, 17, 20 (1974).

[136]BR, *Coming to Grips with Some Major Problems in the Construction Industry* 16 (1974).

[137]*RR*, No. 73-10, at 2-3 (Oct. 29, 1973) (statement of Fred Stevens, NCA president and executive of Stone and Webster).

[138]BR, 2 *Coming to Grips with Some Major Problems in the Construction Industry* 1 (1978).

in their construction contracts was one requiring the contractor to inform users immediately of every collective bargaining demand made on it.[139] In a remarkable paternalistic effort to substitute its will for a pusillanimous contractor's, the Roundtable then urged that in order "to insure that the contractor's views and interests are felt at the bargaining table," members include in their contracts a provision stating that if the contractor subscribes to a multiemployer bargaining organization, the contractor "shall, if User so directs," participate to the fullest extent" in the group's collective bargaining. In order to weaken union workers striking against contractors operating in the locality where industrial users' projects are being built, the Roundtable recommended provisions that would entitle its members to deprive such strikers of alternative employment on the members' projects. Thus it offered as a model provision: "In the event of a labor dispute which threatens adversely to affect the progress or cost of the work hereunder, User reserves the right to restrict additional hiring of employees, to suspend or discontinue the work of the contractor and any subcontractors, or in User's sole discretion to terminate this contract. This paragraph shall be applicable whether or not the contractor or subcontractor is directly involved in said labor dispute."[140]

After laying out this breathtakingly invasive interference with an independent firm's entrepreneurial freedom, the Roundtable, as an afterthought, advised owners that they should "recognize the independent employer status of their contractors and should not attempt to usurp the contractor's prerogatives in his labor relations with his employees."[141] Otherwise, under the NLRA, the user could be held an ally or co-employer "if he becomes excessively involved in the contractor's labor relations decisions."[142] The resulting twofold danger for users would be joint liability for any unfair labor practices committed by contractors and loss of protection against secondary boycotts by unions, which might then become privileged

---

[139]BR, 2 *Coming to Grips with Some Major Problems in the Construction Industry* 3 (1978).

[140]BR, 2 *Coming to Grips with Some Major Problems in the Construction Industry* 4 (1978). In contrast, in 1913, the German construction employers association (Arbeitgeber-Bund für das Baugewerbe) entered into cartel contracts with its counterparts in Sweden, Norway, Denmark, Belgium, Switzerland, and Austria-Hungary in order to insure that striking or locked out workers not be hired during strikes or lockouts. Otto Liebich, *Organisations- und Arbeitsverhältnisse im Baugewerbe: Eine volkswirtschaftliche Studie* 38 (1922).

[141]BR, 2 *Coming to Grips with Some Major Problems in the Construction Industry* 31 (1978).

[142]BR, 2 *Coming to Grips with Some Major Problems in the Construction Industry* 2 (1978).

to picket the user's operations to pressure it to pressure the contractor to resume work.[143]

The self-contradictions inherent in such paternalism were evident in the provisions that, for example, Mobil Oil inserted into its contracts. It required construction firms to take any and all steps to deal with union violations of collective bargaining agreements. A Mobil contractor also "shall decisively exercise his management rights." Nevertheless, Mobil assured the Roundtable's national conference of user groups, such intervention in no way represented a departure from the firm's "philosophy" of not becoming directly involved in the relationship between a contractor and its labor force.[144]

Finally, in order to preempt potential antitrust violations, the Roundtable warned that "to avoid even the appearance of conspiracy it is completely inappropriate for Users to agree among themselves to use any specific contract language."[145] The admonition was curious since the Roundtable's whole reason for existing was to promote, if not to coerce, such agreement first among user-members and then with their construction firms.[146] Internally, the Roundtable adopted a lighthearted attitude toward the risk of antitrust liability. At its second annual members meeting in 1971, it heard one of Blough's White & Case partners explain that "'union activity and joint employer activity to combat it fall outside the antitrust laws.'" Moroever, "'it is no evidence of conspiracy that those who take umbrellas to the ballgame open them when the rain begins.'"[147]

Big business's interest in the development of the construction industry derived from two distinct aspects: rising construction costs, which

---

[143]BR, 2 *Coming to Grips with Some Major Problems in the Construction Industry* 20, 22 (1978).

[144]*RR*, No. 72-12, at 4 (Nov. 28, 1972).

[145]BR, 2 *Coming to Grips with Some Major Problems in the Construction Industry* 23(1978).

[146]To ward off antitrust charges, the Roundtable routinely alleged that it was purely "educational and advisory," lacking authority to issue orders, and composed of members "free to follow or ignore its suggestions." "User teamwork: A New Force in the Industry," *ENR*, Oct. 12, 1972, at 55, 58.

[147]CUAIR, Members Meeting, June 3, 1971, Minutes at 14, in SP, Box 5. The attorney periodically updated his legal advice. He noted that absent an existing labor dispute, it was uncertain whether joint efforts by owners to strengthen contractors' position with regard to a potential labor dispute were protected. Later a White & Case lawyer also advised the Roundtable collectively not to favor or discriminate against contractors or other customers based on whether they support the Roundtable. Haliburton Fales 2d, "Antitrust Implications of Roundtable Activities" 64-65 (Dec. 12, 1975), in BR, 1970: CCH-Antitrust.

resulted in plant costs that rose at an above-average rate, and the troubling suspicion that construction union militance would spread to their own industrial unions. These two aspects could be identical only if rising construction wages were the chief cause of rising plant costs. Although this view was sometimes voiced, CUAIR representatives clearly formulated the distinction. Blough explicitly stressed the "spillover effect" of construction wages into other industries in 1969 at the NAM's Congress of American Industry.[148] He characterized the "inflationary impact of skyrocketing settlements" in construction as "almost unbelievable in magnitude."[149] Two years later he testified to Congress that "the source of wage-push inflation lies primarily...in...construction."[150] When Senator Charles Percy asked him hypothetically "what would have happened to wages in the construction industry if the construction industry were subjected to foreign competition as so many industries are in this country," Blough contested the question's premise by insisting that there was "definitely indirect competition between construction costs abroad and construction costs in this country." For example, every time a shoe manufacturer in Austria sold a pair of shoes, it sold a piece of the factory: "So, whether it is recognized by the construction unions or others in this country, the construction costs abroad are definitely involved in every product...shipped in from abroad."[151]

Similarly, Dow Chemical, which was represented on the Roundtable's Coordinating Committee, warned the construction industry that a continued increase in construction wages would prompt it to stop construction projects, build plants abroad, or carry them out by force account.[152] Indeed, in 1970, Dow helped set an important labor law precedent when it awarded a contract to Helger Construction, Inc., a nonunion firm organized by Gerace Construction, Inc., a union firm, which, because it anticipated a strike by its union workers, could not meet Dow's requirement that it guarantee completion without a work stoppage. By ruling that the employer did not commit an unfair practice by engaging in such a dual union/nonunion ("double-breasted") operation, the NLRB removed one potentially

---

[148]"Wages, Civil Rights Need an Answer," *ENR*, Dec. 11, 1969, at 61.

[149]John Allan, "Inflation Viewed as Stubborn Foe," *NYT*, Dec. 6, 1969, at 55, col. 1, at 59, col. 4.

[150]*Economic Prospects and Policies* at 341.

[151]*Economic Prospects and Policies* at 374.

[152]"Dow Official Warns Industry to Control Its Labor Costs," *ENR*, Apr. 2, 1970, at 54.

troublesome legal obstacle to the conversion of traditional unionized firms to nonunion operations.[153]

Just a few weeks after Dow made its threat, Blough sent a memo to Roundtable members relating various "self-help" measures that members had adopted to escape "the unhealthy rise in construction wage costs...." First on the list was force account maintenance—that is, construction performed by the industrial firm's own employees.[154] In 1969 the "companies seeking to hold the line in construction [we]re so embattled," according to A. H. Raskin, the country's premier labor reporter, "that they [we]re even hinting at the possibility of organizing captive construction firms to build plants if they cannot halt the runaway trend of union rates."[155] Dayton Power & Light created such a company, which lowered costs by having to deal with only one union—and an "independent" one at that.[156] Among force account's advantages was the ability to "avoid mixing $40 a day men with $80 a day men doing the same work in the same plant." In addition to avoiding the unrest triggered by the confrontation of two labor markets, Blough and his anonymous member left unmentioned the obvious advantage of not having to pay anyone $80 a day. They also recommended force account as an effective way to expand the total construction labor force. In adding that the payroll construction workers "[p]resumably...would have affiliation with whatever industrial union is present in the plant,"[157] the CUAIR did not need to mention that often shifting to force account construction would bring about deunionization because many plants operated by Roundtable member were union free. For example, only about 20 percent of Dow Chemical's own employees were unionized—one-half of the weighted average of 41 percent for a group of 78 large corporations.[158]

Vastly more important than inside construction forces was Blough's

---

[153]Gerace Construction, Inc., 193 NLRB 645 (1971). See also below chapter 15.

[154]On force account construction, see Bernard Wysocki, Jr., "Utilities Try Building Own Facilities to Control Costs and Raise Productivity," *WSJ*, July 15, 1975, at 38, col. 1.

[155]A. H. Raskin, "Building Trades: Controls for a Rough Industry?" *NYT*, Sept. 28, 1969, sect. 4, at 4, col. 1 at 3.

[156]*RR*, No. 74-11, at 2 (Nov. 1974).

[157]Roger M. Blough to Members of the Roundtable (Apr. 27, 1970), in SP, Box 5, CUAIR 1969-1970. A few weeks later, the president of American Cyanamid Co. informed Blough that it used payroll employees to do maintenance work in almost all of its plants. Cliff Siverd to Roger Blough (June 2, 1970), in SP, Box 5, File-CUAIR 1969-1970.

[158]Corporate Data Exchange, *Labor Relations* at 14-15.

news item that:

> Several construction users have reported an increasing interest in <u>open bidding for construction work</u>, with merit shop or open shop contractors having an equal opportunity to bid against union shop contractors.
>
> [O]pen shop and merit shop work seems to be growing in relation to 100% building trades projects. Individual open shop firms have increased in both total capacity and complexity of work undertaken. Competitively, total business ratings seem to be moving in the direction of open-shop projects.
>
> Some national contractors are evidencing interest in organizing open-shop affiliates.
>
> The Construction Roundtable is not anti-union and has taken no position against union organizations of any kind. The developments in open bidding, however, is the type of information to which it believes its members are entitled.[159]

This memorandum from April 27, 1970, only a few months after its formation, encapsulated the most far-reaching impact that the Roundtable was to achieve in the coming decades: neither legislation nor restructuring of collective bargaining would prove to be the Archimedian point for mastering construction unions. Instead of reform of collective bargaining, industrial capital chose to contain and roll it back by fostering the expansion of the nonunion sector of construction. In conformity with this thrust, large union construction firms were already preparing to go 'double-breasted,' as the practice of operating nonunion subsidiaries later became known. That market forces may well have triggered this response is not irreconcilable with the Roundtable's then invisible, but now visible, helping hand.

Regardless of whether highly paid building tradesmen were working inside industrial plants or not, Roundtable members were increasingly worried about the "disruptive effect that unrealistically high construction wages have on industrial wage rates." Startled that after 10 years graduate engineers' average salary amounted to only 88 percent of a plumber's wage, the chairman of Eastman Kodak told a local users' meeting in late 1970 that it was hard to justify the five-dollar an hour wage gap between construction and industrial electricians.[160]

That the Roundtable was serious about persuading big business to slow down construction projects if necessary to stiffen contractors' resistance

---

[159]Roger M. Blough to Members of the Roundtable (Apr. 27, 1970), in SP, Box 5, CUAIR 1969-1970.

[160]Remarks by Louis Eilers at Construction Users Meeting (Nov. 23, 1970), included in Memo from Roger Blough to Roundtable Members (Dec. 21, 1970), in SP, Box 5, File-CUAIR 1969-1970.

to unions' demands emerged from letters that Blough sent to the entire membership to alert them to a strike of elevator construction and maintenance workers:

> The Roundtable does not get involved in labor negotiations. Nevertheless, in view of the stakes in this one and the fact that construction users are the ones who will ultimately pay the bill and suffer in other ways from a poor bargain if one is forced, we felt it was in order to advise you of the current situation.
>
> It frequently involves considerable self-restraint not to insist upon an early completion of work such as finishing a bank of elevators in a particular building. But after hearing the facts of this case we believe it is in your own self-interest to be as considerate as you can with your elevator contractor in this particular instance.[161]

In view of the relatively large share that industrial buildings occupy of total industrial capital investments, a common interest in combating above-average cost increases could conceivably have united competing capitals in this regard. By the mid-1970s it was clear that "there has been a long-term shift by industry to favor equipment over fixed plant. This is due in part to more efficient plant design. But it is also due to the cost of industrial construction, which rose 60% between 1970 and 1975—twice the rate of the preceding five years."[162]

The significance of the construction costs of production facilities within the production costs of industrial capital was contested. Here Lefkoe's influential contemporaneous analysis is especially significant since the Roundtable paid him to write it.[163] Lefkoe was hired in May 1968 to "analyze the industry's labor-related problems"[164] by executives of several of

---

[161]Letter from Roger Blough to the Members of the Roundtable (Apr. 20, 1972), in SP, Box 5, File-CUAIR. First among the union's demands was "an extremely complex and restrictive" hiring hall provision. Two months later Blough wrote to the membership that management had reported that user support had been "most helpful" in resisting union demands; he requested that members continue to show self-restraint by refraining from pressuring contractors to accept those demands. Letter from Roger Blough to the Members of the Roundtable (June 27, 1972), in SP, Box 5, File-CUAIR.

[162]Seymour Zucker, "The Danger in the Plant Construction Slump," *BW*, Apr. 5, 1976, at 25. See also USDC, *U.S. Income and Output* 9 (1958).

[163]A DOL memo surveying proposals for dealing with problems in the construction industry accorded Lefkoe's book a prominent place as it did the Roundtable and *Reader's Digest* without knowing that the Roundtable had paid for the other two. Subject: Recent Public Recommendations Made on How to Correct the Problems in the Construction Industry (undated), in in NACP, RG 174: General Records of the Labor Dept., Records of Sec. James D. Hodgson, 1970-1972, 1971, Box No. 94: Commissions, Folder: 1971-Commissions CICBC (Secretary's Working Papers).

[164]M. Lefkoe, *The Crisis in Construction: There Is an Answer* vii (1970). Lefkoe did not identify those who had hired him beyond "the management of several large firms that are concerned

the large corporations that had formed the Labor Law Study Group and, by the time Lefkoe's book appeared, the CUAIR. A business reporter for the *Wall Street Journal* and freelancer for *Fortune*, Lefkoe had previously worked with the driving forces behind the Labor Law group—Day, Soutar, and Atkinson. Intriguingly, Bechtel, Morrison Knudsen, and other large construction firms paid for Lefkoe's services.[165] At its two meetings in August 1969 the CUAIR Coordinating Committee discussed Lefkoe's report.[166] Shortly after its appearance, Soutar also wrote a very positive review of the book, which Blough distributed to the Roundtable's members.[167]

According to Lefkoe, on the one hand, higher construction costs "are an especially important factor in international competition because the United States is forced to rely on modernizing and building new plants and equipment in order to offset lower wage rates abroad." On the other hand, in view of the long period during which the plant could be used, the capital costs would be amortized over such a large volume of output that increased building cost "turns out to be one of the smallest factors of cost per item." As a stylized numerical example, Lefkoe instanced a new plant costing $25 million, one-fourth or $6.5 million of which was accounted for by payroll. Assuming a 25-year amortization period, the difference between a 5 percent and a ten percent wage increase for one year of work amounted to only $325,000 or $13,000 in annual depreciation charges. If the plant produced 1,300,000 widgets annually, the construction workers' wage increase would equal one cent per widget; if widgets cost $10, the wage increase would be reflected in a 0.1 percent unit cost increase; if they cost $100, the increase would be only 0.01 percent. Because these amounts were "almost insignificant" in their own right and especially as compared to the lost sales

---

with and affected by the [construction] industry's problems." After receiving his report in August, 1969, his clients "decided that the report should be made available to the entire construction industry and to firms and organizations outside the industry that are interested in the industry's problems." *Id.*

[165]Telephone interview with Marty Lefkoe, Westport, CT (Dec. 29, 1998). Lefkoe was uncertain 30 years after the events whether nonunion contractors such as Brown & Root also were involved and paid. For background on the Labor Law group, see Gross, *Broken Promise* at 200-209.

[166]CUAIR, CC, Minutes, Aug. 11 and 25, 1969, in BR, 1969, Vol. II-Minutes.

[167]Memo from J. M. Graney to R. M. Blough (June 3, 1970); Memorandum from Roger Blough to Members (July 7, 1970), in SP, Box 5, File-CUAIR 1969-1970. It is unclear where the review appeared, but it may have been an NAM periodical. Soutar questioned Lefkoe's skepticism of users' efforts to change the industry and of employers' efforts to reform the NLRA, but he praised Lefkoe's fundamentalism and deemed most of Lefkoe's provocative hypotheses worthy of action. *Id.*

that the industrial customer would suffer if the contractor had taken a strike to contest the union's demand for a wage increase and the onset of production had been delayed weeks or months, Lefkoe concluded that "in a vast number of instances...industrial and utility firms will *not* save money in the long run if they halt work on construction jobs...to help keep the labor-cost component of their plants...down."[168] Despite this conclusion, which was at odds with the whole thrust of the Roundtable's reason for being, observers agreed that increased government regulation of construction was appropriate in light of "the industry's strategic role in the economy as the principal capital goods sector."[169]

It is possible to specify the interrelations between construction costs and user interest in constraining building trades unions more closely by identifying those industries with the greatest absolute amounts of capital outlays on plant or structures since they were the most important consumers. It is also important, however, to determine whether such outlays also bulked large vis-à-vis these industries' capital expenditures for equipment or machinery; for if plant outlays occupied a relatively insignificant place within a firm's total fixed capital outlays over time, it was unlikely to have been as concerned with increased construction costs and their underlying factors as firms or industries in which those outlays represented a large share of the fixed capital.

The sources and destinations as well as types of capital goods can be located by using capital flow tables to disaggregate input-output data. Data that the Department of Commerce published for 1963 and 1967 revealed that the biggest manufacturing industry consumer of structures was the petroleum refining industry, while the crude petroleum and natural gas extractive industry was much larger still. These two industries also fulfilled the second criterion inasmuch as about two-thirds and four-fifths, respectively, of their fixed capital expenditures were allocated to structures compared to an average of slightly less than three-tenths for manufacturing as a whole. Other industries with significant plant outlays were aircraft, chemicals, food, iron and steel, motor vehicles, nonferrous metals, and paper products. In these industries, however, structures' share in total fixed capital outlays averaged

---

[168]Lefkoe, *The Crisis in Construction* at 112, 113. See also Gordon Bertram & Sherman Maisel, *Industrial Relations in the Construction Industry* 33 (1965).

[169]D. Quinn Mills, "Discussion," *Industrial Relations Research Association Proceedings of the 24th Annual Winter Meeting* 34 (1971). Lefkoe, *The Crisis in Construction* at vii, noted that his clients "did not necessarily agree with all my conclusions and recommendations...."

about one-fourth to one-third. Of outstanding importance, also, was the utilities sector, whose demand not only exceeded that of any industrial branch, but also constituted about two-thirds of its fixed capital expenditures. The communications industry was also a leading source of demand for structures.[170] Table 19 highlights these structure-intensive industries in 1967.

Table 19: Structures as Share of Total New Gross Fixed Capital Formation for Selected Industries, 1967		
Industry	**Value ($000,000)**	**Share (%)**
Utilities	5,469	66
Crude petroleum/gas	2,478	78
Petroleum refining	607	64
Food products	535	28
Iron and steel	486	27
Chemicals	398	24
Motor vehicles	287	31
Aircraft	269	31
Paper	247	22
Nonferrous metals	243	34
Total manufacturing	6,365	28

Source: "Interindustry Transactions in New Structures and Equipment, 1967," 55 (9) *SCB* 9-21, tab. 2 at 10-15 (Sept. 1975).

---

[170]"Interindustry Transactions in New Structures and Equipment, 1967," 55 (9) *SCB* 9-21 (Sept. 1975). These relationships are not invariant over time or across national borders. In the United Kingdom during the 1950s, for example, the petroleum industry represented little demand for structures. O. W. Roskill, Industrial Consultants, *The Building Industry—1962 Onwards: A Survey Report on the Building Industry in the United Kingdom*, tab. 16 at 126 (1962). As the Center to Protect Workers' Rights, *The War on Wage Protection: The Business Offensive* 9 (1979), observed, the steel industry had an additional reason for wanting lower construction costs: "As costs rose, the demand for construction fell. Because steel is the single most costly building material, the lowering demand for construction impacted heavily and adversely upon the steel producers." Its other assertion—that the "steel industry more than any other industrial sector wanted to weaken the construction unions in the sixties"—was supported only by a quotation by the president of U.S. Steel from 1976.

Roundtable members were by and large firms from these very industries. The corporations whose officials initially constituted CUAIR's Policy Group were AT&T, Consumers Power, GE, GM, Kennecott Copper, Standard Oil (New Jersey), and Union Carbide; its Coordinating Committee members were executives of AT&T, Aluminum Company of America, American Electric Power, Dow Chemical, du Pont, General Dyamics, GE, GM, B.F. Goodrich, Humble Oil, International Paper, Owens-Corning Fibreglas, Procter & Gamble, Shell Oil, Texaco, and U.S. Steel.[171] It should come as little surprise that, for example, AT&T assumed a prominent role. Of the more than 100 leading corporate executives filling the Pierre Hotel's Cotillion Room in New York City at CUAIR's second annual members meeting on June 3, 1971—whose after-dinner program included the Secretary of Labor and a member of the CEA—none had more at stake than H.I. Romnes. In his talk on the "Task of the Chief Executive," AT&T's chairman, speaking to an audience of men most of whose firms had "substantial building programs," reported that the Bell System spent $800 million annually on construction costs. He stressed that it was crucial for the CEO to avoid tight building schedules and overtime: "'The top man cools down labor cost pressures....'"[172] Shell Oil, on behalf of its industry, pointed to the long-range considerations by warning in 1971 that growing energy requirements by 1985 "will put a tremendous burden on the construction industry in the late 1970s and early 1980s."[173]

This composition is thus hardly unexpected, but the fact that most of the construction firms in the Roundtable's Contractors Advisory Group and Contractors Task Force were NCA members does give pause.[174] Given the

---

[171]"Owners Use New Vehicle to Fight Inflation," *ENR*, Aug. 21, 1969, at 14-15. By 1976, the large oil corporations were well represented on the Business Roundtable's Policy Committee. Letter from Richard Kibben (Business Roundtable Executive Director—Construction), to author, Mar. 23, 1976.

[172]CUAIR, Members Meeting, June 3, 1971, "Program"; CUAIR, Members Meeting, June 3, 1971, at 5 (quote), in SP, Box 5, File-CUAIR.

[173]CUAIR, CC, Minutes, Oct. 7, 1971, at 2 (David Luckenbill), in BR, 1972-Vol. II, Minutes.

[174]The original Contractors Advisory Group consisted of presidents, chairmen, or owners: George Atkinson (Guy F. Atkinson), Stephen D. Bechtel, Jr. (Bechtel), Robert Dickey III (Dravo), J. Robert Fluor (Fluor), Edwin L. Jones, Jr. (J.A. Jones Construction), John E. Kenney (Foster Wheeler), and H.C. Turner, Jr. (Turner Construction). Bechtel was chairman of the group. The Contractors Task Force consisted largely of vice presidents: R. Coyne (Peter Kiewit Sons'); H. Edgar Lore (Dravo), Donald Grant (Atkinson), James McClary (Morrison-Knudsen), Karl Sippel (Austin), William P. Scott, Jr. (Scott), and R. Eric Miller (Bechtel). "Contractors Assist Roundtable," *ENR*, Sept.

Roundtable's crucial role in creating a critical mass of nonunion construction firms large enough to build large-scale sophisticated industrial projects by encouraging its members and other corporate consumers to contract with antiunion construction firms, a question arises as to why the NCA, which had not abandoned its commitment to union labor, cooperated with the Roundtable, which initially asked it to recommend ways to improve collective bargaining and increase the labor supply.[175] Despite the fact that the Roundtable's "mission," as the current NCA president has remarked, was "putting unions of out business," NCA members had no alternative to cooperating with the Roundtable since these corporations were their main customers.[176] If large industrial firms believed that construction firms were a factor driving up costs, NCA firms had to experience that perception as an expression of their declining competitiveness compelling them either to turn to nonunion labor—which was made difficult if not impossible by the 'sourcing' advantages that unions offered—or to extract from unions a level of productivity (or of unit labor costs) and industrial peace commensurate with that prevailing in the nonunion sector. As a one-time NCA president put it: "'If we don't get the improvement that's necessary to keep our operations economical, we're going to look for other ways of doing things.'"[177]

Although NCA members employed only a small share (2 to 5 percent) of all construction workers (but perhaps as many as 15 percent of all skilled tradesmen),[178] they nevertheless formed "the stronghold of unionism" in the

---

11, 1969, at 17; "User Teamwork: A New Force in the Industry," *ENR*, Oct. 12, 1972, at 55; "NCA Members Ply the World and Find Jobs on Every Continent," *ENR*, Dec. 5, 1974, at 14. By mid-1972, the Advisory Committee's composition was unchanged except that E. F. Wentworth, Jr., chairman of Foster Wheeler had replaced Kenney; on the Contractors Task Force, Sippel and Scott had been replaced by Saul Horowitz, Jr., chairman of HRH Construction, and Walter Limbach, president of Limbach Corp. Construction Users Anti-Inflation Roundtable, "Contractors Advisory Committee" and "Contractors Task Force" (July 21, 1972), in SP, Box 5, File-CUAIR. Soutar, who was a member of the Roundtable's construction committee, stated that R. Eric Miller, who was in charge of labor relations at Bechtel, acted as a kind of NCA liaison with the Roundtable and "never gave us any trouble." Telephone interview with Douglas Soutar, Litchfield Park, AZ (Jan 27, 1999).

[175]"Contractors Assist Roundtable," *ENR*, Sept. 11, 1969, at 17.

[176]Telephone interview with Robert McCormick, Washington, D.C. (Mar. 11, 1999).

[177]"NCA Increases the Pressure to Cut the Fat Out of Labor Costs," *ENR*, Mar. 1, 1973, at 18 (quoting Fred Stevens).

[178]In 1973 NCA firms were reported as offering 10.5 million hours of work per month; in all of 1972, 6.78 billion man-hours of contract construction work were estimated. "NCA Increases the Pressure to Cut the Fat Out of Labor Costs," *ENR*, Mar. 1, 1973, at 18; USDC, *Business Statistics 1973*, at 79 (19th ed., 1973). NCA firms were also reported as employing 75,000 to 150,000 building tradesmen in addition to 100,000 employed by subcontractors; these two groups represented about 3

industry.[179] Given the NCA's traditional commitment to unions, a decision to reduce or eliminate their union connections would have assumed a significance for the whole industry out of proportion to the NCA's specific weight. Other contractors organizations would doubtless have taken such a decision as a signal to forge ahead with an open-shop policy. At the Roundtable's first members meeting in April 1970, the chairman of one of the largest construction firms sounded very much like his customers in supporting legislation to "restore a balance of power between contractors and the unions...."[180] Six months later Stephen Bechtel, Jr. spoke at great length at a Coordinating Committee meeting urging the need to restore management rights with regard to the selection of employees and foremen as well as to "restore the heads of the international unions to a position of greater responsibility and power over the locals." Bechtel also called on the government to expand training programs to alleviate the shortage of skilled workers and to be "more vigilant in enforcing the law, so that hiring halls would not constitute closed shops, and on the NLRB to process employer cases more promptly. Finally, he also wanted the Davis-Bacon Act guidelines altered so that "prevailing wages did not mean the highest wage paid anywhere in the vicinity."[181] The next year, his vice president in charge of labor relations, agreed with the Roundtable that the construction industry was "sick."[182]

Puzzlement as to the relationship between the NCA and the Roundtable is dissolved by understanding that the Roundtable pursued a two-track strategy. On the one hand, its members recognized that construction unions were too entrenched in certain sectors and regions to be dislodged in the near or middle term. The Roundtable's initial modest goals were expressed by three General Dynamics officials in an unpublished 1970 CUAIR task force report. They argued that even if management created a new referral system and regained the right to make work assignments, "the expectable and traditional reaction from the building trades unions will be the

---

to 5 percent of total production worker employment in contract construction in 1970. Damon Stetson, "Builders and Unions Sign an Accord to Curb Strikes," *NYT*, Feb. 15, 1971, at 46, col. 5; USDC, *Business Statistics* at 73.

[179]Northup & Foster, *Open Shop Construction* at 99.

[180]"Report to Members of Construction Users Anti-Inflation Roundtable" at 10 (n.d. [Apr. 1970]), in SP, Box 5, File-CUAIR, 1969-1970 [ ].

[181]BR, CC, Minutes, Oct. 26, 1970, at 3-4, in BR, 1970: Vol. II-Minutes.

[182]CUAIR, Members Meeting, June 3, 1971, Minutes, at 15, in SP, Box 5 (John F. O'Connell).

mounting of new organizing campaigns designed to bring into the union fold the thousands of craftsmen not now unionized."[183] Consequently, the Roundtable incessantly declared that "whatever the future may bring, it is imperative that the strength and expertise of contractors at the bargaining table be greatly improved, with the support and encouragement of construction users."[184] On the other hand, the Roundtable also sought to undermine unions' sources of power (such as the hiring hall) and to promote nonunion building firms, initially in the South, in the industrial construction sector that its own members dominated.[185]

The Roundtable's greatest success—facilitating nonunion penetration of the industrial construction—was a self-help measure that could be implemented despite big business's failures in Congress and in restructuring collective bargaining or the construction industry. However, the Roundtable's focus on the hiring hall as the root of all evil had to remain rhetorical as long as no practical alternatives were available and the construction industry's discontinuities made retention by employers of hundreds of thousands of skilled craftsmen on the payroll year-round infeasible.[186]

---

[183]Anthony Alfino, Algie Hendrix, & Carl Oles, "Manpower Supply in the Construction Industry" 46 (Aug. 11, 1970), in BR, CCH: 1970.

[184]*RR*, No. 73-9, at 4 (Sept. 28, 1973).

[185]The Roundtable denied this latter claim. For example, in a draft letter (sent to Blough and 11 other Roundtable leaders) from one of its executives to the Legislative Affairs Officer of the DOL, who had written to the Roundtable on August 29, 1973 requesting a response to questions posed in a resolution of the Texas Building Trades Department, it asserted: "The Roundtable has carefully refrained from interfering in collective bargaining between construction companies and construction unions. In direct reply to the words in the resolution, The Roundtable has made no 'promises or threats...to firms encouraging them to contract with construction companies that are non-union.'" [ ] to R. Ray Randlett, Sept. 21, 1973, in SP, Box 6, File BR-General. A member of the Roundtable's Construction Committee reported to it in 1980 that the NCA had told him and other members that it gave no credence to rumors that the Roundtable fostered open-shop work. BR, CCH: 1980, Minutes, Dec. 9, 1980, at 2.

[186]Telephone interview with Robert McCormick, NCA president, Washington, D.C. (Mar. 11, 1999).

Part IV

The Joint Employer-State Struggle

The deterioration of labor relations in our industry has progressed to the point that the very existence of the construction industry as a free enterprise is in jeopardy. In fact, its impact is so far reaching that it poses a threat to our entire economic system.[1]

---

[1]John Graney, "Misplaced Responsibilities," *CLR*, No. 687, Nov. 20, 1968, at E-1-E-3 at E-1. Graney, labor relations manager of Ebasco Services, NCA past president, and future Roundtable official, delivered this address at the National Conference on Construction Problems.

8

The Nixon Administration's Early Initiatives to Regulate the Construction Industry

"It's a serious question whether the country can tolerate or survive the current collective bargaining system in construction."[1]

The Nixon administration did not initiate the national government's preoccupation with construction workers. Chapter 1 detailed how, as the militarization of the economy expanded certain sectors during the Vietnam war, the Johnson administration issued reports of labor shortages. Nevertheless, the effort to suppress construction workers' militant demands for "more" by breaking up their local labor market monopolies did not became a priority until the Nixon administration. Its focus on and stance toward the construction industry may have been prefigured by the fact that three of its cabinet members were or had been construction contractors: Postmaster General Winton Blount, Secretary of Transportation John Volpe, and Secretary of the Interior Walter Hickel.[2]

A few days after Nixon took office, John Dunlop, a Harvard University labor economist who had served in numerous governmental and private capacities dealing with the construction industry since World War II, submitted a confidential memo to Secretary of Labor George Shultz at the latter's request. In it Dunlop judged that at the national level "the centrifugal forces are greater than at any time in the past thirty years." Identifying the relationship between national contractors associations and national unions as the most appropriate strategic point of entry into this "jungle of tangled problems," Dunlop argued that the central substantive problem was the industry's bargaining structure during a period of high employment. At a time when the parties could not even agree seriously to study their problems dispassionately, Dunlop concluded that only the federal government could take the initiative as catalyst, stimulator, and mediator. Despite the critical impasse, all Dunlop proposed at the outset was the formation of a tripartite group to meet periodically to discuss industrial relations and manpower problems.[3] William J. Usery, Jr., a former Machinists Union official who had just joined the Labor Department, sent a memo to Shultz agreeing with Dunlop's judgment that the parties were unable to develop

---

[1] "'Massive Leapfrogging' in Construction Negotiations Reported by CISC Chairman," *CLR*, No. 974, June 12, 1974, at X-1, X-3 (quoting D. Quinn Mills).

[2] *CLR*, No. 691, Dec. 18, 1968, at A-3.

[3] John Dunlop, "[Confidential] Memorandum: The Building and Construction Industry" at 6-8 (Jan. 23, 1969), in NACP, RG 174: General Records of the Labor Dept., Office of the Secretary, Records of the Secretary of Labor George P. Shultz, 1969-1970, Box No. 79: Labor Disputes, Folder: LD 1969: Building & Construction Trades Industry.

problem-solving arrangements on their own, but the new administration did not take any immediate action.[4]

In August 1969, Arthur F. Burns, Nixon's adviser on domestic affairs, "'jolted by the excessive wage settlements in construction,'" began urging the president and his cabinet to consider jawboning or even an incomes policy: "Burns was concerned that the settlements in construction would have a strong secondary effect on industrial firms, communicated...through employees with similar skills and spreading by imitation to regular industrial workers."[5]

Nixon adopted several of Burns's specific construction-related proposals on September 4, 1969, but rejected the proposed suspension of the Davis-Bacon Act, which requires employers on federal government construction projects to pay (typically union) wage rates determined by the Secretary of Labor to be prevailing for the relevant class of workers "on projects of a character similar to the contract work in the city, town, village, or other civil subdivision of the State in which the work is to be performed."[6] Nixon also refused to prohibit contracts requiring exclusive hiring by means of union hiring halls. The president acted on the advice of Labor Secretary Shultz, who opposed such direct intervention.[7] Accepting the view that construction unions "were prime conveyers of the inflationary virus,"[8] Nixon released a statement on the construction industry in which he complained that the "cost of building a home...ha[d] become exorbitant." In what was to become a refrain of public policy, the president, asserting that a "shortage of skilled manpower is at the root of many problems faced by this industry," directed the DOL and the Department of Health, Education and Welfare to provide training and education "in order to achieve a major increase in needed skilled labor for the construction industry." He also ordered federal contracting agencies to set aside 75 percent of planned starts of federally financed public works. Finally, he established a Cabinet Committee on Construction (CCC), consisting of the Secretaries of Commerce, HUD, Labor, and Transportation, the Postmaster General, and CEA chairman, which was charged with ensuring that federal construction activities not exacerbate the industry's problems.[9] *Business Week* interpreted the committee's charge to analyze problems of seasonality as designed to undermine "workers' arguments that they need higher hourly rates to

---

[4]Memorandum from [William J.]Usery [Jr.] to Secretary (Feb. 4, 1969), in General Records of the Labor Dept., Office of the Secretary, Records of the Secretary of Labor George P. Shultz, 1969-1970, Box No. 58: Councils, Folder: 1969 Committee: Cabinet Committee on Construction.

[5]Neil De Marchi, "The First Nixon Administration: Prelude to Controls," in *Exhortation and Controls: The Search for a Wage-Price Policy 1945-1971*, at 295-352 at 310 (Craufurd Goodwin ed., 1971) (quoting from interview with Burns on Mar. 19, 1974).

[6]40 U.S.C. § 276a (1994). See also 29 C.F.R. § 1.2.

[7]De Marchi, "The First Nixon Administration: Prelude to Controls" at 310-11.

[8]Arnold Weber, "The Continuing Courtship: Wage-Price Policy Through Five Administrations," in *Exhortation and Controls* 353-83 at 359.

[9]Richard Nixon, *PPPUS: 1969*, at 352-53 (1971).

offset idleness in 'off seasons.'"[10]

Employers' reactions to these modest initiatives were not favorable. The president of the AGC, Carl Halvorson, lamented that the curtailment failed to get at the root cause—"excessive union power," which had already caused more than 200 economic work stoppages resulting in 328 million man-hours lost. "The answer," according to the AGC, was "to get rid of some of the archaic labor laws which protect the already 'overly protected'" unions.[11]

Then on September 22, 1969, Nixon implemented Shultz's recommendation to establish a tripartite Construction Industry Collective Bargaining Commission (CICBC), composed of equal numbers of union, employer, and public representatives.[12] The president classified the new commission as continuous with earlier "[c]ooperative effort" by labor, management, and the federal government "in times of stress" such as the World War II-era Wage Adjustment Board (WAB).[13] Instead of a direct attack on wages, which played no visible part, the administration emphasized a more efficient dispute resolution process to deal with the "numerous signs of strife and tension in the past several years in an economy of continuing high employment."[14] This euphemism for the high incidence of strikes and tight labor markets was vindicated the very next year, which was called an "industrial relations debacle: a third of all negotiations resulted in work stoppages."[15] (To put the state's concern with this paricular source of production disruption into perspective: at this same time "the frequency of accidents on construction jobs is so great that work injuries annually cost the industry about 4 to 5 times more man-days of wage and salary workers time than are lost because of work stoppages.")[16]

---

[10]"Construction Pay Push Is Raising the Roof," *BW*, Apr. 18, 1970, at 74. See generally, David Martin, "Construction Seasonality: The New Federal Program," 16 (5) *CR* 4-7 (May 1970). On the CCC's slow progress with regard to manpower issues and dissemination of winter building technology, see White House Memorandum for Dr Paul McCracken (undated); Memorandum from Shultz (OMB) to Nixon, "A Report on the Cabinet Committee on Construction" (July 27, 1971), in NPMS, WHCF, SF Ex FG 256, Box 1: CCC, Folder 22: 1/1/71.

[11]"Halvorson, Haggerty at Odds over Factors Underlying President's Cutback Drive," *CLR*, No. 729, Sept. 10, 1969, at A-2-A-4. One of these laws that employers especially resented was Davis-Bacon. See, e.g., Yale Brozen, "The Law that Boomeranged," *NB*, Apr. 1974, at 70-73.

[12]For the drafts of the executive order and memos from Shultz to Nixon and others concerning the CICBC, see NPMS, WHCF, SF Ex FG 257 CICBC [1969-1970], Box 1, Folder 1 [1969-1970].

[13]Nixon, *PPPUS: 1969*, at 735. See also "Nixon Establishes Building Industry Bargaining Panel," *WSJ*, Sept. 23, 1969, at 2, col. 2.

[14]"Nixon Tries New Tack on Industry Problems," *ENR*, Sept. 18, 1969, at 87, 88 (quoting a confidential briefing paper by John Dunlop, a DOL adviser).

[15]D. Q. Mills, "Construction Wage Stabilization: A Historic Perspective," 11 (3) *IR* 352 (Oct. 1972).

[16]BLS, *Compensation in the Construction Industry* 23 (Bull. 1656, 1970).

Two weeks before Nixon's announcement, the Roundtable's Coordinating Committee noted that votes at the CICBC would probably run eight to four in favor of unions, which would use the commission as an excuse for not taking decisive actions themselves. The committee therefore reached a consensus that the Roundtable should not go on record favoring the proposal, and that some effort might be made to achieve its modification, but nothing came of the suggestion.[17]

The first of the CICBC's two major functions was to seek solutions to the industry's problems concerning training and developing manpower, seasonality and instability of employment, and productivity and mobility of the work force. The other was to "develop voluntary tripartite procedures in settling disputes." Its focus on nationalizing the control of labor relations was reflected in Nixon's appointment of leaders of the AGC and the NAHB as employer-members of the commission.[18] Executive Order 11482 expressly included among the commission's objectives "to increase the labor force engaged in the construction industry" and "to strengthen the role of the national labor organizations and national associations of contractors in the dispute settlement process, and to enhance their responsibility for the results of collective bargaining in the industry."[19] Privately, Nixon asserted to the chairman of the Equal Employment Opportunity Commission, in response to a letter from William H. Brown, III expressing his "disgust" at the underemployment of blacks in the building trades in Pittsburgh, that Brown's statement "describes...one of the important reasons" Nixon created the CICBC.[20]

The labor market proposals appeared to be an unexceptionable basis of a nonzero-sum game for all groups, but the unemployment rates for construction workers during these years (6.9, 6.0, 9.7, and 10.4 percent from 1968 through 1971)[21] raised the obvious question as to who would have benefited from an increase in the labor supply. In contrast to the possible response that there might be enough workers in the abstract, but that their skill-mix was inappropriate,

---

[17]CUAIR, CC, Minutes of Sept. 8, 1969, at 4, in BR, 1969: Vol. II: Minutes.

[18]Nixon, *PPPUS: 1969*, at 735-36. A contemporaneous OECD study revealed that the United States was the only country lacking some type of winter payment program for construction workers. Jan Wittrock, *Reducing Seasonal Unemployment in the Construction Industry: Methods of Stabilizing Construction Activity and Employee Income* 230-32 (1967). As long ago as the 1920s, the Department of Commerce had recognized that "bad weather is not the principal cause of seasonal idleness"—but, rather, customs that had been fixed before newer techniques had been developed. U.S. Dept. of Commerce, *Seasonal Operation in the Construction Industries: Summary of Report and Recommendations of a Committee of the President's Conference on Unemployment* vi (1924).

[19]Exec. Order 11482, §§ 3(a) & (b), in 34 Fed. Reg. 14,723-24 (1969).

[20]Letter from William H. Brown, III to Richard Nixon (Sept. 22, 1969); Richard Nixon to William H. Brown, III (Oct. 24, 1969), in NPMS, WHCF, SF, EX FG 257 CICBC [1969-1970], Box 1, Folder 1.

[21]See above Table 6.

contemporaneous empirical studies found no shortage of skilled workers.[22] By 1971, the head of the Plumbers union charged that the Nixon administration was "'busily dismantling the apprenticeship system to benefit nonunion contractors and to flood the industry with surplus manpower. The Labor Department seems determined to increase the labor force in the construction field...whether or not there are any jobs for these new workers.'"[23]

The administration's proposals to nationalize labor-management relations put the cart before the horse by presupposing a stage of industrialization and a corresponding structure of capital accumulation and centralization lacking in construction. After all, the industry was commonly criticized for its retarded state of technological progress and undercapitalized firm structure, which caused the above-average fluctuations characteristic of the industry.[24] Accordingly, a plausible conclusion is that the whole catalog of reforms (except expansion of the labor supply) contemplated a transformation of the industry—otherwise they would have been condemned to failure.

The CICBC's objective of promoting the national scope of collective baragining had numerous obstacles to overcome. An obvious conflict of interest between local unions and their national organizations as well as between local building firms and their national associations was paired with an implied restoration on the national level of a composition of interests presumably designed to make possible an accommodation of the collective bargaining parties. This prospect, in turn, presupposed the ability of both national employers and labor organizations to overcome local resistance.

It may seem surprising that employers treated this offer by the federal government to assist them in this conflict skeptically: "But management members of the industry discount the possibility of any quick or dramatic labor reforms."[25] Especially the CUAIR showed "little enthusiasm for the commission plan, particularly its involvement in local bargaining."[26] Possibly large users wanted to reserve the structure of such involvement exclusively for themselves. The NCA was not represented on the committee.[27] That the NCA was skeptical of intervention in local negotiations should not be surprising since its national

---

[22]Strauss, "Apprenticeship: An Evaluation of the Need"; Howard Foster, "Nonapprentice Sources of Training in Construction," 93 (2) *MLR* 21-26 (Feb. 1970).

[23]*CLR*, No. 813, Apr. 21, 1971, at A-22.

[24]See below chapter 10.

[25]"Nixon May Benefit Construction," *ENR*, Nov. 14, 1968, at 15-16; see also "Nixon's Labor Plan Criticized," *ENR*, Sept. 25, 1969, at 56.

[26]"Nixon Tries New Tack on Industry Problems," *ENR*, Sept. 18, 1969, at 87, 89.

[27]George McGuire of the NCA sent telegrams to Shultz on Sept. 11, 1969 and to Nixon on Sept. 19, 1969 protesting the exclusion of the NCA from the CICBC. Shultz wrote to McGuire on Sept. 17 informing him that an NCA representative would serve as an alternate. NPMS, WHCF, SF, EX FG 257: CICBC [1969-1970], Folder 4: [1969-70].

agreements placed it in conflict with local contractors.

In January 1970, members of Nixon's cabinet began laying the propagandistic groundwork for some form of intervention. Postmaster General Blount agreed with contractors that construction wage increases were "'outrageous,'" but told them that they themselves bore much of the blame "because they had abdicated their managerial responsibilities."[28] Secretary of Housing George Romney echoed these sentiments, quantifying the wage increases as five times higher than in the automobile industry. Labor Secretary Shultz also deplored these developments, but cautioned that the Nixon administration would try to avoid wage and price controls because they would not achieve their ends.[29]

About the same time, the CICBC unanimously adopted the recommendation of a tripartite committee of lawyers, which had been submitted in September, 1969, giving substance to the commission's charge to centralize labor relations.[30] The CICBC recommended that national labor unions and contractor associations be empowered to approve or disapprove their subordinate entities' strike or lockout decisions, assist in local negotiations, and approve local agreements. Such authority would also have severely curtailed the power that the rank-and-file had been exericising with distressing regularity to reject contracts negotiated by their local leaders and to codetermine their working conditions. The lawyers committee, including two union representatives, wrote that although some people argued that statutorily "taking away from the members of the bargaining unit the ultimate right to approve the terms and conditions under which they will provide their labor...violates the inherently democratic traditions of labor unions," the pressing need to "overcome this problem" of increasing contract rejection by the rank and file meant that until the legislative process ran its course "national unions should encourage local members to delegate binding authority to bargaining teams."[31] A spokesman for Shultz, the CICBC chairman, openly admitted that "'the

---

[28]"Building Pay Rises Decried by Blount," *NYT*, Jan. 16, 1970, at 10, col. 3.

[29]"Home Builders Plan Appeal to Nixon," *NYT*, Jan. 20, 1970, at 53, col. 2, at 63, col. 3-4.

[30]"Advisory Recommendations of the Staff Committee to Review Certain Legal Aspects of the Collective Bargaining Structure in Construction" (Sept. 12, 1969), included as Appendix A in "Report of the CICBC September 1969 to January 1972," transmitted by Secretary of Labor Hodgson to President Nixon, Mar. 30, 1972, in NPMS, WHCF, Subject Files, EX FG 257: CICBC [1969-1970], Box 1, Folder 2: (1969-1970).

[31]"Report of the CICBC September 1969 to January 1972," at 5-6, NPMS, WHCF, Subject Files, EX FG 257: CICBC [1969-1970], Box 1, Folder 2: (1969-1970);"Tripartite Commission Adopts Nine-Point Plan to Expand Bargaining Role at National Level," *CLR*, No. 748, Jan. 21, 1970, at A-1; "Report of Staff Committee on Improving Collective Bargaining Process in Construction Industry," *CLR*, No. 749, Jan. 28, 1970, at X-1, X-3 (quote). This proposal was partially embodied in a bill that President Ford vetoed in 1975; see below chap. 14. The two union lawyers on the committee wrote a memo to one of the employers' lawyers two days before the committee submitted its report attempting to show that cases under the 1959 amendments to the NLRA had "frustrated the legitimate leadership role of national unions and have impaired the authority of local union officers duly elected

whole concern there is to avert the growing rejection of contracts by the rank and file....'" The BCTD members of the CICBC approved the recommendation, one source conceding that "'there might be some opposition from local unions,'" but adding that "'in most instances "I don't think there is going to be adverse reaction to this."'"[32]

Such optimism, however, was premature: militantly self-regarding construction workers were still far from prepared to yield one of the institutions supporting their local labor market monopolies. This resistance was clearly on display that year at the Carpenters' quadrennial convention, which adopted by voice vote a resolution strongly opposing these very proposals "that would dilute or reduce the membership's right to approve or disapprove proposed agreements" or to strike.[33]

Prompted by a memo on ending construction inflation from CEA chairman, Paul McCracken,[34] Nixon returned to the control of construction wages again on March 18, 1970, making a detailed statement about the connection between a shortage of new housing construction and "rampant inflation of construction costs." Specifically, he argued that: "To moderate severe increases in the cost of labor, we must increase the labor supply to meet the increasing demand. This means we must assure equal employment opportunity for all in the industry." The "disturbingly short supply" of skilled labor...contributed to recent construction industry wage settlements that exceed progress in labor productivity and increases in the general cost of living. They go well beyond the historical spread between construction wages and settlements in manufacturing industries." The Philadelphia Plan (which established quotas for hiring blacks on federal construction projects) was one means of increasing the labor supply in an industry that "urgently need[ed] reform and

---

by the majority." Memorandum from Louis Sherman and Robert Connerton to Winn John (Sept. 10, 1969), in NACP, RG 174: General Records of Labor Dept., Office of the Secretary, Records of the Secretary of Labor George P. Shultz, 1969-1970, Box No. 53: Commissions, Folder: 1969 Commission CICBC (Jan.-Sept.).

[32]"Ratification Votes in Trades Opposed," *NYT*, Jan. 21, 1970, at 19, col. 1. The labor members were the presidents of the Carpenters, Operating Engineers, Plumbers, and the BCTD. Robert Semple, Jr., "President Forms a Panel to Solve Building Disputes," *NYT*, Sept. 23, 1969, at 1, col. 5, at 56, col. 7.

[33]*Proceedings of the Thirty-First General Convention of the United Brotherhood of Carpenters and Joiners of America* 303 (1970).

[34]McCracken used the phrase "disturbingly short supply" in referring to construction labor. Memo from McCracken to President on Ending Construction Inflation at 7 (Mar. 14, 1970) (Administratively Confidential), in NACP, RG 174: General Records of the Labor Dept., Records of the Secretary of Labor George P. Shultz, 1969-1970, Box No. 173: International Committee-Cabinet Committee on Oil Imports, Folder: 1970-Committee: CCC (Except May 5). See also Memorandum from John Ehrlichman to Richard Nixon (Mar. 16, 1970) (suggesting that Nixon mention the need to encourage the most effective management in the construction industry), in NPMS, WHCF, SF, Ex FG 257 CICBC [1969-1970], Box 1, Folder 1.

modernization"; it did "not need harassment, unwarranted interference, or political denunciation [but] d[id] need...—most of all—more trained workers." Nixon also directed federal agencies to include in their construction contracts a clause requiring the employment of apprentices or trainees in accordance with established apprentice-journeyman ratios.[35]

Despite its aggressive tone, the speech merely provoked *The New York Times* to editorialize that the gains from Nixon's action to revive the construction industry "may be more than offset by the incentive the Nixon moves have given the overfat unions in the building trades to step up their wage demands. Restraint has always been a stranger to these unions. Last year they fed the inflation fires by signing three-year agreements providing increases of 40 to 50 per cent for a half-million construction workers."[36] In fact, the Nixon administration, as one of its cabinet members confessed to the CUAIR's first members meeting on April 6, "was unable to offer an immediate solution to the high construction wage settlements, indicating that preaching had not turned down that trend and that intervention by a predecessor had exploded."[37] And in the same vein, ten days later, Shultz's undersecretary, Hodgson, reported to him that an approach that Dunlop had developed for inducing the parties to agree on principles—focused on wage parity within regions and wage increases from 1969 as the cap for those in 1970—was also no "answer to a maiden's prayer."[38]

Analysis of the further course of state efforts to check construction wages will be shifted here to focus on two aspects of state intervention that helped structure the ways in which labor-capital conflicts were prosecuted: (1) the Nixon administration's measures to combat racially motivated employment discrimination in order to channel black workers into the construction labor force to undermine construction unions' labor market monopoly; and (2) a program to promote the industrialization of residential construction. Whereas the first program served to increase the supply of labor and disrupt unions politically, the second promised to reduce the demand for skilled labor by facilitating the invasion of construction by capital-rich industrial firms.

---

[35]Richard Nixon, *PPPUS: 1970*, at 268-70, 273, 275 (1971). The apprenticeship regulations were later codified at 29 C.F.R. § 5a. The BCTD contested the DOL's authority to issue these regulations. "Building Trades Department Challenges Legality of Proposed Apprenticeship-Journeyman Ratio Regulation," *CLR*, No. 801, Jan. 27, 1971, at A-2. On the Philadelphia Plan, see below chapter 9.

[36]"Spur to Housing," *NYT*, Mar. 18, 1970, at 46, col. 1.

[37]"Report to Members of Construction Users Anti-Inflation Roundtable" at 15 (n.d. [Apr. 1970]), in SP, Box 5, File-CUAIR 1969-1970 [   ].

[38]Hodgson to Shultz, Subject: Proposals for Dealing with Excessive Wage Increases in the Construction Industry (Apr. 16, 1970), in NACP, RG 174: General Records of the Labor Dept., Office of the Secretary, Records of the Secretary of Labor George P. Shultz, 1969-1970, Box No. 167: CICB-WH Fellows, Folder: 1970 Commissions-CIBC (April-May).

9

Fighting Racist Unions' Militance by Fighting Race Discrimination

[A]lmost the only device and symptom of originality displayed by American employers in disciplining their labor force has been that of playing one race against another.[1]

In our union we don't care whether you're an Irishman, a Jew, or a Nigger.[2]

What more do these people want?[3]

These fellows defend the integrity of their crafts the way horse fanciers defend the blood line of their favorites. Where the horsemen have controlled breeding, the union fellows have apprenticeship.[4]

The history of the exclusion of black workers from the building trades and from building trades unions goes back to the nineteenth century. The ability of construction unions to restrict the number of skilled workers in their industries played an important role in preserving their members' bargaining power regardless of the race or ethnicity of the excluded, but it exerted its most concentrated and baneful impact on blacks, and that exclusion, in turn, was the most destructively divisive for the U.S. working class as a whole.[5] Affirmative action was necessary to exclude black building tradesmen because the heavy reliance on slaves as a source of craftsmen in the antebellum South had created a relatively favorable distribution of skills for entry into the industry in the latter part of the nineteenth century.[6] Thus,

---

[1]John R. Commons, *Races and Immigrants in America* 150 (1920 [1907]).

[2]Philip Foner, *Organized Labor and the Black Worker* 1619-1973, at 247 (1974) (citing *Fortune*, June 1942, at 73, quoting William Hutcheson, president of Carpenters union, although no such quotation is there).

[3]"Building Trades Warn: Won't Budge Much," *ENR*, Oct. 2, 1969, at 13 (quoting George Meany defending the building trades' civil rights record).

[4]Speech by Virgil Day to the Cleveland Engineers Society, in CUAIR *Report*, Dec. 7, 1970, at 2.

[5]The exclusion, for example, of Jewish carpenters and painters from unions in New York City at the beginning of the twentieth century forced them into the alteration and repair sectors of the building industry, which they also organized to a degree. Melech Epstein, *Jewish Labor in U.S.A.: An Industrial, Political, and Cultural History of the Jewish Labor Movement 1882-1914*, at 372-74 (1950); Philip Zausner, *Unvarnished: The Autobiography of a Union Leader* (1941). On the exclusion of Italians by the Bricklayers and Masons, see Edwin Fenton, "Immigrants and Unions: A Case Study: Italians and American Labor, 1870-1920," at 378-429 (Ph.D. diss., Harvard U., 1957); Edwin Fenton, "Italian Immigrants in the Stoneworkers' Union," 3 (2) *LH* 188-207 (Spring 1962).

[6]Sterling Spero & Abram Harris, *The Black Worker: The Negro and the Labor Movement*

although the building trades unions' reaction to the possibility of the influx of a large number of new members was similar to that of other craft unions such as shipping and railroading, blacks' situation was exacerbated precisely by the fact that their skills presented an excellent opportunity to be integrated into the organized labor movement.[7]

Some unions, for example in the trowel trades, "organized Negroes as a matter of self-defence. ... But the race psychology of a local union often counteracts the wholesome effect of the international union's stand."[8] In other trades, such as carpentry and painting, for which blacks' slave experience made them well qualified, they were often segregated into separate locals. In the South, where employers preferred, for example, black bricklayers because their wages were lower, unions' function was to prevent such hiring.[9] The extreme reluctance with which the Painters organized black workers is captured by an article that a district organizer in Birmingham, Alabama, published in the union's journal in 1902: "While we as individuals may oppose the negro, he is here, as he is in the majority of Southern cities, and no power of our labor organizations can deprive him of making a living."[10]

---

5 (1969 [1930]); F. Ray Marshall & Vernon Briggs, Jr., *The Negro and Apprenticeship* 37 (1967); *The Negro Artisan: A Social Study* 8, 158-76 (Atlanta U. Pubs. No. 7, W.E.B. Du Bois ed., 1902); Lorenzo Greene & Carter Woodson, *The Negro Wage Earner* 316-24 (1930); Herbert Northrup, *Organized Labor and the Negro* 19 (1944); Foner, *Organized Labor and the Black Worker* at 125.

[7]Philip Foner, *History of the Labor Movement in the United States: From the Founding of the American Federation of Labor to the Emergence of American Imperialism* 355-56 (1955). For an historical account of the policies of building trades unions toward blacks, see Ira De A. Reid, *Negro Membership in American Labor Unions* 39-48 (n.d. [1930]); F. Wolfe, *Admission to American Trade Unions* 19, 112-34 (1912); Sterling Spero & Abram Harris, *The Black Worker: The Negro and the Labor Movement* 22, 56, 59-60, 70, 76-85, 159-61; Robert Weaver, *Negro Labor: A National Problem* 28-32 (1946); Herman Block, "Craft Unions and the Negro in History," 43 (1) *JNH* 10-33 (Jan. 1958); Ray Marshall, *The Negro and Organized Labor* 101-102, 109-32 (1965); *idem, The Negro Worker* 63-81 (1967); Herbert Hill, "The Racial Practices of Organized Labor: The Contemporary Record," in *The Negro and the American Labor Movement* 286-357 at 293-320 (Julius Jacobson ed., 1968). For more general treatment, see Herbert Hill, "The Racial Practices of Organized Labor—The Age of Gompers and After," *Employment, Race and Poverty* 365-402 (Arthur Ross & Herbert Hill, eds., 1967); John Hutchinson, "The AFL-CIO and the Negro," in *id.*, at 403-31.

[8]Spero & Harris, *Black Worker* at 69. In 1881, the Bricklayers' convention guaranteed black members of locals a travelling card, but locals retained discretion not to admit them. Harry Bates, *Bricklayers' Century of Crafstmanship: A History of the Bricklayers, Masons and Plasterers' International Union of America* 52 (1955). For a strong antiracist statement regarding the exclusion of blacks by the international president, William Bowen, see *Fifth Biennial and Fifty-Seventh Report of the President and Secretary of the Bricklayers, Masons and Plasterers' International Union of America: For the Term Ending June 30, 1928*, at xlii-xlvii (n.d.).

[9]Industrial Commission, 7 *Reports: On the Relations and Conditions of Capital and Labor Employed in Manufactures and General Business* 488-89 (H. Doc. No. 495, 56th Cong., 2d Sess., 1901) (testimony of Thomas Rennie, superintendant, Graniteville Mfg. Co., S. Carolina).

[10]J. R. Camp, "A Business Proposition: For the Sunny South: Organize and Educate the Negro," 15 (5) *PJ* 70 (May 1902).

The high point of racial exclusion was reached in the trades based on more recent technological developments such as the plumbing and electrical trades. The IBEW's constituion did not expressly exclude blacks, but "it was the general understanding and practice...that they were not to be accepted as members." After it was discovered that a chapter of black workers in Florida had been admitted as a result of inadequate information in 1899, its charter was revoked. As late as 1921, the annual convention voted that blacks were not ripe to be organized.[11] Where outright exclusion did not suffice, racist unions could rely on state licensing laws and boycotts of plumbing supply stores in the North and the South that sold fixtures to black plumbers to bar the few who had managed to learn the trade.[12]

In 1935, of 37,536 building trades union members in Manhattan, only 1,008 were black, of whom 635 belonged to the Hod Carriers.[13] These trends continued until the advent of the modern civil rights movement.[14] As late as 1967, Ray Marshall found that there were "virtually no Negroes" in the Electricians, Plumbers, Ironworkers, Sheet Metal Workers, or Elevator Constructor unions "in any Southern city and outside of a few exceptions, the most notable of which is New York, there are very few in most Northern or Western cities."[15] Table 20 shows the evolution of black participation in the building trades after World War II.

The proportion of black plumbers and electricians was minuscule throughout this period. They were also under-represented among carpenters and painters. Only in the trowel trades and among construction laborers were blacks over-represented. Even this concetration was largely driven by their domination of these occupations in the South.[16]

---

[11]Michael Mulcaire, "The International Brotherhood of Electrical Workers: A Study in Trade Union Structure and Functions" at 37-39 (Ph.D. diss., Catholic U. of America, 1923).

[12]Northrup, *Organized Labor and the Negro* at 17-47; Spero & Harris, *Black Worker* at 59-60, 477-81.

[13]Charles Franklin, *The Negro Labor Unionist of New York* 168-71 (1968 [1936]).

[14]Greene & Woodson, *The Negro Wage Earner* at 316, 322, 324; Weaver, *Negro Labor* at 28-32; Mark Kruman, "Quotas for Blacks: The Public Works Administration and the Black Construction Worker," 16 (1) *LH* 37-51 (Winter 1975). Racism was not unique to the building trades unions. Even segments of the CIO, at the high point of its southern organizing campaign after World War II, discriminated against black workers while recruiting them as members; for example, the bathrooms in the CIO organizing hall in Memphis were segregated. Michael Honey, *Southern Labor and Black Civil Rights: Organizing Memphis Workers* 256 (1993).

[15]Marshall, *The Negro Worker* at 64. For details, see *id.* at 63-91. For an extended argument that racial discrimination in construction stemmed largely from the membership's and not the leadership's attitudes, and that public policy mistakenly focused on integrating a blue-collar industry—which was not even the most discriminatory manual trade—at a time when white-collar occupations were both far more segregated and the future growth areas for employment, see Mills, *Industrial Relations and Manpower in Construction* at 143-77.

[16]Herbert Northrup & Howard Foster, *Open Shop Construction*, tab. XII-1 at 323-25, tab. XII-2 at 329-30 (1975).

Table 20: Blacks as a % of All Workers in Selected Building Trades, 1950-1970			
Trade	1950	1960	1970
Electricians	1.1	1.5	2.9
Plumbers	3.0	3.3	4.6
Carpenters	3.8	4.4	5.2
Painters	5.4	6.8	9.0
Masons, tile setters, & stone cutters	10.4	11.4	15.2
Plasterers & cement finishers	19.3	21.7	27.4
Total selected trades	4.8	5.6	6.9
Laborers	25.3	25.9	22.2

Source: USBC, *Census of Population: 1950*, Vol. II: *Characteristics of the Population*, Pt. I: *United States Summary*, tab. 128 at 1-276, 277 (1953); USBC, *Census of Population: 1960*, Vol. I: *Characteristics of the Population*, Pt. 1: *United States Summary*, tab. 205 at 1-544, 545 (1964); US BC, *1970 Census of Population*, Vol. I: *Characteristics of the Population*, Pt. 1: *United States Summary*, Sect. 2, 1-749, 750, 755, 756 (1973).

To be sure, it might not be in members' economic interest to exclude blacks, who could then work at lower rates in the nonunion sector, thus possibly threatening the competitive viability of the union sector. But this argument could lose some of its force when applied to the technologically newer trades: here unions could plausibly exclude blacks from employment altogether by denying them access to union-controlled apprenticeship programs. To the extent that firms were not in a position to escape the effects of such 'artificial' restrictions on the supply of labor by introducing more capital-intensive construction methods, they would have had an interest in encouraging an enlarged supply of skilled tradesmen.[17] Moreover, where, as in Chicago in the 1910s and 1920s, unions succeeded in imposing a closed shop on construction, skilled black tradesmen migrating from the South could be excluded with impunity: their only choice was to perform less

[17]"Building Trades Feel Pressure to Admit Negroes as Apprentices," *WSJ*, Oct. 16, 1967, at 1, col. 6; "Crafts Ease Their Stand on Bias," *BW*, Dec. 9, 1967, at 133-34; "Racial Progress in the Building Trades," *AL*, Sept. 1968, at 37-43; "Effort to Train Blacks for Construction Jobs Falters in Pittsburgh," *WSJ*, July 24, 1969, at 1, col. 4; "Negro Drive for Jobs in Construction Unions Is Gaining Momentum," *WSJ*, Sept. 26, 1969, at 1, col. 6; AFL-CIO, *Report of the Proceedings of the Fifty-Fifth Convention, 1969*, at 176-83 (1969); "Organized Labor's Excellent Racial Policy," *The Lather*, Nov. 1969, at 7-10.

skilled work in other industries.[18]

Despite only tepid initiatives by the Kennedy administration, which owed its advent to overwhelming black electoral support, the civil rights movement used the rhetorical political opening to launch a series of well-publicized demonstrations against the building trades unions, which it viewed as chiefly responsible for the exclusion of blacks from well-paid jobs in an expanding industry at highly visible construction sites across the country. The struggle moved to a higher level after the election in 1964 of Lyndon Johnson, whose administration sought to reconcile its labor and black constituents while recognizing that it could no longer neglect the latter's grievances against the former.[19] Black workers excluded from unions or deprived of employment opportunities by unions found potentially powerful legal recourse in Title VII of the Civil Rights Act of 1964, which made it an unlawful employment practice for a labor union to discriminate, or to cause or attempt to cause an employer to discriminate, against any person on the basis of race.[20] The construction industry and unions quickly became the target of more protest and litigation than any other.[21]

The early litigation provides a good sense of the range and pervasiveness of the discrimination.[22] In February 1966 the United States filed the first construction industry lawsuit under the new law against the Building and Construction Trades Council of St. Louis and electricians, laborers, plumbers, pipefitters, and sheet metal workers locals there. The suit arose out of work performed on the National Park Service Gateway Arch. In order to satisfy the nondiscrimination provisions of federal contracts, the general contractor entered into a subcontract with a black plumbing contractor, who employed black workers, who were members of a non-AFL-CIO union. The unions, which refused to work together with non-AFL-CIO members, in an effort to remove the nonunion contractor and his employees, violated the NLRA by engaging in an unlawful secondary boycott.[23] By 1967, the plumbers and

---

[18]James Grossman, *Land of Hope: Chicago, Black Southerners and the Great Migration* 182, 216-17 (1991 [1989]).

[19]Jill Quadagno, *The Color of Welfare: How Racism Undermined the War on Poverty* 62-78 (1994).

[20]§ 703(c), 78 Stat. 253, 255-56 (1964).

[21]William Gould, *Black Workers in White Unions: Job Discrimination in the United States* 281-84 (1977), speculates on why blacks focused on construction when other industries lacked superior records.

[22]In order to underscore the intractability of racist white construction unions, a noted black author stated in 1964 that Vice President Johnson had made a secret visit to New York during the summer of 1963 to settle the dispute over discrimination in the building trades. During a marathon 35-hour session with union leaders Johnson was unable to persuade them: "'I failed.... No one can move these people. They simply don't mean to do it.'" In 1964 the White House did not fully confirm or deny the report. "Lomax Says Chaos Looms in Negro Drive for Rights," *NYT*, Apr. 13, 1964, at 20, col. 3-6.

[23]IBEW Local 1, 164 NLRB 313 (1967); United States v. Building and Construction Trades

pipefitters had agreed to cease discriminating and to implement "a community
relations program designed to dispel from the minds of Negroes any notion that they
are not welcome in this Local equally with white persons," and to cooperate in
operating remedial and preparatory training programs for blacks.[24] The trial against
the electricians and sheet metalworkers unions, which virtually monopolized work
in St. Louis, revealed that when the suit was filed, all the members of both locals,
numbering more than 2,500, were white; the electricians local did not accept its first
black apprentice or refer for employment its first blackworker until 1966.[25]

     These patterns and practices were replicated throughout the United States
and formed the basis of numerous other suits filed in the 1960s and 1970s.[26] In the
mid-1960s, in Pittsburgh, for example, no nonwhite members were reported in the
Asbestos Workers, Boilermakers, Plumbers, Sign Painters, Steamfitters, Stone and
Marble Masons, Tile Setters, Elevator Constructors, Terrazo Helpers, Plumbers
Laborers, or Marble Polishers and Helpers locals. Similarly, in New York City, none
of the 4,000 Construction Steamfitters, 3,300 Sheet Metal Workers, or 3,000
Construction Plumbers was black.[27] Of Local 28 of the Sheet Metal Workers'
International Association of Greater New York *The New York Times* wrote: "No
Northern union has resisted demands for the elimination of Jim Crow practices more

---

Council of St. Louis, 271 F. Supp. 447 (E.D. Mo. 1966). Intriguingly, in November 1966, the council
met with the Midwest Contractors Association, which employed black workers, to discuss possible
collective bargaining and the employees' admission into the unions, but the employers voted not to
continue these discussions—in part because the wage scale of the black workers' union (Local 99 of
the Congress of Independent Unions (CIU)), which the black contractors had organized in 1960, was
at least two dollars lower than that of the AFL-CIO unions. United States v. Sheet Metal Workers
International Association, Local Union 36, 416 F.2d 123, 128 n.9 (8th Cir. 1969). According to Ray
Marshall, *The Negro Worker* 66 (1967), the CIU (which he erroneously calls the "Congress of
Industrial Unions"), was integrated. The complex conflict between black employers and unions was
shaped in part by the consequences of the discrimination to which black contractors were themselves
exposed: "To some extent...their personal interest may work at cross purposes with a central goal of
national labor policy, the inclusion of minority workers. [U]nion membership is an essential element
in minority demands, and yet most minority contractors are anxious to continue employing nonunion
workers so that they are not deprived of one of their few competitive cost advantages." Gould, *Black
Workers in White Unions* at 283-84.

     [24]United States v. Sheet Metal Workers International Association, Local Union 36, 416 F.2d
123, 125 (8th Cir. 1969). See also "Bias Suits Force Big Changes," *ENR*, June 29, 1967, at 54.

     [25]United States v. Sheet Metal Workers International Association, Local Union 36, 280
F.Supp. 719, 721 (E.D. Mo. 1968); United States v. Sheet Metal Workers International Association,
Local Union 36, 416 F.2d at 127-28. Local 1 represented 95 percent of all electricians employed in
major residential, commercial, and industrial construction projects in St. Louis City and County, while
Local 36 had collective bargaining agreements with most sheet metal contractors in the area. *Id.* at 129
n.12.

     [26]For a partial listing, see GAO, *Federal Efforts to Increase Minority Opportunities in Skilled
Construction Craft Unions Have Had Little Success* 56-67 (HRD-79-13, 1979).

     [27]Marshall, *The Black Worker* at 63-78.

stubbornly...."[28] Until 1964, when an agreement was reached and approved by a New York State trial court following an enforcement proceeding brought by the State Commission for Human Rights, Local 28 had never admitted a black as a member or apprentice in its entire 76-year history. The court specifically rejected the union's last-ditch effort to retain some version of the key mechanism undergirding the exclusion of blacks—namely, that 80 percent of the trainees participating in the apprenticeship program, which was the "only realistic way of becoming a member," were relatives of members.[29]

Why black workers might have found building trades unions lacking credibility on the issue of their racial exclusionism is evident from the obfuscation deployed by the president of the Ironworkers at the union's convention in 1968. Conceding the "widespread belief that all building and construction trades discriminate against minorities," John Lyons nevertheless found it

hard to say why such a concept developed, other than to possibly oversimplify what is probably the national feeling by stating that the average citizen feels or has heard that it is hard to get into a building trades union. These two conclusions have been put together to develop a general line of thought that if they are true, then building trades unions must necessarily discriminate. I believe the existence of the first concept "that a building trades union is hard to get into" is the result of the necessities of maintaining uniform wage rates and working conditions in an industry as diverse and widespread as...construction.... If building trades unions were going to exist at all over the years, they had to be, by the very nature of our industry, militant organizations. Further, if they are going to continue on into the future, they must remain militant organizations. The maintenance of a militant type of organization quite obviously gives to those not within the industry, an impression of a barrier. The impression of a barrier to admittance into building trades unions or to the possibilities of employment in the building industry...exists to a far greater extent among the Negro than it does among the White citizens. This, more than any other single factor, bears upon the low number of Negroes.[30]

---

[28]"Union Bias Breakthrough," *NYT*, Aug. 25, 1964, at 32, col. 2 (editorial).

[29]State Commission for Human Rights v. Farrell, 252 NYS2d 649, 652 (N.Y. Sup. Ct. 1964); Robert Tomasson, "Union Must Drop Father-Son Rule," *NYT*, Aug. 25, 1964, at 1, col. 5, at 15, col. 3. In 1922 Samuel Gompers acknowledged in testimony that since 1920 the Plumbers union in New York City had closed the book and that only members' sons and brothers were permitted to enter. *Mr. Gompers Under Cross-Examination: Excerpts from the Testimony of Mr. Gompers Before the Committee of the New York Legislature Investigating Housing Conditions (Lockwood Committee)* 6798 (1922). The then largest study of occupational mobility revealed that in 1962 13.7 percent of construction craftsmen were offspring of fathers who were also construction craftsmen—the highest degree of self-recruitment in any nonagricultural manual occupation. Similarly, 13.9 percent of the sons of construction craftsmen were construction craftsment. Peter Blau & Otis Duncan, *The American Occupational Structure* tab. 2.8 at 39, tab. 2.2 at 28 (1967).

[30]"Report of the General President John H. Lyons to the Thirty-Third Convention of the International Association of Bridge, Structural and Ornamental Iron Workers," 58 (10) *Ironworker* 1, 29 (Oct. 1968).

   In contrast, a remarkable metamorphosis on the race issue was on display in the Plumbers union, whose general president, Peter T. Schoemann, articulated a program that rapidly underwent radical change. Two months before Title VII went into effect in mid-1965, he had declared to the members that the national union's three-word policy with regard to admitting blacks to apprenticeship and membership, "Take them in," was the better part of valor because: "Neither the old labor injunctions nor the American Plan of the 20's nor Taft-Hartley nor 'right-to-work' laws, nor anything else I can think of, can inflict such injury on us as clumsy regulation of apprenticeship and hiring practices in the name of equal opportunity."[31]

   At the union's 1966 convention, Schoemann was still beholden to a mythical explanation of racial underrepresentation that he found useful to analogize to the breaking of the color line in major league baseball in 1947 after which "the opportunity was there, it was up to each individual young man to take advantage of it." But if, unlike black baseball players, few blacks were employed in plumbing, Schoemann wondered whether that "sociological fact...is traceable not to widespread discrimination, but rather to a simple lack of interest or inclination? If this is the case, then we are not going to criticize any racial group for not wanting to be plumbers and pipe fitters, and I sure wish they would quit criticizing us for not having more of their own people."[32]

   The next year, Schoemann resumed his rearguard defense of his union's racially-biased nepotistic training practices: "Well, is there something indecent about giving reasonable preference to sons of union members on apprenticeship entrance? Is there something unclean about a contractor taking his own son into his own shop in preference to a Negro boy whom some academic Liberal in a Washington office thinks he ought to take in instead?"[33] In a "gloves-off" speech to building trades unionists, Schoemann then asserted that "the civil rights organizations and their allies have more political power to break down our hiring practices and our union security than the NAM, the Chamber of Commerce, the National Right-to-Work Commitee and all big business tycoons and conservative senators and congressmen who ever existed." Schoemann assured his audience that the union's view "on this racial issue is shared by the large American middle class and by the great majority of our fellow citizens. They are not for any spoon feeding or coddling or giving special breaks to

---

   [31]"Schoemann Urges Full Compliance with Civil Rights Law," *CLR*, No. 503, May 12, 1965, at A-14, A-16.

   [32]"UA President Schoemann's Convention Keynote Address," *CLR*, No. 568, Aug. 10, 1966, C-1, C-3, C-4.

   [33]Peter Schoemann, "Enough Is Enough," 79 (4) *UAJ* n.p. [inside front cover], n.p. [inside back cover] (Apr. 1967). Schoemann's implicit analogy between plumbers and plumbing contractors inadvertently uncovered the illogical structure of Title VII, which does not prohibit discrimination against self-employeds.

anybody because of the color of their skin."[34] Finally, the plumbers' leader warned that the mere fact that the labor movement had always been in the vanguard of progressive social movements in the past did not mean that

we ought to be in the forefront of an effort to seek out and recruit members of the minority race for the skilled trades. We have been in the forefront of certain social fights in the past, but I think you will always find that it was something that benefited our membership rather directly, because in our type of building trades craft unionism, we are not social revolutionaries. We are business unionists, we are bread-and-butter trade unionists, and within the construction industry, we are the agency whose job it is to protect the standards.

For this reason we would hope that the employers would be giving us more support than they have been.[35]

By the end of 1967, Schoemann announced union support for some measure of affirmative action. Ostensibly, his change of direction was inspired by the insight that the union's stake in society would be jeopardized if "those at the bottom of the ladder" created "upheavals" in their search for another society."[36] In the spring of 1968 Schoemann told a group of his union's delegates at a BCTD meeting that this acceptance of affirmative action was tactical, involving merely other means. The ultimate goal, serving the welfare of 300,000 member plumbers by protecting institutions such as the hiring hall and apprenticeship, remained constant: "If we want to remain free, if we want to keep our apprenticeship programs out of the hands of the federal government...it is absolutely imperative that we institute affirmative action programs." Schoemann did not conceal that, unlike the "impersonal corporation," which could promote affirmative action by spending some money, union plumbers "are among the people who will be threatened economically by the rise of the Negro multitudes. We are the ones who will have to make some sacrifice...." His advice, however, was that: "the way to take the castor oil is take it in a big dose now."[37]

Schoemann's transformation culminated in an article he wrote in the May 1968 issue of the Plumbers' journal calling on unions to make a large contribution to the elimination of racism. In past legislative struggles:

We stood with the little people, with the people who worked with their hands, with the people who worked for others. We did not stand with the financiers, and the giant corporations. Consequently, we were counted on the liberal side of most political arguments, and the

[34]Peter Schoemann, "Equal Employment Opportunity: A Statement of Principles," 79 (7) *UAJ* n.p. [inside front cover]-n.p. [inside back cover] at 61, 63 (July 1967).

[35]Schoemann, "Equal Employment Opportunity" at 64-inside back page.

[36]Peter Schoemann, "Some Reflections on Thanksgiving," 79 (11) *UAJ* n.p. [inside front page]-n.p. [inside back page] at inside back page (Nov. 1967).

[37]Peter Schoemann, "United Association and Affirmative Action," 80 (4) *UAJ* n.p. (Apr. 1968).

liberals in Congress, in the state legislatures and the general public could usually be found on our side, and we on theirs.   ...

Now, rather suddenly, all of that has changed. We find ourselves embroiled in a social crisis where we are no longer the little people. It is a case of the "haves" and the "have nots" and we are definitely numbered among the "haves." We do not belong there as much as a lot of other people who make more money than we do, but considering where the protest and the trouble are coming from, we are definitely "haves."

And so it turns out, that just as we are winning more economic security than we ever had, we are finding ourselves deprived of a certain kind of security, a psychological security that we enjoyed right up until the onset of the newest revolution. For there was indeed a kind of security in being always the underdog and feeling that we had no direction to go but up. Today we still have plenty of room for going up, but it is not nearly so important for the moment as the people who are coming up from below.[38]

To be sure, this rare piece of introspection, concluding that the "innocence of our trade union childhood is over," was not driven by altruism or perhaps even by solidarity. For as Schoemann observed, with the election of black mayors in Cleveland and Gary and the prospect of black majorities in more than a dozen of the largest cities, union plumbers had to hold present to mind that: "Most of our bread and butter is located right in the heart of those cities."[39]

State efforts to eliminate racist barriers to employment were neither simply a humanist solution of the "American Dilemma" nor a response to demands by black men for equal access to "'manly' jobs with...high status implications" of especial importance to those either denied employment altogether or shunted into low-paid, menial jobs.[40] They reflected employers' interests insofar as this integration was to be structured so that the concomitant changes in the size and qualitative structure of the labor supply favored long-term and cyclical profitability. Herbert Northrup, a longtime advocate of employers against unions, explained this kill-two-birds-with-one-stone approach at the November 19, 1968 National Conference on Construction Problems sponsored by the Chamber of Commerce. After bemoaning the building unions' "tremendous power" as reinforced by the "union-government power axis," Northrup saw a ray of hope: "The civil rights issue may well provide a means of solving some construction problems.... Minority groups are the best potential sources of...craftsmen in view of the college orientation of white youth today. ... I look on the civil rights problem not only as one that must be solved for its own sake because

[38]Peter Schoemann, "Affirmative Action: Initial Response Encouraging," 80 (5) *UAJ* n.p. [inside front page]-n.p. [inside back page] at inside front page-56 (May 1968).

[39]Schoemann, "Affirmative Action: Initial Response Encouraging" at 56. On Schoemann's negative reaction to the Philadelphia Plan—an "illegal and unworkable" initiative requiring the union to "utilize certain workers, whether qualified or not"—see "UA Head Blasts Union Critics," *ENR*, Aug. 28, 1969, at 109.

[40]"Excerpts from Testimony of Herbert Hill on Equal Opportunity Contract Compliance," *CLR*, No. 690, Dec. 11, 1968, at C-1, C-3. See generally, Quadagno, *The Color of Welfare* at 61-78.

in a free enterprise [sic], everyone...deserves equal rights and equal opportunity, but also as a means of helping to alleviate the shortage of construction craftsmen and to relieve the country of a situation which should not and cannot endure."[41]

A few months later, Peter Pestillo, at GE official at the Roundtable, in an internal working paper asked not only whether the civil rights issue could be "used to drive a wedge into the restrictions on apprentice training," but also: "Can Negro contractors be used to serve as a new source of construction labor?" Unfortunately, he concluded, they generally lacked some of the skills needed for major construction projects.[42] But the theme absorbed the Roundtable, which repeatedly revisited it. In October 1970, for example, its Coordinating Committee debated the extent to which the "Roundtable should seek to use the minority question." Opponents of such a tactic feared that token compliance with minority guidelines might remove all pressure against inflation.[43] Since it might prove difficult to manufacture public outrage over the increasing cost of building chemical or rubber plants, B. F. Goodrich's representative on the Coordinating Committee ventured that "it might be more politically palatable to tie the attack on spiraling costs in the construction industry to their effect upon social needs, including employment of minorities...."[44]

Once again *Fortune* made itself the spokesperson of this new strategy to undercut construction unions. An October 1969 editorial ("'Black Mondays' Are Good for Us") praised black "militants" for having forced the closure of projects in which "the monopoly power of the building-trades unions" had excluded Blacks.[45] *Fortune* viewed the introduction of black construction workers as a means of rolling back the unions' "notoriously high wage levels" to a level that no longer stemmed from an "artificially contrived labor shortage." At the same time the magazine assured its readers that the incessantly growing pie was after all large enough for all workers: "The white union members have no legitimate cause for complaint; there will be plenty of jobs for everyone. The President's Committee on Urban Housing...estimated last year that two million more construction workers will be

---

[41]Herbert Northrup, " Restrictive Practices and Racial Barriers" at 9, 11, in *Papers Presented at the National Conference on Construction Problems* (Nov. 18-19, 1968). The paper is also available as "'Restrictive Practices in Construction': Remarks of Herbert R. Northrup of University of Pennsylvania," *CLR*, No. 687, Nov. 20, 1968, at F-1-F-4. On the conference, see above chapter 7.

[42]Peter J. Pestillo, "Construction Problems: In Search of a Solution" at 11-12 (Mar. 14, 1969), in BR, 1969: CCH.

[43]BR, CC, Minutes, Oct. 26, 1970, at 7, in BR, 1970: Vol. II-Minutes.

[44]BR, CC, Minutes, Dec. 1, 1970, at 4, in BR, 1970: Vol. II-Minutes.

[45]On the course of some of these campaigns, see "U.S. Steel Won't Halt Building in Pittsburgh over Negroes' Demands," *WSJ*, Aug. 28, 1969, at 4, col. 3; Elwood Hain, Jr., "Black Workers Versus White Unions: Alternative Strategies in the Construction Industry," 16 *WLR* 37-76 (1969); Irwin Dubinsky, "Trade Union Discrimination in the Pittsburgh Construction Industry," 6 (3) *UAQ* 297-311 (Mar. 1971); *idem, Reform in Trade Union Discrimination* (1973); *Challenge* 6 (7-8) (Oct.-Nov. 1969). On the first black Monday in Chicago, see Seth King, "4,000 Negroes in Chicago Rally in Bid for Skilled Building Jobs," *NYT*, Sept. 23, 1969, at 56, col. 3.

needed by 1975. In today's full-employment economy, the only substantial pool of jobless males to meet that need is in the black community."[46] Several months later the boom phase of the business cycle turned into a crisis/depression; by 1975 fewer construction workers were employed than at the time of *Fortune*'s prognosis, and the *Wall Street Journal* reported on its front page: "Nonunion Firms Get an Increasing Share of Construction Work."[47]

The coordinated approach of antiunionism and antiracism was unveiled at the NAM's Congress of American Industry in New York City in December 1969. Roger Blough, representing the CUAIR, and Arthur Fletcher, Assistant Secretary of Labor for Wage and Labor Standards, and one of the highest ranking Blacks in the Nixon administration, presented a "package" for cutting construction costs and "a warning that the civil rights headaches of unions and contractors have just begun...." Fletcher declared that the federal government would insure that collective bargaining in the 1970s would "require the presence of a third party at the table"; on behalf of minority groups, he would push the civil rights agenda from the social to the economic sphere by "sharing the wealth by sharing the jobs." One of his chief methods of desegregating the labor supply was the elimination of the "'nonsense requirements' of apprenticsehip...."[48] Within liberal circles of black academics and politicians it was "common knowledge" at the time that Fletcher's function in the DOL was "to crack the building trades unions."[49] Indeed, Fletcher was an "early advocate of Davis-Bacon suspension as a tool for opening up construction work to minorities" by improving "the competitive position of ABC contractors bidding on federal and federal-aid projects...."[50]

---

[46]"'Black Mondays' Are Good for Us,'" *Fortune*, at 86 (Oct. 1969).

[47]James Hyatt, "Nonunion Firms Get an Increasing Share of Construction Work," *WSJ*, Dec. 18, 1975, at 1, col. 6. As Jonathan Grossman, *The Department of Labor* 222-23 (1973), noted: "The drive for more blacks in the 'hard hat' trades was initiated when business was booming. Later...the building slump brought unemployment.... Unions that have therefore been reluctant to set aside future openings for blacks fight even harder when the jobs of members seem in jeopardy." See also 98 (6) *MLR* 85-86 (June 1975).

[48]"Wages, Civil Rights Need an Answer," *ENR*, Dec. 11, 1969, at 61. For an excellent contemporaneous analysis, which has stood the test of time, see Pacific Studies Center, "Black Monday," *PRWET*, Nov.-Dec. 1969, at 18-23. Although described as reprinted from *Ramparts*, it was published there later and lacked the CUAIR membership list. "Black Monday's Sunday Allies," *Ramparts*, Jan. 1970, at 34-38.

[49]Interviews at Metropolitan Area Research Council (New York City, Jan. 1971). See generally, Arthur Fletcher, "The Black Dilemma If Nixon Wins," *WSJ*, Sept. 25, 1972, at 12, col. 3.

[50]"Administration Works on a Plan to Stabilize Wages," *ENR*, Mar. 18, 1971, at 186. The president of one construction union urged Nixon to dismiss Fletcher on the grounds that Fletcher had stated that the real reason for Nixon's suspension of the Davis-Bacon Act was not to control inflation, but rather "to weaken and even destroy the great construction unions....'" "Union Leader Urges Labor Aide's Ouster," *NYT*, Apr. 5, 1971, at 31, col. 3 (quoting Edward Carlough of Sheet Metal Workers). Fletcher had purportedly told a group of nonunion contractors on March 12, 1971, that "'the union grip on the processes of government has been weakened.'" *Id.*

Federal government intervention assumed a more concrete shape at the end of the 1960s when the Nixon DOL began implementing Executive Order No. 11246 of Sept. 24, 1965, which required that all federal contracts include language forbidding contractors to "discriminate against any employee or applicant for employment because of race, creed, color, or national origin."[51] On June 27, 1969, Arthur Fletcher issued an order on the "Revised Philadelphia Plan for Compliance with Equal Opportunity Requirements of Executive Order 11246 for Federally-Involved Construction."[52] (An earlier Philadelphia Pre-Award Plan of Nov. 30, 1967 had been suspended because the Comptroller General had issued an opinion that it violated competitive bidding principles.)[53]

Why the Nixon administration revived and implemented an affirmative action program in construction that the Johnson administration had abandoned is a question that has occupied political scientists and historians. Joan Hoff has argued that the Philadelphia Plan "allowed the Nixon administration to keep the focus on the racism of the northern craft unions...rather than switching it to the equally racist hiring practices of the southern textile industries." This tactic frustrated the hopes of prominent Democrats that a Republican focus on the South would have precluded successful application of Nixon's southern strategy.[54] This explanation tracks the resolution passed by the annual convention of the BCTD on September 22, 1969, the day before the Revised Philadelphia Plan was issued. In addition to defending its overall record in admitting blacks, attacking the discriminatory employment practices of the news media, and declaring that it was "unalterably opposed to the quota system,"[55] the BCTD called the plan "a part of a pattern of conduct formulated by political strategists in the Nixon administration to divide the labor movement while slowing the process of implementing the civil rights program on voting and education

---

[51]Exec. Order No. 11246, § 202(1), 30 Fed. Reg. 12,319, 12,320 (1965). See also Contractors Association of Eastern Pennsylvania v. Shultz, 311 F. Supp. 1002, 1005 (E.D. Pa. 1970); "Building Trades Feel New Pressure to Admit Negroes as Apprentices," *WSJ*, Oct. 16, 1967, at 1, col. 6. Exec. Order No. 11246 superseded Exec. Order No. 11925, 26 Fed. Reg. 1977 (1961), which it largely repeated; Michael Sovern, *Legal Restraints on Racial Discrimination in Employment* 104 (1966).

[52]DOL, "Memorandum: Revised Philadelphia Plan" (June 27, 1969). The memorandum was also reprinted in 115 Cong. Rec. 39,951-56 (1969).

[53]DOL, "Memorandum: Revised Philadelphia Plan" at 4. For a concise analysis of the various government-imposed and consensual plans in various cities, see Gould, *Black Workers in White Unions* at 297-315.

[54]Joan Hoff, *Nixon Reconsidered* 91-92 (1994). See also J. Larry Hood, "The Nixon Administration and the Revised Philadelphia Plan for Affirmative Action: A Study in Expanding Presidential Power and Divided Government," 23 (1) *Presidential Studies Q.* 145-67 at 163 n.11 (Winter 1993).

[55]Damon Stetson, "Building Unions Spur Negro Jobs," *NYT*, Sept. 23, 1969, at 1, col. 6, at 56, col. 5; "Excerpts from Building Trades Statement on Hiring Minorities," *NYT*, Sept. 23, 1969, at 56, col. 3.

in the South."[56]

Nixon himself savored the "delicious prospect of setting organized labor and the civil rights establishment at each other's throats." Nevertheless, his sponsorship of the affirmative action Philadelphia Plan, ironically, split his southern strategy coalition of Republicans and conservative Democrats, while Blacks accused him of undermining the Plan's compuslory features in favor of meaningless "hometown" programs designed to pay back the construction unions for their support for the Indochina war.[57]

In trying to explain why Nixon would have pursued a program that was bound to alienate his newly won hard-hat voters while propitiating Blacks, 90 percent of whom had voted against him in 1968, Jill Quadagno points to his desire to counteract criticism from the civil rights movement of his Supreme Court nominees and his opposition to school busing, the threat of racial violence in connection with violent demonstrations at construction sites, and above all "a political calculus designed to keep the core Democratic constituencies at odds" with each other while the administration appeared moderately in the middle. Quadagno also roots the Philadelphia Plan in the Nixon administration's expansion of a federal housing program and the concomitant employment boom for construction workers. Although the federal government could have geared the job growth to "alleviate the tensions between African Americans and the unions...[it] focused instead on increasing the labor supply to reduce spiraling wages" because "[o]nly by flooding the labor market with skilled workers could wages be reduced." The extraordinary efforts that the DOL undertook to expand apprenticeship programs outside of the unions' control resulted in "new trainees flooding a recession-dampened market"; consequently, instead of the predicted labor shortage, construction unemployment "skyrocketed."[58]

The ostensible occasion for these efforts was blacks' underrepresentation in the skilled trades, which was in part concealed by their overrepresentation in the category of "laborers." Thus the Equal Employment Opportunity Commission (EEOC) issued data based on reports from so-called referral unions (locals that had agreements with employers to refer workers) showing that in 1967 blacks nationally accounted for 30.5 percent of all laborers; in the so-called trowel trades, they accounted for 9.6 percent of bricklayers and 14.0 percent of plasterers. Their share in the skilled occupations, however, was minuscule: plumbers, 0.2 percent; elevator constructors, 0.4 percent; electrical workers, 0.6 percent; carpenters, 1.6 percent; iron

[56]"Resolution 270," reprinted in *The Philadelphia Plan: Congressional Oversight of Administrative Agencies (The Department of Labor): Hearings Before the Subcommittee on Separation of Powers of the Senate Committee on the Judiciary*, 91st Cong., 1st Sess. 179 (1970).

[57]Hugh Graham, *The Civil Rights Era: Origins and Development of National Policy 1960-1972*, at 325, 340-41, 344 (1990).

[58]Quadagno, *Color of Welfare* at 79, 81-82, 84. Quadagno's analysis is so indebted to Nixon administration documents in the National Archives that it at times incorrectly conflates draft documents with implemented programs.

workers, 1.7 percent; painters, 3.7 percent; and operating engineers, 4.0 percent.[59]

Because Philadelphia, which had witnessed the first protests by Blacks in 1963 against their underrepresentation in construction,[60] was the site of the test case, the program was called the Philadelphia Plan. Fletcher based the order—which prohibited awarding federal construction contracts in excess of $500,000 in the Philadelphia area "unless the bidder submits an acceptable affirmative action program which shall include specific goals of minority manpower utilization" for iron workers, plumbers and pipefitters, steamfitters, sheetmetal workers, electrical workers, roofers, and elevator construction workers—on the finding that enforcement of the executive order had

posed special problems in the construction trades. Contractors and subcontractors must hire a new employee complement for each construction job and out of necessity or convenience they rely on the construction craft unions as their prime or sole source of their labor. Collective bargaining agreements and/or established custom between contractors and subcontractors and unions frequently provide for, or result in, exclusive hiring halls; even where the collective bargaining agreement contains no such hiring hall provisions..., as a practical matter, most people working in these classifications are referred to the jobs by the unions. Because of these hiring arrangements, referral by a union is a virtual necessity for obtaining employment in union construction projects, which constitute the bulk of commercial construction.

Because of the exclusionary practices of labor organizations, there traditionally has been only a small number of Negroes employed in these seven trades. ... At the end of 1967, less than one-half of one percent of the membership of the unions representing employees in these seven trades were Negro, although the population in the Philadelphia area

---

[59]*NYT*, Jan. 25, 1970, sect. 1, at 71, col. 5. The referral unions' membership accounted for about three-fifths of all construction union membership. Between 1969 and 1972, total minority membership in the building trades unions increased from 13.2 percent to 15.6 percent, but gains in the skilled trades were far below average. By 1971, blacks accounted for 2.0 percent of elevator constructors, 3.8 percent of plumbers, 5.6 percent of electrical workers, 6.7 percent of sheet metal workers, and 8.3 percent of iron workers. *ENR*, Oct. 16, 1969; Herbert Hammerman, "Minority Workers in Construction Referral Unions," 95 (5) *MLR* 17-26, tab. 5 at 21 (May 1972); *idem*, "Minorities in Construction Referral Unions—Revisited," 96 (5) *MLR* 43-47, tab. 2 at 44 (May 1973); "U.S. Mandates New Minority Hiring Goals in 21 Localities," *ENR*, July 11, 1974, at 17. For an explanation of the weaknesses of these data, especially for comparisons over time, see Robert Glover & Ray Marshall, "The Response of Unions in the Construction Industry to Antidiscrimination Efforts," in *Equal Rights and Industrial Relations* 121-40 at 121-25 (Leonard Hausman et al. eds., 1977. For data on various large cities, see F. Ray Marshall & Vernon Briggs, Jr., *The Negro and Apprenticeship* 48, 85, 114, 138, 152, 160, 177, 183 (1967). Ironically, as blacks' share of laborers fell from 31 to 22 percent between 1960 and 1973, the inflow of young white men was associated with stabilization of the skilled-unskilled construction wage differential, which had been narrowing. Harold Wool, "Future Labor Supply for Lower Level Occupations," 99 (3) *MLR* 22-31 at 24 (Mar. 1976).

[60]Marshall & Briggs, *The Negro and Apprenticeship* at 87-92. On violent clashes in 1969 in Chicago, Pittsburgh, and Seattle, see "Federal Agencies Move in to Put Out Fire of Racial Unrest in Chicago Construction," *CLR*, No. 730, Sept. 17, 1969, at A-4. See also Michael Stern, "Effort to Train Blacks for Construction Jobs Falters in Pittsburgh," *WSJ*, July 24, 1969, at 1, col. 4.

during the past several decades included substantial numbers of Negroes.[61]

The racist mentality that the compulsory Philadelphia Plan had to circumvent or overcome was nicely captured in congressional testimony by the executive director of the General Building Contractors Association of Philadelphia, the self-professed "oldest trade association in any industry in North America." In listing this enlightened organization's actions to promote integration in construction, he highlighted the fact that "a few months ago we employed a young Negro lady as a secretary in our association office"[62]—at a time when thousands of black workers were in the streets shutting down projects to lend force to their demands for equal access to jobs. The cavalier attitude adopted by the mainstream union movement can also be gauged by George Meany's understanding of affirmative action in 1967: "If we run into boys that have the educational qualifications to take the apprenticeship of the various trades, I think we should make it as easy as possible for them to acquire the skills...."[63]

Following public hearings in August and the issuance of an opinion by the Attorney General confirming the legality of the DOL order,[64] Fletcher issued an implementing and amendatory order on September 23, 1969. Based on new data, he found that although minorities accounted for 30 percent of all Philadelphia-area construction workers and 12 percent in the skilled trades, in the designated trades minority participation varied between a low of 0.51 percent among plumbers and pipefitters and 1.76 percent among electricians—a figure "far below that which should have reasonably resulted from participation in the past without regard to race, color and national origin." In addition to determining that more than 2,000 qualified minority workers were available in these trades, Fletcher made the politically crucial finding that firms could add significant numbers of skilled minority workers to their work forces "without adverse impact upon the existing labor force." Based on a 2.5 percent annual retirement rate, a 1 percent annual death or disability occurrence rate, and a further 3 percent annual leave rate for other reasons, he calculated that "each construction craft should have approximately 7.5% new job openings each year without any growth in the craft." Projected craft-specific growth rates extrapolated from the previous six years' figures generated estimates of annual vacancy rates ranging from 9.6 percent among elevator construction workers to 11.2 percent among iron workers. This political leeway was supposed to enable contractors to commit to hiring minority workers, on the basis of one minority craftsman for each non-minority craftsman, in such numbers that after four years they would account for 19

---

[61]DOL, "Memorandum: Revised Philadelphia Plan" at 2-3.

[62]*Philadelphia Plan: Congressional Oversight* at 66, 67 (testimony of Harry Taylor).

[63]"Union-Government Consultation, Not Conflict, on Tough Issues Urged at BTD Convention," *CLR*, Dec. 6, 1967, No. 637, at A-1, A-4.

[64]Letter from the Attorney General to the Secretary of Labor (Sept. 22, 1969).

to 25 percent of all employees in those trades.[65] Indeed, an assistant attorney general in the civil rights division of the Department of Justice candidly testified to the Senate Judiciary Commitee that "the entire plan...assumes an expansion of the rate of construction."[66]

Fletcher expressly characterized the jobs created by the Philadelphia Plan as "a major thrust of the Administration in dealing with employment problems of the disadvantaged of our major urban areas."[67] As his Assistant Secretary was announcing the implementation, Secretary of Labor Shultz, cautioning that the DOL would use "all due process possible," urged local leaders to "be sensitive to the potentially explosive nature" of the problems.[68] In order to increase the minority share, the government proceeded to increase the share of black apprentices.[69] When a year later the Plan had "not begun to produce even minimal gains toward its modest goal of breaking the color barrier in six construction trades," the DOL prepared to sue contractors as unions accused Nixon and the contractors of "trying to lower wages and standards...and to cause friction between two normally Democratic allies, labor

---

[65]DOL, Office of the Assistant Secretary, "Order: Establishment of Ranges for the Implementation of the Revised Philadelphia Plan for Compliance with Equal Employment Opportunity Requirements of Executive Order 11246 for Federally-Involved Construction" 3-16 (quotes at 12, 9, 14) (Sept. 23, 1969). See also "Negro Drive for Jobs in Construction Unions Is Gaining Momentum," *WSJ*, Sept. 26, 1969, at 1, col. 6. On the fate of the Philadelphia Plan a quarter-century later in the wake of "harder times," see Louis Uchitelle, "Union Goal of Equality Fails the Test of Time," *NYT*, July 9, 1995, § 1, at 1, col. 1.

[66]*The Philadelphia Plan: Congressional Oversight* at 105 (testimony of Jerris Leonard).

[67]"Statement by Assistant Secretary Arthur A. Fletcher on Philadelphia Plan Guidelines" 2 (USDL 10-696, Sept. 23, 1969).

[68]"Statement by Secretary Shultz on Phildelphia Plan Guidelines," Sept. 23, 1969 (USDL 10-964). See also *ENR*, Oct. 2, 1969, at 16.

[69]On the regulations regarding equal employment opportunity in apprenticeship and training, see 29 C.F.R. § 30 (1972). According to Byron Calame, "Labor Agency Seeks to Void Unions' Right to Veto On-the-Job Training of Minorities," *WSJ*, Dec. 21, 1970, at 7, col. 1, union influence was supposed to be reduced. On the disputes over the implementation of this program in New York City, see Thomas Ronan, "Construction Men Sign Trainee Pact," *NYT*, Dec. 11, 1970, at 1, col. 2; William Farrell, "City Plan for Minority Building Workers Assailed," *NYT*, Dec. 22, 1970, at 26, col. 5. See also Alex Maurizi, "Minority Membership in Apprenticeship Programs in the Construction Trades,"25 *ILRR* 200-206 (Jan 1972); Gladys Gruenberg, "Minority Training and Hiring in the Construction Industry," 22 (8) *LLJ* 522-36 (Aug. 1971). Since empirical studies revealed that only a fraction of skilled tradesmen went through a formal apprenticeship, some doubted the effectiveness of this state strategy: "[I]t is almost certainly true that for some of the union spokesmen, hearty endorsement of apprenticeship as an entry method is motivated in part by a desire to close nonapprenticeship routes to minorities." William Franklin & Robert Glover, "Entry into the Building Trades Unions: A Comparison of Apprenticeship and Other Routes," in *Labor & Manpower* 77-103 at 101. See also Strauss, "Apprenticeship: An Evaluation of the Need"; Edgar Weinberg, "Reducing Skill Shortages in Construction," 92 (2) *MLR* 4 (Feb. 1969); Howard Foster, "Nonapprenticeship Sources of Training in Construction," 93 (2) *MLR* 21-26 (Feb. 1970); *idem*, "Apprenticeship Training in the Building Trades: A Sympathetic Assessment," 22 (1) *LLJ* 3-12 (Jan 1971).

and minority groups."[70]

The timing of this antidiscrimination campaign was, to be sure, not completely coincidental: at the height of the Vietnam War boom employers were no longer enamored of the law of supply and demand in the labor market. President Nixon himself repeatedly defended the Philadelphia Plan on this basis. At a news conference on September 26, 1969, he stated that "it is essential that black Americans, all Americans, have an equal opportunity to get into the construction unions. There is a shortage in construction workers."[71] (A new watchword appeared five years later: "Manpower shortages may push women into construction work.")[72]

Despite the limited success of the Philadelphia Plan,[73] at the March 1971 annual convention of the AGC,[74] Fletcher boastfully announced complete victory:

I am here to announce what is already a fact.

The old order is not only under pressure to change; the order is collapsing. ... The era of arrogance and discrimination by some trade unions has ended. Corrupted by their sense of power, they have overreached. ... We are within a year of a great influx of minority workers into the construction trades, as the citadel of labor supply control plus over discrimination is being destroyed. ... I want to explain my announcement to you that the era of union domination of the employment pattern in the construction industry is over. ... The union grip on the processes of government has been weakened considerably if not broken. ...

When I came into office, the union movement in the construction industry thought it could control the Congress, the courts and the President. It has been demonstrated since then that, not only do they not control these institutions, but their practices of discrimination make all of their institutions very vulnerable. They have lost public support because of the outrageous abuse of their power, both in terms of demands for heavy wage increases, and in the effort which they have made to preserve the segregated character of some of the unions.

---

[70]Paul Delaney, "Nixon Plan for Negro Jobs in Construction Is Lagging," *NYT*, July 20, 1970, at 1, col. 5, at 18, col. 7. See also Elliot Carlson, "The Philadelphia Plan to Integrate Unions Called Failure by Some," *WSJ*, Dec. 3, 1970, at 1; Richard Rowan & Lester Rubin, *Opening the Skilled Construction Trades to Blacks: A Study of the Washington and Indianapolis Plans for Minority Employment* (1972).

[71]"The President's News Conference of September 26, 1969," in Nixon, *PPPUS: 1969*, at 748, 755. See also "Statement about Congressional Action on the Philadelphia Plan," in *id.* at 1040.

[72]"Manpower Shortages May Push Women into Construction Work," *ENR*, May 9, 1974, at 24-26.

[73]Glover & Marshall, "The Response of Unions in the Construction Industry to Antidiscrimination Efforts" at 131, pointed out that a central defect in the plan was that it required employers to hire black workers without requiring unions to admit them; as a result, blacks became attached to temporary jobs rather than to the labor market.

[74]Fletcher gave the same speech to the ABC's annual legislative conference and to the Roundtable's national meeting of local user groups. "Administration Works on a Plan to Stabilize Wages," *ENR*, Mar. 18, 1971, at 186; CUAIR *Report*, May 28, 1971, at 1, 3.

And that is why I am here to announce the end of the...era of union dominance in the construction industry.[75]

Although Nixon's construction industry policies could hardly have satisfied building trades union leaders, the nomination in 1972 of Senator George McGovern as the Democratic presidential candidate, purportedly drove them to support Nixon's reelection. Finding McGovern "wholly unacceptable," but claiming that Nixon "now understands the complexities of the construction industry and sympathizes with the most fundamental concerns of the construction workers," nine union presidents extolled Nixon's "belief in the dignity of honest work and his opposition to policies which would sap and undermine the fundamental strength of American character."[76] (The worst point that the president of the Ironworkers could make against McGovern was that he had "condemn[ed] wages as a means of attaining an income" by supporting a guaranteed annual income.)[77] Nixon's appointment in 1973 of Peter Brennan, president of the Building and Construction Trades Council of Greater New York and a long-time opponent of affirmative action and other means of rectifying racial discrimination against blacks by construction unions, as Secretary of Labor not only betokened backsliding in the effort to integrate, but also represented an attempt, in the words of a future black chairman of the NLRB, by the administration "to establish a firmer foundation for its newly won blue-collar constituency" by "cleverly widen[ing] the cleavage between the industrial unions...and the more conservative crafts, whose social vision does not extend further than the next wage increases for their white memberships."[78] By late 1973, Brennan urged that the Philadelphia Plan be

---

[75]"Address by Assistant Secretary of Labor Arthur Fletcher at Annual Convention of Associated General Contractors," *CLR*, No. 808, Mar. 17, 1971, at D-1, D-2.

[76]"Chiefs of Nine Building Trades Unions Endorse Candidacy of Nixon for Second Term in Office," *CLR*, No. 887, Sept. 27, 1972, at A-6, A-7. Supporting Nixon were the presidents of the Ironworkers, Plumbers, Lathers, Bricklayers, Masons, Operating Engineers, Plasterers, Laborers, Asbestos Workers, and Marble Workers unions; the presidents of the Carpenters, Electrical Workers, Painters, Sheet Metal Workers, Boilermakers, Roofers, Elevator Constructors, and Granite Cutters unions remained neutral. They were "understood to be happy with the Construction Industry Stabilization Committee, which has imposed wage restraints in their industry but not so strenuously or arbitrarily as has the Pay Board in other industries." Philip Shabecoff, "9 Heads of Building Unions Back Nixon for Re-election," *NYT*, Sept. 27, 1972, at 34, col. 1. Brennan organized similar support in New York City; Damon Stetson, "200 Labor Chiefs in City Form Nixon Committee," *NYT*, Sept. 28, 1972, at 52, col. 7.

[77]John Lyons, "The President's Page," 72 (10) *Ironworker* 2-4 at 3 (Oct. 1972).

[78]William Gould, "Moving the Hard-Hats In," 216 (2) *Nation* 41 (Jan. 8, 1973). This important issue concerning discrimination was overlooked in an otherwise insightful letter to the editor calling attention to the inconsistency of the appointment of a construction union leader by a president beholden to the CUAIR. Daniel Wilton, "Brennan as Labor Secretary," *NYT*, Dec. 7, 1972, at 36, col. 4. See also "Brennan Appointment to Secretary of Labor Draws Varied Reactions from Labor, Civil Rights Groups," *CLR*, No. 897, Dec. 6, 1972, at A-16.

terminated in favor of voluntarily negotiated "hometown" systems, which the Nixon administration introduced after it had "made political peace with the 'hard hat' unions during the 1972 Congressional election campaigns," and most of which failed to meet their minority hiring goals.[79]

Union resistance to integrationist policy was ambiguous. Even if the racism underlying such opposition originally represented a defensive reaction—which employers cultivated—against the use of blacks and other minorities as strikebreakers and wage-depressants, it took on a social-psychological life of its own, which could be reactivated even when it lacked any "rational" basis.[80] The prominence of such discriminatory policies in building trades unions originated in special features of the construction industry.

First, because unions in the organized sector of the industry performed the function of furnishing the required number of workers with the requisite skills, they exercised a degree of control over the selection process that most unions lacked. Although this arrangement was, given the structure of the industry, favorable to employers, it would have stood in the way of an industrial revolution of construction. In connection with efforts to promote such a development, unions regarded the policy of racial integration as a means of accelerating the dissolution of union power. As Lefkoe, the Roundtable's hired analyst, after emphasizing the necessity of transferring the labor-supply system to employers, stated: "Employment would be open to any qualified person, but it is likely that 'ghetto' residents and members of minority groups would be a prime source of manpower. Many organizations have already been set up to aid members of these two groups in obtaining employment, and contractors would use these organizations to help recruit employees." If the unions tried to prevent the hiring of non-members, then, according to Lefkoe, the firms would gain a progressive image: "[T]he fact that a great many of the workers being hired were members of minority groups would enable contractors to obtain a considerable amount of assistance from the courts; from federal, state and municipal agencies; and from powerful civil rights organizations." [81]

Second, the particularly frequent and sharp cyclical oscillations in construction—which workers experienced to an extraordinary degree in the form of unemployment—historically prompted unions to seek to keep the reserve army of workers as small as possible. That black workers were particularly hard hit by this phenomenon stemmed from the fact that unions' demands pertained only to their own members; to the extent that no other union took up the struggle for Blacks, unions virtually drive them into employers' waiting arms.

---

[79]"The Snags in Trying to Get Minorities Hired," *BW*, Dec. 1, 1973, at 86; Gould, *Black Workers in White Unions* at 297-315.

[80]On the extent to which racially discriminatory policies are expressions of members' attitudes in democratically run locals, see Orley Ashenfelter, "Racial Discrimination and Trade Unionism," Working Paper No. 17 at 7-13 (Indus. Rel. Sect., Princeton U., Nov. 1969).

[81]Lefkoe, *Crisis in Construction* at 159 (quote), 161 (quote), 169, 173.

To be sure, the union movement did initiate certain programs that signaled a change of direction. For example, by early 1969, the AFL-CIO invested in a program to rehabilitate ghetto housing in St. Louis with people from the neighborhood.[82] Yet during the first Nixon administration Blacks were able to increase their share of skilled construction workers only modestly. According to data collected by the EEOC, from 1969 to 1972 black membership in the higher paid mechanical trades (such as boilermakers, electrical workers, elevator constructors, iron workers, plumbers, and sheetmetal workers) rose only from 1.6 percent to 2.2 percent.[83] Halting progress toward integration in the early 1970s was due not only to union resistance, but to employers' flagging interest resulting from depressed conditions in the construction industry.[84] Table 21 shows the relative increase of black men in the crafts:

One defense that the unions mounted against attacks on their willingness to admit blacks to apprenticeship was to belittle the contribution that such formal training could make toward alleviating black unemployment: even if blacks achieved the 15-percent share of 50,000 annual openings set by civil rights groups, it would, given the across-the-board 50-percent dropout rate, have amounted to only 3 percent of the total number of unemployed nonwhite males under 21.[85] When the DOL issued regulations in 1971 setting goals for recruiting minority workers into apprenticeship programs, the BCTD protested on the grounds that the proportion of nonwhites was already high and above their share of the adult male work force. The union umbrella organization added this revealing ideological broadside: "This attempt at social engineering is a poorly disguised effort to restructure our economic society to the whims of a handful of federal mandarins. We prefer free choice by free men, and we are certain that the vast majority of Americans, white and non-white alike, prefer such freedom."[86]

---

[82]"Program to Train Area Residents During Urban Improvement Project Established in St. Louis," *CLR*, Jan. 8, 1969, No. 694, at A-6.

[83]"Blacks Made Slight Progress Between 1969-1972 in Entering Building Trades," *CLR*, No. 978, July 10, 1974, at B-1. In 1967, the even lower shares varied from 0.2 percent among plumbers and sheet metal workers to 3.9 percent among boilermakers. "Top-Paid Crafts Have Fewest Negroes, Laborers Most, EEOC Survey Shows," *CLR*, No. 732, Oct. 1, 1969, at B-8, B-10.

[84]John Landon & William Peirce, "Discrimination, Monopsony, and Union Power in the Building Trades: A Cross-Sectional Analysis," *Proceedings of the IRRA: 24th Annual Winter Meeting* 245-61 (1971); idem, "Discrimination, Monopsony, and Union Power in the Building Trades," 95 (4) *MLR* 24-26 (Apr. 1972); Benjamin Wolkinson, *Blacks, Unions and the EEOC: A Study of Administrative Futility* 10-16 (1973); Jonathan Grossman, *The Department of Labor* 222-23 (1973).

[85]"Excerpt of Remarks of AFL-CIO Secretary-Treasurer William F. Schnitzler at Apprenticeship and Training Conference," *CLR*, No. 616, July 12, 1967, at C-1, C-2.

[86]"AFL-CIO Building Trades Department Blasts Federal Aprrentice Regs," *CLR*, No. 804, Feb. 17, 1971, at A-12, A-14.

Table 21: Black Men as a % of All Male Craft Workers, 1962-1974			
Occupation	1962	1974	Year of Highest % if not 1974
All craft workers	4.7	7.4	
Masons	12.7	18.2	
Carpenters	5.4	6.0	6.7 (1970)
Cement finishers	27.8	30.4	42.0 (1966)
Crane/hoist operators	10.0	17.9	19.6 (1969)
Electricians	2.3	4.4	
Machinists	1.5	5.6	6.2 (1973)
Auto mechanics	9.0	7.9	10.6 (1973)
Painters	8.3	11.1	
Plumbers	3.9	5.6	6.0 (1972)

Source: Stuart Garfinkle, "Occupations of Women and Black Workers, 1962-74," 98 (11) *MLR* 25-35, tab. 4 at 30 (Nov. 1975).

Many observers have either overlooked these realities or left the impression that humanistic-progressive management and union leaders were, unfortunately, not always able to prevail over their reactionary subordinates.[87] Similarly misleading were analysts who fell into an illusory politics by proposing to offer accurate prognoses to workers to prove to them that increasing their supply by several hundred thousand would exert no negative impact on their employment situation.[88]

Although it has been an axiom of radical working class politics since the nineteenth century that white workers can never be free so long as black workers remain subordinates, the situation, at least in the North, was fundamentally different from that in the South even as late as the 1950s or 1960s. As the historian of race and unionism in Memphis astutely observes: "[A]s long as... exclusionary practices prevailed among white workers, employers had little reason to fear labor challenges to the 'southern way of life.' Furthermore, should any such challenges arise, workers faced the likelihood of repression, since the white community had largely sacrificed the civil rights protections embodied in the Bill of Rights in the process of imposing a racial dictatorship over blacks. When workers did begin to demand change, the

---

[87]E.g., Marshall & Briggs, *Negro and Apprenticeshp* at 34, 242-43.

[88]Herbert Hill, "Racial Inequality in Employment: The Patterns of Discrimination," 357 *AAAPSS* 30-47 at 43-44 (Jan. 1965).

repressive exercise of state power...provided the ultimate guarantor of the South's racial and class system."[89] Nothing even remotely analogous characterized the political-economic structure of the North during the Vietnam war era. As long as the building trades unions monopolized the labor market in the large cities, it is difficult to discern how, in light of their superior wages and control over working conditions, they, as business unionists, were in any appreciable economic way injured by their exclusionary policies toward blacks.

Ironically, however, the very decline of the unions in the 1980s underscored the robustness of this counterintuitive argument: despite the threats and plans by big business and the state to undermine the unions by flooding the labor market with black workers, the spectacular expansion of the nonunion sector in fact never relied on that labor force. Indeed, during the rest of twentieth century, nonunion firms employed even fewer blacks than their union competitors. In a final consequence of the cunning of history, however, racist policies did come to haunt unions; for even if excluding blacks failed to harm the unions in a direct economic way, the political and moral disrepute which they incurred made it easier for their enemies to mold public opinion against them and to deprive them of public (and to some extent even AFL-CIO) support when the Roundtable and the federal government launched their multipronged assaults. Though driven in large part by the same strengths and weaknesses, the exclusion of black workers would ultimately harm the unions less than their failure to organize the much larger group of white labor market competitors.

---

[89]Honey, *Southern Labor and Black Civil Rights* at 42-43.

10

Operation Breakthrough:
Industrialized Housing and the
Threat of Vertical Integration

If the workmen in the building trade are to take combined action to accelerate production, they must as a body be consulted as to the purpose to which their energy is to be applied, and must not be expected to build fashionable houses, when what are required are six-room cottages to house families which are at present living with three persons to a room.[1]

[M]ajor manufacturing concerns are casting an eye on the construction industry to determine whether with new methods, they can take it over.[2]

"We have had a threefold surge in the homebuilding rate since 1969, but there has been no strain on the labor supply." And the reason...is that more and more houses have become manufactured products—"just like everything else"—and the factories that make them can vastly increase production without tapping the limited supply of skilled building tradesmen.[3]

The origins of the federal government program to foster industrialized home building reached back into the 1960s.[4] The account here begins where unions perceived developments as impinging on their capacity to guarantee the best possible conditions for the sale of their members' labor power.

Soon after taking office, Nixon's Secretary of Housing and Urban Development (HUD), George Romney, the former president of the fourth largest U.S. automobile manufacturing firm, announced plans to create low-cost housing in the same way that American Motors had produced cheap automobiles. Operation Breakthrough, which Romney unveiled on May 8, 1969, was designed to use mass production technology to build housing for the poor. From the outset the Nixon administration made it clear that construction unions' restrictions on the size of the work force and on the use of prefabricated materials might subvert the program.[5] Unions' suspicions were scarcely allayed by Operation Breakthrough's forerunner in Detroit—begun in the late 1960s while Romney was the governor of Michigan—in which producers relied on unskilled workers and paid them well below the going

---

[1]R. H. Tawney, *The Acquisitive Society* 153 (1948 [1920]).

[2]Herbert Northrup, "Restrictive Practices and Racial Barriers" at 12, in *Papers Presented at the National Conference on Construction Problems* (Nov. 18-19, 1968).

[3]"A Housing Revolution in Precut Parts," *BW*, Feb. 10, 1973, at 43, 44.

[4]On the congressional authorization of a program of industrialized housing for the poor, see Housing and Urban Development Act of 1968, Pub. L. No. 90-448, §108, 82 Stat. 476, 495.

[5]"Romney Expands Effort to Build Housing for Poor," *NYT*, May 9, 1969, at 1, col. 5.

rates for factory and skilled workers in Detroit. Unions' fears were exacerbated by construction firms' reaction to the government training funds that additionally subsidized the operations: with the help of such low wages and subsidies "they, too, could build cheaper, even with conventional methods."[6]

The unions' response was not long in coming. Three days after Romney introduced Operation Breakthrough, 3,000 delegates to the BCTD national legislative conference booed him when he called on them to end their restrictive practices.[7] Then on the same day (September 23) that the DOL announced implementation of the Philadelphia Plan, HUD Undersecretary Richard Van Dusen warned the BCTD national convention that it had to choose between, on the one hand, restricting membership, resisting technological change, and pushing for higher wages, thus frustrating the administration's plan for decent housing for all, and, on the other, drawing on unemployed minorities, shortening apprenticeships, increasing productivity by embracing Breakthrough's promotion of mass production techniques, and fighting inflation. The BCTD's skepticism was captured by the response of its president, C. J. Haggerty, that unemployment in housing was rapidly rising.[8]

HUD continued to view the building trades unions as a major impediment to the implementation of Operation Breakthrough. A memo to Romney on the subject of reducing construction costs emphasized that because shortages of skilled craftsmen enabled unions to demand large wage increases, it was absolutely essential that the federal government do everything possible to increase the supply. The memo also recommended that in order to avoid the relevant DOL offices that were "dominated" by organized labor, other agencies should set standards for training. Finally, the memo called for the promulgation of an executive order prohibiting the federal government from letting federally funded or assisted contracts in areas where prevailing wage rates exceeded maximum wage rates set by the order.[9] The seriousness with which some in the Nixon administration were pursuing this last recommendation was underscored by the fact that two months later four cabinet members repeated it in a memo to the president.[10]

---

[6]Jerry Flint, "Houses Put on the Assembly Line in Detroit Test," *NYT*, Aug. 4, 1969, at 1, col. 4, at 47, col. 6.

[7]"Romney Jeered at Union Parley," *NYT*, May 13, 1969, at 42, col. 3.

[8]Damon Stetson, "Unions Are Urged to Spur Housing," *NYT*, Sept. 24, 1969, at 18, col. 4, 5.

[9]Memo from Samuel J. Simmons, Equal Opportunity, to George Romney, Subject: Recommendation for the Reduction of Cosntruction Cost (Dec. 15, 1969), in NACP, RG 207: General Records of the Dept of HUD, Office of the Under Secretary, Subject File of Richard Van Dusen, 1969-72, Box No. 24, Folder: EO Equal Opportunity 1969 Part I (1 of 2).

[10]Blount, Stans, Romney, and Volpe, Memorandum for the President, Re: The Need for a more direct attack on the wage-price spiral (Feb. 14, 1970), in NACP, RG 207: General Records of the Dept of HUD, Office of the Under Secretary, Subject File of Richard Van Dusen, 1969-72, WH 1-1-WH 1-2, Box No. 74, Folder: WH 1-1 Memoranda to President 1970-1969 (2 of 2)

At the time of the May 1970 Wall Street demonstrations,[11] Haggerty, the BCTD president, stressed that the federal government had subsidized "non-union cheap labor shenanigans" by keeping afloat unprofitable firms making component parts by enabling them to pay apprentice wages of $4 per day.[12] Even more instructive was his Labor Day message. After sympathizing with members who had expressed their outrage at antiwar demonstrators, Haggerty shifted his focus:

We must not allow our patriotic love for our country, particularly strong in this time of war, to be misinterpreted as a blanket endorsement of public officials or civic leaders whose domestic policies completely contravene our policies and all that we stand for.

Certainly it should not be considered an endorsement of the actions of those who would use their offices to destroy our standards, destroy our working conditions, destroy our training programs and even destroy our prevailing wage structure.[13]

Haggerty also delivered a sobering lecture on self-criticism to his members. Widely reported was his warning that: "Hundreds of millions of dollars of work was lost this year to nonunion contractors explicitly because" union construction workers failed to "deliver a full day's work for a full day's pay" or "honestly and rigidly observe" their contracts, or because "personal whims rather than actual illness or other compelling reasons" produced an above-average rate of absenteeism and quits, and "continuous and devastating work stoppages" resulted from jurisdictional disputes between unions. Portentously, Haggerty added that: "Unless we take drastic action to correct those abuses...our employers will soon turn to other sources for their labor supply."[14] Unsurprisingly, the AGC immediately used Haggerty's admissions against interest as the epigram for its publication attacking restrictive practices.[15]

A few months later Romney confirmed that unions' fears were not baseless.

---

[11]See chapter 11 below.

[12]"AFL-CIO on Breakthrough," *ENR*, May 7, 1970, at 3; 33 (5) *BCTB* (May 1970) [no pagination].

[13]C. J. Haggerty, "Labor Day Is Time for Objective Appraisal as well as Deserved Recognition of Efforts, President Haggerty Says in Annual Message," 23 (8) *BCTB* (Aug. 1970) [no pagination].

[14]Haggerty, "Labor Day Is Time for Objective Appraisal as well as Deserved Recognition of Efforts, President Haggerty Says in Annual Message." See also "Haggerty Questions Jurisdictional Strikes, Absenteeism, and Contract Compliance in His Annual Labor Day Message," *CLR*, No. 780, Sept. 2, 1970, at A-12-A-14; "Honor Pacts or Lose Jobs, Labor Chief Tells Unions," *NYT*, Sept. 4, 1970, at 9, col. 1. On the uniqueness of large-scale political jurisdictional disputes in the United States, see George Barnett, "The Causes of Jurisdictional Disputes in American Trade Unions," 9 (4) *HBR* 400-408 at 404 (Apr. 1931). Barnett emphasized that building tradesmen believed that they could protect their employment by dividing the industry into a large number of sections "in each of which the exclusive right to employment belongs to the men practising that particular trade."

[15]AGC, *Restrictive Practices in the Building Trades* 1 (Sept. 1970), in NACP, RG 174: General Records of the Labor Dept., Office of the Secretary, Records of Sec. James D. Hodgson, Box No. 20: Boards, Folder: 1970-Commissions: CICBC (October).

Ironically, *ENR* reported his predictions in an article headlined, "Nixon Shuns a Wage Confrontation with Labor."

I believe we'll see a reduction in labor costs. ... The American people are sick and tired of paying the tab for upward pressure on costs. This pressure will be brought to a halt though a combination of direct government action, new labor legislation, and the switch to industrialized housing which can be built without having to use highly skilled, high-cost trade union labor requiring years of training. Restrictive trade practices, too, will be eliminated....[16]

The fact that the head of the umbrella organization of building trades unions found it necessary to caution those behind the May demonstrations, which had been used to neutralize the Nixon administration's plans to curb union militance, whereas Nixon's administrator of the state industrialization program announced antiunion measures, makes a brief sketch of that program and the federal government's implementation strategy necessary. To be sure, the program was continuous with the impact that alleged labor shortages, operating through the normal processes of capital accumulation, had already been exerting. Scrutinizing the years from 1956 to 1968, the Department of Commerce observed that: "Shortages of skilled workers in the construction trades and rising wage demands have contributed to increased mechanization in all phases of the construction industry. New building materials and methods have led to greater mechanization of residential and non-residential building construction."[17]

From its inception, Operation Breakthrough, which Nixon characterized as a means of solving the problem of a shortage of construction workers,[18] relied on large industrial firms whose core operations lay outside of construction.[19] Near the end of the Johnson administration, William Chartener, assistant secretary of commerce for economic affairs, had warned that: "It is possible—indeed inevitable

---

[16]"Nixon Shuns a Wage Confrontation with Labor," *ENR*, Jan. 14, 1971, at 13.

[17]U.S. Business and Defense Service Adm., *Growth Pace Setters in American Industry, 1956-68*, at 28.

[18]"Annual Budget Message to the Congress, Fiscal Year 1971," in Nixon, *PPPUS: 1970*, at 46, 66 ([Feb. 2, 1970] 1971).

[19]One of the important indirect benefits of Operation Breakthrough, according to assistant HUD secretary for research and technology Harold Finger, was that "the big corporations are moving into industrial production faster than they would have without Breakthrough." John Herbers, "Housing Plan Turns Out First Factory-Built Unit," *NYT*, May 20, 1971, in NACP, RG 207, General Records of the Dept. of HUD, Records of the Office of the Undersecretary, Operation "Breakthrough," Press Clippings, 1971-73, Box No. 4. See also "Instant City Expert Builds Against All Odds," *ENR*, Oct. 17, 1968 at 36, 41-42; Dorothy Nelkin, *The Politics of Housing Innovation* 102 (1971). Similar plans formulated shortly after World War II remained largely unrealized. James Fitch, *American Building* 344-45 (1948); Glenn Beyer, *Housing and Society* 504 (1965). At that time, too, armaments firms, which were attempting to adjust to demobilization, were to be accorded a significant role.

if present trends continue—that other industries, rich in technological know-how, managerial competence and financial resources, will take advantage of the inability of the construction industry to satisfy its market at a reasonable cost.... It is no secret that a number of major corporations are making plans to move into the field of construction with a new technological look."[20] Johnson's HUD had "decided early in the game that large industrial corporations should bring their research talents and money into the housing field. The chance of a foothold in what will be one of the nation's most comprehensive programs—housing—provided the profit incentive...." The key to success was "figuring schemes to assemble enough units into a marketable package in a given area to interest large industrial corporations, the Kaisers, the GMs, GEs, and others."[21]

The same focus characterized Operation Breakthrough. As a Cabinet Construction Committee memo from December 1969 noted, pointing to recent moves by Boise Cascade and ITT-Levitt, a "distinct trend toward massive capitalization is beginning to take formation." And prescriptively the memo viewed the combined phenomenon of industrialized housing and the formation of large corporate diversified firms in the construction industry as one of the primary mechanisms for reaching national housing goals.[22]

The reason for this orientation lay not only in the fact that the degree of capital concentration and centralization among traditional residential building firms would have been insufficient to finance the huge investments, but also in the fact that they and the unions associated with them would have regarded the plan as a threat to their interests.[23] As the president of the American Institute of Architects

---

[20]"Attacking the Bargaining Crisis," *ENR*, May 30, 1968, at 11-12.

[21]"Instant City Expert Builds Against All Odds," *ENR*, Oct. 17, 1968, at 36, 41-42 at 42

[22]Working Group of the Subcommittee on Industrial Structure, CCC, "The Contract Construction Industry: A New Focus" at 2, 18 (Dec. 16, 1969) (Limited Official Use), in NACP, RG 174: General Records of the Labor Dept., Records of the Secretary of Labor George P. Shultz, 1969-1970, Box No. 173: International Committee-Cabinet Committee on Oil Imports, Folder: 1970-Committee: CCC (May 5).

[23]Nelkin, *Politics of Housing Innovation* at 68; "Is the Crisis a Catastrophe?" *Forbes*, Jan. 1, 1971, at 76. Some authors, committed to a leftwing conspiracy approach, explained the plan as flowing from the need for a new source of profits for the military-industrial complex once it hit up against its limits to growth. Marc Weiss, "Housing Industrial Complex," 4 (1) *PRWET* 23-27 (Nov.-Dec. 1972). On the participation of such aerospace firms as Boeing, Avco, Grumman, Northrop, Raytheon, Aerojet General, and TRW in addition to Ford, GE, Westinghouse, ALCOA, ITT, Kaiser, Hercules, U.S. Steel, Chrysler, Bethlehem Steel, CBS, Borg-Warner, Goodyear Rubber, Jones & Laughlin Steel, see "The Siren Call of Housing," *Forbes*, Jan. 1, 1971, at 119; Donald Schon, "Innovation by Invasion," *IST*, No. 27, at 52-60 (Mar. 1964); "Alcoa Expands Housing Role," *ENR*, July 17, 1969, at 78; "Ford Buys Share of Prefab Firm," *ENR*, Sept. 25, 1969, at 58; *ENR*, Apr. 16, 1970, at 3; *ENR*, May 7, 1970, at 3; *ENR*, Nov. 12, 1970, at 3; Lawrence Meyer, "The Housing Shortage Goes Critical," 80 (7) *Fortune* 136 (Dec. 1969); "Factory Housing Faces More Sticky Obstacles Than Its Boosters See," *WSJ*, Mar. 8, 1971, at 1, col. 6; *WSJ*, Feb. 4, 1971, at 18; "Northrop Holds Talks on Possible Purchase of George A. Fuller Construction Co.," *WSJ*, Sept. 2, 1971, at 8, col.

warned contractors in 1969: "You better do something about it. There are a lot of other people, including the aerospace firms, that can perform your management functions. You can join up or get bent."[24] The close meshing of the federal government with the great national industrial capitals proved to be necessary to overcome the impediments to industrialized housing. For the microeconomic point of the new method of production lay precisely in creating a new spatial division of labor by substituting capital for labor: "Modular production is primarily intended to overcome the skilled labor shortage. Levitt estimates that 250 skilled man-hours in the field will be replaced by less than 150 unskilled and semi-skilled man-hours in the factory...."[25] To be sure, it was misleading of advocates to speak of a shortage when they really had the price of skilled labor power in mind. This substitution process did not per se guarantee an improvement in profitability—the point was whether the increased fixed capital investments could be amortized over sufficient units of output to lower unit costs. This stage was not attained in the United States during the period under review.[26] (Although Romney had predicted that by 1980 two-thirds of all houses would be manufactured in factories, as of 1995 less than one-third of new U.S. single-family homes was factory built.)[27]

The success of such an undertaking presupposed either the agreement or

---

1; "Housing Enters the Era of the Superbuilder," *BW*, Dec. 26, 1970, at 50-53; "Northrop Snaps Up a Big-Name Builder," *BW*, Dec. 25, 1971, at 19 (purchase of Fuller); "Corporate Giants that Soured on Real Estate," *BW*, Feb. 16, 1974, at 96, 98. These articles chronicle many of the firms' precipitate entry and retreat. Despite emphasizing that large corporations had exercised caution in commiting their own capital, William Keating, *Emerging Patterns of Corporate Entry into Housing* 75, 125 (1973), declared that it could be "safely said" that they would soon extend their dominance to the housing industry.

[24]"The AGC Sees No Panacea Ahead," *ENR*, Mar. 27, 1969, at 17-18.

[25]"Housing Enters the Era of the Superbuilder," *BW*, Dec. 26, 1970, at 52-53.

[26]"Making Modular Units Is Easy, Making Money at It Isn't So Easy," *WSJ*, Sept. 7, 1972, at 1, col. 6. Ironically, modular builders complained: "'Large tract builders putting up 100 to 500 homes at a time have what is almost an assembly line in the field—we can't beat that.'" "Modular Housing Takes a Beating," *BW*, May 13, 1972, at 148. For international comparisons, see W. Roest, *Bouw en economische groei* 56 (1973); Alexander Pike, "Failure of Industrialized Building and Housing Programs," 37 (2) *AD* 507 (Nov. 1967). For an example of the inability to make accurate prognoses, see Battelle Memorial Institute, *The State of the Art of Prefabrication in the Construction Industry* 83 (1967). A principal obstacle to cheap modular housing was the high cost transportation. "The Modules Look for a Cheaper Ride," *BW*, May 22, 1971, at 22-23. As early as 1972, one critic awarded Romney the Edsel Award. 1 (3) *Impact* 3 (Nov. 1972). HUD maintained a file with scores of critical materials. NACP, RG 207: General Records of the Dept. of HUD, Records of the Office of the Undersecretary, Operation "Breakthrough," Company and Subject File, 1971-73, Box No. 3, Folder: Criticism.

[27]"Secretary Romney Predicts Two-Thirds of All U.S. Housing Will Be Factory-Produced by 1980," *CLR*, No. 799, Jan. 13, 1971, at A-3; "And Now for the Homeburger," *Economist*, Aug. 10, 1996, at 19. As Peter Williamson, "Tomorrow's Housing," ENR, Apr. 30, 1974, at 137-44 at 139, noted: "Unfortunately for would-be industrialized builders, there are no markets to justify the capital outlay for a $1-million or $2-million factory."

weakening of construction unions since the industrialization program would have triggered not only an enormous process of dequalification and thus of labor power devaluation, but also construction-industry-wide disemployment.[28]   A way, therefore, had to be found to induce unions to accept a situation in which fewer and fewer skilled workers would be employed.[29] To be sure, this program was based on an empirical assumption that was contested even at the time—namely, that residential construction was largely unionized.[30]   If, as other contemporary authorities observed, 80 percent of housing was built by nonunion workers, "the union wage spiral was not a direct factor in pushing up the price of housing," especially since unorganized construction workers' wages amounted to only half of union rates.[31] By 1974, the domination of residential construction by non-and

---

[28]On the displacement of skilled on-site construction workers by factory workers with three weeks of training, see David Shipler, "Small Plant Taking Big Step in Prefabs," *NYT*, Oct. 27, 1970, at 47, col. 1. The Sheet Metal Workers International Association in San Francisco agreed that journeymen working in fabricating shops would be paid $5 an hour instead of the $9.41 paid for on-site construction. "Metalworkers' Union, California Employers Set Lower Shop Wage," *WSJ*, July 9, 1971, at 24, col. 4.

[29]"A Steeper Labor Cost Spiral in '71, Lower in '72," *ENR*, Sept. 17, 1970, at 88-103 at 103; *The Report of the President's Committee on Urban Housing: Technical Studies* 2:49 (1968).

[30]Howard Foster, "Unions, Residential Construction and Public Policy," 12 (4) *QREB* 45-55 (Winter 1972); *idem, Manpower in Homebuilding: A Preliminary Analysis* 42-48 (1974). A vice president of the NAHB testified before Congress in 1969 that 50 percent of housing units and almost all apartment houses were built by union labor. *Situs Picketing: Hearings Before the Special Subcommittee on Labor of the House Committee on Education and Labor,* 91st Cong., 1st Sess. 126 (1969) (testimony of Louis Barba). In 1952, a survey of 16 cities revealed that almost 100 percent of workers on commercial, industrial, public, and semi-public work were unionized, whereas in nonapartment residential construction the share varied from 100 percent in Chicago, St. Louis, and Cleveland to 25 percent in Indianapolis, Cincinnati, and Columbus. William Haber & Harold Levinson, *Labor Relations and Productivity in the Building Trades* 35-36 (1956). William Tobin, the chairman of the NAHB labor department testified before Congress in 1951 that 24 percent of local affiliated associations operated in cities with 100 percent unionization of residential construction and 22 percent in cities with no unionization. *To Amend the National Labor Relations Act, 1947, with Respect to the Building and Construction Industry: Hearings Before the Subcommittee on Labor and Labor Management Relations of the Senate Committee on Labor and Public Welfare,* 82d Cong., 1st Sess. 139 (1951). In 1946, when 250,000 organized workers were employed in residential construction, 73 percent of building trades locals reported that they negotiated agreements covering most of residential construction in their areas; in only eight cities did all of the unions claim to control a majority of residential construction. BLS, *Union Wages and Hours in the Building Trades* 24 (Bull. 910, 1947). In 1939, the BLS reported that the consensus among unions and contractors was that nearly all large residences in the cities surveyed were constructed by union labor. In only four cities did union rates prevail in virtually all residential construction; in 12 to 16 cities union rates were estimated to prevail in half of small residential jobs; in 47 to 52 cities, less than half. BLS, *Union Wages, Hours, and Working Conditions in the Building Trades* 37 (Bull. 674, 1940). A BLS survey from 1936 revealed that 57 percent of workers in residential construction were unionized compared to 72 percent in nonresidential construction. Edward Sanford, "Wage Rates and Hours of Labor in the Building Trades," 45 (2) *MLR* 281-300 at 297 (Aug. 1937).

[31]Lenhart, "Construction Wage-Stabilization Efforts" at 2215.

"militantly anti-union" firms had motivated the United Brotherhood of Carpenters to try to organize homebuilding, just as it had resolved, with some success, in 1970 to organize in-plant and erection employees of firms manufacturing prefabricated housing.[32] On another track, however, the Carpenters' resistance to the use of prefabricated materials as limiting on-site work provoked builders, including such a vertically integrated firm as Boise Cascade, supported by the Chamber of Commerce of the United States and the Business Roundtable, to file unfair labor practice charges under the NLRA.[33]

According to the well-informed insider, Daniel Quinn Mills, the federal government's error set in motion an unwanted self-fulfilling prophecy:

There is little doubt that the federal government has inadvertently facilitated the organization of industrial housing by the unions. The government largely misunderstood the labor relations situation in homebuilding, believing organization by the unions to be greater than it is, and publicized as critical a somewhat minor problem of union acceptance of prefabricated housing. In order to resolve the supposed dispute, the government sought labor agreements to facilitate on-site acceptance by the unions. ... In the process, the building trades obtained further representation in the housing production industry.[34]

If this view was correct, then the policy could be traced back to a deal that the Nixon administration had entered into with construction unions and parts of the industry. Mills's reference to a "minor problem" appears, however, to have been an understatement; after all, even in the factories supplying the industrialized housing industry that were organized by (construction) unions, workers' wages were barely more than half of those of skilled building tradesmen.[35]

---

[32]"Carpenters Launch Major Organizing Drive for Residential Construction," *CLR*, No. 951, Jan. 2, 1974, at A-9; "General Executive Board Policy Statement on Prefabricated Housing," 90 (4) *Carpenter* 2, 3, 36 (Apr. 1970). At least one modular house manufacturer's production-line workers were members of the United Brotherhood of Carpenters. "Stirling Homex Plans to Ship Housing Units to Markets by Water," *WSJ*, Mar. 1, 1971, at 8.

[33]E.g., Chamber of Commerce of the United States v. NLRB, 574 F.2d 457 (9th Cir. 1978). See generally, Douglas Leslie, "Right to Control: A Study in Secondary Boycotts and Labor Antitrust," 89 *HLR* 904-20 (1976).

[34]Daniel Quinn Mills, *Industrial Relations and Manpower in Construction* 267-68 n.54 (1972). Felician Foltman, in reviewing this book, characterized Mills, based on his career activity, as a spokesman for the construction industry as a whole. 26 (3) *ILRR* 1030-31 (Apr. 1973).

[35]"Metalworkers' Union, California Employers Set Lower Shop Wage," *WSJ*, July 9, 1971, at 24, col. 4. Eastern European state-socialist countries acknowledged the progressive aspect of the higher degree of the socialization of the forces of production associated with such dequalification processes. R. Richta et al., *Politische Ökonomie des 20. Jahrhunderts* 54-55 (1971); Edward Kuminek, "Changes in the Output of the Building Industry as a Factor in the Development of Home-Building," in *The Economic Problems of Housing: Proceedings of a Conference Held by the International Economic Association* 228-35 at 234 (Adela Nevitt ed., 1967) (discussing Poland). Although unions in capitalist societies as working-class protective organizations cannot trust

The second important reason for the necessity of 'collaboration' between the federal government and the large industrial firms investing in the construction industry was to weaken the the alliance of local governments, construction unions, and unionized building firms standing in the way of a thorough national industrialization of residential construction.[36] Within the sector investing in construction three groups of firms can be distinguished: (1) those whose technological basis offered specific advantages in industrialized building; (2) those without such possibilities, but that bought up larger traditional construction companies with the aim of using large investments to enable them to acquire such a technological basis; and (3) those manufacturing various components for the construction industry that were induced to integrate forward into building because of the difficulties that union restrictions might cause them in selling their products to contractors.[37]

That this state-promoted industrialization movement did not achieve the successes that had been widely predicted was due to several factors: (1) the level of short-term profits was, in view of the long-term uncertainties, not high enough

---

modernized versions of the compensation theory that promise new and better employment to those displaced by mechanization, every national labor movement that aspires to transcend the status of a factor of production chasing after special interests must also seek to promote a humane development of the forces of production. Thus in view of the chronic shortage of decent housing for low-income workers, construction unions that flatly reject methods of production that would alleviate this dearth undermine classwide goals. For an example of a pseudo-communist analysis that ignores this contradiction, see "Construction Unions Attacked," 6 (10) *Challenge* 13 (Jan. 1970). On the world's leading example of a union that paid as much attention to the projects its members built as to the conditions under which they built them, see Pete Thomas, *Taming the Concrete Jungle: The Builders Laborers' Story* (1973). Under the leadership of Jack Mundey, its Communist secretary, the Builders Labourers Federation of New South Wales instituted green bans on environmentally harmful projects and struck at a university that fired a homosexual and refused to hold a women's liberation course. Such actions prompted the *Sydney Morning Herald* to declare that: "'There is something highly comical in the spectacle of builders' labourers, whose ideals in industrial relations do not rise above strikes, violence, intimidation and the destruction of property, setting themselves up as arbiters of taste and protectors of the national heritage.'" Jon Tinker, "Tin-Hatted Conservationist," 62 (901) *New Scientist* 620-24 at 620 (June 6, 1974). On the judicial deregistration of the union for exceeding the scope of its legitimate activity, see Master Builders' Ass'n of New South Wales v. Australian Bldg. Constr. Employees and Builders' Labourers Fed'n, 23 FLR 356 (1973-1974).

[36]Weiss, "Housing Industrial Complex" at 25-26; James O'Connor, *The Fiscal Crisis of the State* 83-84 (1973).

[37]"Some New Approaches to Industrialized Housing," *JH*, No. 8, at 431-39 (Sept. 1967); Lefkoe, *Crisis in Construction* at 11. The best example of a firm falling into the last group was Boise Cascade, whose constructiion activity proved unsuccessful. "Housing Builds Boise Cascade," *ENR*, Dec. 12, 1968, at 28, 33-34; A. Richard Immel, "Sales of Scenic Lots for Vacation Homes Run into Many Woes," *WSJ*, Dec. 24, 1970, at 1, col. 1; "Boise Cascade Says It Had 4th Period Loss, Profit in '70 Plummeted," *WSJ*, Feb. 4, 1971, at 18, col. 6; "Boise Cascade to Incur $44 Million Charge in 2nd Period Writeoffs, Writedowns," *WSJ*, June 21, 1971, at 10, col. 1; "Corporate Giants that Soured on Real Estate," *BW*, Feb. 16, 1974, at 96, 98.

to justify the further withdrawal of this capital by industrial firms from more profitable spheres of investment; (2) the rapid and (as always) unexpected sequence of phases of the business cycle (1967-69: boom; 1969-71: crisis and depression; 1972-73: inflationary boom; 1973-75: inflationary crisis and depression) prevented the planning and implementation of an expensive state program that had to be secured for the long term; and (3) undermining the livelihoods of hundreds of thousands of small building contractors together with the workers relying on them for employment became a politically delegitimizing impediment.[38] That resistance stemmed not only from small business owners is shown by the fact that construction lenders were also seen as having "no interest in new and more economic production methods or lower prices for new housing since they are typically identical with mortgage lenders having a great stake in capital values in the existing housing supply."[39]

This analysis makes it implausible to identify Operation Breakthrough as derived from or corresponding to the interests of capital in general without recourse to dubious a priori or a posteriori constructions.[40] This non-correspondence may derive from the fact that aggregate capitalist interests cannot be articulated from the standpoint of an individual branch.

Such agnosticism can be contrasted with the contemporaneous approach of the Maoist Progressive Labor Party: "There are 870,000 contractors in this country. Most are small and have a hard time staying in business. Big Business could easily set up a few big construction firms that would force most of the small fry out. This is the whole direction of the Big Business plan."[41] Here was paired a reckless overestimation of the "power of the monopolies" with neglect of the conditions of production for profit. The group's approach was, moreover, inconsistent since it in effect demanded that workers together with small contractors ward off the threat of big business, although it also reported that the 870,000 contractors were "united against the men."

The possible results of such tactics can be imagined using Lefkoe's contemporaneous insider-analysis commissioned by the Roundtable. Lefkoe observed a certain opposition of interests between general and specialty contractors, which led to the latter's refusal to coordinate their wage negotiations: "Each

---

[38]On these "mittelstandspolitischen" reasons, see C. Offe & V. Ronge, "Fiskalische Krise, Bauindustrie und die Grenzen staatlicher Aufgabenrationalisierung," 1 (2) *Leviathan* 214 (May 1973).

[39]Leo Grebler, *Production of New Housing* 150 (1950). See also "An Historical Evaluation of Industrialized Housing—Building Systems in the U.S.," in *The Report of the President's Committee on Urban Housing: Technical Studies* 2:184; Fitch, *American Building* at 334-35.

[40]Claus Offe, *Strukturprobleme des kapitalistischen Staates* 65-105 (1973); Joachim Hirsch, *Staatsapparat und Reproduktion des Kapitals* 217-30, 252-61 (1974).

[41]"Construction Workers," 7 (4) *PL* 52 (Feb. 1970). See also 6 (7-8) *Challenge* (Oct.-Nov. 1969).

specialty group is as anxious as the union it deals with to promote and retain the on-site work it does. Thus, certain types of specialty contractors and the unions they deal with often join forces in opposing technological advances that would take work they perform from the site to the factory."[42] Even if specialty contractors had created a united front with the general contractors (AGC) against national wage contracts (of the NCA-members), which continued in force, so that workers striking under local contracts might have found employment elsewhere, the former tended to appeal to their industrial customers for help—in the hope that they would suspend the projects in order to resist the workers' wage demands.

Of overriding importance in this context is that many of the firms participating in Operation Breakthrough formed the Roundtable, which established that resistance as its highest priority.[43] After Lefkoe attempted to explain microeconomically why such behavior on the part of the large construction customers would be irrational, he demonstrated how capital exists only individually:

The argument that client firms should be willing to act against their own economic self-interest in order to help "the economy as a whole" probably will not get very far. It will be seen by the executives of most of the client firms as a not very well disguised way of asking them to reduce their own companies' profits in order to increase the profits of those *other* companies which are being called "the economy as a whole."[44]

Lefkoe then warned those who did not understand that customers would use that call for help to bring the industry under their control: "Unfortunately contractors...almost a century ago did not understand any better than contractors today that if the business community is going to provide money..., it also is going

---

[42]Lefkoe, *Crisis in Construction* at 38. Some of Lefkoe's incisive analyses about the construction industry contrast sharply with the bizarre and ignorant assertions that he makes about the NLRA and labor law in general. His point of departure—quoted by him at length from a monograph, published by Lefkoe Consulting, Inc., *Organized Labor's Use of Coalition Bargaining: The Noose Gets Tighter*—is the allegation that underlying labor law is the"almost universal acceptance of...numerous economic and historical myths about capitalism," in particular the theory that "employees are 'exploited'...by employers, who band together to drive wages down to the level of bare subsistence." Lefkoe, *The Crisis in Construction* at 57-58. His outlandish claims about the relentlessly pro-union Taft-Hartley Act are especially inapt since he alleges that the government is "the primary source of union coercive power," whereas in fact the NLRB did not even exercise jurisdiction over construction unions until Taft-Hartley, which curtailed building trades unions' power—which had flourished without protection by the Wagner Act—by outlawing and enjoining secondary action. *Id.* at 55-79. Under the name Morty Lefkoe, he has moved on to the business of new age self-improvement consulting. http://www.decisionmaker.com/bio.html
[43]Lefkoe, *Crisis in Construction* at 93-96; Weiss, "Housing Industrial Complex" at 26.
[44]Lefkoe, *Crisis in Construction* at 114-15.

to make sure that its assistance is used properly and for its benefit."[45]

Fortune later understood this novel strategy, observing that initially the CUAIR "had to buck considerable suspicion among contractors. Ordinarily customers do not interfere with the business of a supplier; if they dislike his product or price, they go elsewhere. But here was something new in U.S. business—big companies were encouraged to intervene in the affairs of suppliers who had lost control of their costs. Contractors soon saw that their long-term interests were served by the arrangement."[46] As an entrepreneurial strategy for medium-sized and small firms, Lefkoe suggested vertical and/or horizontal integration, which would not only have done away with the opposition between general and specialty contractors, but also prompted the rationalization movement to apply modular methods, which could, in turn, have reduced the number of skilled workers. Thus Lefkoe imagined a strong trend toward capital concentration and centralization, which would bring about the disemployment of many union members, whereas others "would be willing to renounce...union membership in return for year-round employment at union wage rates." Further advantages would accrue to the new construction firms in the form of the restoration of management prerogatives associated with the disappearance of unions.[47]

From this analysis of the forces operating within the industry it emerges that collaboration of workers with small building contractors in order to thwart an invasion by industrial capital could have led to catastrophic consequences. To be sure, many firms, especially in large cities such as New York, were apparently prepared to undertake this effort—hence the May demonstrations, which, however, hardly expressed the political standpoint that the Progressive Labor Party strategy would have ascribed to it.

---

[45]*Id.* at 119-20. Lefkoe was referring to the so-called American Plan in San Francisco in the beginning of the 1920s, which undermined the power of local building firms and unions; that such a scenario had lost none of its currency was demonstrated by Lefkoe's reference to the NAM and the Roundtable. *Id.* at 116-20; see also below ch. 14.

[46]Gilbert Burck, "A Time of Reckoning for the Building Unions," *Fortune*, June 4, 1979, at 82, 88.

[47]Lefkoe, *Crisis in Construction* at 136-43, 148, 162 (quote), 168.

11

Construction Workers' Counter-Demonstrations Supporting the U.S. Invasion of Cambodia and Neutralizing the Nixon Administration: The End of the '60s

The union craftsman, while not exactly a Wall Street banker or a prosperous physician, does have a large stake in preserving our society with its institutions against the destructive forces of revolutionary change. ... In a way, the craft union is more hateful than Wall Street to the brainstrusters of the Left.... If, Brothers, we must beware the Right because we are labor, we must beware the Left because we are very fortunate labor in a very blessed country.[1]

[T]he press and television have...attached something demeaning and brutal to the name [hard hat]. Why? Because a few construction workers in New York, goaded beyond endurance by the sight of unwashed, uncombed, unkempt young rebels desecrating a flag so many fought to protect in World War II, reacted in a very human way. They used their fists, fists calloused by honest work, fists used to paying taxes and saluting the flag.[2]

The building-trades counter-demonstrations in Manhattan in May 1970 in the wake of the open U.S. invasion of Cambodia, the killing of four students at Kent State University by the National Guard on May 4, and the student-led antiwar demonstrations became a crucial symbolic political event in the complex struggle over construction unionism. For *Business Week*, suddenly much more than symbols was at stake: events had consolidated "the academic community against the war, against business, and against government. This is a dangerous situation. It threatens the whole economic and social structure of the nation."[3] The magazine intoned similarly solemn words about the construction workers' "almost surreal performance"—what it called "Three days that shook the establishment."[4]

National leaders of the building trades unions, unlike some of their industrial counterparts, had long displayed chauvinist zeal in supporting U.S. war-making in Vietnam.[5] In 1965, the National Legislative Conference of the BCTD, 4,200 building trades union leaders representing more than 3,500,000 workers, unanimously passed a resolution supporting President Johnson's conduct of the war,

---

[1]Peter Schoemann, "Enough Is Enough," 79 (4) *UAJ* n.p. [inside front cover], n.p. [inside back cover] (Apr. 1967).

[2]M. A. Hutcheson, "If Hard Hats Stand for Hard-Working Old-Fashioned Patriotism, So Be It," 91 (5) *Carpenter* 40 (May 1971).

[3]"Handling the Student Protest Movement," *BW*, May 16, 1970, at 140.

[4]"Three Days that Shook the Establishment," *BW*, May 16, 1970, at 24.

[5]To be sure, polls indicated that overall a somewhat larger proportion of union members favored more U.S. military action in Vietnam than of the population at large. Derek Bok & John Dunlop, *Labor and the American Community* 61 (1970).

and calling on their 8,000 local unions and 525 state and local councils to "counteract the senseless [antiwar] demonstrations" by promoting a "better understanding" of the war goals.[6] In 1966 Maurice Hutcheson, who had inherited his general presidency of the Carpenters from his father William, analogized the right to dissent regarding the war in Vietnam to the right to cry "fire" in a crowded theater.[7] To be sure, that year also witnessed the AFL-CIO convention adopt a resolution pledging the organization's "unstinting support...of all measures the Administration might deem necessary to halt Communist aggression...."[8] In 1967, the president of the BCTD told its annual convention that "we should stay until we do win, decisively and totally."[9]

The year 1970 also marked the high point in labor militance during the Vietnam era. The United States had not experienced such a level of strikes, strikers, and striker-days across a broad spectrum of industries (including and especially construction) since the historically unprecedented postwar wave of 1946.[10] In March mail workers ignited the first strike in the history of the postal service, which originated in New York City, was illegal, nationwide, and, after the federal government had failed to keep mail moving with the National Guard, successful. April witnessed wildcat strikes by Teamsters in various locals in blatant disregard of their national president's orders. "The truculence of the 1970 wearer of a union button," according to *The New York Times*, was driven by the "melting away of wage envelopes in a period of high corporate profits...."[11]

In the wake of these pioneering labor eruptions and the nationwide seismic reaction to the invasion of Cambodia, student demonstrations took place on May 6, 1970 at various locations in New York City including Wall Street. Construction workers made their first appearance by raining down bottles, beer cans, and asphalt on demonstrators from a building on Broadway.[12] Medical students and construction workers, according to the front-page caption of "New York's Picture Newspaper," "tangle[d] after medics, gathering for antiwar rally at Battery, reportedly made obscene gestures at workers showing American flag."[13] Strikes at and closings of colleges and universities, followed by the decision of the New York City Board of

---

[6]"Our Firm Stand: Viet Nam Resolution," 18 (12) *BCTB* (Dec. 1965) [no pagination]. See also "AFL-CIO Building Trades Convention Acts on 30 Resolutions in San Francisco," 109 (1) *IOE* 11-13 at 13 (Jan. 1966).

[7]M. A. Hutcheson, "When the Right to Dissent Becomes a Disservice," 85 (1) *Carpenter* 40 (Jan. 1966).

[8]"Sixth AFL-CIO Convention Examines Labor's Future," 109 (1) *IOE* 8-10 at 9 (Jan. 1966).

[9]"Haggerty Opens Building Trades Convention," *CLR*, No. 636, Nov. 29, 1967, at A-6, A-8.

[10]BLS, *Analysis of Work Stoppages, 1970* (Bull. 1727, 1972).

[11]A. H. Raskin, "Strike Fever Speeds Up Wage-Price Spiral," *NYT*, Apr. 5, 1970.

[12]Sandor Polster, "Protests Are Peaceful," *NYP*, May 6, 1970, at 2, col. 1; Pete Hamill, "Hard Hats and Cops," *NYP*, May 12, 1970, at 47, col. 1-2.

[13]*NYDN*, May 7, 1970, at 1.

Education to close all public schools on Friday, May 8, as a memorial to the students killed at Kent State, enhanced protesters' availability and visibility. Construction workers' first major ground-level intervention occurred on May 7 at a rally of 2,000 protestors at Wall and Broad, when about 50 of them from a nearby project "waded into the crowd and began to pummel demonstrators." As the protestors left and marched up Broadway, construction workers "began to pelt the marchers with rocks and cans" from the upper floors of a building.[14] *New York Post* columnist Pete Hamill described them standing "up there, bellies bulging defiantly" after having hit a woman passerby with their beer cans and clumps of asphalt.[15]

The first counter-demonstration by construction workers, many of whom were employed building the World Trade Center, was directed against a Wall Street student protest on May 8. With building activity "intense" as a result of work at the Trade Center and other major office buildings, and airport and institutional construction, "'[r]ight now there's 120 per cent employment of construction labor in New York in the key trades.'" The tight labor market and abundant overtime made for prosperous times.[16] Hundreds of such construction workers, whose highest priority, to judge by their actions, was to remedy the tattered prestige of the American flag—their displeasure was triggered, inter alia, by the fact that the headquarters of the *Wall Street Journal* was unflagged, an abuse that they alleviated by hoisting one of their own—"some armed with lead pipes and crowbars, ranged freely through the financial district for almost three hours," beating up many demonstrators without prompting much interest from the police, who reportedly knew and drank with them.[17] While kicking a person they had knocked onto the ground, one of a group of construction workers said: "'This Commie kid deserves to be killed.'" A Sullivan & Cromwell lawyer who tried to intervene wound up in the hospital.[18] The *New York Post*, which for days devoted its front and second and third pages to the demonstrations, editorially denounced the workers as "mobsters" and "hard-hat rightist brutalitarians."[19] Vice President Agnew justified their acts by distinguishing between the motives of violent leftists and those of construction workers: "if at times they lose their tempers and throw a punch or two...theirs is not

---

[14]Sandor Polster, "Order Schools Closed Friday," *NYP*, May 7, 1970, at 1, col. 5, at 2, col. 3.

[15]Pete Hamill, "In the Heart of the Beast," *NYP*, May 7, 1970, at 49, col. 1 at 3.

[16]Alan Oser, "Building Costs Push Steadily Upward," *NYT*, June 14, 1970, sect. 8, at 1, col. 1 at 4 (quoting Saul Horowitz, Jr., president, HRH Construction Co.).

[17]Homer Bigart, "Thousands in City March to Assail Lindsay on War," *NYT*, May 16, 1970, at 11, col. 3; Michael Drosnin, "After 'Bloody Friday,' New York Wonders If Wall Street Is Becoming a Battleground," *WSJ*, May 11, 1970, at 10, col. 3 at 4 (quote); Pete Hamill, "Hard Hats and Cops," *NYP*, May 12, 1970, at 47, col. 1-3; John Brooks, *The Go-Go Years* 6-10 (1973).

[18]Sandor Polster, "Workmen Smash into Students Here," *NYP*, May 8, 1970, at 1, col. 5, at 2, col. 3-4.

[19]"Hard Hats and Broken Heads," *NYP*, May 9, 1970, at 26, col. 1-2.

an aggressive anger...eager to invade the property of others...."[20]

Agnew's praise of property-loving workers suppressed the fact that a "roving band of 500 construction workers," after "storm[ing]" City Hall and forcing an inferior force of police, "'in the interest of safety,'" to raise the flag from its half-mast position that Lindsay had ordered in memory of the Kent State students, "bulled their way into the [Pace] college lobby, smashing huge glass plate windows and slugging terrified students...gathering signatures for an antiwar petition." At least 12 were hospitalized.[21]

A *New York Times* reporter concluded that the workers' patriotic rhetorical flights might have struck the "more cynical bystander...[as] an easy price to pay for an unexpected day off from work. But to anyone who spent hours in the march constantly hearing of this special devotion to the physical presence of the flag, this fervor seemed composed of deeper strains ranging from the mystical to the primitive."[22] (Union construction workers' reverence for the flag is indeed venerable: as early as 1886, the Bricklayers Union passed a resolution both disavowing any affiliation with organizations governed by socialist, communist, or anarchist views and urging that "'the flag bearing the stars and stripes is the flag that should be recognized as the standard of all labor organizations.'")[23] A "thin, gentle-looking woman," whom three construction workers punched in the ribs—"'If you want to be treated like an equal we'll treat you like one'"—when she tried to stop one of them from going after a student with a pair of iron clippers, concluded: "'They believe passionately that the students are destroying the country. They are very sincere and its [sic] very scarey.'"[24] So passionately sincere was one 29-year-old structural ironworker, an ex-Marine who was earning $348 a week on the U.S. Steel building at Liberty Street and Broadway, that he was able to "run after and beat people with long hair" despite having recently broken three toes when a steel beam fell on his foot: "'it was probably the only day my foot didn't hurt me a bit. I had other things on my mind.'"[25]

In the course of the next two weeks similar patriotic outbursts occurred. On

---

[20]Spiro Agnew, "In Defense of Hard Hats," 70 (8) *Ironworker* 2-3 at 2 (Aug. 1970) (reprinted from the St. Louis *Globe Democrat*).

[21]Jean Crafton et al., "500 Storm City Hall to Raise Flag," NY*DN*, May 9, 1970, at 3, col. 1-3. Perversely, the *Daily News* editorialized that Lindsay had "brought much of this trouble on himself" because in the previous four years he had "hampered and hobbled the police...in the matter of curbing disorderly crowds." "We Do Not Condone," NY *DN*, May 12, 1970, at 39, col. 1.

[22]Francis Clines, "Workers for Nixon and Flag Come out in Force," *NYT*, May 24, 1970, sect. 4 at 2, col. 4.

[23]Harry Bates, *Bricklayers' Century of Craftsmanship: A History of the Bricklayers, Masons and Plasterers' International Union of America* 75-76 (1955).

[24]Leonard Katz, "'They Came at Us Like Animals,'" *NYP*, May 9, 1970, at 8, col. 1 at 3.

[25]Timothy Lee, "Construction Workers—Who They Are, What They Believe," *NYP*, May 16, 1970, at 21, col. 1-2.

May 11, 1,500 to upwards of 5,000 construction workers and longshoremen "roamed through Lower Manhattan in organized bands," throwing punches at bystanders.[26] A "huge lunchtime crowd lined the streets...cheering the workmen as if they were a conquering army."[27] Even as five police unions responded to charges about their passivity in the face of construction workers' violence by asserting that "'New York City stands today on the brink of anarchy,'"[28] Hamill accused them of having "collaborated with the construction workers in the same way that Southern sheriffs used to collaborate with the rednecks...beating up freedom riders."[29] The same day a member of Ironworkers Local 455 exclaimed to 3,000 students at City College that the construction workers he had seen were "'black shirts and brown shirts of Hitler's Germany'"; his own local, in contrast to others whose members had terrorized students, was fully integrated and the majority opposed the war.[30] In its account of the May 11th demonstration, the *Daily World*, the organ of the Communist Party U.S.A., which had initially failed to identify the May 8th attackers as workers, finally reported that 1,000 construction workers had "again rampaged."[31] Its editor, apparently incapable of believing that genuine proletarians could have "defiled the honor of every workingman and working woman," repeatedy had recourse to skeptical quotation marks in mentioning the "goon attacks of 'construction workers'"; these "'construction workers' [sic] forays... smelled like Hitler's street gangs."[32]

The marching construction workers' demand on May 12 was the impeachment of "'the red Mayor,'"[33] while the following day's watchword was "'Down With Lindsay, Up With Nixon.'"[34] By this time, Hamill reported, "the troops of the New Bullyism" had been joined by "all those white collar workers one always sees lounging at street corners on Broad St. at lunchtime, making sucking sounds

---

[26]Sandor Polster, "Cops Nip Violence in Workers March," *NYP*, May 11, 1970, at 1, col. 6 (quote); Edward Kirkman & Joseph McNamara, "5,000 Demonstrators Rap Mayor," NY*DN*, May 12, 1970, at 3, col. 1.

[27] Michael Drosnin, "Construction Men Stage Another March in Wall Street Area," *WSJ*, May 12, 1970, at 12, col. 2.

[28]Anthony Mancini, "Police Unions: Wait for Facts," *NYP*, May 11, 1970, at 1, col. 4, at 2, col. 1. Mayor Lindsay had called for an investigation into reports that the police had received advance warning of the workers' plans. Cy Egan, "Mayor Calls Police Brass on the Carpet," *NYP*, May 9, 1970, at 1, col. 1.

[29]Hamill, "Hard Hats and Cops."

[30]Anthony Burton, "Builds a Bridge to Students," NY*DN*, May 12, 1970, at 3, col. 3, 5.

[31]Vicki Morris, "Day of Mourning, Day of Marching," *DW*, May 9, 1970, at 3, col. 4; "1,000 Stage Pro-War Mob Attacks at City Hall," *DW*, May 12, 1970, at 12, col. 3.

[32]"Goon Squads and Cops," *DW*, May 12, 1970, at 7, col. 1. The next day it continued to use quotation marks in describing the "'construction workers' [who] roamed the financial district at will...." "Business Students in Wall St. Peace Rally," *DW*, May 13, 1970, at 3, col. 2 at 4.

[33]Sandor Polster, "Cops Split Protest Groups," *NYP*, May 12, 1970, at 3, col. 3 at 5.

[34]Sandor Polster, "Marchers Go Uptown," *NYP*, May 13, 1970, at 1, col. 1.

with their mouths as girls go by. They were there in their Robert Hall suits and the dandruff on the shoulders, the army of the $125-a-week clerks inflamed now by the excitement of doing something that...would give them an opportunity to strike out at all the privileged, at all the pampered...."[35] On the 15th, as the U.S. Attorney announced that the federal government was investigating the violent attacks as possible violations of antiwar demonstrators' civil rights, 3000 construction workers were marching 15 abreast up Broadway to City Hall Park led by motorcyclists in black leather jackets and accompanied by a 12-piece brass band. With the help of a bull horn, a Brooklyn Republican assemblyman praised the workers for their "'pride in America.'"[36]

Construction workers' intervention attained its organized high point on May 20. In the words of *The New York Times*:

> Marching under a sea of American flags, helmeted construction workers led tens of thousands of noisy but peaceful demonstrators...in a rally and parade supporting the Vietnam policies of President Nixon and assailing Mayor Lindsay and other opponents of the war in Indochina.
>
> Staged by the Building and Construction Trades Council of Greater New York to demonstrate "love of country and love and respect for our country's flag," the noontime rally...drew a crowd estimated to number 60,000 to 150,000.[37]

Peter Brennan, president of the 200,000-member Council, set the tone by instructing the cheering sea of war and Nixon supporters that "'this flag is more than just a piece of cloth.'"[38] Such rhetoric prompted Hamill to express his disbelief that Brennan would ever hold a rally calling for integration of construction unions.[39]

The timing and genesis of the May 20th demonstration are instructive. According to a statement made the previous day by David Livingston, the president of District 65, Wholesale, Retail, Office and Processing Union and one of the organizers of a labor-student coalition antiwar rally scheduled for May 21, after an erroneous report had appeared in the press the previous week setting the rally for May 20, Brennan announced that the Building and Construction Trades Council demonstration would take place at the same place and time. Livingston denounced Brennan's demonstration as "'the closest thing to civil insurrection we've had in this city. Maybe civil insurrection is too strong, but it's damn close. ... It's clearly a call

---

[35]Peter Hamill, "USA Alla Way," *NYP*, May 13, 1970, at 51, col. 1.

[36]Sandor Polster, "U.S. Probing Violence Here," *NYP*, May 15, 1970, at 1, col. 1, at 2, col. 1-2.

[37]Homer Bigart, "Huge City Hall Rally Backs Nixon's Indochina Policies," *NYT*, May 21, 1970, at 1, col. 6.; Frank Prial, "Antiwar Protests Go On; Nixon Backers March Here," *NYT*, May 14, 1970, at 20, col. 5.

[38]Sandor Polster, "Pro-War Rally Draws Huge Crowd," *NYP*, May 20, 1970, at 5, col. 5.

[39]Peter Hamill, "The Flag," *NYP*, May 20, 1970, at 53, col. 1 at 2.

for war, and it's a call for violence...."[40] The May 21st antiwar rally organized by unions representing automobile, clothing, hospital, and municipal workers included a sizable proportion of blacks, but overall was only one-third as large as the building trades demonstration.[41]

Brennan, whom Nixon later rewarded with an appointment as Secretary of Labor, both denied that his organization had had anything to do with the violence during the demonstration on May 8 and proudly announced that letters and calls to the unions ran twenty to one in favor of the workers' spontaneous action against antiwar demonstrators who "'spat at the American flag.'"[42] The president of the national Painters Union telegraphed brother Brennan: "We support without reservation the patriotic stand you have taken in support of our country and the flag."[43]

The reality-content of the demonstrators' political orientation can be gauged by their signs, which variously referred to Lindsay as "a Commy rat, a faggot, a leftist, an idiot, a neurotic, an anarchist and a traitor," and fantasized that "'Mao Lindsay's Red Guards are SDS Bums.'"[44] For some the confrontation seemed to be an ersatz for a lost war: "'We've got to beat these Communists somewhere. So we're fighting them.'"[45] That the "Commie bastard" they "stomped" was a Sullivan & Cromwell lawyer did not appear to faze them.[46] The quasi-surrealistic politics were underscored by the fact that the construction workers viewed as their enemies a group of students from elite business schools with short hair and ties who were "'expressing views as members of the Establishment'" and appreciatively listened to Wall Street bankers sympathetically assure them that business opposed the war because the accompanying inflation was destroying the economy.[47] Indeed, the construction

---

[40]Abel Silver & Sandor Polster, "Unions Split on Marches," *NYP*, May 19, 1970, at 1, col. 4, at 2, col. 1, 3.

[41]Sandor Polster, "Students and Unions Rally Against War," *NYP*, May 21, 1970, at 3, col. 5-6.

[42]Damon Stetson, "Unions Differ on Indochina War," *NYT*, May 13, 1970, at 18, col. 6, 7; Emanuel Perlmutter, "Head of Building Trades Unions Here Says Response Favors Friday's Action," *NYT*, May 12, 1970, at 18, col. 1 (quote).

[43]84 (6) *PATJ* 5 (June 1970). See also S. Frank Raftery, "Construction Workers Help prove that Real Patriotism Still Lives," 84 (7) *PATJ* n.p. [inside front page] (July 1970).

[44]Bigart, "Thousands in City March," at 11, col. 4. On May 20, demonstrators also carried placards declaiming that "We Hate Our Commie Mayor." Pete Hamill, "Lion in the Streets," *NYP*, May 21, 1970, at 43, col. 1 at 2.

[45]Francis Clines, "For the Flag and for Country, They March," *NYT*, May 21, 1970, at 22, col. 3 (quoting a printer).

[46]Michael Drosnin, "After 'Bloody Friday,' New York Wonders If Wall Street Is Becoming a Battleground," *WSJ*, May 11, 1970, at 10, col. 3 at 4.

[47]Homer Bigart, "2 Protest Groups Meet on Wall St.," *NYT*, May 13, 1970, at 1, col. 1 (short hair and ties), at 18, col. 5-6 (bankers); Homer Bigart, "Thousands Assail Lindsay in 2d Protest by Workers," *NYT*, May 12, 1970, at 1, col. 5, 6 ("Establishment").

workers may have understood more about capitalism than Brown Brothers Harriman & Co. partner and ex-Treasury Undersecretary Robert Roosa, who declared to the students that "'when we are relieved of the cost of this war, there will be full employment for everyone.'"[48] The workers' enmity becomes even more bizarre in light of the signs some carried reading, "God Bless the Establishment."

The street theater prompted this interpretation from *Times* columnist Russell Baker: "As a battle cry for the working man, 'God Bless the Establishment' makes sense only if we view it as absurdist, as a tacit announcement that the reasons labor is in the street applying workingman's boot to collegiate kidney are so diffuse, so complex, so far beyond rational explanation that the question can only be answered with the Lennonesque put on, 'God Bless Wall Street, Country Club, Grosse Pointe and All.'" [49] In the crowd, whose "swagger" was "built of a kind of joy at being what participants saw as the first counter-response from a long-suffering middle America," was a black construction worker who opined that "'Communism must be fought every place.'"[50] However, a sample of the 300 to 400 black construction workers in lower Manhattan "revealed sentiment against the 'make-believe patriotism'" of their white counterparts.[51] Moreover, the New York chapter of the National Afro-American Labor Council, likening the beatings administered by construction workers to "'repressive violence against blacks,'" warned that it would "not tolerate the beatings of any heads at any construction site in...any...black communities hereabouts.'"[52]

The newspaper of historical record drove home the larger political-economic point by quoting a student: "'I'm scared. If this is what the class struggle is all about,' he added, surveying the flag-waving workers, 'there's something wrong somewhere.'"[53] This insight was perhaps designed to sober dreamy left-wing students, who had missed the cue that "the evidence is inescapable that in the United States—for reasons known only to some Higher Being—labor and management despite their disagreements, have learned to work better with each other than anywhere else in the world."[54] Editorially, too, *The New York Times* delighted in

---

[48]Michael Drosnin, "Police Keep Workers and Business Students Apart at Peace Rally," *WSJ*, May 13, 1970, at 14, col. 3. Epistemologically much more modest was David Rockefeller, chairman and CEO of Chase Manhattan Bank, who told visiting students that with 100,000 shareholders, 25,000 employees and untold customers, he felt that he lacked "'the authority to express political sentiment on behalf of this bank.'"

[49]Russell Baker, "Observer: Passions in Search of an Understanding," *NYT*, May 17, 1970, § 4 at 18, col. 3. For further examples of the demonstrators' irrational slogans , see Francis Clines, "Hard Hats on the March—Fists Swinging," *NYT*, May 17, 1970, § 4 at 9, col. 3.

[50]Francis Clines, "Workers Find Protest a 2-Way Street," *NYT*, May 13, 1970, at 18, col. 3.

[51]"The Blacks in the Hardhats," *NYP*, May 14, 1970, at 4, col. 1.

[52]"Blacks Unionists Blast Beatings of War Foes," *NYP*, May 19, 1970, at 36, col. 3 (quotes); Hugh Wyatt, "Black Leaders Give Warning to Hard Hats," NY*DN*, May 20, 1970, at 30, col. 1.

[53]Bigart, "Huge City Hall Rally," at 22, col. 2.

[54]"The Building Trades," *AL*, Oct. 1968, at 18-22, 53-55, 57 at 57. For the European leftist

confirming that the extremes had met: "The building-tradesmen, of course, are in the forefront of those who deplore...the decay of law and order. They have now joined the revolutionaries and bombthrowers on the left in demonstrating that anarchy is fast becoming a mode of political expression."[55] Perversely, these demonstrations by what some New York "'Establishment'" lawyers called "'labor fascists' in the Wall Street area" finally prompted members of major law firms to protest the war.[56] Even the *Wall Street Journal* editors eschewed "the irrational shouting of a mob."[57]

Despite this considerable journalistic attention, the key question remained unasked: why was this apparently slumbering patriotism suddenly transmogrified into manifest political action only after five years of large-scale U.S. warfare in Indochina?[58] The construction industry's leading trade journal reported that the demonstrations were "spontaneous," but hints also surfaced casting doubt such claims.[59] The first report in *The New York Times* quoted a Wall Street broker who had observed with binoculars two men in gray suits and hats directing the construction workers with hand motions.[60] A reporter for the then liberal *New York Post*, which covered the demonstrations in much greater detail than the *Times*, discovered that Ralph L. Clifford, a radical right-winger who published the *New York Graphic*, had been guiding the workers. Clifford, who stated that he greatly admired Joseph McCarthy and the John Birch Society, distributed a leaflet calling Lindsay a "'One World socialist Mayor.'" Moreover, these demonstrators, many of whom were drunk, received twice their daily wages from their employers just to demonstrate.[61] The *Wall Street Journal* reported that one construction worker, "who said his life would be in danger if he was identified, claimed the attack was organized by shop stewards with the support of some contractors. He said one contractor offered his men cash bonuses to join the fray."[62]

---

view of U.S. construction unions as "communist eaters," see Gerhard Armanski, Peter Schulze, & Peter Tergeist, "Ökonomische und soziale Krise in den USA: 2. Teil," *Links*, No. 68, July-Aug. 1975, at 19-21 at 20.

[55]"Violence on the Right," *NYT*, May 9, 1970, at 24, col. 1-2.

[56]Thomas Brady, "1,000 'Establishment' Lawyers Join War Protest," *NYT*, May 15, 1970, at 21, col. 5.

[57]"Toward Peace and Quiet," *WSJ*, May 12, 1970, at 22, col. 1 (editorial).

[58]See Philip Foner, *U.S. Labor and the Vietnam War* 103-108 (1989).

[59]"Construction Workers Back Nixon's Cambodia Policy," *ENR*, May 28, 1970, at 57.

[60]Homer Bigart, "War Foes Here Attacked by Construction Workers," *NYT*, May 9, 1970, at 1, col. 5, at 10, col. 5.

[61]Richard Schwartz, "Man in Gray & the Violence," *NYP*, May 12, 1970, at 3, col. 1-2, at 90, col. 1-4; telephone interview with Richard Schwartz, New York City (1970). See also Tom Draper, "Pay for Hard-Hats," *NYT*, May 21, 1970, at 34, col. 5 (letter questioning who was paying workers whose contracts strictly provided wages only for hours worked).

[62]Michael Drosnin, "After 'Bloody Friday,' New York Wonders If Wall Street Is Becoming a Battleground," *WSJ*, May 11, 1970, at 10, col. 3 at 4. See also "The Sudden Rising of the Hardhats," *Time*, May 25, 1970, at 20-21.

If construction firms were financing these days of controlled proletarian rage, they refused to acknowledge their complicity. Workers at the major building sites admitted having taken time off to demonstrate or "battle with students" without loss of any wages. Yet when asked by the *New York Post*, all of the general contractors and subcontractors at the large construction sites in downtown Manhattan—including the World Trade Center, where 2,200 workers were employed, and the U.S. Steel building, one of the whose subcontractors was American Bridge, a wholly owned subsidiary of U.S. Steel, whose former president, Roger Blough, was directing big business's campaign against high construction wages—denied any knowledge of what their employees "do as citizens of the United States, because of their own conscience" on their lunch hour.[63]

A prominent sociologist found "some similarity to the plot of the motion picture 'Z,'"[64] but an explanation was still lacking as to why construction firms should have been especially interested in giving away some of their profits in order to provide public support for Nixon's invasion of Cambodia and to gain publicity for their employees' claims that the Mayor of New York City was a communist and homosexual.[65] Further mystery emanated from Fred Cook's article in *The Nation*, which confirmed that construction firms had co-organized the demonstrations, but also pointed out that immediately before the Cambodia invasion the Nixon administration had developed plans to undermine the building trades unions—a step that might have been expected to please employers. Pressure on the unions seemed to come from a second side inasmuch as 30 to 40 percent of their members working in lower Manhattan had traveled to New York from other states; they supposedly feared that Mayor Lindsay's "open union" campaign would disemploy them by transferring their jobs to black and Puerto Rican New Yorkers. The most enlightening aspect of Cook's article was his reference to the offer of support that George Meany, the AFL-CIO president, had made to Nixon immediately after the

---

[63]"The Great Hardhat Mystery," *NYP*, May 19, 1970, at 3, col. 2, at 93, col. 1 (quoting Carl Eckhardt, assistant project manager for Otis Elevator at the World Trade Center). At the peak, more than 5,000 workers were on site at the World Trade Center. "World Trade Center," 25 (7) *Laborer* 8-11 (July 1971).

[64]Richard Hamilton, *Class and Politics in the United States* 498 n.103 (1972). See also Jay Borland, "'Hard-Hats' Scored," *NYT*, May 14, 1970, at 36, col. 5 (letter): "Is it possible...that trade unionism's just and single-minded pursuit of a living wage created among its members a pig-headed insularity that borders on fascism?" A confidential memorandum, dated March 11, 1970, allegedly from the office of Vice President Spiro Agnew, included an implication that the Nixon administration would promote demonstrations by construction workers in New York and other cities to support its Indochina war policies. Agnew denied the genuineness of the memo, which also dealt with cancelling the 1972 national election and repealing the Bill of Rights. *Scanlan's Monthly*, Aug. 1970, at 1; James Naughton, "Agnew Attacks Memo as Fraud," *NYT*, July 22, 1970, at 22, col. 1.

[65]*ENR* reported: "No one in the New York Building Trades Employers Association or in the Building and Construction Trades Council of Greater New York...would comment on rumors that the demonstrators had contractor or union support." "Hard Hat Workers Take Hard Line on War," *ENR*, May 14, 1970, at 11.

Cambodia invasion; Brennan then implemented this offer. From this perspective the demonstrations represented a kind of horse trade by means of which the unions sought to ward off the federal government's campaign against them. Cook, who regarded the demonstrations as characterized by "the classic elements of Hitlerian street tactics," was unable to provide a plausible answer to the question as to why the companies would have financed such a counter-move.[66]

By May 26 Nixon had already received Brennan and other union leaders at the White House.[67] Indeed, "Brennan's leadership of the New York City hardhats' 1970 march to support the decision to invade Cambodia" earned eternal gratitude from Nixon, who nurtured "'fantastic and deep psychological and emotional attachment for Brennan because of Cambodia,' says a Republican on Capitol Hill. 'I remember then that it seemed I was virtually alone,' Mr. Nixon recalled..., 'and one day a very exciting thing happened: The hardhats marched in New York City. And for the first time the press began to realize that...the people supported doing what is right.'"[68] Nixon's embrace of the rampaging hardhats offended the *Wall Street Journal*. Immediately after the White House meeting, the newspaper opined editorially that since neither Nixon nor anyone in his administration publicly condemned the "enraged mobs...it is possible to imagine that the Administration considers kicking bystanders in the head...less reprehensible than, say, throwing stones at armed, helmeted National Guardsmen."[69] And George Meany later used the incident against Brennan. When President Ford asked Brennan to stay on as Secretary of Labor after Nixon's resignation, Meany not only called him "completely unacceptable" to labor, but demeaned him personally: "He was not a national labor leader. He was a local building trades fellow, who had very, very little experience. I don't even think he knew where the White House was until Chuck Colson brought him down here for that hard-hat publicity stunt."[70]

The May 1970 demonstrations can be understood in the context of the joint

---

[66]Fred Cook, "Hard-hats: The Rampaging Patriots," *Nation*, June 15, 1970, at 712-19 at 712, 717-18. Cook's mention of the companies' reliance on government contracts was too unspecified to bear any explanatory weight. For background on the possibility that white construction workers' animus against Mayor Lindsay may have been sparked by his having held up city construction contracts in a dispute over building trades unions' exclusion of black workers, see William Gould, *Black Workers in White Unions: Job Discrimination in the United States* 310-15 (1977). The General Secretary of the Communist Party, U.S.A., Gus Hall, suggested that "those secret operators" who "secretly organized the march, for their purposes" were "big real-estate interests." Hall failed to name them, but later singled out the Chase Manhattan Bank and the Rockefeller interests and others who profited from the war. Gus Hall, *Hard Hats and Hard Facts* 4-5, 13 (1970).

[67]Michael Hanrahan, "Hard Hats to Be Nixon's Guests," NY*DN*, May 26, 1970, at 2, col. 1; Robert Semple, Jr., "Nixon Meets Heads of 2 City Unions; Hails War Support," *NYT*, May 27, 1970, at 1, col. 6.

[68]Byron Calame, "'Pistol Pete' vs. Labor's Bureaucracy," *WSJ*, June 22, 1973, at 8, col. 4.

[69]"No Time for Ambiguity," *WSJ*, May 28, 1970, at 12, col. 1-2.

[70]"Brennan to Stay on as Secretary of Labor," *CLR*, No. 986, Sept. 4, 1974, at A-16.

state-employer efforts to control construction wages. Local unions, which were most negatively affected by these proposals, had begun to discuss this connection even before the demonstrations. For example, in early 1970 an official of the Bricklayers and Masons Union in Detroit wrote that the construction unions "are being boxed in by the strongly united Contractors' Association, bolstered by sharpened attacks by the Nixon administration."[71] Shortly after the May demonstrations, references appeared to the reticence suddenly characterizing the Nixon offensive, which had just begun.[72] In connection with the newest revelations about construction wages ("Be a construction worker and—make $26,000 a year"), *ENR* voiced the suspicion that Nixon would not intercede "because of the administration's apparent political interest in middle-income blue collar workers."[73]

Employers' soon suspected that construction unions' Cambodian strategy of restricting Nixon's initiatives against them had proved successful. Already on the morning of Brennan's audience with Nixon in May, Arthur J. Fox, Jr., the editor of *ENR* sent Nixon a telegram stating that Nixon was about to commend Brennan for peacefully demonstrating "with some of the same construction workers who terrorized citizens of new York just a week before." Fox conceded that the construction workers might be with Nixon on Cambodia, but requested that Nixon ask Brennan what they were contributing to Nixon's fight against inflation.[74]

Big business harbored similar suspicions. At a small meeting of Roundtable members in early October 1970 "[t]here was a general consensus that the Administration is having a love affair with labor and the 'hard hats.'"[75] Later that month at the fall meeting of the Business Council, its chairman, Fred Borch, who was also GE chairman, conceded that he partly had in mind Nixon's "recent praise of the 'hard-hat' construction workers for supporting the Administration's Vietnam policy" when the Council criticized the president for failing to control inflation in general and to eliminate construction unions' restrictions on productivity and access to employment.[76]

Fortune, too, was unable to conceal its disappointment that the building unions' clever tactics had for the time being enabled them to block possible adverse action by the Nixon administration. The president, in the magazine's view, could have made political capital out of the unjustified wage increases, but "his hard-hat supporters may have boxed him in. As one prominent Administration official puts

---

[71]Eugene Tolot, "Building Trade in Crisis," 9 (1) *LT* 30 (Jan.-Feb. 1970).

[72]Calame, "'Pistol Pete' vs. Labor's Bureaucracy."

[73]"Be a Construction Worker and—Make $26,000 a Year," *ENR*, Sept. 17, 1970, at 55.

[74]"He Didn't Get the Message," *ENR*, June 4, 1970, at 60.

[75][ ], "File Memorandum: Roger's Round Table" (Oct. 5, 1970), in SP, Box 5, File-CUAIR 1969-1970.

[76]Albert Hunt, "Business Council's Inflation Gripes May Renew Nixon Leadership Issue," *WSJ*, Oct. 19, 1970, at 4, col. 1.

it, 'the hard-hats' well staged and organized support of Nixon foreign policy, obviously planned at high levels, has made it impossible to get through to the President. The hard-hats knew exactly what they were doing, and the gains they could exact.'"[77] These arguments are consistent with the hypothesis that the May demonstrations were a calculated arrangement.

For public consumption, the Manhattan demonstrations helped establish an image of union construction workers as the violent right wing of the labor movement.[78] Even weeks after the demonstrations, national construction union leaders continued to praise the "'hard hats'" as mirroring "the feeling of the great percentage of Americans" who were relieved that someone had finally stood up and shown that "'we have put up with about all we are going to take' from the radical left; the peaceniks; the revolutionaries; the anti-establishment nuts...."[79] However, in the realm of semi-occluded Washington in-fighting, the ostensibly pro-Nixon street militance succeeded in temporarily diverting state attention from implementing the strategy of preventing construction unions—and especially locals—from taking full advantage of tight labor markets.

---

[77]Gilbert Burck, "The Building Trades versus the People," 82 (4) *Fortune* 95-97, 159-60, at 96-97 (Oct. 1970).

[78]Joshua Freeman, "Hardhats: Construction Workers, Manliness, and 1970 Pro-War Demonstrations," 26 (4) *JSH* 725-44 (Summer 1993). Manhattan was by far the main but not the only site of such violent prowar demonstrations. "Fights at Arizona Peace Rally," *NYT*, June 1, 1970, at 48, col. 5.

[79]John Lyons, "The President's Page," 70 (8) *Ironworker*, n.p. (inside front cover, inside back cover) (Aug. 1970). See also "Campus, Radical Troubles U.S., Canada in Anniversary Period," 90 (7) *Carpenter* 8-9, 12 (July 1970), which included fotos titled, "'Hard Hats' Show Patriotic Support," discoursed at length about the "mobs of the new left," but said nothing about the demonstrations.

12

Multi-Employer and Regional Bargaining

[F]acing labor is now not a localized employer group...but a group of organized employers, bound together nationally...with a unified point of view. ... Furthermore, they are better prepared to go outside of the ranks of the industry itself to join with the employers in other industries in a movement aimed finally at undermining labor standards and pushing American industrial life back to the chaos of 1929-1933.[1]

The construction industry, as the Roundtable noted, was "grotesquely fragmented": 70 percent of firms employing seven or fewer workers employed 20 percent of the labor force, while the two percent employing 100 or more accounted for 75 percent of construction work.[2] Such size-structural fragmentation, reflected in and amplified by geographic collective bargaining fragmentation, prompted a spate of proposals for strengthening employers' negotiating positions. These efforts culminated in the introduction on October 20, 1971, by Representative (and later presidential candidate) John B. Anderson (R. Ill.) of a short bill, the Construction Industry Stabilization Act of 1971, which would have directed the CISC to prepare a plan for reforming the industry's bargaining structure with a view to expanding and consolidating collective bargaining units on an areawide basis. However, it died without any congressional action.[3]

Similarly stillborn was a much more detailed bill that Anderson introduced three weeks later (the Construction Industry Bargaining Stabilization Act), which would have empowered a tripartite Construction Industry Bargaining Commission to create geographic bargaining areas; failure to negotiate within such areas would have become an employer and union unfair labor practice under the NLRA. It would also have been an unfair labor practice for employers during negotiations to lockout unless they locked out all unions representing workers subject to the negotiations; similarly, unions would have committed an unfair labor practice by engaging in a strike during negotiations unless all workers subject to the negotiations struck.[4]

Crucial to the success of Anderson's plan were the dual provisions of expanded collective bargaining units and common contract expiration dates, which,

---

[1]Building Trades Department, A. F. of L., *Negotiating the Construction Code: History of Participation by Building Trades Organizations in Code Making Under NRA* 25 (n.d. [1936]) (prepared by Solomon Barkin).

[2]BR, "Efficiency at the Construction Job Site: Final Report" at 3 (Dec. 1977), in BR, 1977 CCH, File: CICE.

[3]H.R. 11387, 92d Cong., 1st Sess. § 3 (1971).

[4]H.R. 11716, 92d Cong., 1st Sess. (1971).

according to Anderson, jointly "would reduce considerably the current ability of unions to strike in one area and then travel to another county to work until employers are forced to capitulate." He observed that the bill was even more important for entitling employer groups to "bargain collectively without the constant threat that unions will settle on the side with weaker members of the group and undermine their bargaining position." The bill's attractiveness also lay in enabling employers to "keep wage rates in line without the heavy-handed intervention of the government."[5]

The very brief congressional life of Anderson's bills belies the long and intense pre-legislative and extra-congressional struggles among numerous employer organizations over the issue of larger bargaining units. Examining this background sheds light on the crucial role that this subject played in employers' strategies and the sharp conflicts among them that it triggered.

To understand this aspect of the debate it is necessary to recall that collective bargaining in construction was decentralized by area and craft. Nevertheless, a "remarkably standard pattern" resulted: "Unlike other industries, few contracts are negotiated directly by a local union representative with a single employer. In most situations, employers in a relatively confined geographic area have banded together to form an association to represent contractors...in a particular craft operation. Generally, the structure of bargaining is on a city-by-city, craft-by-craft basis." The areas encompassed by these bargaining amalgamations may have encompassed a city, metropolitan area, several counties, or parts of a state. An employer association representing only one craft may have been unconcerned with the impact of its collective bargaining agreement on other crafts, but to the extent that its members employed several crafts, the association may have tried to coordinate bargaining. The decentralizing forces on the union side were much more prominent. National unions rarely took part in local negotiating, although they may have consulted if they foresaw a settlement as creating a pattern that might have decisively influenced other agreements.[6]

Though fragmented—1,400 collective agreements were set to expire in 1971—not all construction industry bargaining was localized. Elevator constructors and sprinkler fitters engaged in national bargaining while boilermakers and operating engineers bargained regionally and statewide respectively. A further peculiarity of the industry was national contractors' infrequent participation in wage negotiations with local contractors, the results of which they generally accepted. However, national firms did enter into "'national contracts' with the International President of a craft union." Such agreements insured firms that abiding by locally

---

[5]"Anderson Introduces Bill in Congress to Mandate Regional Bargaining Law for Construction Industry," *CLR*, No. 841, Nov. 3, 1971, at A-9, A-10.

[6]U.S. BLS, *Work Stoppages in Contract Construction, 1962-73*, at 10-11 (Bull. 1847, 1975).

negotiated wages would immunize them against strikes. This capacity to work through local strikes and thus to provide employment for craftsmen, in turn, exerted pressure on local contractors to settle with striking unions.[7] When national agreements permitted national contractors to work during a strike against local contractors over terms of a new agreement, the national contractor was obliged to pay the new wage rate back to the date of the strike or the date from which the new rates became effective in the locality.[8] Large local unions also often opposed national agreements because they deprived locals of the ability to secure terms from the national contractor that they could extract from local contractors.[9]

Intervention to broaden the scope of collective bargaining was in large part designed to undermine the efficacy of strike action by cohesive and democratically structured local unions. As Dunlop's "principal disciple,"[10] Mills, pointed out in early 1971: "rank-and-file union members have been willing to support lengthy strikes, and to sustain them until their demands are met. Union leadership has often been reluctant to press wage demands which seem exorbitant by past practices, but, facing re-election and a militant membership, they have been unwilling to counsel moderation. The suggestions of public officials regarding wage restraint are far less heeded by the rank and file than by union leadership, and in the largely democratic local building trades unions the rank and file dominate wage policy."[11] Since local building trades unions' peculiar power derived from "the decentralized structure of the construction labor market,"[12] it was unclear how legislative mandates to bargain regionally or nationally could succeed without a prior broadening of those labor markets to encompass more than the large city or several-county area within which most contractors operate. Thus greater mobility by firms was a prerequisite.[13]

---

[7]Michael Moscow [untitled speech], in 117 Cong. Rec. 24389, 24390 (1971).

[8]John Dunlop, "The Industrial Relations System in Construction," in *The Structure of Collective Bargaining: Problems and Perspectives* 255-77 at 266 (Arnold Weber ed., 1961).

[9]Mills, *Industrial Relations and Manpower in Construction* at 36-37; Mills, "Chapter 2: Construction" at II-32. The rise of large national construction firms in the late nineteenth century produced other patterns. Their ability to "organize migration constituted a grave threat in every locality in which they obtained work. [W]hen the Omaha local union of bricklayers entered into a general strike for the eight-hour day in 1888, the local bosses obtained the support of Norcross Brothers, which was currently engaged in the construction of a court house in Omaha...and which found that it could not obtain local bricklayers.... The Norcross manager and the local contractors advertised for bricklayers 'all over the country.'" National firms could also "avail themselves of the existence of lower standards in the localities in which they obtained contracts in order to depress the terms of employment of workers whom they hired directly elsewhere and whom they sent into the localities where the work was to be performed." Ulman, *Rise of the National Trade Union* at 56.

[10]"John Dunlop and CISC Allay Feverish Collective Bargaining," *ENR*, July 6, 1972, at 25.

[11]D. Q. Mills, "Wage Determination in Contract Construction," 10 (1) *IR* 72-85 at 75 (Feb. 1971).

[12]DOL, Manpower Administration, *Training and Entry into Union Construction* at 38.

[13]Kenneth McCaffree, "Regional Labor Agreements in the Construction Industry," 9 *ILRR*

The movement for wide-area collective bargaining can be traced back to the energetic efforts of John C. Garvin, the labor relations consultant, whose relentless promotion of regional bargaining began in 1966.[14] In September, 1970, Garvin, who also never missed a chance to tout his seminal role,[15] sent a copy of a talk on rectifying the imbalance in collective bargaining he had just given to yet another group of builders to the vice president of Kaiser Industries, an NCA member. Given the overwhelming support the participants had given his proposal, Garvin told Walter Farrell that it was time for the Roundtable to join the effort. Noting that he was "getting a little bit tired of pleading for support," Garvin added that with or without this help, "John Garvin will organize a National Federation...."[16]

Beginning about 1967, various national contractors organization began drafting wide-area, multi-employer bargaining proposals. Interest in such legislation may have been intensified by the experience in British Columbia. There, in the wake of union success in divide-and-conquer, whipsaw tactics, which led to contractors' being "badly whipped" in 1968 and large wage increases, more than 850 firms assigned their collective bargaining functions to the Construction Labour Relations Association of British Columbia; in 1970, the association persuaded the provincial government to enact legislation creating a limited form of certification of an employers organization as its members binding bargaining agent.[17]

The San Francisco management-side labor law firm of Littler, Mendelson & Fastiff was heavily involved in drafting legislation.[18] One of its clients was the Plumbing-Heating-Cooling Contractors of California, for which it drafted a multi-employer certification bill in 1970, which the firm also furnished to R. Eric Miller, vice president in charge of labor relations at Bechtel. The bill would have amended the NLRA to make it an employer unfair labor practice to fail or refuse to bargain exclusively through such a certified multi-employer agent or to negotiate directly

---

595 (1956).

[14]See above chapter 1. For confirmation of Garvin's role, Thomas Dailey, "Multiemployer Bargaining's Demise," *ENR*, Nov. 15, 1984, at 28 (Lexis).

[15]On Oct. 21, 1969, he gave a handwritten note of his plan to Secretary Shultz in Los Angeles. NACP, RG 174: General Records of the Labor Dept., Office of the Secretary, Records of Sec. George P. Shultz, 1969-1970, Box No. 53: Commissions, Folder: 1969-Commissions CICBC (Oct.).

[16]Letter from John C. Garvin to Walter Farrell (Sept. 30, 1970), in SP, Box 5, File-Construction-Multi Employer Bargaining. Garvin's plan was noteworthy in providing for "a union shop clause in all labor Agreements...." John C. Garvin, "Review and Updare of a Plan for Regional Bargaining in the Construction Industry" at 10, in *id.*

[17]Construction Labour Relations Association of B.C., "Background" (quote at 2) (n.d. [ca. 1973]), in SP, Box 5, File-Multi-Employer Bargaining.

[18]By 1999, Littler, Mendelson purported to be the largest U.S. law firm devoted exclusively to labor and employment law with more than 400 lawyers and numerous offices around the country. http://www.littler.com. In 1970, it had been an eight-lawyer firm. 1 *Martindale-Hubbell Law Directory* 1288B (1970).

with a labor union; correlatively, the proposal would have made it a union unfair labor practice to fail to bargain with such a multi-employer agent. This draft would also have directed the NLRB to determine an appropriate bargaining unit designed to assure an effective unit to the employers in the construction industry; the NLRB would have been required to include in the unit all local and national contractors that had or might seek to have a contractual relationship with unions representing the contractors' employees in a single trade or craft within the unions' area or jurisdiction. If a multiemployer entity filed a petition with the Board alleging that it had collective bargaining relationships with unions in a specific geographic area or that it represented a representative number of local and national contractors in that area, then the Board was required to certify it as the exclusive representative if it found the allegations to be true.[19]

In the accompanying letter to Miller, the law firm explained that the proposal would "require that national agreement contractors participate in local bargaining and bind such contractors to the locally negotiated agreement. It is my understanding that the NCA has objected to participating in local negotiations and being bound by the local agreements. However, you have indicated that this position is being reconsidered and that NCA members may wish to participate in, and be bound by, local negotiations. I am cognizant of the fear that local contractors may attempt to discriminate against national contractors." To allay such fears, the law firm offered, if necessary, to "impose express statutory standards...for insuring fairness on the part of the agent to all contractors which it represents"—in other words, a statutory counterpart to the judicially created union duty of fair representation. Littler, Mendelson conceded that the amended NLRA would "supersede the terms of the national agreements which authorize...contractors to continue working during a strike, and the multi-employer agent could require that contractor lock out in support of the local bargaining position." However, the proposal would also protect such contractors who engaged in a lockout or were otherwise delayed by a labor dispute by prohibiting the project owner from penalizing or replacing them with nonunion firms. While recognizing the "restraints on the freedom of decision" that the legislation would impose on contractors, the law firm urged Miller to regard them as the "quid pro quo for enhanced power in the employers' relationship with the construction unions."[20]

A more explicit explanation of the role of national contractors was included in the law firm's memorandum. The proposal commented on there made it an unfair labor practice for a national contractor to authorize its employees to work through a lockout lawfully ordered by the multi-employer agent. Littler, Mendelson

---

[19]Littler, Mendelson & Fastiff, "Draft Legislation Re Multi-Employer Certification" (Apr. 10, 1970), in SP, Box 5, File-Construction-Multi Employer Bargaining.

[20]Letter from [ ], Littler, Mendelson to R. Eric Miller at 2, 3, 5 (Apr. 10, 1970), in SP, Box 5, File-Construction-Multi Employer Bargaining.

revealed that this proposal was "intended to...bring the national contractors' power to the aid of the employers in a strike-lockout situation while allowing them to continue their bargaining relationship with the national unions rather than local unions." Although the draft legislation neither required national contractors to participate in local bargaining nor bound them to locally negotiated agreements, it did subject them to the multi-employer agent's control in case of a strike of lockout, thus superseding national agreements authorizing national contractors to work through local strikes.[21]

Toward the end of April, the law firm wrote to its client, the Plumbing-Heating-Cooling Contractors of California, enclosing letters that it had received from the Mechanical Contractors Association of America (MCAA) and the National Electrical Contractors Association (NECA) reacting to the California initiative. Whereas the MCAA was supportive, the NECA took the position that the drafts that national organizations of specialty contractors had been working on for three years had already drafted the best possible bill, enactment of which the Californians would only delay. The law firm, however, detected several defects in the specialty contractors' draft, of which the MCAA and NECA were the principal backers in addition to the International Association of Wall and Ceiling Contractors, Mason Contractors Association of America, Ceiling and Interior Systems Contractors, National Association of Plumbing-Heating-Cooling Contractors, Painting and Decorating Contractors of America, Sheet Metal and Air Conditioning Contractors National Association, as well as the AGC. These groups characterized their members as comprising "the reasonable employers who employ the great majority of workers" in the BCTD. In contrast, the nonunion sector of the AGC opposed it.[22]

First, the draft authorized only the NLRB to enforce breaches of the obligation to bargain exclusively through the certified multi-employer agent rather than conferring a private right of action on contractors. Second, the specialty contractors would have made the multi-employer agent's jurisdiction coterminous with that established by the unions. Counsel, however, insisted that unions would

---

[21][ ], Littler, Mendelson, "Memorandum Re Proposed Legislative Changes to Authorize Effective Multi-Employer Bargaining" 2-3, 8-10 (Apr. 1, 1970), attachment to letter from Blough to Members of Coordinating Committee (July 17, 1970), in SP, Box 5, File-Construction-Multi Employer Bargaining.

[22]Letter from [ ] to James Carter (Apr. 21, 1970); letter from [ ] to James A Carter (Apr. 23, 1970); "Associations Supporting Multi-Employer Legislation," attachment to letter from Roger Blough to Members of Coordinating Committee (July 17, 1970) (quote), in SP, Box 5, File-Construction-Multi Employer Bargaining. The California-based movement included the Lathing & Plastering Contractors, Roof Contractors Association, Associated Roofing Contractors, Plumbing-Heating & Air Conditioning Council, Plumbing-Heating-Cooling Contractors Association of the Greater Bay Area, San Francisco Electrical Contractors Association, as well as the AGC of California. Memorandum from James R. Lucas to Western Industrial Contractors Association (May 12, 1970), in SP, Box 5, File-Construction-Multi Employer Bargaining (including the reference to opposition by the nonunion segment of the AGC).

seek to gerrymander such areas to benefit themselves. Worse still, the law firm revealed that lack of employer class solidarity was a major obstacle that the specialty contractors' proposal did nothing to alleviate: "it could be expected that those employers who are presently a thorn in the side of employer associations would continue to be so if the unions and such employers have the opportunity to carve out such jurisdictions." This acute problem of collective action also formed the draft's third weakness: by failing to make financial support for the multi-employer agent mandatory, it ensured that the employers' side would "remain plagued by the 'free-loaders' who refuse to participate in the financial support of employer associations...." The only other non-statutory methods of financing were also counterproductive: hinging it on union agreement to establishing industry funds or risking the acrimony that would be engendered by authorizing multi-employer agents to sue free riders. Consequently, Littler, Mendelson saw no viable alternative to statutory-compulsory funding. The fourth and final weakness was potentially fatal: the specialty contractors ignored the difficulties created by construction firms bound by national contracts. When the law firm raised this issue, the NECA vice president replied that "we would never be able to secure the cooperation" of the NCA on this legislation. While agreeing that this prognosis might ultimately prove correct, counsel urged that "we must make every effort to meet with representatives of NCA to see whether a mutually acceptable approach is possible." The reason was obvious: "The Under Secretary of Labor, Hodgson, told me categorically that multi-employer legislation could not be adopted over the opposition of the NCA.... I am also informed that NCA opposes the legislation as proposed by the national associations." The law firm therefore requested its client's authorization to meet with various associations, including both the NCA and Blough or Graney of the CUAIR, to determine whether the specialty contractors' proposal "should be amended prior to its presentation to the Administration and eventual introduction in the House and Senate."[23]

By mid-1970 the Roundtable began taking an intense interest in these multi-employer bargaining proposals. At a meeting in early July, Blough asked an executive of Morrison-Knudsen Company, a large international construction firm and NCA member, to furnish him with material on the AGC's position on the issue. On July 17, Blough sent to Coordinating Committee members materials on the AGC's as well as on the subcontractors' and Californians' proposals.[24]

The AGC's position was straightforward: it wanted parity between unions and employers under the NLRA. Under the AGC's proposal, the multi-employer

[23]Letter from [ ], Littler, Mendelson to J. D. Mack (Apr. 27, 1970), in SP, Box 5, File-Construction-Multi Employer Bargaining.
[24]Letter from [ ], Morrison-Knudsen Co., to Roger M. Blough (July 14, 1970); letter to Members of Coordinating Committee from Roger Blough (July 17, 1970), in SP, Box 5, File-Construction-Multi Employer Bargaining.

group with the longest continuous history of collective bargaining with unions in a specific geographic area "would have the right to bargain for certain kinds of union construction in the locality of a local union. This would be done by making it an unfair labor practice for a...union...to make an agreement with others that deviates from the historic groups." Unions would also be prohibited from striking the historic group members without striking all other employers performing the same kind of work with the union's members.[25] Finally, the AGC proposal, which included a controversial common national expiration date for agreements, dispensed with member ratification of agreements and entitled employers to refuse to employ strikers who sought work outside of the jurisdiction of the unions on strike.[26]

The subcontractors' proposal emphasized a somewhat different concern. Surprisingly, rather than focusing on unions' leapfrogging tactics, these specialty contractors noted that requiring all local unions to negotiate through one multiemployer representative "eliminates the disrupting influence on collective bargaining resulting from employers who are or seek to be signatories to a contract with the union from seeking a preferential collective bargaing agreement to that enjoyed by other union signatories. Such preferential agreements, whether providing greater or lesser benefits to the employees involved, create unwarranted pressures on other employers...." The specialty contractors were willing to let the geographic scope of these bargaining units correspond to the jurisdiction of the union involved whether it covered a metropolitan area or an entire state: "The employees of all employers in a particular trade have a close community of interest which transcends the particular employer for whom they happen to be working at any given time. Thus, differences in the wages, hours, and other terms and conditions of employment of employees in the unionized portion of this industry cannot be justified by the fact that an employee happens to be working for one union employer one week and a different union employer another week."[27]

As activity surrounding the draft legislation became more intense in late 1970, the CUAIR began to pay more attention to it. On October 5, the day before the Roundtable was to take up the issue, some of its key members met with several executives of Union Carbide, du Pont, and others at the Harvard Club in Manhattan. Even within this small group unanimity did not prevail. It was reported that with Dunlop's assistance the Nixon administration would probably create a commission

---

[25]"Section 1," attachment to letter from Blough to Members of Coordinating Committee (July 17, 1970), in SP, Box 5, File-Construction-Multi Employer Bargaining.

[26][AGC], "An Outline of Proposed Legislation for Restructuring Construction Industry Collective Bargaining" (Aug. 7, 1970), in CUAIR, CC, Minutes, Oct. 6, 1970, in BR, 1970-Vol. II: Minutes.

[27]"Section 2: Explanation of Proposed Legislation," attachment to letter from Blough to Members of Coordinating Committee (July 17, 1970), in SP, Box 5, File-Construction-Multi Employer Bargaining.

to form larger collective bargaining units: "the AGC favored multiple bargaining, after initial opposition, and they may be in bed with Dunlop on all of this. It is a blow to the NCA who appear to be against multiple bargaining." At least one consideration favoring wider bargaining units was the experience, according to a du Pont construction official, that "there was no way to win a strike nowadays without multiple bargaining" in construction. He mentioned that when 500 pipefitters had recently struck his firm for several weeks in Wilmington, Delaware, only 30 were unemployed: "He particularly specified the interstate highway system and low unemployment rates as advantages to relocation of strikers." When one Roundtable member stressed the "role of the open shop in combating union power," the du Pont official responded that "contractors, particularly in the southeast, probably couldn't do 20% of their work on an open shop basis, primarily because of lack of police protection." In response to a remark that contractors unanimously favored wage and price controls, another member stressed the construction and transportation industries' support for controls and multiple bargaining stood in opposition to basic manufacturing's position: "and all these stem from the union power problem which requires basic legislation long-range. The problem here is one of immediacy which legislation cannot correct over night."[28]

The next day an outline of one of the proposed bills was circulated and discussed at length at the meeting of the Roundtable Coordinating Committee. Representatives of contractors associations attended the October 6 meeting to discuss the proposals. The NCA representative, explaining that the organization wanted to eliminate whipsawing, wished to discover whether it could count on users' support.[29] As one key Roundtable figure explained to Kenneth McGuiness, associate and acting general counsel of the NLRB during the Eisenhower administration and head of Labor Policy Association—yet another antiunion big business group, which represented the Roundtable in labor matters[30]—the situation was fluid, complicated, and even confused, yet the CUAIR was very critical of wide-area bargaining as a means of combating union control of the labor market:

[T]he construction industry is still pushing toward area-wide and industry-wide bargaining on a multi-employer basis, and in the process is probably accelerating union power at a rate beyond what they envision. True, they do get away from the anarchy of local union power, but in turn move from the frying pan to the fire by transferring responsibility to the international union, or at least that is their hope. Granted that the structure of the construction industry and the premises from which their logic takes off are different from

---

[28][ ], "File Memorandum: Roger's Round Table" (Oct. 5, 1970), in SP, Box 5, File-CUAIR 1969-1970.

[29]CUAIR, CC, Minutes, Oct. 6, 1970, at 4-5 (Phillip Lyon), in BR, 1970-Vol. II: Minutes.

[30]David Jacobs, "Labor and Social Legislation in the United States: Business Obstructionism and Accommodation," 23 (2) *LSJ* 52 (June 1998) (Lexis).

those on the manufacturing side of industry, the trend is ominous from our point of view.

This subject obviously involves union power, on which LPA is working. This is an immediate manifestation of the problem and may require special attention by LPA. ... [T]hose proposing the bill, the contractors associations, are at odds among themselves on the subject just as we are on the construction users side. This is a clear and present danger since the Administration will shortly be coming out with some similar centralized form of bargaining in the construction industry, to, be administered by a board or commission.[31]

While the CUAIR continued to study various legislative proposals,[32] an ad hoc subcommittee on multi-employer certification of the Council of Construction Employers (CCE), a horizontal association of national specialty contractors and the AGC,[33] met in September and October, issuing an internal interim report documenting the "sharpness of disagreement" among its member organizations. "The only areas of agreement," as the report put it, included: a ban on selective strikes or lockouts; inapplicability of the legislation to nonunion firms; a ban on ratification of final agreements by either union or employer membership; opposition to making it an unfair labor practice for employers to refuse to employ, or continue to employ, employees engaged in bargaining unit strikes; permitting separate project agreements subject to approval by multi-employer agent; and employers' entitlement to refuse to employ strikers on work outside the striking unions' jurisdiction. The members could not agree on these points: a common expiration date for all labor agreements; whether the statute's provisions should be enforced by the NLRB or courts; whether the Secretary of Labor or the NLRB should be authorized to establish the geographical bargaining areas; the size of these areas; whether to certify a single entity to represent all local unions and employers or existing general and specialty bargaining units.[34]

On the last day of 1970, a high-ranking member of the CUAIR Coordinating Committee, who also served on the Chamber of Commerce task force on industry-wide bargaining, sent a letter to Soutar and others commenting on Nixon's December 4 speech before the NAM in which the president had called for consolidated regional bargaining in construction. Noting that he and other corporate executives had been anticipating such administration endorsement for two

---

[31]Letter from [   ] to Kenneth C. McGuiness (Oct. 6, 1970), in SP, Box 5, File-Construction-Multi Employer Bargaining.

[32]Letter with attachment from J. M. Graney to Coordinating Committee Members (Oct. 21, 1970), in SP,Box 5, File-Construction-Multi Employer Bargaining.

[33]According to Cullen & Feinberg, *The Bargaining Structure in Construction* at 21, the CCE had existed informally since August 1968, but did not go public until May 1972; designed to become the voice of unionized construction firms, it was dissolved in 1978.

[34]Council of Construction Employers, "Interim Report of Ad Hoc Subcommittee on Multi-Employer Certification Legislation" (Oct. 28, 1970), in SP, Box 5, File-Construction-Multi Employer Bargaining.

months, he added: "Those of us who have resisted coalition or industry-wide bargaining were concerned lest our union friends take such a plan for construction as encouragement for their efforts to broaden bargaining units in the rest of industry."[35] The apprehension that such initiatives for construction might later be imposed on manufacturing firms continued to haunt Roundtable executives, especially ones who ran corporations that prided themselves on having prevented company-wide organization by resisting or bargaining with unions plant by plant. As a subordinate Roundtable participant noted in analyzing a wide-area bargaining bill: "I don't like federal policy which escalates industrial conflict even if only in construction. We in General Electric wouldn't like such a policy to 'spill over.'"[36]

At the end of August, Blough circulated to Coordinating Committee members a copy of the latest draft of the bill, which proved to be almost identical to the one that Representative Anderson filed in November as H. R. 11716. It turned out to be the only such bill introduced (together with the shorter bill he filed in October). Blough called the subject "one which constantly comes to our attention," and suggested that the Roundtable "again consider it from a policy point of view."[37] Blough and other Roundtable officials had met in July with Anderson, who was chairman of the House Republican Conference, and other House Republican members of the Task Force on Labor Management Relations, to discuss CUAIR's work.[38] Nevertheless, the CUAIR disagreed fundamentally with the focus of wide-area bargaining in general and Anderson's bill in particular. One CUAIR participant found it even "more defective in its procedures and safeguards" than some of the other drafts. Significantly, he singled out its lack of adequate protection for nonunion contractors. But his reasons for recommending that the Roundtable oppose the bill went to the core of all proposals for wide-area bargaining legislation:

First, it represents a belief that big bargaining is the answer. What we need is lower, not fewer, settlements.... Second, I think fooling around with bargaining unit sizes diverts us from our basic tasks. The hiring hall is the real problem; small work forces not small bargaining units is what's wrong. Congress would do better to start there.[39]

---

[35]Letter from [ ] to James Davenport and others, copy to R. Blough and others (Dec. 31, 1970), in SP, Box 5, File-Construction-Multi Employer Bargaining.

[36]Memo from [ ] to [ ] (Sept. 20, 1971), in SP, Box 5, File-Construction-Multi Employer Bargaining.

[37]Blough to Members of the Coordinating Committee (Aug. 31, 1971), in SP, Box 5, File-Construction-Multi Employer Bargaining.

[38]Letter from [ ] to Representative Sherman P. Lloyd (July 27, 1971), in SP, Box 5, File-Construction-Multi Employer Bargaining.

[39]Memo from [ ] to Virgil Day (Sept. 20, 1971), in SP, Box 5, File-Construction-Multi Employer Bargaining.

The Roundtable not only lacked control over the drafting of Anderson's bill, it was not even well informed as to when Anderson would file what and on behalf of which groups he was acting. On October 19, the day before Anderson filed his first bill, Trumbull Blake, the director of the construction division at du Pont—a firm at the forefront of the corporate movement to support large-scale nonunion industrial construction—and a member of the CUAIR task force on the Anderson bill, wrote Soutar that as he understood the situation, Anderson was "marking time to give AGC, NCA, NECA and MCA[A] an opportunity to take a common position supporting the legislation or, alternatively a common position recommending changes." Blake did not know whether the unions supported the bill or not.[40] The Roundtable was apparently so far removed from congressional inner workings that two days after Anderson had actually introduced his first bill, Bechtel's and the NCA's liaison with the CUAIR circulated an out-of-date draft of the bill to Blough, Day, and Bechtel's principal owner, S. D. Bechtel, Jr., with the annotation that Anderson was reported to be considering attaching it as an amendment to another bill and to introduce it as in independent bill. Four days later he sent the same memo to Soutar.[41]

After having had six weeks to study the longer version of Anderson's bill, the Roundtable remained unpersuaded of its usefulness. As its in-house consultants, Graney and McGlaun, informed Soutar, the bill "seems to embrace the premise that larger bargaining groups in construction would eliminate the principal impediment to unequal bargaining strength.... It would not come to grips with what in our opinion are the real problems, such as the hiring hall and manpower in construction."[42]

The bills that Anderson introduced had undergone a long gestation period lasting more than a year and including "extensive consultations" with the AGC, MCAA, NCA, as well as the CCE and the BCTD. Preliminary work began in 1970 after the NCA had "indicated a willingness to give up its national agreement protection against economic strikes if a system of area-wide (as against local) bargaining could be developed on a multi-craft basis and if NCA would be accorded a role in bargaining process and retain the right to employ men directly."[43] In September 1971, *ENR* reported that the bill, which was still circulating within the construction industry, would not be introduced until management agreed to it.

[40]Letter from T. Blake to Douglas Soutar (Oct. 19, 1971), in SP, Box 5, File-Restructuring Bargaining in Construction Industry.

[41]Memo from [   ] to J. F. O'Connell (Oct. 22, 1971); Memo from [   ] to D. H. Soutar (Oct. 26, 1971), in SP, Box 5, File-Restructuring Bargaining in Construction Industry.

[42]Memorandum from J. M. Graney and W. McGlaun to Douglas Soutar (Dec. 27, 1971), in SP, Box 5, File-Construction-Multi Employer Bargaining.

[43]John E. Quinn, "Construction Industry Bargaining Stabilization Act," NCA, *Bulletin* #71-276, at 1 (Aug. 16, 1971), in SP, Box 5, File-Restructuring Bargaining in Construction Industry.

While the AGC sought to achieve that unanimity, Anderson's staff continued to meet with Dunlop and the CICBC.[44] Two months before the bill was introduced, the NCA had learned that Anderson "had been persuaded to delay introducing the legislation while the wage freeze is in effect. The reason given for the delay is that, if introduced now, the Building Trades Union would vigorously oppose it to the extent that the Administration might feel it necessary to disavow any support, thus assuring almost certain defeat of the Bill." The author of the NCA memorandum added that he could not "completely follow this reasoning."[45]   Just a few days before Anderson introduced the shorter CISC bill, *ENR* had reported that he was filing it first because, as an economic stabilization measure, it would be referred to the House Banking and Currency Committee, thus avoiding the House Labor Committee, where the longer bill, which still lacked management's unanimous support, might get lost.[46]   In the event, both bills were referred to the Labor Committee and Congress took no action on either one.

A regional bargaining bill that the CICBC was reported as having been preparing during its almost two-year existence was never introduced,[47] but a draft was circulated within the construction industry and the Roundtable.   Thus in response to a telegram that a well-placed CUAIR official sent on Feburary 15, 1972 to several CUAIR participants requesting their comments and positions regarding the Anderson bill and "the new draft bill" in time for the February 18th Roundtable

---

[44]"Construction Gets Areawide Bargaining Bill," *ENR*, Sept. 23, 1971, at 45.

[45]"Construction Industry Bargaining Stabilization Act (Anderson Bill)," undated memo sent to Douglas Soutar by [   ], NCA (Oct. 20, 1971), in SP, Box 5, File-Restructuring of Bargaining in Construction Industry. Anderson lacked specific recollection of the bills, but when prompted, agreed that it was plausible that they came to naught because the Nixon administration did not want to antagonize the construction unions. Telephone interview with John B. Anderson, Washington, D.C. (Mar. 30, 1999).

[46]"Stabilization Committee May Get a Bigger Job," *ENR*, Oct. 14, 1971, at 65.

[47]The initiative was purportedly beset by constitutional and administrative difficulties. "Anderson Introduces Bill in Congress to Mandate Regional Bargaining Law for Construction Industry," *CLR*, No. 841, Nov. 3, 1971, at A-9, A-10. The report that Secretary of Labor Hodgson transmitted to Nixon in March 1972 seemed to suggest that, apart from having met 17 times, the CICBC had accomplished very little. Following Nixon's speech on Dec. 4, 1970, it prepared several draft proposals to modify the geographic scope of collective bargaining, but as of January, 1972, the time at which the report ended, it was still drafting. "Report of the CICBC September 1969 to January 1972," at 2, 8-9 (Mar. 30, 1972), in NPMS, WHCF, Subject Files, EX FG 257: CICBC [1969-1970], Box 1, Folder 2: (1969-1970). The impression that the CICBC accomplished little is reinforced by a memo that Under secretary of Labor Hodgson sent to CEA chairman McCracken in mid-1970 lamenting that his efforts to interest the CICBC in issuing a statement on construction wage settlements "were not rewarding." Memorandum from Hodgson to McCracken (May 28, 1970), in NACP, RG 174: General Records of the Labor Dept., Records of the Secretary of Labor George P. Shultz, 1969-1970, Box No. 173: International Committee-Cabinet Committee on Oil Imports, Folder: 1970-Committee: CCC (Except May 5).

meeting on this subject,[48] a Bechtel official telegraphed back:

we favor some legislation to reshape bargaining process in construction including wide area multi-craft, multi-employer bargaining. Anderson bill not perfect but better than CICBC draft which has following deficiencies from our viewpoint. Firstly eliminates craft board concept. Secondly dependent on voluntary action. Thirdly does not allow national contractor participation in bargaining process to extent needed. [W]ith the inbalance [sic] of bargaining strength and existing fragmentation of the construction bargaining process the problems will not be alleviated through voluntary means.[49]

The demise of Anderson's bill may have been linked to the ambivalence that both employers and unions displayed toward larger bargaining units. Why employers might seek such units when faced with tight local labor markets was clear. A study of consolidated bargaining in California in the mid-1960s observed that construction employers around 1940, "[i]n taking a long-run view...may well have considered that regional bargaining was one way to cope with the power that the building trades might again acquire in the circumstances of a boom."[50] The AGC, which complained that industry stabilization disappeared when, some time after the Korean War, "international unions lost control over their locals," supported Anderson's bill.[51] Nevertheless, both the CUAIR Coordinating Committee and its contractors task force were divided over areawide bargaining in general and Anderson's bill in particular even before it had been introduced.[52] Despite the risks associated with construction unions' locally based power—whose "demands...are formulated and struck for locally"[53]—employers were also skeptical of wider units. For example, at the time that the Eightieth Congress was developing antiunion legislation that resulted in the Taft-Hartley amendments to the NLRA in 1947, one of the bills would have curtailed industry-wide bargaining by making it an unfair labor practice to bargain with respect to places of employment not located within the same labor market.[54] In 1968, too, the Chamber of Commerce-sponsored

---

[48]Telegram from [   ] to Trumbull Blake, Walter Farrell, James Graham, and [   ] (Feb. 15, 1972); in SP, Box 5, File-CUAIR; draft memo from Blough to coordinating committee members (enclosing draft of CICBC bill) (undated, mid-Feb. 1972), in SP, Box 5, File-Restructuring of Bargaining in Construction Industry.

[49]Telegram from [   ] to [   ] (Feb. 16, 1972), in SP, Box 5, File-Construction Multi-Employer Bargaining.

[50]Gordon Bertram, *Consolidated Bargaining in California Construction: An Appraisal of Twenty-Five Years' Experience* 7 (1966).

[51]*Economic Stabilization Legislation: Hearings Before the Senate Committee on Banking, Housing and Urban Affairs*, 92d Cong., 1st Sess. 279 (1971) (statement of William Dunn, executive director, AGC).

[52]CUAIR, CC, Minutes, Oct. 7, 1971, at 3 (Roger Blough), in BR, 1971, Vol. II-Minutes.

[53]"The Wages of the Building Zoom," *BW.*, July 19, 1969, at 89, 90.

[54]Robert Rankin & Winfried Dallmayr, *Freedom and Emergency Powers in the Cold War*

meeting heard suggestions that broader-based bargaining was not a panacea: Herbert Northrup warned that it "tends to bring all wages and benefits to the top, adding to the inflationary impact."[55] (Even at the end of the 1970s, Mills remained skeptical of regional bargaining, observing that if it merely substituted "large, crisis-creating work stoppages for several separate and more tolerable stoppages," it could hardly help stabilize the industry.)[56]

After "intensive consideration" over a period of months, the CUAIR candidly, for internal consumption, set forth the advantages and risks of broadening the scope of collective bargaining. Anderson's approach was designed both to "prevent advantages accruing to workmen who strike contractors in Area A while working conveniently in adjacent Area B" and to "prevent contractors in the area from working during strikes or subsequently under arrangements at variance with that concluded by the single bargaining agencies." However, opponents within the Roundtable pointed to:

Apprehension that the area to be determined by legislated procedures and the bargaining to be enforced upon all contractors and unions in the area by certification may promote undesirable local bargaining results, may restrict competition from outside the area, may adversely react against competition from non-union contractors, and may tend to result in bargaining areas which are unnecessarily large and which may even extend to industry-wide bargaining, which they consider highly undesirable.[57]

The salient point here was that some Roundtable members feared that an exclusive focus on improving contractors' position in collective bargaining would detract from promoting the nonunion sector. In addition, the larger the area, the greater the risk that more production might be stopped by a strike; thus, perversely, the end result might even greater union power and larger rather than smaller settlements. Ultimately, the Coordinating Committee was apparently unable to overcome its members' divergent views; the policy that it proposed internally in March 1972 was so platitudinous that it presumably satisfied no one: encouragement of more comprehensive local bargaining but only voluntarily and without legislative intervention; support for "geographical areas of sufficient size to accomplish a livable economic result from the standpoint of unions, employees, and contractors both during and after possible work stoppages." Its most forthright stand favored national contractors' participation in local bargaining. The

---

101(1964).

[55]"Men for All Seasons?" *BW*, Dec. 7, 1968, at 117, 188 (quoting Herbert Northrup).

[56]Daniel Quinn Mills, "Labor Relations and Collective Bargaining," in *The Construction Industry: Balance Wheel of the Economy* 59-82 at 74 (Julian Lange & Daniel Quinn Mills eds., 1979).

[57]"Roundtable Policy re Broadening Area Collective Bargaining in Construction" at 1 (Mar. 27, 1972), in CUAIR, CC Meeting, Mar. 17, 1972, attached to Minutes, in SP, Box 5.

Coordinating Committee was so deadlocked that it took several revisions before it could even agree on deleting the word "organized" from the proposal to encourage local user groups to "assist [organized] local contractor groups to increase total effectiveness in contract negotiation and...administration."[58]

The CUAIR appreciated the legislation's obvious purpose to roll back "the power of unions in running labor relations," but after "long, intense consideration" by its Coordinating Committee, the group objected to governmental imposition of regional bargaining on the ground that it might "promote undesirable local bargaining results,...restrict competition from contractors outside the area,...adversely react against competition from non-union contractors...."[59] The CUAIR's skepticism toward government controls flowed from its argument that only structural changes could deal with root causes. Perhaps an even stronger impediment to CUAIR acceptance of legislated area-wide construction bargaining was the concern that it would spill over into the industrial sector, forcing users—many of which had energetically prevented unions from organizing all their plants—to engage in such geographically expanded collective bargaining as well.[60]

The Roundtable's rejectionist position diverged even from that of the NCA, which among construction employer groups was most closely aligned with it and had come to accept the need for some form of compulsory wider-area bargaining. The most plausible explanation for this divergence is two-fold: first, regardless of its potentially salutary impact on the construction industry, industrial employers did not want to set a precedent for federal imposition of wide-area bargaining units on the manufacturing sector, in which many large firms pursued a strategy of confining unions to individual plants rather than expanding bargaining units; and second, whereas unionized construction firms focused on the goal of increasing their bargaining power vis-à-vis unions, the Roundtable's dual-track strategy was equally dedicated to expanding the nonunion construction sector, a goal that the NCA and specialty contractor associations did not yet share in 1970-72. Later, however, when "the stampede-like growth of the open shop...rendered Garvin's dream an idea whose time has come and gone,"[61] the Roundtable's intransigence seemed prescient.

---

[58]"Roundtable Policy re Broadening Area Collective Bargaining in Construction" at 1-2 (Mar. 27, 1972), in CUAIR, CC Meeting, Mar. 17, 1972, attached to Minutes, and Minutes at 6, in SP, Box 5. The statement was also published in CUAIR *Report,* No. 72-4 at 1-2 (Apr. 11, 1972).

[59]"Construction Users Roundtable Urges Area Bargaining—But Not Legislated Solution," *CLR,* No. 872, June 14, 1972, at A-12, A-13, A-16.

[60]CUAIR, CC, Minutes, Feb. 18, 1972, at 6, in BR, 1972: Vol. II-Minutes.

[61]Thomas Dailey, "Multiemployer Bargaining's Demise," *ENR,* Nov. 15, 1984, at 28 (Lexis) (vice president of Perini Corporation).

13

The Nixon Administration's Wage Controls

"We may have killed the goose that laid the golden egg...."[1]

On July 23, 1970, soon after he had succeeded George Shultz as the Secretary of Labor, James Hodgson prepared talking points for Nixon's meeting that day with the CICBC. He noted that the principal sensitive issue for the CICBC was wage controls: most employer representatives wanted them, whereas unions were "chilly" toward selective controls applied only to the construction industry. Whatever differences separated management and labor on this issue: "All realize the Administration opposes the controls concept." As if concluding that controls were a dead end, Hodgson stressed to Nixon that the administration had to double or triple the flow of manpower into construction in order to undercut the basis of the wage increases.[2]

Big business, however, preferred not to wait for the long-term effects of an increased supply of construction labor. At the October 1970 meeting of the elite Business Council, expressing concern that wage increases were exceeding productivity increases, corporate executives were "particularly concerned with what [Westinghouse board chairman Donald] Burnham called 'exorbitant' increases in the wages of construction workers. He said these wage increases spilled over into other areas of the economy.'" The president of Continental Can Company created a concrete image of the infection mechanism by reporting at the closed-door session that "plumbers, electricians and other construction union members who came into industrial plants to work were making $2.70 to $4 an hour more than the regular employees of the plant. That 'creates pressure' for wage increases in industry...."[3]

A sense of an onrushing convergence of views was reinforced by the speech that John Dunlop gave to the AGC midyear board meeting on Oct. 14, 1970. Even Dunlop, known in his capacity as international union leaders' strongest supporter as "the Hardhats' Machiavelli,"[4] deemed wage increases in 1969-70 "outrageous."[5]

---

[1] Haynes Johnson & Nick Kotz, *Unions* 131 (1972) (quoting Martin Ward, president of the Plumbers Union).

[2] Secretary of Labor to Dwight Chapin (July 23, 1970), in NPMS, WHCF, SF, Ex FG 257 CICBC [1969-1970], Box 1, Folder 1 [1969-1970].

[3] Eileen Shanahan, "Business Group Asks U.S. to Discourage Pay Rises," *NYT*, Oct. 18, 1970, at 1, col. 2, 54, col. 1.

[4] "John Dunlop and CISC Allay Feverish Collective Bargaining," *ENR*, July 6, 1972, at 25, 27.

[5] Telephone interview with John T. Dunlop, Harvard University (Jan. 7, 1999).

He therefore announced that he had reluctantly concluded that an industry with almost a million employers lacked the capacity to control behavior at full employment; accordingly, national legislation would be required to restructure bargaining.[6] He proposed legislation to broaden the geographic scope of collective bargaining in order to combat the tendency of localized bargaining to encourage strikes and leap-frogging wages, intensify imbalance of bargaining power under full employment, limit mobility, and prevent local units from "having a proper perspective of national and regional interests."[7] When the CUAIR Coordinating Committee discussed Dunlop's initiative a few weeks later, Bechtel's labor relations manager agreed that legislation was necessary because the private sector had proved unable to solve the problem.[8] And the next month Blough reported to the committee that Dunlop had told him that the ease with which striking workers could get other jobs was a cause of inflation that could be reduced by letting the NLRB structure bargaining units and national union presidents bring their constructive influence to bear on national settlement methods.[9]

In fact, a draft bill to broaden the geographic scope of collective bargaining in construction was circulating at this time in the Nixon admininstration. In transmitting the draft to the Secretary of Labor, the executive director of the CICBC, Michael Moskow, noted that Dunlop had stated that national contractors would go along with it if they deemed the geographic bargaining areas wide enough to serve their interests. The draft bill's congressional finding struck a note that resonated with employers: mobility in the industry had reached such an extent that "when a work stoppage occurs in one locality the parties have access to work opportunities in neighboring localities, thus reducing normal economic pressure for resolving their differences" and promoting high wage settlements. The collective bargaining commission that the draft would have established was empowered to broaden the scope of collective bargaining "to balance the power between the parties." Only one collective bargaining agreement would have been authorized in each geographic area, and strikes and lockouts during negotiations would have to have been area-wide.[10]

---

[6]"Speech by Dr. John T. Dunlop on Restructuring Bargaining in the Construction Industry," *DLR*, No. 236, at E-1, E-2 (Dec. 7, 1970). The BCTD reported in November on Dunlop's "personal views," which were focused on overcoming fragmentation. "Dunlop Says Construction Bargaining 'Fragmented,'" 23 (11) *BCTB* (Nov. 1970).

[7]"Dunlop Sketches Views on Machinery to Restructure Collective Bargaining," *CLR*, No. 786, Oct. 14, 1970, at A-9.

[8]CUAIR, CC, Minutes, Nov. 4, 1970, at 5, in BR, 1970-Vol. II: Minutes.

[9]CUAIR, CC, Minutes, Dec. 1, 1970, at 5, in BR, 1970-Vol. II: Minutes.

[10]Draft Bill to Broaden Scope of Collective Bargaining in Construction Industry and Create Collective Bargaining Commission, §§ 2(a), 5(d), 9(a), 10(a), in NACP, RG 174: General Records of the Labor Dept., Office of the Secretary, Records of Sec. James D. Hodgson, 1970-1972, 1971, Box No. 20: Boards, Folder: 1970-Commissions CICB (October). In early 1972 Blough circulated for comment to the members of the CUAIR Coordinating Committee a confidential copy of this bill (dated

In the event, the administration never introduced such a bill and no such provisions were ever enacted.

Animated perhaps by the CEA's "Second Inflation Alert" focusing on the "huge" 22.1 percent increase in third-quarter first-year construction wage-bargaining settlements as a cause of unemployment among 324,000 workers,[11] Nixon's initiative toward the end of 1970 seemed to assume a more concrete form ready for codification.[12] In explaining his administration's economic policy to restrain war-related inflation to the annual meeting of the NAM on December 4, 1970, Nixon illustrated the wage side by reference to the construction industry, "in which one out of three negotiations has led to a strike" and "major construction wage settlements are more than double the national average for all manufacturing." He announced that "[u]nless the industry wants government to intervene in wage negotiations on Federal projects to protect the public interest," "the structure of collective bargaing must be changed." Specifically he called for the replacement of destabilizing craft-by-craft and city-by-city patterns by "more consolidated bargaining" of regional scope.[13]

In connection with Nixon's NAM speech, the business press reported that a "formula for braking runaway construction wages by creating areawide bargaining units will almost certainly be the first Administration-sponsored labor bill to go before the new Congress. The bill's No. 1 position reflects the Nixon Administration's order of priorities. Slowing down the headlong pace of wage increases in the building trades is essential to curbing inflation, Administration spokesmen emphasize." *Business Week* reported that the bill's outlines were embodied in a report that Dunlop had submitted to the CICBC. Its key feature was the creation of a National Labor-Management Commission, which would have recommended, independently of the NLRB, the size of construction industry bargaining units; the point would have been to overcome the fragmentation that "limits both the employer's ability to resist local union demands and the international union's ability to influence local union decisions." The proposal's most radical provision would have barred contractors from operating in a certified bargaining area during a construction strike: "Such a bar would make it impossible for striking construction workers to find jobs with a competitor who has not been struck, a current practice that eases the pressure on the striking construction worker

---

Dec. 16, 1971), calling it the first draft of a new bill prepared by the DOL apparently as a substitute for Anderson's bill. Memorandum from Roger Blough to Members (Feb. 7, 1972), in BR, CCH: 1972.

[11]"'Second Inflation Alert'—A Report by the President's Council of Economic Advisers," *CLR*, No. 793, Dec. 2, 1970, at E-1, E-2. The construction wage data were based on a small number of settlements.

[12]Michael Moskow, "New Initiatives in Public Policy for the Construction Industry," IRRA, *Proceedings of the Twenty-Fourth Annual Winter Meeting* 25-33 (1971).

[13]"Remarks at the Annual Meeting of the National Association of Manufacturers," in Nixon, *Presidential Papers: 1970* at 1088, 1092.

while increasing it on his employer." *Business Week* noted that this section would give legal force to the efforts by the Roundtable to persuade large corporations voluntarily to close their construction projects during strikes in solidarity with construction employers.[14]

Such state intervention could have disadvantaged NCA members, which, as national firms, worked through local strikes, creating a clear conflict with local contractors,[15] but would have been an effective means for aiding certain sectors of the industry by interdicting some of local unions' central defensive tools. That such a program also played into the hands of the national construction unions made its enactment more plausible. Nevertheless, *Business Week* reported, "few people connected with the industry appear to take the threats very seriously." Moreover, administration and industry sources stated that the proposals "would have, at most, only long-range impact on construction wages. They also note that Nixon would not do anything too drastic without the approval of the building trades because of their political clout."[16]

The press also reported at the time on a possible repeal of the Davis-Bacon Act, which since 1931 had provided for locally prevailing (generally union) wages to be paid by contractors operating under federal government construction contracts.[17] Local officials had been beseeching Nixon to suspend the law. In July, 1970, for example, the mayor of Kansas City had included such a request in a letter to the president explaining that after contractors had agreed to 137 percent wage

---

[14]"A Way to Fence In Construction Pay," *BW*, Dec. 5, 1970, at 53; see also Byron Calame, "Growing Inflation in Building Trades Is Under Scrutiny," *WSJ*, Dec. 7, 1970, at 2.

[15]Michael Moscow, "The Wage-Price Dilemma in Construction," 117 Cong. Rec. 24,389 (1971). See also Calame, "Growing Inflation in Building Trades Is Under Scrutiny," *WSJ*, Dec. 7, 1970, at 2.

[16]"Building Trades Don't Scare Easily," *BW*, Dec. 12, 1970, at 15.

[17]40 U.S.C. §§276a-276a-5; Calame, "Growing Inflation in Building Trades." See generally, D. Gujurati, "The Economics of the Davis-Bacon Act,"40 (3) *JB* 303-16 (July 1967); John Gould, *Davis-Bacon Act: The Economics of Prevailing Wage Laws* (1971). Amusingly, one of the most severe charges that antiunion critics leveled was: "Decreased morale arises when nonunion workmen who had been working on a Davis-Bacon job complete it and go back to working for a company at decreased pay rates." Armand Thieblot, *The Davis-Bacon Act* 86 (1975). Despite craft unions' traditional voluntarist or anti-statist stance, even before the Great Depression, William Hutcheson, the president of the Carpenters union, urged members to urge Congress to pass a prevailing wages law. United Brotherhood of Carpenters and Joiners of America, *Proceedings of the Twenty- Second General Convention* 61 (1928). Yet in 1936 he still opposed the AFL's call for a government mandated 30-hour week. Louis Stark, "A.F. of L. Demands 30-Hour Week Law," *NYT*, Nov. 28, 1936, at 1, col. 6. See generally, George Higgins, "Voluntarism in Organized Labor in the United States, 1930-40" (Ph.D. diss., Catholic U., 1944); Michael Rogin, "Voluntarism: The Political Functions of an Antipolitical Doctrine," *ILRR*, 15 (4):521-35 (July 1962). Voluntarism rests on the principle that capital and not the state should be the major addressee of labor's demands "because legislation could affect the lives of men at work in a very few points—and those not vitally important for progressively improving conditions." Samuel Gompers, 1 *Seventy Years of Life and Labor* 210 (1925).

increases on government supported projects, laborers had struck for similar raises on private work.[18] Arthur Burns, the new chairman of the Federal Reserve Board, who favored an incomes policy, had urged Nixon to suspend the Davis-Bacon Act to "wave a big stick at the building trades unions to hold down their unconscionably inflationary wage settlements...." Nixon had included an announcement of this suspension in a draft of his NAM speech, but deleted it at the suggestion of George Shultz, Nixon's former Secretary of Labor and then director of the Bureau of the Budget, "who argued that antagonizing the hard-hat unions would be bad politics."[19]

That the administration's restraint was overdetermined was clear from a memo that Hodgson sent to Shultz at the end of 1970 on wage stabilization in construction: "Attempts to establish wage controls are doomed to ultimate failure. They work only in a period of unified national purpose...."[20] Such objections did not mean that these measures would not have had capital-friendly effects, but merely that they were not effective short-term anti-inflation tools (since only wages were relevant from the perspective of wage cost-push inflation).[21] If the objections were accurate, then the Nixon administration was possibly pursuing longer-term aims—otherwise the whole program would have to be dismissed as pure rhetoric.

Instead of introducing the Dunlop bill during the first months of 1971, the Nixon administration engaged in the maneuvering that led to creating the Construction Industry Stabilization Committee (CISC).[22] A hint of changes to come emerged in blunt comments by Labor Secretary Hodgson on January 8. His department may have had a "hands-off policy...as far as saying what wage increases are justified," but "I only say what is not justified and I am damn sure that the construction industry is not entitled to the wage increases it has been getting." Exactly how to end "the 'chaos'" in construction collective bargaining was, however, not easy to determine. Repeal of the Davis-Bacon Act would have little impact since private industry bargaining, which encompassed the vast bulk of construction work, set prevailing wages. One major reason that construction wages could "have gone beyond what is good for the nation, for the economy, for the industry itself" was that: "because of the small size of bargaining units...a

---

[18]Letter from Ilus Davis to Nixon (July 13, 1970), in NACP, RG 174: General Records of the Labor Dept., Office of the Secretary, Records of Sec. James D. Hodgson, 1970-1972, 1971, Box No. 21: Commissions-Construction, Folder: 1970-Commissions CICB (August).

[19]Rowland Evans, Jr. & Robert Novak, *Nixon in the White House: The Frustration of Power* 370-71 (1971).

[20]Memorandum from Hodgson to Shultz re Implementation of Construction Industry Wage-Stabilization Concept (12/31/71 [sic; must be 1970]), in NACP, RG 174: General Records of the Labor Dept., Office of the Secretary, Records of Sec. James D. Hodgson, Box No. 20: Boards, Folder: 1970-Commissions: CICBC (October).

[21]Paul Samuelson, Economics 807 (8th ed. 1970).

[22]For an insider account, see Mills, "Construction Wage Stabilization" at 350-65.

construction worker can now go on strike in one town and then commute to a job in another town near by until the employer is forced to capitulate." But the kinds of union curbs that might have remedied this problem (such as statewide bargaining) would not be forthcoming from a Congress controlled by Democrats.[23] Exposed to such strike power—one insider observed that "the 'strike' during which the union's members are all at work" was "rather bizarre, but common" in construction[24]—no wonder that the Council of Construction Employers had urged creation of a national stabilization agreement including a no-strike pledge and arbitration.[25]

Despite Hodgson's admission that repealing the Davis-Bacon Act would serve little purpose, the suggested talking points that he prepared for Nixon's meeting on January 18 with the CICBC included the warning that if the parties failed to devise a voluntary plan to lower wage settlements, the administration would have to consider measures such as suspending the law.[26] At his meeting with the CICBC and other union and management officials, Nixon appealed to them to devise a plan within 30 days that would "seriously modify the wage-price spiral" in construction. Hodgson, who was also chairman of the CICBC, emphasized that Nixon considered the 15.7 percent construction wage increases during the first nine months of 1970 in tandem with an 11 percent unemployment rate a "crisis" requiring immediate action.[27] Later in January, Hogdson returned to the theme: "The continued high level of strikes and the continued high settlements have convinced us that there is something wrong and that the whole industry bargaining structure is in need of revision. The cries of anguish and indignation that we hear, both from inside and outside the industry, confirm this conviction."[28]

---

[23]Philip Shabecoff, "Hodgson Says President Seeks Curbs on Construction Wages," *NYT*, Jan. 9, 1971, at 12. In 1971, private construction accounted for 72.8 percent of the $110.0 billion of value of new constructionput in place; federally owned projects accounted for only 3.6 percent, and state and locally owned for the rest. *Economic Report of the President* tab. C-38 at 292 (1975). By 1977, projects directly covered by the Davis-Bacon Act accounted for only 4.3 percent; some of the remainder was indirectly covered. General Accounting Office, *The Davis-Bacon Act Should Be Repealed* 3 (HRD-79-18, 1979).

[24]D. Quinn Mills, "Chapter 2: Construction," in *Collective Bargaining: Contemporary American Experience* II-42 (Gerald Somers ed. 1979).

[25]"Nixon Makes Appeal to Building Industry on Wage-Price Spiral," *WSJ*, Jan. 19, 1971, at 8 (the CCE appeal was made in June 1970).

[26]Memorandum from Hodgson for the President Re January 18, 1971 meeting witht he CICBC (Jan. 16, 1971), in NACP, RG 174: General Records of the Labor Dept., Records of Sec. James D. Hodgson, 1970-1972, 1971, Box No. 94: Commissions, Folder: 1971-Commissions CICBC (Secretary's Working Papers).

[27]"Nixon Makes Appeal to Building Industry on Wage-Price Spiral," *WSJ*, Jan. 19, 1971, at 8.

[28]"Labor Secretary Hodgson Cautiously Optimistic over Prospects for Coming Year in Construction," *CLR*, No. 801, Jan. 27, 1971, at A-16, A-17.

Within days of the January 18 meeting, the CICBC set up a working group to propose something like a stabilization board. Since Dunlop, the key member of the working group, had publicly endorsed adoption of the approach used by the 1961 Missile Site Construction Commission, of which he had also been a member, observers surmised that a similar approach would be worked out: unions and employers would agree to refrain from strikes and lockouts for a set period, during which they would try to reach a collectively bargained settlement at the local level. If they failed, a tripartite commission would propose its own settlement; even if the parties did reach a settlement on their own, the commission would still review it for its potential inflationary impact, and require further bargaining or offer its own settlement. In exchange for such a restriction of their bargaining power, unions reportedly sought two concessions: a "promise of no Federal threats to force the unions to speed up the acceptance of black and other minority group apprentices" and retention of the Davis-Bacon Act. For their part, contractors sought a conflicting measure—a modification of the Davis-Bacon Act so that prevailing wages reflected average (rather than the highest) contract settlements.[29]

Construction workers and their unions suffered a propagandistic set back at the end of January when the president of the United Automobile Workers, Leonard Woodcock, proposed the creation of a wage-price review board before which dominant unions and firms would have to justify wage and price increases. In this connection he observed that "'there is no question that the wage increases

---

[29]Philip Shabecoff, "Building Leaders Move to Control Pay-Price Spiral," *NYT*, Jan. 22, 1971, at 1, col. 5, at 15, col. 1-2. Later and throughout the remainder of the twentieth century employers pushed to weaken or repeal the Davis-Bacon Act. Although the Reagan administration introduced several regulatory changes, Congress failed to act. See generally, GAO, *The Davis-Bacon Act Should Be Repealed* (HRD-79-18, 1979); Center to Protect Workers' Rights, *The War on Wage Protection: The Business Offensive* (1979); Center to Protect Workers' Rights, *The GAO on Davis-Bacon: A Fatally Flawed Study* (1979); Building & Construction Trades Dept, AFL-CIO v. Donovan, 712 F.2d 611 (D.C. Cir. 1983); Building & Construction Trades Dept, AFL-CIO v. Martin, 961 F.2d 269 (D.C. Cir. 1992); Center to Protect Workers' Rights, *The Davis-Bacon Act: A Response to the Cato Institute's Attack* (n.d. [1993]); *CUH*, Oct. 1993, at 1 (urging repeal). In a masterpiece of ambiguity, the Roundtable stated that although repeal remained the primary objective, "this objective should not be misconstrued as an attempt to push back wages to inequitably low wages." BR, 2 *Coming to Grips with Some Problems in the Construction Industry* 25-26 (1978). To the extent that nonunionism has become the norm, union rates no longer prevail—especially since the Reagan administration promulgated a revised regulation that eliminated the rule in effect since 1935 under which the rate paid to 30 percent of the workers of a certain class in a certain area was defined as prevailing if no rate was paid to 50 percent; absent a 30 percent wage rate, a weighted average was used. Since 1983, if no rate is paid to 50 percent, the weighted average becomes the prevailing wage. 29 CFR § 1.2(a). Test surveys of construction wages that the BLS carried out in 1998 revealed that only 5 percent of construction workers in Tucson and 17 percent in Jacksonville, Florida were unionized. BLS, *Tucson, AZ Wages and Benefits: Construction Industry Test Survey, April 1998*, at 2 (Bull. 2510-2, 1998); BLS, *Jacksonville, FL Wages and Benefits: Construction Industry Test Survey, April 1998*, at 2 (Bull. 2510-1, 1998).

in the construction industry are excessive.'" Like the Westinghouse chairman, he supported the claim by reference to the fact that outside electricians working on projects in UAW plants sometimes received wages two or three dollars higher than UAW electricians, who often were more skilled.[30]

Nixon's hard line at the January 18th meeting was supposed to "give the union leaders, many of whom privately were agreeable to a stabilization program, the political cover to take some meaningful steps."[31] However, because the BCTD was divided over a voluntary stabilization of wages, it preferred leaving it up to the administration to impose controls.[32] At his February 17th news conference, Nixon, characterizing construction as "a sick industry" with 16 percent annual wage increases, stated that in the absence of a voluntary plan to restrain wages and prices, the federal government would take action.[33] By this time it was clear that "[f]or many observers, particularly in the business sector, construction wages were the fuse on an already unstable labor market situation that posed the threat of a classic wage-push inflationary spiral."[34] On February 23, less than a month after the first national conference of the Construction Action Council of the U.S. Chamber of Commerce focused on the need for repeal or suspension,[35] Nixon issued a presidential proclamation suspending the Davis-Bacon Act in an effort to "weaken union bargaining positions and reduce wage increases."[36]

---

[30]Philip Shabecoff, "A Wage-Price Review Board Is Recommended by Woodcock," *NYT*, Jan. 27, 1971, at 13, col. 1.

[31]Michael Moskow, "Construction Industry Wage Controls During the Nixon Administration," IRRA, *Proc. of the Fiftieth Annual Meeting*, 1:182-90 at 186 (1998).

[32]"Building Unions Decline to Move on Nixon's Plea for a Wage-Price Plan," *WSJ*, Feb. 12, 1971, at 2.

[33]"The President's News Conference of February 17, 1971," in Richard Nixon, *PPPUS: 1971*, at 158, 165 (1972).

[34]Arnold Weber & Daniel Mitchell, *The Pay Board's Progress: Wage Controls in Phase II* 2 (1978).

[35]"U.S. Chamber Conference Discusses Repeal or Suspension of Davis-Bacon," *CLR*, No. 802, Feb. 3, 1971, at A-17.

[36]Moskow, "Construction Industry Wage Controls During the Nixon Administration" at 186. D. Q. Mills, "Construction Wage Stabilization: A Historic Perspective," 11 (2) *IR* 350-65 at 352, 353 (Oct. 1972), reported that discussions on collective bargaining reform under the auspices of the CICBC "reached their culmination" at the AFL-CIO Executive Council's February 1971 meeting: "Draft documents were prepared embodying the concept of an Executive Order very similar" to the one that Nixon issued in March, "but with somewhat more stringent provisions...." The discussions revealed that "substantial government action was necessary" because "national leadership in the industry was incapable of applying effective restraints to local collective bargaining." Although "the stage was set for federal action to stabilize bargaining in construction through a tripartite board acting under federal law..., without prior notice to the industry leadership, the Administration" suspended the Davis-Bacon Act. Nine years later, days after Reagan's election, even the president of the NCA proposed urging the new administration, which had already declared that it would not repeal Davis-Bacon, to "'use the threat of repeal to extract a concession from the building trades that we enter some sort of national

The sea change in construction employers' attitude toward government labor regulation was symbolized by the fact that just a few years earlier the high degree of employer organization had been regarded as the basis of employers' acceptance of Davis-Bacon as removing wages from competition on government projects.[37] In the meantime, however, "[d]espite the President's romance with the hard hats after the Cambodian venture, 'the mess in construction,' as Administration officials referred to it, was becoming increasingly painful."[38] The presidential proclamation adduced the following interrelated elements as constituting the national emergency justifying suspension:

Construction industry collective bargaining settlements are excessive and show no signs of decelerating.

Increased unemployment and more frequent and longer work stoppages in the construction industry have accompanied the excessive and accelerating wage demands....

The excessive and accelerating wage settlements in the construction industry have affected collective bargaining in other industries, thus contributing to inflation in the overall economy.

This combination of factors in the construction industry has threatened the basic stability of the construction industry and thus the Nation's economy.

Construction industry employers and employee representatives have been unable voluntarily to agree upon any arrangement which would ameliorate these conditions.

The Federal Government is planning to expand its direct and financially-assisted construction, in part to reduce unemployment....

The Federal Government anticipates that a larger portion of total resources will be devoted to construction activity as the economy expands.

The Davis-Bacon Act...frequently require[s] contractors...to pay the high negotiated wage settlements...thereby sanctioning and spreading the high rates and thus inducing further acceleration contributing to the threat to the Nation's economy.[39]

In his accompanying statement, Nixon underscored that the fragmented bargaining structure "makes competition between local unions for higher wages particularly intense. It makes strikes on particular projects more likely since alternative work is often available nearby." To be sure, the president portrayed construction workers as the chief losers in the inflationary vicious cycle as the higher wages they sought to compensate for increased unemployment merely

---

bargaining program to get some control over wages.'" "Wage Restraint: What Next?" *ENR*, Nov. 27, 1980, at 72 (quoting Maurice Mosier).

[37]David Johnson, "Prevailing Wage Law," *Labor, Management and Social Policy* 231-62 at 233 (Gerald Somers ed., 1963).

[38]Harry Lenhart, Jr., "Construction Wage-Stabilization Efforts Provide Tests for Nixon's Phase 2," 3 *NJ* 2209-23 at 2215 (Nov. 6, 1971).

[39]Proclamation 4031, 36 Fed. Reg. 3457-58 (1971).

slowed down building, thus disemploying even more workers.[40]

Generally construction firm associations were dissatisfied, calling the suspension inadequate and ineffective.[41] In particular the AGC, which preferred a wage freeze rolling construction wages back to those in place at the end of 1970,[42] labelled the suspension, which the Nixon administration hoped would impel unions and employers to develop a stabilization plan voluntarily, "'disappointing, inadequate and totally ineffective in bringing stability to the construction industry."[43] But the AGC did avail itself of what it perceived as heightened public awareness of construction inflation, which the Davis-Bacon Act suspension had intensified, to propose a Construction Labor Relations Act. The same annual convention in early March 1971 that acted to "expand its efforts to help contractors organize and maintain open shop operations," proposed removing the construction industry from the NLRA and placing it under a new federal statute that would have repealed Davis-Bacon outright, prohibited exclusive hiring halls, required multitrade and multiemployer bargaining, eliminated restrictive practices, and precluded union rank and file ratification of labor contracts.[44] The AGC's initiative was, however, overshadowed by the construction wage stabilization regime that Nixon announced only a few days later.[45]

The limited impact of the suspension of the Davis-Bacon Act was signalled the next day by the Secretary of Transportation, who observed that in large metropolitan areas only few nonunion contractors were large enough to bid on federal projects in any event. John Volpe also bluntly warned that if the suspension failed to exert the requisite "psychological impact," "wage-price controls would

---

[40]"Statement on Suspending Davis-Bacon Act Provisions for Federal Construction Projects," in Nixon, *PPPUS: 1971*, at 199, 200-201.

[41]"Davis-Bacon Suspension Draws Mixed Reactions from Unions and Contractors Around the Country," *CLR*, No. 805, Feb. 24, 1971, at AA-7. Mills recognized that the Nixon administration "apparently believed its suspension would weaken the building trades unions and result in lower wage increases in 1971 negotiations," but stated categorically that "no national construction employer or union leader believed that suspension...could have more than a marginal effect on 1971 negotiations. Quite the contrary, employer representatives stated that the suspension would be of no value in the most organized areas, especially the large cities of the North and West...." Mills, "Construction Wage Stabilization" at 353.

[42]"AGC Prods Nixon and Paves Way to Industry Labor Reform," *ENR*, Mar. 18, 1971, at 55; "AGC Chief Healy Will Press Labor on Its 'Fair Day's Work' Pledge," *ENR*, Mar. 18, 1971, at 64, 65.

[43]"President Takes First Firm Step to Stop Building Costs Escalation," *WSJ*, Feb. 24, 1971, at 3.

[44]"AGC Prods Nixon and Paves Way to Industry Labor Reform," *ENR*, Mar. 18, 1971, at 55.

[45]"A Labor Bill for Construction," *ENR*, Mar. 18, 1971, at 200 (editorial); "The Trouble with Labor is Management," *ENR*, Feb. 24, 1972, at 64 (editorial). No such bill appears to have been introduced in Congress in 1971.

have to be imposed...."[46] The Roundtable vigorously applauded the suspension, calling it "politically courageous."[47]

Following suspension, Nixon found himself "picketed by angry groups of construction workers" around the country. "Suspension of Davis-Bacon," reported the *Wall Street Journal*, "seemed to have undone all the administration's careful cultivation of the blue collar vote."[48] While workers expressed a "bewildered and resentful feeling of betrayal," Peter Brennan, president of the Building and Construction Trades Council in New York, erstwhile Nixon favorite, and soon to become his Secretary of Labor, called the suspension outright "'union busting.'"[49] The NCA and AGC believed that suspension would have little impact on bargaining during 1971; both major employers organizations "expressed bitter disappointment over Nixon's refusal to resort to controls to halt the wage spiral."[50]

A few days after the suspension of Davis-Bacon, Carl Madden, chief economist of the Chamber of Commerce, addressed the annual meeting of the ABC. With great rhetorical gusto he lambasted the "labor anarchy" threatening to break out of the construction industry and to engulf the entire economy and society: "The wage push in building amounts to an unabashed and unique giant consumer robbery. Recently, one State Building Trades president said, 'There is no reason why a union man should not be earning $30,000 a year. ... If Ralph Nader and his co-workers...really want to protect consumers from exploitation, they could do no better than train their big guns on the wage monopoly in our nation's biggest industry." Distraught by the unaccustomed experience of being on the short end of the labor market's supply-demand lever "artificially created" by unions, the Chamber official, citing Heath Larry, the vice chairman of U.S. Steel, characterized the issue as "'whether a democracy predicated upon a free market economy, can really cope with the problem.' The problem of skyrocketing construction settlements is incredible; it is pulling settlements sought in other industries upwards like a magnet...."[51]

Having succeeded in gaining attention for the "crisis" in construction,[52] one

---

[46]"Volpe Warns Firms, Unions of Controls Unless They Agree to Curb Building Costs," *WSJ*, Feb. 25, 1971, at 10, col. 1.

[47]CUAIR *Report*, May 28, 1971, at 2 (Blough); CUAIR, Members Meeting, June 3, 1971, Minutes at 8, 12, in SP, Box 5.

[48]John Pierson, "Wage-Price Curbs for Building Industry Are Nixon Victory, But Impact Is Unclear," *WSJ*, Mar. 30, 1971, at 3, col. 1, at 2.

[49]Robert Tomasson, "Nixon Now Target of U.S. Hard Hats," *NYT*, Mar. 17, 1971, sect. 1, at 18, col. 1.

[50]"The Hard Hats Are Talking Tougher," *BW*, Mar. 13, 1971, at 105.

[51]Carl Madden, "Construction Wages: The Great Consumer Robbery," *CLR*, No. 808, Mar. 17, 1971, at E-1, E-2.

[52]A Nixon cabinet member offered this explanation to the Roundtable as to why Nixon restored the law after a month. CUAIR, Members Meeting, June 3, 1971, Minutes at 20. Secretary

month after suspending the Davis-Bacon Act, Nixon revoked his suspension[53] on the same day (March 29) that he issued Executive Order 11588 establishing the CISC. The statutory warrant for the president's creation of the CISC was the Economic Stabilization Act of 1970, which the Democratic Congress had enacted the previous August as an amendment to the Korean War-era Defense Production Act of 1950—more to embarrass the Nixon administration than in the expectation that it would be implemented.[54] It authorized the president to issue orders and regulations that "he may deem appropriate to stabilize prices, rents, wages, and salaries at levels not less than those prevailing on May 25, 1970," and empowered him to provide for "such adjustments as may be necessary to prevent gross inequities."[55]

The executive order recited that suspension of the Davis-Bacon Act had induced "national leaders of labor and management" to agree to "participate with the Government in fair measures to achieve greater wage and price stability," but that they had been "unable to agree on any voluntary arrangement."[56] Union leaders, according to the *Wall Street Journal*, were prepared to submit to the controls voluntarily, "but wanted government pressure to convince their rank-and-file."[57] Indeed, six weeks earlier *The New York Times* had reported that the national construction union officers had "made it clear that they could not impose a wage freeze on their own members even if they wanted to, since their unions are largely decentralized...." They were, in effect, telling the Nixon administration that it "must impose any solution on the construction industry...."[58] Accordingly, "[t]he real question," the *Times* editorialized a few days after Nixon had issued his executive order, "is still whether the local unions, long accustomed to grabbing everything in reach, can be persuaded to moderate their appetite," while other wages and prices

---

of Labor Hodgson told Nixon that the CISC's successes in reducing wage increases and strikes "testify to your wisdom in suspending the Davis-Bacon Act. Without this action the parties would never have given the subject the necessary attention." Hodgson to Nixon (n.d.), in NPMS, WHCF, SF Ex FG 315, Box 1, Folder 8: [Ex] FG 315, CISC [1971-1972].

[53]Proclamation 4040, 36 Fed. Reg. 6335 (1971).

[54]Arnold Weber, *In Pursuit of Price Stability: The Wage-Price Freeze of 1971*, at 5 (1973).

[55]Economic Stabilization Act of 1970, Pub. L. No. 91-379, § 202, 84 Stat. 796, 799-800 (1970).

[56]EO 11588, 36 Fed. Reg. 6339 (1971). For a detailed description of the CISC's initial operations, see Lenhart, "Construction Wage-Stabilization Efforts."

[57]John Pierson, "Wage-Price Curbs for Building Industry Are Nixon Victory, But Impact Is Unclear," *WSJ*, Mar. 30, 1971, at 3, col. 1.

[58]Philip Shabecoff, "Building Unions Expect a Freeze on Pay and Prices," *NYT*, Feb. 16, 1971, at 1, col. 1, at 49, col. 1. For further assertions by national union leaders that "their members...would not allow them to" accept wage controls voluntarily, see Philip Shabecoff, "Nixon Expected to Order Building Wage-Price Curb," *NYT*, Mar. 27, 1971, at 1, col. 1.

remain uncontrolled and "living costs continue to soar."[59] In the event, the CISC gave national union presidents "considerably more influence" over locals.[60]

This power struggle and divergence of interests between national and local unions were not new. Going back to the nineteenth century, the building trades unions' "peculiar political organization...differ[ed] from practically all other American trade unions in the small degree to which centralization of function in the national union...developed." The national unions' weakness and inability to control local unions were rooted "in the method used to enforce their policies on the employers"—namely, the joint closed shop locally organized by city building trades councils.[61] Immediately following World War II, too, construction union leaders, according to Dunlop, had shared building employers' wish "to prevent construction wage rates from exploding.... [B]ut the absence of all wage controls would make it almost impossible to hold local unions in line who were in a strong bargaining position to extract very substantial increases from their local contractors." National union leaders were motivated not by "altruism," but by "attention to longer run self-interest. This self-interest could more easily be achieved with the sanction of government controls than in its absence when local unions would be most difficult to control."[62]

Nixon's order provided that "Associations of contractors and national and international unions shall jointly establish craft dispute boards...to determine whether wages and salaries are acceptable." The standard of acceptability was "adjustments...normally considered supportable by productivity improvement and cost of living trends, but not in excess of the average of the median increases in wages and benefits...negotiated in major construction settlements in the period 1961 to 1968." The executive order also permitted the CISC to consider "[e]quity adjustments...to restore traditional relationships among crafts in a single locality and within the same craft in surrounding localities." These boards were then required to inform the tripartite (union-employer-public) CISC of all their actions. Implementation of any wage increase before the board and/or the committee approved it was a violation of the executive order. If the board or the CISC found a wage increase unacceptable, the Secretary of Labor and the states were prohibited from taking into consideration any such excess increase in making wage

[59]"Rocky Road to Pay Stability," *NYT*, Apr. 2, 1971, at 38, col. 1 (editorial). See also A. H. Raskin, "Construction: Controls of a Sort for a Runaway Industry," *NYT*, Apr. 4, 1971, sect. 4, at 2, col. 4.

[60]"John Dunlop and CISC Allay Feverish Collective Bargaining" at 25.

[61]George Barnett, "The Causes of Jurisdictional Disputes in American Trade Unions," 9 (4) *HBR* 400-408 at 404-405 (Apr. 1931).

[62]John Dunlop & Arthur Hill, *The Wage Adjustment Board: Wartime Stabilization in the Building and Construction Industry* 43 (1950).

determinations under Davis-Bacon or similar federal or state statutes.[63]   This prohibition, by effectively freezing the existing Davis-Bacon wage rate for the craft and locality in question, permitted nonunion contractors to pay lower wages on government projects.[64]

Tying wage increases to productivity increases presupposed, as do all incomes policies, that wage workers were willing to "accept that the existing division of wealth and income derived from it was basically fair."[65]   Such acquiescence was tantamount to acknowledgment by the union movement of a overriding community of interest between labor and capital transcending conjunctural disputes.[66] Yet as one of the CISC managers noted later, the reason that the private sector in the United States did not implement wage-price controls without government intervention was precisely the lack of labor-management cohesion or trust necessary to enforce such stabilization.[67]

Such lack of trust vis-à-vis employers and government regulators soon seemed fully justified. After the CISC had been busy for weeks stabilizing wages, the Nixon administration was still only "slowly...preparing to place some restraints on construction prices and on the compensation received by management in the industry." Even after unions complained about this blatant inequity, the *Wall Street Journal* reported: "Some of those involved in carrying out the order have conceded that the restraints to be applied to management probably would be tough enough only to ensure continued union participation in the overall scheme."[68] When the

---

[63]EO 11588, §§ 1, 2, 3(a), 4(c), 5(a), 6(a), 6(b), 36 Fed. Reg. at 6339-41. Approval by a board of wage increases had to be unanimous. 36 Fed. Reg. 19580, 19582 (1971) (to be codified at 29 C.F.R. §2001.42(a)). When Nixon issued another executive order in October to create the machinery to administer Phase II of the general wage and price stabilization program that he had put into effect in August, he brought the CISC within the framework of the new regime; this order also repealed § 6 of EO 11588, which contained the guidelines for wage increases. EO 11627, § 14, 36 Fed. Reg. 20139, 20144 (1971). The NCA wrote to Nixon urging not only that the NCA be represented on the CISC (which it was), but that John R. Van de Water be considered for chairman and John Garvin for one of the public members. Letter from J. R. Fluor to Richard Nixon (Apr. 6, 1974), in NPMS, WHCF, SF Ex FG 315, Box 1, Folder 8: [Ex] FG 315 CISC [1971-1972]. Van de Water, a management consultant who advised employers on how to resist unionization, became NLRB chairman under Reagan. Gross, *Broken Promises* at 249-50. For a list of CISC members and alternates, see Lenhart, "Construction Wage-Stabilization Efforts" at 2210.

[64]John Pierson, "Wage-Price Curbs for Building Industry Are Nixon Victory, But Impact Is Unclear," *WSJ*, Mar. 30, 1971, at 3, col. 1.

[65]Andrew Shonfield, *Modern Capitalism: The Changing Balance of Public and Private Power* 217 (1969 [1965]).

[66]Leo Panitch, *Social Democracy and Industrial Militancy: The Labour Party, the Trade Unions and Incomes Policy, 1945-1974*, at 3-4 (1976).

[67]Daniel Quinn Mills, *Government, Labor, and Inflation: Wage Stabilization in the United States* 90-91 (1975).

[68]Byron Calame, "New Controls on Building Industry Prices, Management Pay Readied by

Interagency Committee on Construction finally proposed regulations at the end of June, the *Journal* observed that they seemed to "Be Weak on Policing" because they "[f]orced the buyers of private construction to take legal action on their own to make contractors pass along any savings resulting from the stabilization committee's disapproval of inflationary union wage settlements."[69]

Employer reaction was mixed. The AGC "completely and wholeheartedly" supported the initiative, although it would have preferred "a stronger measure such as a wage-price freeze...."[70] Big business industrial users, however, had been dissatisfied with Nixon's approach even before he announced it. In February the CUAIR Coordinating Committee perceived great danger that government-imposed controls might spread to other industries.[71] In March, "[w]hen there were strong indications that the CISC would be formed and blessed by the Nixon administration, opposition...developed in management quarters outside the construction industry. This opposition was expressed most vocally by Roger M. Blough...." The CUAIR leader "met with President Nixon to express his concern over establishing a wage stabilization agency for the construction industry that ceded authority to the parties to the problem," but "was unsuccessful in dissuading Nixon...."[72] All Blough got for his troubles was a "Dear Roger" letter from the president assuring him that the administration had not become complacent about inflation.[73]

Only a few weeks after the CISC's creation, *The New York Times* found "near unanimity" among construction workers that the Nixon administration's criterion limiting noninflationary wage increases to 6 percent (the average increase in union contract wages and benefits between 1961 and 1968) was "was unfair and unworkable and would be resisted."[74] Both Labor Secretary Hodgson and CISC chairman Dunlop declared that Executive Order 11588 did not impose a fixed ceiling on negotiated wage increases, which would all have to be evaluated individually. Rather, the CISC's objectives were to moderate wage increases below the average 18 percent for the first year of contracts recorded in 1970 and to reduce

---

Nixon Panel," *WSJ*, June 16, 1971, at 6, col. 3.

[69]"Romney Panel Proposes Curbs on Construction Prices and Bosses' Pay," *WSJ*, June 28, 1971, at 3, col. 2. Two months later, after the general wage-price freeze had gone into effect, the committee had still not implemented regulations. Byron Calame, "Construction-Industry Panel May Be Model for Stabilizing Pay, Prices After Nov. 12," *WSJ*, Aug. 18, 1971, at 30, col. 1.

[70]Pierson, " Wage-Price Curbs for Building Industry."

[71]CUAIR, CC, Minutes, Feb. 16, 1971, at 4, in BR, 1971-Vol. II: Minutes.

[72]Weber & Mitchell, *The Pay Board's Progress* at 23. The authors, who were, respectively, a public member and chief economist of the Nixon Pay Board, offered no source to document this meeting.

[73]Letter from Richard Nixon to Roger [Blough] (June 15, 1971), in NPMS, WHCF, SF Ex FG 315, Box 1, Folder 8: [Ex] FG 315 CISC [1971-1972].

[74]"Construction Men Seem Confused on Wage Order," *NYT*, May 4, 1971, at 26, col. 3.

the incidence of strikes from one-third of all construction negotiations to 5 to 10 percent.[75] Hodgson stated that it would be impossible until 1973 at the earliest to hold wage increases down to 6 percent. He characterized the media's exclusive focus on that criterion as "'distorting'" because it neglected the other guideline—applying equity to preserve or restore traditional relationships between wages in various construction unions.[76]

Initially, big business did not uniformly judge the CISC a success. As early as April, the chairman and CEO of General Electric complained to Nixon that equity adjustments could lead to a continual ratcheting up of wages. Thinking of the impact on his own company's profits, Fred Borch noted that in renegotiating all of its major metal agreements that year, GE would have little chance of achieving reasonable settlements "if 'outsized' annual increases in construction bear an apparent federal stamp of approval."[77] In June, the chairman and CEO of du Pont wrote to the Cabinet Committee on Construction, complaining about the CISC decision involving painters in Little Rock. Charles B. McCoy asserted that the decision brought to a halt meaningful bargaining by unions "while they pick new high targets for 'equity judgments.'"[78] In his sharp-tongued reply, Herbert Stein, a member and soon to become chairman of the CEA, informed McCoy that he had thought that the CISC's purpose was precisely to halt the outcome of the "'meaningful collective bargaining' that we had been getting." He then lamented that in response to businessmen's urging of a cogent incomes policy without controls—the administration should tell unions what was right—it had created the CISC and "we've had nothing but complaints about it from businessmen ever since." Finally Stein asked rhetorically whether businessmen thought that the government could set up a voluntary or involuntary wage control system without

---

[75]"Stabilization Order Sets No Fixed Limits on Negotiated Boosts, Dunlop and Hodgson Assert," *CLR*, No. 817, May 19, 1971, at AA-1, AA-2. That same day Congress amended the Economic Stabilization Act to prohibit the president from exercising his authority "with respect to a particular industry or segment of the economy unless the President determines, after taking into account the seasonal nature of employment, the rate of employment or underemployment, and other mitigating factors, that prices or wages in that industry or segment of the economy have increased at a rate which is disproportionate to the rate at which prices or wages have increased in the economy generally." Act of May 18, 1971, Pub. L. No. 92-15, § 3(a)(2), 85 Stat. 38 (1971).

[76]"Hodgson Says Construction Pay Curbs Are Working," *NYT*, May 18, 1971, at 78, col. 3-6.

[77]Letter from Fred Borch to Richard Nixon (Apr. 13, 1971), in NACP, RG 174: General Records of Labor Dept., Office of the Secretary, Records of Secretary James D. Hodgson, 1970-72, 1971, Box No. 105: Committees to Interdepartmental (Miscellaneous to Construction Industry Stabilization), Folder: 1971-Committee: Construction Industry Stabilization (June-). Secretary Hodgson's reply of June 14, 1971, failed to engage Borch's criticisms. *Id.*

[78]McCoy to Cabinet Committee on Construction (June 21, 1971), in NPMS, WHCF, SF, EX FG 315, Box 1, Folder 8: [EX] FG 315, CISC [1971-1972].

union participation.[79] The fact that du Pont, a key Roundtable member and pioneer in "patronizing open shop contractors and loudly espousing their virtues,"[80] was at odds with the Nixon administration over so central an element of wage controls as the cooptation of unions reveals the limits of capital's capacity for implementing its agenda. The president of the NCA, too, conveyed to Nixon his serious concern about the slow pace of the wage stabilization program especially in light of its request earlier in the year for an outright wage and profit freeze.[81] Blough reported to the members of the Coordinating Committee in September 1971 that the executive order establishing the CISC contained nothing that attempted to cure the industry's chronic problems.[82]

In the event, the CISC took credit for having reduced the average increase in settlements to 11 percent in 1971 and the number of strikes by two-thirds.[83] First-year wage increases in major union settlements declined from 17.6 percent in 1970 to 12.6 percent in 1971, 6.9 percent in 1972, and 5.2 percent in 1973. In the wake of general wage and price controls introduced by Nixon on August 15, 1971, convergence between construction and the rest of the economy was reflected in the corresponding increases for manufacturing—8.1, 10.9, 6.6, and 5.9 percent. Similarly, life-of-contract wage increases in construction amounted to 14.9, 10.8, 6.0, and 5.2 percent in 1970, 1971, 1972, and 1973, respectively; in manufacturing the corresponding increases were 6.0, 7.3, 5.6, and 4.9 percent.[84] By 1972, collectively bargained wage increases in construction had fallen below those in the rest of the economy.[85] This convergence may have defused complaints by industrial

---

[79]Herbert Stein to C.B. McCoy (June 25, 1971), in NPMS, WHCF, SF, EX FG 315, Box 1, Folder 8: [EX] FG 315, CISC [1971-1972].

[80]"Man of the Year: H. Edgar Lore: Moving an Industry Toward Unity," *ENR*, Feb. 15, 1979, at 34-40 at 38.

[81]Letter from Benjamin Forst to Richard Nixon (June 22, 1971), in NPMS, WHCF, SF Ex FG 315, Box 1, Folder 8: [Ex] FG 315 CISC [1971-1972].

[82]Memorandum from Roger Blough to Members (Sept. 20, 1971), in BR, CCH: 1971.

[83]"CISC Public Members Assert Construction Wage Increases Down Due to Stabilization Committee," *CLR*, No. 849, Jan. 5, 1972, at A-21. The CISC's mission was both easier and more complicated than that of its counterparts during World War II and the Korean War because wage controls in 1971 were imposed "in the aftermath of a construction boom (not prior to the expansion), in the context of a very rapid wage inflation (not prior to its development), in a period of falling demand and loosening labor markets (rather than the opposite), and in the context of a very badly distorted wage structure." Mills, "Construction Wage Stabilization" at 355-56.

[84]*Oversight on Economic Stabilization: Hearings Before the Subcommittee on Production and Stabilization of the Senate Committee on Banking, Housing and Urban Affairs*, 93d Cong., 2d Sess. 466 (1974) (statement of John Dunlop).

[85]Weber & Mitchell, *The Pay Board's Progress*, tab. 10-11 at 302. See also Clark Ross, "The Construction Wage Stabilization Program," 17 *IR* 308-14 (1978). The *Wall Street Journal* nevertheless complained editorially: "Wages aren't going up quite as fast as they were before the committee began business, but an observer has to look closely to see the difference." "Stability in

unions that the CISC was allowing construction workers larger wage increases than the Pay Board was authorizing for manufacturing workers. Industrial union leaders charged that such discrimination was a payback for construction unions' support for the Republican party.[86]

Because international union presidents were appointed to the craft boards, the latter were regarded as "a device that will give the general presidents of the building trades unions more leverage over their locals."[87] Indeed, this "long-sought control over rebellious local building-trades barons," coupled with a warning that the union leaders, during the post-freeze Phase II after November 1971, "would be thrown to the mercy of the less sympathetic Nixon Pay Board if they didn't cooperate," was the chief means by which Dunlop succeeded in inducing them to acquiesce in the scaled-back wage increases.[88] By mid-1972, *Business Week* could report that "the building-trades leadership has gone on an offensive against high wage demands and restrictive work practices. The controls program has given the union leaders a clout they did not have before. They can now insist on a moderation that they consider necessary for the welfare of the industry—and for workers' jobs...."[89] The industry's leading magazine, *ENR*, rhapsodized that a "fantastic aspect of CISC is hearing a top AFL-CIO official close to the workings of CISC openly boast of the way it has been knocking down excessive demands of locals...."[90]

As a device designed to empower the national union bureaucracies to prevent workers and their local unions from continuing to secure above-average wage increases, the CISC functioned as the paradigm of an "incomes policy to thwart or reverse episodes of worker militancy and, in so doing, to reduce real wages...." Pursuit of a policy violative of "the traditional trade union objective of advancing the real incomes of members" was acceptable to national union officials only by virtue of a "quid pro quo" in the form of "measures of institutional protection designed to compensate unions for the loss of support of their members

---

Construction," *WSJ*, Dec. 6, 1971, at 12, col. 1 at 2.

[86]Jerry Flint, "Big Construction Raises Backed by Panel in Secret," *NYT*, Jan. 28, 1972, at 15, col. 1; Philip Shabecoff, "Pay Unit Reports Accord on Construction Wages," *NYT*, Jan. 29, 1972, at 17, col. 1; "Construction Panel Told to Give Data," *NYT*, Feb. 29, 1972, at 15, col. 1; "Abel Heats Up an Ancient Union Feud," *BW*, Mar. 11, 1972, at 106. Philip Ross, "The Influence of the Construction Unions on the Wage-Price Freeze," in *Negotiation-Arbitration '72*, at 67-74 (Luke Power et al. eds., 1972), argued that the CISC was merely window dressing.

[87]Lenhart, "Construction Wage-Stabilization Efforts" at 2223.

[88]Byron Calame & James Gannon, "John Dunlop Is Likely to Stress Pay Control, Back Room Bargaining," *WSJ*, Jan. 15, 1973, at 1, col. 6, at 19, col. 2.

[89]"New Ideas Shake Building Trades," *BW*, May 13, 1972, at 124.

[90]"John Dunlop and CISC Allay Feverish Collective Bargaining," *ENR*, July 6, 1972, at 25, 27.

with increased organization authority....'"[91]

Despite the CISC's success in slashing construction wage increases, some free-market economists opposed the CISC's operation. For example, Hendrik Houthakker, who had resigned as a member of Nixon's CEA in July 1971, called the "'whole organization...just an extension of the unions.... All these labor arbitrators are aligned with the unions....'" Consequently, the CISC accepted as a given the structure that Houthakker saw as producing the "inflationary wage settlements"—namely, the lack of free entry into the unions, which held back the labor supply.[92]

In the period after the introduction of wage controls the rate of increase of nominal wages slowed down; in that sense the intervention into construction wages could be interpreted as a trial balloon since the post-August 15, 1971 general wage controls produced a similar effect.[93] After that date the government considered using the CISC—which continued in force[94]—as a model for other industries, but

---

[91]Robert Flanagan, David Soskice, & Lloyd Ulman, *Unionism, Economic Stabilization, and Incomes Policies: European Experience* 37 (1983).

[92]Lenhart, "Construction Wage-Stabilization Efforts" at 2222.

[93]Mills, "Construction Wage Stabilization" at 355-56; Philip Shabecoff, "Hodgson Says President Seeks Curbs on Construction Wages," *NYT*, Jan. 9, 1971, at 12; "Nixon Makes Appeal to Building Industry on Wage-Price Spiral," *WSJ*, Jan. 19, 1971, at 8; "Building Unions Decline to Move on Nixon's Plea for a Wage-Price Plan," *WSJ*, Feb. 12, 1971, at 2;"President Takes First Firm Step to Stop Building Costs Escalation," *WSJ*, Feb. 24, 1971, at 3; "Volpe Warns Firms, Unions of Controls Unless They Agree to Curb Building Costs," *WSJ*, Feb. 25, 1971, at 10; Philip Shabecoff, "Nixon Expected to Order Bulding Wage-Price Curb," *NYT*, Mar. 27, 1971, at 1, col. 1-2; "A Destructive Misunderstanding," *WSJ*, Mar. 25, 1971, at 8, col. 1 (editorial); "Construction Men Seem Confused by Wage Order," *NYT*, May 4, 1971, at 26, col. 3; "First Approval of Building Industry Pay Settlement Is Given by Wage-Price Panel," *WSJ*, Apr. 9, 1971, at 2, col. 3; "Hodgson Says Construction Pay Curbs Are Working," *NYT*, May 18, 1971, at 78, col. 3; Byron Calame, "New Controls on Building Industry Prices, Management Pay Readied by Nixon Panel," *WSJ*, June 16, 1971, at 6, col. 3; "Construction Pay Panel Refuses to Sanction 31.6% Plumbers Boost," *WSJ*, June 24, 1971, at 15, col. 6; "Romney Panel Proposes Curbs on Construction Prices and Bosses' Pay," *WSJ*, June 28, 1971, at 3, col. 2; Elliot Carlson, "Panel nears Pay Stabilizing Breakthrough; Philadelphia Carpenters Average 11% Raise," *WSJ*, July 9, 1971, at 3, col. 2; "Stability in Construction," *WSJ*, Dec. 6, 1971, at 12, col. 1 (editorial); "U.S. Bid to Stabilize Construction Wages Menaced by Dispute over Deferred Wages," *WSJ*, May 5, 1971, at 3, col. 2. On the operation of the controls, see *Economic Report of the President* ch. 2 (1973).

[94]EO No. 11627, § 14 (Oct. 15, 1971); "Stabilization Committee Remains in Business," *CLR*, No. 830, Aug. 18, 1971, at AA-1. The Pay Board authorized the CISC to administer Pay Board policies by amended order No. 2, which, inter alia, required the CISC to apply its policy on economic adjustments to the money value of changes in work rules. CUAIR *Report*, Jan. 28, 1972; "CISC, Pay Board Reach Accord on 'Substantive Policies,'" *CLR*, No. 853, Feb. 2, 1972, at AA-1. Publication was delayed at the CISC's request until the Pay Board published it unilaterally. 37 Fed. Reg. 8140-41 (1972); Arnold Weber & Daniel Mitchell, *The Pay Board's Progress: Wage Controls in Phase II* at 228 n.22 (1978). On the antagonistic relationship between the two entities, see *id.* at 226-32. Virgil Day of the Roundtable was one of three Pay Board representatives on the joint subcommittee

fundamental differences became manifest:

> The government's construction setup...had something to offer the national leaders of the building-trades unions in return for their cooperation in the scheme. They were assured of a key role in the running of the individual review board for their craft.... And this has enabled many of them to exercise greater control over troublesome locals and rebellious local leaders who have traditionally made life difficult for national construction union officials.
>
> The stabilization-committee approach would have much less appeal to the heads of major industrial unions such as the United Auto Workers Union or the United Steelworkers Union.... While few building-trades unions have agreements that are negotiated by their president, for instance, the heads of the UAW and USW regularly handle the major bargaining for their members.[95]

Michael Moskow, Deputy Under Secretary of Labor for Economic Affairs and Program Coordination and executive director of the CICBC, characterized the CISC in June 1971 as a "system of self-regulation with implicit but real sanctions"—"a halfway house between purely voluntary restraint and outright controls." Instead of prescribing rigid guidelines or fixed wage increases, this regime permitted "'equity adjustments' in order to restore traditional differentials with other crafts in the same locality and with the same crafts in neighboring localities." The Nixon administration, aiming to "turn a race into an orderly procession...at a slower pace" but to insure that everyone would "end up in the traditional order," wished to avoid "serious morale and productivity problems...to say nothing of the likelihood of strikes against the government."[96] The CISC viewed the construction industry as beset by structural wage distortions: derangement of customary relationships among crafts during the 1960s had triggered a destabilizing process of "competitive readjustment." The result was a "leapfrogging process" that generated wage increases "well out of line with the rest of the labor market."[97]

---

established to assure conformity between the Pay Board and the CISC. CUAIR *Report*, Jan. 25, 1972, at 1. The CISC was also continued for Phase III of the Economic Stabilization Program by EO No. 11695, § 5 (Jan. 11, 1973). In late 1971, Congress again amended the Economic Stabilization Act, requiring the president to "issue standards as a guide for determining levels of wages, salaries, prices...." These standards "shall...provide for...such general exceptions and variations as are necessary to foster orderly economic growth and to prevent gross inequities, hardships, serious market disruptions, domestic shortages of raw materials, localized shortages of labor, and windfall profits" and "call for generally comparable sacrifices by business and labor...." Economic Stabilization Act Amendments of 1971, Pub. L. No. 92-210, § 2, 85 Stat. 743, 744 (1971).

[95]Byron Calame, "Construction-Industry Panel May Be Model for Stabilizing Pay, Prices After Nov. 12," *WSJ*, Aug. 18, 1971, at 30, col. 1 at 2.

[96]Untitled speech *reprinted in* 117 Cong. Rec. 24,388-90 (1971).

[97]Weber & Mitchell, *The Pay Board's Progress* at 112.

High ranking government officials privately remarked in 1971 that the plan was to "squeeze the equity adjustments out of the system as quickly as possible and then get down to the six percent figure by the end of next year or early in 1973."[98] Equity adjustments, however, proved to be complicated. The root of the perceived conflict was so-called coercive comparisons, which created "an interdependence between some wage rates so strong that if the traditional connection is broken, the consequences—often in the form of a strike—are nearly always detrimental to the efficiency of the labor market." For example, where the wage rates of plumbers and electricians in a town had been the same for decades, the CISC viewed limiting the electricians to a 6 percent increase when the plumbers had bargained for 15 percent the previous year as counterproductive. The intra-working class equity question was exacerbated by the belief that "wage rate connections in the construction industry are, perhaps, the most coercive in the economy."[99]

Despite the fact that by late 1972 the CISC was still holding to wage increases of about 6 percent, the CUAIR's skepticism, at least for internal consumption, seemed to be based on the suspicion that some sort of sleight-of-hand was at work since that "6% figure represents an actual savings in cents per hour of only 5 cents compared to the construction wage record of the 1967-1971 period; during that period...wages [increases] averaged approximately 52 cents per hour compared to the present figure of 46 cents to 47 cents...." This revelation prompted the Coordinating Committee to conclude that a cents-per-hour standard would be a more appropriate measure for purposes of controlling construction wages, although it might be inappropriate as a general wage standard because it reduced wage "desired wage differentials" based on skill, experience, education, and responsibility.[100]

After the CISC had been operating for two years, Nixon reminded the national conference of the BCTD that at the time he had established the CISC "the top international presidents, who are always in there fighting for that last buck right down the line, said, we have got to do a better job" because "exorbitant" wage increases had been "driving jobs away from organized labor into nonunion labor." Now, however, Nixon could certify that with reduced wage rate increases construction had become "responsible" and was "no longer a sick industry."[101]

As Phase III of the control program progressed, the CISC began to relax its wage standards. An informal ceiling of 35-cent per hour building trade wage increases in early 1973 soon gave way to efforts to limit raises to 45 cents as unions

---

[98]Lenhart, "Construction Wage-Stabilization Efforts" at 2215.

[99]Lenhart, "Construction Wage-Stabilization Efforts" at 2217 (quoting Moskow).

[100]CUAIR, CC, Minutes, Nov. 2, 1972, at 3-5, in BR, 1972, Vol. II-Minutes.

[101]"Remarks at the National Conference of Building and Construction Trades Department, AFL-CIO," in Richard Nixon, *PPPUS: 1973*, at 290, 291-92 (Apr. 16, 1973 [1975]).

pointed to the absence of tightened controls in other sectors.[102]   At the same time, Representative Anderson introduced yet another bill to promote area-wide collective bargaining, but it too died without action.[103] A year later, in the wake of Congress's failure to extend construction wage controls and the expiration of the CISC on April 30, 1974, Dunlop and Mills warned of renewed "'massive leapfrogging.'" Freed of government constraints, unions, according to *Business Week*, began engaging in "unusually militant negotiating." To the extent that "a few significant moves by unions to cede away restrictive rules for more pay and fringes" emerged, the reason was "the same everywhere: Open-shop construction, a few years ago limited to home-building, is now spreading through all forms of commercial and industrial construction. Largely because of the high costs of restrictive rules, contractors using only union labor are losing construction projects to competitors who meet union wage scales but are not bound by rules that add to manpower needs and reduce productivity."[104] As controls expired in 1974, reports surfaced of union leaders' fear that a "militant rank-and-file will push them to settlements so high that employers will have new opportunities to recruit nonunion hands at wages below the new, higher union scale."[105] Nevertheless, just a few weeks earlier, the BCTD had voted unanimously against extending wage controls.[106] That year the differentials in median wage rates between union and nonunion contractors ranged from 50 percent to well over 100 percent in various trades and regions.[107]

The Roundtable agreed with many that it was "unthinkable" to end all controls. But, as Virgil Day, chairman of the group's Construction Committee, observed, another national tripartite board would be acceptable only if it strengthened and extended coordinated bargaining and eliminated "insupportable practices...." Regardless of what arrangements replaced the CISC, Day insisted that

---

[102]"Building Pay: A Leaky Ceiling," *BW*, June 9, 1973, at 82.

[103]H. R. 8298, 93d Cong., 1st Sess (May 31, 1973). It would have authorized the CISC to devise a reform plan. The same fate befell the much more complex bill that he introduced six years later; H.R. 3779, 96th Cong., 1st Sess. (1979).

[104]"An End to Labor Stability in Building Wages," *BW*, June 29, 1974, at 46. See also Leonard Silk, "Labor's Turn at Bat," *NYT*, June 19, 1974, at 61, col. 7; "A Grudging Retreat from Work Rules," *BW*, June 2, 1975, at 20-21. Dunlop stated later that Congress had simply grown tired of controls and refused to consider his plans for retaining controls only in a few sectors such as construction and health care. Telephone interview with John Dunlop, Cambridge, Mass. (Jan. 7, 1999).

[105]Edward Cowan, "Controls Ending in High Inflation," *NYT*, Apr. 28, 1974, at 1, col. 6, at 42, col. 5. See also Edward Cowan, "Democrats Favor Price-Curb Action," *NYT*, Apr. 25, 1974, at 1, col. 4, at 17, col. 1.

[106]Philip Shabecoff, "Meany Attack on Nixon Cheered by Construction Union Leaders," *NYT*, Apr. 2, 1974, at 14, col. 1.

[107]Northrup, *Open Shop Construction Revisited*, tab. XI-14 at 499.

coordinated wide-area bargaining "'in the hope of making the contractor co-equal with labor'" remained the most important component.[108] By early 1974 the Roundtable and contractors' groups were still unable to attain unanimity concerning the optimal post-CISC approach. Among the possibilities considered by the Construction Committee were repeal of the Davis-Bacon Act and "strengthening open shop contracting through legislation directed at union violence."[109] The committee also noted that "unions need legislated controls to maintain control over their locals."[110] Day, who remained chairman of the Construction Committee even after he left GE to become associated with the corporate law firm of Vedder, Price, warned at the February 19 meeting that if a new construction wage explosion occurred, it might become "an imminent necessity for major users to consider again all their options including the possibility of mounting their own construction forces...." Despite the CISC's impending demise, members could articulate no objective more concrete than that construction wage controls should be continued, but only if accompanied by a strengthening of collective bargaining: "'Otherwise,' as one contractor asserted, 'we might as well forget controls.'"[111]

The Roundtable was unable to achieve any of its desiderata legislatively or administratively, but its spectacular success in the immediate and middle-term in promoting the antiunion sector and shrinking the union sector of construction proved to be far more valuable and enduring. Perhaps this perspective explains why in the Roundtable's annual meeting summary report Blough, despite complaining about wage increases and hundreds of strikes in the preceding year, offered no plan other than voluntary action such as a stronger national alliance of contractor associations.[112]

---

[108]*RR*, No. 73-10, at 3 (Oct. 29, 1973). The Construction Committee expressed similar views in 1974. *RR*, No. 74-2, at 2-3 (Feb. 28, 1974); *RR*, No. 74-4, at 2 (Apr. 26, 1974).

[109]BR, CC, Minutes, Jan. 16, 1974, at 6, in BR, CCH: 1974.

[110]BR, CC, Minutes, Mar. 1, 1974, at 6, in BR, CCH: 1974.

[111]BR, CC, Minutes, Feb. 19, 1974, at 2, in BR, CCH: 1974.

[112]*RR*, June 17, 1974, at 2.

Part V

The Outcome

"The nonunion competition is devastating to us and anyone who doesn't think so is a total idiot."[1]

---

[1]Haynes Johnson & Nick Kotz, *Unions* 144 (1972) (quoting Edward Carlough, president of the Sheet Metal Workers Union).

14

The Unions' Failure to Stave Off the Open Shop Legislatively During the Ford Interregnum

In the past the building trades unions were led mostly by chiefs of advanced age who politicially were somewhat to the right of William McKinley.[1]

The deep recession of 1974-75, which undermined what some viewed as burgeoning rank and file insurgence outside of construction,[2] seemed at first to render the expiration of wage controls moot. Yet by 1975, a year after the CISC had been terminated, 18 percent construction unemployment did not deter unions from seeking 6 to 8 percent wage increases.[3] *Business Week* complained editorially: "The trouble is that the international headquarters of the unions cannot get the word through to the locals that do the actual bargaining. After years of maintaining tight control of construction labor supply through their hiring halls, the locals see no reason to give up what they consider a good thing."[4] A construction employers' association official agreed: "'The irony of the thing is that at the international level, the unions recognize the situation...but the locals are willing to commit suicide, though they are starting to see that the problem affects them at the local level.'"[5] And with understanding for the predicament of local construction firms, Professor Albert Rees, the director of the Council on Wage and Price Stability during the Ford administration, explained wage movements as rooted in a lack of employer solidarity: "'[I]t's hard for employers to show backbone,' when in some areas—such as Washington state—giant contractors sign national agreements and employ workers who are on strike against local contractors."[6]

Nationalizing the scope of collective bargaining and empowering national

---

[1]Philip Shabecoff, "Picketing the Issue in Construction Fight," *NYT*, Mar. 13, 1977, sect. 3, at 2, col. 3 at 6.

[2]Kim Moody, *An Injury to All: The Decline of American Unionism* 83-94 (1996 [1988]).

[3]James Hyatt, "Construction Workers, Despite Dearth of Jobs, Still Seek Pay Boosts," *WSJ*, Apr. 10, 1975, at 1, col. 6.

[4]"Stranglehold on Building," *BW*, June 2, 1975, at 80 (editorial).

[5]"The Hidden Dynamite in Construction Wages," *BW*, May 5, 1975, at 33, 34 (quoting Dwight Hall, labor relations director of a builders' group in Ohio and Pennsylvania).

[6]"The Hidden Dynamite in Construction Wages," *BW*, May 5, 1975, at 34. Congress established the Council, which had no enforcement powers, shortly after the end of wage controls to study, hold hearings on, monitor, and alert the government and public to inflationary developments. Pub. L. No. 93-387, 88 Stat. 750 (1974).

union officials to check the demands and strike-happiness of workers and their local unions continued to preoccupy Dunlop after he became Secretary of Labor in the Ford administration. Arguably he was seeking to induce union leaders to act in the unions' long-term interest. In any event, management regarded his efforts to facilitate area-wide bargaining—which the unorthodox new president of the Carpenters advocated, believing that depression-like conditions in the mid-1970s would weaken members' resistance to the restructuring—as an attempt to "'salvage what's left of the unionized segment of the industry.'"[7]

Dunlop's ability to refocus state management of labor relations was amply on display in June 1975 when he testified before Congress on a bill (H.R. 5900) to amend the NLRA to exempt construction union action (common situs picketing) against general contractors who operated with nonunion subcontractors from the statute's ban on secondary pressure. He tried to make the amendment, which the unions had unsuccessfully been pursuing for a quarter-century, more palatable by introducing "the principle that authorization of such picketing by the appropriate national union be required."[8]

In the aftermath of demonstrations in April 1975 by thousands of union construction workers in Washington, D.C. for government relief of the depression-level unemployment,[9] *ENR* reported on the "atmosphere of confusion generated by a surprise proposal," which it interpreted as "the opening thrust in a major new campaign to strengthen the control of the building trades international unions over their locals." Employers, who had expected Dunlop to support the original bill, were "pleased" because they "felt the injection of a completely new issue into the debate would slow the legislative process."[10] The Roundtable Construction Committee, which as early as April had engaged in intense discussion of the new common situs picketing drive and decided that the Roundtable should undertake an immediate program to counter it (including reenergizing the campaign against the

---

[7]"Dunlop Warned on Labor Pact Talks," *ENR*, Aug. 19, 1976, at 14, 15 (quoting management attorney Lawrence Zimmerman); "Carpenters' Sidell Calls for Better Construction Bargaining," *ENR*, Mar. 13, 1975, at 25. This judgment overlaps with that of a late 1960s' left-wing period piece, which called him one of the "most powerful...underground lobbyists...commonly regarded as chief spokesman in Washington for the construction trades unions. Dunlop is credited with having devised the strategy which brought these warring unions together, and won them unprecedented wage increases." James Ridgeway, *The Closed Corporation: American Universities in Crisis* 76 (1968).

[8]*Equal Treatment of Craft and Industrial Workers: Hearings Before the Subcommittee on Labor-Management Relations of the House Committee on Education and Labor*, 94th Cong., 1st Sess. 10 (1975). See also "Dunlop Asks Congress to Broaden Rights of Unions Picketing Construction Sites," *WSJ*, June 6, 1975, at 4.

[9]"Construction Workers Mass in Capital to Demand Jobs," *NYT*, Apr. 22, 1975, at 19, col. 1.

[10]"Situs Picketing Legislation Faces Some New Obstacles," *ENR*, June 12, 1975, at 8.

Davis-Bacon Act),[11] was also surprised by Dunlop's qualification of the bill, but still found it damaging.[12]

Union leaders, in contrast, were put in "an immediate bind. Privately they support Dunlop's goal of centralizing power in the internationals, but they are afraid to speak out for fear of creating serious political problems with their local unions."[13] One reason some local union leaders could have been expected to acquiesce in or support area-wide bargaining was its potential for reducing competition for higher wage demands, which threatened the re-electability of those officials who failed to negotiate increases as high as those gained by neighboring locals or other trades.[14]

At the end of his prepared statement to the House committee Dunlop, who had been associated with virtually every federal government initiative involving construction labor relations since World War II, added this personal observation:

> I have come to the conclusion over the past decade that the legal framework of collective bargaining in the construction industry is in need of serious review. ... A vastly enhanced role for national unions and national contractor associations, working as a group, is essential...if the whipsawing and distortions of the past are to be avoided and if the problems of collective bargaining structure, productivity, and manpower development are to be constructively approached....[15]

Specifying his position in the course of questioning, Dunlop—who was also chairman of the Collective Bargaining Committee in Construction, which Ford had established on April 1, 1975 and was charged with facilitating local coordinated and larger area bargaining[16]—testified that "until collective bargaining gives a greater role to national unions and national employer organizations you will not mitigate this tendency of the industry to have an upward rise in wage and benefit levels which is greater than other industries [sic]."[17] A month later Dunlop repeated his statement at parallel Senate hearings.[18]

---

[11]BR, CC, Minutes, Apr. 22, 1975, at 4, in BR, CCH: 1975.

[12]BR, CC, Minutes, June 17, 1975, at 4-5, in BR, CCH: 1975 (Jack Turner).

[13]"Situs Picketing Legislation Faces Some New Obstacles," *ENR*, June 12, 1975, at 8.

[14]Paul Hartman & Walter Franke, "The Changing Bargaining Structure in Construction: Wide-Area and Multicraft Bargaining," 33 (2) *ILRR* 170-84 at 175 (Jan. 1980).

[15]*Equal Treatment of Craft and Industrial Workers: Hearings Before the Subcommittee on Labor-Management Relations of the House Committee on Education and Labor*, 94th Cong., 1st Sess. 11 (1975).

[16]EO 11849, 40 Fed. Reg. 14887 (1975). Blough opined that the CBCC could have gotten a little more authority, "but perhaps the unions wanted it that way." BR, CC, Minutes, Apr. 22, 1975, at 4, in BR, CCH: 1975.

[17]*Equal Treatment of Craft and Industrial Workers* at 37.

[18]*Equal Treatment of Craft and Industrial Workers, 1975: Hearings Before the Subcommittee on Labor of the Senate Committee on Labor and Public Welfare*, 94th Cong., 1st Sess.

The impetus that Dunlop's energetic involvement gave to the new initiative prompted intense and wide-ranging debate at the Roundtable's Construction Committee. On June 17 Blough reported that Dunlop wanted legislation that would both tie down local bargaining in an area to prevent a single contractor from going over the edge and setting a precedent for the whole area and give national union presidents more authority over the locals. Luckenbill of Shell Oil used the opportunity to stress that the Roundtable's position on the Anderson bill in 1972 was still valid: mandatory multi-employer bargaining certification was well conceived, but it created the counterbalancing problem of giving unions a high degree of power. For that reason voluntary action was superior and multicraft bargaining should be confined to reasonably small geographic areas with high-density populations. The basis for the Roundtable's preference for voluntarism soon became evident: when Douglas Soutar warned that Dunlop's objective of legislating the restructuring of collective bargaining in construction would set a precedent that other industries might not want, Blough added: "You're looking at a piece of the new philosophy of national planning; no question about that." The reason for the Roundtable's ambivalence toward more centralized bargaining transcended the issue of government intervention. As Blough and Construction Committee vice chairman Rex Reed (of AT&T) observed, "intense thinking would be required to resolve the dichotomy between desiring greater power for the national leaders of the building trades and strengthening bargaining at the local level."[19] The members then heard D. Quinn Mills, who was invited to attend this meeting, counter the thrust of the discussion by arguing that it was not possible for national unions and contractor organizations to affect local negotiations on a voluntary basis.[20]

At the same meeting the Construction Committee also delved into the common situs picketing question. At this point the Roundtable was so pessimistic that when it heard Peter Cockshaw—the publisher of a construction labor newsletter whom it had invited—declare that the bill had a good chance of passage, Blough asked: "'Then shall we fold our tent?'" Seeing some hope, Cockshaw urged the group to drop everything else to fight the bill. Nor did Cockshaw omit the larger context against which that struggle had to be understood. The establishment by union contractors of nonunion affiliates and the development of strong open-shop competition in areas where it had never been expected prefigured a "tremendous shake up" nationally: "Open-shop work has become too attractive, and offers the user such cost savings, that it cannot be overlooked as an alternative to unionized work." Relativizing this movement, Luckenbill "interposed that there were not yet many

---

8-9 (1975).

[19]BR, CC, Minutes, June 17, 1975, at 3-4, in BR, CCH: 1975. Earlier, too, the Roundtable had supported wide-area, but opposed regional bargaining. BR, CC, Minutes, Oct. 4, 1973, at 12, in BR, 1973-Vol. II: Minutes.

[20]BR, CC, Minutes, June 17, 1975, at 10, in BR, CCH: 1975.

open shop contractors equipped to take on major industrial construction in the northeastern region of the nation."[21]

The Construction Committee resumed its intense discussion of legislative and voluntary approaches to construction labor-management relations at its next meeting on July 15, but members were preoccupied with the situs picketing bill, on which the group formed a task force. The possible spillover of such picketing against non-construction firms prompted several members (such as Goodyear and International Paper) to take action on their own. Pittsburgh Plate Glass, for example, paid for an advertisement in the *Washington Post*.[22]

In response to a request from the House committee, Dunlop submitted language incorporating his suggestion into the common situs picketing bill.[23] At the same time, the subcommittee chairmen having expressed their enthusiasm, Dunlop also transmitted a draft bill that the *Wall Street Journal* touted as bolstering international union leaders' "control over their often rambunctious locals."[24] On the eve of the bill's introduction in September as the Construction Industry Stabilization Act of 1975 (H.R. 9500) and the Construction Industry Collective Bargaining Act of 1975 (S. 2305), *Business Week* wildly exaggerated it as potentially leading to a "voluntary, but permanent incomes policy for the building trades unions," which national union leaders would be willing to accept "in exchange for greater power over their members."[25]

In fact, however, the bill was a very modest initiative creating a mechanism through which "responsible leaders...can meet to discuss" industry problems. As the House Education and Labor Committee report stressed, the bill's "principal force lies in the power of persuasion...." Its limited scope did not encompass nonunion employers, and participation was "essentially voluntary," the only sanction being a 30-day delay of the right to strike or picket; it contained no unfair practices or prohibitions. The bill would have created a tripartite (labor-management-neutral) Construction Industry Collective Bargaining Committee (CICB Committee). Local labor unions would have been required to give notice to their national organizations 60 days before expiration of local collective bargaining agreements; if the CICB Committee took jurisdiction of a dispute, the parties were not permitted to strike or

---

[21]BR, CC, Minutes, June 17, 1975, at 5,7 in BR, CCH: 1975. Cockshaw also stated that Vice President Rockefeller favored enactment of the situs picketing bill.

[22]BR, CC, Minutes, July 15, 1975, at 3-4, in BR, CCH: 1975. On the legal advice that Roundtable received that ambiguities in the bill could trigger shut-downs of user operations, see BR, CC, Minutes, Oct. 21, 1975, at 5-6, in BR, CCH: 1975.

[23]*Equal Treatment of Craft and Industrial Workers, 1975: Hearings Before the Subcommittee on Labor of the Senate Committee on Labor and Public Welfare*, 94th Cong., 1st Sess. 8 (1975).

[24]Walter Mossberg, "Overhaul of Construction Bargaining Is Aim of Bill Labor Agency Is Drafting," *WSJ*, July 25, 1975, at 2.

[25]"Incomes Policy Breakthrough," *BW*, Sept. 8, 1975, at 87.

lockout for 30 days.[26] Once the CICB Committee took jurisdiction, the bill specified that no new collective bargaining agreement between a local union and employer "shall be of any force or effect unless such new agreement...is approved in writing" by the national union.[27] Republican opponents belittled the bill's allegedly principal achievement: national unions, they argued, already had "the power to intervene in local disputes and to veto local settlements through their constitutional prerogatives." That they refrained from exercising that power "is possibly dictated by internal political pressures, which this does nothing to remove."[28]

These Republican skeptics identified a significant political weakness of this approach. Even Dunlop in his congressional testimony conceded this point albeit concealed behind three exceptions: "In general, with the exception of the Electrical Workers, the negotiation and enforcement of collective bargaining agreements and the conduct of strikes (except where strike fund are requested) are carried on by local unions or district councils and local chapters of contractor associations, except where the separate and diverse constitutional powers and procedures of the national unions to intervene may be exercised."[29] And earlier, too, Dunlop had asserted that construction unions "are strongly centralized in the sense that the national union can practically control the local unions within wide limits. The traditions of discipline are well established. The national union may have to authorize any strike to be legal under the constitution; the national may place a local in supervision for violation of policy. There are important exceptions to this generalization even in the most centralized union. Some locals are recalcitrant. Political considerations within the national union may dictate caution on the part of the national officers." Nevertheless, looking back at the experience of government controls during World War II, Dunlop had noted that the "strong centralization of most unions in the

---

[26]H.R. Rep. No. 509: Construction Industry Collective Bargaining Act of 1975, 94th Cong., 1st Sess. 3-5 (1975). Mike Davis, *Prisoners of the American Dream: Politics and Economy in the History of the US Working Class* 133, 134 (1987 [1986]). sensationally but incorrectly described this initiative as a "sweeping settlement" imposing "the sacrifice of the rights of local members to strike...."

[27]H. R. 9500, 94th Cong., 1st Sess. § 5(c) at 7 (Sept. 10, 1975).

[28]H.R. Rep. No. 509: Construction Industry Collective Bargaining Act of 1975, at 12 (minority views of Rep. John Ashbrook).

[29]*Construction Industry Collective Bargaining Act of 1975: Hearings Before the House Committee on Education and Labor,* 94th Cong., 1st Sess. 3 (1975) (statement of John Dunlop). Dunlop's associate and student, Mills, stated in 1972 that most of the international building trades unions had constitutional authority "to approve local strikes (and thus the issues over which strikes may occur), but in many unions such authority can be exercised only when strike benefits are requested." Mills, *Industrial Relations and Manpower in Construction* at 32. In 1979 he noted again that "most of the eighteen international unions have authority in their constitutions to approve local strikes (and thereby the issues over which the strike may occur), but in many the authority exists only when strike benefits are requested." Daniel Quinn Mills, "Labor Relations and Collective Bargaining," in *The Construction Industry: Balance Wheel of the Economy* 59-82 at 68 (Julian Lange & Daniel Quinn Mills eds., 1979).

industry was utilized in the Wage Adjustment Board to require all applications of local unions for wage increases to be submitted through the national union."[30]

In fact, the CICBC reported in 1970 that 13 of 18 national construction unions had authority to approve local strikes, although five of them possessed this power only if locals requested strike funds.[31] Several construction unions had a long tradition of national union control of local strikes.[32] For example, the Brickayers, going back to the nineteenth century, developed such structures "as a protection for contractors whose business operations extended over the entire country. In return for union wages and working conditions, the union "promised that if grievances affecting a national contractor could not be settled locally they should be referred to the international union, work continuing until a decision was given. As a result, [t]he business agent, shop steward, or dissatisfied worker no longer had the power to 'pull the job.'"[33] In the 1970s, the union constitution provided that the executive board "shall have full and complete power over all strikes...."[34]

The IBEW, too, had long insured that locals not engage in strikes too often by using a constitutional procedure: if the executive board did not sustain a strike decision, the local could appeal by seeking approval by two-thirds of the locals, thus making the strike legal and forcing the issue of strike funds; by 1893, the constitution was amended to prohibit locals from soliciting funds from other locals without the executive board's authorization.[35] In the early 1960s, the IBEW's revocation of the charter of a Baltimore local for striking without the international president's approval and in defiance of his repeated orders to return to work was judicially upheld. The Fourth Circuit observed that: "The calling of a strike is such a momentous step in a labor controversy that it is usually subjected to strict control by international unions. The strike is a weapon that can bring the employer to his

---

[30]Dunlop & Hill, *Wage Adjustment Board* at 9-10. In the mid-1950s, a BLS study of the constitutions of 133 national unions revealed that 97 (with 85.5 percent of all union members) either required national organization authorization before locals could strike or made strike benefits dependent on such authorization. "Strike-Control Provisions in Union Constitutions," 77 *MLR* 497-500, tab. 1 at 498 (1954).

[31]"Report of Staff Committee on Improving Collective Bargaining Process in Construction Industry," *CLR*, No. 749, Jan. 28, 1970, at X-1, X-3.

[32]The Electrical Workers and Hod Carriers were exceptions. George Janes, *The Control of Strikes in American Trade Unions* 15-51 (1916). But see Theodore Glocker, *The Government of American Trade Unions* 118 (1913) (stating that strike funds were usually controlled locally in the building trades).

[33]William Haber, *Industrial Relations in the Building Industry* 288 (1930).

[34]Bricklayers, Masons and Plasterers International Union of America, *1972 Constitution and Rules of Order*, art. IV, sect. 2, at 16.

[35]Michael Mulcaire, "The International Brotherhood of Electrical Workers: A Study in Trade Union Structure and Functions" 103-104 (Ph.D. diss., Catholic U., 1923).

knees; but the effect on the employer can be too devastating for the union's own good. ... It is widely felt that vesting control in the international over the strike weapon assures that generally only intelligent and responsible use of it will be made after the greater interests of the international and the general economy have been considered."[36]   The IBEW constitution in the 1970s provided that no local "shall cause or allow a stoppage of work in any controversy of a general nature before obtaining consent of the I[nternational]. P[resident]."[37]

The Sheet Metal Workers' constitution provided that the "authority or consent of the International Association shall not be required for a local union to call a strike following the termination or expiration of a collective bargaining agreement," but two-thirds of the members present at a special meeting had to approve local strikes by secret ballot. With respect to disputes not arising out of a notice to terminate or reopen an agreement, the general president was empowered to order locals and their members to refrain from striking or to return to work "if, in his judgment, such strike or threatened strike" violated an existing collective bargaining agreement or the union constitution. Payment of strike benefits was, moroever, discretionary with the president.[38]   The Operating Engineers constitution stated merely that strike benefits "shall continue for such period of time as in the judgment of the General President may be necessary."[39]

In contrast, the provisions relating to strike and lockout law in the Painters' constitution did not confer any substantive powers on the international.[40]   The Carpenters' constitution required a majority of the affected members to vote for a strike and empowered the general executive board to terminate strike support if it believed that support for the strike had ceased. It also required locals to try to meet with and "bring about an adjustment," while a vague but capacious provision also empowered the general president to "take such action as may be necessary in the interests" of the union after he himself failed to "adjust the trouble by negotiation or arbitration."[41]

In the event, at the September 10th hearing on H.R. 9500 before the House Education and Labor Committee, Secretary Dunlop presented a wide-ranging justification for the need to modify the structure of collective bargaining in construction. The expiration of the Economic Stabilization Act on April 30, 1974,

---

[36]Parks v. IBEW, 314 F.2d 886, 905 (4th Cir. 1963), cert. denied, 372 U.S. 976 (1963).

[37]IBEW, *Constitution*, art. 17, sect. 13, at 63 (1974).

[38]*Constitution & Ritual of the Sheet Metal Workers' International Association*, art. 30, sect. 2(a), at 136 (quotes), sect. 3(b) at 137 (1974).

[39]International Union of Operating Engineers, *Constitution*, art. 19, sect. 3, at 70 (1972).

[40]*Constitution of the International Brotherhood of Painters and Allied Trades* sect. 252-58 at 129-30 (1970).

[41]*Constitution and Laws of the United Brotherhood of Carpenters and Joiners*, sect. 59A, H, I, M, P at 61-64 (1971).

"without provision for an orderly transition to a period without controls," had led, in the context of the Nixon impeachment proceedings, to "disrespect for national leadership," a 60 percent increase in construction strikes from 1973 to 1974, and a recrudescence of "excessive wage and benefit increases." Consequently, in 1974, not only did wage increases in major construction collective bargaining agreements exceed those in manufacturing, but renewed "distortions" in some crafts and localities were "preparing the way for a return to the excessive wage inflation of the late 1960's to the detriment of the industry, its workers and enterprises, and to the country as a whole." The chief defect in the bargaining structure, according to Dunlop, lay in its failure to consider "wider interests in local bargaining, resulting in whipsawing negotiations, distortions of appropriate wage relationships, inefficient manpower utilization, and costly strikes."[42]

Associations of employers operating under union contracts generally supported the legislation. The CCE, an association of 12 national employers' associations, suffering under the coexistence of "leapfrog bargaining," "horrendous unemployment," and the "ever-increasing inability" of union contractors to "obtain work," argued that both labor and capital were structurally incapable of extricating themselves from their self-created dilemma and required state intervention: "Although the majority in both labor and management are aware that economic suicide is being committed, little can be done about it without remedial legislation."[43]

As an association of the country's and world's largest construction firms, operating in national and international markets, the NCA may have lacked standing to press such grievances, but its support for the bill derived from its desire to deal with the "chaotic conditions" caused by the combination of unions' "propensity" to outdo one another's wage demands and their "immense power" in contrast to that of contractors. Whatever glimmer of hope the NCA saw in the bill was rooted in the possibility that it "may provide a basis for the shifting of power from the local level, where such power, in many cases, has been demonstrably abused, to a national level, where a far more responsible application of the power can be expected. With national contractor organizations and international unions injecting themselves into the local negotiations, the process can be expected to be conducted in a far less provincial, self-interested manner." But the NCA was acutely aware of the bill's shortcomings: "A real solution...requires a major infusion of more power into the management side. The ability of the building and construction trades to fragment the power of the contractors, and to strike one contractor while the strikers work for other contractors must be significantly reduced. Contractors

---

[42]*Construction Industry Collective Bargaining Act of 1975: Hearings Before the House Committee on Education and Labor*, 94th Cong., 1st Sess. 4, 5 (1975) (statement of John Dunlop).

[43]*Construction Industry Collective Bargaining Act of 1975: Hearings Before the House Committee on Education and Labor*, 94th Cong., 1st Sess. 47, 49 (1975) (statement of Harry Taylor, president, CCE).

must be permitted to bargain as units and to arrive at their settlements with the unions as one. Only then will a reasonable parity exist in the bargaining power of the two parties, and only then will the industry begin to stabilize."[44]

However, not all employer organizations supported the initiative. The AGC insisted on the insertion of a variety of other provisions that it had unsuccessfully sought to enact during the Nixon administration.[45] The most far-reaching of them would have conferred exclusive bargaining agent status on multiemployer bargaining groups so that all employers of union workers working on like work would have been covered. This measure would have barred employers from continuing to employ workers whose union was striking other members of the multiemployer group. The AGC's goal was to bar interim, national, and project agreements, which "prejudice the ability of the multi-employer bargaining group to reach a reasonable settlement with the union."[46] Nor did Dunlop gain many converts when he told the Roundtable's annual national conference of local user groups in November that the common situs picketing bill's net effect would not be great. He argued that it would simply make union jobs more completely unionized and nonunion jobs more exclusively nonunion.[47]

Among the hostile antiunion reactions to the bill by far the most radical and even bizarrely ideological came from the Chamber of Commerce. In his testimony before the Senate Labor Committee, the chairman of the Chamber's Labor Relations Committee attacked the transfer of power to national unions on the grounds that: "It seems to imply to me that we do not really believe in democracy in the trade union movement, that the local people who are closer to the constituency in the unions, either will not or do not exercise restraint, I would assume because of the pressures of constituency, and therefore we are going to turn it over to national leaders who are less susceptible to the pressures."[48] The image of the Chamber of Commerce as the defender of grassroots union militance, which construction employers, industrial capital, and the state had all been decrying as destroying itself and the economy, may defy belief, but it underscores employers' bind: they saw their profits and macroeconomic stability threatened by the bargaining power associated with democratic control of local unions, but they also feared the consequences that might result from restricting members' legal rights

---

[44]*Construction Industry Collective Bargaining Act of 1975: Hearings Before the House Committee on Education and Labor* at 79-80 (letter of Maurice Mosier, exec. vice president, NCA).

[45]See above chapter 12.

[46]*Construction Industry Collective Bargaining Act of 1975: Hearings Before the House Committee on Education and Labor* at 54-55 (statement of Laurence Rooney, exec. committee, AGC).

[47]*CUH*, Nov. 1975, at 2.

[48]*Construction Industry Collective Bargaining Act of 1975: Hearings Before the Subcommittee on Labor of the Senate Committee on Labor and Public Welfare*, 94th Cong., 1st Sess. 124 (1975) (statement of Robert Thompson).

against union officials.[49] Similarly, the NCA, whose members were the premier firms operating in and creating a national market and collective bargaining, attributed "many of the construction industry's basic problems to the Landrum-Griffin law that...shifted to local unions much of the power previously vested in the parent international unions."[50]

While *Business Week* repeated its assertion about a "voluntary, but permanent, incomes policy" immediately after the bill was introduced,[51] it also reported that even employers' groups supporting the bill expressed disappointment that it failed to mandate the kind of wide area and multicraft coordinated bargaining that Anderson's bill had included in 1971: "These moves would have reduced intraregional wage competition and would have protected contractors against whipsaw tactics by different craft unions."[52] The business and trade press quoted an administration official as perceiving the bill's deepest flaw in its failure to deal with the industry's basic structural bargaining problems:

"You need an approach that gives contractors more power in bargaining.... You have to allow contractors to join together effectively in negotiating and that would take an antitrust exemption. You have to deal with the unions' ability to divide and conquer. You have to prevent situations where a union can strike a contractor and then its members work elsewhere during a strike. It is the feeling of local contractors that this is largely an AFL-CIO-approved bill."[53]

---

[49]Similarly, five years earlier, when the AGC proposed that unions be prohibited from submitting labor agreements to their membership to ratify because frequent rejections forced management to make higher offers, the Roundtable observed that many industrial managers "would prefer to retain this element of union democracy while conceding the occasional hardship the contractors cite." CUAIR, "Report - Legislative Issues" at 3 (n.d. [ca. 1970]), in SP, Box 5, File-CUAIR 1969-1970. Bechtel's current vice president and labor relations manager still expressed skepticism about the AGC's proposal. Telephone interview with Kenneth Hedman, San Francisco (Mar. 12, 1999).

[50]"Single Labor Law Suggested for Construction," *ENR*, July 10, 1975, at 57. D. Q. Mills, "The Construction Industry," 21 *LLJ* 498, 500 (1970), agreed with the NCA that Landrum-Griffin, 29 U.S.C. §§ 401-531, had restrained international unions' use of their power to intervene in local negotiations. As the Roundtable formulated the intra-employer dispute: "A number of observers have concluded that the Landrum-Griffin provision allowing union members to bring suit for damages against their union officials has been a deterrent to more aggressive action by international union officials in restraining irresponsible and disruptive actions by local unions." Nevertheless, "some elements of the industry" did not support a proposal to revise the law to limit the right to sue. BR, "The Impact of Local Union Politics" 7 n.1 (Rep. C-7, Mar. 1993 [June 1982]).

[51]"Dunlop's Attack on 'Leapfrogging,'" *BW*, Sept. 15, 1975, at 28.

[52]"Dunlop's Attack on 'Leapfrogging,'" *BW*, Sept. 15, 1975, at 28; see also "Dunlop Bill Seeks Voluntary Wage Stability," *ENR*, Sept. 11, 1975, at 9, 10. According to *Business Week* the regional bargaining provisions were deleted "because union objections would have prevented quick passage." "Dunlop's Attack on 'Leapfrogging,'" *BW*, Sept. 15, 1975, at 29.

[53]"Dunlop Bill Seeks Voluntary Wage Stability," *ENR*, Sept. 11, 1975, at 10. The same

Although even its chief sponsor conceded that the bill was a modest beginning,[54] the House report clearly stated its ultimate goal: "The national organizations are in effect being conscripted to perform a function that furthers the national labor policy. Their functions will often be to restrain the subordinate bodies and their members. The actions taken might well be politically unpopular."[55] The NCA believed that such actions would be more than merely unpopular. While agreeing that internationals "act more responsibly than the locals," it questioned whether the provision conferring "veto power over out-of-line settlements has real teeth. 'I find it hard to believe that that an international union is going to say 'no' to an agreement that a local union and local contractor have reached.'"[56]

Since construction employers opposed relaxation of the ban on common situs picketing that would have enhanced unions' ability to shut down construction sites[57]—and that would, in *ENR*'s words, have been the greatest threat to the expansion of the open shop[58]—the deal that had been worked out with President Ford entailed enactment of both H.R. 5900 and H.R. 9500. As late as October Virgil Day explained to the Roundtable that it was unrealistic to have great expectations that the bill would fail.[59] Yet even after Congress met Ford's demand by passing a bill that merged both bills and retained Dunlop's language requiring national unions to authorize common situs picketing,[60] employers' opposition to the picketing provision (forcefully backed by Ronald Reagan, Ford's rival for the Republican presidential nomination) prompted Ford to break the deal and veto the bill, unleashing a scathing response from the labor movement and Dunlop's

---

quotation appeared in "Dunlop's Attack on 'Leapfrogging,'" *BW*, Sept. 15, 1975, at 29.

[54]121 Cong. Rec. 32,082 (1975) (Rep. Frank Thompson).

[55]H.R. Rep. No. 509: *Construction Industry Collective Bargaining Act of 1975*, 94th Cong., 1st Sess. 4 (1975).

[56]"Dunlop's Attack on 'Leapfrogging,'" *BW*, Sept. 15, 1975, at 28 (quoting Maurice Mosier, NCA executive vice-president).

[57]The NCA, for example, had opposed an earlier situs picketing bill. *Situs Picketing: Hearings Before the Special Subcommittee on Labor of the House Committee on Education and Labor*, 91st Cong., 1st Sess. 86-87 (1969). Interestingly, District 50 of the United Mine Workers, which had several thousand members in heavy and highway construction, opposed the bill on the same grounds as so-called independent unions—namely, that it would enable the building trades unions to pressure contractors to get rid of them. *Id.* at 85, 133-42 (testimony of Don Mahon, exec. Secretary, National Federation of Independent Unions, and Elwood Moffett, president of District 50).

[58]"50 to 60% of U.S. Construction May Be Open Shop," *ENR*, Sept. 18, 1975, at 41. Nevertheless, *ENR* conceded editorially: "Clearly, building trades' president Robert A. Georgine and the unions he represents have a legitimate complaint against the legal niceties of labor law that let contractors use corporate entities and contractual arrangements as shields against labor disputes they have knowingly invited or created." *ENR*, July 31, 1975, at 56.

[59]BR, CC, Minutes, Oct. 21, 1975, at 6, in BR, CCH: 1975.

[60]H.R. 5900, § 101(c), in H. Rep. No. 697: *Economic Rights of Labor in the Construction Industry*, 94th Cong., 1st Sess. 3 (1975).

resignation. Ford's economic advisers' argument that the proposed wage stabilization provision could be dispensed with "because a depressed market would help keep construction wage increases down" seemed misplaced given the coexistence of 20 percent unemployment and average wage increases of 10 percent in new collective bargaining agreements.[61]

Union firms working with the Roundtable hoped that now that unions had lost common situs picketing, collective bargaining could be strengthened.[62] Unions, however, had not abandoned the issue. And the Roundtable, which began reorganizing opposition to the bill in July 1976 after presidential candidate Carter embraced picketing,[63] resolved to use "the fullest possible resources" to oppose the new bill.[64] The unions' loss of influence by the late 1970s was symbolized by the defeat of the bill, refiled in 1977 after Carter's election, in the House 217-205.[65] The NCA also opposed the bill on the grounds that common situs picketing rights were too high a price to pay for the weak collective bargaining provisions.[66] Republicans still objected to the collective bargaining provisions as ineffective and not giving national unions any powers they did not already possess.[67] Construction unions' lobbying failure was a harbinger of much harsher defeats.

---

[61] 121 Cong. Rec. 42,015-6 (1975); "Too Much Union Power," *BW*, Dec. 8, 1975, at 94 (editorial); Edward Cowan, "9 Labor Leaders Quit Ford Panel," *NYT*, Jan. 9, 1976, at 1, col. 5; "Building Unions Quit Bargaining Panel Set Up by Ford, Warn of Primaries Fight," *WSJ*, Jan. 9, 1976, at 2; "Ford's Veto Sends Labor into a Fury," *BW*, Jan. 12, 1976, at 24-25 (quote). For extended coverage of the veto and its aftermath, see *CLR*, No. 1053, Dec. 31, 1975, at AA-1-10. The vast majority of the mail that Ford received urging a veto resulted from a campaign by the antiunion National Right to Work Committee. A. H. Raskin, "Hard Hats and Their Focal Role," *NYT*, Jan. 4, 1976, sect. 3, at 1, col. 1., at 9, col. 5-6.

[62] BR, CC, Minutes, Jan. 20, 1976, at 3, in BR, CCH: 1976 (Donald Grant of Atkinson Co.).

[63] BR, CC, Minutes, July 20, 1976, at 6, in BR, CCH: 1976.

[64] BR, CC, Minutes, Feb. 15, 1977, at 3, in BR, CCH: 1977.

[65] 123 Cong. Rec. 8713 (1977) (H.R. 4250).

[66] *Equal Treatment of Craft and Industrial Workers, 1977: Hearings Before the Subcommittee on Labor of the Senate Committee on Human Resources*, 95th Cong., 1st Sess. 574-622 (1977) (statement of Maurice Mosier, NCA president). See also Philip Shabecoff, "Picketing the Issue in Construction Fight," *NYT*, Mar. 13, 1977, sect. 3, at 2, col. 3. The *Times* editorially adopted this view: "Stabilized Construction," *NYT*, Sept. 4, 1975, at 34, col. 1; "One Labor Bill...That Should Be Two," *NYT*, Nov. 22, 1975, at 28, col. 2. The *Times* continued to oppose the bill because it would have legalized secondary boycotts: if the unions wished to avoid this constraint, they were free to merge into a single union, thus rendering their picketing permissible primary activity. "An Uncommonly Bad Bill," *NYT*, Mar. 12, 1977, at 22, col. 1.

[67] H. Rep. No. 96: *Equal Treatment of Craft and Industrial Workers*, 95th Cong., 1st Sess. 50 (1977).

15

Unions and the Anti-Union Movement

Programs that are too ambitious (for example, attempts to impose open-shop conditions nationally or in other ways to shift dramatically the locus of power in the industry) will also lead to extensive conflicts, chaos, and, ultimately, very meager results.[1]

This judgment in 1972 by one of the best informed and networked construction industry analysts, who also occupied a central role in state efforts to regulate labor-management relations, underscores how risky social science predictions are. For even as Daniel Quinn Mills was writing this final sentence of his influential book, *Industrial Relations and Manpower in Construction*, antiunion forces were already in the process of successfully "impos[ing] open-shop conditions nationally" and "in other ways...shift[ing] dramatically the locus of power in the industry." In mid-1972 *Business Week* ominously reported that union overreaching had already set in motion a self-destructive downward spiral: the large volume of unemployment partly provoked by high wages had created "a reserve of crafts willing to work 'temporarily' on nonunion projects, usually at union wages but without extras and with fewer benefits. More important for cost savings, they are forgoing the ordinary contractual limits on what and how much a craftsman can do."[2]

Mills's error was not grounded in contemporary ignorance of the prevalence of a menacing nonunion sector. He himself was well aware while writing his book that "a vigorous movement among nonunion contractors had developed and was spreading across the nation from its first foothold in the mid-Atlantic states."[3] Nevertheless, as late as the end of 1975 he called the claim that construction had become 60 percent nonunion was "grossly exaggerated"; he estimated that construction was closer to 80 percent unionized.[4]

---

[1] Daniel Quinn Mills, *Industrial Relations and Manpower in Construction* 282 (1972).

[2] "Open Shops Build Up in Construction," *BW*, July 1, 1972, at 14.

[3] Mills, *Industrial Relations and Manpower in Construction* at 57.

[4] "Troubled Unions: Meaning to Builders, Workers, Home Buyers," *USNWR*, Nov. 24, 1975, at 73 (Lexis). In a recent interview, Mills conceded that neither he nor the unions had fully appreciated the threat before the mid-1970s. He stated that until that time unions did not believe that the open shop was a problem outside of the South and Southeast; they also mistakenly believed both that many of those working in open shops outside the South were in fact union members trying to make a living and that if the threat ever materialized, unions could organize those firms top-down. Although disputes over the size of settlements approved by the CISC from 1971 to 1974 did not involve this issue, Mills recollected that contractors often referred to the open-shop threat, but that unions pooh-poohed the notion. Indeed, the mechanical trades (plumbers, electricians, operating engineers, and sheet metal workers), because their labor market control was greater, did not accept the

Fighting Back or Giving Back?

I feel that over the last twenty years...there have been...an awful lot of people of the same skills who could do the job that the automobile workers do and be delighted to do it, if there was no feeling of class consciousness or unions or anything else, for a lot less than we have been getting our automobiles produced for.[5]

In their history of the Operating Engineers during this period, Mangum and Walsh pointed to the prerequisites of an open-shop breakthrough: qualified contractors willing to operate outside of union structures and able to underbid union firms with an available and sufficient pool of skilled nonunionists. They found that price-sensitive corporate customers formed the market for nonunion firms, unions created the requisite cost advantage by virtue of their large wage increases, while the general and especially construction recessions of the 1970s and 1980s fashioned a work force ready to work without union protections for lower wages. They then identified the chief reasons for the expansion of nonunion construction: the shift of construction from urban union centers to suburbs, exurbs, and the South and Southwest, where unions had always been weaker; unions' failure to make timely concessions; proemployer labor law administration; the increasing domination of what were once union-oriented contractor associations (especially the AGC) by non- and antiunion contractors; and the increased use of double-breasting.[6]

A depressed economy promptly fulfilled the prerequisite of working-class insecurity. By May 1975, when the official unemployment rate among construction workers nationally reached 21.8 percent, the highest rate since the BLS began collecting such data in 1950, "a staggering 50% or more" beset some skilled trades in many big cities.[7] Local unions' willingness, by the mid-1970s, to abandon work

---

reality of the threat until later in the 1970s, whereas the basic trades (carpenters and bricklayers) recognized the danger by the mid-1970s. Although the Roundtable purported to be interested primarily in reducing the cost of construction regardless of the impact on unions, Mills speculated that weakening unions was in its own right also one of the Roundtable's goals. Telephone interview with Daniel Quinn Mills, Harvard Business School (Jan. 4, 1999).

[5]Paul Samuelson, "Discussion," in *The Impact of the Union* 252 (D. McCord Wright ed., 1956 [1951]).

[6]Garth Mangum & John Walsh, *Union Resilience in Troubled Times: The Story of the Operating Engineers, AFL-CIO, 1960-1993*, at 149-64 (1994). For a local case study from an antiunion perspective, see Herbert Northrup, "Arizona Construction Labor: A Case Study of Union Decline," 11 (2) *JLR* 161-79 (Spr. 1990).

[7]*ENR*, June 12, 1975, at 3; James Hyatt, "Construction Workers, Despite Dearth of Jobs, Still Seek Pay Boosts," *WSJ*, Apr. 10, 1975, at 1, col. 6 (quote); Robert Bednarzik, "The Plunge of Employment During the Recent Recession," 98 (12) *MLR* 3-11 at 9 (Dec. 1975); "Georgine Calls Jobless Tally Too Low," *ENR*, Jan. 29, 1976, at 47; BCTD, *1976 National Jobs Conference* 22-25 (1976).

rules, such as organized coffee breaks, to reduce the gap between union and nonunion firms' costs suggested that labor market pressures had begun to make themselves felt.[8] As the president of the Bricklayers, Thomas Murphy, conceded: "'Look, nobody minds when a man has a cup of coffee.... It's when he comes down from the ninth story to have the coffee that we look bad.'"[9] Such acquiescence in the lowering of their standards suddenly qualified as "fighting back...in ways that would have seemed unimaginable" a few years earlier.[10] The president of the Operating Engineers announced to the AGC: "'Hedge-hopping, leapfrogging and this business of a strike a month have got to go.'"[11] The president of the Plumbers declared that only one work rule should prevail: "A man shows up on time, works the full time required and does the job efficiently. If he doesn't, he gets fired."[12] Such comments prompted Edgar Lore, vice chairman of Dravo, to remark at a Roundtable Construction Committee meeting that it was significant that the Plumbers president was "exhibiting genuine concern about the noncompetitiveness of union construction labor."[13] The pressure of unemployment and nonunion expansion prompted one senior BCTD staff person to observe in 1976: "'Five years ago our people were robber barons.... But now all that has changed. We are trying to be reasonable.'"[14] Change, however, did not occur fast enough for the Roundtable, where Lore said bluntly that his greatest disappointment about bargaining in 1976 was that most contractors had not availed themselves of "an opportunity provided by the economic situation and insist[ed] on work-rule changes in new labor agreements."[15]

As the unemployment rate among bricklayers in New York City soared to 80 to 90 percent, their union took wage cuts of 33 percent (from $14.52/hour including fringe benefits) for renovation, rehabilitation, small residential, and shopping center work to meet nonunion competition.[16] In Miami, union plumbers took a two-dollar

---

[8]"A Big Concession on Work Rules," *BW*, Jan. 26, 1976, at 82; "A Healthy Response," *BW*, Jan. 26, 1976, at 104 (editorial). By 1976 coffee breaks had been eliminated from most contracts in Florida. *CUH*, Dec. 1976.

[9]Jerry Flint, "Trade Unions Losing Grip on Construction," *NYT*, Dec. 12, 1977, at 1, col. 3, at 40, col. 4. The current president of the NCA stated that he could tell stories about how workers on the World Trade Center made a good living coming down from the 99th floor. Telephone interview with Robert McCormick, Washington, D.C. (Mar. 9, 1999).

[10]Helen Dewar, "Construction Unions: Backs to a Wall They Helped Build," *WP*, June 19, 1978, at A1 (Lexis).

[11]"AGC Wants Craft Boards and NCA Liaison," *ENR*, Nov. 25, 1976, at 10 (quoting J. C. Turner of the Operating Engineers).

[12]"Troubled Unions: Meaning to Builders, Workers, Home Buyers," *USNWR*, Nov. 24, 1975, at 73 (Lexis).

[13]BR, CC, Minutes, Oct. 19, 1976, at 5, in BR, CCH: 1977.

[14]Lee Dembart, "Building Unions Eye Bargaining Shift," *NYT*, Feb. 14, 1976, at 8, col. 4.

[15]BR, CC, Minutes, Sept. 21, 1976, at 5, in BR, CCH: 1977.

[16]"Union Take Pay Cut," *ENR*, Dec. 18, 1975, at 16; Joseph Fried, "City's Building Industry Faces Still Harder Times," *NYT*, Feb. 15, 1976, at 1, col. 3, at 66, col. 2. Such an accommodation was

an hour pay cut, while carpenters and laborers in St. Louis gave up double-time for overtime for the first time in 70 years.[17] Some employers alleged that such mass unemployment "may make some workers 'psychopathic'" enough to commit sabotage so that work had to be done twice.[18] When 33 percent unemployment among the 60,000 members of the Philadelphia Building & Construction Trades Council prompted unions to take wage cuts (ranging from 6.5 to 34 percent in addition to time and one-half instead of double time for Saturday work) in 1976 in exchange for work rehabilitating abandoned government-owned housing, the anti-union ABC, ironically, complained that the move "'will undercut our people.'"[19] The concessions forced by massive unemployment prompted the *Economist* to call construction workers "fallen aristocrats."[20]

By the end of 1977, with unemployment in bricklayer locals in New York City at 85 percent,[21] the newspaper of record accorded the sea change in construction the status of major national news. Under a front page headline—"Trade Unions Losing Grip on Construction"—*The New York Times* quoted the BCTD's president: "By the thousands, workers 'put their union cards in their pockets or their shoes and go to work nonunion' because that is the only way they can find jobs...."[22] The same day, *Business Week* declared: "The increasing use of nonunion work forces in construction has now reached the point where it is exerting a major downward pressure on labor costs." The combination of high construction unemployment and nonunion competition had finally forced construction wage increases below those in manufacturing: the former fell 10 quarters in a row—from 9.9 percent in the first quarter of 1975 to 6.6 percent in the third quarter of 1977. This relative wage depression made itself felt in another respect: for the first time in recent history, construction could no longer boast of the highest average weekly blue-collar

---

not unprecedented. In 1940, for example, in their drive to organize the residential sector, unions in Philadelphia, Detroit, St. Louis, and Pittsburgh established wage rates between normal urban union rates and nonunion residential construction rates. "The Building Trades," 48 (1) *AF* 26-27 (July 1940). The Bricklayers' campaign to control one-and two-family residential construction in Philadelphia, Washington, D.C., St. Louis, Detroit, Boston, Cincinnati, and Columbus on the eve of World War II was, ironically, driven by the "menacing situation" that arose when members who left the union to work at lower wages in residential construction "provided a possible field" for organizing by the CIO Construction Workers Union. Bates, *Bricklayers' Century of Craftsmanship* at 245.

[17]"The Building Trades Give Some Ground," *BW*, May 16, 1977, at 48.

[18]Priscilla Meyer, "Sabotage on the Rise at Construction Sites in New York City," *WSJ*, Jan. 20, 1976, at 6, col. 3.

[19]"Labor Accepts Less to Win Housing Jobs," *BW*, Aug. 2, 1976, at 23, 24.

[20]"Construction Workers: Fallen Aristocrats," *Economist*, Aug. 28, 1976, at 26.

[21]Jerry Flint, "Bricklayers' Union Fights to Hold Its Share in a Slumping Business," *NYT*, Dec. 4, 1977, sect. 1, at 69, col. 3.

[22]Jerry Flint, "Trade Unions Losing Grip on Construction," *NYT*, Dec. 12, 1977, at 1, col. 3.

earnings.[23]

The depression doubtless induced the president of the Plumbers to appear at a Roundtable meeting to propose a voluntary forum for leading union and contractor officials to monitor collective bargaining and use their prestige to preclude unsound settlements.[24] In 1978, with the unemployment rate among New York City electricians approaching 50 percent, the seniority-based layoff system resulted in many unionists' losing their mortgaged houses as their prolonged unemployment outlasted their unemployment benefits. The IBEW therefore negotiated a work-sharing program requiring the base work force not subject to layoffs to take annual eight-week unpaid furloughs.[25] Yet even at the height of this depression—total new construction put in place, adjusted for inflation, was 23 percent lower in 1975 than in 1973 and 11 percent lower than in 1965, while new construction as a share of GNP fell from 11.8 percent in 1965 to 7.9 percent in 1975[26]—*Business Week* warned that economic recovery "could revive the militancy that is typical of construction unions in tight labor markets."[27]

As "nonunion companies exploited industry downturns that heightened competition for jobs," the BCTD for the first time ever established an organizing arm. Breaking with their top-down tradition of pressuring contractors to hire only union members through the union hiring hall, the unions resolved in the late 1970s to organize workers of nonunion firms.[28] Instead of organizing employers at specific construction sites, unions such as the IBEW began focusing on "control of the labor pool within a local union jurisdiction...by organizing employees individually and thereby controlling the availability of the work force." Where such campaigns were successful, employers were forced either to rely on the union for a supply of workers or to leave the union's jurisdiction.[29]

---

[23]"Open-Shop Construction Picks Up Momentum," *BW*, Dec. 12, 1977, at 108. For the year ending November 1977, average weekly earnings in construction ($307.43) fell behind those in mining ($326.35). *Id.*

[24]*CUH*, Dec. 1977, at 3 (Martin Ward).

[25]*WSJ*, June 6, 1978, at 1, col. 5. Significantly, the IBEW had to strike over the plan because employers had contended that the plan "directly attacks their right to manage their businesses. They say it would create inefficiency by breaking up work forces that the contractors had each trained and built up over the years." Lesley Oelsner, "Electricians' Strike Begins to Hurt at Some New York Building Sites," *NYT*, Apr. 8, 1978, at 27, col. 1 at 2.

[26]Patrick MacAuley, "Economic Trends in the Construction Industry, 1965-80," 27 (5) *CR*, May-June 1981, at 7-18, tab. 1 at 8, tab. 2 at 9.

[27]"The Building Trades Play It Cool—for Now," *BW*, May 17, 1976, at 33.

[28]WSJ, Apr. 11, 1978, at 1, col. 5 (quote); Jerry Flint, "Building Unions Plan Organizing Campaign," *NYT*, Dec. 1, 1977, at A18, col. 1; "Open-Shop Construction Picks Up Momentum," *BW*, Dec. 12, 1977, at 108. On the top-down method, see Garth Mangum, *The Operating Engineers: The Economic History of a Trade Union* 250-51 (1964). On the bottom-up organizing campaign in Las Vegas begun in 1997, which was once again being touted as a break with tradition, see below.

[29]Jane Lewis & Bill Mirand, "Creating an Organizing Culture in Today's Building and

By early 1975, after a decade's warnings and complaints, the normal cyclical workings of the economy had also prompted *ENR* to announce: "Manpower shortages have nearly disappeared."[30] Even at lower wages, nonunion contractors could "attract the highly skilled craftsman if that craftsman has been out of work long enough and his family is suffering."[31] And although the number of strikes continued at a high level in the construction industry, the vast increase in unemployment did affect unions' "ability to involve a large number of workers for a long period of time."[32]

Emblematic of the sea change in labor relations was the special project agreement into which "job-starved" unions in northern Michigan entered in 1976 with the Shell Oil Company for building a small addition to a natural gas processing plant. Three years earlier, when Shell had used nonunion labor to build the plant in a small town, 350 state troopers were brought in to deal with violent mass demonstrations. In 1976, when Shell announced that it would let one union and nonunion prime contractor compete for the job, the unionized firm warned that it could not secure the work unless the unions abandoned all productivity-impeding practices. The result was full freedom for the employer to decide staffing size, elimination of premium time payments for Saturday work scheduled to make up for work lost because of bad weather during the week, and of travel pay and coffee breaks. Yet Dunlop and representatives of employers associations voiced concern that proliferation of such special project agreements with their differing terms in adjoining regions could further destabilize collective bargaining, conferring unfair advantages on certain employers.[33]

Another illustration of depression-driven concessions was a three-year agreement between the North East Florida Building and Construction Trades Council and Davy International, the U.S. subsidiary of a large British international construction firm, which had won the bid for a $200 million Occidental Chemical Company plant. In exchange for providing virtually full employment for a thousand members of seven unions, the employer secured a two-year wage freeze, elimination of double-time for overtime, and reimbursement of travel expenses. But the chief concession was "an iron-clad agreement against a strike," which was replaced by arbitration enforceable by a back-to-work court order. "'This is something we never have liked,'" according to the business agent of the Operating Engineers local. "'The

---

Construction Trades: A Case Study of IBEW Local 46," in *Organizing to Win: New Research on Union Strategies* 297-308 at 300 (Kate Bronfenbrenner et al. eds, 1998). See also Brian Condit et al., "Construction Organizing: A Case Study of Success," in *id.* at 309-19.

[30]"Manpower Shortages Have Nearly Disappeared," *ENR*, Mar. 20, 1975, at 171.

[31]"Open-Shop Construction Picks Up Momentum," *BW*, Dec. 12, 1977, at 108.

[32]David Lipsky & Henry Farber, "The Composition of Strike Activity in the Construction Industry," 29 (3) *ILRR* 388-404 at 401 (Apr. 1976).

[33]A. H. Raskin, "Craft Unions Ease Rules to Obtain Building Work," *NYT*, Aug. 22, 1976, sect. 1, at 26, col. 6.

tried and true method of settling disputes is the withdrawal of the labor supply. This contract eliminates our atomic bomb.'"[34]

The complete reversal of construction market shares was glaringly on display in Houston: in 1977 nonunion firms accounted for almost three-quarters of new industrial construction, whereas a decade earlier union firms had controlled 90 percent of such work.[35] In response to such dramatic deterioration, the national unions by 1976-77 had begun to develop an innovative strategy of negotiating national contracts for all trades in certain branches such as heavy construction, industrial building, and nuclear power plant construction. The point was to standardize terms and conditions such as hours, overtime, and crew sizes in order to "circumvent local work rules...." Such agreements would continue to permit wages to be set locally, but wage increases would be offset by national work standards, thus making union employers more competitive.[36] Nevertheless, in 1979, *Fortune* could gleefully announce that "excessive wage increases," high unemployment, and the vast expansion of the nonunion construction sector had brought on "A Time of Reckoning for the Building Unions."[37] The same year Secretary of Labor Ray Marshall observed that construction workers' hourly wage increases during the previous decade had been 25 percent lower than the average for all workers.[38]

Nevertheless, construction unions retained considerable reserves of strength. For example, in the early 1980s, at the low point of the deepest post-World War II depression, when the union construction sector embraced only 40 percent of the industry or 10 percentage points lower than a decade earlier, *Forbes* declared that the building trades unions "still look invincible": in 1981, for example, their collectively bargained wage increases averaged a "whopping 13.5%" or 4.5 percent more than the all-industry average.[39]

That sphere of invincibility, however, was narrowing. In October 1976, after the open shop movement and unemployment had become more pervasisve, the NCA voted unanimously to eliminate the union shop requirement in its union agreements until the BCTD negotiated a single multicraft industrial construction agreement establishing uniform standards that would replace individual special

---

[34]Douglas Sease, "Construction Unions in Jacksonville, Fla., Strike Novel Accord," *WSJ*, Aug. 28, 1977, at 3, col. 4 at 5.

[35]"Open Shop Construction Keeps Growing Bigger, Getting Stronger," *ENR*, Oct. 27, 1977, at 20-24.

[36]"National Constructors Seek New Industrial Labor Pact," *ENR*, Oct. 21, 1976, at 15-16; "Construction Works to Loosen the Rules," *BW*, Mar. 21, 1977, at 32-33; "Construction Unions, Contractors Agree to Cut Labor Strife at Nuclear Plant Sites," *WSJ*, Apr. 19, 1978, at 14, col. 2.

[37]Gilbert Burck, "A Time of Reckoning for the Building Unions," *Fortune*, June 4, 1979, at 82-96, at 82.

[38]Ray Marshall, "'Uniquely Vulnerable' Construction Workers," *NYT*, May 17, 1979, at 22, col. 1 (letter to editor).

[39]Anne Field, "Hard Hats Soften Up," *Forbes*, Mar. 15, 1982, at 110.

projects agreements. The decision signaled the unions that if they failed to accommodate the large national companies, the latter would "'abandon their union-only policy in favor of an outright open shop position or a "double-breasted" stance....'"[40]

The spread of the nonunion sector became so pervasive by the end of 1976 that, when John Oliver of du Pont, the chairman of the Roundtable's Construction Committee, solicited members' suggestions for the group's 1977 agenda, he received this almost embarrassing response from Shell Oil Company's manager of construction relations:

The rapid growth of merit shop work in some areas (e.g. Florida, Alabama) is making it difficult to stimulate local owner interests in Building Trades activities, and to maintain viable local unionized contractor associations. This can result in unreasonable Building Trades settlements, which will ultimately impact the merit shop work. This is likely to be a growing problem. It is sometimes reflected in conflict between the local user group and local union contractor associations, because the latter feel that the users are interested solely in promoting merit shop activity.[41]

The success of the two-track strategy of strengthening construction firms' bargaining power and eliminating collective bargaining altogether was nicely captured by the director of the Cleveland construction employers association. As he told the Roundtable's national conference of local user group in 1977: in the Midwest a "more effective factor in moderating construction labor settlements than user groups and the Business Roundtable is the growth of open shop competition with unionized construction."[42]

By the end of 1977, the BCTD realized that even under the Carter administration no common situs picketing relief would be forthcoming from Congress. At the same time, as major labor law reform legislation passed the House and moved to the Senate, where a majority would have voted for it if an employer-backed filibuster had been broken, the NAM announced the creation of the Council on a Union-Free Environment.[43] President Georgine then declared at the BCTD convention that it would directly confront the nonunion movement, which, in conjunction with the enormous pool of unemployed, had caused significant defections by members.[44] The BCTD "decided that it was time to wage

---

[40]"NCA Votes to Lift Union Shop Clause," *CLR*, No. 1097, Nov. 3, 1976, at A-12, A-13.

[41]Letter from W. A. Gabig to John Oliver (Dec. 3, 1976), in BR, 1977 CCH, File: Miscellaneous.

[42]*CUH*, June 1977, at 3 (Norman Prusa).

[43]D. Quinn Mills, "Flawed Victory in Labor Law Reform," *HBR*, May-June 1979, at 92 (Lexis).

[44]"Building Trades Launch Organizing Drive to Combat Expanding Open Shop," *CLR*, No.

an all-out war against the growth of the open shop"—by which it meant that it would finally embark on the organizing in which unions in other industries had always engaged.[45] The fact that the "once sacred power generating stations, including large nuclear plants, are being awarded to Brown and Root, to Daniels, to Zachary [sic], and others, with little or no hesitation by clients who only a few years ago would never have considered such a practice" must have contributed to impelling the building trades unions to this unprecedented step.[46] Amusingly, the AGC—about one-half of whose members were engaged in nonunion operation[47]—denounced the announcement as a move to "'crush rather than compete with'" the nonunion sector.[48]

Reeling from "one of the most devastating blows" that building trades unions had ever suffered, Carpenters president Sidell recalled that in 1974 organizing had focused on residential construction, whereas in 1978 "we are concerned with open shop conditions in every segment of our construction jurisdiction in practically every area of the United States and Canada.... The battle lines have been drawn and we must now decide whether we will procrastinate or...launch the counteroffensive necessary to turn back the open shop threats that this day jeopardizes [sic] our very existence."[49] The Carpenters had always been "an advocate of the free enterprise system," but: "There seems to be developing a form of class warfare in our continent. Business, management or capital...is not content to play their traditional role. ... They...will not be happy until they achieve their goal of a 'union free environment.' This is not a slogan nor an idle threat—it is their goal—to destroy the labor movement...."[50]

The year 1978 also saw presidents of half of the construction unions sign

---

1153, Dec. 7, 1977, at A-17, A-18. See also "President Robert A. Georgine's Keynote Address to Building and Construction Trades Department Convention," *ibid.*, at D-1.

[45]*Proceedings of the Thirty-Third General Convention of the United Brotherhood of Carpenters and Joiners of America* 409-10 (1978) (address of Robert Georgine, president, BCTD). The building trades' new bottom-up organizing, if it was correctly depicted, may have been both an unlawful labor practice and almost optimally designed to alienate nonunion workers. The IBEW organizing director was quoted as saying that open-shop workers would have to be recruited like those of old: "'If they didn't want to be union we intimidated them and coerced them and put a union card in their back pocket.'" "Trades to Organize in Atlanta," *ENR*, Nov. 24, 1983, at 62 (quoting Michael Lucas).

[46]*Proceedings of the Thirty-Third General Convention of the United Brotherhood of Carpenters and Joiners of America* 412 (1978) (address of Robert Georgine, president, BCTD).

[47]*CUH*, June 1978, at 3.

[48]"AGC, ABC Rap Building Trades' Organizing Campaign to Combat Open Shop Competition," *CLR*, No. 1154, Dec. 14, 1977, at A-19, A-20.

[49]*Proceedings of the Thirty-Third General Convention of the United Brotherhood of Carpenters and Joiners of America* 28, 29 (1978).

[50]*Proceedings of the Thirty-Third General Convention of the United Brotherhood of Carpenters and Joiners of America* 29 (1978).

the AGC Basic Trades Collective Bargaining Impasse Settlement Plan, which privately implemented part of Dunlop's 1975 antistrike bill. Under the plan, local bargainers notified their national organization of an impasse 15-20 days before the contract's expiration; if the local rejected the international's recommendations, the local was to refrain from striking until the international met with local bargaining committees.[51] Such accommodation throws into relief Georgine's later rhetorical blast: "'the real purpose of the Roundtable is to destroy local unions and take away the gains they have made through the collective bargaining process.'"[52]

Against the backdrop of the vast gains made by the nonunion sector and NCA's changed by-laws permitting members to open nonunion subsidiaries, the NCA in May 1978 finally achieved the single multicraft national agreement that it had been seeking since 1963, which was to supersede various special project and single-craft national agreements. Members' nonunion subsidiaries were not covered by the agreement unless they became union shops and signed the agreement.[53] The agreement, which initially covered eleven southern states and eight unions, declared overtime undesirable and not to be worked outside of unusual circumstances, reduced the scope of supra-statutory premium overtime rates, prohibited all strikes and slow downs arising out of jurisdictional disputes, eliminated travel expenses and time, prohibited all rest periods, organized coffee breaks, and other nonworking time, and entitled the employer to "utilize the most efficient methods or techniques of construction, tools or other labor-saving devices...." The agreement also prohibited all strikes, picketing, honoring of picket lines, and lockouts—with one exception: in the case of an area strike over renegotiation of the local collective bargaining agreement, it permitted the union to refuse to refer workers and the employer to shut down the project, thus achieving the Roundtable's long sought-after goal of enabling national contractors to support local contractors by not hiring their striking workers. To be sure, NCA members may not always have been grateful for the right to lockout on behalf of local contractors: at one nuclear power plant project in Washington State in 1976, a long strike-lockout, which was settled on the union's terms, cost the NCA members millions of dollars. Perhaps most importantly with regard to meeting nonunion competition, it permitted one-third of a craft work force to consist of apprentices and subjourneymen paid 60 percent of the journeyman wage.[54]

---

[51]"A New Plan for Resolving Bargaining Impasses," *ENR*, Dec. 14, 1978, at 76.

[52]"Business Roundtable: New Lobbying Force," 35 (38) *CQ* 1964-67 at 1964 (Sept. 17, 1977).

[53]"NCA and Labor Wrap Up New Kind of Labor Pact," *ENR*, May 25, 1978, at 8-9.

[54]For the text, see "National Industrial Construction Agreement," *CLR*, No. 1176, May 24, 1978, at C-1-C-8, which inexplicably omitted the text of the provision on subjourneymen, which, however, was reprinted in BR, "Subjourneymen in Union Construction" 25 (Rep. D-1, Nov. 1992 [Feb. 1982]); see also "Union Firms to Fight Open Shop," *ENR*, Nov. 26, 1981, at 31. By 1981, the

The trend toward regional collective bargaining was underscored by the NCA's decision in 1979 to admit to membership unionized firms performing smaller-scale regional industrial construction. If, as some observers believed, the open shop movement had brought about a deterioration in local bargaining—which by the end of the 1970s had ceased in several states and trades[55]—admission of regional contractors might enable the NCA to push more vigorously for regional bargaining. This shift reflected the sea change that the growth of the nonunion sector had brought about in a few years: in 1968, the NCA president had rejected regional bargaining as a solution to labor-management problems on the grounds that it would require "a vast, nationwide unscrambling and restructuring of our industry's collective bargaining forms and patterns." A decade later, when a new structure had already imposed itself on the industry, homilies about the efficacy of "restraint" had obviously lost their plausibility.[56] A reported spread of wide-area bargaining by 1980, at least in the Midwest, coupled with elimination of post-negotiation ratification by the membership, may have created the basis for the removal of decisionmaking from the rank-and-file for which capital, the state, and some national union leaders had hoped from the beginning.[57]

The defeat of Labor Law Reform in Congress in 1978—against which the Roundtable mobilized significant resources[58]—which would have imposed a modest deterrent on employers who violated workers' rights under the NLRA and made organizing somewhat less burdensome, registered an epochal decline in unions' capacity to effectuate their relatively narrow national legislative agenda. In the wake of employers' defensive victory, the AFL-CIO began to perceive corporations as having returned to the age of class warfare.[59] To this real class struggle the

NICA had been extended to four Rocky Mountain states, but to no unions other than the original eight—the plumbers, carpenters, operating engineers, ironworkers, laborers, asbestos workers, boiler makers, and cement masons. At expiration in 1985, it covered 10 unions and 27 states. "NCA Industrial Pact Expires," *ENR*, May 2, 1985, at 50. On the Washington lockout, see Mills, "Chapter 2: Construction" at II-31-32.

[55]"Man of the Year: H. Edgar Lore: Moving an Industry Toward Unity," *ENR*, Feb. 15, 1979, at 34-40 at 37 (mentioning the Carolinas, Vermont, and parts of New Mexico, Georgia, Texas, and Florida).

[56]"NCA Asks Labor to Shape Up," *ENR*, Oct. 24, 1968, at 81.

[57]Paul Hartman & Walter Franke, "The Changing Bargaining Structure in Construction: Wide-Area and Multicraft Bargaining," 33 (2) *ILRR* 170-84 (Jan. 1980). The AGC, which supported local bargaining, feared the multitrade national industrial agreement that the NCA sought to achieve. "AGC Takes the Offensive on Many Fronts," *ENR*, Oct. 21, 1976, at 59. The BCTD began advocating such national agreements in preference to ad hoc project agreements, which they perceived as undercutting local contracts, yet 20 years later they still abounded. "BCTD Issues Project Labor Agreement Language," *LRR*, June 2, 1997, at 151.

[58]*CUH*, Sept. 1977.

[59]Thomas Ferguson & Joel Rogers, "Labor Law Reform and Its Enemies," *Nation*, Jan. 6-14, 1979, at 19-20; Barbara Townley, *Labour Law Reform in US Industrial Relations* (1986); James

BCTD responded with rhetorical class warfare. Georgine, who spoke of a "'terrible conspiracy'" as early as 1972,[60] accused the Roundtable of seeking the "'total annihilation' of organized labor."[61] Denouncing the Roundtable's "'master strategy,'"[62] the BCTD issued a special report in 1979 highlighting the union busting activities activities of the Business Roundtable, which it charged with executing the plan, laid out more than a decade earlier, "to destroy the 17 building trades unions" and "to slash the wages of union carpenters, plumbers and electricians."[63] Chief among the Roundtable's tactics was prevailing on local user groups to "push union contractors to be unreasonable in contract negotiations"; it also urged project owners to restrict additional hiring or to discontinue work to prevent striking unions from strengthening their bargaining position by sending their striking members out to work on nonstruck projects.[64] The attack on this latter tactic seemed especially incongruous: as early as 1973, in order to remove one of local contractors' central objections to national agreements, construction unions had entered into a national agreement with the NCA that entitled both the union and the employer to stop work in the face of a local economic strike, thus enabling NCA members to support struck local contractors. Back then, unions touted the provision as designed to "promote smooth labor relations...."[65]

By 1981, the NCA reported that the oil and chemical industries were using nonunion firms 40 to 50 percent of the time, while the paper industry was building 70 to 80 percent of its new mills with nonunion workers. The president of the AGC warned the BCTD's convention that year that unless unions eased their work rules, within a decade practically all construction would be nonunion and "reorganized on an industrial basis." The corporate antiunionists became so self-confident that Charles D. Brown, du Pont's construction director, boasted: "'We prefer the open-shop culture, where a contractor is limited only by his ability to manage and the initiative of his craftsmen....'" But he also allowed as "if unions 'clean up their act where we are still building union, then we might think about using them on new

---

Gross, *Broken Promise: The Subversion of U.S. Labor Relations Policy, 1947-1994*, at 236-39 (1995).

[60]Haynes and Kotz, *Unions* at 138.

[61]"Unions Say Roundtable Seeks to Destroy Labor," *ENR*, Sept. 6, 1979, at 62.

[62]"Building Trades Declare War As They Fight for Survival," *ENR*, Oct. 18, 1979, at 66.

[63]BCTD, "Special Report: The Builders," *reprinted in CLR*, No. 1243, Sept. 12, 1979, at D-1-D-8, at D-2. For later attacks of a similar nature, see "The Roundtable Is Hit Again," *ENR*, May 1, 1980, at 67 (Operating Engineers' president accuses Roundtableof "blackmailing" unions and union firms into lower wage settlements).

[64]BCTD, "Special Report: The Builders," *reprinted in CLR*, No. 1243, Sept. 12, 1979, at D-4.

[65]"New Work Rules Contract Designed to Make Smooth Labor Relations, Make Union Employers More Competitive," 27 (12) *Laborer* 2, 3 (Dec. 1973).

jobs.'"[66] Even in the Far West, long a citadel of unionism, John F. O'Connell, former Bechtel labor relations manager and president and NCA president, told the Roundtable, if trends continued, in five years "no contractor would be able to stay in business...unless he has access to the open shop alternative."[67]

Depression-level unemployment rates in 1982-83—rising in excess of 90 percent for occupations such as bricklayers in parts of Alabama, Illinois, and New York—put an end to wage settlements that in *Business Week*'s words had "defied logic...."[68] The Roundtable declared that freezes and rollbacks in more than one-third of collective bargaining agreements in 1983 had reduced the overall increase in construction wages to its lowest level in 20 years, while the first half of 1984 saw an aggregate decrease of 45 cents per hour.[69] In connection with these depression-induced wage reverses, Charles Brown told his fellow members on the Roundtable Construction Committee: "Maybe we should wash our mouths out with soap when we talk about wage increases. ... The stage is now set and the marketplace will determine what happens."[70]

How far unions had backtracked from their outbursts of rhetorical class struggle became clear at a 1982 meeting that explored ways of halting the decline of union construction. Organized by the AGC, the National Conference on Union Construction heard Georgine signal the demise of construction union militance by conceding that strikes were "'the most ridiculous thing that exists on a construction site today,'" for which there was "'absolutely no justification.'"[71]

Also attending was Charles Brown, who represented the Business Roundtable. As general manager of du Pont's engineering department he had carried through on threats to cancel contracts with union firms whose employees refused to work on sites where nonunion firms also operated (which ousting Brown jocularly called "'market recovery in reverse'").[72] As chairman of the Roundtable's construction committee task force, he led its Construction Industry Cost Effectiveness Project (CICEP)—which had been sparked by concerns that allegedly declining productivity and above-average rising costs in construction had caused users to become less competitive because they replaced facilities less quickly than

---

[66]"Building Trades Lose Ground," *BW*, Nov. 9, 1981, at 103 (Lexis). The AGC president was Thomas Dailey.

[67]BR, CC, Minutes, Feb. 19, 1980, at 3, in BR, Minutes.

[68]"Construction Contracts are Yielding to Reality," *BW*, June 28, 1982, at 45 (Lexis). On the previous extent of such hazard pay provisions, see BLS, *Contract Clauses in Construction Agreements, 1972-73*, tab. 75 at 44 (Bull. 1819, 1974); BLS, *Contract Clauses in Construction Agreements* 40 (Bull. 1864, 1975).

[69]*CUH*, Jan. 1984; *CUH*, June 1984.

[70]BR, CC, Minutes, Jan. 18, 1983, at 4, in BR, CCH: 1983.

[71]"Union Sector Weighs Its Future," *ENR*, Aug. 26, 1982, at 118.

[72]BR, CC, Minutes, Jan. 18, 1983, at 5-6 (Brown), in BR, Minutes.

they should have[73]—many of whose 223 recommendations were designed to eliminate union inroads into management prerogatives. In 1977, the Construction Committee decided to undertake a "major, long-term study" of the industry; it was entrusted to a task force, which was at first chaired by Dow Chemical's construction manager, Jack Turner, and then by Brown. The CICEP involved more than 250 people and published two dozen reports, of which the Roundtable distributed two million free copies.[74] These achievements prompted *ENR* to name Brown Construction Man of the Year in 1983. The Roundtable was able to create a huge audience for its plans for revamping construction by distributing two million free copies of the various CICEP reports.[75]

In 1985 the Roundtable could report to its members that Georgine had told the annual BCTD convention that the U.S. loss of world market dominance, by making construction costs an important economic factor, had "driven owners into the arms of the nonunion contractor."[76] By the 1980s, many of the project's 223 recommendations formed the basis of the working conditions concessions that the construction unions had been forced to yield.

After a delay in securing a new agreement and doubts about its scope and effectiveness contributed to a decline in NCA membership from 55 in 1982 to 32 in 1987, the NCA reached its most comprehensive National Construction Stabilization Agreement (NCSA) ever with the BCTD in 1987, two years after the previous one had expired.[77] Covering all 15 construction unions and the Teamsters, it contained not only by then familar provisions eliminating coffee breaks and premium overtime, but also a no-strike prohibition enforcible by liquidated damages of $10,000 per shift.[78] The NCA's Labor Relations Committee concluded in 1991 that the NCSA had helped in "keeping non-union firms out of pro-union

---

[73]"Roundtable Tackles Construction Cost Effectiveness," *ENR*, Dec. 20, 1979, at 179. Brown told union leaders that "'unreasonably high'" construction costs were "choking off modernization and expansion, and pricing owners' products out of the market...." *CUH*, Jan. 1983, at 1.

[74]BR, "Chapter 2" at 12-16.

[75]"Industry Study Moves to Operational Phase," *ENR*, Dec. 16, 1982, at 132; "Man of the Year: Charles Brown," *ENR*, Feb. 10, 1983, at 52 (Lexis); Robert Jortberg & Thomas Haggard, *CII: The First Ten Years* 12 (1993) (2 million copies). Erlich, *With Our Hands* at 160, argued that: "On a day-to-day basis...every national union has accepted the Roundtable framework."

[76]*CUH*, Sept. 1985.

[77]"NCA Industrial Pact Expires," *ENR*, May 2, 1985, at 50. By 1999, membership had shrunk to ten. Telephone interview with NCA president Robert McCormick, Washington, D.C. (Mar. 9, 1999).

[78]"Peter Waldman, "Construction Industry Group, Labor Set Pact to Cut Job Losses to Nonunion Crews," *WSJ*, Feb. 18, 1987 (Westlaw); Jay Kraker, "NCA, Building Trades Set Model Project Pact," *ENR*, Feb. 26, 1987, at 50. Enforcement under the NCSA is illustrated by an incipient walk-off by Ironworkers at a Boeing construction project in Washington State: "the potential $10,000 per shift penalty brought an immediate halt to the action." NCA, *Bulletin*, #92-36 at 2 (Apr. 17, 1992).

areas," but had not penetrated the South or other nonunion areas.[79] Nevertheless, according to the NCA president, the agreement has essentially eliminated all significant grounds for employers' complaints especially in conjunction with the virtual disappearance of strikes.   And despite their advances in industrial construction, nonunion firms failed to penetrate the multibillion dollar power plant and infrastructure megaprojects.[80]

At the same time, it was reported from Los Angeles that unions were "desperately trying to stave off an onslaught" of nonunion contractors paying wages and benefits "substantially below union scale." Key to this development was an invasion by large national open-shop commercial and industrial construction firms such as Brown & Root, Daniel International, and Becon Construction (Bechtel's nonunion subsidiary). And undergirding the whole displacement process was a "general reduction in the skill level required.... Merit-shop contractors say that they can underbid their union competition by paying wages that are close to the union scale to a few key workers, who oversee many other workers who have lesser skills and are lower paid." This phenomenon of "cut-throat competition" unleashed repeated cycles of lower wages and lower profits in an effort to become the low bidder. As a result, whereas originally firms could increase their profitability "by going non-union and bidding against union firms," once most competitors were also nonunion, a typical firm's "profit margin is no better than when the industry was an all-union operation."[81]

By 1990 construction unions' efforts to cooperate with management to regain market share had matured to the point that strikes, *ENR* gloated, had become "so few that the Bureau of Labor Statistics no longer counts them."[82] The Reagan administration had in fact cut back on the collection and publication of strike data, but the BLS did continue to keep track of the dwindling volume of strikes. All strike indicators fell sharply following 1974 as "increasing competition from nonunion firms" made militance much riskier.[83] From 1984 to 1988, when the BLS tracked only strikes involving 1,000 or more workers, no year witnessed more than seven such construction strikes or 20,000 strikers participating in them; construction during those years never accounted for more than 6 percent of such strikers or 4 percent of striker-days.[84] To be sure, aggregate strike activity trended

---

[79]NCA, *Bulletin* #92-36, at 2 (Apr. 17, 1992).

[80]Telephone interview with Robert McCormick, Washington, D.C. (Mar. 9, and 11, 1999).

[81]Leslie Berkman, "Construction Unions Try to Stem Job Losses," *LAT*, Mar. 16, 1986, pt. 4 at 1, col. 1 (Lexis).

[82]Hazel Bradford, "Toning Up Union Muscle," *ENR*, Apr. 26, 1990, at 36.

[83]BLS, *Analysis of Work Stoppages, 1978*, at 4 (Bull. 2066, 1980).

[84]Calculated according to BLS, *Handbook of Labor Statistics*, tab. 141 at 544-45 (Bull. 2340, 1989). See also "Industry Saw Far Fewer Strikes in 1988," *ENR*, Mar. 2, 1989, at 5. The more comprehensive time-series presented in tables 16a and 16b were discontinued after 1981 and replaced

toward and reached record lows in the 1980s and 1990s, but construction workers' quiescence was even more pronounced.[85] From 1984 to 1997, when the BLS classified work stoppages involving 5,000 or more workers as "major," only four construction strikes (one each in 1984, 1989, 1991, and 1996) reached this threshold; during 10 of these 14 years none did.[86] Between 1993 and 1997, the eight construction strikes involving 1,000 or more strikers accounted for only 5 percent of all such strikes; in turn, the 22,900 participating strikers accounted for only 2 percent of all strikers and 1 percent of striker-days.[87]

The Roundtable's enduring political-economic impact made itself evident at the end of the century in its capacity to shape union leaders' action framework. Attending the Roundtable's annual national construction conference in 1998, the Carpenters' new young president blamed his own and the other building trades unions for their decline: "'We thought we could be exclusive [and] kept people out of the union, but not out of the trade,'" said Douglas McCarron, but "'[f]air competition drives you to be better [and] there is no doubt that the Business Roundtable put a competitive edge back in the industry.'"[88]

---

by a series tracking only strikes involving 1,000 or more workers. In 1982, construction accounted for 39 percent of such strikes, 14 percent of the strikers, and 7 percent of striker-days. BLS, *Handbook of Labor Statistics* tab. 124 at 410 (Bull. 2217, 1985). By 1985, however, only 1,800 construction workers took part in one such strike.

[85]In 1997, only 29 strikes involving 1,000 or more workers were recorded compared to 424 in 1974; only 4,497,000 striker-days, accounting for 0.01 percent of all working time, were reported in 1997 compared to 52,761,000 and 0.29 percent in 1970. "Major Work Stoppages, 1997," BLS, *News* (USDL 98-57, Feb. 12, 1998). In the years after tables 16a and 16b end, construction strikes, strikers, and striker-days as a proportion of all strikes, strikers, and striker-days dropped to record or near-record lows. BLS, *Handbook of Labor Statistics*, tab. 132 at 401-404 (Bull. 2175, 1983).

[86]In 1996, 6,500 bricklayers in Chicago struck for a week; in 1991, 7,100 Philadelphia carpenters struck for three days; in 1989, 12,000 operating engineers struck for five days in Ohio; in 1984, 10,000 laborers struck for 10 days in Illinois. In 1986, the threshold was set at 10,000 workers; two Teamsters strikes in construction have been omitted. "Major Work Stoppages in 1984," 37 (3) *CWD* 41-43 (Mar. 1985); "Major Work Stoppages, 1985," BLS, *News* (USDL 86-74, Feb. 26, 1986); "Major Work Stoppages, 1986," 39 (3) *CWD* 27-29 (Mar. 1987); "Major Work Stoppages in 1987," 40 (3) *CWD* 35-37 (Mar. 1988); "Major Work Stoppages, 1988," BLS, *News* (USDL 89-80, Feb. 23, 1989); "Major Work Stoppages, 1989," BLS, *News* USDL 90-81, Feb. 16, 1990); "Major Work Stoppages, 1990," 43 (3) *CWD* 34-36 (Mar. 1991); "Major Work Stoppages, 1991," BLS, *News* (USDL 92-53, Feb. 4, 1992); "Major Work Stoppages, 1992," BLS, *News* (USDL 93-36, Feb. 3, 1993); "Major Work Stoppages, 1993," BLS, *News* (USDL 94-69, Feb. 10, 1994); "Major Work Stoppages, 1994," BLS, *News* (USDL 95-25, Jan. 27, 1995); Michael Cimini, "Major Work Stoppages in 1995," 48 (2-3) *CWC* 150-54 at 152 (Feb.-Mar. 1996); "Major Work Stoppages, 1996," BLS, *News* (USDL 97-44, Feb. 12, 1997); "Major Work Stoppages, 1997," BLS, *News* (USDL 98-57, Feb. 12, 1998).

[87]Calculated according to unpublished annual compilations by BLS of individual strikes (faxed to author Dec. 29, 1998). BLS resumed these annual compilations for internal purposes in 1993. Telephone interview with Fehmida Sleemi, BLS, Washington, D.C. (Dec. 29, 1998).

[88]William Krizan, "Roundtable Listens to Unions," *ENR*, Nov. 23, 1998, at 13 (Westlaw).

Employers and union officials continued in the 1980s to blame local democracy for the market-induced decline of unionism. *ENR* quoted contractors and even union journeymen as stating that a "'radical minority' controls many votes, often preventing moderation in contract terms," while a plumbers' business agent added: "'Do you see successful businesses operating this way, with branch offices that don't have to listen to the parent company?'" With ignorance added to autonomy and radical democracy, no wonder that plumbers failed to understand that the labor market's limit was lower than the sky: "some members don't even understand that contractors have to be the low bidder to get jobs."[89] Decentralized local autonomy vis-à-vis international union bureaucracies, when paired with internal democracy and skilled workers' ability to resist employer overreaching, encouraged an alliance of construction firms, corporate customers, government economic managers, and national construction union leadership to reduce construction workers' scope for interfering with all these other actors' plans.[90]

By the late 1990s, employers' collective bargaining complaints and proposals of the 1960s and 1970s had been stood on their head: national construction union leaders, arguing that locals, bereft of regional coordination, were being "splintered...whipsawed by region wide employers," systematically consolidated them into regional councils, which then coordinate all collective bargaining.[91]   Ironically, this initiative prompted the proemployer Republican chairman of the House Subcommittee on Employer-Employee Relations to assert that the locals' loss of control over collective bargaining necessitated amendments to the Landrum-Griffin Act.[92]   Taking as his point of departure that the "labor movement derives its strength from democracy and unions lacking democracy at the intermediate and local level cannot serve in full measure their economic, social, and political function in a democratic society," Representative Harris Fawell introduced a bill in 1998 requiring that intermediate union bodies engaged in collective bargaining be elected by secret ballot by the members.[93]

Typical of the steps that unions have taken to make themselves and their employers "more competitive" is the Market Recovery Program for Union Construction that the BCTD and the National Construction Employers Council

---

[89]"Union Construction in Trouble," *ENR*, Nov. 5, 1981, at 26 (Lexis).

[90]For an insider's account of local autonomy and democracy, see Robert Cook, "Work in the Construction Industry: A Report from the Field," in 2 *Research in Social Problems and Public Policy* 207-41 at 213-14 (1982).

[91]Hearing on "Impediments to Union Democracy," Pt. II: "Right to Vote in the Carpenters Union?" Hearings Before the Subcommittee on Employer-Employee Relations of the House Committee on Education and the Workforce, 105th Cong., 2d Sess. (June 25, 1998) (Westlaw) (statement of Douglas McCarron, general president., United Brotherhood of Carpenters).

[92]144 Cong. Rec., Oct. 13, 1998, at E2108.

[93]H. R. 4770, §§ 2, 5, 105th Cong., 2d Sess. (1998).

(consisting of the AGC, NCA, and ten subcontractors' organizations) developed in 1982-83 to create a "new relationship...to something more appropriate for the construction industry of today and tomorrow."[94] Against the backdrop of the drastic decline in union workers and contractors since 1971, but also deflecting criticism that the program was designed to cut wages, the organizations contended that union contractors did not always demand lower wages as part of their wishlist of "necessary adjustments." Instead: "Working conditions such as organized breaks, travel time and overtime appear to be the key to competitiveness." Wages were cut only where "the deterioration of union construction had been allowed to progress until it no longer dominates the local market" and sheer union survival required wage reductions.[95] As the Roundtable industrial customers, "in a quest for lower building costs, awarded more jobs to nonunion contractors," the *Wall Street Journal* reported, the union sector shrank and "cutthroat competition among such firms drove down wages."[96] The overall success of this accommodationist approach was reflected in the fact that the 1984 and 1985 collective bargaining years produced the lowest average wage increases in 40 years, which were attributed to the Market Recovery Program and the pressure of increased use of subjourneymen.[97]

Inexplicably, the introduction of subjourneymen, which as a symbol of everything allegedly progressive about nonunion construction was perched at the top of the list of critical recommendations made by the contractor committee of the CICEP,[98] nevertheless found little favor with the union contractors that had fought for it. The Roundtable asserted in its 1982 CICEP report devoted to this subject: "The major economic advantage enjoyed by open-shop contractors is the ability to use a high percentage of semiskilled workmen, paid accordingly. This not only brings lower labor costs, but also creates a source of manpower to train into experienced journeymen." In nonunion firms typically 40 percent or more of craft workers are helpers.[99] Remarkably, although the NCA secured in its National Industrial Construction Agreement a provision permitting members to hire a work force consisting of as many as one-third subjourneymen paid only 60 percent of the journeyman wage, it was among the least used provisions because employers found

---

[94]BCTD, "Market Recovery Guidebook for Union Construction" 1 (1985). As early as 1980, Blough spoke of a persistent feeling that if the NCEC failed to remain viable, restructuring of collective bargaining by legislative fiat might become the order of the day again. BR, CC, Minutes, Dec. 9, 1980, at 3, in BR, CCH: 1980.

[95]BCTD, "Market Recovery Guidebook for Union Construction" at 6.

[96]Robert Tomsho, "Labor Squeeze: With Housing Strong, Builders Often Find Skilled Help Lacking," *WSJ*, Jan. 27, 1994, at A1 (Westlaw).

[97]"Wage Hikes Hit Rock Bottom," *ENR*, Jan. 10, 1985, at 60; "Wage Hikes Stall at 1.6% in '85," *ENR*, Jan. 9, 1986, at 52.

[98]"Industry Study Moves to Operational Phase," *ENR*, Dec. 16, 1982, at 132.

[99]Business Roundtable, "Subjourneymen in Union Construction" 4 (quote), 6 (Rep. D-1, Nov. 1992 [Feb. 1982]).

it "'easier to just call the hiring hall and get so many journeymen....'"[100] Nevertheless, the mere fact that unions yielded on the issue of subjourneymen so soon after Georgine had declared categorically that "'the argument that there should be a difference between skilled and unskilled work within a craft is not workable,'" reveals how quickly the basis of their contrary position must have collapsed.[101]

By the middle of the Reagan administration, rhetorical class struggle against the Roundtable had turned into real class cooperation with the Roundtable. The unions may have viewed themselves as having had little choice at a time when their loss of control over the labor market was reflected in the significant proportion of their membership that found it necessary to seek employment in nonunion firms.[102] In response to a survey, members of the unionized Mechanical Contractors Association of America reported in 1983 that one-half of Davis-Bacon work and 43 percent of industrial work in their areas had become nonunion. Ominously, a large majority stated that owners and general contractors did not even permit union firms to bid. Many of these specialty contractors, complaining that work rule concessions could not compensate for high wages, were considering nonunion or dual-shop operations. Almost half reported that in many areas union plumbers were working at nonunion wages and even forming their own nonunion businesses.[103]

At the Roundtable's 28th national user conference in 1984, unions "acknowledged publicly for the first time that they were working to reduce labor inefficiencies outlined in the Roundtable reports." The BCTD secretary-treasurer Joseph Maloney admitted that two years earlier the Roundtable had challenged unions by portraying them as "'only aroused enough to rearrange the deck chairs on the Titanic.'" But in the meantime, he insisted, unions had made "'more changes in local labor agreements than were made in the prior 82 years.'" Indeed, he claimed that the Market Recovery Program for Union Construction corrected most

---

[100]"Union Firms to Fight Open Shop," *ENR*, Nov. 26, 1981, at 31 (quoting NCA president Maurice Mosier). BR, "Subjourneymen in Union Construction" at 11, was unable to find "any substantial use of subjourneymen" on any NCA building project operating under the agreement permitting their use. The only reason adduced by for nonuse of subjourneymen is contractors' and owners' fears of causing "labor unrest...." *Id.* at 16. Bourdon & Levitt, *Union and Open-Shop Construction* at 59-60, found that 75 percent of the union firms they surveyed favored introduction of a helper classification. Herbert Northrup, "The 'Helper' Controversy in the Construction Industry," 13 (4) *JLR* 421-35 at 432 (Fall 1992), who relentlessly mocks unions for their alleged "King Canute performance attempting to stop the economic tides of the future with political action that cannot withstand public examination," fails to explain why union employers fail to take advantage of subjourneymen provisions after securing them.

[101]"Union Construction in Trouble," *ENR*, Nov. 5,1981, at 26 (Lexis). The Roundtable also touted the use of subjourneymen as helping union contractors "meet minority employment goals...." BR, "Subjourneymen in Union Construction" at 15.

[102]Marc Silver, *Under Construction: Work and Alienation in the Building Trades* 89-90 (1986).

[103]*CUH*, Jan. 1984.

of the 57 inefficient local labor practices identified by the CICEP. In particular, Maloney stressed, unions were entering into project agreements that made union firms more competitive by permitting them to use subjourneymen. Having made all those concessions, however, the BCTD complained that construction owners continued their "'adversarial approach'" to unions. In a warning that by this time must have rung hollow, Maloney advised the Roundtable that further efforts to achieve "a union-free business environment might result in 'a phoenix rising from the ashes' that might be less to their liking."[104] For its part, the Roundtable welcomed the Market Recovery Program as an implementation of the organization's CICEP,[105] which it declared was not an antiunion attack.[106]

Maloney's mere presence at the Roundtable users conference signaled a remarkable turn of events; his confessions and conciliatory attitude revealed the sea change in labor-management relations that the Roundtable had promoted. Just five years earlier, Maloney had publicly accused the Roundtable of using its members' combined assets of three-quarters of a trillion dollars—"no greater concentration of economic power has every [sic] been placed in the hands of one centralized group in this Nation's political history"—to target the entire trade union movement after having eliminated construction unions' gains. [107]

Maloney's boss, Georgine, somewhat obliquely and face-savingly, tried to explain at one of the seemingly endless series of congressional hearings on construction labor law why by 1983 unions had had to make certain concessions. Because a dynamic industry had been subject to technological change over the half-century since collective bargaining had begun,

many of the things that we bargained for in the earlier years were carried over from collective bargaining agreement to collective bargaining agreement.

Over the past 10 or 12 years the employers have brought those things to our attention. As in any free collective bargaining system, it's a lot more difficult to get out of an agreement something that you have in it, that employees feel that is a benefit of theirs, even though it may not really apply to what the technological situation is today.

---

[104]"Roundtable Study Shaving Costs," *ENR*, Dec. 13, 1984, at 58 (Lexis) (quotes).

[105]Business Roundtable, "CICE: The Next Five Years and Beyond" 5 (1988).

[106]*CUH*, May 1983, at 1 (Thomas Stephenson, vice president-construction, Alcoa).

[107]Maloney correctly recorded the numerous Supreme Court cases, some not even related to construction, that the Roundtable had helped finance. He also correctly noted the Roundtable's simultaneous promotion of stronger contractor bargaining and open-shop construction. "Address by Joseph F. Maloney, Secretary-Treasurer, AFL-CIO Before the Convention of the New Jersey State Building and Construction Trades Council" (quote at 26) (Atlantic City, June 15, 1979) (copy on file at BR). To be sure, Maloney's account was confused in claiming that local Roundtable user groups "brought extensive pressure to bear on local contractors to form local or regional bargaining units," yet portraying this step as a "necessary concession in particular to the specialty contractors who had been seeking the strength of numbers for years." *Id.* at 4-5.

So we have, over the past 10 years, entered into all kinds of specialized agreements and project agreements...that...make all the starting times the same, quitting times the same, the overtime pay the same, and all those kinds of things, in order to make our contractors more competitive.[108]

Georgine misled his congressional interlocutors by suggesting that the point of contention between masters and men had been mere uniformity. What employers in fact wanted was more working time and work for less wages—no coffee breaks, work to begin promptly at starting time, and no premium overtime pay at all for work outside the core weekday, first shift hours, or in excess of eight hours on a given day. Whether abandonment of control over the workday and of supra-statutory overtime pay (such as double-time) represented merely the accommodation of modern conditions, which no longer require such frills, or amounted to the surrender of integral elements of healthful working conditions and the value of labor power under the pressure of high unemployment (20.0 percent in 1982 and 18.4 percent in 1983)[109] and loss of a quasi-monopoly of the labor market, is precisely the question that labor union officials did not publicly confront.[110] Yet hazard pay for working more than 75 feet above the ground, which some employers insisted on eliminating, hardly seems a luxury in an occupation as extraordinarily dangerous as structural ironwork. And while employers were complaining that strong unions could extract superfluous double wages for overtime, Congress was discussing an increase in the statutory overtime rate from 50 to 100 percent on the grounds that it was necessary to bring employers' marginal costs in line with the

---

[108]*Oversight Hearing, Developments in Labor Law Affecting the Construction Industry: Hearing Before the Subcommittee on Labor-Management Relations of the House Committee on Education and Labor*, 98th Cong., 1st Sess. 12 (1983) (testimony of Robert Georgine). Four year earlier, Georgine had been accommodating enough to call construction wage increases in the late 1960s "'unreasonable.'" "The Building Trades Storm the Guideline," *BW*, June 18, 1979, at 48 (Lexis). An earlier study explained that "no great difficulty is encountered in accounting for the tenacity of antiquated regulations. They remain...because the skilful business agent knows that rules of this type can be conceded by the union in an emergency without any real loss to the workers, and that at the same time the employer may be willing to make a considerable sacrifice in order to have the rules abandoned." Montgomery, *Industrial Relations in the Chicago Building Trades* at 146.

[109]*Handbook of U.S. Labor Statistics* 86 (2d ed.; Eva Jacobs ed. 1998).

[110]An activist carpenter and director of the Northeast Regional Council of Carpenters, when asked whether such abandoned terms and conditions of employment had been an extravagance resulting from overreaching or elements of construction workers' social wage, replied that although "overreaching" was a loaded term, when a union controls 80 percent of the labor market, it is able to achieve terms otherwise unavailable. Telephone interview with Mark Erlich, Jamaica Plain, MA, Nov. 20, 1998. More blunt is his admission that "the increasingly antiunion climate in the late 1970s and early 1980s" was exacerbated by the "unyielding defense of well-established but nonproductive practices on union job sites added to the problem. Contracts retained archaic work rules even though they were costly and compromised the competitiveness of signatory contractors." Grabelsky & Erlich, "Recent Innovations in the Building Trades" at 176-77.

full marginal social costs of working overtime.[111]

Yet when unions originally struggled for these terms of employment, they did not regard them as merely creating uniformity, but as crucial to control over the quality and pace of work: "Nowhere has the tension between the contractor's goal of maximized production and the carpenter's desire for craft pride exploded more intensely than in the age-old conflict over speed and rest breaks." When Boston area carpenters, for example, finally negotiated a five-minute coffee break for the first time in 1958, contractors strenuously resisted what their employees viewed as "a struggle to preserve workers' dignity."[112] And even antiunion sources confirmed the need for at least some of these practices. While attacking alleged abuses, *ENR* conceded: "Almost every union contract provides for coffee breaks, morning and afternoon, and most contractors approve, because they say the breaks could decrease fatigue and increase efficiency."[113] Even the Roundtable, which deemed coffee breaks longer than 10 minutes "excessive," agreed that pauses "are now so ingrained in the American work scene that most observers accept a break of some sort for the construction worker sometime during the first part of his shift." The organization insisted, however, that to be cost-effective, breaks should not be included in collective bargaining agreements; instead, contractors should grant them when they have the flexibility in terms of the work flow.[114]

Contractors and owners, according to a Business Roundtable survey from the early 1980s, also attached great significance to "nonproductive work time" such as unauthorized breaks, late starts, early quits, and excessive time for washing up and putting away tools. More respondents (80 percent) identified them than any other "inefficient work practices" not authorized or actually prohibited by collective bargaining agreements.[115] These sharply conflicting value-laden characterizations of the nature of the dispute reflect the diametrically opposed political economy of labor and that of capital.

The view from the building site was emphatic. One skilled ironworker noted in the early 1980s that project agreements "often make our time start and end at our workplace rather than when we come through the gate. Since on these huge

---

[111]Ronald Ehrenberg & Paul Schumann, "The Overtime Pay Provisions of the Fair Labor Standards Act," in *The Economics of Legal Minimum Wages* 264-95 (Simon Rottenberg ed. 1981); *To Revise the Overtime Compensation Requirements of the Fair Labor Standards Act of 1938: Hearings Before the Subcommittee on Labor Standards of the House Committee on Labor and Education*, 96th Cong., 1st Sess (1979).

[112]Erlich, *With Our Hands* at 154-55.

[113]Edward Young, "Low Productivity: The Real Sin of High Wages," *ENR*, Feb. 24, 1972, at 18-23 at 21.

[114]BR, "Constraints Imposed by Collective Bargaining Agreements," 5, 7 (Rep. C-4, Oct. 1991 [Sept. 1982]).

[115]BR, "Local Labor Practices" (Rep. C-5, Jan. 1988 [Apr. 1982]).

sites we may be working anywhere from ten to twenty minutes' walk from the gate, this amounts to about a one-half hour gain for the contractor and loss to us." The elimination of double-time for overtime also elicited a different view from workers: "'I don't want overtime. We work our life away as it is. The whole reason we bargained for double time in the first place was to make it too expensive for the contractors. Instead of working us longer hours they'd have to hire more men.'"[116] Ironically, although the CICEP report, reminding owners and contractors of "some physiological fundamentals," emphasized that overtime increased fatigue and injuries and reduced productivity, construction firms appear more interested in eliminating premium pay for overtime than the overtime itself.[117] Even more ironically, although the Roundtable had been preaching against scheduled overtime as multidimensionally disruptive since 1974, a survey of its membership in 1999 revealed that almost 90 percent of chemical and petrochemical firms found it difficult to recruit workers for their construction projects despite offering them guaranteed overtime.[118]

Even the strategy of concessionary bargaining to save what was left of the union sector soon revealed itself to be a trap as nonunion contractors were in a position to beat their competitors in the race to the bottom that atomized labor markets invariably unleash.[119] Despite this inherent contradiction, national construction unions embarked on a concessionary strategy. The Carpenters' Operation Turnaround, begun in 1982, prompted the AGC's director of collective bargaining services to praise the "'phenomenal...change in attitude,'" which reflected the union's willingness to accept much of the blame for the ascension of nonunion construction. This mood swing did not, however, extend to "healthier" Carpenters locals, especially on the West coast; nor did any national union except the Plumbers endorse the plan.[120] In 1983, the Carpenters' international president at a meeting that he requested with members of the Roundtable's Construction

---

[116]Robert Cook, "Work in the Construction Industry" at 233. Cook, a former sociologist at Yale, was quoting another worker. On the origin of premium overtime rates in the nineteenth century as a method of preventing employers from extending the workday and of spreading work to the unemployed, see Haber, *Industrial Relations in the Building Trades* at 228-89; Richard Schneirov & Thomas Suhrbur, *Union Brotherhood, Union Town: The History of the Carpenters' Union of Chicago 1863-1987*, at 135 (1988). On the struggle over the start of the working day and the entitlement to wages for time spent walking from the gate to the work station, see Marc Linder, "Class Struggle at the Door: The Origins of the Portal-to-Portal Act of 1947," 39 *BLR* 53-180 (1991).

[117]BR, "More Construction for the Money" 54 (Jan. 1983) (quote); BR, "Scheduled Overtime Effect on Construction Projects" (Rep. C-2, Nov. 1980).

[118]BR, *Coming to Grips with Some Major Problems in the Construction Industry* 1 (1974); "Construction Industry Faces Worker Shortage," 160 *LRR* 53 (Jan. 18, 1999).

[119]Grace Palladino, *Dreams of Dignity, Workers of Vision: A History of the International Brotherhood of Electrical Workers* 266 (1991).

[120]"Carpenters' Drive on Track," *ENR*, Jan. 13, 1983, at 62.

Committee pointedly asked whether the Roundtable was seeking a union-free environment, but admitted that the union needed to become competitive.[121]

To be sure, not all construction unions adopted an accommodationist strategy.[122] In Columbus, Ohio, for example, Local 189 of the Plumbers Union, which had seen its control of the labor market dwindle since the later 1960s, took innovative action in 1978-79 when Kroger Food Stores refused to let union contractors bid on a warehouse it was building. After an injunction interfered with the union's picket line, which had succeeded in shutting down the site, Local 189, supported by members' families and other building tradesmen, interrupted business as usual at local Kroger stores. In one store they filled up carts with perishables and left them in the checkout line. After Kroger secured an injunction, unionists collected and converted their cash into $20 bills and bought low-priced items in order to exhaust stores' small change. Following another injunction, unions bought up all the bread (which they donated to the poor) and other special items at a store to make it less attractive to shoppers. Then they converted their cash into pennies to make purchases (again donated to charities) that would take so long to transact that customers in the long lines left in anger. After enduring weeks of these tactics, Kroger agreed to use union workers.[123]

In 1985, the BCTD was able to pressure General Motors, which was worried about long-term labor relations in the plant, to antagonize nonunion contractors in Tennessee, which had expected to build GM's huge billion Saturn plant there; instead, all contractors had to agree to recognize unions as the exclusive bargaining representative of all craft employees, who had to be hired through the union hiring hall even if Tennessee's anti-union shop law permitted them not to become members. Although the project implemented the CICEP recommendations, the IBEW bargained to exempt itself from provisions permitting the use of up to 40 percent subjourneymen and eliminating supra-statutory premium wages for overtime.[124] Nevertheless, unlike the project agreements that the BCTD had negotiated in the 1960s and 1970s, which secured higher wages than those prevailing locally in order to draw the requisite labor supply, Saturn project wages

---

[121]BR, CC, Minutes, Sept. 20, 1983, at 6-7 (Patrick Campbell).

[122]According to Mills, "Labor Relations and Collective Bargaining" at 61, unions had secured a notable success in almost completely organizing pipeline and gas distribution construction in the late 1970s. On construction union organizing strategies in the 1980s: *Labor Research Review*, No. 12: "Up Against the Open Shop: New Initiatives in the Building Trades" (Fall 1988).

[123]Richard Schneirov, *Pride and Solidarity: A History of the Plumbers and Pipefitters of Columbus, Ohio, 1889-1989*, at 126-27 (1993).

[124]"Saturn Project Pact Infuriates Open Shop," *ENR*, Dec. 12, 1985, at 56; "Say It Ain't So, Saturn," *ENR*, Dec. 12, 1985, at 64 (editorial). ABC unsuccessfully sought a ruling from the NLRB that the contractor was engaging in an unlawful secondary boycott. William Krizan, "Saturn Site Squabble Squashed," *ENR*, April 10, 1986, at 54.

were 10 percent below local scale.[125]

The next year, using much more confrontational tactics, including protests in front of the Japanese embassy in Washington, D.C., and successful lobbying of Congress to eliminate special tax breaks, unions persuaded Toyota and its Japanese construction manager, Ohbayashi, to change its plans and enter into an agreement similar to Saturn's for building Toyota's large plant in Kentucky after some contracts had already been let to nonunion firms. Fearing that they might never secure another all-union project in the area or in the automobile industry, construction unions had taken the risky step of refusing to refer workers to the project despite unemployment rates as high as one-third in some trades.[126] Emboldened by these victories, Georgine announced that after having given so many concessions, the unions had decided that in addition to making union firms more competitive, it was also vital to make it harder for nonunion contractors to win contracts. Ironically, the aforementioned 1987 no-strike agreement with the NCA was an integral element of this more aggressive tactic.[127]

Local action in California became especially militant. In 1987, after a $350 million contract to modernize a steel plant jointly owned by USX and a Korean firm had been awarded to low-bidding BE&K, the Alabama-based leader of the open shop movement, local construction unions engaged in a wide variety of protests to prevent the project from becoming the largest nonunion construction job in California history. BE&K, while denying union charges that its wages would be one-fourth of the locally prevailing rate, admitted that "'we won't pay them like lawyers.'" Ironically, United Steel Workers union members who agreed to wage reductions to preserve their jobs at the Pittsburg, California mill, sympathized with the union construction workers, who had offered to work for 80 percent of their regular rate, but viewed the no-strike clause in their collective bargaining agreement as precluding any effective assistance. When the Contra Costa County board of supervisors finally rejected the county Building and Construction Trades Council's appeal from a decision to exempt the project from environmental review, the unions' last obstacle to completion was removed.[128] Nevertheless, the same year, half of the building trades union membership in the San Francisco area agreed to

---

[125]Grabelsky & Erlich, "Recent Innovations in the Building Trades" at 177.

[126]William Krizan, "Building Trades Target Toyota," *ENR*, July 17, 1986, at 82; Jay Kraker, "Toyota Plant Plows Ahead with No Sign of Union Pact," *ENR*, Nov. 27, 1986, at 65; Maria Recio et al., "Toyota Flip-Flops, Signs Union Pact at Ky. Plant," *ENR*, Dec. 4, 1986, at 10; "No Winner," *ENR*, Dec. 4, 1986, at 56 (editorial); William Krizan & James Schwartz, "Toyota Pact Breaks New Ground," *ENR*, Dec. 11, 1986, at 60.

[127]William Krizan, "Building Trades Plan Toyota-Type Fights," *ENR*, Feb. 5, 1987, at 42.

[128]Henry Weinstein, "Workers Are Steeling Themselves to Fight Non-Union Upgrading of Pittsburg Plant," *LAT*, Mar. 16, 1987, pt. 1, at 3, col. 2 (Lexis) (quote); UPI, Nov. 4, 1987 (Lexis); Jay Mathews, "Town Fights Korean Venture," *WP*, Dec. 6, 1987, at H2 (Lexis); Chris Chrystal, "Steel Plant Targeted for Labor Protest," UPI, Mar. 14, 1988 (Lexis).

a five-cent per hour check-off to fund a computer system to track government permits for construction; the unions then protested every suspected nonunion contractor regardless of the project's size. The local ABC conceded that the tactic was "causing trouble."[129] Unions in other parts of the country also strenuously resisted BE&K's efforts to enter the construction market.[130]

In several localities activist construction unions have been successful in inducing cities to enact ordinances requiring employers that bid for public construction contracts to pay prevailing wages, provide health insurance, pay workers' compensation premiums and unemployment insurance tax, and treat workers as employees. In Massachusetts, Cambridge, Worcester, Boston, and other cities passed such labor standards measures in the latter half of 1990s.[131] Antiunionists' objections to such initiatives are telling. Herbert Northrup, the most prominent academic critic of construction unions, lamenting the fact that such an ordinance led Cambridge to reject a $27,000 lower bid from a nonunion firm, asserted that such programs "are based on union demands for monopoly. Unable to compete with the open-shop contractors on an economic basis, the construction unions seek to offset economic considerations with political initiatives. ... The question...is whether politically assisted monopoly will smother economics with the public as the big loser."[132] Northrup's fixation on individual firms' costs and product prices blinds him to the costs to workers caused by such a profit-über-alles perspective. The possibility that the workers producing such cheap output may not receive adequate medical care or even income to sustain themselves in excellent condition for the duration of a normal working life is disqualified as a value-laden "political" detour around the neutral "economic" arbiter of societal well-being. Similarly suppressed is the fact that to the extent that health care providers increase insurance costs to employers with health plans to pay for the expense of care for uncovered persons, such employers are subsidizing nonunion firms.[133]

---

[129]"Bay Area Unions Get Tough," *ENR*, Sept. 10, 1987, at 39.

[130]In Illinois in the mid-1990s, unions were held liable for $544,000 in damages for having threatened an unlawful secondary strike against a construction company that hired BE&K to work on a refinery. BE&K Constr. Co. v. Will & Grundy Counties Bldg Trades Councils, 156 F.3d 756 (7th Cir. 1998).

[131]"Boston Mayor Signs Ordinance Establishing Labor Standards for Public Jobs," *DLR*, June 30, 1998, at D13 (Lexis).

[132]Northrup, "Construction Union Programs to Regain Jobs" at 11. A 1990 Contra Costa County, California, ordinance that required employers on private industrial construction projects costing more than $500,000 to pay prevailing wages as set by state law for public works was held pre-empted by the NLRA: "A precedent allowing this interference with the free-play of market forces...could redirect efforts of employees not to bargain with employers, but instead, to seek to set minimum wage and benefit packages with political bodies." Chamber of Commerce of the United States v. Bragdon, 64 F.3d 497, 504 (9th Cir. 1995).

[133]"Health Care Affecting Competition," *ENR*, July 19, 1990, at 13 (Lexis).

One accommodationist tactic that construction unions have devised defies the traditional pattern. "Job-targeting" has been championed by the IBEW in its dealings with the NECA. The local union increases membership dues across the board in order to finance a fund that bridges the gap between the regular union rate and the lower target rate, which enables the employer to compete with lower-wage nonunion firms. The workers on the job-targeted projects nevertheless receive the full union rate. Rather than singling out a particular group of union members for a lower standard of living who in no way differ from other members, job-targeting is a solidarity-driven technique for sharing losses equally.[134] Job-targeting could be viewed as a belated response to the collapse of the 1960s building boom that disemployed enough workers to make the nonunion sector viable: when many unions refused to conform union wage rates to these depression-like conditions, workers hid their union cards and worked for nonunion firms at even lower wages.[135] By the 1980s, some unions hid the lower rates which they were finally conceding to union employers.[136]

By the 1990s, unions also finally began to take organizing more seriously. They were reported to be "quietly...assembling their troops for an all-out bottom-up organizing blitz" designed to raise nonunion workers' standards rather than defensively lowering union standards.)[137] The BCTD's COMET (Construction Organizing Membership Education Training) program, which encourages unemployed unionists to work for and organize nonunion firms, alarmed even the Roundtable, which warned its members that this "significant change from traditional organizing...bears close watching."[138] In Las Vegas, the Building Trades Organizing Project, a pilot project begun in 1997, was so successful that the BCTD in 1999 not only approved it as a permanent program, but agreed to expand it to other cities. Union membership there increased by 35 percent, or 7,000 members, in 1997-98, making it the country's fastest-growing union construction market.[139]

Finally, one strategy that harks back to a long-forgotten cooperative tradition—often as a response to open-shop drives[140]—is the formation by

---

[134]Herbert Northrup & Augustus White, "Subsidizing Contractors to Gain Employment: Construction Union 'Job Targeting,'" 17 *BJELL* 62 (1996). Herbert Northrup, "Construction Union Programs to Regain Jobs: Background and Overview," 18 (1) *JLR* 1-15 at 8 (Winter 1997), reports that the IBEW began discouraging the practice in 1995 because it depressed wages, although the Plumbers and Sheet Metal Workers continued to use it.

[135]Bourdon & Levitt, *Union and Open-Shop Construction* at 5.

[136]Grabelsky & Erlich, "Recent Innovations in the Building Trades" at 178, observe that such "clever" market recovery programs "tended to drive wages down in the local union market."

[137]William Krizan, "Building Trades Plan Big Organizing Drive," *ENR*, May 3, 1993, at 6.

[138]*CUH*, July 1993, at 2.

[139]*Las Vegas Review-Journal*, Jan. 27, 1999, at 1D (Lexis); 160 *LRR* 158 (Feb. 8, 1999).

[140]In 1910, the Bricklayers, supported by the other building trades, struck in Alton Illinois, and with a start-up capital of $5,000 bid on and won contracts below cost, thus forcing out open-shop

metropolitan building and construction trades councils of their own construction companies. Modeled after a similar program in Milwaukee, the Detroit council in 1993 established Building Trades Contracting Inc., whose purpose is to underbid nonunion firms, especially contractors hiring nonunion subcontractors, and to employ its members regardless of profitability.[141]

The Role of Labor Law

Capital has assumed to itself the right to own and control labor for the accomplishment of its own greedy and selfish ends.[142]

Contrary to a commonplace of the literature on the industry, the NLRB has played a significant part in construction labor relations. From 1959—the year in which the Landrum-Griffin amendments adjusted certain aspects of the NLRA to construction—through mid-1998, the NLRB conducted 9,343 representation elections in the industry, of which unions won 5,002 or 54 percent. In 1989, for example, construction unions accounted for a record 14 percent of all union election victories.[143] On the enforcement side, as well, construction is one of the Board's prime targets. In 1997, 13 percent of all employer unfair labor practice cases received by the NLRB, but more than half of all unfair labor practice cases involving union violations of the NLRA's secondary boycott, jurisdictional dispute, and picketing provisions stemmed from construction.[144]

One tactic that construction unions have deployed with great skill in connection with organizing campaigns is "salting" an employer's work force with union organizers. Because it has been a "clever tactic," that is, cheap for union and costly for antiunion employers, firms have fought it through NLRB litigation.[145] After the U.S. Supreme Court unanimously rebuffed employers' efforts to persuade the NLRB and courts that such organizers were not covered or protected by the

---

employers; a similar strategy prevailed the following year in Aberdeen, S. Dakota. William Weyforth, *The Organizability of Labor* 81-82 (1917). For other examples, see BLS, *Beneficial Activities of American Trade-Unions* 207, 209-10 (Bull. No. 465, 1928).

[141]*CUH*, Oct. 1993, at 2.

[142]Harry Bates, *Bricklayers' Century of Craftsmanship* 106-107 (1955) (quoting from the preamble to the Bricklayers' 1865 constitution).

[143]These data are tabulated from the NLRB, *Annual Report*; from 1960 forward the data appeared in appendix table 16; in 1959, in appendix table 17; the data for 1998 appeared in BNA, 159 *LRR* 466-67 (Dec. 14, 1998).

[144]Calculated according to *Sixty-Second Annual Report of the National Labor Relations Board for the Fiscal Year Ended September 30, 1997*, tab. 5 at 114-15 (1998).

[145]Herbert Northrup, "'Salting the Contractors' Labor Force: Construction Unions Organizing with NLRB Assistance," 46 (3) *ILRR* 469-92 at 484 (Apr. 1993).

NLRA against antiunion discrimination,[146] employers pursued a dual strategy. First, they lobbied Congress to overturn the Supreme Court's ruling by amending the NLRA to exclude these organizers.[147] While they have thus far failed to secure enactment of such a provision, they have had more success narrowing the protected scope of salting judicially. For example, one federal appellate court has ruled that an employer is not engaged in unlawful discrimination if it refuses to hire a "salt" pursuant to a general policy not permitting its employees to hold a second job.[148]

The salience of salting highlights the issue of the responsibility that labor law bears for the shrinkage of construction unions. Some analysts have argued that, since the relative costs as between union and nonunion construction moved in favor of the former during the 1980s, the decline in union density should have been reversed, whereas in fact it intensified; seeing no other causal factor in play, they find it plausible to attribute the accelerated decline to the increase in double-breasting and abrogation of prehire agreements, the cost of which was markedly lowered by several landmark legal decisions in the 1970s.[149] This legal deregulation is viewed as merely different in form from that in other industries (such as trucking), which has brought about a deterioration in working conditions.[150] Others modify this judgment by including employers' increasing ability to evade prehire agreements in the indictment. They conclude that construction unions have consequently shared the fate of industrial unions—concessions vis-à-vis employers that continue to bargain with them and retreat into ever narrower bastions impervious to attack by nonunion firms.[151]

To understand such arguments, it is necessary to review briefly the history

---

[146]NLRB v. Town & Country Electric, Inc., 513 U.S. 1125 (1995).

[147]Truth in Employment Act of 1997, H.R. 758 and S. 328, 105th Cong., 1st Sess. (1997). The Senate bill would amend the provision in the NLRA that prohibits employers from interfering, restraining, or coercing employees in the exercise of their right to self-organize by adding that it shall not "be construed as requiring an employer to employ any person who seeks or has sought employment with the meployer in furtherance of the objectives of an organization other than the employer." S. 328, § 4.

[148]Architectural Glass & Metal Co. v. NLRB, 107 F.3d 426 (6th Cir. 1997).

[149]Steven Allen, "Unit Costs, Legal Shocks, and Unionization in Construction," 16 (3) *JLR* 367-77 (Summer 1995); Allen, "Developments in Collective Bargaining in Construction in the 1980s and 1990s" at 24. When the NLRB stated in 1973 that double-breasting was "not uncommon" in construction, it referred to a single case involving a dual entity electrical contractor in New Mexico one of which performed residential and the other commercial work. Peter Kiewit Sons' Co., 206 NLRB 562 (1973) (Westlaw) (citing Central New Mexico Chapter, Nat'l Elec. Contractors Ass'n, 152 NLRB 1604 (1965)).

[150]Dale Belman & Michael Belzer, "The Regulation of Labor Markets: Balancing the Benefits and Costs of Competition," in *Government Regulation of the Employment Relationship* 179- at 206 (Bruce Kaufman ed. 1998).

[151]Stephen Evans & Roy Lewis, "Union Organisation, Collective Bargaining and the Law: An Anglo-American Comparison of the Construction Industry," 10 *CLLJ* 473-504 (1989).

of NLRA/NLRB regulation of the construction industry. The NLRB declined jurisdiction over the construction industry under the original Wagner Act.[152] One basis for the Board's action was the deviant structure of the construction industry: occasional, short-term employment for many employers. It also declined jurisdiction "because the industry was substantially organized and hence had no need of the protection afforded by the act." The consequence was the Board's development of labor law without reference to the construction industry's peculiarities.[153] Ironically, in the first cases after the enactment of Taft-Hartley (whose union unfair labor practices clearly implicated construction unions),[154] the respondent-chargee employers and respondent-chargee union argued in the alternative that the work at issue was not covered interstate commerce and that the Board should not exercise jurisdiction, whereas the union and employer charging parties in those cases supported jurisdiction.[155]

After considerable complaint from unions and employers about "serious problems" arising from the NLRA's applicability to construction, Congress included several special provisions in the act's 1959 amendments. The most important provision, sanctioning prehire agreements—which would otherwise subject both union and employer to liability for commission of unfair labor practices for recognizing a union as exclusive bargaining representative of a group of workers a majority of whom have not selected that union as its representative—was included because "[r]epresentation elections in a large segment of the industry are not feasible to demonstrate such majority status due to the short periods of actual employment by specific employers."[156] Congress's justified validation of the preexisting consensual collective bargaining practice thus:

Since the vast majority of building projects are of relatively short duration, such labor

---

[152]Brown & Root, 51 NLRB 820 (1943).

[153]S. Rep. No. 187: *Labor-Management Reporting and Disclosure Act of 1959*, 86th Cong., 1st Sess. 27 (1959).

[154]Peter Pestillo, a GE official actively involved in the organization of the Roundtable, offered this unconventional private analysis of Taft-Hartley's impact on construction: "Operating then in a climate of a Republican Congress determined to aid the general business community and aided by the fact that the unions in the building trades have traditionally been Republicans, the construction unions fared pretty well. They got a secondary union shop arrangement, exclusive hiring halls and, most important, a proviso section 8(e)." Peter J. Pestillo, "Construction Problems: In Search of a Solution" at 7 (Mar. 14, 1969), in BR, 1969: CCH.

[155]Ozark Dam Constructors, 77 NLRB 1136 (1948) (a joint venture including Brown & Root, Peter Kiewit Sons, and Morrison Knudsen); Local 74, United Brotherhood of Carpenters & Joiners of America, 80 NLRB 533 (1948). In Starrett Brothers & Eken, 77 NLRB 275 (1948), the employer did not contest coverage of the construction industry, but the affected employees were largely white-collar. See also "NLRB to Rule Over Construction Trades," 1(2) *BCTB* 1 (Feb. 1948).

[156]S. Rep. No. 187: *Labor-Management Reporting and Disclosure Act of 1959* at 55-56.

agreements necessarily apply to jobs which have not been started and may not even be contemplated. ... One reason for this practice is that it is necessary for the employer to know his labor costs before making the estimate upon which his bid will be based. A second reason is that the employer must be able to have available a supply of skilled craftsmen ready for quick referral. A substantial majority of the skilled employees in this industry constitute a pool of such help centered about their appropriate craft union. If the employer relies upon this pool of skilled craftsmen, members of the union, there is no doubt under these circumstances that the union will in fact represent a majority of the employees eventually hired.[157]

The prehire provision is now codified in the NLRA: "It shall not be an unfair labor practice...for an employer engaged primarily in the building and construction industry to make an agreement covering employees engaged (or who, upon their employment, will be engaged) in the building and construction industry with a labor organization of which building and construction employees are members...because...the majority status of such labor organization has not been established under...section 159...prior to the making of such agreement...."[158]

In 1971, the Nixon NLRB effectively invalidated this prehire provision by holding in *R.J. Smith Construction Company* that an employer did not commit an unfair labor practice by unilaterally abrogating a validly executed prehire agreement at any time before the union achieves majority support in the bargaining unit.[159] To be sure, in 1973 the D.C. Circuit Court of Appeals vacated the Board's order on the grounds that it frustrated congressional purpose to render prehire agreements "voidable at will" and "virtually unenforceable." The case—in which the employer had refused to negotiate, granted selected wage increases, fired its only union members, and refused to comply with the agreement's hiring hall and union security provisions—proved that the Board's interpretation permitted an employer to avoid a prehire agreement "by discouraging union membership through flagrant unfair labor practices, thereby insuring that the union never attains a majority."[160]

Because the court's action failed to deter the Board from adhering to its

---

[157]S. Rep. No. 187: *Labor-Management Reporting and Disclosure Act of 1959* at 28. See also H. R. Rep. No. 741: *Labor-Management Reporting and Disclosure Act of 1959*, 86th Cong., 1st Sess. 19 (1959). Even a Republican member of the Reagan Board conceded: "There may very well be many more instances in which the work force majority assembled after a prehire agreement is executed does not support a union. But the diminishment of unionization in the construction industry does not in and of itself justify allowing an employer to test majority support in an 8 (a)(5) proceeding." John Deklewa & Sons, 282 NLRB 1375 (1987) (Stephens, concurring) (Lexis).

[158]29 U.S.C. § 158(f).

[159]R. J. Smith Construction Co., 191 NLRB 693 (1971).

[160]Local No. 150, International Union of Operating Engineers, 480 F.2d 1186, 1190 (D.C. Cir. 1973).

R..J. Smith rule, the issue continued to be litigated.[161] After the D.C. Circuit had once again reversed the Board in another case, the U.S. Supreme Court in 1978 afforded tepid sanction to the Board's approach by concluding that "the Board's construction of the Act, although perhaps not the only tenable one, is an acceptable reading of the statutory language and a reasonable implementation of the purposes of the relevant statutory sections."[162] Finally, in 1987, the Reagan Board, in spite of urgings to the contrary by the ABC and National Right to Work Legal Defense Fund as amici curiae and at oral argument, expressly overruled *Smith*. Concluding that the earlier doctrine did not square with the statutory language or history and failed to serve the legislature's objectives of labor relations stability and employee free choice, it held in *John Deklewa & Sons* that construction employers did commit an unfair labor practice in repudiating prehire agreements. However, the NLRB also ruled that, unlike nonconstruction employers, a construction employer is not required to bargain with the union as its employees' exclusive bargaining representative after the prehire agreement expires. Under *Smith* the so-called conversion doctrine had been favorable to unions: if they could show majority status for a relevant period, the prehire agreement could be converted to a standard agreement protected under section 9(a) as entered into by the exclusive majority bargaining representative.[163]

---

[161]International Association of Bridge, Structural and Ornamental Iron Workers, Local 3 v. NLRB, 843 F.2d 770, 774 (3f Cir. 1987).

[162]NLRB v. Local No. 103, International Association of Bridge, Structural and Ornamental Iron Workers, 434 U.S. 335, 341 (1978). The case was of additional interest because the employer had breached the prehire agreement by double-breasting. The issue before the court was whether the union had committed an unfair labor practice by peacefully picketing the nonunion subsidiary's work site for more than 30 days in violation of § 8(b)(7), which prohibits picketing an employer for more than 30 days to force it to recognize the union as its employees' bargaining representative unless the union is already the certified representative; under the Board's precedents, the ban did not extend to enforcement of an existing collective bargaining agreement. *Id.* at 354 (Stewart, J., dissenting). The Court's underlying motivation may have been its bias in favor of Taft-Hartley's support for individual worker free choice as opposed to the Wagner Act's support for collective bargaining: "Privileging unions and employers to execute prehire agreements in an effort to accommodate the special circumstances in the construction industry may have greatly convenienced unions and employers, but in no sense can it be portrayed as an expression of employees' organizational wishes." *Id.* at 349.

[163]In various cases the Board had found evidence of majority status in an enforced union security clause, union membership of a majority of the bargaining, or exclusive hiring hall referrals. Because the union now enjoyed an irrebuttable presumption of majority status, conversion also created a bar to any election petitions by employers or employees. John Deklewa & Sons, 282 NLRB 1375 (1987), *enforced sub. nom.* International Association of Bridge, Structural and Ornamental Iron Workers, Local 3 v. NLRB, 843 F.2d 770 (3d Cir. 1988); *cert. denied*, 488, U.S. 889 (1988). Robert Pleasure, "Construction Industry Labor Law: Contract Enforcement After *Deklewa* and Consumer Boycotts After *DeBartolo* and *Boxhorn*," 10 *IRLJ* 40-50 at 46 (1988), tried to explain the Board's reversal as continuous with the Reagan administration's deregulatory aspirations. However, the Board may simply have been trying to reduce the volume of disputes and cases generated by the *Smith* rule,

The fact that under *Deklewa* unions lose the presumption of majority status at the time of contract expiration, thus entitling employers to walk away and cease bargaining, prompted BCTD president Georgine to characterize the decision as "even more disadvantageous for unions than were the previous rules."[164] Indeed, the BCTD has even called for overturning it legislatively while the AGC pushed for its continuation.[165] In the immediate aftermath of *Deklewa* construction unions continued to lobby for amendments to the NLRA that would also have made it unlawful for an employer to repudiate a prehire agreement unless a majority of bargaining unit employees had voted against the union in an NLRB-certified election.[166]

The Board has also fashioned other rules to accommodate the construction industry's peculiar features such as intermittent employment for short periods on different projects for many employers.[167] Perhaps the most unusual special rule

---

which because of union allegations of de facto conversion, had not turned out to be the bright-line rule the Board had envisioned. Telephone interview with Matt Glasson, construction union attorney, Cedar Rapids, IA (Dec. 29, 1998). Not all circuit courts of appeal adopted *Deklewa* as a reasonable interpretation of the NLRA; the two that have retained the pre-*Deklewa* rule, the Fourth and Eleventh Circuits, have jurisdiction over the most open-shop regions—the South and Southeast. Local Union 48 Sheet Metal Workers v. S.L. Pappas & Co., 106 F.3d 970 (11th Cir. 1997), *reh'g en banc denied*, 114 F.3d 1204 (1997); Industrial Turnaround Corp., 115 F.3d 248 (4th Cir. 1997).

[164]*The Construction Industry Labor Law Amendments: Hearing Before the Subcommittee on Labor-Management Relations of the House Committee on Education and Labor*, 100th Cong., 1st Sess. 11 (1987) (testimony of Robert Georgine). The BCTD's attorney, Larry Cohen, conceded that *Deklewa*'s ruling that "an employer may not unilaterally walk away" from a prehire agreement during its term was "a gain." *Id.* at 29.

[165]Steven Setzer, "H.R. 281 Scope May Be Clarified," *ENR*, Mar. 12, 1987, at 58; Steven Setzer, "Unions Rally the Troops for Congressional Blitz," *ENR*, Apr. 16, 1997, at 114; "NLRB Considers Prehire Policy," *ENR*, Nov. 25, 1996, at 16. ENR editorially supported the decision as "A Reasonable Compromise," *ENR*, Mar. 5, 1987, at 48. Life and the law under *Deklewa* have generally not borne out unions' initial negative reaction. Telephone interview with construction union attorney Matt Glasson, Cedar Rapids, IA (Dec. 29, 1998). By the same token, an open-shop coalition conceded that employers could "live" with *Deklewa*. *The Construction Industry Labor Law Amendments: Hearing Before the Subcommittee on Labor-Management Relations of the House Committee on Education and Labor*, 100th Cong., 1st Sess. at 109, 132 (statement of the National Coaltion to Defeat H.R. 2181).

[166]*The Construction Industry Labor Law Amendments: Hearing Before the Subcommittee on Labor-Management Relations of the House Committee on Education and Labor* at 5. H.R. 114, 103d Cong., 1st Sess. (1993), which made no progress after Congressman Clay introduced it, appears to be the last prounion bill designed to deal with prehire agreements and double breasting.

[167]Despite the virtually universal view that construction workers typically work for several employers each year, data from several construction industry pension and benefit funds suggest otherwise. In 1993, 58 percent of the workers with the Massachusetts Laborers Benefit Fund worked for only one employer (working on average 1,033 hours). Data for a Bricklayers and an Electricians fund in 1992 revealed similar proportions—58 percent and 63 percent, respectively. Commission on the Future of Worker-Management Relations, *Fact Finding Report* 95 n.5 (1994).

pertains to eligibility for elections: in addition to workers employed during the payroll period immediately preceding the date on which the Board orders an election, all bargaining unit employees are eligible "who have been employed for a total of 30 days or more within the period of 12 months, or who have had some employment in that period and have been employed 45 days or more within the 24 months immediately preceding the eligibility date for the election..., and who have not been terminated for cause or quit voluntarily prior to the completion of the last job for which they were employed...."[168] Such a proworker rule can in no way be interpreted as having impeded unionism.

The legal origins of permissible double-breasting[169] are associated with the efforts of a Midland, Michigan general contractor, Gerace Construction, to secure additional work in 1969-70. Gerace, a union contractor and AGC member, had been in business for 12 years with annual revenues of about $5 million derived from projects ranging in value from $100,000 to $1 million. Its president, Francis Gerace, was concerned that beginning in 1969 he had been unable to obtain jobs valued at less than $100,000 because "union jurisdictional problems had unduly increased labor costs." He therefore considered forming a nonunion entity, unfettered by craft classifications, to recapture the smaller jobs that Gerace Construction had lost. Gerace was galvanized into action in 1970 by news of a remodeling job for Dow Chemical Company. Gerace decided to create a nonunion entity when he could not fulfill Dow's requirement that he guarantee completion without work interruption because he feared a strike after expiration of his collective bargaining agreement. Gerace owned a majority of the shares in Helger Construction Company, the new nonunion entity, which was initially managed by a Gerace employee. A Gerace trailer became the office of Helger, which also rented its power tools and equipment from Gerace. Gerace reserved for himself authority to decide to what extent Helger would compete with Gerace.[170]

Based on these fact findings, the NLRB trial examiner then focused on the issue of whether the two businesses constituted a single employer; the principal factors were common ownership, common management, financial dependence, operational integration, interchange of employees, and, above all, common control of labor relations. He found entrepreneurial unity based on common ownership and direction and Helger's financial reliance on Gerace, and especially on the joint

---

[168]Daniel Construction Co., 167 NLRB 1078, 1081 (1967). This decision slightly modified Daniel Construction Co., 133 NLRB 264 (1961), and was upheld by Steiny & Co., 308 NLRB 1323 (1992).

[169]For a detailed but (proemployer) biased account, see Herbert Northrup, Robert Williams, & Douglas McDowell, *Doublebreasted Operations and Pre-Hire Agreements in Construction: The Facts and the Law* (1987). See also Joseph Bucci & Brian Kirwin, "Double Breasting in the Construction Industry," 10 *CL* 1 (Jan. 1990).

[170]Gerace Construction Inc., 193 NLRB 645, 646-49 (1971).

determination of Helger's employment and labor relations policies by Gerace's directors. Status as a single employer was, however, not dispositive of the issue of whether Helger's employees were accretions to Gerace's pre-existing appropriate bargaining unit. But the trial examiner quickly concluded that they were accretions based on the traditional criteria, many of which were identical with those used to determine entrepreneurial unity (operational integration, centralization of managerial and administrative control, proximity, similarity of working conditions, skills, and functions, common control over labor relations, collective bargaining history, and interchange of employees). Because the trial examiner found that "Helger was organized to do work which Gerace Construction was equipped to do, had done, and which its principal, Francis Gerace, wanted to do and in order that the Employer's obligations under the contracts between Grace Construction and the [unions] could be circumvented." Consequently, the employer had violated its duty to bargain in good faith and had interfered with the workers' rights to collectively bargain by failing to apply the terms of the pre-existing agreements to Helger's employees.[171]

On the other hand, the trial examiner dismissed the complaint that the employer had discriminated against the workers to discourage union activity or dissipate the unions' majority status. He hinged this conclusion largely on the finding that the formation of Helger had not deprived Gerace employees of any work they would otherwise have performed. The fact that Helger offered below-union wage rates did not constitute discrimination, but at most contract breach. The remedy required the employer to recognize the union only prospectively as the exclusive bargaining representative at Helger; the trial examiner refused to award backpay because it "would be foolish for the Board to close its eyes to the realities of the operations of the construction industry. The employees who accepted work with Helger knew that they were accepting work with a firm which was operating nonunion.... To give them backpay would be to award them a windfall...."[172]

Even this meager obstacle placed in the way of double-breasting was removed by the NLRB itself when it reviewed the decision. The Board was apparently willing to let Gerace-Helger bootstrap itself into dual existences by virtue of manipulable formalities (such as separate workers compensation policies and separate membership in the AGC and ABC); even more irrationally, the Board deployed circular reasoning to find insufficient common control of labor relations by reference to the very outcomes that Gerace desired—namely, that "[u]nlike Gerace, Helger operates an open shop without regard to craft lines and pays employees less than Gerace's contract rates." Because it found that Gerace and Helger were separate employers with separate bargaining units, the Board

---

[171]Gerace Construction Inc., 193 NLRB at 649-51 (quote at 651).

[172]Gerace Construction Inc., 193 NLRB at 651, 652 (quote).

concluded that the employers had no obligation to recognize the union at Helger.[173]

When *Road & Streets* reported on double-breasting in 1972 in the aftermath of the *Gerace* case, the practice appeared to be limited to two contractors.[174] Gerace boasted, accurately as it turned out, that his case was a "'landmark decision, which is why I'm an instant celebrity.'" Emblematically, Nello Teer, the owner of the other firm, Nello Teer Company of North Carolina, the next year became the president of the AGC, once a largely union-oriented organization, in which open shop firms had become a force to be reckoned with. Teer himself identified one of the movement's major problems—wages and benefits inferior to those of the union sector. Although equalization, he conceded, appeared to deprive open-shop employers of their chief advantage, there would still be "no union hampering management's right to manage."[175]

Gerace may have set the precedent, but the contractor involved was small even though he worked for Dow, a leading force among the Roundtable's corporate users pushing for nonunion construction. The enduring importance of double-breasting jurisprudence is associated with a charge filed in 1972 against Peter Kiewit Sons. Its higher profile stemmed both from the fact that the U.S. Supreme Court ruled on it and that Kiewit was "one of the world's largest construction concerns," whose owner was very wealthy, prominent, and politically well-connected.[176] Peter Kiewit Sons (Kiewit) and South Prairie Construction Company were both wholly owned subsidiaries of Peter Kiewit Sons, Inc. (Inc.). Local 627 of the Operating Engineers had represented Kiewit workers building highways in Oklahoma since 1960. During contract negotiations in 1970 an official of Kiewit, which was the only union highway contractor in the state, told the union that if it could not induce more contractors to sign the collective bargaining agreement, it would stop bidding and leave Oklahoma. While the 1970-73 agreement was in effect, Inc. decided that it could no longer bid competitively because nonunion

---

[173]Gerace Construction Inc., 193 NLRB at 645-46. The Board has continued to use the circular argument; e.g., United Constructors, 233 NLRB 904, 913 (1977).

[174]In fact, a month after *Gerace*, the NLRB specifically noted the similarities to that case in deciding Frank N. Smith Associates, Inc., 194 NLRB 212 (1971).

[175]"Open Shop—Problem or Solution?" *Roads & Streets*, Apr. 1972, at 107, 108.

[176]Peter Kiewit's estimated personal wealth of $150-$200 million made him "perhaps the leading figure in Nebraskan social and business circles. His "$400 million dollar empire was amassed through building...public works projects...." He owned a daily newspaper and a television station in Omaha, and was board chairman of railroad, telephone, banking, and gas companies. George Goodman, "Peter Kiewit, 79, Builder in West; Public Works Created an Empire," *NYT*, Nov. 4, 1979, sect. 1 at 44, col. 1. In 1967, President Johnson named him, together with George Meany, Walter Reuther, Whitney Young, Jr., and other public figures to the President's Committee on Urban Housing. *Report of the President's Committee on Urban Housing: A Decent Home* iii (1968). Kiewit was the 12th largest U.S. contractor in 1972, gaining new contracts valued at $436 million. "The ENR 400: Top Contractors Increase Domestic Work," *ENR*, Apr. 12, 1973, at 46, 51.

contractors were paying 50 cents to one dollar less per hour in wages. Kiewit's continuing presence, according to its vice president and Inc. director, would require "a company that wasn't burdened by the union agreement." To that end, Inc. activated South Prairie, another wholly owned subsidiary, which built highways in other states without a union work force. In 1972, South Prairie successfully bid on one of the largest highway contracts in Oklahoma history. The administrative law judge (ALJ) found that Inc. set Kiewit's labor policies and also gave South Prairie its instructions; most of South Prairie's supervisors had previous worked for Kiewit in the same capacity. She also found that Inc. brought South Prairie in "for the specific purpose of circumventing Peter Kiewit's statutory duty to honor the agreement." The ALJ concluded that Kiewit and South Prairie formed a unit appropriate for collective bargaining and that they violated their duty to apply the collective bargaining agreement to South Prairie's employees; she therefore ordered them to make those workers whole. The NLRB, however, dismissed the complaint. Asserting that common control of labor policies was a critical factor in determining whether both employers were a single enterprise, the Board conclusorily held that: "Although Inc. determined that South Prairie would operate on a nonunion basis, South Prairie's labor policy determinations within that framework are set by South Prairie's president, whereas Kiewit's labor policies are determined by an official of Inc."[177] The same three Board members, two Republicans and a conservative former Regional Office director appointed during the Eisenhower administration, had also decided *Gerace*.[178]

Two years later, the D.C. Circuit vacated the Board's order. Although the court observed that centralized control of labor relations was not "'critical' in the sense of being the sine qua non of 'single employer' status," it emphasized that Inc.'s exercise of control in imposing the nonunion framework on South Prairie "constitutes a very substantial qualitative degree of centralized control of labor relations." In addition, however, the court found strong evidence in favor of substantial interrelation of operations and common management.[179] The Board's proemployer bias had been amply on display in its assertion that the union was merely "'attempting to seize upon common corporate ownership to achieve initial representation without engaging in an organization campaign.'"[180] Gerard Smetana, the Roundtable's chief labor law litigator, warned the group that the appellate decision prevented contractors from using double-breasting to avoid the economic consequences that lawful subcontractor agreements posed.[181]

---

[177]Peter Kiewit Sons' Co., 206 NLRB at

[178]Gross, *Broken Promise* at 195, 219-21.

[179]Local No. 627, International Union of Operating Engineers v. NLRB, 518 F.2d 1040, 1046 (quote), 1047 (D.C. Cir. 1975).

[180]Local No. 627, International Union of Operating Engineers v. NLRB, 518 F.2d at 1049.

[181]*CUH*, Nov. 1975, at 4.

The Supreme Court affirmed the D.C. Circuit's ruling that Kiewit and South Prairie were a single employer—but only on the grounds that Congress had charged the appellate courts and not the Supreme Court with the primary responsibility of denying or enforcing Board orders. However, it vacated the lower court's ruling that the two firms' employees formed an appropriate bargaining unit on the grounds that the court had invaded the Board's statutory jurisdiction instead of permitting the NLRB to determine the appropriate unit.[182] In the interim before the Board decided the case, one perceptive commentator, offering a "somewhat cynical and speculative reading," asked: "Was the Supreme Court hinting that the Board could insulate future 'double breasted' decisions from reversal on the basis of unit, rather than single employer, grounds?"[183] On remand in 1977, the Board did indeed determine that the operations of South Prairie, which were exclusively involved in highway construction, and Kiewit, which also included such heavy construction work as airports, mills, and railroad bridges, were "not so closely intertwined in all respects" as to create one community of interests.[184] The Court of Appeals, which is restricted by the NLRA to determining whether the Board has determined an (not the most) appropriate bargaining unit, is required to affirm unless it finds that the Board's determination is arbitrary and unreasonable. In 1979 it affirmed.[185]

Since that time the Board has approved double-breasting "except in those few instances in which an ill-planned employer...blatantly transferred unit work to a jointly owned and supervised nonunion firm."[186] In contrast, the NLRB deems

---

[182]South Prairie Construction Co. v. Local No. 627, International Union of Operating Engineers, 425 U.S. 800 (1976).

[183]Tim Bornstein, "The Emerging Law of the 'Double Breasted' Operation in the Construction Industry," 28 *LLJ* 77-88 at 87 (1977).

[184]Peter Kiewit Sons' Co., 231 NLRB 76, 78 (1977).

[185]Local No. 627, International Union of Operating Engineers v. NLRB, 595 F.2d 844 (D.C. Cir. 1979).

[186]Stephen Belfort, "Labor Law and the Double-Breasted Employer: A Critique of the Single Employer and Alter Ego Doctrines and a Proposed Reformulation," 1987 *Wisc. L. Rev.* 67, 82. One such exception was Appalachian Construction, Inc., 235 NLRB 685 (1978), where the Board's finding that the same people conducted day-to-day supervision prompted it to see that the "subcontract was nothing more than an attempt to deceive the Union and thereby circumvent their obligations under the labor agreement." The contingency in juridical-economic development is signaled by the fact that during the pendency of the Kiewit litigation, even astute legal observers argued that it was unclear "whether the 'double breasted' movement is likely to gather great momentum and to become a movement of national importance or whether it will be utilized only by a handful of smaller contractors in isolated markets. The emerging law on this sensitive issue appears to favor the contractor, but it is still in such an early and tentative stage of development that it would be premature to assume that the would-be 'double breaster' can proceed to organize a non-union affiliate in the secure knowledge that the NLRB and courts will smile upon his efforts—far from it." Bornstein, "The Emerging Law of the 'Double Breasted' Operation in the Construction Industry" at 77. See also

irrelevant employers' admission that their chief purpose in creating the nonunion entity is to avoid the uncompetitive consequences of their labor contracts.[187] By the mid-1980s, the consolidation of this proemployer jurisprudence prompted union lawyers to conclude that the Board mechanically approved double-breasting "so long as the same person does not exercise the day-to-day control of labor relations" regardless of common control and ownership or of joint use of the same offices, equipment and technicians. From the union perspective, therefore, "the NLRB has made a joke of collective bargaining in the construction industry. ... By manipulating their...corporate structure, contractors can work either union or nonunion as they choose."[188]

By 1986, 20 of the 25 largest U.S. construction firms operated dual shops,[189] the most prominent example being the purchase in 1977 by Fluor, an NCA member and one of the largest construction firms, of nonunion Daniel.[190] To nullify this administrative and judicial promotion of the antiunion movement, the BCTD sought to persuade Congress to amend the NLRA to make double-breasting an unfair labor practice. Bills were filed, hearings held, and reports issued on the subject during the 1980s.[191] In 1986, a bill embodying that provision passed the House 229-173. Unions undertook their biggest push in the 100th Congress, when the Construction Industry Labor Law Amendments of 1987, passed the House again 227-197.[192] The perception that the NLRB and the courts had eroded the illegality

---

Robert Penfield, "The Double-Breasted Operation in the Construction Industry," 27 *LLJ* 89-93 at 93 (1976).

[187]Belfort, "Labor Law and the Double-Breasted Employer" at 86.

[188]Robert Connerton, "Collective Bargaining: A Process Under Siege," in *American Labor Policy: A Critical Appraisal of the National Labor Relations Act* 246-58 at 254 (Charles Morris ed. 1987) (general counsel, Laborers Int'l). The president of the NCA, Robert McCormick, observed that unions' weakened position combined with the fact NCA member firms no longer sign local contracts (and therefore no longer have other collective bargaining agreements in force in the same geographic area) has meant that since the late 1970s employers have not had to resort to "tricks" to engage in double-breasted operations. Telephone interview with Robert McCormick, Washington, D.C. (Mar. 9, 1999).

[189]*The Construction Industry Labor Law Amendments: Hearing Before the Subcommittee on Labor-Management Relations of the House Committee on Education and Labor*, 100th Cong., 1st Sess. 11 (1987) (testimony of Robert Georgine).

[190]"Fluor Acquires 96% of Daniel," *ENR*, June 9, 1977, at 15; *CUH*, July 1977.

[191]*Developments in Labor Law Affecting the Construction Industry: Hearing Before the Subcommittee on Labor-Management Relations of the House Committee on Education and Labor*, 98th Cong., 1st Sess. (1983); H.R. 6043, 98th Cong., 2d Sess. (1984); H. R. Rep. No. 311: *Construction Industry Labor Law Amendments of 1985*, 99th Cong., 1st Sess. (1985).

[192]H. R. Rep. No. 137: *Building and Construction Industry Labor Law Amendments of 1987*, 100th Cong., 1st Sess (1987). See also S. Rep. No. 314: *Construction Industry Labor Law Amendments of 1987*, 100th Cong., 2d Sess. (1988); H.R. 931 and S. 807, 101st Cong., 1st Sess. (1989). The Senate never voted on any of these bills.

of "sham" double-breasting prompted bipartisan support for amendments to "restore the law's original intent."[193] S. 492/H. R. 281 would have amended the NLRA's definition of "employer" by adding: "In the construction industry, any two or more business entities performing or otherwise conducting or supervising the same or similar work, in the same or different geographical areas, and having, directly or indirectly (A) substantial common ownership; (B) common management; or (C) common control; shall be deemed a single employer." It would then have applied this definition to a new provision added to section 8(d) of the NLRA, which defines the employer's obligation to bargain in good faith: "Whenever the collective bargaining involves employees of a business entity comprising part of a single employer in the construction industry...the duty to bargain collectively...shall include the duty to apply the terms of a collective bargaining agreement between such business entity and a labor organization to all other business entities comprising the single employer within the geographical area covered by the agreement."[194]

Congressional testimony in 1987 on double-breasting by union and management officials underscored their respective positions as supplicants and power-holders. Georgine, representing the BCTD, confided to the Senate Labor Subcommittee that the building trades unions "are sympathetic to the need of our employers to remain competitive, and I am proud of the record of the building trades over the last decade in actively pursuing the elimination of non-competitive work practices...." He then explained the unions' view that the NLRA "dictates that workers and management must together negotiate solutions to the non-competitive aspects of collective bargaining agreements, and the Act should prohibit employers from unilaterally solving such problems through a decision to become double-breasted." All that the statutory protection boiled down to was labor's entitlement to "the opportunity to attempt to preserve our jobs through collectively bargained modifications, or concessions if you will...."[195]

The NCA, whose members had created nonunion entities to compete on the basis of nonunion wages and working conditions, strongly opposed the bill.[196]

---

[193]133 Cong. Rec. S 1918 (Feb. 5, 1987) (statement of Sen. D'Amato, Rep.) (Lexis).

[194]S. 492, § 2, 100th Cong., 1st Sess. (1987).

[195]*Construction Industry Labor Law Amendments of 1987: Hearing Before the Subcommittee on Labor of the Senate Committee on Labor and Human Resources*, 100th Cong., 1st Sess. 57 (1987). If all that were at stake was servants' right to petition their masters to acquiesce in the latter's demands for lower wages and inferior working conditions, it is unclear what the unions hoped to gain. After all, even under the proposed amendments, employers could still lawfully negotiate with them to impasse and then implement those wages and conditions; the unions would then have to strike to determine which side controlled the labor market—the same option available to them whenever employers create sham double-breasted operations.

[196]*The Construction Industry Labor Law Amendments: Hearing Before the Subcommittee on Labor-Management Relations of the House Committee on Education and Labor*, 100th Cong., 1st

Asserting that neither construction companies nor the law could alter the fact that "it is ultimately the construction user who determines the division between union and non-union market share," their general counsel told Congress that in the sector that was—whether "for reasons of competitive cost, geographic considerations, perceived productivity factors, or simple preference"—"owner determined as open shop," failure to establish open-shop subsidiaries would have "totally foreclosed" that market to their firms.[197]

The NCA's view was fully corroborated by the CEO of du Pont, the corporate user that since 1970 had perhaps done most to support the Roundtable-inspired assault on construction unions. (For example, in 1983, du Pont, which awarded contracts to both union and non union low-bidding qualified contractors, cancelled five contracts with unionized firms after other unions had honored the picket set up by pipefitters at the separate gate for nonunion workers.)[198] Richard Heckert sought to place the anti-dual shop bill in the larger framework of U.S. industry's worldwide competitiveness. From the end of World War II until the 1970s, the fact that union contractors "had a virtual monopoly" on industrial projects did not concern industrial customers: because U.S. manufacturers faced little competition from non-U.S. producers, at least in the U.S. market, "construction costs were not a major constraint as we expanded capacity": being "in the same boat," no U.S. producer "suffered a competitive disadvantage." But in the 1970s, under the dual impact of an increase in construction costs and especially construction labor costs in excess of the already high general rates of inflation and the increasing competitiveness of non-U.S. producers with lower capital and operating costs, the "situation could not continue long without the loss of domestic business and jobs in capital-intensive industries." Fortunately, for U.S. capital, by the 1970s "free market economics finally worked and some sorely needed alternatives began to develop. In addition to the few open-shop contractors who were scaled to do major work, many large union contractors acquired new open-shop capabilities. It became possible to award construction contracts on the basis of comeptitive costs."[199]

Sess. 220-22 (1987) (NCA written submission).

[197]*Construction Industry Labor Law Amendments of 1987: Hearing Before the Subcommittee on Labor of the Senate Committee on Labor and Human Resources*, 100th Cong., 1st Sess. 202, 205-206 (1987) (statement of Concerned General Counsel of Major U.S. Construction Companies). At least one NCA member, Ebasco Services, announced at the BCTD annual convention in 1990 that it had shed its nonunion subsidiaries and remained successful. "Health Care Affecting Competition," *ENR*, July 19, 1990, at 13 (Lexis).

[198]*CUH*, Feb. 1983, at 2.

[199]*Construction Industry Labor Law Amendments of 1987: Hearing Before the Subcommittee on Labor of the Senate Committee on Labor and Human Resources*, 100th Cong., 1st Sess. 111 (1987) (statement of Richard Heckert). The competition after the 1960s was described by the National Coalition to Defeat S. 492 as "preclud[ing] manufacturers from continuing to transfer their

The happy end for du Pont was that by 1987, its $2 billion annual capital budget was equally split between union and open shops: "Construction costs came down as open shops submitted bids at a lower unit cost, and union shops reduced their bids to stay competitive." The anti-dual shop amendment, however, would "break what the free market fixed." Because the result would be the closing of the contractor's union or nonunion entity, du Pont and other manufacturers would lose: as the pool of available contractors bidding shrank, "competitive bidding would inevitably become less intense."[200] In the welter of all this big-picture discussion of the centrality of cost- and especially wage-cutting to competitiveness, Senator Metzenbaum was unable to elicit an adequate response from his interlocutor to this facetiously thought-provoking question: "Why doesn't Du Pont form a separate operation and get some cheap executives. [Laughter]"[201] What du Pont in fact got was cheap engineers. The NCA reported in 1991 that du Pont in the course of an unprecedented cost-cutting program expected to lay off more than 550 engineers and professional support staff in Delaware. To leap into the breach, BE&K, one of the most prominent exponents of the antiunion construction movement, which had a five-year relationship with du Pont, planned to open an office in Delaware employing more than 200 people.[202]

Regardless of the economic advantages conferred on construction employers by the administrative and judicial rulings facilitating the establishment of nonunion entities by unionized firms, considerable force attached to Northrup's speculation that "if the Kiewit decision had gone the other way, the vacuum would have been filled by unionized companies becoming fully open shop, and by newly created companies formed to work open shop. The market has worked in this manner. Undoubtedly, it will continue to do so."[203] Indeed, although Northrup made this the-laws-of-economics-are-stronger-than-the-laws-of-men argument in 1995 in criticizing Steven Allen's efforts to single out the law of double-breasting as the primary explanation of the continued decline of the building trades unions in the 1980s, Allen had already conceded the point in 1987 at the time of congressional debates over amendments to the NLRA to make double-breasting an unfair labor practice: "'If this law is passed, the unionized contractors, who are already declining in number, will simply stop signing new contracts, and more

---

construction costs to the consumer." *Id.* at 296.

[200]*Construction Industry Labor Law Amendments of 1987: Hearing Before the Subcommittee on Labor of the Senate Committee on Labor and Human Resources*, 100th Cong., 1st Sess. 112 (1987) (statement of Richard Heckert).

[201]*Construction Industry Labor Law Amendments of 1987: Hearing Before the Subcommittee on Labor of the Senate Committee on Labor and Human Resources*, 100th Cong., 1st Sess. 163 (1987).

[202]NCA, *Bulletin*, #92-36 (Apr. 17, 1992).

[203]Herbert Northrup, "Doublebreasted Operations and the Decline of Construction Unionism," 16 (3) *JLR* 379-85 at 383 (Summer 1995).

construction will go to the non-union sector.'"[204]

Thanks in part to the intense lobbying that the Roundtable—which rhetorically asked its members to consider the possibility that next manufacturing firms would be prohibited from maintaining union and nonunion plants[205]—mobilized, the anti-double-breasting proposals were not enacted. But construction unions succeeded in keeping the issue alive by means of the Clinton administration's Commission on the Future of Worker-Management Relations. In connection with its focus on the socially deleterious impact of the trend toward treating employees as contingent workers, the commission recommended that the threshold coverage definitions of "employee" and "employer" in all federal labor and tax legislation be made uniform and rooted in the economic realities of employment relations. Within this framework the commission also recommended that the NLRB expand the single employer doctrine to prevent union construction firms from spinning off subsidiaries to do the same kind of work free from collective bargaining obligations.[206]

Membership and Wages

Evidently a fair percentage of the plumber's work can be done by less-skilled men; otherwise the plumbers would not fear their competition so greatly.[207]

Some sense of the enormous membership reduction that the construction unions have suffered since the 1960s can be gleaned from Table 22, which shows their average per capita membership paid to the AFL-CIO in 1965 and 1995.

Among the larger craft unions, the boilermakers, bricklayers, carpenters, ironworkers, painters, and plasterers all experienced membership losses ranging between 30 and 61 percent. Among unions virtually all of whose members worked in construction, only the plumbers and operating engineers were able to increase their membership even slightly. These figures become much more stark in contrast with the 45 percent increase in the number of construction workers between 1965 and 1995.[208]

---

[204]Warren Brookes, "Construction Unions on Self-Destructive Campaign," *San Francisco Chronicle*, May 5, 1987 (Westlaw).

[205]*CUH*, Feb.-Mar. 1987.

[206]Commission on the Future of Worker-Management Relations, *Final Report*, chapter 5 (1995). John Dunlop chairmanship of the commission preordained this outcome.

[207]J. Seidman, J. London, B. Karsh, D. Tagliacozzo, *The Worker Views His Union* 62 (1958).

[208]From 1965 to 1995, production or nonsupervisory workers in construction rose 45 percent (from 2,749,000 to 3,993,000). Calculated according to *Handbook of U.S. Labor Statistics* 139 (2d ed.; Eva Jacobs ed. 1998).

Table 22: Construction Union Membership, 1965 and 1995			
Union	1965	1995	Change (%)
Asbestos	12,000	12,000	0
Boilermakers	108,000	42,000	-61
Bricklayers	120,000	84,000	-30
Carpenters	700,000	378,000	-46
Electrical	616,000	679,000	10
Elevator Constructors	12,000	20,000	67
Ironworkers	132,000	82,000	-38
Laborers	403,000	352,000	-13
Operating Engineers	270,000	298,000	10
Painters	160,000	95,000	-41
Plasterers	68,000	29,000	-57
Plumbers	217,000	220,000	1
Roofers	22,000	21,000	-5
Sheet Metal	100,000	106,000	6

Source: BNA, *Directory of U.S. Labor Organizations: 1997 Edition*, at 81-82 (C. Gifford ed., 1997); BNA, *Directory of U.S. Labor Organizations: 1986-87 Edition*, at 61-65 (Courtney Gifford ed., 1986)

The minimal diminution in the number of unions contradicts repeated predictions over the years of mergers that would reduce the building trades unions to four to six by the end of the century. The persistence of small and overlapping unions results, no doubt, primarily from internal resistance by officials who would lose their positions. Nevertheless, employers would presumably not welcome the additional bargaining strength that union amalgamation would effect. Moreover, the tens of thousands of specialty contractors may guard craft lines as jealously as unions.[209]

---

[209]In the 1920s, the Communist William Z. Foster declared that the existence of 22 building trades unions was "not only incredibly stupid but also, in view of the rapid concentration of the enemy's forces, a criminal betrayal of the workers' interests." W. Z. Foster, *Misleaders of Labor* 321 (1927). See also W. Cummins, "Industrial Unionism in the Building Trades of the United States," 15

A 1980 Census Bureau special survey revealed that 31.6 percent of employed wage and salary workers in the construction industry were in labor organizations.[210] Viewed occupationally, 33.0 percent of carpenters, 48.7 percent of other construction craft workers, and 32.9 percent of construction laborers were union members.[211]

Questions that have been included in the CPS annually since 1983 also underscore the ongoing sharp decline in construction union membership. In 1983, 27.5 percent of employed wage and salary workers in construction were union members; by 1998, the share had fallen to 17.8 percent. This decrease resulted from the fact that while construction employment rose 44.7 percent, from 4,109,000 to 5,946,000, union membership fell 6.6 percent, from 1,131,000 to 1,056,000. This pattern of stagnating membership despite explosive growth in employment deviates strongly from developments in manufacturing: there, a 3.7 percent increase in employment accompanied by a catastrophic 41.0 percent decline in membership depressed the unionization rate from 27.8 percent to 15.8 percent in 1998.[212] More ominous is that the proportion of union workers receiving less than the union wage in construction rose markedly during the 1980s.[213]

In certain trades, however, union density has remained far above average. Structural metal workers, electricians, and plumbers occupied the highest rungs with rates of 65, 43, and 37 percent in 1995, down from 74, 46, and 43 percent, respectively, in 1985.[214] At the other extreme, only 10 percent of painters and roofers were organized in 1996.[215]

---

(4) *ILR* 568-80 (Apr. 1927). When the CIO tried to organize construction workers along industrial lines, it found contractors as resistant as workers. "C.I.O. Makes Sorties in Building Field," *NYT*, Mar. 21, 1940, at 1, col. 3, at 20, col. 3-4.

[210]BLS, *Earnings and Other Characteristics of Organized Workers, May 1980*, tab. 6 at 20 (Bull. 2105, 1981).

[211]BLS, *Earnings and Other Characteristics of Organized Workers, May 1980*, tab. 2 at 10.

[212]32 (1) *EE*, tab. 53 at 209 (Jan. 1985); BLS, "Union Members in 1998," tab. 3 (USDL 99-21, Jan. 25, 1999).

[213]Steven Allen, "Declining Unionization in Construction: The Facts and the Reasons," 41 (3) *ILRR* 343-59, tab. 3 at 349 (Apr. 1988). This series, which ran from 1973 to 1981, showed stability through 1978, at which point the share jumped from 30.0 percent to 45.6 percent by 1981. Allen's data also show that the unionization rate among blue-collar construction workers declined from 47.3 percent in 1966 to 44.8 percent in 1970; large declines then occurred between 1977 and 1978 (41.1 to 36.6 percent) and 1981 and 1983 (39.0 to 32.0 percent). *Id.* tab. 1 at 345. Allen does not explain the timing. Allen, "Developments in Collective Bargaining in Construction in the 1980s and 1990s" at 15, tab. 3 at 37, also points out that the organization rate among all construction employees fell steadily from 42 percent in 1970 to 22 percent in 1987, when it leveled off.

[214]Barry Hirsch & David Macpherson, *Union Membership and Earnings Data Book: Compilations from the Current Population Survey* tab. 14a at 104-105, tab. 14c at 128-29 (1996).

[215]Center for the Protection of Workers' Rights, *The Construction Chart Book: The U.S. Construction Industry and Its Workers* chart 14c (2d ed. 1998). These proportions are somewhat lower

Although the decline in unionization has gone hand in hand with a diminution of the gap between union and nonunion wages, the union premium remains significant.[216] The CPS also reveals that in 1983 the usual weekly earnings of full-time wage and salary workers in construction were $522 for union members or 74 percent higher than the $300 that their nonunion counterparts received; by 1998, the premium was smaller albeit still large—59 percent ($790 and $496). The premium has thus increased relative to the premium for all private sector nonagricultural employees, which declined by one-half, from 39 percent to 26 percent.[217] Private employer surveys for 1996 reveal even larger gaps: a weighted average hourly wage (including benefits) for all crafts of $15.28 for nonunion journeymen compared to $28.39 for union workers or 86 percent higher. Remarkably, the ten components of wages that employers decried most bitterly—overtime, shift premium, show-up pay, manning restrictions, fringes paid on hours paid, time paid not worked, and subsistence, premium, holiday, and travel pay—amounted to only $2.27 or 17 percent of the total difference of $13.11.[218] In individual occupations the decline in the union-nonunion wage gap varied but not in any obvious conformity with differential rates of union density. Thus, from 1985 to 1995, the gap in weekly earnings fell from 80 to 53 percent among bricklayers, 65 to 53 percent among carpenters, from 75 to 66 percent among painters, from 58 to 30 percent among structural metal workers, and from 73 to 65 percent among laborers; among electricians and plumbers, however, the gap actually rose—from 41 to 45 percent and 61 to 68 percent, respectively.[219]

More interesting still is the Roundtable's admission that even from customers' and employers' perspective, "the absence of travel and/or subsistence pay provisions is not necessarily advantageous. In cases where employees are drawn from a union whose jurisdiction includes both an urban and distant rural areas, it may be very difficult to attract sufficient numbers of skilled craftsmen in the more distant areas without travel/subsistence pay."[220] Implicit in this logic is

---

than those presented by Hirsch & Macpherson although they are derived from the CPS.

[216]According to Allen, "Developments in Collective Bargaining in Construction in the 1980s and 1990s" at 18-19, tab. 4 at 38, the gap rose from 37.7 percent in 1967 to a peak of 55.3 percent in 1977, falling back to 38.8 percent by 1981; another series, beginning in 1983, fell from 39.6 percent to 29.0 percent in 1992. According to Hirsch & Macpherson, *Union Membership and Earnings Data Book* tab. 6 at 16, the union-nonunion mean hourly wage gap rose from 55 percent in 1973 to 67 percent in 1977 before falling to 42 percent by 1981, after which it fluctuated between 42 and 58 percent.

[217]32 (1) *EE*, tab. 55 at 211 (Jan. 1985); 45 (1) *EE*, tab. 43 at 218 (Jan. 1998); BLS, "Union Members in 1998," tab. 4 (USDL 99-21, Jan. 25, 1999).

[218]Northrup, "Construction Union Programs to Regain Jobs" at 4.

[219]Hirsch & Macpherson, *Union Membership and Earnings Data Book*, tab. 14a at 104-105, 108, tab. 14c at 128-29, 132.

[220]BR, 2 *Coming to Grips with Some Major Problems in the Construction Industry* 54

the conclusion that the abandonment of these wage components must have caused either employers to make do with less skilled workers or craftsmen to acquiesce in totally uncompensated longer commutes to and from work or disruption of their nonwork lives.

Despite huge gaps in wage and benefit levels,[221] and the epidemic violation of labor standards laws by nonunion firms that deprive workers of overtime, social security, unemployment and workers compensation, and OSHA protection by unlawfully misclassifying them as self-employed,[222] management audaciously asserts that unions lack any appeal: "'There are no sweatshops left. In fact there are no union war cries left that people can identify with.'"[223] Yet if even the Roundtable could be appalled that construction was so dangerous that in 1979 injuries accounted for 6.5 percent of the total cost of industrial, commercial, and utility construction, is it implausible that workers themselves in the 1990s would regard their places of employment as sweatshops from which they required protection when those costs had risen to between 7.9 and 15.0 percent?[224]

The decline in the degree of unionization beginning in the 1970s suggests that construction unions were no longer seeking to extend their scope, but rather were preoccupied with defending positions in various geographic areas and sub-branches against open-shop inroads. This restrictive strategy raises the question as to whether it remained true that: "For the well-established employers, it is...important to have a floor under competitive labor costs. Otherwise, the threat is always present of a competitor securing cost advantages through undercutting labor standards."[225] This argument was hardly obsolete, but its applicability may have been confined to regions and sub-branches that traditionally counted as

---

(1978).

[221]Benefits, especially pensions and health plans, in nonunion firms are "less common and generous...." Northrup, *Open Shop Construction Revisited* at 578 (quote); 'The Hidden Issue in Bargaining," *ENR*, June 24, 1984, at 56.

[222]According to the House Committee on Government Operations, "[c]onstruction appears to be the industry most widely affected" by employers' misclassification of workers as independent contractors. H. Rep. No. 1053: *Contractor Games: Misclassifying Employees as Independent Contractors*, 102d Cong., 2d Sess. 2 (1992). See generally, *Exploiting Workers by Misclassifying Them as Independent Contractors: Hearing Before the Employment and Housing Subcommittee of the House Committee on Government Operations*, 102d Cong., 1st Sess. (1991).

[223]"Union Construction in Trouble," *ENR*, Nov. 5, 1981, at 26 (Lexis) (quoting Dale Kirkland, executive director, NECA, northern California).

[224]John Everett & Peter Frank, Jr., "Costs of Accidents and Injuries to the Construction Industry," *JCEM*, June 1996, at 158-64. For an overview of the extraordinarily high workers' compensation premiums in the various states, see Mary Powers, "Insurance: Programs Cut into Workers' Comp Cost," *ENR*, Sept. 28, 1998, at 32-33.

[225]Frank Pierson, "Building-Trades Bargaining Plan in Southern California," 70 (1) *MLR* 14 (Jan. 1950). See also Haber, *Industrial Relations in the Building Industry* at 255; Bertram and Maisel, *Industrial Relations* at 40.

organized.

Further discontent may arise from the fact that while average hourly earnings of production or nonsupervisory workers in construction rose 164 percent from $6.06 in 1972 to $16.00 in 1997, those of their counterparts in manufacturing and the total private economy rose 245 percent (from $3.82 to $13.17) and 231 percent (from $3.70 to $12.26), respectively. Thus, while hourly construction wages exceeded those in manufacturing and the total private economy by 59 percent and 64 percent, respectively, in 1972, by 1997 the excess had declined to 21 percent and 31 percent, respectively. Weekly earnings adjusted for inflation put into sharper relief the absolute and relative decline of construction wages. Average weekly earnings in construction increased from $235.89 in 1973 to $622.40 by 1997; but the $511.69 in constant (1982) dollars in 1973 represented the high point, from which the sum fell by more than 26 percent to a low of $377.07 by 1992, rising only slightly to $382.78 by 1997. Workers in other sectors also experienced real weekly earnings declines, but much smaller ones: 6 percent in manufacturing (from $361.08 in 1973 to $340.18 in 1997), and 17 percent in the total private economy (from $315.38 to $260.89). Accordingly, the excess of deflated weekly construction over manufacturing and total private-sector earnings fell from 42 and 62 percent in 1973 to 13 and 47 percent, respectively, by 1997.[226] That the increasing weight of the low-wage nonunion construction sector is reflected in the relative and absolute deterioration of the industry's wages is suggested by the fact that construction unemployment, though remaining high, moderated vis-à-vis aggregate unemployment.[227]

The proposition that sweatshops are alive and well in open shop construction found its most credible support in an absolutely unimpeachable witness, Ted C. Kennedy, cofounder and chairman of BE&K, one of the largest construction firms in the United States, former president of ABC, and one of the leading spokesmen of the open shop movement, who in 1982 was finally coopted into the Roundtable's Contractors Advisory Committee.[228] In the most brutally blunt public speech ever delivered by a construction employer, Kennedy told the Engineering and Construction Conference of the American Institute of Chemical Engineers in 1992:

---

[226]Calculated according to *Handbook of U.S. Labor Statistics* at 152-53.

[227]Between 1948 and 1975, the ratio of the unemployment rate in construction to the aggregate rate averaged 2.2:1; between 1976 and 1997 it declined to 2.05. Likewise, unemployment in construction as a proportion of total unemployment declined from 10.6 percent to 9.6 percent. Calculated according to *Handbook of U.S. Labor Statistics* at 85-86.

[228]"ABC Works to Erase Nonunion Image," *ENR*, Oct. 18, 1979, at 31, 34, 35; BE&K, "1998 Corporate Overview"; telephone interview with Ted C. Kennedy (Birmingham, AL, Nov. 20, 1998); BR, CC, Minutes, Feb. 16, 1982, at 7.

We shift the cost of benefits to our employees. We eliminate any wage increases. We retire the older, more expensive talent. We reclassify people as probationary, and we abandon any meaningful retirement plan except social security. We do it all in the name of competitiveness and a free market. We are without a doubt the biggest whores in the business. ... And if we contractors and engineers are the biggest prostitutes, you owners are the pimps and procurers. You've reveled in the competitive world of union and merit shop contractors fighting it out for market share. You've sat back and watched with glee as we beat each other down.... The average wage increase in the merit shop industry over the last 10 years is less than 10 cents per hour per year. Few craftsmen have any kind of meaningful retirement program. Fewer still have any kind of medical or hospitalization [sic] beyond workman's compensation. And, if they have a heart attack, we'll probably have to take up a collection for the burial. And our idea of job security—as long as the sun is shining and there's a weld to be made. But, if either stops, your severance pay is just as long as it takes you to get to the gate. We'll train you—on your own time.... You'll be exposed to one of the more dangerous occupations, but if the law doesn't protect you, in all likelihood—we won't either. ... You owners are sitting there watching us degrade what is supposed to be our most valuable commodity—our people. And, as the wages fall, the benefits disappear and more and more leave the industry, you take refuge by saying, "it's the American way—the competitive market place at work—the free enterprise system in action." B-a-l-o-n-e-y!!!!! It's shortsighted...and destined to turn over our industry to others—outside the United States. How in the world do we attract bright, energetic, young people into a business where they can't earn a retirement; they can't expect to work a full year; they may get a 10 cents per hour per year raise; and other benefits are virtually nonexistent. ... I detest monopolies. And one of the more positive moves in the last 20 years is the rise of the merit shop movement as a viable competitor to the union monopoly. But, as valuable as the breakup of the monpoly was, we contractors and you owners have absolutely abandoned the responsibility that goes with increased competition. The increased competition has provided a large portion of its cost savings at the expense of the individual employees' well-being. ... But, it does not need to be. We could all raise craft wages a reasonable amount, provide benefits we're not ashamed of, create a career for young people instead of a revolving door.... As long as owners believe that efficiency and cost effectiveness are directly related to low wages and minimal fringe rates, we are going to have continuing high turnover.... As long as contractors continue to treat their employees as seasonal harvest hands instead of skilled professionals, we cannot expect to maintain a work force of skilled 20-year veterans.... If either the contractors or the owners believe that this type of work force can compete with the Germans, or Scandinavians, or Japanese in the 21st century, you need to take a drug test![229]

Conditions like these, in which a few experienced and highly paid skilled workers supervise a dozen or more narrowly trained, semi-skilled, and low-waged 18- to 25-year-olds, exacerbated by employers' misclassification of their employees

---

[229]Ted C. Kennedy, "Managing Change in 21st Century" 3-8 (Engineering & Construction Conference of the Am. Institute of Chemical Engineers, San Francisco, Sept. 15, 1992) (manuscript made available by Ted C. Kennedy).

as self-employed in order to avoid employment taxes and labor standards statutes, and a piecework system that induces workers to drive themselves at a pace that cannot be sustained for more than 10 or 15 years, lend credence to unionists' claims that open-shop "'[m]anagement will blow it themselves.... They'll push and push and push until there'll be a rebellion.'"[230] As even John Dunlop, who prided himself on working on problems that took at least a decade to solve, conceded, the "conflict of interest" between unions' desire for broadly trained craft workers and employers' preference for narrow specialists "is not readily solved...."[231]

Even construction unions' worst enemies profess a desire to retain them. The Roundtable, presumably buoyed by the experience of pitting nonunion and newly chastened union firms against each other, proclaimed in 1982 that a construction industry that wishes to "remain vigorous...cannot afford the demise of the union sector...which offers experienced and capable contractors and a skilled manpower pool. The long-term interests of owners, contractors and labor will be best served by a competitive balance between the union and open-shop sectors."[232] But a decade later, when the Roundtable asserted that the union sector had shrunk to 25 to 30 percent from 75 to 80 percent in the early 1970s,[233] it made clear how limited a union role it was willing to tolerate. Reacting to the "union tool box of intimidation tactics" such as corporate campaigns, mass picketing, salting, job targeting, local prevailing-wage ordinances, and environmental permit "extortion," designed to re-expand unionization, the Roundtable declared that "the business community must take measures now to insure that the merit-based, free-enterprise system is preserved and strengthened to keep American business competitive in a fiercely competitive global marketplace." Unsurprisingly, it especially called on owners to support the antiunion ABC.[234]

The decline in union membership in the private sector in general and in construction in particular by the end of the century reached such precarious low points that even Herbert Northrup, who has devoted 60 years to combating them and the last 25 to touting open shop construction, was moved to concede that "it may well be that unions have declined below the level that is best for the public

---

[230]Erlich, *With Our Hands* at 189-91, 173 (quoting a union carpenter). Early in the nineteenth century, a leading orthodox political economist observed: "Workmen...when they are liberally paid by the piece, are very apt to overwork themselves, and to ruin their health and constitution in a few years. A carpenter in London, and in some other places, is not supposed to last in his vigour above eight years." J. R. McCullough, *The Principles of Political Economy, with some Inquiries Respecting Their Application* 347 (5th ed., 1864 [1825]; reprint 1965).

[231]John Dunlop, "Labor-Management Relations," in *Design and the Production of Houses* 259-301 at 282 (Burnham Kelly ed., 1959).

[232]BR, "Subjourneymen in Union Construction" 4 (Rep. D-1, Nov, 1992 [Feb. 1982]).

[233]"Roundtable Sees Union Tactics as Anti-Competitive," 40 (3) *Contractor* 1 (Mar. 1, 1993) (Westlaw).

[234]William Krizan, "Roundtable Paper Targets Unions," *ENR*, June 1, 1992, at 15.

good."[235] After watching building trades unions lose much of their membership since the 1970s, *ENR*, too, has reminded its readers periodically that the industry "needs a viable union sector. Unions help to make sure that the standard of living for the industry's millions of workers fall no further than it has. And they can act as a watchdog and voice for construction workers in general." To be sure, even *ENR* has in mind "more businesslike" unions,[236] that are "much more willing to put any rule on the negotiating table."[237] Indeed, *ENR* editorially praised unions for the "vigorous peaceful market competition" with nonunion firms, from which "owners stand to gain most."[238]

A quarter-century after their meteoric rise and efforts to specialize and deskill their workers, nonunion firms' chief problems remains their failure to train an adequate supply of labor. *ENR* bluntly conceded that "[i]f not for a series of economic recessions and a feast of skills available from former union workers, that sector's every-which-way, on-the-job or not-at-all training would have strangled its ability to compete."[239]

The irony that antiunion firms have parasitically flourished by undermining the union labor market is compounded by the fact that, the nonunion sector, which had trumpeted union racism as one of the key elements of its propaganda campaign against the building trades unions in the 1960s and 1970s, not only made no progress in integrating its work force, but also became marginally more white than its union foes: from 1977-78 to 1989 whites as a share of all union construction workers declined from 90.6 to 89 percent, while the share in the nonunion sector remained stagnant at 91 percent.[240] Indeed, how little progress the entire governmental civil rights thrusts of the late 1960s and early 1970s secured for black workers in the skilled construction crafts can be gauged by the proportions of blacks among such trades at the 1980 and 1990 census of population displayed in Table 23.[241]

---

[235]Herbert Northrup, "'New' Union Approaches to Membership Decline: Reviving the Policies of the 1920s?" 12 *JLR* 333-47 at 344 (Fall 1991).

[236]"A More Businesslike Union," *ENR*, Sept. 1, 1997, at 58 (editorial). See also "Union Construction Needs Help," *ENR*, Nov. 5, 1981, at 104 (editorial) ("A strong union sector helps keep wages and working conditions at decent levels on nonunion as well as union jobs..."); "BMW Corporate Attack May Not Be a Winner," *ENR*, Apr. 12, 1993, at 94 (editorial) ("unions deserve credit for representing members' interests in a competent and peaceful manner. They also sent a valuable message to international firms seeking to do business in the U.S. that at least one segment of our society militantly guards wages, benefits and working conditions of workers").

[237]Sherrie Winston, "Building Trades Sharpen Skills, Toughen Tactics and Organize," *ENR*, Sept. 1, 1997, at 28 (Lexis).

[238]"Roundtable Draft paper Shows Market Rumblings," *ENR*, June 1, 1992, at 58.

[239]"Open Shop at Critical Stage," *ENR*, Feb. 5, 1996, at 30.

[240]Steven Allen, "Developments in Collective Bargaining in Construction in the 1980s and 1990s" at 5 (NBER Working Paper No. 4674, 1994).

[241]See generally, GAO, *Federal Efforts to Increase Minority Opportunities in Skilled*

Table 23: Blacks as a % of Selected Construction Crafts, 1980 and 1990		
Craft	1980	1990
Brick- & stonemason, tile setter	14.9	12.8
Carpenter	5.1	5.1
Electrician	4.9	6.0
Painter	9.8	9.1
Plumber	6.6	7.1
Structural metal worker	5.2	5.7

Sources: USBC, *1980 Census of Population*, Vol. 1: *Characteristics of the Population*, Chapter D: *Detailed Population Characteristics*, Pt. 1: *United States Summary*, tab. 277 at 1-181 (Mar. 1984); USBC, *1990 Census of Population and Housing Equal Employment File* (CD-90-EEO-1, Jan. 1993).

Some observers have attributed the shrinkage of the union sector during the last quarter of the twentieth century to a relatively simple mechanism—"the market has again done its job of checking the abuse of private power...." The CISC also "performed well in breaking the wage spiral more quickly and less painfully than it could otherwise have been done, but basically sanity has been restored to construction bargaining by old-fashioned competitive forces."[242]

The displacement of unions of skilled workers by less skilled nonunionists presupposes some restructuring of the work processes that rendered once scarce and monopolizable skills redundant. If, as the Roundtable claimed in the early 1980s, "[a]t least 40 to 50% of construction work requires a minimum of skill and can be efficiently and safely done by helpers or subjourneymen," loss of control over the labor market by unions of the skilled would not be surprising.[243] To some extent the trade press focuses on this very point:

Among specialty contractors, innovations in materials and equipment may be playing the greatest role in allowing open shop firms into the marketplace. For example, "You don't have to know how to calk a joint or sweat lead to put hot water-heating and sanitary sewer systems in a house anymore" says a management source. "It's plastic pipe.

Construction Craft Unions Have Had Little Success (HRD-79-13, 1979). For somewhat higher proportions for all minorities based on the CPS earning files for 1996, see CPWR, *The Construction Chart Book: The U.S. Construction Industry and Its Workers* chart 17a (2d ed. 1998).

[242]DOL, Labor-Management Services Adm., *The Bargaining Structure in Construction: Problems and Prospects* 69 (1980) (prepared by Donald Cullen & Louis Feinberg).

[243]BR, "Subjourneymen in Union Construction" at 17.

All you need is a hacksaw, a can of glue and a little sense."[244]

Union activists also concede that the simplification brought about by preassembled materials and modular components, produced in factories by industrial workers, has gradually transformed the traditional skilled fabricator into a less skilled installer. Many nonunion contractors, in order to "speed up production...have broken down the crafts into dozens of repetitive tasks and teach a worker only to install toilets, hang doors or build chimneys."[245] Whether the accelerated fragmentation of the crafts into numerous subspecialties will mean that workers who are no longer masters of a whole trade will, like the deskilled before them, decide that, unable to rely on their collective skill, they can defend their working conditions and living standards only with the aid of a union's political-economic power remains to be seen.[246] When, however, such division of labor is combined with antiunion contractors' admission that "'our pay is substandard. We're paying less than Wal-Mart,'" a renaissance of unionism is hardly implausible.[247]

---

[244]"Union Construction in Trouble," *ENR*, Nov. 5, 1981, at 26, 27.

[245]Robert Tomsho, "Labor Squeeze: With Housing Strong, Builders Often Find Skilled Help Lacking," *WSJ*, Jan. 27, 1994, at A1 (Westlaw). See also Mark Erlich, "Who Will Build the Future?" *Labor Research Rev.*, No. 12, Fall 1988, at 1-19 at 8. Erlich laments that deskilling of carpenters, at least in the long run, "seems to be a foregone conclusion." Erlich, *With Our Hands* at 226.

[246]E.g., Joan Scott, *The Glassworkers of Carmaux: French Crafstmen and Political Action in a Nineteenth-Century City* 106 (1974).

[247]Mary Powers, "Groups Grapple with Training," *ENR*, Feb. 26, 1996, at 9 (quoting Jeff Masters, executive director, Alabama chapter of ABC).

16

Cycles of Open-Shop Drives

The current predicament of the seventeen building trades unions is both astonishing and portentous. A dozen or so years ago they were enthroned in what seemed like an impregnable monopoly position. They ran the U.S. construction industry, the nation's largest, like a conquering army. Today they are in disorderly retreat...preparing to do battle for their existence.[1]

Since the 1960's, unionized construction has declined from about 80 percent to about 20 percent of the total market. ... We have observed the virtual de-unionization of many construction markets, with calamitous results for builders, owners, users, customers, unions and workers. ... The erosion of union strength has unleashed a chaotic and destructive competition throughout the industry.[2]

The antiunion drive that large industrial customers organized in the Roundtable initiated in the late 1960s raises the issue of the conditions under which such strategies can succeed. To shed light on the question, earlier twentieth-century movements to oust construction unions will be analyzed. This retrospective is all the more appropriate since Lefkoe, whom Roundtable members hired to analyze the industry, in the course of making ominous predictions about the consequences of intervention by larger users, referred to the domination of the construction industry in San Francisco by large corporate customers in the 1920s as an example of what inevitably happens when contractors request help from their customers in dealing with unions. His conclusion was that contractors in San Francisco and Chicago "[u]nfortunately...did not understand any better than contractors do today that if the business community is going to provide money (directly or in the form of losses due to shutdowns) and other forms of assistance, it is also going to make sure that its assistance is used properly and for its benefit. This help, regardless of the orginal intent, is likely...to result in substituting one 'dictatorship' for another."[3]

During that earlier period, open-shop drives in construction, far from being initiated by small contractors or even even large metropolitan commerical firms,

---

[1]Gilbert Burck, "A Time of Reckoning for the Building Unions," *Fortune*, June 4, 1979, at 82.

[2]Jeffrey Grabelsky & Fred Kotler, "Unions Impose Stability on a Turbulent Construction Industry," *NYT*, Oct. 31, 1994, at A14, col. 4-6 (letter to editor).

[3]Lefkoe, *The Crisis in Construction: There Is an Answer* 115-20 (quote at 119-20) (1970). In a footnote, Lefkoe added that after he had written the quoted passage the CUAIR was formed, but that he did not expect that it would accomplish much on its own because it would fail to deal with the construction industry's basic problems. *Id.* at 120 n. **.

were the instruments of nonconstruction capital.[4] The most significant aspect of these early drives to attain "[n]othing less than the entire destruction of the power of the unions" in construction relates to their origins: the initiating, motive, and financial force behind these movements lay, for the most part, outside of the industry itself, in national or local general employers' associations.[5] Chief among them was the Citizens' Industrial Association of America, an arm of the NAM. In 1903 it launched "a mass attack upon unionism which partook of a crusade against unionism in general" and which by 1908 "had stopped unionism in its tracks" especially in smaller towns.[6] This historical review of successful campaigns against construction unionism underscores the ahistorical nature of partisan attacks in the late 1960s and early 1970s that spoke of "the closed-shop practices the building unions have been making ironclad since the days of the medieval guilds."[7]

One of the earliest versions of the movement in construction emerged in San Francisco in 1904 in the wake of an earlier drive against waterfront workers; after losing momentum on account of the large amount of reconstruction work following the 1906 earthquake, the open-shop movement was taken over by the Chamber of Commerce before passing into the hands of the Law and Order Committee and finally the Industrial Association of San Francisco (IASF) during the 1910s.[8] Of the employers behind the Law and Order Committee the U.S.

---

[4]William Haber, *Industrial Relations in the Buildiung Industry* 252 (1930), noted that it was often claimed that if influenced by capitalists from other branches, contractors would endorse the closed shop more widely. The aggressive open-shop campaign directed by the National Erectors' Association against the International Association of Bridge and Structural Ironworkers (beginning in 1906) did not contradict this claim insofar as the erection firms were closely connected to and supported by steel firms well known for their extreme antiunion views and actions. Luke Grant, *The National Erectors' Association and the International Association of Bridge and Structural Ironworkers* (1971 [1915]); Haber, *Industrial Relations* at 454; Clarence Bonnettt, *History of Employers' Associations in the United States* 137-50 (1956).

[5]F.W. Hilbert, "Employers' Associations in the United States," in *Studies in American Trade Unionism* 183-217 at 217 (quote), 208-17 (Jacob Hollander & George Barnett eds., 1906). Robert Christie, *Empire in Wood: A History of the Carpenters' Union* 155-69 (1956), argued that contractors in large cities launched an open shop movement in the first decade of the twentieth century not to destroy unions, but to regulate their racketeering and extortionism and to ensure that employers not be victimized by them.

[6]Selig Perlman & Philip Taft, *History of Labor in the United States, 1896-1932*, at 129, 136 (1935) (quote); Albion Taylor, *Labor Policies of the National Association of Manufacturers*, in 16 (1) *UISSS* 121 (Mar. 1927); U.S. Senate, Committee on Education and Labor, *Violations of Free Speech and Rights of Labor*, Report No. 6, Pt. 6: *Labor Policies of Employers' Associations*, Pt. III: *The National Association of Manufacturers*, 76th Cong., 1st Sess. 27-32 (1939); Philip Foner, 3 *History of the Labor Movement in the United States: The Policies and Practices of the American Federation of Labor, 1900-1909*, at 32-60 (1964).

[7]A. H. Raskin, "Unused Inflation Curb," *NYT*, Mar. 1, 1971, at 29, col. 1.

[8]U.S. Senate, Committee on Education and Labor, *Violations of Free Speech and Rights of Labor*, Report No. 1150, Pt. 2: *Employers' Associations and Collective Bargaining in California*, Pt.

Secretary of Labor reported in 1919 that the basic motive underlying their internationally infamous campaign to prosecute and impose capital punishment on the militant labor unionist Tom Mooney was the desire to operate their businesses on an open-shop basis.[9] The IASF was responsible for the most vigorously enforced of the second wave of open-shop drives, which took place during the years following World War I.[10] This broad antiunion movement was launched in the midst of the aftershocks of the war and the deep cyclical crisis of 1921: "Many employers,...preparing for a war of extermination against organized labor...seized their opportunity the moment production and prices began to fall and unemployment reduced the bargaining power of the workers."[11] The NAM's postwar Open Shop Movement, which was "predicated upon a coming boom in real estate, which had already given an indication of attaining great momentum,"[12] was given both "a running start" and a "tone" by the steel oligopolies' "success in smashing" the steelworkers' 1919 strike.[13] A contemporary history adduced the following reasons for the success of this second open-shop drive:

Firstly, the employers had enriched themselves enormously during and immediately after the war, and did not lack the funds for fighting organized labor. Secondly, never before in the history of the United States was the government so completely in the hands of big business, trusts, and corporations, as after the war. Thirdly, by the end of 1920 the army recruited for the war was demobilized and millions of soldiers came back to the factories

---

II: *Organized Antiunionism in California Industry Prior to the Passage of the National Labor Relations Act*, 77th Cong., 2d Sess. 79-91 (1942); U.S. Senate, Committee on Education and Labor, *Hearings on S. Res. 266: Violations of Free Speech and Rights of Labor*, Pt. 60, 76th Cong., 3d Sess. 21,943-73, 22,111-48 (1940); San Francisco Chamber of Commerce, *Law and Order in San Francisco* (1916); Robert Knight, *Industrial Relations in the San Francisco Bay Area, 1900-1918* (1960).

[9]*Connectiontion of Certain Department of Labor Employees with the Case of Thomas J. Mooney: Letter from the Secretary of Labor*, H. Doc. No. 157, 66th Cong., 1st Sess. 15 (1919). See generally, Philip Foner, 7 *History of the Labor Movement in the United States: Labor and World War I, 1914-1918*, at 74-95 (1987).

[10]For accounts of events in San Jose, California and Minnesota, see "Extracts from Secretary Dobson's Supplementary Report, Delivered to the Saratoga Springs, N.Y., Convention: So-Called 'Open-Shop' Warfare," 27 (11) *BMP* 241-42 (Nov. 1924).

[11]George Soule, *Prosperity Decade: From War to Depression: 1917-1929*, at 200 (1968 [1947]).

[12]Senate Committee on Education and Labor, *Violations of Free Speech and Rights of Labor*, Rep. No. 1150 Pt. 2 at 91.

[13]Irving Bernstein, *The Lean Years: A History of the American Worker 1920-1933*, at 148 (1966 [1960]). See generally, Savel Zimand, *The Open Shop Drive: Who Is Behind It and Where Is It Going?* (1921); "Who Is Paying for the Open Shop Movement?" 28 (5) *JEWO* 239 (May 1929); Allen Wakstein, "The Origins of the Open-Shop Movement, 1919-1920," 51 *JAH* 460-75 (1964); *idem*, "The National Association of Manufacturers and Labor Relations in the 1920s," 10 (2) *LH* 163-76 (Spr. 1976). On the strike, see Commission of Inquiry, the Interchurch World Movement, *Report on the Steel Strike of 1919* (1920).

looking for their old jobs.[14]

The objective pressures of the business cycle sufficed to weaken the labor movement as the steep rise in unemployment was accompanied by a sharp fall in wages. Table 24 shows this development during World War I and its aftermath. Alone from 1920 to 1921, real wages fell by more than 13 percent as unemployment more than quadrupled.[15] This "liquidation...was extensive and thorough"; the increase in productivity and decline in wages "helped to protect profit margins and to restore confidence.... In the construction industry the decrease in costs evidently played an important role. While high building costs had tended to cause postponement of construction projects in 1919-20, the reduction in costs in 1920-21...led to an early recovery in construction."[16]

In view of this cyclical development as well as of the renewed entrepreneurial onslaught, it is not surprising that the growth in union membership, which had been almost uninterrupted since the turn of the century, was suddenly converted into a 26-percent plunge from 1920 to 1923: 1920—5,110,800; 1921—4,815,000; 1922—4,059,400; 1923—3,780,000.[17] The even sharper fall in wages in nonunion firms put unions under greater pressure to accede to employers' demands for increased physical productivity.[18]

Nor had the preceding years, as the BLS noted, been golden for construction workers: "The great discrepancy in the increases of prices of building materials and the cost of living as compared with wage rates in the building industry during the years 1913 to 1920 was reflected in the decrease in the number of suitable workingmen's dwellings available during that period."[19] Despite this clear empirical refutation, employers' open-shop propaganda in the 1920s sought to inflame public opinion against construction unions by attributing the housing shortage to their work rules and high wages.[20] Such rhetoric constituted another

---

[14]Anthony Bimba, *The History of the American Working Class* 293-94 (1936 [1927]).

[15]See generally, V.W. Lanfear, *Business Fluctuations and the American Labor Movement 1915-1922* (1924). On declining real wages during World War I, see DOL, Div. of Public Works and Construction Development, *Economics of the Construction Industry* 186 (1919).

[16]R.A. Gordon, "Cyclical Experience in the Interwar Period: The Investment Boom of the 'Twenties," in Universities-National Bureau Committee for Economic Research, *Conference on Business Cycles* 163-215 at 173 (1951).

[17]Leo Wolman, *The Growth of American Trade Unions 1880-1923*, at 33 (1924). See also idem, "Labor," in President's Conference on Unemployment, 2 *Recent Economic Changes in the United States: Report of the Committee on Recent Economic Changes* 425-93 at 480-82 (1929).

[18]Lloyd Ulman, "The Development of Trades and Labor Unions," in *American Economic History* 395 (Seymour Harris ed., 1961).

[19]"Trend of Wages, Prices of Materials, Cost of Living in the Building Industry," 15 (6) *MLR* 1277-79 at 1277 (Dec. 1922).

[20]Lewis Lorwin, *The American Federation of Labor: History, Policies, and Prospects* 203

similarity between the American Plan and the antiunion movement of the 1970s.[21]

Table 24: Wages and Unemployment, 1916-1922					
Year	Full-Time Equivalent Earnings ($)	% of Time Lost by Unemployment	Money Earnings ($)	Cost of Living (1910-14=100)	Real Earnings (in 1910-1914 $)
1916	826	4.2	791	111.2	711
1917	956	3.8	920	130.8	703
1918	1,107	4.3	1,059	153.5	689
1919	1,260	6.9	1,173	176.8	663
1920	1,448	5.0	1,376	204.7	672
1921	1,347	21.0	1,064	182.4	583
1922	1,330	14.4	1,138	171.0	665

Source: Stanley Lebergott, "Earnings of Nonfarm Employees in the U.S., 1890-1946," 43 (241) *JASA* 76 (Mar. 1948).

The local expression of the open-shop movement of interest here arose in the San Francisco construction industry. The IASF, formed on November 8, 1921, embodied the determination of "[l]arge employers in the city in the building materials, manufacturing, retailing, railroad, banking, and insurance industries, as well as the Chamber of Commerce...to destroy the powerful building trades, the decisive element in the local labor movement. Since they considered the contractors unreliable on the open shop, they established a permit system...."[22] Thus the peculiarity of the American Plan in its application to construction—and at the same time the aspect that constitutes its historical relevance for the analysis of the 1970s—is that not construction firms but, rather, their large industrial and finance customers, drove the movement.[23]

(1933).

[21]"Because of the housing shortage and the high rents the building trades were a particularly vulnerable point for an attack which needed the support of public opinion. It was charged that the high cost of building was due to the wages paid and to the restrictive union rules and practices of the various craft unions...." Soule, *Prosperity Decade* at 202.

[22]Bernstein, *Lean Years* at 154.

[23]Christie, *Empire in Wood* at 235; Louis Adamic, *Dynamite: The Story of Class Violence*

Nor was this structural relationship unique to San Francisco. A similar development also began in 1921 in Chicago. There a "Citizens' Committee" of antiunion industrial and finance capitalists recommended to a group of national building companies, which had feared strikes in other cities if they complied with the decisions of this antiunion committee, that they either submit or temporarily withdraw from the Chicago construction market. To be sure, the Citizens' Committee to Enforce the Landis Award never achieved the degree of control in Chicago that the IASF secured in San Francisco. Its genesis was also more serendipitous, and its reign, which included the importation of more than 25,000 workers, was briefer.[24]

The particular virulence of the intervention in San Francisco may be explained by the earlier development of the construction industry and class conflict there. In the period from 1849 to 1869, this growth was, as in other cities, relatively slow: "The master retained a farily permanent force of men. Moreover, he worked with them, and directed the task himself. The line that divided master and journeyman was relatively indistinct." The city's rapid growth during the last third of the nineteenth century (1869-1896) transformed the industry: "Building construction was one of the first industries in San Francisco to feel the effects of large-scale production. Large construction projects called for contractors with considerable capital and large forces of workers." This transformation led to the ouster of the old masters by general contractors who insured that "the customary relationships of master and journeyman" disappeared.[25]

As a result, construction unions became autonomous vis-à-vis the general labor movement. This separation found its organizational expression in the Building Trades Council (BTC) headed by the leader of the United Brotherhood of Carpenters and Joiners. During the period from the turn of the century to the

---

in America 264 (rev. ed., 1934).

[24]Royal Montgomery, *Industrial Relations in the Chicago Building Trades* 235, 275-309 (1927); Haber, *Industrial Relations in the Building Industry* at 387-99. By 1929, it was estimated that 81 percent of building trades workers in Chicago were organized—the city's highest. Carroll Christenson, "Collective Bargaining in Chicago : 1929-30: A Study of the Economic Significance of the Industrial Location of Trade-Unionism," tab. 1 at 2 (Ph.D diss. U. Chicago, 1931), reprinted in *Collective Bargining in Chicago 1929-30: Social Science Studies*, No. 27 (1933). An in some respects deviant movement took place in Seattle in 1919-20. Led by the Assocated Industries, the open shop American Plan encompassed virtually all industries. Although the "core" of the drive was the plan "to destroy the unions altogether, and with them workers' collective control over the work process," the Associated Industries consciously sought to accommodate "some of the needs unions sought to meet for their members, specifically the financial erosion of working-class living standards after the war." The Seattle Master Builders' Association, for example, after eliminating the closed shop, actually increased carpenters' wages. Dana Frank, *Purchasing Power: Consumer Organizing, Gender, and the Seattle Labor Movement, 1919-1929,* at 100 (1994). This account does not describe the changes that occurred after construction employers seized control over the work process.

[25]Frederick Ryan, *Industrial Relations in the San Francisco Building Trades* 9, 13 (1935).

founding of the IASF, the BTC enjoyed "a bargaining advantage over the employers in that changes were instituted by the workers."[26] Here it is necessary to distinguish between the union members and the organization that P. H. McCarthy led effectively but autocratically.[27] Construction employers' acquiescence was explained by the fact that they "would organize readily into trade associations from which immediate benefits in limiting competition...could be derived, but to form a central organization to oppose the demands of the workers appeared to be a useless endeavor so long as an increase in costs could be passed on to the builder."[28]

Counterforces opposed to this arrangement stemmed from two sides: industrial and finance capital in San Francisco, which feared that the city would soon be overtaken by Los Angeles as the economic center of California,[29] and union members themselves, whose standard of living had suffered under the BTC's rule. After construction wages had remained almost unchanged from 1907 to 1917, the situation came to a head in 1920 during the next set of collective bargaining negotiations. Although the cost of living had risen 96 percent between 1913 and 1920 compared to a 71.7 percent rise in wages, employers demanded a nominal reduction in wages in view of the depressed economy. After the Chamber of Commerce and contractors made it clear to the BTC that "employers would receive the support of the bankers and industrial leaders" if the unions refused to agree to arbitration, McCarthy yielded. The Arbitration Board—the chief arbitrator was the archbishop of San Francisco although the Catholic church was one of the city's largest building customers—issued an award reducing wages by 7.5 percent. McCarthy's withdrawal from the arbitration proceedings triggered a lockout, in the course of which the BTC accepted the arbitration award. This action, in turn, prompted the membership, in its first referendum in 17 years, to reject the proposal by a two-thirds majority. The newly formed Conference Committee of the Allied Building Trades Unions called for a general strike, to which workers outside of the

---

[26]Ryan, *Industrial Relations in the San Francisco Building Trades* at 15, 112 (quote). See generally, Michael Kazin, *Barons of Labor: The San Francisco Building Trades and Union Power in the Progressive Era* 82-107 (1989).

[27]Commission on Industrial Relations, 6 *Industrial Relations: Final Report and Testimony*, Sen. Doc. No. 415, 64th Cong., 1st Sess. 5,169-401 (1916); Ira Cross, "Collective Bargaining and Trade Agreements in the Brewery, Metal, Teaming, and Building Trades of San Francisco, California," 4 (4) *UCPE* 233-364 at 331-42 (1918); L. O'Donnell, "The Greening of a Limerick Man: Patrick Henry McCarthy, " 9 (2) *Eire-Ireland* 119-28 (1976).

[28]Ryan, *Industrial Relations in the San Francisco Building Trades* at 118.

[29]The *Wall Street Journal* reported in 1922 that earlier contactors had been "ready to resist the tyranny of McCarthy, but a majority of local bankers, who were for industrial peace at any price, coerced them into submitting to the czar's exactions...." "Dethronement of a Czar," in [Wall Street Journal], *A History of Organized Felony and Folly: The Record of Union Labor in Crime and Economics* 99-101 at 100 (1923 [1922]).

building trades remained indifferent.[30]

By early August, *ENR* reported that the "American Plan is now an accepted fact in San Francisco except among certain unions and the building trades council leaders...."[31] Even as the workers voted to end the strike on August 27, five-sixths of them also voted against adopting the American Plan.[32] The following month the Building Construction Branch of the Rank and File Federation of Workers was established, the preamble to whose constitution declared: "This organization is founded upon the understanding that the industrial society of today is divided into two classes, the working class and the master class, and that as long as these two classes exist, there shall be a neverceasing struggle between them." Its "ultimate aim" was "complete control of the natural resources of the earth and of the machinery of production in order that those who toil shall reap the full product of their labor," but its more immediate goal was the abolition of organization along craft lines by means of transferable working cards, which would eliminate jurisdictional disputes. Although the revolt "had stirred up reactions within the workers that were entirely foreign to the philosophy of 'business unionism,'" what had united the workers was opposition to McCarthy's autocratic methods, and when he resigned in January 1922, the workers returned to the old unions.[33]

It was in the context of this strike activity that the American Plan originated in San Francisco. The tradition of a city-wide militant antiunion employers' association went back to the turn of the century, and, under the name Citizens' Alliance of San Francisco, turned its attention to the building unions in 1904. Such organizations were typical of the period when rapid urban growth, fueled by unrestricted immigration and the development of concentrated large industry sustained such demand for urban construction that building workers attained a "unique bargaining position." Many of the large corporate sponsors of the IASF were identical with those forming the Law and Order Committee of the Chamber of Commerce formed in 1916 to destroy unionism in San Francisco. Their complaints focused on restraints that union rules had imposed on the construction industry, leading to higher costs and higher prices, and preventing the requisite flow

---

[30]Ryan, *Industrial Relations in the San Francisco Building Trades* at 132-61, 144 (quote); "Builders in Lockout Against San Francisco Unions," 86 (22) *ENR* 970 (June 2, 1921); "Lower Wages in Building Industry at San Francisco," 86 (15) *ENR* 660 (Apr. 14, 1921).

[31]"San Francisco Building Situation Gradually Improving," 87 (6) *ENR* 259 (Aug. 11, 1921).

[32]"San Francisco Building Situation Clears Up," 87 (16) *ENR* 427 (Sept. 8, 1921).

[33]Ryan, *Industrial Relations in the San Francisco Building Trades* at 221 (quote), 163 (quote), 164-65. Emblematic of McCarthy's rule was his reaction to a painters' strike in 1914 that the BTC had not authorized: he urged the Building Trade Employers' Association to threaten a lockout of all unions. *Id.* at 127. See also Commission on Industrial Relations, 6 *Industrial Relations* at 5,473-84.

of capital into building.[34]

To induce building contractors to derecognize the unions as collective bargaining partners, the IASF reimbursed them for all monetary losses. Many large industrial customers such as Standard Oil Company of California offered additional premiums to encourage construction firms to hire nonunion workers. In order to overcome the resistance of numerous contractors who either were themselves former union members or allegedly feared union countermeasures, the IASF had two means of pressure at its disposal: denial of credit and withholding of construction materials.[35] The IASF then entered into form contracts with the individual workers, which required them to "produce a full day's output" defined as "that amount of work which would ordinarily be performed by a skilled, experienced [worker] devoting his entire time, energies, and attention to his work" despite the fact that the contract provided that, if injured, the worker could not sue the IASF; instead, his recourse was merely to file a workers' compensation claim against "the immediate employers" to whom the IASF had assigned him.[36]

In order to execute the American Plan, the IASF "had to flood the labor market with nonunion labor." It achieved this end by importing workers and introducing "virtually unlimited apprentices."[37] By mid-1924, the IASF's trade schools had graduated 1,000 apprentices and were training 700 more; by the next year, painters, plasterers, and plumbers were suffering from their low-wage competition.[38] The American Plan's initial success can be gauged by the fact that by 1922 the building industry was almost 100 percent covered.[39] In addition, from 1920 to 1923 the manual trades in San Francisco were transformed from more than 90 percent organized to 85 percent open shop.[40]

The IASF's withholding of construction materials from contractors who continued to operate union shops ultimately led to a series of state and federal prosecutions, which culminated in a decision handed down by the U.S. Supreme Court in 1925. In November 1923, a federal district court for the Northern District of California, in an action brought by the United States Government to restrain the

---

[34]Senate Committee on Education and Labor, *Violations of Free Speech and Rights of Labor*, Rep. No. 1150 Pt. 2 at 83-90, 84 n.46 (quote); Ryan, *Industrial Relations in the San Francisco Building Trades* at 134-38.

[35]Haber, *Industrial Relations in the Building Industry* at 415-19.

[36]"Building Trades—San Francisco: Bonus Contract of the Industrial Association of San Francisco," 16 (1) *MLR* 107-109 at 108 (Jan. 1923).

[37]Senate Committee on Education and Labor, *Violations of Free Speech and Rights of Labor*, Rep. No. 1150 Pt. 2 at 96.

[38]Ryan, *Industrial Relations in the San Francisco Building Trades* at 190

[39]1 (2) *AP* (Oct. 1922) (no pagination).

[40]Robert Dunn, *The Americanization of Labor: The Employers' Offensive Against the Trade Unions* 48-49 (1927).

IASF, the Builders' Exchange, and other entities, from executing an conspiracy in restraint of interstate commerce, issued a decree enjoining the IASF and other defendants from "requiring any permit for the purchase of materials or supplies produced without the state, and coming here in interstate commerce, or for making, as a condition for the issuance of a permit, any regulation that will interfere with the free movement of plumbers' or other supplies produced without the state."[41]

Two years later, however, the U.S. Supreme Court unanimously reversed the decree. The U.S. Government had pleaded that the purpose of the conspiracy "was to take away from employers the right to employ men upon any other terms than those of the so-called American Plan." The defendants' power to "coerce manufacturers outside of the State to withhold the materials manufactured by them from anyone within the State who did not submit to the will of the conspirators" was evidenced by the fact that "90 percent of the new building work in San Francisco was being done by members of the defendant."[42] The Court's recitation of the background focused on the fact that unions, which represented 99 percent of all building workers, had enforced "many restrictions...which the employers, and a large body of other citizens, considered to be unreasonable, uneconomic and injurious to the building industries, resulting...in decreased production, increased cost and generally retarded progress." These restrictions included the number of apprentices, amount of work, use of labor-saving devices, and "interfering with the legitimate authority of the employer." After the failure of efforts to persuade strikers to return to work in 1921, "mass-meetings were held by representative citizens in large numbers and from all walks of life. At thse meetings it was resolved that the work of building must go forward...." The Supreme Court reversed the lower court, however, because the IASF's aim was not restraint of interstate trade, "but was a purely local matter, namely, regulation of building operations within a limited local area, so as to prevent their domination by the labor unions." Moreover, the means used did not implicate interstate commerce, in part because most of the building materials were produced in California.[43]

To "crush the building trades unions completely," the IASF used its initial fund of $1,250,000, which consisted of contributions from members including large oil companies, banks, railroads, and utilities such as Standard Oil, Wells Fargo Bank, Southern Pacific Railroad, Pacific Gas and Electric, and the Emporium, whose capital in large part consisted of buildings and structures and which were therefore particularly interested in establishing a new order in the San Francisco

---

[41]United States v. Industrial Ass'n of San Francisco, 293 F. 925, 928 (D. N.D. Cal. 1923). See also "Federal Court in San Francisco Finds Builders' Exchange 'Guilty' in 'American Plan' Conspiracy Case," 26 (12) *BMP* 269-72 (Dec. 1923).

[42]Industrial Association of San Francisco v. United States, 268 U.S. 64, ***7, 10 (1925) (Brief of United States).

[43]Industrial Association of San Francisco, 268 at 72-84.

building industry.[44]

The IASF's demagogic character, which it shared with other antiunion movements before and since, emerged clearly in its assurance from the outset that the American Plan "is not aimed at the destruction of unions, but has adopted the fundamental policy that dealings shall be with individual employees only and agreements will not be made with unions."[45] In fact, however, as contemporaries understood: "It was born to defeat the unions. Its work has been primarily to recruit and protect strike breakers...."[46] Significantly, as early as 1922 the IASF itself called attention to the fact that: "If the open shop is to be a complete success it is absolutely necessary that it be universally adopted. An open-shop policy in one city and a closed-shop policy in an adjoining city tends to demoralize building conditions in both places."[47] To this end, the IASF held a conference in Salt Lake City, reinforcing the spread, by October 1921, of the American Plan to Los Angeles and other west coast cities.[48]

An overall evaluation of the IASF is confronted with contradictory material. A prevalent opinion takes the position that the IASF failed to replace the control functions that unions necessarily exercise in a modern industrial society: "With the elimination of union control, the stabilizing influences and functions, which have been attributed to building trade unions, were no longer available. ... Although the attempt was clearly made to remove wages and other economic conditions from competition, under the American Plan no effective substitute for the trade unions was developed."[49] This position is inconsistent—an inconsistency, to be sure, inherent in the American Plan itself—insofar as the elimination of these special union functions would have had to be linked to a restructuring of the construction industry, which was not even contemplated.

Two especially important functions are self-supervision at work and responsibility for supplying the requisite quantity and quality of labor power.

---

[44]Senate Committee on Education and Labor, *Violations of Free Speech and Rights of Labor*, Rep. No. 1150, Pt. 2, at 94 (quote); Haber, *Industrial Relations in the Building Industry* at 431, 575 n.39.

[45]"American Plan Probable Result of San Francisco Strike," 87 (3) *ENR* 128 (July 21, 1921).

[46]Haber, *Industrial Relations in the Building Industry* at 432.

[47]Brief for Appellee, Industrial Association of San Francisco v. United States, 268 U.S. 64 (1925) (quoting from official IASF publication dated Apr. 13, 1922, at 114).

[48]87 (17) *ENR* 711 (Oct. 27, 1921); "A $100,000,000 Year: Los Angeles an Open Shop Town," *Constructor*, 4 (1):55 (Jan. 1922); "Open Shop Thriving: Lack of Jurisdictional Craft Disputes Effect Large Saving," *Constructor* at 86 (efficiency in Tucson rose 30 to 40 percent by virtue of using unskilled labor where closed shop demanded skilled labor); "Open Shop Working Well," 5 (6) *Constructor* 53-54 (June 1923) (Duluth); "Labor Situation: Work Successfully Manned Under Open Shop," 5 (10) *Constructor* 46 (Oct. 1923) (AGC "licked" unions in New Orleans).

[49]Gordon Bertram & Sherman Maisel, *Industrial Relations in the Construction Industry* 26-27 (1955).

Whereas unions' retention of the former function depends on the craft character of the labor processes, the second is rooted in the relatively low level of capital accumulation and centralization. Since the IASF failed to intervene in the immediate process of production at all—"[a]lthough the initiative and directing control in determining wages, hours and working conditions is no longer with the employers...the employers in the building trades still have complete freedom in conducting their business"—it was scarcely surprising that it had to "depend on the voluntary assistance of the unions in policing the job. ... The Industrial Association seems to have taken advantage of the opportunity to use the unions as 'job stewards.' The unions complain to the Association and the latter chastizes the employer if it sees fit. The position of the union is not unlike that of the minority party in a government. Its function is to spy on industrial conditions and, on any violation of the code of conduct, to make a protest to the party in power."[50] In this context, the IASF, feeling "strong enough to dominate the local industry monopolistically without the cooperation of the trade union leaders," could be viewed as a forerunner of a version of fascist corporativism.[51]

To be sure, one essential element was lacking: the American Plan arose at a time when construction unionists in San Francisco were fighting an autocratic bureaucracy, which was not even able to achieve a wage increase to compensate for the rate of inflation. The very fact that a frontal attack on unions would solidarize the membership would have to have given pause.

It is characteristic of class-oriented movements such as the American Plan that they attempt to portray themselves as standing above the classes whose interests coincide with those of society as a whole.[52] Thus in 1923 the IASF, after a jury had acquitted 34 building material dealers on charges of having violated the state antitrust law by having refused to sell to union contractors, declared that the result "should redound materially and permanently to the benefit of every community that seeks to free its industry from autocratic class control and to secure the ultimate good of all labor, union and non-union, as well as of industry itself." The IASF asserted that the jury, to whom the defendants had argued that San Francisco had prospered under the American Plan, had upheld the "doctrine that the general good of the whole community must be put above advantage to any one class."[53] In claiming that civic improvement was its sole motivation, the IASF portrayed itself as having acted reluctantly only after conditions in the construction

---

[50]Haber, *Industrial Relations in the Building Industry* at 437, 434.

[51]William Z. Foster, *Misleaders of Labor* 194 (1927). Cf. Paul Crosser, *Ideologies and American Labor* 152 (1941); Franz Neumann, *Behemoth: The Structure and Practice of National Socialism 1933-1944*, at 337-40 (1966 [1942]).

[52]Lefkoe, *Crisis in Construction* at 114.

[53]"San Francisco Material Dealers Acquitted of Charges," 90 (22) *ENR* 977 (May 31, 1923). The article erroneously referred to a jury trial before the California Supreme Court.

industry had reached the point at which "intervention of some outside party that had strength enough to whip both employers and workers into shape was inevitable...."[54]

The long-term practical effect of the American Plan, even in San Francisco, is less clear. As the national president of the Bricklayers union wrote three decades later: "By 1924, the building boom had created such a demand that all union men had no difficulty in getting work at the union scale, although no agreements were concluded until 1926. By that time the influence of the Association was on the wane and subsequently was reduced to a paper organization."[55] Although the IASF agreed to suspend its permit system in 1927, its "almost complete domination of labor" continued until 1933, when federal legislation began to confer collective bargaining rights.[56]   Nationally, too, the open-shop campaign "in the long run...had little influence on the membership and status of the building unions...."[57]

Nevertheless, writing a few years after the IASF's demise, the Senate Committee on Education and Labor affirmed that it was

an example par excellence of local association success in denying labor its collective-bargaining rights. From a local viewpoint, it achieved what so many of its predecessors had failed of accomplishment, namely, the destruction of effective organization among the city's two most unified groups of workers and, consequently, the complete dominance of all organized labor. Alone of all the local employers' associations, through its relentless enforcement of the permit plan, it achieved complete restraint not only of labor, but also of the entire building industry.[58]

The view that the American Plan was ultimately a failure neglects the influence that the effective displacement of union counterpower had on the wage formation process. Table 25 compares the development of hourly wages, the cost of living, and real wages of construction workers in San Francisco and nationally, clearly showing that San Francisco construction workers' nominal hourly wages stagnated during the decade after the introduction of the American Plan, whereas nationally construction workers experienced a 46 percent increase (until the high point in 1931). While wage costs in San Francisco were favorable to enterprises there, the workers' real hourly wages rose much more slowly than nationally and, especially after 1924, only as a result of the decline in the cost of living.[59]   In

---

[54]Ryan, *Industrial Relations in the San Francisco Building Trades* at 170-71.

[55]Bates, *Bricklayers' Century* at 204.

[56]Senate Committee on Education and Labor, *Violations of Free Speech and Rights of Labor*, Rep. No. 1150, Pt. 2, at 95. The IASF collapsed in 1937. *Id.* at 89.

[57]Soule, *Prosperity Decade* at 202.

[58]Senate Committee on Education and Labor, *Violations of Free Speech and Rights of Labor*, Rep. No. 1150, Pt. 2 at 98.

[59]The real hourly wage data must be used cautiously since they ignore unemployment and short hours, which are vital determinants of wages during depressions. The average annual earnings

absolute terms, the IASF "maintained a wage scale lower than that of any closed-shop city in the country."[60]

	San Francisco			United States		
Year	Hourly Wages	Cost of Living	Real Hourly Wages	Hourly Wages	Cost of Living	Real Hourly Wages
	1913=100					
1920	177	185	96	194	203	96
1921	158	163	97	198	181	109
1922	160	158	99	185	169	109
1923	162	162	100	205	172	119
1924	168	160	105	221	173	128
1925	170	164	104	230	177	130
1926	172	161	107	245	179	137
1927	172	160	107	253	175	145
1928	172	161	107	255	173	147
1929	172	160	107	258	173	149
1930	172	151	114	269	169	159
1931	172	138	125	270	154	175
1932	162	128	127	230	138	167
1933	156	110	142	224	131	171

Table 25: Construction Wages in San Francisco and the United States, 1920-1933

Source: Ryan, *Industrial Relations in the San Francisco Building Trades* at 182; William Haber & Harold Levinson, *Labor Relations and Productivity in the Building Trades* at 205.

per full-time construction employee attained in 1920 were not definitively surpassed until 1942: "The effect of the depression was so comprehensive, so catastrophic...that real earnings in 1930-34 were almost identical with those in 1890-94...." Lebergott, "Earnings of Nonfarm Employees in the U.S., 1890-1946" at 84, 75, 77.

[60]Haber, *Industrial Relations in the Building Industry* at 440.

Cleveland in the 1920s witnessed a similar development, which formed a link in the general "American Plan" campaign supported by the NAM, which focused on attacking building trades unions.[61] One of the campaign's most spectacular manifestations was the Bethlehem Steel Corporation's announcement that it would refuse to sell fabricated steel to building contractors in New York and Philadelphia operating on a union shop basis even if the result were a suspension of building in those cities.[62] In Cleveland, as in other well-organized cities, this emphasis derived from the circumstance that these unions

presented one of the most serious obstacles to the campaign of the open-shop movement. Among the most powerful unions in the labor movement, their strength sprang from various economic factors inherent in the building industry, and was considerably increased by the fact that the twenties saw a boom in the building industry and a great demand for skilled labor.

Strong and successful, the building-trades unions gave great impetus, both by their example and by their activities, to unionization in other industries. This fact was recognized by the unions and the open-shop associations.[63]

Since the contractors themselves were often less than enthusiastic about opposing unions where the latter helped standardize wage costs, the NAM American Plan recognized that the support of all businesses would have to be enlisted to place pressure on the contractors, especially the large ones, to adhere to antiunion policies.[64] The American Plan held out the prospect that political and

---

[61]For the organization's own presentation of the campaign, see its *Open Shop Bulletin*, which appeared in 27 issues from November 1920 to March 1932, as well as its *Open Shop Encyclopedia for Debaters: A Reference Book for Use of Teachers, Students and Public Speakers* (Noel Sargent compiler, 3d ed., 1922 [1921]). For a sample of AFL opinion on the drive, see Samuel Gompers, "'Open Shop' Hypocrisy Exposed," 28 (2) *AF* 109-11 (Feb. 1921); "Open Shop—Survival of Outworn Industrial Era," 28 (2) *JEWO* 62-63, 112 (Feb. 1929); "The Case for Employer Violence—Substantive Record," 28 (3) *JEWO* 121, 165 (Mar. 1929); "Turning the Clock Back in the Key Industries," 28 (4) *JEWO* 179, 222 (Apr. 1929); "Who Is Paying for the Open Shop Movement?" 28 (5) *JEWO* 239 (May 1929). For a left-wing view, see Jay Lovestone, *The Government—Strikebreaker: A Study of the Role of Government in the Recent Industrial Crisis* (1923). On the open-shop movement in Wheeling, West Virginia, begun in June, 1921, to break a two-month strike by building trades unionists who had refused to accept a 20 percent wage cut after expiration of their agreements, see John Hennen, *The Americanization of West Virginia: Creating a Modern Industrial State 1916-1925*, at 110 (1996).

[62]Gompers, "'Open Shop' Hypocrisy Exposed" at 110.

[63]U.S. Senate, Committee on Education and Labor, *Violations of Free Speech and Rights of Labor*, Rep. No. 6, Pt. 5: *Labor Policies of Employers' Associations*, Pt. II: *The Associated Industries of Cleveland*, 76th Cong., 1st Sess. 25 (1939); see also *id.* at 8-18.

[64]For materials reprinted from the "Hand Book of the Ninth Semi-Annual, American Plan-Open Shop Conference," held in Detroit in 1926, and from the "Proceedings of Eighth Semiannual American Plan-Open Shop Conference," held in San Diego in 1925, which explicitly pointed to the

economic benefits would accrue to business at large from a successful struggle against organized labor. The ideological transparence of the alleged impact of the open shop left nothing to be desired: "Removes subconscious class antagonisms"; "Makes effective the slogan 'The best man wins'"; "Increases capital investments due to increased safety of returns"; "Class consciousness is removed": "Irritating forces that would divide society are put in quarantine"; "It recognizes that certain subversive activities in this country are inspired movements that emanate from abroad"....[65] At the same time, the American Plan promised lower building costs.[66] On this basis it proved possible to recruit a large number of industrial firms and banks to oppose a construction strike in 1926; by raising a $5 million fund in support of the employers, a "Citizens' Committee" enabled them to gain favorable terms, although the unions "still retained much of their power."[67]

In this respect, too, the open-shop movement in Cleveland proved to be representative of the national movement in construction inasmuch as a temporary blow was struck at a well-organized body of workers in one city without causing irreparable damage. Although these forces registered no significant advances, neither did the unions make any inroads into previously nonunion areas or sectors. The fact that the open-shop movement failed to gain ground during the depression of the 1930s underscores the unions' relative strength.[68] The movement's ultimate failure, however, may be traced back to the rise of industrial unionism in the 1930s and the insight on the part of industrial capital that antiunionism as a social principle had, for the time being at least, outlived its usefulness.

The American Plan's "harmonious coercion" did not so much peter out during the 1920s as yield to "the gentler methods of paternalistic welfare capitalism" as "[e]mployers could not decide whether their interests were better served simply by keeping labor disorganized or by putting it into organizations under their control. ... Employers were unsure whether to regard the worker as a displaceable cog in the productive machine or as an indispensable consumer of industry's rising output, his wage as a cost item to be kept low or as an income

---

need to mobilize "[f]inancial and building interests" as well as "[b]usiness men" in general to restrict contracts to antiunion contractors, see *id.* at 211-12, 220-21.

[65]*Id.* at 205, 207.

[66]*Id.* at 27, 205, 220. Although it is difficult to assess the claim that unions contributed to unnecessary increases in building costs during the 1920s, in the long run, increased productivity cannot result from mere oligopsonistic advantages in the labor market; rather, more efficient construction methods would have to be forthcoming, and there is no indication that American Planners were preparing any technological breakthroughs. They seem to have restricted themselves to wresting control of the skilled labor supply from unions and coordinating it among cities. *Id.* at 211-12.

[67]*Id.* at 27-29.

[68]William Haber, "Building Construction," in *How Collective Bargaining Works* 183-228 at 205 (Harry Millis ed., 1942).

factor to be pushed high."[69]

Since the IASF prepared no new structures that would have transformed this external intervention from an emergency into a permanent component of institutionalized labor relations, and since it also failed to create a new framework within which the old relations between unions and contractors could have developed, it is easy to understand why labor relations scholars in the 1930s regarded the American Plan as lacking a future (collective bargaining was in fact resumed in 1936): "If the Association had developed its original program of maintaining a balance of power between two equals so as to strengthen the employers and temper the power of the unions, its efforts would indeed have been commendable. The policy of the Association, however, has been to establish what it calls a 'benevolent individualism.'"[70]

This view resembles that held by construction employers associations, the Roundtable, and government policymakers in the 1960s and 1970s, who did not seek to crush the building trades unions, but pleaded for state intervention to recreate a 'lost equilibrium' between construction labor and capital such as it still existed in other industries. Such a position overlooked the fact that the balance of forces between labor and capital in these industries was crucially determined by the state of capital accumulation and centralization and technological development. State intervention that circumvented these determinants by establishing a corresponding juridical superstructure without having touched the production process itself could not help missing its alleged goal. Because it is unimaginable that under the political realities of the 1970s an entire sector of national unions accounting for 20 percent of total AFL-CIO membership would have been crushed by direct political means, the most effective open-shop movement would have sought to realize its goal primarily by means of a structural transformation of the construction industry. For in the long run no labor union is immune to the development of the forces of production even if it may be in a position temporarily to stop the process or to negotiate better terms for adoption of the next wave of industrialization.

Unlike the American Plan's explicit anti-Bolshevist thrust,[71] the open-shop movement of the 1970s was much less straightforwardly ideological—in large part because it succeeded in constructing its union opponents as greedy rather than politically subversive—and more concerned with a practical transformation of the construction industry. Roundtable activities can be interpreted as analogous to those of the American Plan, but crucial differences separate them. The Roundtable

---

[69]Bernstein, *Lean Years* at 145-46.

[70]Haber, *Industrial Relations in the Building Industry* at 437.

[71]Philip Foner, 8 *History of the Labor Movement in the United States: Postwar Struggles, 1918-1920*, at 172-73 (1988).

was an incomparably more sophisticated, influential, systematic, and serious national force. To be sure, it never sought or attained the kind of direct power over a metropolitan construction market that the IASF wielded in San Francisco during the 1920s. Nevertheless, its voluble demands for restraining construction unions' allegedly arbitrary or monopoly power or even eliminating their basis achieved a much more lasting and broad-based impact. The Roundtable was unable to secure enactment of its national legislative agenda, but it did thwart the AFL-CIO's congressional initiatives. Its most important accomplishment, undermining unions' quasi-monopoly of the large-scale industrial construction so vital to Roundtable members' accumulation strategies, was a self-help measure undertaken largely without state assistance. As was the case with the IASF, however, the Roundtable's successes may lack a firm foundation because they were not based on a thoroughgoing restructuring of the construction industry. So long as a deviant firm-size-structure and centralization of capital remain coupled with noncontinuous employment and a nonindustrialized craft production system, uncommonly strong unions and above-average wages will remain a threat.

Appendix: War and Construction Wages

In peace or in war the building and construction industry occupies a strategic place in the economy.[1]

    The efforts that the state and employers' organizations concentrated on controlling construction wages during the Vietnam War raise a question as to whether some necessary relationship between the structure of wartime economies and the demand for construction workers resulting in faster wage growth in that sector is a constant or whether historical circumstances peculiar to the 1960s and 1970s accounted for that disparity. A brief account of relevant developments during World War II and the Korean War sheds some light on this question.[2]

    During the so-called defense period (1939-1941) and the war itself the gap between building and manufacturing wages narrowed. In particular, from 1940 to 1943, hourly earnings in manufacturing rose 45 percent compared with 30 percent in private building construction; consequently, hourly manufacturing earnings as a share of those in construction rose from 69 to 77 percent. The gap in gross weekly earnings narrowed even more: manufacturing as a proportion of construction rose from 79 to 90 percent between 1940 and 1943 although the gap widened again somewhat during the early postwar years.[3] Table 26 shows the course of hourly and weekly earnings from 1937 to 1947.[4]

    That construction wages lagged behind those in manufacturing during the militarization of the U.S. economy requires explanation especially since construction employment rose much more rapidly (although it failed to maintain its peak level as long as manufacturing because its expansion was a prerequisite for expansion of manufacturing).[5] In part this difference resulted from building trades unions' extraordinary acquiescence in federal "wage stabilization" programs.

---

[1]John Dunlop & Arthur Hill, *The Wage Adjustment Board: Wartime Stabilization in the Building and Construction Industry* 3 (1950).

[2]On the Emergency Construction Wage Commission during World War I, when the federal government entered into agreements with unions for the first time, see Alexander Bing, *War-Time Strikes and Their Adjustment* 14-19 (1921).

[3]*Economic Report of the President* 107-108 (1949).

[4]For a description of the wage data, see USDC, *Business Statistics: 1953 Biennial Edition* 220 n.5 (1953). The wage data for construction refer to private building construction, which accounted for about three-fifths of total construction employment during the years in question. BLS, *Construction in the War Years 1942-45*, at 7, 10 (Bull. 915, 1948); BLS, *Construction and Housing, 1946-47*, at 14 (Bull. 941, 1948).

[5]Milton Derber & Sidney Netreba, "Money and Real Weekly Earnings During Defense, War, and Reconversion Periods," 64 (6) *MLR* 983-86 (June 1947); H. Wagner, "Die zyklischen Überproduktionskrisen der Industrieproduktion in den USA in den ersten beiden Etappen der allgemeinen Krise des Kapitalismus (1914 bis 1958) (Schluß)," *JW*, 1965, pt. II, at 26-102.

Table 26: Employment and Weekly and Hourly Earnings in Manufacturing and Construction, 1937-1947

Year	Employment				Average Gross Weekly Earnings			Average Hourly Earnings		
	Manufac-turing (000)	Index (1939 = 100)	Con-struc-tion (000)	Index (1939 = 100)	Manu-facturing ($)	Con-struc-tion ($)	Ratio	Manufac-turing ($)	Con-struc-tion ($)	Ratio
1937	10,606	105	1,112	97	24.05	30.14	0.80	0.62	0.90	0.69
1938	9,253	92	1,055	92	22.30	29.19	0.76	0.63	0.91	0.69
1939	10,078	100	1,150	100	23.86	30.39	0.79	0.63	0.93	0.68
1940	10,780	107	1,294	113	25.20	31.70	0.79	0.66	0.96	0.69
1941	12,974	129	1,790	156	29.58	35.14	0.84	0.73	1.01	0.72
1942	15,051	149	2,170	189	36.65	41.80	0.88	0.85	1.15	0.74
1943	17,381	172	1,567	136	43.14	48.13	0.90	0.96	1.25	0.77
1944	17,111	170	1,094	95	46.08	52.18	0.88	1.02	1.32	0.77
1945	15,302	152	1,132	98	44.39	53.73	0.83	1.02	1.38	0.74
1946	14,515	144	1,661	144	43.74	56.24	0.78	1.08	1.48	0.73
1947	15,901	158	1,921	167	49.25	63.30	0.78	1.22	1.68	0.73

Source: The Economic Report of the President: To the Congress, January 7, 1949, tab. C-8, C-9, C-10 at 106-108 (1949).

In anticipation of war, a "vast" increase in public construction had led to a virtual doubling of employment in that sector to almost one million workers between May 1940 and May 1941. As a result of the loss of skilled labor during the Depression, shortages, especially in remote areas, caused employers to offer premium wages, such as double-time rates for all hours over eight per day, in connection with regular extra-shift operations, to recruit workers. To avoid obstacles to rapid completion of projects and a crazy quilt of provisions in various localities, the Office of Production Management (OPM) and certain government agencies engaged in defense construction entered into a "Memorandum of Stabilization Agreement" with the BCTD months before the United States entered World War II. Under this July 22, 1941 agreement, the unions "gave up more advantageous overtime rates,"[6] accepting instead a uniform overtime rate of time and a half for all hours over 8 per day.[7] In addition, the BCTD agreed "that there shall be no stoppage of work on account of jurisdictional disputes, or for any other cause. All grievances and disputes shall be settled by conciliation and arbitration."[8] In exchange, the federal government agreed to maintain the established specialty subcontracting system and apprenticeship program.[9]

Construction unions' decision to submit to these early and voluntary controls has been traced back "to the fact that the unions secured unprecedented recognition from the Federal Government that they represented the workers of the construction industry."[10] A year later, on May 22, 1942—before Congress enacted a general statutory wage stabilization program on October 2, 1942—in the wake of rising and varying wage rates especially on large projects in isolated areas, the BCTD entered entered into a Wage Stabilization Agreement with the federal contracting agencies that wage rates paid pursuant to collective bargaining agreements as of July 1, 1942 would remain in effect for at least one year; these rates were also to apply under subsequent renewals of collective bargaining agreements unless they were so old as to have been out of line with general wage prevailing on July 1, 1942, applied to localities where changing local conditions required revised rates, or failed to take into account abnormal changes in conditions. To determine whether such wage rate revision was necessary, the agreement also provided for the creation of a Wage Adjustment Board, which was

---

[6]Dunlop & Hill, *Wage Adjustment Board* at 18-19.

[7]"Memorandum of Stabilization Agreement Between Certain Government Agencies Engaged in Defense Construction and the Building and Construction Trades Department of the American Federation of Labor," ¶ 1 (July 22, 1941), *reprinted in* Dunlop & Hill, *Wage Adjustment Board* at 138.

[8]"Memorandum of Stabilization Agreement," ¶ 3, *reprinted in* Dunlop & Hill, *Wage Adjustment Board* at 138.

[9]"Memorandum of Stabilization Agreement," ¶ ¶4, 7, *reprinted in* Dunlop & Hill, *Wage Adjustment Board* at 138, 139.

[10]Dunlop & Hill, *Wage Adjustment Board* at 20.

directed to consider existing collective bargaining agreements in making such determinations.[11] Construction union presidents were in part motivated to accept this second voluntary wage stabilization program because they "were genuinely concerned over the prospects of getting wages so high that they would have to be sharply reduced later. They had lived through the period of wage reductions after World War I and did not wish to see it repeated."[12]

The Wage Adjustment Board for the Building Construction Industry, which initially consisted of equal numbers of union and contracting agency representatives, and, as of October 13, 1943, of equal numbers of union, industry, and public representatives, was empowered to investigate and recommend wage rate adjustments and was required to "consider requests for wage adjustments when presented by local labor organizations with the approval of the international or national labor organization and submitted through and approved by" the BCTD.[13] Entrusting the initiation of wage increase requests to unions, thus bypassing employers, was unique among wartime wage controls; it was prompted by the need to create uniform area wage rates even in localities lacking a contractors association. The mechanism also "required a degree of supervision by the international unions over the wage demands of their locals."[14] The voluntary origins of the Board, which came into existence on May 29, 1942 and was dissolved on Feb. 24, 1947—formal controls thus lasted one and a half years longer than general wage controls—had a lasting impact in that it always enjoyed "an unusually large measure of support from the leadership of the unions."[15]

What advantages accrued—or at least did the national union leadership imagine would accrue—from its compliant attitude toward state intervention? This compliance was significantly reflected in the extraordinary extent to which building unions adhered to their no-strike pledge. Thus although strike activity in general subsided during World War II, no work stoppage at all involving more than 10,000 workers occurred in construction between August 1941 and June 1946; during this period, 103 such strikes took place in other industries, including 42 strikes between U.S. entry into the war and V-E day. Even excluding strikes conducted by CIO unions and the United Mine Workers and focusing only on AFL unions, building trades strikes as a share of all AFL-union strikes declined to 12 percent between

---

[11]"Building and Construction Trade Wage Stabilization Agreement" (May 22, 1942), *reprinted in* Dunlop & Hill, *Wage Adjustment Board* at 141-42.

[12]Dunlop & Hill, *Wage Adjustment Board* at 27.

[13]Secretary of Labor, Order No. 101 (May 29, 1942), *reprinted in* Dunlop & Hill, *Wage Adjustment Board* at 143-44. For the change in the Board's composition, see National War Labor Board, General Order No. 13 (Oct. 13, 1943), *reprinted in id.* at 146.

[14]Dunlop & Hill, *Wage Adjustment Board* at 31-32.

[15]Dunlop & Hill, *Wage Adjustment Board* at 127.

1942 and 1945 from 17 percent for the period between 1935 and 1941.[16] In return, the OPM, under the co-directorship of Sidney Hillman, head of the Amalgamated Clothing Workers (AFL), granted building trades unions exclusive collective bargaining rights: "Every new employee hired on the vast construction projects of the government automatically had to become a member of an AFL union."[17]

The very fact that the WAB enhanced the position of the international unions vis-à-vis the locals was presumably welcomed by the national leaders in light of the decentralizing tendencies generated by the Depression. Dunlop explicitly confirmed this motivation of using state intervention as a means of undermining the position of the local union leadership for the immediate postwar years when the national unions supported continuation of controls:

[T]here was a genuine concern among...contractors and union leaders to prevent construction wage rates from exploding under postwar construction conditions. There was certain to be a shortage of skilled tradesmen in many areas.... Many...union leaders had experienced the 1919-1922 period and wished to avoid the problems for a labor union accompanying sharp wage cuts. The union leaders were desirous of moderate increases, but the absence of all wage controls would make it almost impossible to hold local unions in line who were in a strong bargaining position to extract very substantial increases from their local contractors. The attitude of the union leaders was not altruism; it was attention to longer run self-interest. This self-interest could more easily be achieved with the sanction of government controls than in its absence when local unions would be most difficult to control.[18]

It is unclear whether this strategy in fact led to any significant long-term increase in national union strength. Indeed, it is even unclear whether this struggle took place between the national and local union leadership or between the leadership and the rank and file. From Dunlop's contemporaneous insider's account the latter interpretation draws some credence: "Many local officers paid heavily for their cooperation with the government's stabilization and production policies by defeat in union elections in 1944-45."[19] With respect to the problems envisaged by the leadership based on the unions' experience in the aftermath of World War I, it appears (at least in retrospect) that its view was shortsighted; for it did not enter into formal agreements with the federal government until the height

---

[16]BLS, *Handbook of Labor Statistics: 1947 Edition*, tab. E-4, E-8, and E-9 at 137, 145, 147-48 (Bull. No. 916, 1948).

[17]Sidney Lens, *Left, Right and Center: Conflicting Forces in American Labor* 330 (1949). See also "Negro Workers Barred by Hillman-AFL Deal," 2 (17) *UCWN* 2 (Oct. 1, 1942).

[18]Dunlop & Hill, *War Adjustment Board* at 43. Cf. BR, *Coming to Grips with Some Problems in the Construction Industry* 36 (1975): "During World War II, the unions and their employers had developed an atmosphere of cooperation as both were represented on the Wage Adjustment Board...."

[19]Dunlop, "The Decontrol of Wages and Prices" at 5.

of war construction had been reached.[20] Although this tactic may at first sight appear to have been successful—if it was even planned—since the upward pressure on wages could have been expected to diminish in any event, thus making wage controls almost superfluous, the middle-term goal was to avoid wage cuts and the accompanying effects on union membership resulting from a postwar recession; in fact, however, construction employment, unlike that in manufacturing, quickly passed its World War II peak. Since unions were aware of the possibility of a relative scarcity of skilled craftsmen and its impact on wages,[21] they would have been in a position to negotiate wage increases that would have improved on the stagnating real wages that obtained between World War II and the Korean War.

The other advantage that national unions may have anticipated from recognition by the federal government was the opportunity to increase the degree of organization (or, alternatively, to preserve a given level despite an influx of large numbers of workers not previously employed in the industry). Such an expectation would have been reasonable in light of the increasing importance of public construction. Building trades unions may, for example, have feared that a large public housing program, conducted along industrial lines, would have posed a threat since the CIO was trying to organize workers along those lines in residential construction.[22] Given the problems surrounding calculation of the degree of organization in construction, it is difficult to offer a precise answer to the question of whether union strength grew in the wake of World War II. But despite the existence of some indications that the degree of organization did rise in certain sectors, since the postwar public housing boom never materialized, the role played by the federal government's recognition remains unclear.[23]

As it did during World War II, but not during the Indochina War, Congress programmatically reshaped the economy during the Korean War. The Defense Production Act of 1950 declared that U.S. foreign and military policy "requires diversion of certain materials and facilities from civilian use to military and related purposes." To "prevent economic disturbances, labor disputes, interferences with

---

[20]*Construction Volume and Costs, 1915-56*: Supplement to 3 *CR* 44-52 (1957).

[21]"Construction Workers—How Many and at What Wages," *ENR*, Feb. 7, 1946, at 123-36.

[22]Harry Bates, *Bricklayers' Century of Craftsmanship* 244-45 (1955); Lewis Lorwin, *American Federation of Labor: History, Policies, and Prospects* 459 (1933); William Haber, "Building Construction," in *How Collective Bargaining Works* 183-228 at 199 nn. 37-39 (Harry Millis ed., 1942).

[23]According to Garth Mangum, *The Operating Engineers* 249 (1964), "local unions of the operating engineers did not make concerted efforts to organize...highway construction until after World War II." Herbert Northrup & Howard Foster, *Open Shop Construction* 123-27 (1975), argue that the Davis-Bacon Act exerted a positive effect on organizing. Howard Foster, *Manpower in Homebuilding: A Preliminary Analysis* 44 (1974), claimed that the time between World War II and the Korean War "probably represents the high-water mark of union representation...for the past four decades" in residential construction.

effective mobilization of national resources, and impairment of national unity and morale," Congress empowered the president to stabilize wages and salaries, and prohibited the payment and receipt of wages in contravention of regulations promulgated under the act.[24] Though far from the total war of the years 1942-45, the "partial mobilization," economic "forced draft," and wage controls, sharply distinguished the Korean War from the quasi-free market approach during the Johnson administration's prosecution of the Vietnam war.[25] The BCTD and nine national contractors associations on February 9, 1951 requested that the Wage Stabilization Board[26] establish an agency similar to the World War II-era WAB. The grounds for a separate agency were: the need to avoid conflicts with Davis-Bacon Act wage determinations; the inapplicability of general wage regulations to workers subject to intermittent employment and employment by numerous employers; the existence of thousands of collective bargaining agreements; and the tradition of separate treatment during World War II.[27] The tripartite Construction Industry Stabilization Commission, created on May 18, 1951, was authorized to "stabilize wages on the basis of areas traditionally established for collective bargaining purposes."[28] Unlike the situation during World War II, however, unions did not give a no-strike pledge, while the Commission was not officially authorized to settle disputes (as the CISC was in the 1970s).[29] Increases in hourly earnings in construction approximated those in manufacturing.[30] Two weeks after taking office, President Eisenhower suspended wage controls on February 6, 1953.[31]

---

[24]Defense Production Act of 1950, Pub. L. No. 774, §§ 2, 401, 402(b)(1), 405(b), 64 Stat. 798, 799, 803, 803, 807.

[25]Almost 50 percent of national production was scheduled for war purposes during World War II compared to 20 percent for the Korean War. L. Reed Tripp, "Problems and Concepts of Wage Stabilization," 1 *History of the Wage Stabilization Program 1950-1953*, at 8-32 at 8-9 (Abraham Weiss, Hilda Callaway, & Harry Weiss eds., 1953).

[26]The Wage Stabilization Board was created by EO 10,161, § 403, 15 *FR* 6105, 6106 (1950).

[27]Gertrude Schroeder, "Construction," in 1 *History of the Wage Stabilization Program 1950-1953*, at 466-76 at 467 (Abraham Weiss, Hilda Callaway, & Harry Weiss eds., 1953).

[28]16 *FR* 6640 (July 7, 1951). See generally, "Wage Policies of the WSB: A Symposium," 7 (2) *ILRR* 174-245 (Jan. 1954); "Construction Industry Stabilization Commission Established," 4 (6) *BCTB* 1 (June1951); Bruno Stein, "Wage Stabilization in the Korean War Period: The Role of Subsidiary Wage Boards," 4 (2) *LH* 161-77 at 173-75 (Spr. 1963).

[29]D. Quinn Mills, "Wage Stabilization in the Construction Industry: An Historical Perspective," 23 *LLJ* 462-68 (1972).

[30]D. Q. Mills, "Construction Wage Stabilization: A Historic Perspective," 11 (3) *IR* 350-64 at 355 (Oct. 1972). Wage increases for 1951 were limited to 10 percent above those in effect on the day the Korean War began; for 1952, the formula allowed an additional 15 cents per hour or about 6 percent. Samuel Hill, "Policies of Commission," in [U.S. Wage Stabilization Board], *History of the Construction Industry Stabilization Commission of the Wage Stabilization Board* 20-64 at 30 (n.d. [1953]); Schroeder, "Construction" at 473-74.

[31]EO 10434.

A Note on Sources

Because full bibliographical data are provided in the footnotes, a formal bibliography is superfluous. This note describes one of the book's most important primary sources—the archival materials of the Construction Users Anti-Inflation Roundtable/Business Roundtable. The Roundtable has organized a substantial volume of material dealing with its construction-related activities in a large number of loose-leaf binders at its office in Washington, D.C. For the years 1969 through 1973, there are two binders per year: one is labelled, "Construction Committee History," the other, "Volume II--Minutes." (The binder for 1968, the year before the CUAIR was founded, includes important papers relating to the events leading to the organization's formation.) From 1974 on, the "Construction Committee History" and "Minutes" are consolidated in one binder. The "Construction Committee History" includes internal memoranda, reports, letters, and other materials. The "Minutes" include the minutes of all the meetings of the CUAIR's Coordinating Committee (1969-72) and the Business Roundtable's Construction Committee (1972 forward). The Roundtable provided access to all of these materials, without restriction, for note-taking, although it prohibited photocopying. The materials are not otherwise open to the public.

A complementary collection of Roundtable materials is available at the Kheel Center for Labor-Management Documentation & Archives at Cornell University. They were deposited by Douglas Soutar, former vice president for industrial relations at the American Smelting and Refining Company and a key figure in national labor-management relations and at the Roundtable. Located in Boxes 5 and 6 of Collection 5914, the construction industry papers include minutes of Roundtable annual meetings, draft reports, letters, memoranda, and notes. As a condition of access to the papers, Soutar requires users to agree "to adhere to the rights of privacy of individuals mention [sic] in these papers during their lifetime and honor the confidentiality of any minutes or other privileged organizational documents for 25 years from whence they were drawn...." No such organizational documents were used, but in a few instances the identities of living people who are quoted or paraphrased have had to be withheld to comply with the conditions imposed by Soutar. Empty square brackets [ ] in a footnote indicate that a name has been withheld. In most cases these persons' identities are inconsequential, but in others identifying the corporations that they managed would have shed additional light on those firms' labor-management strategies.

Index